Spreadsheet

Modeling and

Decision

Analysis

A Practical Introduction to Management Science

Cliff T. Ragsdale

Virginia Polytechnic Institute
and State University

COURSE TECHNOLOGY, INC.
ONE MAIN STREET, CAMBRIDGE, MA 02142
AN INTERNATIONAL THOMSON PUBLISHING COMPANY

I(T)P

Albany • Bonn • Boston • Cincinnati • London
Madrid • Melbourne • Mexico City • New York
Paris • San Francisco • Singapore • Tokyo
Toronto • Washington

Spreadsheet Modeling and Decision Analysis: A Practical Introduction to Management Science is published by Course Technology, Inc.

Managing Editor	Mac Mendelsohn
Production Editor	Pale Moon Productions
Text and Cover Designer	Mike Fender Design

© 1995 Course Technology, Inc.
A Division of International Thomson Publishing, Inc.

For more information contact:
Course Technology, Inc.
One Main Street
Cambridge, MA 02142

International Thomson Publishing Europe
Berkshire House 168-173
High Holborn
London WCIV 7AA
England

Thomas Nelson Australia
102 Dodds Street
South Melbourne, 3205
Victoria, Australia

Nelson Canada
1120 Birchmount Road
Scarborough, Ontario
Canada M1K 5G4

International Thomson Editores
Campos Eliseos 385, Piso 7
Col. Polanco
11560 Mexico D.F. Mexico

International Thomson Publishing GmbH
Königswinterer Strasse 418
53227 Bonn
Germany

International Thomson Publishing Asia
211 Henderson Road
#05-10 Henderson Building
Singapore 0315

International Thomson Publishing Japan
Hirakawacho Kyowa Building, 3F
2-2-1 Hirakawacho
Chiyoda-ku, Tokyo 102
Japan

Trademarks

Course Technology and the open book logo are registered trademarks of Course Technology, Inc.

I(T)P The ITP logo is a trademark under license.

Microsoft is a registered trademark, and Excel and Windows are trademarks of Microsoft Corporation. Screen shots are reprinted with permission from Microsoft Corporation.

Some of the product names and company names used in this book have been used for identification purposes only and may be trademarks or registered trademarks of their respective manufacturers and sellers.

Disclaimer

Course Technology, Inc. reserves the right to revise this publication and make changes from time to time in its content without notice.

ISBN 0-538-87049-4

Printed in the United States of America

10 9 8 7 6 5 4

READ THIS BEFORE YOU BEGIN

TO THE STUDENT

You will need the Excel data files to work through the Questions and Problems included in this text. The data files may be downloaded directly using the following internet web site:

http://www.thomson.com/swcp/mm/ragsdale.html

If it is not possible for you to download the files directly, your instructor will make the files available to you.

TO THE INSTRUCTOR

If it is not possible for your students to download their own data files directly, you may order a copy of the disk files. Call the ITP Academic Resource Center at 800-423-0563 and request ISBN 0-7600-3469-9. Adopters of this book are granted the right to distribute the files on the Data Disks to any student who has purchased a copy of this book. You are free to post all these files to a network or to standalone workstations, or simply to provide copies of the disks to your students. The instructions in this book assume that the students know which drive and directory contain the data files.

OVER THE PAST DECADE, electronic spreadsheets have become the standard tool business people use to model and analyze quantitative problems. A quick glance through the advertisements in most newspapers and computer magazines reveals that a spreadsheet package is usually included as part of the standard bundle of software that comes with many new computers. For those of us interested in the field of management science and operations research (MS/OR), this represents an exciting opportunity. The latest versions of these spreadsheet packages contain powerful analytical tools that we could only dream about a decade ago. Now, literally millions of people are using these spreadsheet programs as a standard part of their daily work activities to build models of the decision problems they face.

Given the pervasive use of spreadsheets in the business world, it seems logical to use spreadsheets as the means for introducing students to the concepts and tools typically covered in the introductory MS/OR course. This simultaneously develops students' skills with a standard tool of today's business world (spreadsheets) and opens their eyes to how a variety of MS/OR techniques can be used in this modeling environment. Using spreadsheets in this class also helps to capture students' interests and adds a new dimension of relevance to MS/OR as they see how this material can be applied with popular commercial software being used in the business world. This approach also increases the likelihood that students will actually use these MS/OR techniques in their future business careers.

This book provides an introduction to the most commonly used MS/OR techniques and shows how these tools can be implemented using Microsoft Excel 5.0 for Windows. While other spreadsheet packages can be used to accomplish the same objective, Excel currently offers the best collection of built-in analytical capabilities and, therefore, is the preferred choice for this book. Prior experience with Excel is certainly helpful, but is not a requirement for using this text. In general, a student familiar with Windows and the spreadsheet concepts presented in most introductory computer courses should have no trouble using this text. Step-by-step instructions and screen shots are provided for each example, and software tips are sprinkled throughout the text as needed. (Copies of Excel can be ordered from Course Technology, Inc. at attractive educational discount prices.)

PHILOSOPHY

In recent years, much has been written in the MS/OR magazines and even more has been said in discussions at academic meetings about how the introductory MS/OR course should be taught. One seemingly unanimous opinion is that the material covered should be tied to real-world applications. I have tried to address this issue throughout the text by using scenarios that are as realistic as possible for an introductory text to illustrate the concepts and mechanics of various MS/OR topics. Additionally, nearly every chapter contains a feature titled "The World of Management Science" that summarizes an article describing actual applications of the techniques discussed in that chapter. Numerous end-of-chapter problems and more challenging case problems—often based on real applications—are included throughout the book.

Another opinion voiced by some in our discipline hails spreadsheets as a way to remove the "algebraic curtain" from the MS/OR curriculum. This is an opinion that I do not fully share. I agree that it is unwise to use the introductory MS/OR course as a stage on which the instructor performs amazing feats of "mathemagics" that leave students absolutely mystified as to what is going on. I also agree that it is unwise to use this class to drill students in the algebraic details of algorithms that pre-date the introduction of the personal computer. However, I think it is equally unwise to abandon all discussion of the mathematical foundations upon which all MS/OR techniques rely.

For example, the constraints in many optimization problems can be expressed in a number of algebraically equivalent ways—some of which are easy to implement in spreadsheets and some of which are not. The constraints for more complicated optimization problems often require some algebraic manipulation in order to uncover a structure or pattern in the constraints that allows them to be implemented efficiently. Thus, an effective modeler needs to be comfortable with the algebraic representation and manipulation of constraints. Similarly, it is well-known that the way in which some optimization problems are formulated often determines whether or not you will be able to solve the problem in a realistic amount of time. A clear discussion of this issue requires the use of some basic mathematical symbols.

There is less emphasis on mathematical derivations and computation in this book than in more traditional MS/OR books. However, the use of mathematics is not abandoned entirely. This book uses mathematical symbols to do what they are best at (that is, conveying general concepts and ideas about modeling) and uses spreadsheets to do what they are best at (that is, implementing models and crunching numbers). I have found this approach to be very effective in helping students develop the ability to think about models in mathematical terms at a somewhat abstract level and implement their thoughts in a very practical way via spreadsheets.

ORGANIZATION

The text is laid out in a fairly traditional format, beginning with an overview of MS/OR in chapter 1. Chapters 2 through 8 cover various topics in deterministic modeling techniques (linear programming, sensitivity analysis, networks, integer programming, goal programming and multiple objective optimization, and nonlinear programming). Chapters 9 through 11 cover predictive modeling and forecasting techniques (regression analysis, discriminant analysis, and time series analysis). Chapters 12 through 14 cover stochastic modeling techniques (simulation and queuing theory). Chapter 12 introduces the concepts of simulation using only the inherent capabilities built into Excel. Chapter 13 is an alternate version of chapter 12 that introduces the concepts of simulation using a popular spreadsheet add-in called @RISK (pronounced "at Risk"). Most instructors will likely cover only one of these chapters, depending on whether or not their students have access to @RISK. Chapters 15 and 16 cover project management and decision theory, respectively.

The material in the text could be covered in a variety of ways. After covering chapter 1, a quick refresher on spreadsheet fundamentals (entering and copying formulas, basic formatting and editing, etc.) is always a good idea. (*Microsoft Excel 5.0 for Windows—Illustrated Brief Edition*, also published by Course Technology, is an excellent aid for this type of refresher and can be bundled with this text at an attractive discount price.) Following this, an instructor could cover the material on optimization, forecasting, or simulation depending on his or her personal preferences. The chapters on queuing, project management and decision analysis all make general references to simulation and, therefore, probably should not precede the discussion of that topic.

INNOVATIVE FEATURES

Aside from its strong spreadsheet orientation, this book contains a number of other unique features that distinguishes it from more traditional MS/OR texts. In keeping with its focus on model formulation and implementation, the details of algorithmic procedures such as the simplex method are kept to a minimum. In the chapter on networks, I abandoned traditional discussions of the stepping stone algorithm and the northwest corner rule in favor of showing how network flow problems can be formulated and solved as linear programming problems. Instead of having a separate chapter on inventory models, I used examples from this area to illustrate potential uses of nonlinear programming and simulation.

This book also includes a unique chapter on discriminant analysis. Traditionally, we have taught students how to use regression analysis to forecast or predict the value of a continuous-valued dependent variable using a set of independent variables. However, many business problems exist in which the dependent variable takes on a discrete set of values. Many students have no idea of how to approach such a problem. Worse, those who have been exposed to expert systems might try to apply this relatively expensive technology to solve to a classification problem that could be handled more easily and efficiently using discriminant analysis.

INSTRUCTOR'S RESOURCE KIT

An Instructor's Resource Kit (ISBN: 0-7600-3329-3) is available to adopters of this book. This kit includes an instructor's manual with solutions to all the problems and cases, transparency masters for all of the figures in the book, and a test bank consisting of multiple choice and short answer problems for each text chapter. A computerized format for the test bank (ISBN: 0-7600-3301-3) is also available. Call the ITP Academic Resource Center at 800-423-0563 to request these items.

ACKNOWLEDGMENTS

I am indebted to a number of individuals who made important contributions to the development and completion of this book. Everyone at Course Technology has been a constant source of support and motivation throughout the project. I am especially grateful to my managing editor, Mac Mendelsohn, whose experience, judgment, guidance, encouragement, and professionalism were simply invaluable. Additionally, I would like to thank my production editor, Robin Geller, for her consistently positive attitude and perseverance in keeping the project on schedule, and my copy editor, Kathy Finnegan, for keeping my grammar tidy and my writing clear and to the point. I am grateful to my good friend Jon Fleming for producing much of the artwork in the text, and to Catherine Griffin and John Swope for providing numerous suggestions for improvement from a student's perspective.

My sincere thanks go to each of the following reviewers of this text who provided extremely helpful guidance and assistance throughout the project. Their ideas, suggestions, and contributions are reflected throughout the text. David Ashley, University of Missouri at Kansas City, provided summaries of the articles found in "The World of Management Science" feature throughout the text and also created the queuing template used in chapter 14. Larry Weatherford, University of Wyoming, performed an enormous amount of work in helping to revise chapter 12 and convert this material to make use of @RISK in chapter 13. Jack Yurkiewicz, Pace University, contributed many of the end-of-chapter cases and helped to improve the realism of many examples throughout the text. Bob Nau, Duke University, provided many of the ideas on data structuring found in chapter 3 and made important contributions to the material on sensitivity analysis and networks in chapters 4 and 5. Mike Middleton, University of San Francisco, developed and provided the TreePlan decision tree add-in found in chapter 16. Doug Morrice, University of Texas at Austin, provided insightful critiques of each chapter and suggested the inventory control example used in the simulation chapters. Janet M. Wagner, University of Massachusetts at Boston, provided many encouraging reviews and made several important suggestions for improving chapter 8 on nonlinear programming.

I would also like to acknowledge the contributions of my good friend and colleague Antonie Stam, University of Georgia, to the material on discriminant analysis in chapter 10. Articles written by Andrew Seila, University of Georgia, and Jerry Banks, Georgia Tech, provided inspiration for some of the early drafts of the simulation material in chapters 12 and 13. Also, Dan Fylstra, of Frontline Systems, provided some of the information in chapter 8 regarding the options for solving nonlinear programming problems.

I am very grateful to Chuck Taylor, my department head at Virginia Tech, for his advice on numerous issues and for his thoughtfulness in arranging my teaching schedule in support of this project. I am also grateful to the secretaries in our department, Sylvia Seavey, Tracy McCoy, and Teena Long, for their efficient administrative assistance throughout this project.

I must also thank K. Roscoe Davis and Patrick G. McKeown, both of the University of Georgia, who wrote the management science book that first piqued my interest in this area and who have since become valued mentors and friends. I would also like to thank Margaret Thomas, University of Central Florida, who did more to encourage an insecure undergraduate psychology major than she will ever know.

Last, but certainly not least, I would like to thank my wife, Kathy, for her unending patience, support, encouragement, and love throughout this project. "Many daughters have done nobly, but you exceed them all . . . ."

FINAL THOUGHTS

I hope you enjoy the spreadsheet approach to teaching MS/OR as much as I do and that you find this book to be very interesting and helpful. Any comments, questions, suggestions, or constructive criticism you have concerning this text are most welcome and can be sent to me at the e-mail address given below.

Cliff T. Ragsdale
e-mail: CRAGS@VTVM1.CC.VT.EDU

CONTENTS

Introduction to Modeling and Decision Analysis

THIS BOOK is titled *Spreadsheet Modeling and Decision Analysis: A Practical Introduction to Management Science*, so let's begin by discussing exactly what this title means. By the very nature of life, all of us must continually make decisions that we hope will solve problems and lead to increased opportunities for ourselves or the organizations for which we work. But making good decisions is rarely an easy task. The problems faced by decision makers in today's competitive, fast-paced business environment are often extremely complex and can be addressed by numerous possible courses of action. Evaluating these alternatives and choosing the best course of action represents the essence of **decision analysis**.

During the past decade, millions of business people discovered that one of the most effective ways to analyze and evaluate decision alternatives involves using electronic spreadsheets to build computer models of the decision problems they face. A **computer model** is a set of mathematical relationships and logical assumptions implemented in a computer as a representation of some real-world decision problem or phenomenon. Today, electronic spreadsheets provide the most convenient and useful way for business people to implement and analyze computer models. Indeed, most business people would probably rate the electronic spreadsheet as their most important analytical tool apart from their brain! Using a **spreadsheet model** (a computer model implemented via a spreadsheet), a business person can analyze decision alternatives before having to choose a specific plan for implementation.

This book introduces you to a variety of techniques from the field of management science that can be applied in spreadsheet models to assist in the decision analysis process. For our purposes, we will define **management science** as a field of study that uses computers, statistics, and mathematics to solve business problems. It involves applying the methods and tools of science to management and decision making. Management science is also sometimes referred to as operations research or decision science. See Figure 1.1 for a summary of how management science has been applied successfully in a number of real-world situations.

HOME RUNS IN MANAGEMENT SCIENCE

In the last decade, scores of operations research and management science projects have saved companies millions of dollars and have improved government services. Here are some of the "home runs" culled from the book *Excellence in Management Science Practice* (Prentice Hall, 1991).

- 1981: A computer-aided dispatching system at ChevronUSA allowed each dispatcher to handle 400 loads per day, compared with the industry average of 150. Running on an IBM 3033, the system could solve a typical dispatching problem in less than a second. Benefit: Chevron cut transportation costs by 3%.

- 1982: General Dynamics Corp.'s Data Systems Division developed a model to help it make an information system (IS) capacity planning decision. The model showed that computer throughput would be 23% higher if existing tape drives were replaced with drives that were 60% faster.

- 1982: The Arizona Department of Transportation developed a decision-support system for allocating maintenance funds to the roughest roads while staying within budget. The system has been adopted by Alaska, Colorado, Kansas, Finland, and Saudi Arabia.

- 1984: The New York City Department of Sanitation used several management science techniques to improve the deployment of street cleaners, garbage trucks, and inspectors, turning the department's embarrassingly poor performance into a national model. Benefits: Then-Mayor Ed Koch said the streets were much cleaner, and refuse collection productivity increased 17%.

- 1986: Weyerhaeuser Co. developed an interactive computer model that helps lumberjacks cut each log to maximize profits and minimize waste. The model considers variables such as the log's length, diameter, curvature, taper and knots. Benefit: The company increased profits by $100 million.

- 1987: General Motors Corp.'s Delco Electronics Division developed a PC-based planning system to identify the best way to ship 300 types of components to 30 assembly plants. Benefit: GM cut logistics costs by 26%, saving $2.9 million a year.

Source: Betts, Mitch, "Efficiency Einsteins," *ComputerWorld* (March 22, 1993) 64. Copyright 1993 by CW Publishing, Inc., Framingham, MA 01701. Reprinted from *ComputerWorld*.

Figure 1.1: Examples of successful management science applications

In the not too distant past, management science was a highly specialized field that generally could be practiced only by those who had access to mainframe computers and who possessed an advanced knowledge of mathematics and computer programming languages. This characterization is true of most, if not all, of the success stories listed in Figure 1.1. However, the proliferation of powerful personal computers (PCs) and the development of easy-to-use electronic spreadsheets have made the tools of management science far more practical and available to a much larger audience. Virtually everyone who uses a spreadsheet today for model building and decision making is a practitioner of management science—whether they realize it or not. So it is only a matter of time before we begin to hear success stories about "home runs" being hit by spreadsheet-based applications using the tools of management science discussed in this book.

THE MODELING APPROACH TO DECISION MAKING

The idea of using models in problem solving and decision analysis is really not new, and is certainly not tied to the use of computers. At some point, all of us have used a modeling approach to make a decision. For example, if you have ever moved into a dormitory, apartment, or house you undoubtedly faced a decision about how to arrange the furniture in your new dwelling. There were probably a number of different arrangements to consider. One arrangement might give you the most open space but require that you build a loft. Another might give you less space but allow you to avoid the hassle and expense of building a loft. To analyze these different arrangements and make a decision, you did not build the loft. You more likely built a **mental model** of the two arrangements, picturing what each looked like in your mind's eye. Thus, a simple mental model is sometimes all that is required to analyze a problem and make a decision.

For more complex decision problems, a mental model might be impossible or insufficient and other types of models might be required. For example, a set of drawings or blueprints for a house or building provides a **visual model** of the real-world structure. These drawings help illustrate how the various parts of the structure will fit together when it is completed. A road map is another type of visual model because it assists a driver in analyzing the various routes from one location to another.

You have probably also seen car commercials on television showing automotive engineers using **physical**, or **scale**, **models** to study the aerodynamics of various car designs in order to find the shape that creates the least wind resistance and maximizes fuel economy. Similarly, aeronautical engineers use scale models of airplanes to study the flight characteristics of various fuselage and wing designs. And civil engineers might use scale models of buildings and bridges to study the strengths of different construction techniques.

Another common type of model is a **mathematical model**, which uses mathematical relationships to describe or represent an object or decision problem. Throughout this book we will study how various mathematical models can be implemented and analyzed on computers using spreadsheet software. But before we move to an in-depth discussion of spreadsheet models, let's look at some of the more general characteristics and benefits of modeling.

CHARACTERISTICS AND BENEFITS OF MODELING

Although this book focuses on mathematical models implemented in computers via spreadsheets, the examples of non-mathematical models given earlier are worth discussing a bit more because they help illustrate a number of important characteristics and benefits of modeling in general. First, the models mentioned earlier are usually *simplified* versions of the object or decision problem they represent. To study the aerodynamics of a car design, we do not need to build the entire car complete with engine and stereo. Such components have little or no effect on aerodynamics. So, although a model is often a simplified representation of reality, the model is useful as long as it is valid. A **valid** model is one that accurately represents the relevant characteristics of the object or decision problem being studied.

Second, it is often *less expensive* to analyze decision problems using a model. This is especially easy to understand with respect to scale models of big-ticket items such as cars and planes. Besides the lower financial cost of building a model, the analysis of a model can help avoid costly mistakes that might result from poor decision making. For example, it is far less costly to discover a flawed wing design using a scale model of an aircraft than after the crash of a fully loaded jet liner.

Frank Brock, former executive vice president of the Brock Candy Company, related the following story about blueprints his company prepared for a new production facility. After months of careful design work he proudly showed the plans to several of his production workers. When he asked for their comments, one worker responded, "It's a fine looking building Mr. Brock, but that sugar valve looks like it's about twenty feet away from the steam valve." "What's wrong with that?" asked Brock. "Well, nothing," said the worker, "except that I have to have my hands on both valves at the same time!"[1] Needless to say, it was far less expensive to discover and correct this "little" problem using a visual model before pouring the concrete and laying the pipes as originally planned.

Third, models often deliver needed information on a *more timely basis*. Again, it is relatively easy to see that scale models of cars or airplanes can be created and analyzed more quickly than their real-world counterparts. Timeliness is also an issue when vital data will not become available until some later point in time. In these cases, we might create a model to help predict the missing data to assist in current decision making.

Fourth, models are frequently helpful in examining things that would be *impossible to do* in reality. For example, human models (crash dummies) are used in crash tests to see what might happen to an actual person if a car hits a brick wall at a high speed. Likewise, models of DNA can be used to visualize how molecules fit together. Both of these are difficult, if not impossible, to do without the use of models.

Finally, and probably most importantly, models allow us to gain *insight* and *understanding* about the object or decision problem under investigation. The ultimate purpose of using models is to improve decision making. As you will see, the process of building a model can shed important light and understanding on a problem. In some cases, a decision might be made while building the model as a previously misunderstood element of the problem is discovered or eliminated. In other cases, a careful analysis of a completed model might be required to "get a

---

1. Colson, Charles, and Jack Eckerd, *Why America Doesn't Work* (Denver, Colorado: Word Publishing, 1991) 146-47.

handle" on a problem and gain the insights needed to make a decision. In any event, it is the insight gained from the modeling process that ultimately leads to better decision making.

MATHEMATICAL MODELS

As mentioned earlier, the modeling techniques in this book differ quite a bit from scale models of cars and planes or visual models of production plants. The models we will build use mathematics to describe a decision problem. We use the term "mathematics" in its broadest sense, encompassing not only the most familiar elements of math, such as algebra, but also the related topic of logic.

Now, let's consider a simple example of a mathematical model:

$$PROFIT = REVENUE - EXPENSES \qquad \text{1.1}$$

Equation 1.1 describes a simple relationship between revenue, expenses, and profit. It is a mathematical relationship that describes the operation of determining profit—or a mathematical model of profit. Of course, not all models are this simple, but, taken piece by piece, the models we will discuss are not much more complex than this one.

Frequently, mathematical models describe functional relationships. For example, the mathematical model in equation 1.1 describes a functional relationship between revenue, expenses, and profit. Using the symbols of mathematics, this functional relationship is:

$$PROFIT = f(REVENUE, EXPENSES) \qquad \text{1.2}$$

In words, the above expression means "profit is a function of revenue and expenses." We could also say that profit *depends* on (or is *dependent* on) revenue and expenses. Thus, the term PROFIT in equation 1.2 represents a **dependent variable**, whereas REVENUE and EXPENSES represent **independent variables**. Frequently, compact symbols are used to represent variables in an equation like 1.2. For example, if we let Y, X_1, and X_2 represent PROFIT, REVENUE, and EXPENSES, respectively, we could rewrite equation 1.2 as:

$$Y = f(X_1, X_2) \qquad \text{1.3}$$

The notation $f(\cdot)$ represents the function that defines the relationship between the dependent variable Y and the independent variables X_1 and X_2. In the case of determining PROFIT from REVENUE and EXPENSES, the mathematical form of the function $f(\cdot)$ is quite simple because we know that $f(X_1, X_2) = X_1 - X_2$. However, in many other situations we will model, the form of $f(\cdot)$ will be quite complex and might involve many independent variables. But regardless of the complexity of $f(\cdot)$ or the number of independent variables involved, many of the decision problems encountered in business can be represented by models that assume the general form:

$$Y = f(X_1, X_2, ..., X_k) \qquad \text{1.4}$$

In equation 1.4, the dependent variable Y represents some bottom-line performance measure of the problem we are modeling. The terms $X_1, X_2, ..., X_k$ represent different independent variables that play some role or have some impact in determining the value of Y. Again, $f(\cdot)$ is the function (possibly quite complex) that specifies or describes the relationship between the dependent and independent variables.

The relationship expressed in equation 1.4 is similar to what occurs in most spreadsheet models. Consider a simple spreadsheet model that calculates the monthly payment for a car loan, shown in Figure 1.2.

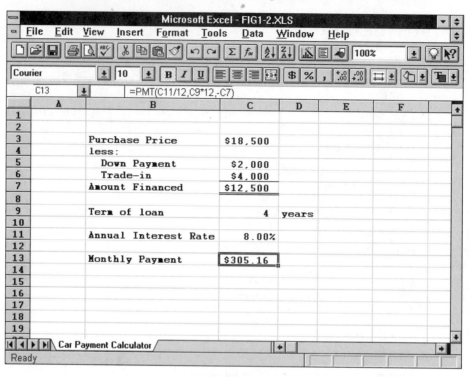

Figure 1.2: *Example of a simple spreadsheet model*

The spreadsheet in Figure 1.2 contains a variety of input cells (for example, purchase price, down payment, trade-in, term of loan, annual interest rate) that correspond conceptually to the independent variables X_1, X_2, ..., X_k in equation 1.4. Similarly, a variety of mathematical operations are performed using these input cells in a manner analogous to the function $f(\cdot)$ in equation 1.4. The results of these mathematical operations determine the value of some *output cell* in the spreadsheet (for example, monthly payment) that corresponds to the dependent variable Y in equation 1.4. Thus, there is a direct correspondence between equation 1.4 and the spreadsheet in Figure 1.2. This type of correspondence exists for most of the spreadsheet models in this book.

CATEGORIES OF MATHEMATICAL MODELS

Not only does equation 1.4 describe the major elements of mathematical or spreadsheet models, it also provides a convenient means for comparing and contrasting the three categories of modeling techniques presented in this book—Prescriptive Models, Predictive Models, and Descriptive Models. Figure 1.3 summarizes the characteristics and techniques associated with each of these categories.

Model Characteristics

Category	Form of $f(\cdot)$	Values of Independent Variables	Management Science Techniques
Prescriptive Models	known, well-defined	known or under decision maker's control	Linear Programming, Networks, Integer Programming, CPM, Goal Programming, EOQ, Nonlinear Programming
Predictive Models	unknown, ill-defined	known or under decision maker's control	Regression Analysis, Time Series Analysis, Discriminant Analysis
Descriptive Models	known, well-defined	unknown or uncertain	Simulation, Queuing, PERT, Inventory Models

Figure 1.3: Categories and characteristics of management science modeling techniques

In some situations, a manager might face a decision problem involving a very precise, well-defined functional relationship $f(\cdot)$ between the independent variables $X_1, X_2, \ldots, X_k$ and the dependent variable Y. If the values for the independent variables are under the decision maker's control, the decision problem in these types of situations boils down to determining the values of the independent variables $X_1, X_2, \ldots, X_k$ that produce the best possible value for the dependent variable Y. These types of models are called **Prescriptive Models** because their solutions tell the decision maker what actions to take. For example, you might be interested in determining how a given sum of money should be allocated to different investments (represented by the independent variables) in order to maximize the return on a portfolio without exceeding a certain level of risk.

A second category of decision problems is one in which the objective is to predict or estimate what value the dependent variable Y will take on when the independent variables $X_1, X_2, \ldots, X_k$ take on specific values. If the function $f(\cdot)$ relating the dependent and independent variables is known, this is a very simple task—simply enter the specified values for $X_1, X_2, \ldots, X_k$ into the function $f(\cdot)$ and compute Y. In some cases however, the functional form of $f(\cdot)$ might be unknown and must be estimated in order for the decision maker to make predictions about the dependent variable Y. These types of models are called **Predictive Models**. For example, a real estate appraiser might know that the value of a commercial property (Y) is influenced by its total square footage (X_1) and age (X_2), among other things. However, the functional relationship $f(\cdot)$ that relates these variables to one another might be unknown. By analyzing the relationship between the selling price, total square footage, and age of other commercial properties, the appraiser might be able to identify a function $f(\cdot)$ that relates these two variables in a reasonably accurate manner.

The third category of models you are likely to encounter in the business world are called **Descriptive Models**. In these situations, a manager might face a decision problem that has a very precise, well-defined functional relationship $f(\cdot)$ between the independent variables $X_1, X_2, \ldots, X_k$ and the dependent variable Y.

However, there might be great uncertainty as to the exact values that will be assumed by one or more of the independent variables X_1, X_2, ..., X_k. In these types of problems, the objective is to describe the outcome or behavior of a given operation or system. For example, suppose a company is building a new manufacturing facility and has several choices about the type of machines to put in the new plant, as well as various options for arranging the machines. Management might be interested in studying how the various plant configurations would affect on-time shipments of orders (Y) given the uncertain number of orders that might be received (X_1), and the uncertain due dates (X_2) that might be required by these orders.

THE PROBLEM-SOLVING PROCESS

Throughout our discussion, we have said that the ultimate goal in building models is to assist managers in making decisions that solve problems. The modeling techniques we will study represent a small but important part of the total problem-solving process. To become an effective modeler, it is important to understand how modeling fits into the entire problem-solving process.

Because a model can be used to represent a decision problem or phenomenon, we might be able to create a visual model of the phenomenon that occurs when people solve problems—what we call the problem-solving process. Although a variety of models could be equally valid, the one in Figure 1.4 summarizes the key elements of the problem-solving process and is sufficient for our purposes.

Figure 1.4: A visual model of the problem-solving process

Identify Problem → Formulate and Implement Model → Analyze Model → Test Results → Implement Solution

← ← unsatisfactory results ← ←

The first step of the problem-solving process, identifying the problem, is also the most important. If we do not identify the correct problem, all the work that follows will amount to nothing more than wasted effort, time, and money. Unfortunately, identifying the problem to solve is often not as easy as it seems. We know that a problem exists when there is a gap or disparity between the present situation and some desired state of affairs. However, we usually are not faced with a neat, well-defined problem. Instead, we often find ourselves facing a "mess"![2] Identifying the real problem involves gathering a lot of information and talking with many people to increase our understanding of the mess. We must then sift through all this information and try to identify the root problem or problems causing the mess. Thus, identifying the real problem (and not just the symptoms of the problem) requires insight, some imagination, time, and a good bit of detective work.

The end result of the problem identification step is a well-defined statement of the problem. Simply defining a problem well will often make it much easier to solve. Having identified the problem, we turn our attention to creating or formulating a model of the problem. Depending on the nature of the problem, we might use a mental model, a visual model, a scale model, or a mathematical model. Although this book focuses on mathematical models, this does not mean that mathematical models

---

2. This characterization is borrowed from chapter 5, James R. Evans, *Creative Thinking in the Decision and Management Sciences* (Dallas, Texas: South-Western Publishing, 1991), 89-115.

are always applicable or best. In most situations, the best model is the *simplest* model that accurately reflects the relevant characteristic or essence of the problem being studied.

We will discuss several different management science modeling techniques in this book. It is important that you not develop too strong a preference for any one technique. Some people have a tendency to want to formulate every problem they face as a model that can be solved by their favorite management science technique. This simply will not work.

As indicated in Figure 1.3, there are fundamental differences in the types of problems a manager might face. Sometimes the values of the independent variables affecting a problem are under the manager's control; sometimes they are not. Sometimes the form of the functional relationship $f(\cdot)$ relating the dependent and independent variables is well-defined, and sometimes it is not. These fundamental characteristics of the problem should guide your selection of an appropriate management science modeling technique. Your goal at the model formulation stage is to select a modeling technique that fits your problem, rather than trying to fit your problem into the required format of a preselected modeling technique.

After you select an appropriate representation or formulation of your problem, the next step is to implement this formulation as a spreadsheet model. We will not dwell on the implementation process now because that is the focus of the remainder of this book. After you verify that your spreadsheet model has been implemented accurately, the next step in the problem-solving process is to use the model to analyze the problem it represents. The main focus of this step is to generate and evaluate alternatives that might lead to a solution of the problem. This often involves playing out a number of scenarios or asking several "What if?" questions. Spreadsheets are particularly helpful in analyzing mathematical models in this manner. In a well-designed spreadsheet model, it should be fairly simple to change some of the assumptions in the model to see what might happen in different situations. As we proceed, we will highlight some techniques for designing spreadsheet models that facilitate this type of "what if" analysis. "What if" analysis is also very appropriate and useful when working with nonmathematical models.

The end result of analyzing a model does not always provide a solution to the actual problem being studied. As we analyze a model by asking various "What if?" questions, it is important to test the feasibility and quality of each potential solution. The blueprints Frank Brock showed to his production employees represented the end result of his analysis of the problem he faced. He wisely tested the feasibility and quality of this alternative before implementing it, and discovered an important flaw in his plans. Thus, the testing process can give important new insights into the nature of a problem. The testing process is also important because it provides the opportunity to double check the validity of the model. At times we might discover an alternative that appears to be too good to be true. This could lead us to find that some important assumption has been left out of the model. Testing the results of the model against known results (and simple common sense) helps ensure the structural integrity and validity of the model. After analyzing the model we might discover that we need to go back and modify the model.

The last step of the problem-solving process, implementation, is often the most difficult. By their very nature, solutions to problems involve people and change.

For better or for worse, most people resist change. However, there are ways to minimize the seemingly inevitable resistance to change. For example, it is wise, if possible, to involve anyone who will be affected by the decision in all steps of the problem-solving process. This not only helps develop a sense of ownership and understanding of the ultimate solution, but it also can be the source of important information throughout the problem-solving process. As the Brock Candy story illustrates, even if it is impossible to include those affected by the solution in all steps, their input should be solicited and considered before a solution is accepted for implementation. Resistance to change and new systems can also be eased by creating flexible, user-friendly interfaces for the mathematical models that are often developed in the problem-solving process.

Throughout this book, we focus mostly on the model formulation, implementation, analysis, and testing steps of the problem-solving process, summarized in Figure 1.4. Again, this does not imply that these steps are more important than the others. If we do not identify the correct problem, the best we can hope for from our modeling effort is "the right answer to the wrong question," which does not solve the real problem. Similarly, even if we do identify the problem correctly and design a model that leads to a perfect solution, if we cannot implement the solution, we still have not solved the problem. Developing the interpersonal and investigative skills required to work with people in defining the problem and implementing the solution are as important as the mathematical modeling skills you will develop by working through this book.

SUMMARY

This book introduces you to a variety of techniques from the field of management science that can be applied in spreadsheet models to assist in decision analysis and problem solving. This chapter discussed how spreadsheet models of decision problems can be used to analyze the consequences of possible courses of action before a particular alternative is selected for implementation. It described how models of decision problems differ in a number of important characteristics and how you should select a modeling technique that is most appropriate for the type of problem being faced. Finally, it discussed how spreadsheet modeling and analysis fit into the problem-solving process.

REFERENCES

Forgione, G. "Corporate MS Activities: An Update." *Interfaces*, vol. 13, no. 1, 1983.

Grayson, C. "Management Science and Business Practice." *Harvard Business Review*, vol. 51, 1973.

Hall, R. "What's So Scientific About MS/OR?" *Interfaces*, vol. 15, 1985.

Wysoki, R. "OR/MS Implementation Research: A Bibliography." *Interfaces*, vol. 9, no. 2, 1979.

Business Analysts Trained in Management Science Can Be a Secret Weapon in a CIO's Quest for Bottom-Line Results

Source: Betts, Mitch, "Efficiency Einsteins," *ComputerWorld*, (March 22, 1993): 64. Copyright 1993 by CW Publishing, Inc., Framingham, MA 01701. Reprinted from *ComputerWorld*.

EFFICIENCY NUTS. Perhaps you've seen one at a cocktail party, explaining that the host could disperse that crowd around the popular shrimp dip if he would just divide the dip into three bowls and place them around the room.

As she sketches the improved traffic pattern on the back of a paper napkin, you notice that her favorite word is "optimize"—a sure-fire sign she has been trained in the field of "operations research" or "management science."

These folks are driven to solve logistics problems, a trait that may not make them sparkle on the party circuit but may be exactly what today's information systems departments need to deliver more business value. Experts say smart information systems (IS) executives will learn to exploit the talents of these mathematical wizards in their quest to boost a company's bottom line.

"If IS departments had more participation from operations research analysts, they would be building much better, richer IS solutions," declares Ron J. Ponder, chief information officer (CIO) at Sprint Corp. in Kansas City, Mo., and former CIO at Federal Express Corp. Ponder and others say analysts trained in operations research or management science can turn ordinary information systems into money-saving decision-support systems and are ideally suited to be members of the business process re-engineering team.

"I've always had an operations research department reporting to me, and it's been invaluable. Now I'm building one at Sprint," Ponder says. As someone who has a Ph.D. in operations research and who built the legendary package-tracking systems at Federal Express, Ponder is a true believer in something that many IS professionals have never even heard of.

MATHEMATICAL REASONING

So what is operations research? It's the use of advanced analytical techniques (such as mathematical models) to improve or optimize the performance of an organization. Management science is virtually the same, only academic research papers in this field have a higher ratio of text to equations. Together, they go by the acronym OR/MS.

In either case, OR/MS analysts just love to solve business problems—and the more complex the puzzle, the more they like it. A classic example is the crew scheduling problem at United Airlines. How do you plan the itineraries of 8,000 pilots and 17,000 flight attendants when there is an astronomical number of combinations of planes, crews, and cities?

The OR/MS analysts at United came up with a client/server-based scheduling system, called Paragon, that seeks to minimize the amount of paid time that crews spend waiting for flights. Their model even factors in constraints such as union rules and Federal Aviation Administration regulations. It is expected to save the airline at least $1 million a year.

Over the years, some of the best CIOs have had operations research backgrounds. For example, Joseph T. Brophy, the award-winning former CIO at The Travelers Corp., previously worked as an operations research analyst on the Polaris submarine weapons system.

Operations research got its start in World War II, when the military had to make decisions about allocating scarce resources to various military operations. Since then, the analytic sciences have spread throughout business and government, from designing efficient drive-thru window service for Burger King Corp. to ultra-sophisticated computerized stock trading.

Somewhere along the way, perhaps in the 1970s, the operations research and IS disciplines went on separate tracks. "The IS profession has had less and less contact with the operations research folks . . . and IS lost a powerful intellectual driver," says Peter G. W. Keen, executive director of the International Center for Information Technologies in Washington, D.C.

The split is ironic, considering that one of the first business applications for computers in the 1950s was to solve operations research problems for the petroleum industry. A technique called linear programming was used to figure out how to blend gasoline for the right flash point, the right viscosity and the right octane and in the cheapest possible way.

The 1990s may be an ideal time for the two disciplines to rebuild some bridges, Keen and other observers say. Today's OR/MS professionals are involved in a variety of IS-related fields, including inventory management, electronic data interchange, computer-integrated manufacturing, network management and practical applications of expert systems and neural networks.

Furthermore, each side needs something the other side has. OR/MS analysts need the corporate data to plug into their models, and the IS folks need to plug the OR/MS models into their strategic information systems. Meanwhile, CIOs need to build smart applications that enhance the bottom line and make them heroes with the chief executive officer.

NOT PEOPLE PERSONS

However, Keen says, there are some barriers to collaboration. Some OR/MS professionals lack communication skills and tend to focus on esoteric mathematics rather than real-world business problems. "On the other hand, they are very, very bright people. If you can get them away from what I call 'rigor without relevance' and get them onto relevant projects, their rigor is very valuable," Keen says.

Perhaps the biggest barrier is an undercurrent of rivalry between some IS and OR/MS groups as they compete for internal customers, budgets, and glory. But failure to cooperate could be suicidal for both professions, experts says. At a time when some OR/MS groups are facing budget cuts and CIOs are getting fired left and right, it would behoove the two camps to cooperate on some CEO-pleasing "home runs," says consultant Donald B. Brout, president of Quality Technology Decisions, Inc. in New York.

"Operations research and management science have a lot to offer the CIO," says Brout, who has a background in both management science and IS. "We can all be heroes."

OR/MS analysts can develop a model of the way a business process works now and simulate how it could work more efficiently in the future, he says. Therefore, it makes sense to have an OR/MS analyst on the interdisciplinary team that tackles business process re-engineering projects.

In essence, OR/MS professionals add more value to the IS infrastructure by building "tools that really help decision makers analyze complex situations," says Andrew B. Whinston, director of the Center for Information Systems Management at the University of Texas at Austin.

Thomas M. Cook, president of American Airlines Decision Technologies, Inc. in Forth Worth, Texas, puts it in even stronger terms. IS departments typically believe their job is done if they deliver accurate and timely information. But Cook says that adding OR/MS skills to the team can produce *intelligent* systems that actually recommend *solutions* to business problems.

One of the big success stories at Cook's operations research shop is a "yield management" system, which decides how much to overbook and how to set prices for each seat so that a plane is filled up and profits are maximized. The yield management system, which deals with more than 250 decision variables, accounts for a whopping 5% of American Airlines' revenue. The airline's Sabre reservation system "got a lot of great press, but the value of things like yield management might even dwarf Sabre's benefits," Brout says.

WHERE TO START

So how can the CIO start down the road toward collaboration with OR/MS analysts? Brout says that if the company already has a group of OR/MS professionals, the IS department can draw on their expertise as internal consultants. Otherwise he says, the CIO can simply hire a few OR/MS wizards, throw a problem at them and see what happens. The payback may come surprisingly fast. As one former OR/MS professional put it: "If I couldn't save my employer the equivalent of my own salary in the first month of the year, then I wouldn't feel like I was doing my job."

Questions and Problems

1. What is meant by the term decision analysis?

2. Define the term computer model.

3. What is the difference between a spreadsheet model and a computer model?

4. Define the term management science.

5. What is the relationship between management science and spreadsheet modeling?

6. What kinds of spreadsheet applications would not be considered management science?

7. In what ways do spreadsheet models facilitate the decision-making process?

8. What are the benefits of using a modeling approach to decision making?

9. What is a dependent variable?

10. What is an independent variable?

11. Can a model have more than one dependent variable?

12. Can a decision problem have more than one dependent variable?

13. In what ways are prescriptive models different from descriptive models?

14. In what ways are prescriptive models different from predictive models?

15. In what ways are descriptive models different from predictive models?

16. How would you define the words description, prediction, and prescription? Carefully consider what is unique about the meaning of each word.

17. Identify one or more mental models you have used. Can any of them be expressed mathematically? If so, identify the dependent and independent variables in your model.

18. Consider the spreadsheet model shown in Figure 1.2. Is this model descriptive, predictive, or prescriptive in nature, or does it not fall into any of these categories?

19. What are the steps in the problem-solving process?

20. Which step in the problem-solving process do you think is most important? Why?

21. Must a model accurately represent every detail of a decision situation to be useful? Why or why not?

22. If you were presented with several different models of a given decision problem, which would you be most inclined to use? Why?

CHAPTER 2

Introduction to Optimization and Linear Programming

OUR WORLD is filled with limited resources. The amount of oil we can pump out of the earth is limited. The amount of land available for garbage dumps and hazardous waste is limited and, in many areas, diminishing rapidly. On a more personal level, each of us has a limited amount of time in which to accomplish or enjoy the activities we schedule each day. Most of us have a limited amount of money to spend while pursuing these activities. Businesses also have limited resources. A manufacturing organization employs a limited number of workers. A restaurant has a limited amount of space available for seating.

Deciding how best to use the limited resources available to an individual or a business is a universal problem. In today's competitive business environment, it is increasingly important to make sure that a company's limited resources are used in the most efficient manner possible. Typically, this involves determining how to allocate the resources in such a way as to maximize profits or minimize costs. **Mathematical programming** (MP) is a field of management science that finds the optimal, or most efficient, way of using limited resources to achieve the objectives of an individual or a business. For this reason, mathematical programming is often referred to as **optimization**.

APPLICATIONS OF MATHEMATICAL OPTIMIZATION

To help you understand the purpose of optimization and the types of problems in which it can be used, let's consider several examples of decision-making situations in which MP techniques have been applied.

Determining Product Mix. Most manufacturing companies can make a variety of products. However, each product usually requires different amounts of raw materials and labor. Similarly, the amount of profit generated by the products varies. The manager of such a company must decide how many of each product to produce in order to maximize profits or to satisfy demand at minimum cost.

Manufacturing. Printed circuit boards, like those used in most computers, often have hundreds or thousands of holes drilled in them to accommodate the different electrical components that must be plugged into them. To manufacture these boards, a computer-controlled drilling machine must be programmed to drill in a given location, then move the drill bit to the next location and drill again. This process is repeated hundreds or thousands of times to complete all the holes on a circuit board. Manufacturers of these boards would benefit from determining the drilling order that minimizes the total distance the drill bit must be moved.

Routing and Logistics. Many retail companies have warehouses around the country that are responsible for keeping stores supplied with merchandise to sell. The amount of merchandise available at the warehouses and the amount needed at each store tends to fluctuate, as does the cost of shipping or delivering merchandise from the warehouses to the retail locations. Large amounts of money can be saved by determining the least costly method of transferring merchandise from the warehouses to the stores.

Financial Planning. The federal government requires individuals to begin withdrawing money from individual retirement accounts (IRAs) and other tax-sheltered retirement programs no later than age 70.5. There are various rules that must be followed to avoid paying penalty taxes on these withdrawals. Most individuals want to withdraw their money in a manner that minimizes the amount of taxes they must pay while still obeying the tax laws.

CHARACTERISTICS OF OPTIMIZATION PROBLEMS

These examples represent just a few areas in which MP has been used successfully. We will consider many other examples throughout this book. However, these examples give you some idea of the issues involved in optimization. For instance, each example involves one or more *decisions* that must be made: How many of each product should be produced? Which hole should be drilled next? How much of each product should be shipped from each warehouse to the various retail locations? How much money should an individual withdraw each year from various retirement accounts?

Also, in each example restrictions, or *constraints*, are likely to be placed on the alternatives available to the decision maker. In the first example, when determining the number of products to manufacture, a production manager is probably faced with a limited amount of raw materials and a limited amount of labor. In the second example, the drill should never return to a position where a hole has already been drilled. In the third example, there is a physical limitation on the amount of merchandise a truck can carry from one warehouse to the stores on its route. In the fourth example, laws determine the minimum and maximum amounts that can be withdrawn from retirement accounts without incurring a penalty. Many other constraints also can be identified for these examples. Indeed, it is not unusual for real-world optimization problems to have hundreds or thousands of constraints.

A final common element in each of the examples is the existence of some goal or *objective* that the decision maker considers when deciding which course of action is best. In the first example, the production manager can decide to produce several different product mixes given the available resources, but the manager will probably choose the mix of products that maximizes profits. In the second example, a large number of possible drilling patterns can be used, but the ideal pattern will probably involve moving the drill bit the shortest total distance. In the third example, there are numerous ways merchandise can be shipped from the warehouses to supply the stores, but the company will probably want to identify the routing that minimizes the total transportation cost. Finally, in the fourth example, individuals can withdraw money from their retirement accounts in many ways without violating the tax laws, but they probably want to find the method that minimizes their tax liability.

EXPRESSING OPTIMIZATION PROBLEMS MATHEMATICALLY

From the preceding discussion we know that optimization problems involve three elements: decisions, constraints, and an objective. If we intend to build a mathematical model of an optimization problem, we will need mathematical terms or symbols to represent each of these three elements.

DECISIONS

The decisions in an optimization problem are often represented in a mathematical model by the symbols $X_1, X_2, \ldots, X_n$. We will refer to $X_1, X_2, \ldots, X_n$ as the **decision variables** (or simply the variables) in the model. These variables might represent the quantities of different products the production manager can choose to produce. They might represent the amount of different pieces of merchandise to ship from a warehouse to a certain store. They might represent the amount of money to be withdrawn from different retirement accounts.

The exact symbols used to represent the decision variables are not particularly important. You could use $Z_1, Z_2, \ldots, Z_n$ or symbols like Dog, Cat, and Monkey to represent the decision variables in the model. The choice of which symbols to use is largely a matter of personal preference and might vary from one problem to the next.

CONSTRAINTS

The constraints in an optimization problem can be represented in a mathematical model in a number of ways. Three general ways of expressing the possible constraint relationships in an optimization problem are:

A less than or equal to constraint: $\qquad f(X_1, X_2, ..., X_n) \leq b$

A greater than or equal to constraint: $\qquad f(X_1, X_2, ..., X_n) \geq b$

An equal to constraint: $\qquad f(X_1, X_2, ..., X_n) = b$

In each case, the **constraint** is some function of the decision variables that must be less than or equal to, greater than or equal to, or equal to some specific value (represented above by the letter b). We will refer to $f(X_1, X_2, ..., X_n)$ as the left-hand-side (LHS) of the constraint and to b as the right-hand-side (RHS) value of the constraint.

For example, we might use a less than or equal to constraint to ensure that the total labor used in producing a given number of products does not exceed the amount of available labor. We might use a greater than or equal to constraint to ensure that the total amount of money withdrawn from a person's retirement accounts is at least the minimum amount required by the IRS. You can use any number of these constraints to represent a given optimization problem depending on the requirements of the situation.

OBJECTIVE

The objective in an optimization problem is represented mathematically by an objective function in the general format:

MAX (or MIN): $\quad f(X_1, X_2, ..., X_n)$

The **objective function** identifies some function of the decision variables that the decision maker wants to either MAXimize or MINimize. In our earlier examples, this function might be used to describe the total profit associated with a product mix, the total distance the drill bit must be moved, the total cost of transporting merchandise, or a retiree's total tax liability.

The mathematical formulation of an optimization problem can be described in the general format:

MAX (or MIN): $\qquad f_0(X_1, X_2, ..., X_n)$ **2.1**

Subject to: $\qquad f_1(X_1, X_2, ..., X_n) \leq b_1$ **2.2**

$$\vdots$$

$\qquad f_k(X_1, X_2, ..., X_n) \geq b_k$ **2.3**

$$\vdots$$

$\qquad f_m(X_1, X_2, ..., X_n) = b_m$ **2.4**

This representation identifies the objective function (equation 2.1) that will be maximized (or minimized) and the constraints that must be satisfied (equations 2.2 through 2.4). Subscripts added to the f and b in each equation emphasize that the functions describing the objective and constraints can all be different. The goal in optimization is to find the values of the decision variables that maximize (or minimize) the objective function without violating any of the constraints.

MATHEMATICAL PROGRAMMING TECHNIQUES

Our general representation of an MP model is just that—general. There are many kinds of functions you can use to represent the objective function and the constraints in an MP model. Of course, you should always use functions that accurately describe the objective and constraints of the problem you are trying to solve. Sometimes the functions in a model are linear in nature (that is, form straight lines or flat surfaces); other times they are nonlinear (that is, form curved lines or curved surfaces). Sometimes the optimal values of the decision variables in a model must take on integer values (whole numbers); other times the decision variables can assume fractional values.

Given the diversity of MP problems that can be encountered, many techniques have been developed to solve different types of MP problems. In the next several chapters, we will look at these MP techniques and develop an understanding of how they differ and when each should be used. We will begin by examining a technique called **linear programming** (LP), which involves creating and solving optimization problems with linear objective functions and linear constraints. LP is a very powerful tool that can be applied in many business situations. It also forms a basis for several other techniques discussed later and is, therefore, a good starting point for our investigation into the field of optimization.

AN EXAMPLE LP PROBLEM

We will begin our study of LP by considering a simple example. You should not interpret this to mean that LP cannot solve more complex or realistic problems. LP has been used to solve extremely complicated problems, saving companies millions of dollars. However, jumping directly into one of these complicated problems would be like starting a marathon without ever having gone out for a jog—you would get winded and could be left behind very quickly. So we'll start with something simple.

Blue Ridge Hot Tubs manufactures and sells two models of hot tubs: the Aqua-Spa and the Hydro-Lux. Howie Jones, the owner and manager of the company, needs to decide how many of each type of hot tub to produce during his next production cycle. Howie buys prefabricated fiberglass hot tub shells from a local supplier and adds the pump and tubing to the shells to create his hot tubs. (This supplier has the capacity to deliver as many hot tub shells as Howie needs.) Howie installs the same type of pump into both hot tubs. He will have only 200 pumps available during his next production cycle. From a manufacturing standpoint, the main difference between the two models of hot tubs is the amount of tubing and labor required. Each Aqua-Spa requires 9 hours of labor and 12 feet of tubing. Each Hydro-Lux requires 6 hours of labor and 16 feet of tubing. Howie expects to have 1,566 production labor hours and 2,880 feet of tubing available during the next production cycle. Howie earns a profit of $350 on each Aqua-Spa he sells and $300 on each Hydro-Lux he sells. He is confident that he can sell all the hot tubs he produces. The question is, how many Aqua-Spas and Hydro-Luxes should Howie produce if he wants to maximize his profits during the next production cycle?

FORMULATING LP MODELS

The process of taking a practical problem—such as determining how many Aqua-Spas and Hydro-Luxes Howie should produce—and expressing it algebraically in the form of an LP model is known as **formulating** the model. Throughout the next several chapters you will see that formulating an LP model is as much an art as a science.

STEPS IN FORMULATING AN LP MODEL

There are some general steps you can follow to help make sure your formulation of a particular problem is accurate. We will walk through these steps using the hot tub example.

1. Understand the problem. This step appears to be so obvious that it hardly seems worth mentioning. However, many people have a tendency to jump into a problem and start writing the objective function and constraints before they really understand the problem. If you do not fully understand the problem you face, it is unlikely that your formulation of the problem will be correct.

The problem in our example is fairly easy to understand: how many Aqua-Spas and Hydro-Luxes should Howie produce to maximize his profit, while using no more than 200 pumps, 1,566 labor hours, and 2,880 feet of tubing?

2. Identify the decision variables. After you are sure you understand the problem, you need to identify the decision variables. That is, what are the fundamental decisions that must be made in order to solve the problem? The answers to this question often will help you identify appropriate decision variables for your model. Identifying the decision variables means determining what the symbols X_1, X_2, ..., X_n represent in your model.

In our example, the fundamental decision Howie faces is this: how many Aqua-Spas and Hydro-Luxes should be produced? In this problem we will let X_1 represent the number of Aqua-Spas to produce and X_2 represent the number of Hydro-Luxes to produce.

3. State the objective function as a linear combination of the decision variables. After determining the decision variables you will use, the next step is to create the objective function for the model. This function expresses the mathematical relationship between the decision variables in the model to be maximized or minimized.

In our example, Howie earns a profit of $350 on each Aqua-Spa ($X_1$) he sells and $300 on each Hydro-Lux ($X_2$) he sells. Thus, Howie's objective of maximizing the profit he earns is stated mathematically as:

MAX: $350X_1 + 300X_2$

For whatever values might be assigned to X_1 and X_2, the above function calculates the associated total profit that Howie would earn. Obviously, Howie wants to maximize this value.

4. State the constraints as linear combinations of the decision variables.

As mentioned earlier, there are usually some limitations on the values that can be assumed by the decision variables in an LP model. These restrictions must be identified and stated in the form of constraints.

In our example, Howie faces three major constraints. Because only 200 pumps are available and each hot tub requires one pump, Howie cannot produce more than a total of 200 hot tubs. This restriction is stated mathematically as:

$$1X_1 + 1X_2 \leq 200$$

This constraint indicates that each unit of X_1 produced (that is, each Aqua-Spa built) will use one of the 200 pumps available—as will each unit of X_2 produced (that is, each Hydro-Lux built). The total number of pumps used (represented by $1X_1 + 1X_2$) must be less than or equal to 200.

Another restriction Howie faces is that he has only 1,566 labor hours available during the next production cycle. Because each Aqua-Spa he builds (each unit of X_1) requires 9 labor hours and each Hydro-Lux (each unit of X_2) requires 6 labor hours, the constraint on the number of labor hours is stated as:

$$9X_1 + 6X_2 \leq 1,566$$

The total number of labor hours used (represented by $9X_1 + 6X_2$) must be less than or equal to the total labor hours available, which is 1,566.

The final constraint specifies that only 2,880 feet of tubing is available for the next production cycle. Each Aqua-Spa produced (each unit of X_1) requires 12 feet of tubing, and each Hydro-Lux produced (each unit of X_2) requires 16 feet of tubing. The following constraint is necessary to ensure that Howie's production plan does not use more tubing than is available:

$$12X_1 + 16X_2 \leq 2,880$$

The total number of feet of tubing used (represented by $12X_1 + 16X_2$) must be less than or equal to the total number of feet of tubing available, which is 2,880.

5. Identify any upper or lower bounds on the decision variables.

Often, simple upper or lower bounds apply to the decision variables. You can view upper and lower bounds as additional constraints in the problem.

In our example, there are simple lower bounds of zero on the variables X_1 and X_2 because it is impossible to produce a negative number of hot tubs. Therefore, the following two constraints also apply to this problem:

$$X_1 \geq 0$$

$$X_2 \geq 0$$

Constraints like these are often referred to as nonnegativity conditions, and are quite common in LP problems.

SUMMARY OF THE LP MODEL FOR THE EXAMPLE PROBLEM

The complete LP model for Howie's decision problem can be stated as:

$$\text{MAX:} \quad 350X_1 + 300X_2 \qquad \qquad \textbf{2.5}$$

$$\text{Subject to:} \quad 1X_1 + 1X_2 \leq 200 \qquad \qquad \textbf{2.6}$$

$$9X_1 + 6X_2 \leq 1{,}566 \qquad \qquad \textbf{2.7}$$

$$12X_1 + 16X_2 \leq 2{,}880 \qquad \qquad \textbf{2.8}$$

$$1X_1 \qquad \geq 0 \qquad \qquad \textbf{2.9}$$

$$1X_2 \geq 0 \qquad \qquad \textbf{2.10}$$

In this model, the decision variables X_1 and X_2 represent the number of Aqua-Spas and Hydro-Luxes to produce, respectively. Our goal is to determine the values for X_1 and X_2 that maximize the objective in equation 2.5 while simultaneously satisfying all the constraints in equations 2.6 through 2.10.

THE GENERAL FORM OF AN LP MODEL

The technique of linear programming is so-named because the MP problems to which it applies are linear in nature. That is, it must be possible to express all the functions in an LP model as some weighted sum (or linear combination) of the decision variables. So, an LP model takes on the general form:

$$\text{MAX (or MIN):} \quad c_1X_1 + c_2X_2 + \ldots + c_nX_n \qquad \qquad \textbf{2.11}$$

$$\text{Subject to:} \quad a_{11}X_1 + a_{12}X_2 + \ldots + a_{1n}X_n \leq b_1 \qquad \qquad \textbf{2.12}$$

$$\vdots$$

$$a_{k1}X_1 + a_{k2}X_2 + \ldots + a_{kn}X_n \geq b_k \qquad \qquad \textbf{2.13}$$

$$\vdots$$

$$a_{m1}X_1 + a_{m2}X_2 + \ldots + a_{mn}X_n = b_m \qquad \qquad \textbf{2.14}$$

Up to this point, we have suggested that the constraints in an LP model represent some type of limited resource. Although this is frequently the case, in later chapters you will see examples of LP models in which the constraints represent things other than limited resources. The important point here is that *any* problem that can be formulated in the above fashion is an LP problem.

The symbols c_1, c_2, ..., c_n in equation 2.11 are called **objective function coefficients** and might represent the marginal profits (or costs) associated with the decision variables X_1, X_2, ..., X_n, respectively. The symbol a_{ij} found throughout equations 2.12 through 2.14 represents the numeric coefficient in the ith constraint for variable X_j. The objective function and constraints of an LP problem represent different weighted sums of the decision variables. The b_i symbols in the constraints, once again, represent values that the corresponding linear combination of the decision variables must be less than or equal to, greater than or equal to, or equal to.

You should now see a direct connection between the LP model we formulated for Blue Ridge Hot Tubs in equations 2.5 through 2.10 and the general definition of an LP model given in equations 2.11 through 2.14. In particular, note that the various symbols used in equations 2.11 through 2.14 to represent numeric constants (that is, the c_j, a_{ij}, and b_i) were replaced by actual numeric values in equations 2.5 through 2.10. Also, note that our formulation of the LP model for Blue Ridge

Hot Tubs did not require the use of equal to constraints. Different problems require different types of constraints, and you should use whatever types of constraints are necessary for the problem at hand.

SOLVING LP PROBLEMS: AN INTUITIVE APPROACH

After an LP model has been formulated, our interest naturally turns to solving it. But before we actually solve our example problem for Blue Ridge Hot Tubs, what do you think is the optimal solution to the problem? Just by looking at the model, what values for X_1 and X_2 do you think would give Howie the largest profit?

Following one line of reasoning, it might seem that Howie should produce as many units of X_1 (Aqua-Spas) as possible because each of these generates a profit of $350, whereas each unit of X_2 (Hydro-Luxes) generates a profit of only $300. But what is the maximum number of Aqua-Spas that Howie could produce?

Howie can produce the maximum number of units of X_1 by making no units of X_2 and devoting all his resources to the production of X_1. Suppose we let $X_2 = 0$ in the model in equations 2.5 through 2.10 to indicate that no Hydro-Luxes will be produced. What then is the largest possible value of X_1? If $X_2 = 0$ then the inequality in equation 2.6 tells us:

$$X_1 \leq 200 \qquad \text{2.15}$$

So we know that X_1 cannot be any greater than 200 if $X_2 = 0$. However, we also have to consider the constraints in equations 2.7 and 2.8. If $X_2 = 0$ then the inequality in equation 2.7 reduces to:

$$9X_1 \leq 1,566 \qquad \text{2.16}$$

If we divide both sides of this inequality by 9, we find that the previous constraint is equivalent to:

$$X_1 \leq 174 \qquad \text{2.17}$$

Now consider the constraint in equation 2.8. If $X_2 = 0$ then the inequality in equation 2.8 reduces to:

$$12X_1 \leq 2,880 \qquad \text{2.18}$$

Again, if we divide both sides of this inequality by 12, we find that the previous constraint is equivalent to:

$$X_1 \leq 240 \qquad \text{2.19}$$

So, if $X_2 = 0$, the three constraints in our model imposing upper limits on the value of X_1 reduce to the values shown in equations 2.15, 2.17, and 2.19. The most restrictive of these constraints is equation 2.17. Therefore, the maximum number of units of X_1 that can be produced is 174. In other words, 174 is the largest value X_1 can take on and still satisfy all the constraints in the model.

If Howie builds 174 units of X_1 (Aqua-Spas) and 0 units of X_2 (Hydro-Luxes) he will have used all of the labor that is available for production ($9X_1 = 1,566$ if $X_1 = 174$). However, he will have 26 pumps remaining ($200 - X_1 = 26$ if $X_1 = 174$) and 792 feet of tubing remaining ($2,880 - 12X_1 = 792$ if $X_1 = 174$). Also, notice that the objective function value (or total profit) associated with this solution is:

$$\$350X_1 + \$300X_2 = \$350*174 + \$300*0 = \$60,900$$

From this analysis, we see that the solution $X_1 = 174$, $X_2 = 0$ is a *feasible solution* to the problem because it satisfies all the constraints of the model. But is it the *optimal solution*? In other words, is there any other possible set of values for X_1 and X_2 that also satisfies all the constraints *and* results in a higher objective function value? As you will see, the intuitive approach to solving LP problems that we have taken here cannot be trusted because there actually is a *better* solution to Howie's problem.

SOLVING LP PROBLEMS: A GRAPHICAL APPROACH

The constraints of an LP model define the set of feasible solutions—or the **feasible region**—for the problem. The difficulty in LP is determining which point or points in the feasible region correspond to the best possible value of the objective function. For simple problems with only two decision variables, it is fairly easy to sketch the feasible region for the LP model and locate the optimal feasible point graphically. Because the graphical approach can be used only if there are two decision variables, it has limited practical use. However, it is an extremely good way to develop a basic understanding of the strategy involved in solving LP problems. Therefore, we will use the graphical approach to solve the simple problem faced by Blue Ridge Hot Tubs. Chapter 3 shows how to solve this and other LP problems using a spreadsheet.

To solve an LP problem graphically, you first must plot the constraints for the problem and identify its feasible region. This is done by plotting the *boundary lines* of the constraints and identifying the points that will satisfy all the constraints. So how do we do this for our example problem (repeated below)?

MAX:	$350X_1 + 300X_2$	**2.20**
Subject to:	$1X_1 + 1X_2 \leq 200$	**2.21**
	$9X_1 + 6X_2 \leq 1{,}566$	**2.22**
	$12X_1 + 16X_2 \leq 2{,}880$	**2.23**
	$1X_1 \geq 0$	**2.24**
	$1X_2 \geq 0$	**2.25**

PLOTTING THE FIRST CONSTRAINT

The boundary of the first constraint in our model, which specifies that no more than 200 pumps can be used, is represented by the straight line defined by the equation:

$$X_1 + X_2 = 200 \qquad \textbf{2.26}$$

If we can find any two points on this line, the entire line can be plotted easily by drawing a straight line through these points. If $X_2 = 0$ we can see from equation 2.26 that $X_1 = 200$. Thus, the point $(X_1, X_2) = (200, 0)$ must fall on this line. If we let $X_1 = 0$, from equation 2.26, it is easy to see that $X_2 = 200$. So the point $(X_1, X_2) = (0, 200)$ must also fall on this line. These two points are plotted on the graph in Figure 2.1 and connected to form the straight line representing equation 2.26.

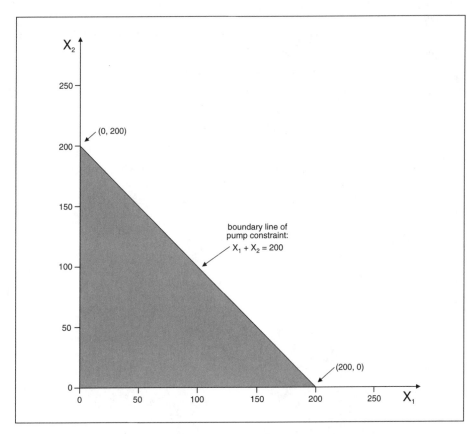

Figure 2.1: Graphical representation of the pump constraint

Note that the graph of the line associated with equation 2.26 actually extends beyond the X_1 and X_2 axes shown in Figure 2.1. However, we can disregard the points beyond these axes because the values assumed by X_1 and X_2 cannot be negative (because we also have the constraints given by $X_1 \geq 0$ and $X_2 \geq 0$).

The line connecting the points (0, 200) and (200, 0) in Figure 2.1 identifies the points (X_1, X_2), which satisfy the *equality* $X_1 + X_2 = 200$. But recall that the first constraint in the LP model is the *inequality* $X_1 + X_2 \leq 200$. Thus, after plotting the boundary line of a constraint we must determine which area on the graph corresponds to feasible solutions for the original constraint. This can be done easily by picking an arbitrary point on either side of the boundary line and checking whether it satisfies the original constraint. For example, if we test the point $(X_1, X_2) = (0, 0)$ we see that this point satisfies the first constraint. Therefore, the area of the graph on the same side of the boundary line as the point (0, 0) corresponds to the feasible solutions of our first constraint. This area of feasible solutions is shaded in Figure 2.1.

PLOTTING THE SECOND CONSTRAINT

Some of the feasible solutions to one constraint in an LP model usually will not satisfy one or more of the other constraints in the model. For example, the point $(X_1, X_2) = (200, 0)$ satisfies the first constraint in our model, but it does not satisfy the second constraint, which requires that no more than 1,566 labor hours be used (because 9*200 + 6*0 = 1,800). So, what values for X_1 and X_2 will simultaneously satisfy both of these constraints? To answer this question, we need to plot the second constraint on the graph as well. This is done in the same manner as before—by locating two points on the boundary line of the constraint and connecting these points with a straight line.

The boundary line for the second constraint in our model is given by:

$$9X_1 + 6X_2 = 1{,}566 \tag{2.27}$$

If $X_1 = 0$ in equation 2.27, then $X_2 = 1{,}566/6 = 261$. So the point $(0, 261)$ must fall on the line defined by equation 2.27. Similarly, if $X_2 = 0$ in equation 2.27 then $X_1 = 1{,}566/9 = 174$. So the point $(174, 0)$ must also fall on this line. These two points are plotted on the graph and connected with a straight line representing equation 2.27, as shown in Figure 2.2.

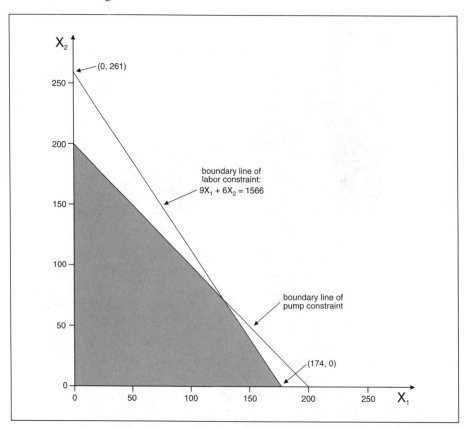

Figure 2.2: Graphical representation of the pump and labor constraints

The line drawn in Figure 2.2 representing equation 2.27 is the boundary line for our second constraint. To determine the area on the graph that corresponds to feasible solutions to the second constraint, we again need to test a point on either side of this line to see if it is feasible. The point $(X_1, X_2) = (0, 0)$ satisfies $9X_1 + 6X_2 \leq 1{,}566$. Therefore, all points on the same side of the boundary line satisfy this constraint.

PLOTTING THE THIRD CONSTRAINT

To find the set of values for X_1 and X_2 that satisfies *all* the constraints in the model we need to plot the third constraint. This constraint requires that no more than 2,880 feet of tubing be used in producing the hot tubs. Again, we will find two points on the graph that fall on the boundary line for this constraint and connect them with a straight line.

The boundary line for the third constraint in our model is:

$$12X_1 + 16X_2 = 2,880 \qquad\qquad \textbf{2.28}$$

If $X_1 = 0$ in equation 2.28, then $X_2 = 2,880/16 = 180$. So the point $(0, 180)$ must fall on the line defined by equation 2.28. Similarly, if $X_2 = 0$ in equation 2.28, then $X_1 = 2,880/12 = 240$. So the point $(240, 0)$ must also fall on this line. These two points are plotted on the graph and connected with a straight line representing equation 2.28, as shown in Figure 2.3.

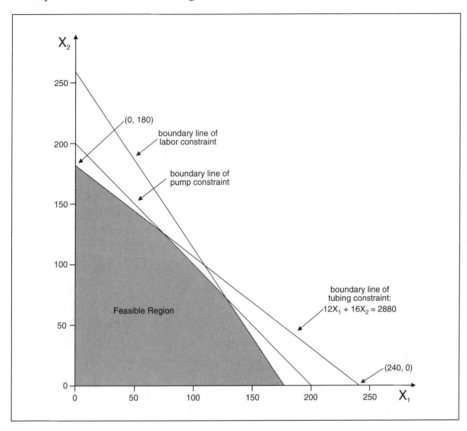

Figure 2.3: Graphical representation of the feasible region

Again, the line drawn in Figure 2.3 representing equation 2.28 is the boundary line for our third constraint. To determine the area on the graph that corresponds to feasible solutions to this constraint, we need to test a point on either side of this line to see if it is feasible. The point $(X_1, X_2) = (0, 0)$ satisfies $12X_1 + 16X_2 \leq 2,880$. Therefore, all points on the same side of the boundary line satisfy this constraint.

THE FEASIBLE REGION

It is now easy to see which points satisfy *all* the constraints in our model. These points correspond to the shaded area in Figure 2.3, labeled "Feasible Region." The **feasible region** is the set of points or values that the decision variables can assume and simultaneously satisfy all the constraints in the problem. Take a moment now to carefully compare the graphs in Figures 2.1, 2.2, and 2.3. In particular, notice that when we added the second constraint in Figure 2.2 some of the feasible solutions associated with the first constraint were eliminated because these solutions did not satisfy the second constraint. Similarly, when we added the third constraint in Figure 2.3 another portion of the feasible solutions for the first constraint was eliminated.

PLOTTING THE OBJECTIVE FUNCTION

Now that we have isolated the set of feasible solutions to our LP problem, we need to determine which of these solutions is best. That is, we must determine which point in the feasible region will maximize the value of the objective function in our model. At first glance, it might seem that trying to locate this point is like searching for a needle in a haystack. After all, as shown by the shaded region in Figure 2.3, there are an *infinite* number of feasible solutions to this problem. Fortunately, we can easily eliminate most of the feasible solutions in an LP problem from con-sideration. It can be shown that if an LP problem has an optimal solution with a finite objective function value, this solution will always occur at a point in the feasible region where two or more of the boundary lines of the constraints intersect. These points of intersection are sometimes called **corner points** or **extreme points** of the feasible region.

To see why the finite optimal solution to an LP problem occurs at an extreme point of the feasible region, consider the relationship between the objective function and the feasible region of our example LP model. Suppose we are interested in finding the values of X_1 and X_2 associated with a given level of profit, such as $35,000. Then, mathematically, we are interested in finding the points (X_1, X_2) for which our objective function equals $35,000, or where:

$$\$350X_1 + \$300X_2 = \$35,000 \hspace{4em} \textbf{2.29}$$

This equation defines a straight line, which we can plot on our graph. Specifically, if $X_1 = 0$ then, from equation 2.29, $X_2 = 116.67$. Similarly, if $X_2 = 0$ in equation 2.29, then $X_1 = 100$. So, the points $(X_1, X_2) = (0, 116.67)$ and $(X_1, X_2) = (100, 0)$ both fall on the line defining a profit level of $35,000. (Note that all the points on this line produce a profit level of $35,000.) This line is shown in Figure 2.4.

Now suppose we are interested in finding the values of X_1 and X_2 that produce some higher level of profit, such as $52,500. Then, mathematically, we are interested in finding the points (X_1, X_2) for which our objective function equals $52,500, or where:

$$\$350X_1 + \$300X_2 = \$52,500 \hspace{4em} \textbf{2.30}$$

This equation also defines a straight line, which we could plot on our graph. If we do this, we'll find that the points $(X_1, X_2) = (0, 175)$ and $(X_1, X_2) = (150, 0)$ both fall on this line, as shown in Figure 2.5.

FINDING THE OPTIMAL SOLUTION USING LEVEL CURVES

The lines in Figure 2.5 representing the two objective function values are some-times referred to as **level curves** because they represent different levels or values of the objective. Note that the two level curves in Figure 2.5 are *parallel* to one another. If we repeat this process of drawing lines associated with larger and larger values of our objective function, we will continue to observe a series of parallel lines shifting away from the origin (that is, away from the point (0, 0)). The very last level curve we can draw that still intersects the feasible region will determine the maximum profit we can achieve. This point of intersection, shown in Figure 2.6, represents the optimal feasible solution to the problem.

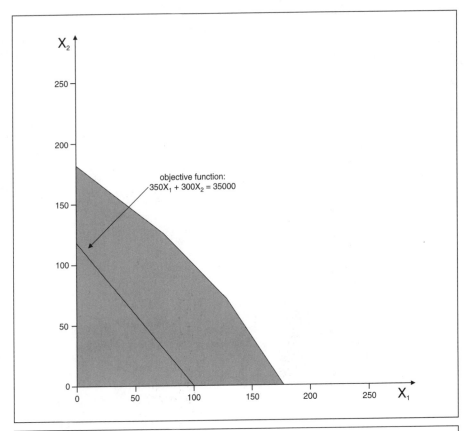

Figure 2.4: *Graph showing values of X_1 and X_2 that produce an objective function value of $35,000*

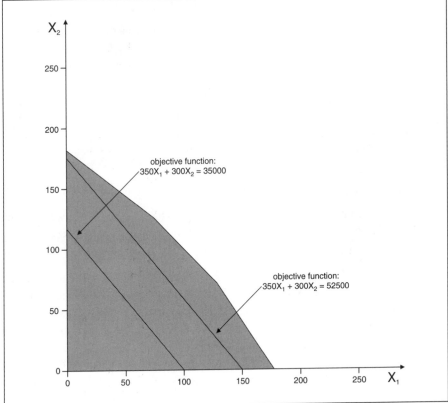

Figure 2.5: *Parallel level curves for two objective function values*

Figure 2.6: Graph showing optimal solution where the level curve is tangent to the feasible region

As shown in Figure 2.6, the optimal solution to our example problem occurs at the point where the largest possible level curve intersects the feasible region at a single point. This is the feasible point that produces the largest profit for Blue Ridge Hot Tubs. But how do we figure out exactly what point this is and how much profit it provides?

If you compare Figure 2.6 to Figure 2.3, you see that the optimal solution occurs at the point where the boundary lines of the pump and labor constraints intersect (or are equal). Thus, the optimal solution is defined by the point (X_1, X_2) that simultaneously satisfies equations 2.26 and 2.27, which are repeated below:

$$X_1 + X_2 = 200$$

$$9X_1 + 6X_2 = 1,566$$

From the first equation we easily conclude that $X_2 = 200 - X_1$. If we substitute this definition of X_2 into the second equation we obtain:

$$9X_1 + 6(200 - X_1) = 1,566$$

Using simple algebra, we can solve this equation to find that $X_1 = 122$. And because $X_2 = 200 - X_1$ we can conclude that $X_2 = 78$. Therefore, we have determined that the optimal solution to our example problem occurs at the point $(X_1, X_2) = (122, 78)$. This point satisfies all the constraints in our model and corresponds to the point in Figure 2.6 identified as the optimal solution.

The total profit associated with this solution is found by substituting the optimal values of $X_1 = 122$ and $X_2 = 78$ into the objective function. Thus, Blue Ridge Hot

Tubs can realize a profit of $66,100 if it produces 122 Aqua-Spas and 78 Hydro-Luxes ($350*122 + $300*78 = $66,100). Any other production plan would result in a lower total profit. In particular, note that the solution we found earlier using the intuitive approach (which produced a total profit of $60,900) is inferior to the optimal solution identified here.

FINDING THE OPTIMAL SOLUTION BY ENUMERATING THE CORNER POINTS

Earlier we indicated that if an LP problem has a finite optimal solution, this solution will always occur at some corner point of the feasible region. So, another way of solving an LP problem is to identify all the corner points, or extreme points, of the feasible region and calculate the value of the objective function at each of these points. The corner point with the largest objective function value is the optimal solution to the problem.

This approach is illustrated in Figure 2.7, where the X_1 and X_2 coordinates for each of the extreme points are identified along with the associated objective function values. As expected, this analysis also indicates that the point $(X_1, X_2) = (122, 78)$ is optimal.

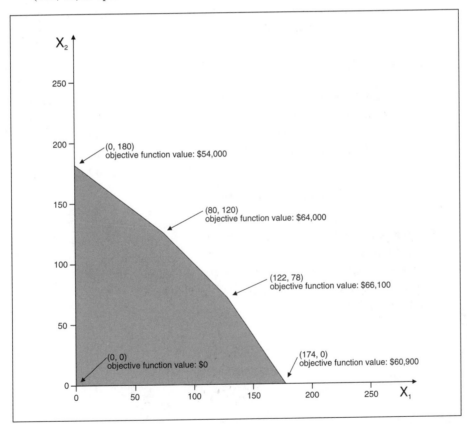

Figure 2.7: Objective function values at each extreme point of the feasible region

Enumerating the corner points to identify the optimal solution is often more difficult than the level curve approach because it requires that you identify the coordinates for *all* the extreme points of the feasible region. If there are many intersecting constraints, the number of extreme points can become rather large, making this procedure very tedious. Also, a special condition exists for which this procedure will not work. This condition, known as an **unbounded solution**, will be described shortly.

SUMMARY OF GRAPHICAL SOLUTION TO LP PROBLEMS

To summarize this section, a two-variable LP problem is solved graphically by performing these steps:

1. Plot the boundary line of each constraint in the model.

2. Identify the feasible region, that is, the set of points on the graph that simultaneously satisfy all the constraints.

3. Locate the optimal solution by one of the following methods:

   a. Plot one or more level curves for the objective function and determine the direction in which parallel shifts in this line produce improved objective function values. Shift the level curve in a parallel manner in the improving direction until it intersects the feasible region at a single point. Then find the coordinates for this point. This is the optimal solution.

   b. Identify the coordinates of all the extreme points of the feasible region and calculate the objective function values associated with each point. If the feasible region is bounded, the point with the best objective function value is the optimal solution.

SPECIAL CONDITIONS IN LP MODELS

Several special conditions can arise in LP modeling: *alternate optimal solutions, redundant constraints, unbounded solutions,* and *infeasibility*. The first two conditions do not prevent you from solving an LP model and are not really problems—they are just anomalies that sometimes occur. On the other hand, the last two conditions represent real problems that prevent us from solving an LP model.

ALTERNATE OPTIMAL SOLUTIONS

Some LP models can actually have more than one optimal solution, or **alternate optimal solutions**. That is, there can be more than one feasible point that maximizes (or minimizes) the value of the objective function.

For example, suppose Howie can increase the price of Aqua-Spas to the point where each unit sold generates a profit of $450 rather than $350. The revised LP model for this problem is:

$$
\begin{aligned}
\text{MAX:} \quad & 450X_1 + 300X_2 \\
\text{Subject to:} \quad & 1X_1 + 1X_2 \leq 200 \\
& 9X_1 + 6X_2 \leq 1{,}566 \\
& 12X_1 + 16X_2 \leq 2{,}880 \\
& 1X_1 \geq 0 \\
& 1X_2 \geq 0
\end{aligned}
$$

Because none of the constraints changed, the feasible region for this model is the same as for the earlier example. The only difference in this model is the objective function. Therefore, the level curves for the objective function are different from what we observed earlier. Several level curves for this model are plotted with its feasible region in Figure 2.8.

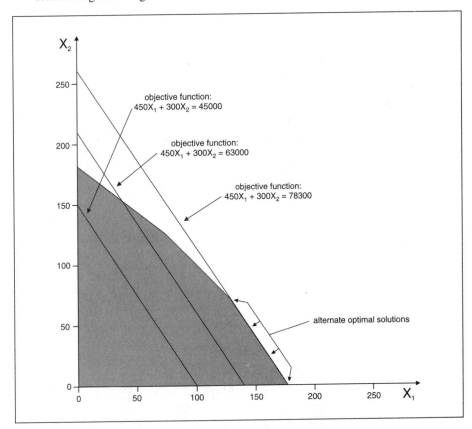

Figure 2.8: Example of an LP problem with an infinite number of alternate optimal solutions

Notice that the final level curve in Figure 2.8 intersects the feasible region along an *edge* of the feasible region rather than at a single point. All the points on the line segment joining the corner point at (122, 78) to the corner point at (174, 0) produce the same optimal objective function value of $78,300 for this problem. Thus, all these points are alternate optimal solutions to the problem. If we used a computer to solve this problem, it would identify only one of the corner points of this edge as the optimal solution.

The fact that alternate optimal solutions sometimes occur is really not a problem because this anomaly does not prevent us from finding an optimal solution to the problem. In fact, in chapter 7, Goal Programming and Multiple Objective Optimization, you will see that alternate optimal solutions are sometimes very desirable.

REDUNDANT CONSTRAINTS

Redundant constraints present another special condition that sometimes occurs in an LP model. A **redundant constraint** is a constraint that plays no role in determining the feasible region of the problem. For example, in the hot tub example, suppose that 225 hot tub pumps are available instead of 200. The earlier LP model can be modified as follows to reflect this change:

MAX: $350X_1 + 300X_2$

Subject to:

$$1X_1 + 1X_2 \leq 225$$
$$9X_1 + 6X_2 \leq 1{,}566$$
$$12X_1 + 16X_2 \leq 2{,}880$$
$$1X_1 \qquad \geq 0$$
$$1X_2 \geq 0$$

This model is identical to the original model we formulated for this problem *except* for the new upper limit on the first constraint (representing the number of pumps that can be used). The constraints and feasible region for this revised model are shown in Figure 2.9.

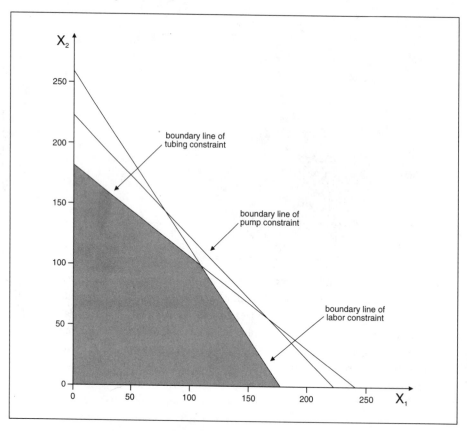

Figure 2.9: Example of a redundant constraint

Notice that the pump constraint in this model no longer plays any role in defining the feasible region of the problem. That is, as long as the tubing constraint and labor constraints are satisfied (which is always the case for any feasible solution), then the pump constraint will also be satisfied. Therefore, we can remove the pump constraint from the model without changing the feasible region of the problem—the constraint is simply redundant.

The fact that the pump constraint does not play a role in defining the feasible region in Figure 2.9 implies that there will always be an excess number of pumps available. Because none of the feasible solutions identified in Figure 2.9 fall on the boundary line of the pump constraint, this constraint will always be satisfied as a strict inequality ($1X_1 + 1X_2 < 225$) and never as a strict equality ($1X_1 + 1X_2 = 225$).

Again, redundant constraints are not really a problem. They do not prevent us (or the computer) from finding the optimal solution to an LP problem. However, they do represent "excess baggage" for the computer; so if you know that a constraint is redundant, eliminating it will save the computer this excess work. On the other hand, if the model you are working with will be modified and used repeatedly, it might be best to leave any redundant constraints in the model because they might not be redundant in the future. For example, from Figure 2.3 we know that if the availability of pumps is returned to 200, then the pump constraint again will play an important role in defining the feasible region (and optimal solution) of the problem.

UNBOUNDED SOLUTIONS

When attempting to solve some LP problems, you might encounter situations in which the objective function can be made infinitely large (in the case of a maximization problem) or infinitely small (in the case of a minimization problem). As an example, consider this LP problem:

MAX: $X_1 + X_2$

Subject to: $X_1 + X_2 \geq 400$

$-X_1 + 2X_2 \leq 400$

$X_1 \geq 0$

$X_2 \geq 0$

The feasible region and some level curves for this problem are shown in Figure 2.10. From this graph, you can see that as the level curves shift farther and farther away from the origin, the objective function increases. Because the feasible region is not bounded in this direction, you can continue shifting the level curve by an infinite amount and make the objective function infinitely large.

Although, it is not unusual to encounter an unbounded solution when solving an LP model, such a solution indicates that there is something wrong with the formulation—for example, one or more constraints were omitted from the formulation, or a less than constraint was erroneously entered as a greater than constraint.

While describing how to find the optimal solution to an LP model by enumerating corner points, we noted that this procedure will not always work if the feasible region for the problem is unbounded. Figure 2.10 provides an example of such a situation. The only extreme points for the feasible region in Figure 2.10 occur at the points (400, 0) and ($133.\overline{3}$, $266.\overline{6}$). The objective function value at both of these points (and at any point on the line segment joining them) is 400. By enumerating the extreme points for this problem we might erroneously conclude that alternate optimal solutions to this problem exist that produce an optimal objective function value of 400. This is true if the problem involved *minimizing* the objective function. However, the goal here is to *maximize* the objective function value, which, as we have seen, can be done without limit. So, when trying to solve an LP problem by enumerating the extreme points of an unbounded feasible region, you must also check whether or not the objective function is unbounded.

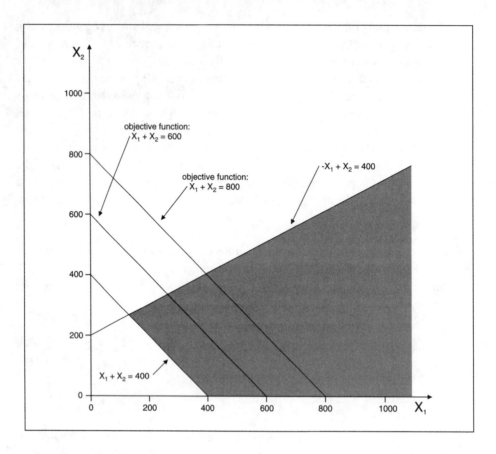

Figure 2.10: *Example of an LP problem with an unbounded solution*

INFEASIBILITY

An LP problem is **infeasible** if there is no way to simultaneously satisfy all the constraints in the problem. As an example, consider the LP model:

MAX:	$X_1 + X_2$		
Subject to:	$X_1 + X_2$	$\leq$	150
	$X_1 + X_2$	$\geq$	200
	X_1	$\geq$	0
	X_2	$\geq$	0

The feasible solutions for the first two constraints in this model are shown in Figure 2.11. Notice that the feasible solutions to the first constraint fall on the left side of its boundary line, whereas the feasible solutions to the second constraint fall on the right side of its boundary line. Therefore, no possible values for X_1 and X_2 exist that simultaneously satisfy both constraints in the model. In such a case, there are no feasible solutions to the problem.

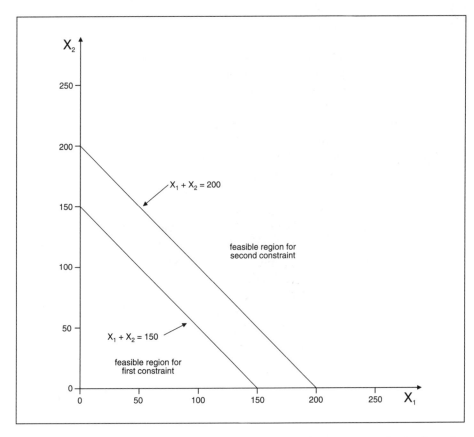

Figure 2.11: *Example of an LP problem with no feasible solution*

Infeasibility can occur in LP problems, perhaps due to an error in the formulation of the model—such as unintentionally making a less than or equal to constraint a greater than or equal to constraint. Or there just might not be a way to satisfy all the constraints in the model. In this case, constraints will have to be eliminated or loosened in order to obtain a feasible region (and feasible solution) for the problem.

Loosening constraints involves increasing the upper limits (or reducing the lower limits) to expand the range of feasible solutions. For example, if we loosen the first constraint in the previous model by changing the upper limit from 150 to 250, there is a feasible region for the problem. Of course, loosening constraints should not be done arbitrarily. In a real model, the value 150 would represent some actual characteristic of the decision problem (such as the number of pumps available to make hot tubs). We obviously cannot change this value to 250 unless it is appropriate to do so—that is, unless we know another 100 pumps can be obtained.

SUMMARY

This chapter provided an introduction to an area of management science known as mathematical programming (MP), or optimization. Optimization covers a broad range of problems that share a common goal—determining the values for the decision variables in a problem that will maximize (or minimize) some objective function while satisfying various constraints. Constraints impose restrictions on the values that can be assumed by the decision variables and define the set of feasible options (or the feasible region) for the problem.

Linear programming (LP) problems represent a special category of MP problems in which the objective function and all the constraints can be expressed as linear combinations of the decision variables. Simple, two-variable LP problems can be solved graphically by identifying the feasible region and plotting level curves for the objective function. An optimal solution to an LP problem always occurs at a corner point of its feasible region (unless the objective function is unbounded).

Some anomalies can occur in optimization problems; these include alternate optimal solutions, redundant constraints, unbounded solutions, and infeasibility.

REFERENCES

Bazaraa, M. and J. Jarvis. *Linear Programming and Network Flows*. New York: Wiley, 1990.

Dantzig, G. *Linear Programming and Extensions*. Princeton, NJ: Princeton University Press, 1963.

Shogan, A. *Management Science*. Englewood Cliffs, NJ: Prentice Hall, 1988.

Winston, W. *Operations Research: Applications and Algorithms*. Belmont, CA: Duxbury Press, 1994.

Questions and Problems

1. An LP model can have more than one optimal solution. Is it possible for an LP model to have exactly *two* optimal solutions? Why or why not?

2. In the solution to the Blue Ridge Hot Tubs problem, the optimal values for X_1 and X_2 turned out to be integers (whole numbers). Is this a general property of the solutions to LP problems? In other words, will the solution to an LP problem always consist of integers? Why or why not?

3. To determine the feasible region associated with less than or equal to constraints or greater than or equal to constraints, we graphed these constraints as if they were equal to constraints. Why is this possible?

4. Are the following objective functions for an LP model equivalent? That is, if they are both used, one at a time, to solve a problem with exactly the same constraints, will the optimal values for X_1 and X_2 be the same in both cases? Why or why not?

   MAX: $2X_1 + 3X_2$

   MIN: $-2X_1 - 3X_2$

5. Which of the following constraints are not linear or cannot be included as a constraint in a linear programming problem?

   a. $2X_1 + X_2 - 3X_3 \geq 50$

   b. $2X_1 + \sqrt{X_2} \geq 60$

   c. $4X_1 - \frac{1}{3}X_2 = 75$

   d. $\dfrac{3X_1 + 2X_2 - 3X_3}{X_1 + X_2 + X_3} \leq 0.9$

   e. $3X_1^2 + 7X_2 \leq 45$

6. Solve the following LP problem graphically by enumerating the corner points.

   MAX: $3X_1 + 4X_2$

   Subject to: $X_1 \qquad \leq 12$

   $X_2 \leq 10$

   $4X_1 + 6X_2 \leq 72$

   $X_1, X_2 \geq 0$

7. Solve the following LP problem graphically using level curves.

   MIN: $2X_1 + 3X_2$

   Subject to: $2X_1 + 1X_2 \geq 3$

   $4X_1 + 5X_2 \geq 20$

   $2X_1 + 8X_2 \geq 16$

   $5X_1 + 6X_2 \leq 60$

   $X_1, X_2 \geq 0$

8. Solve the following LP problem graphically using level curves.

    MAX: $2X_1 + 5X_2$

    Subject to:
    $$6X_1 + 5X_2 \leq 60$$
    $$2X_1 + 3X_2 \leq 24$$
    $$3X_1 + 6X_2 \leq 48$$
    $$X_1, X_2 \geq 0$$

9. Solve the following LP problem graphically by enumerating the corner points.

    MIN: $5X_1 + 20X_2$

    Subject to:
    $$X_1 + X_2 \leq 12$$
    $$2X_1 + 5X_2 \leq 40$$
    $$X_1 + X_2 \leq 15$$
    $$X_1, X_2 \geq 0$$

10. Consider the following LP problem.

    MAX: $3X_1 + 2X_2$

    Subject to:
    $$3X_1 + 3X_2 \leq 300$$
    $$6X_1 + 3X_2 \leq 480$$
    $$3X_1 + 3X_2 \leq 480$$
    $$X_1, X_2 \geq 0$$

    a. Sketch the feasible region for this model.

    b. What is the optimal solution?

    c. Identify any redundant constraints in this model.

11. Solve the following LP problem graphically by enumerating the corner points.

    MAX: $10X_1 + 12X_2$

    Subject to:
    $$8X_1 + 6X_2 \leq 98$$
    $$6X_1 + 8X_2 \leq 98$$
    $$X_1 + X_2 \geq 14$$
    $$X_1, X_2 \geq 0$$

12. Solve the following LP problem using level curves.

    MAX: $4X_1 + 5X_2$

    Subject to:
    $$2X_1 + 3X_2 \leq 120$$
    $$4X_1 + 3X_2 \leq 140$$
    $$X_1 + X_2 \geq 80$$
    $$X_1, X_2 \geq 0$$

13. The Electrotech Corporation manufactures two industrial-sized electrical devices: generators and alternators. Both of these products require wiring and testing during the assembly process. Each generator requires 2 hours of wiring and 1 hour of testing and can be sold for a $250 profit. Each alternator requires 3 hours of wiring and 2 hours of testing and can be sold for a $150 profit. There are 260 hours of wiring time and 140 hours of testing time available in the next production period.

a. Formulate an LP model for this problem.

b. Sketch the feasible region for this problem.

c. Determine the optimal solution to this problem using level curves.

14. Refer to question 13. Suppose that Electrotech's management decides that they need to make at least 20 generators and at least 20 alternators.

a. Reformulate your LP model to account for this change.

b. Sketch the feasible region for this problem.

c. Determine the optimal solution to this problem by enumerating the corner points.

15. Refer to question 14. Suppose that Electrotech can acquire additional wiring time at a very favorable cost. Should it do so? Why or why not?

16. Bill's Grill is a popular college restaurant that is famous for its hamburgers. The owner of the restaurant, Bill, mixes fresh ground beef and pork with a secret ingredient to make delicious quarter-pound hamburgers that are advertised as having no more than 25% fat. Bill can buy beef containing 80% meat and 20% fat at $0.85 per pound. He can buy pork containing 70% meat and 30% fat at $0.65 per pound. Bill wants to determine the most economical way to blend the beef and pork to make hamburgers that have no more than 25% fat.

a. Formulate an LP model for this problem. (Hint: The decision variables for this problem represent the percentage of beef and the percentage of pork to combine.)

b. Sketch the feasible region for this problem.

c. Determine the optimal solution to this problem by enumerating the corner points.

17. The Springer Dog Food Company makes dry dog food from two ingredients. The two ingredients (A and B) provide different amounts of protein and vitamins. Ingredient A provides 16 units of protein and 4 units of vitamins per pound. Ingredient B provides 8 units of protein and 8 units of vitamins per pound. Ingredients A and B cost $0.50 and $0.20 per pound, respectively. The company wants its dog food to contain at least 12 units of protein and 6 units of vitamins per pound.

a. Formulate an LP model for this problem.

b. Sketch the feasible region for this model.

c. Find the optimal solution to the problem by enumerating the corner points.

18. Refer to question 17. How will the optimal solution change if the company requires only 5 units of vitamins per pound rather than 6?

19. A farmer in Georgia has a 100 acre farm on which to plant watermelons and cantaloupes. Every acre planted with watermelons requires 50 gallons of water per day and must be prepared for planting with 20 pounds of fertilizer. Every acre planted with cantaloupes requires 75 gallons of water per day and must be prepared for planting with 15 pounds of fertilizer. The farmer estimates that it will take 2 hours of labor to harvest each acre planted with watermelons and 2.5 hours to harvest each acre planted with cantaloupes. He believes that watermelons will sell for about $4 each, and cantaloupes will sell for about $1 each. Every acre planted with watermelons is expected to yield 100 salable units. Every acre planted with cantaloupes is expected to yield 300 salable units. The farmer can pump about 6,000 gallons of water per day for irrigation purposes from a shallow well. He can buy as much fertilizer as he needs at a cost of $10 per 50-pound bag. Finally, the farmer can hire laborers to harvest the fields at a rate of $5 per hour. If the farmer sells all the watermelons and cantaloupes he produces, how many acres of each crop should the farmer plant in order to maximize profits?

    a. Formulate an LP model for this problem.

    b. Sketch the feasible region for this model.

    c. Find the optimal solution to the problem using level curves.

20. PC-Express is a computer retail store that sells two kinds of microcomputers: desktops and laptops. The company earns $600 on each desktop computer it sells and $900 on each laptop. The microcomputers PC-Express sells are actually manufactured by another company. This manufacturer has a special order to fill for another customer and cannot ship more than 80 desktop computers and 75 laptops to PC-Express next month. The employees at PC-Express must spend about 2 hours installing software and checking each desktop computer they sell. They spend roughly 3 hours to complete this process for laptop computers. They expect to have about 300 hours available for this purpose during the next month. The store's management is fairly certain that they can sell all the computers they order, but are unsure how many desktops and laptops they should order to maximize profits.

    a. Formulate an LP model for this problem.

    b. Sketch the feasible region for this model.

    c. Find the optimal solution to the problem by enumerating the corner points.

CHAPTER 3

Modeling and Solving LP Problems in a Spreadsheet

CHAPTER 2 DISCUSSED how to formulate linear programming (LP) problems and how to solve simple, two-variable LP problems graphically. As you might expect, very few real-world LP problems involve only two decision variables. So the graphical solution approach is of limited value in solving LP problems. However, the discussion of two-variable problems provides a basis for understanding the issues involved in all LP problems and the general strategies for solving them.

For example, every solvable LP problem has a feasible region, and an optimal solution to the problem can be found at some extreme point of this region (assuming the problem is not unbounded). This is true of all LP problems regardless of the number of decision variables. Although it is fairly easy to graph the feasible region for a two-variable LP problem, it is difficult to visualize or graph the feasible region of an LP problem with three variables because such a graph would be three-dimensional. If there are more than three variables it is virtually impossible to visualize or graph the feasible region for an LP problem because such a graph involves more than three dimensions.

Fortunately, several mathematical techniques have been developed to solve LP problems involving almost any number of variables without visualizing or graphing their feasible regions. These techniques are now built in to spreadsheet packages in a way that makes solving LP problems a fairly simple task. So using the appropriate computer software, you can solve almost any LP problem easily. The main challenge is ensuring that you formulate the LP problem correctly and communicate this formulation to the computer accurately. This chapter shows you how to do this using spreadsheets.

SPREADSHEET SOLVERS

The importance of LP (and optimization in general) is underscored by the fact that the latest versions of Excel, Quattro Pro, and Lotus 1-2-3 all come with built-in spreadsheet optimization tools called **solvers**. Several spreadsheet add-in packages are also available to bring the power of optimization to older versions of these spreadsheet packages. This book uses Excel to illustrate how spreadsheet solvers can solve optimization problems. However, the same concepts and techniques presented here apply to other spreadsheet packages as well.

You can also solve optimization problems without using a spreadsheet by using a specialized mathematical programming package. A partial list of these packages includes: LINDO, MPSX, CPLEX, and MathPro. Typically, these packages are used by researchers and businesses interested in solving extremely large problems that do not fit conveniently in a spreadsheet.

SOLVING LP PROBLEMS IN A SPREADSHEET

We will demonstrate the mechanics of using the Solver in Excel by solving the problem faced by Howie Jones, described in chapter 2. Howie owns and operates Blue Ridge Hot Tubs, a company that sells two models of hot tubs: the Aqua-Spa and the Hydro-Lux. Howie purchases prefabricated fiberglass hot tub shells and installs a common water pump and the appropriate amount of tubing into each hot tub. Every Aqua-Spa requires 9 hours of labor and 12 feet of tubing; every Hydro-Lux requires 6 hours of labor and 16 feet of tubing. Demand for these products is such that each Aqua-Spa produced can be sold to generate a profit of $350, and each Hydro-Lux produced can be sold to generate a profit of $300. The company expects to have 200 pumps, 1,566 hours of labor, and 2,880 feet of tubing available during the next production cycle. The problem is to determine the optimal number of Aqua-Spas and Hydro-Luxes to produce in order to maximize profits.

Chapter 2 developed the following LP formulation for the problem Howie faces. In this model, X_1 represents the number of Aqua-Spas to be produced, and X_2 represents the number of Hydro-Luxes to be produced.

$$\text{MAX}: \quad 350X_1 + 300X_2 \qquad \} \text{ profit}$$

$$\text{Subject to}: \quad 1X_1 + 1X_2 \leq 200 \qquad \} \text{ pump constraint}$$

$$9X_1 + 6X_2 \leq 1{,}566 \qquad \} \text{ labor constraint}$$

$$12X_1 + 16X_2 \leq 2{,}880 \qquad \} \text{ tubing constraint}$$

$$1X_1 \qquad\qquad \geq 0 \qquad \left.\begin{array}{c} \\ \\ \end{array}\right\} \begin{array}{l} \text{simple lower bounds} \\ \text{for the decision variables} \end{array}$$

$$1X_2 \geq 0$$

So how do you solve this problem in a spreadsheet? First you must implement, or build, this model in the spreadsheet.

IMPLEMENTING AN LP MODEL IN A SPREADSHEET

The following four steps represent guidelines you can follow in taking an algebraic formulation of an LP problem and implementing it in a spreadsheet:

1. Organize the data for the model on the spreadsheet. The data for the model consist of the coefficients in the objective function, the various coefficients in the constraints, and the right-hand-side (RHS) values for the constraints. There is usually more than one way to organize the data for a particular problem on a spreadsheet, but you should keep in mind some general guidelines. First, the goal is to organize the data so their purpose and meaning are as clear as possible. Think of your spreadsheet as a management report that needs to communicate clearly the important factors of the problem being solved. To this end, you should spend some time organizing the data for the problem in your mind's eye—visualizing how the data can be laid out logically—before you start typing values in the spreadsheet. Descriptive labels should be placed in the spreadsheet to clearly identify the various data elements. Often, row and column structures of the data in the model can be used in the spreadsheet to facilitate model implementation. (Note that some or all of the coefficients and values for an LP model might be calculated from other data, often referred to as the primary data. It is best to maintain primary data in the spreadsheet and use appropriate formulas to calculate the coefficients and values that are needed for the LP formulation. Then, if the primary data change, appropriate changes will be made automatically in the coefficients for the LP model.)

2. Reserve separate cells in the spreadsheet to represent each decision variable in the algebraic model. Although you can use any empty cells in a spreadsheet to represent the decision variables, it is usually best to arrange the cells representing the decision variables in a way that parallels the structure of the data. This is often helpful in setting up formulas for the objective function and constraints. When possible, it is also a good idea to keep the cells representing decision variables in the same area of the spreadsheet. And you should use descriptive labels to clearly identify the meaning of these cells.

3. Create a formula in a cell in the spreadsheet that corresponds to the objective function in the algebraic model. The spreadsheet formula corresponding to the objective function is created by referring to the data cells where the objective function coefficients have been entered (or calculated) and to the corresponding cells representing the decision variables.

4. For each constraint in the algebraic model, create a formula in a cell in the spreadsheet that corresponds to the left-hand-side (LHS) of the constraint. The formula corresponding to the LHS of each constraint is created by referring to the data cells where the coefficients for these constraints have been entered (or calculated) and to the appropriate decision variable cells. Many of the constraint formulas have a similar structure. Thus, when possible, you should create constraint formulas that can be copied to implement other constraint formulas. This not only reduces the effort required to implement a model, but also helps avoid hard-to-detect typing errors.

Note that the preceding steps represent guidelines—not rules. Every LP problem is somewhat different, and a good bit of skill and creativity is involved in setting up effective spreadsheet models for these problems. You might not always follow these guidelines step-by-step for every spreadsheet model you implement, but they should help focus your attention on the important considerations when you build a spreadsheet model for an LP problem. We will now demonstrate how these guidelines can be used to implement a spreadsheet model using our example problem.

A SPREADSHEET MODEL FOR THE EXAMPLE PROBLEM

One possible spreadsheet representation for our example problem is given in Figure 3.1 (and in the file FIG3-1.XLS on your data disk). Let's walk through the creation of this model step-by-step so you can see how it relates to the algebraic formulation of the model.

Figure 3.1: A spreadsheet model for the Blue Ridge Hot Tub production problem

ORGANIZING THE DATA

One of the first steps in building any spreadsheet model for an LP problem is to organize the data for the model on the spreadsheet. In Figure 3.1 we entered the data for the unit profits for Aqua-Spas and Hydro-Luxes in cells B5 and C5, respectively. Next, the number of pumps, labor hours, and feet of tubing required to produce each type of hot tub are entered in cells B8 through C10. The values in cells B8 and C8 indicate that one pump is required to produce each type of hot tub. The values in cells B9 and C9 show that each Aqua-Spa produced requires 9 hours of labor, and each Hydro-Lux requires 6 hours. Cells B10 and C10 indicate that each Aqua-Spa produced requires 12 feet of tubing, and each Hydro-Lux requires 16 feet. The available number of pumps, labor hours, and feet of tubing are entered in cells E8 through E10. Notice that appropriate labels are also entered to identify all the data elements for the problem.

REPRESENTING THE DECISION VARIABLES

As indicated in Figure 3.1, cells B4 and C4 represent the decision variables X_1 and X_2 in our algebraic model. The values of zero in these cells indicate that they are reserved for representing the variables in our model. We will use Solver to determine the optimal values for these cells. Figure 3.2 summarizes the relationship between the decision variables in the algebraic model and the corresponding cells in the spreadsheet.

Decision Variables: X_1 X_2

                         ↓   ↓

Spreadsheet Cells: B4   C4

Figure 3.2: Summary of relationship between the decision variables and corresponding spreadsheet cells

REPRESENTING THE OBJECTIVE FUNCTION

The next step in implementing our LP problem is to create a formula in a cell of the spreadsheet to represent the objective function. We can accomplish this in many ways. Because the objective function is $350X_1 + 300X_2$, you might be tempted to enter the formula =350*B4+300*C4 in the spreadsheet. However, if you wanted to change the coefficients in the objective function, you would have to go back and edit this formula to reflect the changes. Because the objective function coefficients are entered in cells B5 and C5, a better way of implementing the objective function is to refer to the values in cells B5 and C5 rather than entering numeric constants in the formula. The formula for the objective function is entered in cell E5 as:

Formula for cell E5:   =B5*B4+C5*C4

As shown in Figure 3.1, cell E5 initially returns the value 0 because cells B4 and C4 both contain zeros. Figure 3.3 summarizes the relationship between the algebraic objective function and the formula entered in cell E5. By implementing the objective function in this manner, if the profits earned on the hot tubs ever change, the spreadsheet model can be changed easily and the problem can be re-solved to determine the impact of this change on the optimal solution.

Algebraic Objective: 350 X_1 + 300 X_2

                         ↓   ↓   ↓ ↓

Formula in cell E5:   =B5*B4+C5*C4

Figure 3.3: Summary of relationship between the algebraic objective function and spreadsheet representation of the formula

REPRESENTING THE CONSTRAINTS

The next step in building the spreadsheet model involves implementing the constraints of the LP model. Earlier we said that for each constraint in the algebraic model, you must create a formula in a cell of the spreadsheet that corresponds to the LHS of the constraint. The LHS of each constraint in our model is:

LHS of the pump constraint

$$1X_1 + 1X_2 \le 200$$

LHS of the labor constraint

$$9X_1 + 6X_2 \le 1{,}566$$

LHS of the tubing constraint

$$12X_1 + 16X_2 \le 2{,}880$$

We need to set up three cells in the spreadsheet to represent the LHS formulas of the three constraints. Again, this is done by referring to the data cells containing the coefficients for these constraints and to the cells representing the decision variables. The LHS of the first constraint is entered in cell D8 as:

Formula for cell D8:   =B8*B4+C8*C4

Similarly, the LHS of the second and third constraints are entered in cells D9 and D10 as:

Formula for cell D9:   =B9*B4+C9*C4

Formula for cell D10:   =B10*B4+C10*C4

These formulas calculate the number of pumps, hours of labor, and feet of tubing required to manufacture the number of hot tubs represented in cells B4 and C4. Figure 3.4 summarizes the relationship between the LHS formulas of the constraints in the algebraic formulation of our model and their spreadsheet representations.

Figure 3.4: Summary of relationship between the LHS formulas of the constraints and their spreadsheet representations

LHS formula for the pump constraint:	$1 \quad X_1 + 1 \quad X_2$
	↓ ↓ ↓ ↓
Formula in cell D8:	=B8*B4+C8*C4
LHS formula for the labor constraint:	$9 \quad X_1 + 6 \quad X_2$
	↓ ↓ ↓ ↓
Formula in cell D9:	=B9*B4+C9*C4
LHS formula for the tubing constraint:	$12 \quad X_1 + 16 \quad X_2$
	↓ ↓ ↓ ↓
Formula in cell D10:	=B10*B4+C10*C4

We know that Blue Ridge Hot Tubs has 200 pumps, 1,566 labor hours, and 2,880 feet of tubing available during its next production run. In our algebraic formulation of the LP model, these values represent the RHS values for the three constraints. Therefore, we entered the available number of pumps, hours of labor, and feet of tubing in cells E8, E9, and E10, respectively. These terms indicate the upper limits on the values cells D8, D9, and D10 can assume.

REPRESENTING THE BOUNDS ON THE DECISION VARIABLES

Now what about the simple lower bounds on our decision variables represented by $X_1 \geq 0$ and $X_2 \geq 0$? These conditions are quite common in LP problems and are referred to as **nonnegativity conditions** because they indicate that the decision variables can assume only nonnegative values. These conditions might seem like constraints and can, in fact, be implemented like the other constraints. However, Solver allows you to specify simple upper and lower bounds for the decision variables by referring directly to the cells representing the decision variables. Thus, at this point, we have taken no specific action to implement these bounds in our spreadsheet.

HOW SOLVER VIEWS THE MODEL

After implementing our algebraic model in the spreadsheet, we can use Solver to find the optimal solution to the problem. But first, we need to define the following three components of our spreadsheet model for Solver:

1. Target cell—the cell in the spreadsheet that represents the *objective function* in the model (and whether its value should be maximized or minimized)

2. Changing cells—the cells in the spreadsheet that represent the *decision variables* in the model

3. Constraint cells—the cells in the spreadsheet that represent the *LHS formulas* of the constraints in the model (and any upper and lower bounds that apply to these formulas)

These components correspond directly to the cells in the spreadsheet we established when implementing the LP model. For example, in the spreadsheet for our example problem, the target cell is represented by cell E5, the changing cells are represented by cells B4 and C4, and the constraint cells are represented by cells D8, D9, and D10. Figure 3.5 shows these relationships.

Figure 3.5: Summary of
Solver's view of the model

By comparing Figure 3.1 with Figure 3.5, you can see the direct connection between the way we formulate LP models algebraically and how Solver views the spreadsheet implementation of the model. The decision variables in the algebraic model correspond to the changing cells for Solver. The LHS formulas for the different constraints in the algebraic model correspond to the constraint cells for Solver. Finally, the objective function in the algebraic model corresponds to the target cell for Solver. So although the terminology Solver uses to describe spreadsheet LP models is different from the terminology we use to describe LP models algebraically, the concepts are the same. Figure 3.6 summarizes these differences in terminology.

Terms used to describe LP models algebraically	Corresponding terms used by Solver to describe spreadsheet LP models
objective function	target cell
decision variables	changing cells
LHS formulas of constraints	constraint cells

Figure 3.6: Summary of
Solver terminology

USING SOLVER

After implementing an LP model in a spreadsheet, we still need to solve the model. To do this we must first indicate to Solver which cells in the spreadsheet represent the objective function (or target cell), the decision variables (or changing cells), and the constraints (or constraint cells). To invoke Solver in Excel, choose the Solver command from the Tools menu, as shown in Figure 3.7. This displays the Solver Parameters dialog box shown in Figure 3.8. Then complete the options in the Solver Parameters dialog box.

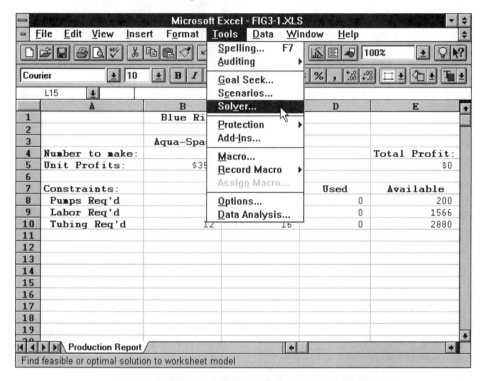

Figure 3.7: Command for invoking Solver

Figure 3.8: The Solver Parameters dialog box

DEFINING THE TARGET CELL

In the Solver Parameters dialog box, specify the location of the cell that represents the objective function by entering it in the Set Target Cell box, as shown in Figure 3.9.

Figure 3.9: Specifying the target cell

Notice that cell E5 is the target cell and that we instructed Solver to set the target cell value equal to the maximum possible value, as specified by the Max button. Select the Min button when you want Solver to find a solution that minimizes the value of the target cell. The Value button finds a solution where the objective function has a specific value.

DEFINING THE CHANGING CELLS

To solve our LP problem, we also need to indicate which cells represent the decision variables in the model. Again, Solver refers to these cells as changing cells. The changing cells for our example problem are specified as shown in Figure 3.10.

Cells B4 and C4 represent the decision variables (or changing cells) for the model. Solver will determine the optimal values for these cells. If the decision variables were not in a contiguous range, we would have to list the individual decision variable cells separated by commas in the By Changing Cells box. Whenever possible, it is best to use contiguous cells to represent the decision variables.

Figure 3.10: Specifying the changing cells

Guess What?

The Guess button in the Solver Parameters dialog box instructs Solver to make an educated guess regarding which cells in the spreadsheet represent the decision variables. Although Solver sometimes guesses correctly, more frequently it is wrong. It is better to tell Solver where the decision variables are located and leave the guesswork out of this process.

DEFINING THE CONSTRAINT CELLS

Next we must define the constraint cells in the spreadsheet and the restrictions that apply to these cells. As mentioned earlier, the constraint cells are the cells in which we implemented the LHS formulas for each constraint in our model. To define the constraint cells, click the Add button shown in Figure 3.10, then complete the Add Constraint dialog box shown in Figure 3.11. In the Add Constraint dialog box, click the Add button again to define additional constraints. Click the OK button when you have finished defining constraints.

Cells D8 through D10 represent constraint cells whose values must be less than or equal to the values in cells E8 through E10, respectively. If the constraint cells were not in contiguous cells in the spreadsheet, we would have to define the constraint cells repeatedly. As with the changing cells, it is usually best to choose contiguous cells in your spreadsheet to implement the LHS formulas of the constraints in a model.

INDICATE LHS FORMULA CELLS

INDICATE RHS VALUE CELLS

Figure 3.11: Specifying the constraint cells

If you want to define more than one constraint at the same time, as in Figure 3.11, all the constraint cells you select must be the same type (that is, they must all be ≤, ≥, or =). Therefore, it is a good idea to keep constraints of a given type grouped in contiguous cells so you can select them at the same time. For example, in our case, the three constraint cells we selected are all less than or equal to (≤) constraints. However, this consideration should not take precedence over setting up the spreadsheet in the way that communicates its purpose most clearly.

DEFINING THE NONNEGATIVITY CONDITIONS

One final specification we need to make for our model is that the decision variables must be greater than or equal to zero. As mentioned earlier, we can impose these conditions as constraints by placing appropriate restrictions on the values that can be assigned to the cells representing the decision variables (in this case, cells B4 and C4). To do this, we simply add another set of constraints to the model, as shown in Figure 3.12.

Figure 3.12: Adding the nonnegativity conditions for the problem

Figure 3.12 indicates that cells B4 and C4, which represent the decision variables in our model, must be greater than or equal to zero. Notice that the RHS value of this constraint is a numeric constant that is entered manually. The same type of constraints can also be used if we placed some strictly positive lower bounds on these variables (for example, if we wanted to produce at least 10 Aqua-Spas and at least 10 Hydro-Luxes). However, in that case it probably would be best to place the minimum required production amounts on the spreadsheet so that these restrictions are clearly displayed. We can then refer to those cells in the spreadsheet when specifying the RHS values for these constraints.

REVIEWING THE MODEL

After specifying all the constraints for our model, the final Solver Parameters dialog box appears, as shown in Figure 3.13. This dialog box provides a summary of how Solver views our model. It is a good idea to review this information before solving the model to make sure you entered all the parameters correctly and to correct any errors before proceeding.

OPTIONS

Solver provides a number of options that affect how it solves a problem. These options are available in the Solver Options dialog box, which you display by clicking the Options button in the Solver Parameters dialog box. Figure 3.14 shows the Solver Options dialog box.

Figure 3.13: Summary of
how Solver views the model

SELECT THIS OPTION

Figure 3.14: The Solver
Options dialog box

Notice the option named Assume Linear Model. If the problem you are trying to solve is an LP problem (that is, an optimization problem with a linear objective function and linear constraints) Solver can use a special algorithm known as the *simplex method* to solve the problem. The simplex method provides an efficient way of solving LP problems and, therefore, requires less solution time. Furthermore, using the simplex method allows for expanded sensitivity information about the solution obtained. (Chapter 4 discusses this in detail.) In any event, when using Solver to solve an LP problem, it is a good idea to select the Assume Linear Model option as indicated in Figure 3.14.

The Max Time and Iterations options determine how much time and effort Solver is allowed in attempting to solve the problem. The default settings for these options work well and should be changed only if Solver runs out of time while trying to solve a particular problem.

The Precision option specifies how much rounding error is allowed in the solutions Solver obtains. Whenever you use a computer to solve a difficult math problem, slight rounding or precision errors can enter the solution. For example, Solver might obtain an optimal solution that requires the use of 200.00000906 pumps, which *technically* violates the upper bound of 200 specified for the number of pumps available. However, because there is no *practical* difference between the value 200 and 200.00000906, you might consider this solution to be close enough or within an acceptable tolerance of satisfying the constraints. This type of precision problem is common and seldom poses a practical problem. If you need a more precise solution to a problem, you can use the Precision option to control the level of precision Solver uses in checking the feasibility of its solutions.

The Tolerance option relates to solving integer programming problems, and is discussed in detail in chapter 6. The Estimates, Derivatives, and Search options are discussed in chapter 8.

SOLVING THE MODEL

After entering all the appropriate parameters and choosing any necessary options for our model, the next step is to solve the problem. Click the Solve button in the Solver Parameters dialog box to solve the problem. When Solver finds the optimal solution, it displays the Solver Results dialog box shown in Figure 3.15. If the values on your screen do not match those in Figure 3.15, click the Restore Original Values option button, click OK, then re-enter the parameters and options.

This dialog box provides options for keeping the solution found by Solver or restoring the spreadsheet to its original condition. Most often you'll want to keep Solver's solution unless there is an obvious problem with it. Notice that the Solver Results dialog box also provides options for generating Answer, Sensitivity, and Limits reports. Chapter 4 discusses these options.

As shown in Figure 3.15, Solver determined that the optimal value for cell B4 is 122 and the optimal value for cell C4 is 78. These values correspond to the optimal values for X_1 and X_2 that we determined graphically in chapter 2. The value of the target cell (E5) now indicates that if Blue Ridge Hot Tubs produces and sells 122 Aqua-Spas and 78 Hydro-Luxes, the company will earn a profit of $66,100. Cells D8, D9, and D10 indicate that this solution uses all the 200 available pumps, all the 1,566 available labor hours, and 2,712 of the 2,880 feet of available tubing.

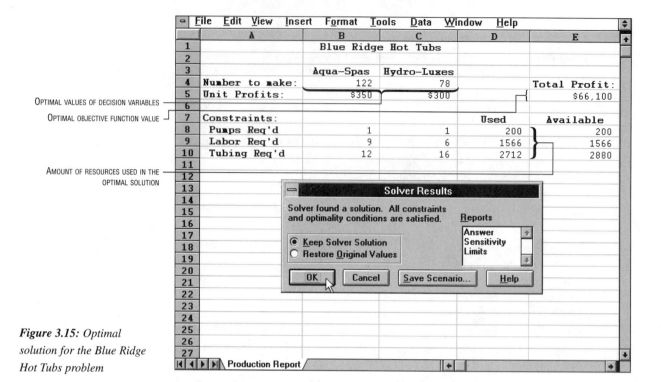

OPTIMAL VALUES OF DECISION VARIABLES

OPTIMAL OBJECTIVE FUNCTION VALUE

AMOUNT OF RESOURCES USED IN THE OPTIMAL SOLUTION

Figure 3.15: *Optimal solution for the Blue Ridge Hot Tubs problem*

SETTING UP AND SOLVING OTHER LP PROBLEMS

Now that you have a basic idea of how Solver works and how to set up an LP model in a spreadsheet, we'll walk through several more examples of formulating LP models and solving them with Solver. These problems will help you develop the skills you need to formulate LP models and will also show you some helpful "tricks of the trade." These problems also highlight the wide variety of business problems in which LP can be applied.

As we proceed, keep in mind that you can set up these problems more than one way. Creating spreadsheet models that effectively communicate their purpose is very much an art—or at least an acquired skill. The spreadsheet models in this chapter represent finished products that involved a great deal of moving and copying data, and inserting and deleting rows and columns.

These example problems should also help you understand what must be done to set up and solve an LP model in a spreadsheet, and give you some ideas for solving the problems at the end of this chapter. When you work through the end of the chapter problems, you will better appreciate how much thought is required to find a good way to implement a given model.

MAKE VS. BUY DECISIONS

As mentioned at the beginning of chapter 2, LP is particularly well suited to problems where scarce or limited resources must be allocated or used in an optimal manner. Numerous examples of these types of problems occur in manufacturing organizations. For example, LP might be used to determine how the various components of a job should be assigned to multi-purpose machines in order to minimize the time it takes to complete the job. As another example, a company might receive an order for several items that it cannot fill entirely with its own production capacity. In such a case, the company must determine which items to produce and which items to subcontract (or buy) from an outside supplier. The following is an example of this type of make vs. buy decision.

The Electro-Poly Corporation is the world's leading manufacturer of slip rings. A slip ring is an electrical coupling device that allows current to pass through a spinning or rotating connection—such as a gun turret on a ship, aircraft, or tank. The company recently received a $750,000 order for various quantities of three types of slip rings. Each slip ring requires a certain amount of time to wire and harness. The following table summarizes the requirements for the three models of slip rings.

	Model 1	Model 2	Model 3
Number Ordered	3,000	2,000	900
Hours of Wiring Required per Unit	2	1.5	3
Hours of Harnessing Required per Unit	1	2	1

Unfortunately, Electro-Poly does not have enough wiring and harnessing capacity to fill the order by its due date. The company has only 10,000 hours of wiring capacity and 5,000 hours of harnessing capacity available to devote to this order. However, the company can subcontract any portion of this order to one of its competitors. The unit costs of producing each model in-house and buying the finished products from a competitor are summarized below.

	Model 1	Model 2	Model 3
Cost to Make	$50	$83	$130
Cost to Buy	$61	$97	$145

Electro-Poly wants to determine the number of slip rings to make and the number to buy in order to fill the customer order at the least possible cost.

DEFINING THE DECISION VARIABLES

To solve the Electro-Poly problem, we need six decision variables to represent the alternatives under consideration. The six variables are:

M_1 = number of model 1 slip rings to make in-house

M_2 = number of model 2 slip rings to make in-house

M_3 = number of model 3 slip rings to make in-house

B_1 = number of model 1 slip rings to buy from competitor

B_2 = number of model 2 slip rings to buy from competitor

B_3 = number of model 3 slip rings to buy from competitor

As mentioned in chapter 2, we do not have to use the symbols X_1, X_2, ..., X_n for the decision variables. If other symbols better clarify the model, you are certainly free to use them. In this case, the symbols M_i and B_i help distinguish the **M**ake in-house variables from the **B**uy from competitor variables.

DEFINING THE OBJECTIVE FUNCTION

The objective in this problem is to minimize the total cost of filling the order. Recall that each model 1 slip ring made in-house (each unit of M_1) costs \$50; each model 2 slip ring made in-house (each unit of M_2) costs \$83; and each model 3 slip ring (each unit of M_3) costs \$130. Each model 1 slip ring bought from the competitor (each unit of B_1) costs \$61; each model 2 slip ring bought from the competitor (each unit of B_2) costs \$97; and each model 3 slip ring bought from the competitor (each unit of B_3) costs \$145. Thus, the objective is stated mathematically as:

MIN: $50M_1 + 83M_2 + 130M_3 + 61B_1 + 97B_2 + 145B_3$

DEFINING THE CONSTRAINTS

Several constraints affect this problem. Two constraints are needed to ensure that the number of slip rings made in-house does not exceed the available capacity for wiring and harnessing. These constraints are stated as:

$2M_1 + 1.5M_2 + 3M_3 \le 10,000$ } wiring constraint

$1M_1 + 2M_2 + 1M_3 \le 5,000$ } harnessing constraint

Three additional constraints ensure that 3,000 model 1 slip rings, 2,000 model 2 slip rings, and 900 model 3 slip rings are available to fill the order. These constraints are stated as:

$M_1 + B_1 = 3,000$ } demand for model 1

$M_2 + B_2 = 2,000$ } demand for model 2

$M_3 + B_3 = 900$ } demand for model 3

Finally, because none of the variables in the model can assume a value of less than zero, we also need the following nonnegativity condition:

$M_1, M_2, M_3, B_1, B_2, B_3 \ge 0$

IMPLEMENTING THE MODEL

The LP model for Electro-Poly's make vs. buy problem is summarized as:

MIN: $50M_1 + 83M_2 + 130M_3 + 61B_1 + 97B_2 + 145B_3$ } total costs

Subject to: $M_1 + B_1 = 3,000$ } demand for model 1

$M_2 + B_2 = 2,000$ } demand for model 2

$M_3 + B_3 = 900$ } demand for model 3

$2M_1 + 1.5M_2 + 3M_3 \le 10,000$ } wiring constraint

$1M_1 + 2M_2 + 1M_3 \le 5,000$ } harnessing constraint

$M_1, M_2, M_3, B_1, B_2, B_3 \ge 0$ } nonnegativity conditions

The data for this model are implemented in the spreadsheet shown in Figure 3.16 (and in the file FIG3-16.XLS on your data disk). The coefficients that appear in the objective function are entered in the range B9 through D10. The coefficients for the LHS formulas for the wiring and harnessing constraints are entered in cells B16 through D17, and the corresponding RHS values are entered in cells F16 and F17. Because the LHS formulas for the demand constraints involve simply summing the decision variables, we do not need to list the coefficients for these constraints in the spreadsheet. The RHS values for the demand constraints are entered in cells B13 through D13.

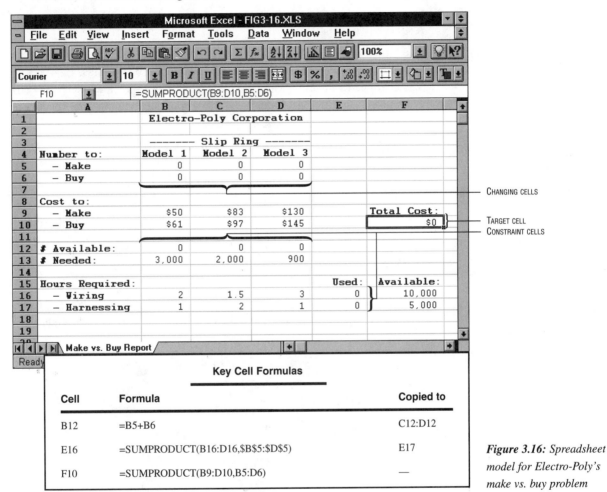

Figure 3.16: Spreadsheet model for Electro-Poly's make vs. buy problem

Cells B5 through D6 contain zeros to indicate that these cells are reserved to represent the six variables in our algebraic model. The objective function could be entered in cell F10 as:

Formula for cell F10:   =B9*B5+C9*C5+D9*D5+B10*B6+C10*C6+D10*D6

In this formula, the values in the range B5 through D6 are multiplied by the corresponding values in the range B9 through D10; these individual products are then added together. Therefore, the formula is simply the sum of a collection of products—or a *sum of products*. It turns out that this formula can be implemented in an equivalent (and easier) way as:

Equivalent formula for cell F10:   =SUMPRODUCT(B9:D10,B5:D6)

The preceding formula takes the values in the range B9 through D10, multiplies them by the corresponding values in the range B5 through D6, and adds (or sums) these products. The SUMPRODUCT() function greatly simplifies the implementation of many formulas required in optimization problems.

Because the LHS of the demand constraint for model 1 slip rings involves adding variables M_1 and B_1, this constraint is implemented in cell B12 by adding the two cells in the spreadsheet that correspond to these variables—cells B5 and B6:

Formula for cell B12:   =B5+B6
(copy to C12 through D12)

The formula in cell B12 is then copied to cells C12 and D12 to implement the LHS formulas for the constraints for model 2 and model 3 slip rings.

The coefficients for the wiring and harnessing constraints are entered in cells B16 through D16. The LHS formula for the wiring constraint is implemented in cell E16 as:

Formula for cell E16:   =SUMPRODUCT(B16:D16,$B$5:$D$5)
(copy to cell E17)

This formula is then copied to cell E17 to implement the LHS formula for the harnessing constraint. (In the preceding formula, the dollar signs denote absolute cell references. An **absolute cell reference** will not change if the formula containing the reference is copied to another location.)

SOLVING THE MODEL

To solve this model we need to specify the target cell, changing cells, and constraint cells identified in Figure 3.16, just as we did earlier in the Blue Ridge Hot Tubs example. Figure 3.17 shows the Solver parameters and options required to solve Electro-Poly's make vs. buy problem.

Figure 3.17: Solver parameters and options for the make vs. buy problem

After we click the Solve button in the Solver Parameters dialog box, Solver finds the optimal solution shown in Figure 3.18.

	A	B	C	D	E	F
						=SUMPRODUCT(B9:D10,B5:D6) [F10]
1			Electro-Poly Corporation			
2						
3			———— Slip Ring ————			
4	Number to:	Model 1	Model 2	Model 3		
5	— Make	3,000	550	900		
6	— Buy	0	1,450	0		
7						
8	Cost to:					
9	— Make	$50	$83	$130		Total Cost:
10	— Buy	$61	$97	$145		$453,300
11						
12	# Available:	3,000	2,000	900		
13	# Needed:	3,000	2,000	900		
14						
15	Hours Required:				Used:	Available:
16	— Wiring	2	1.5	3	9,525	10,000
17	— Harnessing	1	2	1	5,000	5,000
18						
19						

Make vs. Buy Report

Figure 3.18: Optimal solution to Electro-Poly's make vs. buy problem

ANALYZING THE SOLUTION

The optimal solution shown in Figure 3.18 indicates that Electro-Poly should make (in-house) 3,000 model 1 slip rings, 550 model 2 slip rings, and 900 model 3 slip rings (that is, $M_1 = 3,000$, $M_2 = 550$, $M_3 = 900$). Additionally, it should buy 1,450 model 2 slip rings from its competitor (that is, $B_1 = 0$, $B_2 = 1,450$, $B_3 = 0$). This solution allows Electro-Poly to fill the customer order at a minimum cost of $453,300. This solution uses 9,525 of the 10,000 hours of available wiring capacity and all 5,000 hours of the harnessing capacity.

At first glance, this solution might seem a bit surprising. Electro-Poly has to pay $97 for each model 2 slip ring it purchases from its competitor. This represents a $14 premium over its in-house cost of $83. On the other hand, Electro-Poly has to pay a premium of $11 over its in-house cost to purchase model 1 slip rings from its competitor. It seems as if the optimal solution would be to purchase model 1 slip rings from its competitor rather than model 2 slip rings because the additional cost premium for model 1 slip rings is smaller. However, this argument fails to consider the fact that each model 2 slip ring produced in-house uses *twice* as much of the company's harnessing capacity as does each model 1 slip ring. Making more model 2 slip rings in-house would deplete the company's harnessing capacity more quickly, and would require buying an excessive number of model 1 slip rings from the competitor. Fortunately, the LP technique automatically considers such trade-offs in determining the optimal solution to the problem.

A SCHEDULING PROBLEM

Anyone responsible for creating work schedules for a number of employees can appreciate the difficulties in this task. It can be very difficult to develop a *feasible* schedule, much less an *optimal* schedule. Trying to ensure that a sufficient number of workers is available when needed is a complicated task when you must consider multiple shifts, rest breaks, and lunch or dinner breaks. However, some sophisticated LP models have been devised to solve these problems. Although a discussion of these models is beyond the scope of this text, we will consider a simple example of an employee scheduling problem to give you an idea of how LP models are applied in this area.

Air-Express is an express shipping service that guarantees overnight delivery of packages anywhere in the continental United States. The company has various operations centers, called hubs, at airports in major cities across the country. Packages are received at hubs from other locations and then shipped to intermediate hubs or to their final destinations.

The manager of the Air-Express hub in Baltimore, Maryland, is concerned about labor costs at the hub and is interested in determining the most effective way to schedule workers. The hub operates seven days a week, and the number of packages it handles each day varies from one day to the next. Using historical data on the average number of packages received each day, the manager estimates the number of workers needed to handle the packages as:

Day of Week	Workers Required
Sunday	18
Monday	27
Tuesday	22
Wednesday	26
Thursday	25
Friday	21
Saturday	19

The package handlers working for Air-Express are unionized and are guaranteed a five-day work week with two consecutive days off. The base wage for the handlers is $655 per week. Because most workers prefer to have Saturday or Sunday off, the union has negotiated bonuses of $25 per day for its members who work on these days. The possible shifts and salaries for package handlers are:

Shift	Days Off	Wage
1	Sunday and Monday	$680
2	Monday and Tuesday	$705
3	Tuesday and Wednesday	$705
4	Wednesday and Thursday	$705
5	Thursday and Friday	$705
6	Friday and Saturday	$680
7	Saturday and Sunday	$655

The manager wants to keep the total wage expense for the hub as low as possible. With this in mind, how many package handlers should be assigned to each shift if the manager wants to have a sufficient number of workers available each day?

DEFINING THE DECISION VARIABLES

In this problem, the manager must decide how many workers to assign to each shift. Because there are seven possible shifts, we need the following seven decision variables:

X_1 = the number of workers assigned to shift 1

X_2 = the number of workers assigned to shift 2

X_3 = the number of workers assigned to shift 3

X_4 = the number of workers assigned to shift 4

X_5 = the number of workers assigned to shift 5

X_6 = the number of workers assigned to shift 6

X_7 = the number of workers assigned to shift 7

Another way to represent this is:

X_i = the number of workers assigned to shift i, for i = 1, 2, ..., 7

DEFINING THE OBJECTIVE FUNCTION

The objective in this problem is to minimize the total wages paid. Each worker on shift 1 and 6 is paid $680 per week, and each worker on shift 7 is paid $655. All other workers are paid $705 per week. Thus, the objective of minimizing the total wage expense is expressed as:

MIN: $680X_1 + 705X_2 + 705X_3 + 705X_4 + 705X_5 + 680X_6 + 655X_7$ } total wage expense

DEFINING THE CONSTRAINTS

The constraints for this problem must ensure that at least 18 workers are scheduled for Sunday, at least 27 are scheduled for Monday, and so on. We need one constraint for each day of the week.

To make sure that at least 18 workers are available on Sunday, we must determine which decision variables represent shifts that are scheduled to work on Sunday. Because shifts 1 and 7 are the only shifts that have Sunday scheduled as a day off, the remaining shifts, 2 through 6, all are scheduled to work on Sunday. The following constraint ensures that at least 18 workers are available on Sunday:

$$0X_1 + 1X_2 + 1X_3 + 1X_4 + 1X_5 + 1X_6 + 0X_7 \geq 18 \quad \text{} \} \text{ workers required on Sunday}$$

Because workers on shifts 1 and 2 have Monday off, the constraint for Monday should ensure that the sum of the variables representing the number of workers on the remaining shifts, 3 through 7, is at least 27. This constraint is expressed as:

$$0X_1 + 0X_2 + 1X_3 + 1X_4 + 1X_5 + 1X_6 + 1X_7 \geq 27 \quad \text{} \} \text{ workers required on Monday}$$

Constraints for the remaining days of the week are generated easily by applying the same logic used in generating the previous two constraints. The resulting constraints are stated as:

$$1X_1 + 0X_2 + 0X_3 + 1X_4 + 1X_5 + 1X_6 + 1X_7 \geq 22 \quad \text{} \} \text{ workers required on Tuesday}$$

$$1X_1 + 1X_2 + 0X_3 + 0X_4 + 1X_5 + 1X_6 + 1X_7 \geq 26 \quad \text{} \} \text{ workers required on Wednesday}$$

$$1X_1 + 1X_2 + 1X_3 + 0X_4 + 0X_5 + 1X_6 + 1X_7 \geq 25 \quad \text{} \} \text{ workers required on Thursday}$$

$$1X_1 + 1X_2 + 1X_3 + 1X_4 + 0X_5 + 0X_6 + 1X_7 \geq 21 \quad \text{} \} \text{ workers required on Friday}$$

$$1X_1 + 1X_2 + 1X_3 + 1X_4 + 1X_5 + 0X_6 + 0X_7 \geq 19 \quad \text{} \} \text{ workers required on Saturday}$$

All our decision variables must assume nonnegative values. This nonnegativity condition is stated as:

$$X_1, X_2, X_3, X_4, X_5, X_6, X_7 \geq 0$$

A NOTE ABOUT THE CONSTRAINTS

At this point you might wonder why the constraints for each day are greater than or equal to rather than equal to constraints. For example, if Air-Express needs only 19 people on Saturday, why do we have a constraint that allows *more* than 19 people to be scheduled? The answer to this question relates to feasibility. Suppose we restate the problem so that all the constraints are equal to constraints. There are two possible outcomes for this problem: (1) it might have a feasible optimal solution, or (2) it might not have a feasible solution.

In the first case, if the formulation using equal to constraints has a feasible optimal solution, this same solution also must be a feasible solution to our formulation using greater than or equal to constraints. Because both formulations have the same objective function, the solution to our original formulation could not be worse (in terms of the optimal objective function value) than a formulation using equal to constraints.

In the second case, if the formulation using equal to constraints has no feasible solution, there is no schedule where the *exact* number of employees required can be scheduled each day. To find a feasible solution in this case, we would need to make the constraints less restrictive by allowing for more than the required number of employees to be scheduled (that is, using greater than or equal to constraints).

Therefore, using greater than or equal to constraints does not preclude a solution where the exact number of workers needed is scheduled for each shift, if such a schedule is feasible and optimal. If such a schedule is not feasible or not optimal, the formulation using greater than or equal to constraints also guarantees that a feasible optimal solution to the problem will be obtained.

IMPLEMENTING THE MODEL

The LP model for the Air-Express scheduling problem is summarized as:

$$\text{MIN: } 680X_1 + 705X_2 + 705X_3 + 705X_4 + 705X_5 + 680X_6 + 655X_7 \quad \} \text{ total wage expense}$$

Subject to:

$$0X_1 + 1X_2 + 1X_3 + 1X_4 + 1X_5 + 1X_6 + 0X_7 \geq 18 \quad \} \text{ workers required on Sunday}$$

$$0X_1 + 0X_2 + 1X_3 + 1X_4 + 1X_5 + 1X_6 + 1X_7 \geq 27 \quad \} \text{ workers required on Monday}$$

$$1X_1 + 0X_2 + 0X_3 + 1X_4 + 1X_5 + 1X_6 + 1X_7 \geq 22 \quad \} \text{ workers required on Tuesday}$$

$$1X_1 + 1X_2 + 0X_3 + 0X_4 + 1X_5 + 1X_6 + 1X_7 \geq 26 \quad \} \text{ workers required on Wednesday}$$

$$1X_1 + 1X_2 + 1X_3 + 0X_4 + 0X_5 + 1X_6 + 1X_7 \geq 25 \quad \} \text{ workers required on Thursday}$$

$$1X_1 + 1X_2 + 1X_3 + 1X_4 + 0X_5 + 0X_6 + 1X_7 \geq 21 \quad \} \text{ workers required on Friday}$$

$$1X_1 + 1X_2 + 1X_3 + 1X_4 + 1X_5 + 0X_6 + 0X_7 \geq 19 \quad \} \text{ workers required on Saturday}$$

$$X_1, X_2, X_3, X_4, X_5, X_6, X_7 \geq 0 \quad \} \text{ nonnegativity conditions}$$

A convenient way of implementing this model is shown in Figure 3.19 (and in the file FIG3-19.XLS on your data disk). Each row in the table shown in this spreadsheet corresponds to one of the seven shifts in the problem. For each day of the week, entries have been made to indicate which shifts are scheduled to be on or off. For example, shift 1 is scheduled off Sunday and Monday, and on the remaining days of the week. Notice that the values for each day of the week in Figure 3.19 correspond directly to the coefficients in the constraint in our LP model for the same day of the week. The required number of workers for each day is listed in cells B13 through H13 and corresponds to the RHS values of each constraint. The wages to be paid to each worker on the various shifts are listed in cells J5 through J11 and correspond to the objective function coefficients in our model.

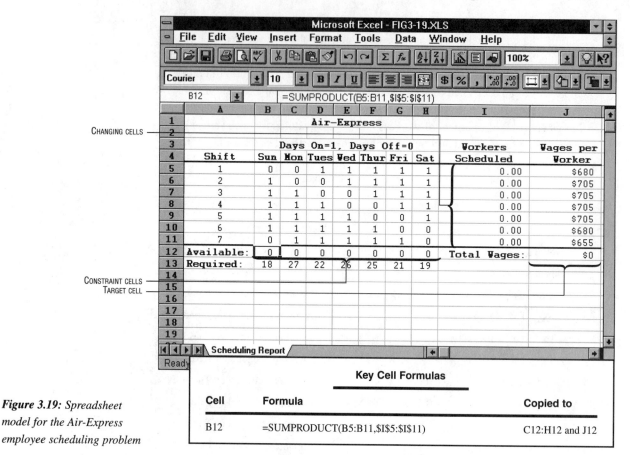

CHANGING CELLS

CONSTRAINT CELLS
TARGET CELL

Figure 3.19: Spreadsheet
model for the Air-Express
employee scheduling problem

Cells I5 through I11 indicate the number of workers assigned to each shift, and correspond to the decision variables X_1 through X_7 in our algebraic formulation of the LP model. The LHS formula for each constraint is implemented easily using the SUMPRODUCT() function. For example, the formula in cell B12 implements the LHS of the constraint for the number of workers needed on Sunday as:

Formula for cell B12:   =SUMPRODUCT(B5:B11,$I$5:$I$11)
(copy to C12 through H12 and J12)

This formula is then copied to cells C12 through H12 to implement the LHS formulas of the remaining constraints. With the coefficients for the objective function entered in cells J5 through J11, the previous formula is also copied to cell J12 to implement the objective function for this model.

SOLVING THE MODEL

Figure 3.20 shows the Solver parameters and options required to solve this problem. The optimal solution is shown in Figure 3.21.

Figure 3.20: Solver parameters and options for the Air-Express scheduling problem

Figure 3.21: Optimal solution to the Air-Express scheduling problem

ANALYZING THE SOLUTION

As shown in Figure 3.21, the optimal solution to this problem ensures that the available number of employees is at least as great as the required number of employees for each day, and that the minimum total wage expense associated with this solution is $22,103. Notice that this solution calls for 5 workers to be assigned to shift 1 ($X_1 = 5.00$), 0.33 workers to be assigned to shift 2 ($X_2 = 0.33$), 6.33 workers to be assigned to shift 3 ($X_3 = 6.33$), and so on. So, although workers generally come in whole units, the solution we obtained suggests that fractional workers be assigned to various shifts. Thus, it would be helpful if we could determine the best possible solution where all the decision variables assume integer values.

Many optimization problems exist in which we might want to restrict the decision variables to assume only integer values. Such problems are known as **integer programming** problems, and they can be quite difficult to solve. We devote an entire chapter to this topic later. However, to appreciate the difficulty in integer programming problems, let's consider how we might obtain an integer solution for our current problem.

One way to get an integer solution to the Air-Express problem is to manually round all the fractional solution values to the next largest integer value. Because we are increasing the number of workers by this process, this should still give us a feasible solution. If all the fractional values in column I in Figure 3.21 are manually rounded to the next largest integer, we obtain the spreadsheet shown in Figure 3.22.

Figure 3.22: An integer solution to the Air-Express problem obtained by rounding up

The solution shown in Figure 3.22 is feasible because the available number of workers in each time period is at least as great as the required number of workers. However, the total wage expense associated with this solution increased from

$22,103 to $23,950. Although rounding up the fractional values gives us a feasible integer solution, we cannot be certain that this is the best possible integer solution to the problem.

From the solution in Figure 3.21, we know that there is no feasible integer solution with an objective function value better than $22,103. If there were, the solution to the original LP problem would have favored this solution over the one it found with an objective function of $22,103. So, although we might not know the optimal integer solution to the problem, we know with certainty that its objective function value is no less than $22,103. In other words, $22,103 is a lower bound on the objective function value for the optimal integer solution to the problem. If the best possible integer solution has an objective function value of no less than $22,103 and we know an integer feasible solution to the problem that has an objective function value of $23,950, the maximum percentage difference between our known integer solution and the optimal integer solution is:

$$\frac{23,950 - 22,103}{22,103} = 8.3\%$$

Thus, even though we do not know if our rounded integer solution is the optimal integer solution, we are certain that it is within 8.3% of the optimal integer solution.

As it turns out, the integer solution we generated by rounding is *not* the optimal integer solution to this problem. A better integer solution, in fact, the *optimal* integer solution, is shown in Figure 3.23. The optimal integer solution to this problem is $X_1 = 4$, $X_2 = 0$, $X_3 = 7$, $X_4 = 0$, $X_5 = 8$, $X_6 = 3$, $X_7 = 11$ with a total wage expense of $22,540. The technique used to obtain this solution is described in chapter 6, which discusses integer programming.

		Days On=1, Days Off=0						Workers	Wages per
Shift	Sun	Mon	Tues	Wed	Thur	Fri	Sat	Scheduled	Worker
1	0	0	1	1	1	1	1	4.00	$680
2	1	0	0	1	1	1	1	0.00	$705
3	1	1	0	0	1	1	1	7.00	$705
4	1	1	1	0	0	1	1	0.00	$705
5	1	1	1	1	0	0	1	8.00	$705
6	1	1	1	1	1	0	0	3.00	$680
7	0	1	1	1	1	1	0	11.00	$655
Available:	18	29	26	26	25	22	19	Total Wages:	$22,540
Required:	18	27	22	26	25	21	19		

Figure 3.23: Optimal integer solution to Air-Express scheduling problem

A BLENDING PROBLEM

Many business problems involve determining an optimal mix of ingredients. For example, major oil companies must determine the least costly mix of different crude oils and other chemicals to blend together to produce a certain grade of gasoline. Lawn care companies must determine the least costly mix of chemicals and other products to blend together to produce different types of fertilizer. The following is another example of this kind of blending problem.

Agri-Pro is a company that sells agricultural products to farmers in a number of states. One service it provides to customers is custom feed mixing, whereby a farmer can order a specific amount of livestock feed and specify the amount of corn, grain, and minerals the feed should contain. This is an important service because the proper feed for various farm animals changes regularly depending on the weather, pasture conditions, and so on.

Agri-Pro stocks bulk amounts of four types of feeds that it can mix to meet a given customer's specifications. The following table summarizes the four feeds, their composition of corn, grain, and minerals, and the cost per pound for each type.

	Percent of Nutrient in			
Nutrient	Feed 1	Feed 2	Feed 3	Feed 4
Corn	30%	5%	20%	10%
Grain	10%	30%	15%	10%
Minerals	20%	20%	20%	30%
Cost per pound	$0.25	$0.30	$0.32	$0.15

Agri-Pro has just received an order from a local chicken farmer for 8,000 pounds of feed. The farmer wants this feed to contain at least 20% corn, 15% grain, and 15% minerals. What should Agri-Pro do to fill this order at minimum cost?

DEFINING THE DECISION VARIABLES

In this problem, Agri-Pro must determine how much of the various feeds to blend together in order to meet the customer's requirements at minimum cost. An algebraic formulation of this problem might use the following four decision variables:

X_1 = pounds of feed 1 to use in the mix

X_2 = pounds of feed 2 to use in the mix

X_3 = pounds of feed 3 to use in the mix

X_4 = pounds of feed 4 to use in the mix

DEFINING THE OBJECTIVE FUNCTION

The objective in this problem is to fill the customer's order at the lowest possible cost. Because each pound of feed 1, 2, 3, and 4 costs $0.25, $0.30, $0.32, and $0.15, respectively, the objective function is represented by:

MIN: $.25X_1 + .30X_2 + .32X_3 + .15X_4$

DEFINING THE CONSTRAINTS

Four constraints must be met to fulfill the customer's requirements. First, the customer wants a total of 8,000 pounds of feed. This is expressed by the constraint:

$X_1 + X_2 + X_3 + X_4 = 8,000$

The customer also wants the order to consist of at least 20% corn. Because each pound of feed 1, 2, 3, and 4 consists of 30%, 5%, 20%, and 10% corn, respectively, the total amount of corn in the mix is represented by:

$.30X_1 + .05X_2 + .20X_3 + .10X_4$

To ensure that *corn* constitutes at least 20% of the 8,000 pounds of feed, we set up the following constraint:

$$\frac{.30X_1 + .05X_2 + .20X_3 + .10X_4}{8,000} \geq .20$$

Similarly, to ensure that *grain* constitutes at least 15% of the 8,000 pounds of feed, we use the constraint:

$$\frac{.10X_1 + .30X_2 + .15X_3 + .10X_4}{8,000} \geq .15$$

Finally, to ensure that *minerals* constitute at least 15% of the 8,000 pounds of feed, we use the constraint:

$$\frac{.20X_1 + .20X_2 + .20X_3 + .30X_4}{8,000} \geq .15$$

SOME OBSERVATIONS ABOUT CONSTRAINTS, REPORTING, AND SCALING

We need to make some important observations about the constraints for this model. First, these constraints look somewhat different from the usual linear sum of products. However, these constraints are equivalent to a sum of products. For example, the constraint for the required percentage of corn can be expressed as:

$$\frac{.30X_1 + .05X_2 + .20X_3 + .10X_4}{8,000} \geq .20$$

or as:

$$\frac{.30}{8,000} X_1 + \frac{.05}{8,000} X_2 + \frac{.20}{8,000} X_3 + \frac{.10}{8,000} X_4 \geq .20$$

or, if you multiply both sides of the inequality by 8,000, as:

$.30X_1 + .05X_2 + .20X_3 + .10X_4 \geq 1,600$

All these constraints define exactly the same set of feasible values for X_1, ..., X_4. Theoretically, we should be able to implement and use *any* of these constraints to solve the problem. However, we need to consider a number of practical issues in determining which form of the constraint to implement.

Notice that the LHS formulas for the first and second versions of the constraint represent the *proportion* of corn in the 8,000 pound order, whereas the LHS in the third version of the constraint represents the *total pounds* of corn in the 8,000 pound order. Because we must implement the LHS formula of one of these constraints in the spreadsheet, we need to decide which number to display in the spreadsheet—the *proportion* (or percentage) of corn in the order, or the *total pounds of corn* in the order. If we know one of these values, we can easily set up a formula to calculate the other value. But, when more than one way to implement a constraint exists (as is usually the case), we need to consider what the value of the LHS portion of the constraint means to the user of the spreadsheet so that the results of the model can be reported as clearly as possible.

Another issue to consider involves *scaling* the model so that it can be solved accurately. For example, suppose we decide to implement the LHS formula for the first or second version of the corn constraint given earlier so that the *proportion* of corn in the 8,000 pound feed order appears in the spreadsheet. The coefficients for the variables in these constraints are *very* small values. In either case, the coefficient for X_2 is 0.05/8,000 or 0.000006250.

As Solver tries to solve an LP problem, it must perform intermediate calculations that make the various coefficients in the model larger or smaller. As numbers become extremely large or small, computers often run into storage or representation problems that force them to use approximations of the actual numbers. This opens the door for problems to occur in the accuracy of the results and, in some cases, can prevent the computer from solving the problem at all. So if some coefficients in the initial model are extremely large or extremely small, it is a good idea to rescale the problem so that all the coefficients are of similar magnitudes.

RESCALING THE MODEL

To illustrate how a problem is rescaled, consider the following equivalent formulation of the Agri-Pro problem:

X_1 = amount of feed 1 *in thousands of pounds* to use in the mix

X_2 = amount of feed 2 *in thousands of pounds* to use in the mix

X_3 = amount of feed 3 *in thousands of pounds* to use in the mix

X_4 = amount of feed 4 *in thousands of pounds* to use in the mix

The objective function and constraints are represented by:

$$\text{MIN}: 250X_1 + 300X_2 + 320X_3 + 150X_4 \qquad \} \text{ total cost}$$

$$\text{Subject to}: \quad X_1 + X_2 + X_3 + X_4 = 8 \quad \} \text{ pounds of feed required}$$

$$\frac{.30X_1 + .05X_2 + .20X_3 + .10X_4}{8} \geq .20 \quad \} \text{ min \% of corn required}$$

$$\frac{.10X_1 + .30X_2 + .15X_3 + .10X_4}{8} \geq .15 \quad \} \text{ min \% of grain required}$$

$$\frac{.20X_1 + .20X_2 + .20X_3 + .30X_4}{8} \geq .15 \quad \} \text{ min \% of minerals required}$$

$$X_1, X_2, X_3, X_4 \geq 0 \qquad \} \text{ nonnegativity conditions}$$

Each unit of X_1, X_2, X_3, and X_4 now represents 1,000 pounds of feed 1, 2, 3, and 4, respectively. So the objective now reflects the fact that each unit (or each 1,000 pounds) of X_1, X_2, X_3, and X_4 costs $250, $300, $320, and $150, respectively. The constraints have also been adjusted to reflect the fact that the variables now represent thousands of pounds of the different feeds. Notice that the smallest coefficient in the constraints is now $0.05/8 = 0.00625$ and the largest coefficient is 8 (that is, the RHS value for the first constraint). In our original formulation, the smallest coefficient was 0.00000625 and the largest coefficient was 8,000. By rescaling the problem, we dramatically reduced the range between the smallest and largest coefficients in the model.

Automatic Scaling

In solving some earlier problems in this chapter, you might have noticed that the Solver Parameters dialog box provides an option called Use Automatic Scaling (see Figure 3.20). If you select this option, Solver attempts to rescale the data automatically before solving the problem. Although this option is effective, you should not rely solely on it to solve all scaling problems that occur in your models.

The Assume Linear Model Option

When the Assume Linear Model option is selected, Solver conducts a number of internal tests to verify that the model is truly linear in the objective and constraints. If this option is selected and Solver's tests indicate that the model is not linear, a dialog box appears indicating that the conditions for linearity are not satisfied. The internal tests Solver applies are not always 100% accurate and sometimes indicate that the model is not linear when, in fact, it is. This often occurs when a model is poorly scaled. If you encounter this message and you are certain that your model is linear, re-solving the model might result in Solver identifying the optimal solution. If this doesn't work, try reformulating your model so that it is more evenly scaled.

IMPLEMENTING THE MODEL

One way to implement this model in a spreadsheet is shown in Figure 3.24 (and in the file FIG3-24.XLS on your data disk). In this spreadsheet, the percentage of the different nutrients found in each type of feed is listed in cells B5 through E7. Cells B11 through E11 contain the costs of the different types of feeds.

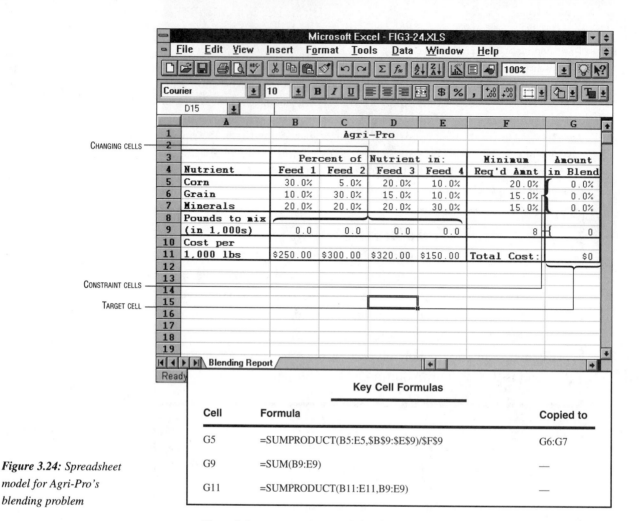

Figure 3.24: Spreadsheet model for Agri-Pro's blending problem

The minimum percentage of the three types of nutrients required by the customer order are entered in cells F5 through F7. Finally, cell F9 contains the total amount of feed (in 1,000s of pounds) required for the order. Notice that the values in column F correspond to the RHS values for the various constraints in the model.

In this spreadsheet, cells B9, C9, D9, and E9 are reserved to represent the decision variables X_1, X_2, X_3, and X_4. These cells will ultimately indicate how much of each type of feed should be mixed together to fill the order.

The objective function for the problem is implemented in cell G11 using the formula:

Formula for cell G11:   =SUMPRODUCT(B11:E11,B9:E9)

The LHS formula for the first constraint involves calculating the sum of the decision variables. This relationship is implemented in cell G9 as:

Formula for cell G9:   =SUM(B9:E9)

The RHS for this constraint is in cell F9. The LHS formulas for the other three constraints are implemented in cells G5, G6, and G7. Specifically, the LHS formula for the second constraint (representing the proportion of corn in the mix) is implemented in cell G5 as:

Formula for cell G5: =SUMPRODUCT(B5:E5,$B$9:$E$9)/$F$9
(copy to G6 through G7)

This formula is then copied to cells G6 and G7 to implement the LHS formulas for the remaining two constraints. Again, cells F5 through F7 contain the RHS values for these constraints.

Notice that this model is implemented in a user-friendly way. Each constraint cell has a logical interpretation that communicates important information. For any given values for the changing cells (B9 through E9) totaling 8,000, the constraint cells (G5 through G7) indicate the *actual* percentage of corn, grain, and minerals in the mix.

Have You Seen LP at Your Grocery Store?

The next time you are at your local grocery store, make a special trip down the aisle where the pet food is located. On the back of just about any bag of dog or cat food, you should see the following sort of label (taken directly from the author's dog's favorite brand of food):

This product contains:

- At least 21% crude protein
- At least 8% crude fat
- At most 4.5% crude fiber
- At most 12% moisture

In making such statements, the manufacturer guarantees that these nutritional requirements are met by the product. Various ingredients (such as corn, soybeans, meat and bone meal, animal fat, wheat, and rice) are blended to make the product. Most companies are interested in determining the blend of ingredients that satisfies these requirements in the least costly way. Not surprisingly, almost all of the major pet food manufacturing companies use LP extensively in their production process to solve this type of blending problem.

SOLVING THE MODEL

Figure 3.25 shows the Solver parameters and options required to solve this problem. The optimal solution is shown in Figure 3.26.

ANALYZING THE SOLUTION

The optimal solution shown in Figure 3.26 indicates that the 8,000 pound feed order is produced at the lowest possible cost by mixing 4,500 pounds of feed 1 ($X_1 = 4.5$) with 2,000 pounds of feed 2 ($X_2 = 2$) and 1,500 pounds of feed 4 ($X_4 = 1.5$).

Figures 3.25: Solver parameters and options for the blending problem

Figures 3.26: Optimal solution to Agri-Pro's blending problem

Cell G9 indicates this produces exactly 8,000 pounds of feed. Furthermore, cells G5 through G7 indicate this mix contains 20% corn, 15% grain, and 21.9% minerals. The total cost of producing this mix is $1,950, as indicated by cell G11.

A PRODUCTION PROBLEM

Many decision problems in production and manufacturing involve determining the best way to allocate scarce resources (labor, materials, machine time, and so on) to produce products in an efficient manner. LP can assist managers in making optimal production decisions. The following problem is an example of what is known as a "cutting stock" problem.

Bellows Lumber Yard, Inc. stocks standard length 25-foot boards, which it cuts to custom lengths to fill individual customer orders. An order has just come in for 5,000 7-foot boards, 1,200 9-foot boards, and 300 11-foot boards. The lumber yard manager has identified six ways to cut the 25-foot boards to fill this order. The six cutting patterns are summarized below:

Number of Boards Produced

Cutting Pattern	7 ft	9 ft	11 ft
1	3	0	0
2	2	1	0
3	2	0	1
4	1	2	0
5	0	1	1
6	0	0	2

One possibility (cutting pattern 1) is to cut a 25-foot board into three 7-foot boards, and not to cut any 9- or 11-foot boards. Note that cutting pattern 1 uses a total of 21 feet of board and leaves a 4-foot piece of scrap. Another possibility (cutting pattern 4) is to cut a 25-foot board into one 7-foot board and two 9-foot boards (using all 25 feet of the board). The remaining cutting patterns have similar interpretations.

The lumber yard manager wants to fill this order using the fewest number of 25-foot boards as possible. To do this, the manager needs to determine how many 25-foot boards to run through each cutting pattern.

DEFINING THE DECISION VARIABLES

The manager of the lumber yard needs to determine the number of times each cutting pattern should be used to cut a 25-foot board. Therefore, this problem requires six variables:

X_i = the number of 25-foot boards that should be cut using pattern i, $i = 2, ..., 6$

That is:

X_1 = the number of 25-foot boards that should be cut using pattern 1

X_2 = the number of 25-foot boards that should be cut using pattern 2

⋮

X_6 = the number of 25-foot boards that should be cut using pattern 6

DEFINING THE OBJECTIVE FUNCTION

The manager's goal is to fill the order using the minimum number of 25-foot boards. The total number of 25-foot boards cut is calculated by summing the decision variables. The objective function for this problem is:

MIN: $X_1 + X_2 + X_3 + X_4 + X_5 + X_6$

DEFINING THE CONSTRAINTS

This problem requires three constraints to ensure that a sufficient number of 7-, 9-, and 11-foot boards is produced. Referring to the table given in the problem, we know that cutting pattern 1 produces three 7-foot boards each time it is used, cutting patterns 2 and 3 each produce two 7-foot boards each time they are used, and cutting pattern 4 produces one 7-foot board each time it is used. Cutting patterns 5 and 6 do not produce any 7-foot boards. Thus, at least 5,000 seven-foot boards will be produced providing that the following relationship is satisfied:

$3X_1 + 2X_2 + 2X_3 + 1X_4 + 0X_5 + 0X_6 \geq 5,000$

Note that the LHS of this constraint equals the number of 7-foot boards that will be produced given any values for X_1 through X_6.

Similar constraints can be developed to ensure that the required number of 9- and 11-foot boards are produced. The constraints for 9- and 11-foot boards, respectively, are:

$0X_1 + 1X_2 + 0X_3 + 2X_4 + 1X_5 + 0X_6 \geq 1,200$

$0X_1 + 0X_2 + 1X_3 + 0X_4 + 1X_5 + 2X_6 \geq 300$

The problem also requires that all the decision variables be nonnegative (or have lower bounds of zero) as:

$X_1, X_2, X_3, X_4, X_5, X_6 \geq 0$

IMPLEMENTING THE MODEL

The LP model for the problem faced by Bellows Lumber Yard is summarized as:

MIN: $X_1 + X_2 + X_3 + X_4 + X_5 + X_6$ } total number of 25-foot boards cut

Subject to:

$3X_1 + 2X_2 + 2X_3 + 1X_4 + 0X_5 + 0X_6 \geq 5,000$ } 7-foot boards required

$0X_1 + 1X_2 + 0X_3 + 2X_4 + 1X_5 + 0X_6 \geq 1,200$ } 9-foot boards required

$0X_1 + 0X_2 + 1X_3 + 0X_4 + 1X_5 + 2X_6 \geq 300$ } 11-foot boards required

$X_1, X_2, X_3, X_4, X_5, X_6 \geq 0$ } nonnegativity conditions

This model is implemented in the spreadsheet shown in Figure 3.27 (and in the file FIG3-27.XLS on your data disk). Each row in this spreadsheet corresponds to one of the cutting patterns. Notice that the coefficients for the LHS of the first constraint appear in column C. The coefficients for the second and third constraints appear in columns D and E.

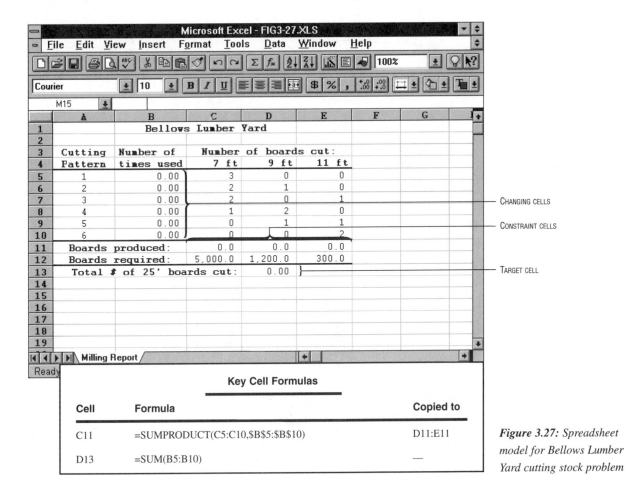

Figure 3.27: Spreadsheet model for Bellows Lumber Yard cutting stock problem

Cells B5 through B10 contain zeros to indicate that these cells are reserved to represent the decision variables X_1, ..., X_6 in the algebraic formulation of our model. That is, cell B5 represents the number of 25-foot boards that should be cut using pattern 1, cell B6 represents the number of 25-foot boards that should be cut using pattern 2, and so on. The objective function for this problem is implemented in cell D13 as:

Formula for cell D13:   =SUM(B5:B10)

The LHS formulas for each constraint are implemented by entering the following formula in cell C11 and copying it to cells D11 and E11:

Formula for cell C11:   =SUMPRODUCT(C5:C10,$B$5:$B$10)
(copy to D11 and E11)

The RHS values for these constraints are entered in cells C12, D12, and E12, respectively.

SOLVING THE MODEL

Figure 3.28 shows the Solver parameters and options required to solve this problem. The optimal solution is shown in Figure 3.29.

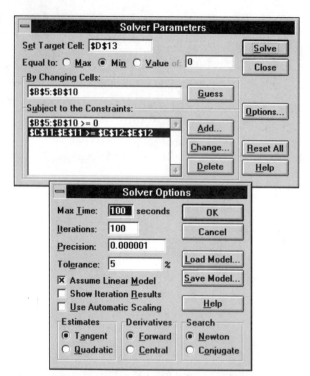

Figure 3.28: Solver parameters and options for the cutting stock problem

Figure 3.29: Optimal solution to Bellows's cutting stock problem

ANALYZING THE SOLUTION

The optimal solution shown in Figure 3.29 indicates that cutting pattern 1 should be used on 1,266.67 of the 25-foot boards, pattern 3 should be used 300 times, and pattern 4 should be used 600 times. The optimal values for the decision variables in the original model are: $X_1 = 1,266.67$, $X_2 = 0$, $X_3 = 300$, $X_4 = 600$, $X_5 = 0$, and $X_6 = 0$. This plan requires that a total of 2,166.67 of the 25-foot boards be cut, and produces exactly the required number of 7-, 9-, and 11-foot boards.

Because there is no way to fill the order using less than 2,166.67 of the 25-foot boards, the lumber yard must cut 2,167 boards to fill the order. The lumber yard most likely will use cutting pattern 1 on 1,267 boards (rather than 1,266.67). This results in cutting 2,167 of the 25-foot boards, and produces a total of 5,001 seven-foot boards.

A TRANSPORTATION PROBLEM

Many transportation and logistics problems businesses face fall into a category of problems known as network flow problems. We will consider one such example here and study this area in more detail in chapter 5.

Tropicsun is a leading grower and distributor of fresh citrus products with three large citrus groves scattered around central Florida in the cities of Mt. Dora, Eustis, and Clermont. Tropicsun currently has 275,000 bushels of citrus at the grove in Mt. Dora, 400,000 bushels at the grove in Eustis, and 300,000 at the grove in Clermont. Tropicsun has citrus processing plants in Ocala, Orlando, and Leesburg with processing capacities to handle 200,000, 600,000, and 225,000 bushels, respectively. Tropicsun contracts with a local trucking company to transport its fruit from the groves to the processing plants. The trucking company charges a flat rate for every mile that each bushel of fruit must be transported. Each mile a bushel of fruit travels is known as a bushel-mile. The following table summarizes the distances (in miles) between the groves and processing plants:

	Distances (in miles) Between Groves and Plants		
Grove	Ocala	Orlando	Leesburg
Mt. Dora	21	50	40
Eustis	35	30	22
Clermont	55	20	25

Tropicsun wants to determine how many bushels to ship from each grove to each processing plant in order to minimize the total number of bushel-miles the fruit must be shipped.

DEFINING THE DECISION VARIABLES

In this situation, the problem is to determine how many bushels of fruit should be shipped from each grove to each processing plant. The problem is summarized graphically in Figure 3.30.

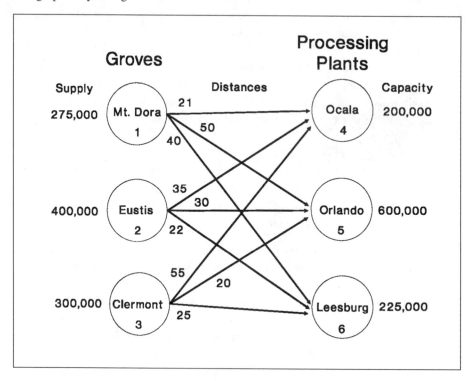

Figure 3.30: Diagram for the Tropicsun transportation problem

The circles (or nodes) in Figure 3.30 correspond to the different groves and processing plants in the problem. Note that a number has been assigned to each node. The arrows (or arcs) connecting the various groves and processing plants represent different shipping routes. The decision problem faced by Tropicsun is to determine how many bushels of fruit to ship on each of these routes. Thus, one decision variable is associated with each of the arcs in Figure 3.30. We can define these variables in general as:

X_{ij} = number of bushels to ship *from* node i *to* node j

Specifically, the nine decision variables are:

X_{14} = number of bushels to ship from Mt. Dora (node 1) to Ocala (node 4)

X_{15} = number of bushels to ship from Mt. Dora (node 1) to Orlando (node 5)

X_{16} = number of bushels to ship from Mt. Dora (node 1) to Leesburg (node 6)

X_{24} = number of bushels to ship from Eustis (node 2) to Ocala (node 4)

X_{25} = number of bushels to ship from Eustis (node 2) to Orlando (node 5)

X_{26} = number of bushels to ship from Eustis (node 2) to Leesburg (node 6)

X_{34} = number of bushels to ship from Clermont (node 3) to Ocala (node 4)

X_{35} = number of bushels to ship from Clermont (node 3) to Orlando (node 5)

X_{36} = number of bushels to ship from Clermont (node 3) to Leesburg (node 6)

DEFINING THE OBJECTIVE FUNCTION

The goal in this problem is to determine how many bushels to ship from each grove to each processing plant while minimizing the total distance (or total number of bushel-miles) the fruit must travel. The objective function for this problem is represented by:

MIN: $21X_{14} + 50X_{15} + 40X_{16} + 35X_{24} + 30X_{25} + 22X_{26} + 55X_{34} + 20X_{35} + 25X_{36}$

The term $21X_{14}$ in this function reflects the fact that each bushel shipped from Mt. Dora (node 1) to Ocala (node 4) must travel 21 miles. The remaining terms in the function express similar relationships for the other shipping routes.

DEFINING THE CONSTRAINTS

Two physical constraints apply to this problem. First, there is a limit on the amount of fruit that can be shipped to each processing plant. Tropicsun can ship no more than 200,000, 600,000, and 225,000 bushels to Ocala, Orlando, and Leesburg, respectively. These restrictions are reflected by the following constraints:

$X_{14} + X_{24} + X_{34} \leq 200{,}000$ } capacity restriction for Ocala

$X_{15} + X_{25} + X_{35} \leq 600{,}000$ } capacity restriction for Orlando

$X_{16} + X_{26} + X_{36} \leq 225{,}000$ } capacity restriction for Leesburg

The first constraint indicates that the total bushels shipped to Ocala (node 4) from Mt. Dora (node 1), Eustis (node 2), and Clermont (node 3) must be less than or equal to Ocala's capacity of 200,000 bushels. The other two constraints have similar interpretations for Orlando and Leesburg. Notice that the total processing capacity at the plants (1,025,000 bushels) exceeds the total supply of fruit at the groves (975,000 bushels). Therefore, these constraints are less than or equal to constraints because not all the available capacity will be used.

The second set of constraints ensures that the supply of fruit at each grove is shipped to a processing plant. That is, all of the 275,000, 400,000, and 300,000 bushels at Mt. Dora, Eustis, and Clermont, respectively, must be processed somewhere. This is accomplished by the following constraints:

$X_{14} + X_{15} + X_{16} = 275{,}000$ } supply available at Mt. Dora

$X_{24} + X_{25} + X_{26} = 400{,}000$ } supply available at Eustis

$X_{34} + X_{35} + X_{36} = 300{,}000$ } supply available at Clermont

The first constraint indicates that the total amount shipped from Mt. Dora (node 1) to the plants in Ocala (node 4), Orlando (node 5), and Leesburg (node 6) must equal the total amount available at Mt. Dora. This constraint indicates that all the fruit available at Mt. Dora must be shipped somewhere. The other two constraints play similar roles for Eustis and Clermont.

IMPLEMENTING THE MODEL

The LP model for Tropicsun's fruit transportation problem is summarized as:

$$\text{MIN:} \quad 21X_{14} + 50X_{15} + 40X_{16}$$
$$+35X_{24} + 30X_{24} + 22X_{26}$$
$$+55X_{34} + 20X_{35} + 25X_{36}$$

} total distance fruit is shipped (in bushel-miles)

Subject to:		
$X_{14} + X_{24} + X_{34} \leq 200{,}000$	} capacity restriction for Ocala
$X_{15} + X_{25} + X_{35} \leq 600{,}000$	} capacity restriction for Orlando
$X_{16} + X_{26} + X_{36} \leq 225{,}000$	} capacity restriction for Leesburg
$X_{14} + X_{15} + X_{16} = 275{,}000$	} supply available at Mt. Dora
$X_{24} + X_{25} + X_{26} = 400{,}000$	} supply available at Eustis
$X_{34} + X_{35} + X_{36} = 300{,}000$	} supply available at Clermont
$X_{ij} \geq 0$, for all i and j	} nonnegativity conditions

The last constraint, as in previous models, indicates that all the decision variables must be nonnegative.

A convenient way to implement this model is shown in Figure 3.31 (and in the file FIG3-31.XLS on your data disk). In this spreadsheet, the distances between each grove and plant is summarized in a tabular format in cells C6 through E8. Cells C13 through E15 are reserved for representing the number of bushels of fruit to ship from each grove to each processing plant. Notice that these nine cells correspond directly to the nine decision variables in the algebraic formulation of the model.

The LHS formulas for the three capacity constraints in the model are implemented in cells C16, D16, and E16 in the spreadsheet. To do this, the following formula is entered in cell C16 and copied to cells D16 and E16:

Formula for cell C16:   =SUM(C13:C15)
(copy to D16 and E16)

These cells represent the total bushels of fruit being shipped to the plants in Ocala, Orlando, and Leesburg, respectively. Cells C17 through E17 contain the RHS values for these constraint cells.

The LHS formulas for the three supply constraints in the model are implemented in cells F13, F14, and F15 as:

Formula for cell F13:   =SUM(C13:E13)
(copy to F14 and F15)

These cells represent the total bushels of fruit being shipped from the groves at Mt. Dora, Eustis, and Clermont, respectively. Cells G13 through G15 contain the RHS values for these constraint cells.

Finally, the objective function for this model is entered in cell F19 as:

Formula for cell F19:   =SUMPRODUCT(C6:E8,C13:E15)

The SUMPRODUCT( ) function multiplies each element in the range C6 through E8 by the corresponding element in the range C13 through E15 and then sums the individual products.

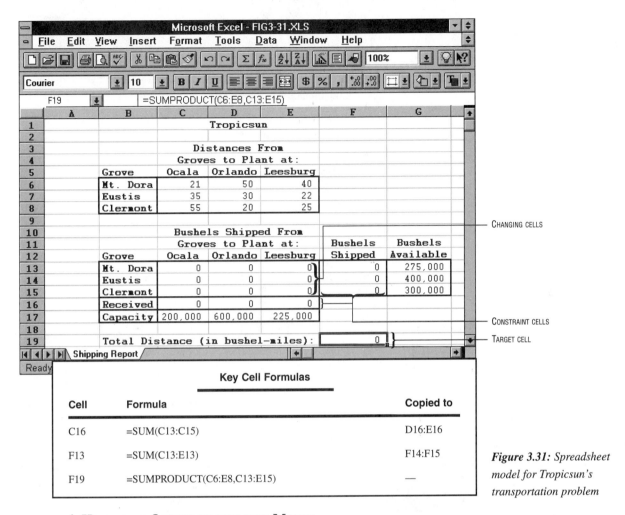

Figure 3.31: Spreadsheet model for Tropicsun's transportation problem

A HEURISTIC SOLUTION FOR THE MODEL

To appreciate what Solver is accomplishing, let's consider how we might try to solve this problem manually using a heuristic. A **heuristic** is a rule-of-thumb for making decisions that might work well in some instances, but is not guaranteed to produce optimal solutions or decisions. One heuristic we can apply to solve Tropicsun's problem is to always ship as much as possible along the next available path with the shortest distance (or least cost). Using this heuristic, we solve the problem as follows:

1. Because the shortest available path between any grove and processing plant is between Clermont and Orlando (20 miles), we first ship as much as possible through this route. The maximum we can ship through this route is the smaller of the supply at Clermont (300,000 bushels) or the capacity at Orlando (600,000 bushels). So we would ship 300,000 bushels from Clermont to Orlando. This depletes the supply at Clermont.

2. The next shortest available route occurs between Mt. Dora and Ocala (21 miles). The maximum we can ship through this route is the smaller of the supply at Mt. Dora (275,000 bushels) or the capacity at Ocala (200,000 bushels). So we would ship 200,000 bushels from Mt. Dora to Ocala. This depletes the capacity at Ocala.

3. The next shortest available route occurs between Eustis and Leesburg (22 miles). The maximum we can ship through this route is the smaller of the supply at Eustis (400,000 bushels) or the capacity at Leesburg (225,000 bushels). So we would ship 225,000 bushels from Eustis to Leesburg. This depletes the capacity at Leesburg.

4. The next shortest available route occurs between Eustis and Orlando (30 miles). The maximum we can ship through this route is the smaller of the remaining supply at Eustis (175,000 bushels) or the remaining capacity at Orlando (300,000 bushels). So we would ship 175,000 bushels from Eustis to Orlando. This depletes the supply at Eustis.

5. The only remaining route occurs between Mt. Dora and Orlando (because the processing capacities at Ocala and Leesburg have both been depleted). This distance is 50 miles. The maximum we can ship through this route is the smaller of the remaining supply at Mt. Dora (75,000 bushels) and the remaining capacity at Orlando (125,000 bushels). So we would ship the final 75,000 bushels at Mt. Dora to Orlando. This depletes the supply at Mt. Dora.

As shown in Figure 3.32, the solution identified with this heuristic involves shipping the fruit a total of 24,150,000 bushel-miles. All the bushels available at each grove have been shipped to the processing plants and none of the capacities at the processing plants have been exceeded. Therefore, this is a *feasible* solution to the problem. And the logic used to find this solution might lead us to believe it is a reasonably good solution—but is it the *optimal* solution? Is there no other feasible solution to this problem that can make the total distance the fruit has to travel less than 24,150,000 bushel-miles?

Figure 3.32: A heuristic solution to the transportation problem

SOLVING THE MODEL

To find the optimal solution to this model we must indicate to Solver the target cell, changing cells, and constraint cells identified in Figure 3.31. Figure 3.33 shows the Solver parameters and options required to solve this problem. The optimal solution is shown in Figure 3.34.

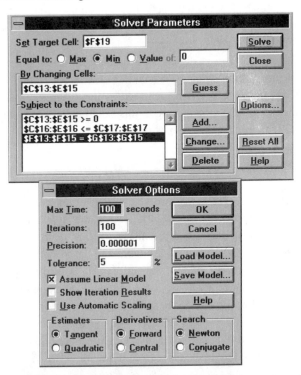

Figure 3.33: Solver parameters and options for the transportation problem

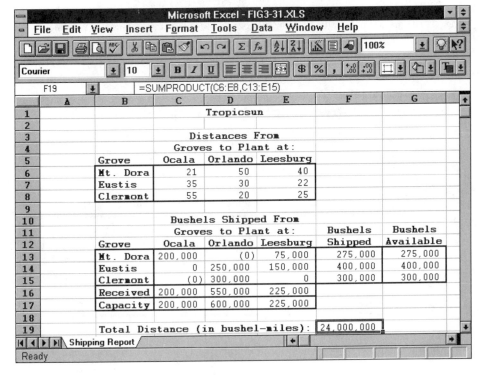

Figure 3.34: Optimal solution to Tropicsun's transportation problem

ANALYZING THE SOLUTION

The optimal solution in Figure 3.34 indicates that 200,000 bushels should be shipped from Mt. Dora to Ocala ($X_{14} = 200,000$) and 75,000 bushels should be shipped from Mt. Dora to Leesburg ($X_{16} = 75,000$). Of the 400,000 bushels available at the grove in Eustis, 250,000 bushels should be shipped to Orlando for processing ($X_{25} = 250,000$) and 150,000 bushels should be shipped to Leesburg ($X_{26} = 150,000$). Finally, all 300,000 bushels available in Clermont should be shipped to Orlando ($X_{35} = 300,000$). None of the other possible shipping routes will be used.

The solution shown in Figure 3.34 satisfies all the constraints in the model and results in a minimum shipping distance of 24,000,000 bushel-miles, which is better than the heuristic solution identified earlier. Therefore, simple heuristics can sometimes solve LP problems, but as this example illustrates, there is no guarantee that a heuristic solution is the best possible solution.

A MULTI-PERIOD PLANNING PROBLEM

Numerous business problems involve decisions that have a ripple effect on future decisions. For example, manufacturing companies typically plan production on a weekly or monthly basis, and the manufacturing plans for one time period can impact the amount of resources available and the inventory carried in subsequent time periods. Similarly, many financial decisions involve multiple time periods because the amount of money invested or spent at one point in time directly affects the amount of money available in subsequent time periods. In these types of multi-period problems it can be difficult to account for the consequences of a current decision on future time periods without an LP model. The formulation of such a model is illustrated in an example from the world of finance.

Taco-Viva is a small but growing restaurant chain specializing in Mexican fast food. The management of the company has decided to build a new location in Wilmington, North Carolina, and wants to establish a construction fund (or sinking fund) to pay for the new facility. Construction of the restaurant is expected to take six months and cost $800,000. Taco-Viva's contract with the construction company requires it to make payments of $250,000 at the end of the second and fourth months, and a final payment of $300,000 at the end of the sixth month when the restaurant is completed.

The company can use four investment opportunities to establish the construction fund; these investments are summarized in the following table:

Investment	Available in Month	Months to Maturity	Yield at Maturity	Risk
A	1, 2, 3, 4, 5, 6	1	1.2%	1
B	1, 3, 5	2	3.5%	3
C	1, 4	3	5.8%	8
D	1	6	11.0%	6

The table indicates that investment A will be available at the beginning of each of the next six months, and funds invested in this manner mature in one month with a yield of 1.2%. Funds can be placed in investment C only at the beginning of months 1 and/or 4, and mature at the end of three months with a yield of 5.8%. The column labeled Risk provides a rating of each investment's level of risk. This rating was made subjectively by the company's chief financial officer on a scale from 1 to 10 (where 1 represents the least risk and 10 the greatest risk).

The management of Taco-Viva needs to determine the investment plan that allows them to meet the required schedule of payments while placing the least amount of money in the construction fund and never having a weighted average risk level greater than 5.

This is a multi-period problem because a six-month planning horizon must be considered. That is, Taco-Viva must plan which investment alternatives to use at various times during the next six months.

DEFINING THE DECISION VARIABLES

The basic decision faced by the management of Taco-Viva is how much money to invest in each investment vehicle during each time period when the investment opportunities are available. To model this problem, we need different variables to represent each investment/time period combination. This can be done as:

$A_1, A_2, A_3, A_4, A_5, A_6$ = the amount of money (in $1,000s) placed in investment A at the beginning of months 1, 2, 3, 4, 5, and 6, respectively

B_1, B_3, B_5 = the amount of money (in $1,000s) placed in investment B at the beginning of months 1, 3, and 5, respectively

C_1, C_4 = the amount of money (in $1,000s) placed in investment C at the beginning of months 1 and 4, respectively

D_1 = the amount of money (in $1,000s) placed in investment D at the beginning of month 1

Notice that all variables are expressed in units of thousands of dollars to maintain a reasonable scale for this problem. So, keep in mind that when referring to the amount of money represented by our variables, we mean the amount in thousands of dollars.

DEFINING THE OBJECTIVE FUNCTION

Taco-Viva's management wants to minimize the amount of money it must initially place in the construction fund in order to cover the payments that will be due under the contract. At the beginning of month 1 the company wants to invest some amount of money that, along with its investment earnings, will cover the required payments without an additional infusion of cash from the company. Because A_1, B_1, C_1, and D_1 represent the initial amounts invested by the company in month 1, the objective function for the problem is:

MIN: $A_1 + B_1 + C_1 + D_1$

DEFINING THE CONSTRAINTS

Two sets of constraints apply to this problem. The first set concerns the flow of funds into and out of the various investments in the different time periods. We refer to these as the cash-flow constraints. Another set of constraints ensures that investments are made in such a way that the weighted average risk never exceeds 5. We refer to these as the risk constraints.

THE CASH-FLOW CONSTRAINTS

To formulate the cash-flow constraints for this problem it is important to clearly identify: (1) when the different investments can be made, (2) when the different investments will mature, and (3) how much money will be available when each investment matures. Figure 3.35 summarizes this information.

	Cash Inflow/Outflow at the Beginning of Month						
Investment	**1**	**2**	**3**	**4**	**5**	**6**	**7**
A_1	−1	1.012					
B_1	−1	<———> 1.035					
C_1	−1	<————————> 1.058					
D_1	−1	<———————————————————————> 1.11					
A_2		−1	1.012				
A_3			−1	1.012			
B_3			−1	<———> 1.035			
A_4				−1	1.012		
C_4				−1	<————————> 1.058		
A_5					−1	1.012	
B_5					−1	<———> 1.035	
A_6						−1	1.012
Req'd Payments (in $1,000s)	**$0**	**$0**	**$250**	**$0**	**$250**	**$0**	**$300**

Figure 3.35: Cash-flow summary table for Taco-Viva's investment opportunities

The negative values, represented by −1 in Figure 3.35, indicate when dollars can flow *into* each investment. The positive values indicate how much these same dollars will be worth when the investment matures, or when dollars flow *out* of each investment. The <———> symbols indicate time periods in which funds neither flow into nor flow out of particular investments. For example, the third row of the table in Figure 3.35 indicates that every dollar placed in investment C during month 1 will be worth $1.058 when this investment matures three months later—at the *beginning* of month 4. (Note that the beginning of month 4 occurs at virtually the same instant as the *end* of month 3. Thus, there is no practical difference between the beginning of one time period and the end of the previous time period.)

Assuming that the company invests the amounts represented by A_1, B_1, C_1, and D_1 at the beginning of month 1, how much money will be available to reinvest or make the required payments at the beginning of months 2, 3, 4, 5, 6, and 7? The answer to this question allows us to generate the set of cash-flow constraints needed for this problem.

As indicated by the second column of Figure 3.35, the only funds maturing at the beginning of month 2 are those placed in investment A at the beginning of month 1 (A_1). The value of the funds maturing at the beginning of month 2 is $1.012A_1$. Because no payments are required at the beginning of month 2, all the maturing funds must be reinvested. But the only new investment opportunity available at the beginning of month 2 is investment A (A_2). Thus, the amount of money placed in investment A at the beginning of month 2 must be $1.012A_1$. This is expressed by the constraint:

$$1.012A_1 = A_2 + 0 \quad \} \text{ cash-flow for month 2}$$

This constraint indicates that the total amount of money maturing at the beginning of month 2 ($1.012A_1$) must equal the amount of money reinvested at the beginning of month 2 (A_2) plus any payment due in month 2 ($0).

Now let's consider the cash flows that will occur during month 3. At the beginning of month 3, any funds that were placed in investment B at the beginning of month 1 (B_1) will mature and be worth a total of $1.035B_1$. Similarly, any funds placed in investment A at the beginning of month 2 (A_2) will mature and be worth a total of $1.012A_2$. Because a payment of $250,000 is due at the beginning of month 3, we must ensure that the funds maturing at the beginning of month 3 are sufficient to cover this payment, and that any remaining funds are placed in the investment opportunities available at the beginning of month 3 (A_3 and B_3). This requirement can be stated algebraically as:

$$1.035B_1 + 1.012A_2 = A_3 + B_3 + 250 \quad \} \text{ cash-flow for month 3}$$

This constraint indicates that the total amount of money maturing at the beginning of month 3 ($1.012A_1 + 1.035B_1$) must equal the amount of money reinvested at the beginning of month 3 ($A_3 + B_3$) plus the payment due at the beginning of month 3 ($250,000).

The same logic we applied to generate the cash-flow constraints for months 2 and 3 can also be used to generate cash-flow constraints for the remaining months. Doing so produces a cash-flow constraint for each month that takes on the general form:

$$\begin{pmatrix} \text{Total \$ amount} \\ \text{maturing at the} \\ \text{beginning of the month} \end{pmatrix} = \begin{pmatrix} \text{Total \$ amount} \\ \text{reinvested at the} \\ \text{beginning of the month} \end{pmatrix} + \begin{pmatrix} \text{Payment due at the} \\ \text{beginning of the month} \end{pmatrix}$$

Using this general definition of the cash-flow relationships, the constraints for the remaining months are represented by:

$$1.058C_1 + 1.012A_3 = A_4 + C_4 \quad \} \text{ cash-flow for month 4}$$

$$1.035B_3 + 1.012A_4 = A_5 + B_5 + 250 \quad \} \text{ cash-flow for month 5}$$

$$1.012A_5 = A_6 \quad \} \text{ cash-flow for month 6}$$

$$1.11D_1 + 1.058C_4 + 1.035B_5 + 1.012A_6 = 300 \quad \} \text{ cash-flow for month 7}$$

To implement these constraints in the spreadsheet, we must express them in a slightly different (but algebraically equivalent) manner. Specifically, to conform to our general definition of an equality constraint ($f(X_1, X_2, \ldots, X_n) = b$) we need to rewrite the cash-flow constraints so that all the *variables* in each constraint appear on the LHS of the equal sign, and a numeric constant appears on the RHS of the equal sign. This can be done as:

$$1.012A_1 - 1A_2 = 0 \qquad \} \text{ cash-flow for month 2}$$

$$1.035B_1 + 1.012A_2 - 1A_3 - 1B_3 = 250 \qquad \} \text{ cash-flow for month 3}$$

$$1.058C_1 + 1.012A_3 - 1A_4 - 1C_4 = 0 \qquad \} \text{ cash-flow for month 4}$$

$$1.035B_3 + 1.012A_4 - 1A_5 - 1B_5 = 250 \qquad \} \text{ cash-flow for month 5}$$

$$1.012A_5 - 1A_6 = 0 \qquad \} \text{ cash-flow for month 6}$$

$$1.11D_1 + 1.058C_4 + 1.035B_5 + 1.012A_6 = 300 \qquad \} \text{ cash-flow for month 7}$$

There are two important points to note about this alternate expression of the constraints. First, each constraint takes on the following general form, which is algebraically equivalent to our previous general definition for the cash-flow constraints:

$$\begin{pmatrix} \text{Total \$ amount} \\ \text{maturing at the} \\ \text{beginning of the month} \end{pmatrix} - \begin{pmatrix} \text{Total \$ amount} \\ \text{reinvested at the} \\ \text{beginning of the month} \end{pmatrix} = \begin{pmatrix} \text{Payment due at the} \\ \text{beginning of the month} \end{pmatrix}$$

Although the constraints look slightly different in this form, they enforce the same relationships among the variables as expressed by the earlier constraints.

Second, the LHS coefficients in the alternate expression of the constraints correspond directly to the values listed in the cash-flow summary table in Figure 3.35. That is, the coefficients in the constraint for month 2 correspond to the values in the column for month 2 in Figure 3.35; the coefficients for month 3 correspond to the values in the column for month 3, and so on. This relationship is true for all the constraints and will be very helpful in implementing this model in the spreadsheet.

THE RISK CONSTRAINTS

The other set of constraints affecting this problem concerns the restriction on the amount of risk the company is willing to allow for this investment. Management indicated that the weighted average risk for all investments should never exceed the value 5. Therefore, we need to create a constraint for each time period that meets this condition.

Let's begin with month 1. Funds can be invested in A_1, B_1, C_1, and/or D_1 during this month, and each investment is associated with a different degree of risk. To calculate the weighted average risk during month 1, we must multiply the risk factors for each investment by the proportion of money in that investment. This is represented by:

$$\text{Weighted average risk in month 1} = \frac{1A_1 + 3B_1 + 8C_1 + 6D_1}{A_1 + B_1 + C_1 + D_1}$$

We can ensure that the weighted average risk in month 1 does not exceed the value 5 by including the following constraint in our LP model:

$$\frac{1A_1 + 3B_1 + 8C_1 + 6D_1}{A_1 + B_1 + C_1 + D_1} \le 5 \qquad \} \text{ risk constraint for month 1}$$

Now let's consider month 2. According to the column for month 2 in our cash inflow/outflow table, the company can have funds invested in B_1, C_1, D_1, and/or A_2 during this month. Thus, the weighted average risk that occurs in month 2 is defined by:

$$\text{Weighted average risk in month 2} = \frac{3B_1 + 8C_1 + 6D_1 + 1A_2}{B_1 + C_1 + D_1 + A_2}$$

Again, the following constraint ensures that this quantity never exceeds 5:

$$\frac{3B_1 + 8C_1 + 6D_1 + 1A_2}{B_1 + C_1 + D_1 + A_2} \leq 5 \quad \} \text{ risk constraint for month 2}$$

The risk constraints for months 3 through 6 are generated in a similar manner, and appear as:

$$\frac{8C_1 + 6D_1 + 1A_3 + 3B_2}{C_1 + D_1 + A_3 + B_3} \leq 5 \quad \} \text{ risk constraint for month 3}$$

$$\frac{6D_1 + 3B_3 + 1A_4 + 8C_4}{D_1 + B_3 + A_4 + C_4} \leq 5 \quad \} \text{ risk constraint for month 4}$$

$$\frac{6D_1 + 8C_4 + 1A_5 + 3B_5}{D_1 + C_4 + A_5 + B_5} \leq 5 \quad \} \text{ risk constraint for month 5}$$

$$\frac{6D_1 + 8C_4 + 3B_5 + 1A_6}{D_1 + C_4 + B_5 + A_6} \leq 5 \quad \} \text{ risk constraint for month 6}$$

Although the risk constraints listed above have a very clear meaning, it is easier to implement these constraints in the spreadsheet if we state them in a different (but algebraically equivalent) manner. In particular, it is helpful to eliminate the fractions on the LHS of the inequalities by multiplying each constraint through by its denominator and re-collecting the variables on the LHS of the inequality. The following steps show how to rewrite the risk constraint for month 1:

1. Multiply both sides of the inequality by the denominator:

$$\left(A_1 + B_1 + C_1 + D_1\right)\frac{1A_1 + 3B_1 + 8C_1 + 6D_1}{A_1 + B_1 + C_1 + D_1} \leq 5\left(A_1 + B_1 + C_1 + D_1\right)$$

to obtain:

$$1A_1 + 3B_1 + 8C_1 + 6D_1 \leq 5A_1 + 5B_1 + 5C_1 + 5D_1$$

2. Re-collect the variables on the LHS of the inequality sign:

$$(1 - 5)A_1 + (3 - 5)B_1 + (8 - 5)C_1 + (6 - 5)D_1 \leq 0$$

to obtain:

$$-4A_1 - 2B_1 + 3C_1 + 1D_1 \leq 0$$

Thus, the following two constraints are algebraically equivalent:

$$\frac{1A_1 + 3B_1 + 8C_1 + 6D_1}{A_1 + B_1 + C_1 + D_1} \leq 5 \quad \} \text{ risk constraint for month 1}$$

$$-4A_1 - 2B_1 + 3C_1 + 1D_1 \leq 0 \quad \} \text{ risk constraint for month 1}$$

The set of values for A_1, B_1, C_1, and D_1 that satisfies the first of these constraints also satisfies the second constraint (that is, these constraints have exactly the same set of feasible values). So, it does not matter which of these constraints we use to find the optimal solution to the problem.

The remaining risk constraints are simplified in the same way, producing the following constraints:

$$-2B_1 + 3C_1 + 1D_1 - 4A_2 \leq 0 \qquad \text{\} risk constraint for month 2}$$
$$3C_1 + 1D_1 - 4A_3 - 2B_3 \leq 0 \qquad \text{\} risk constraint for month 3}$$
$$1D_1 - 2B_3 - 4A_4 + 3C_4 \leq 0 \qquad \text{\} risk constraint for month 4}$$
$$1D_1 + 3C_4 - 4A_5 - 2B_5 \leq 0 \qquad \text{\} risk constraint for month 5}$$
$$1D_1 + 3C_4 - 2B_5 - 4A_6 \leq 0 \qquad \text{\} risk constraint for month 6}$$

Notice that the coefficient for each variable in these constraints is simply the risk factor for the particular investment minus the maximum allowable weighted average risk value of 5. That is, all A_i variables have coefficients of $1 - 5 = -4$; all B_i variables have coefficients of $3 - 5 = -2$; all C_i variables have coefficients of $8 - 5 = 3$; and all D_i variables have coefficients of $6 - 5 = 1$. This observation will help us implement these constraints efficiently.

IMPLEMENTING THE MODEL

The LP model for Taco-Viva's construction fund problem is summarized as:

$$\text{MIN: } A_1 + B_1 + C_1 + D_1 \qquad \text{\} cash invested at beginning of month 1}$$

Subject to:

$$1.012A_1 - 1A_2 = 0 \qquad \text{\} cash flow for month 2}$$
$$1.035B_1 + 1.012A_2 - 1A_3 - 1B_3 = 250 \qquad \text{\} cash flow for month 3}$$
$$1.058C_1 + 1.012A_3 - 1A_4 - 1C_4 = 0 \qquad \text{\} cash flow for month 4}$$
$$1.035B_3 + 1.012A_4 - 1A_5 - 1B_5 = 250 \qquad \text{\} cash flow for month 5}$$
$$1.012A_5 - 1A_6 = 0 \qquad \text{\} cash flow for month 6}$$
$$1.11D_1 + 1.058C_4 + 1.035B_5 + 1.012A_6 = 300 \qquad \text{\} cash flow for month 7}$$
$$-4A_1 - 2B_1 + 3C_1 + 1D_1 \leq 0 \qquad \text{\} risk constraint for month 1}$$
$$-2B_1 + 3C_1 + 1D_1 - 4A_2 \leq 0 \qquad \text{\} risk constraint for month 2}$$
$$3C_1 + 1D_1 - 4A_3 - 2B_3 \leq 0 \qquad \text{\} risk constraint for month 3}$$
$$1D_1 - 2B_3 - 4A_4 + 3C_4 \leq 0 \qquad \text{\} risk constraint for month 4}$$
$$1D_1 + 3C_4 - 4A_5 - 2B_5 \leq 0 \qquad \text{\} risk constraint for month 5}$$
$$1D_1 + 3C_4 - 2B_5 - 4A_6 \leq 0 \qquad \text{\} risk constraint for month 6}$$
$$A_i, B_i, C_i, D_i, \geq 0, \text{ for all } i \qquad \text{\} nonnegativity conditions}$$

To implement this model in a spreadsheet, we begin by entering some of the basic data. Figure 3.36 (and the file FIG3-36.XLS on your data disk) displays the investment options available to Taco-Viva along with their respective returns and risk factors. Cell E12 indicates the maximum allowable weighted average risk.

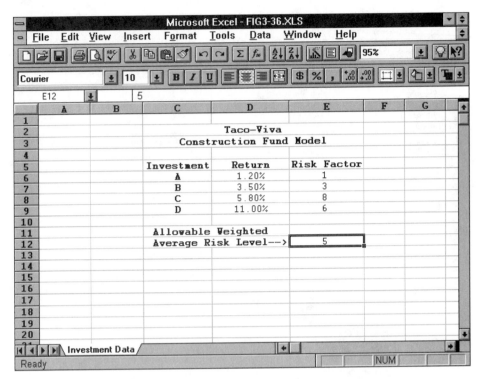

Figure 3.36: Data for Taco-Viva's construction fund problem

Because all the coefficients in the constraints depend directly on these return and risk factor values, we will refer to cells D6 through D9 and cells E6 through E9 in various formulas as we implement our model. Setting up the spreadsheet in this way makes the model flexible and allows Taco-Viva's management to modify any of these values and re-solve the problem easily. For example, it is possible that the yields on one or more of the investments will change before a decision is implemented. Or the company might want to examine how the solution to the problem will change if the maximum allowable risk is increased or decreased.

One approach to implementing this model is shown in Figure 3.37 and Figure 3.38. Figure 3.37 implements the cash inflow/outflow table described earlier. Note that the cash outflows listed in this table are implemented through formulas that refer back to the appropriate cells in Figure 3.36. For example, cell M5 contains the formula:

Formula for cell M5:   =1+D6

If the value in cell D6 changes, the value in cell M5 will be updated automatically with the correct value.

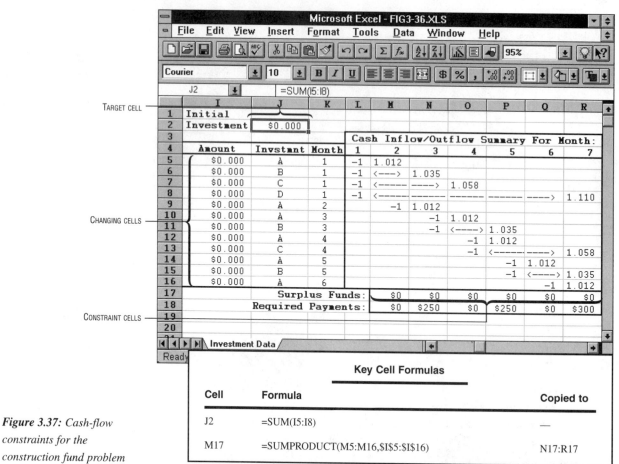

Figure 3.37: Cash-flow constraints for the construction fund problem

Figure 3.38: Risk constraints for the construction fund problem

Key Cell Formulas

Cell	Formula	Copied to
J2	=SUM(I5:I8)	—
S5	=IF(OR(L5=−1,ISTEXT(L5)),VLOOKUP($J5,$C$6:$E$9,3)−$E$12," ")	S5:X16
S17	=SUMPRODUCT(S5:S16,$I$5:$I$16)	T17:X17

Figure 3.38: Continued

Cells I5 through I16 in Figure 3.37 correspond to the different variables in our algebraic formulation of the problem. That is, cell I5 corresponds to the variable A_1, cell I6 corresponds to the variable B_1, and so on. The objective function for the problem is implemented in cell J2 as:

Formula for cell J2:   =SUM(I5:I8)

This formula corresponds directly to the objective function of $A_1 + B_1 + C_1 + D_1$ in our algebraic model.

Earlier we noted that the values listed in columns 2 through 7 of the cash inflow/outflow table correspond directly to the coefficients appearing in the various cash-flow constraints. This property allows us to implement the cash-flow constraints in the spreadsheet conveniently. For example, the LHS formula for the cash-flow constraint for month 2 is implemented in cell M17 through the formula:

Formula in cell M17:   =SUMPRODUCT(M5:M16,$I$5:$I$16)
(copy to N17 through R17)

This formula multiplies each entry in the range M5 through M16 by the corresponding entry in the range I5 through I16 and then sums these individual products. This formula is copied to cells N17 through R17. (Notice that the SUMPRODUCT( ) formula treats blank cells and cells containing labels as if they contained the value zero.) Take a moment now to verify that the formulas in cells M17 through R17 correspond to the LHS formulas of the cash-flow constraints in our algebraic model. Cells M18 through R18 list the RHS values for the cash-flow constraints.

Figure 3.38 shows a split screen that illustrates an easy way to implement the risk constraints for this model. Earlier we noted that the coefficient for each variable in each risk constraint is simply the risk factor for the particular investment minus the maximum allowable weighted average risk value. Thus, the strategy in Figure 3.38 is to generate these values in the appropriate columns and rows of the spreadsheet so that the SUMPRODUCT( ) function can implement the LHS formulas for the risk constraints.

Recall that the risk constraint for each month involves only the variables representing investments that actually held funds during that month. For any given month, the investments that actually held funds during that month have the value −1 or a text entry (that is, some portion of the <----> entries) in the corresponding column of the cash inflow/outflow summary table shown in Figure 3.37. For example, during month 2, funds can be invested in B_1, C_1, D_1, and/or A_2. The corresponding cells for month 2 in Figure 3.37 (cells M6, M7, M8, and M9, respectively) each contain either a text entry or the value −1. Therefore, to generate the appropriate coefficients for the risk constraints, we can instruct the spreadsheet to scan the cash inflow/outflow summary for cells containing text entries or the value −1 and return the correct risk constraint coefficients in the appropriate cells. To do this we enter the following formula in cell S5:

Formula in cell S5:   =IF(OR(L5=–1,ISTEXT(L5)),VLOOKUP
(copy to S5 through X16)   ($J5,$C$6:$E$9,3)–$E$12," ")

To generate the appropriate value in cell S5, the above formula checks if cell L5 is equal to –1 or contains a text entry. If either of these conditions is true, the function looks up the risk factor for the type of investment associated with cell L5 and subtracts the maximum allowable risk factor; otherwise, the function returns a blank space (with a value of zero). This formula is copied to the remaining cells in the range S5 through X16 shown in Figure 3.38.

The values in cells S5 through X16 in Figure 3.38 correspond to the coefficients in the LHS formulas for each of the risk constraints in our algebraic formulation of the model. Thus, the LHS formula for the risk constraint for month 1 is implemented in cell S17 as:

Formula in cell S17:   =SUMPRODUCT(S5:S16,$I$5:$I$16)
(copy to T17 through X17)

The LHS formulas for the remaining risk constraints are implemented by copying this formula to cells T17 through X17.

SOLVING THE MODEL

To find the optimal solution to this model, we must indicate to Solver the target cell, changing cells, and constraint cells identified in Figures 3.37 and 3.38. Figure 3.39 shows the Solver parameters and options required to solve this model. The optimal solution is shown in Figure 3.40.

Figure 3.39: Solver parameters and options for the construction fund problem

Microsoft Excel - FIG3-36.XLS

File Edit View Insert Format Tools Data Window Help

Courier   10   B I U $ %

J2   =SUM(I5:I8)

			Cash Inflow/Outflow Summary For Month:						
Amount	Invstmnt	Month	1	2	3	4	5	6	7
($0.000)	A	1	-1	1.012					
$635.843	B	1	-1	<--->	1.035				
$108.621	C	1	-1	<------	----->	1.058			
$0.000	D	1	-1	<------	------	------	------	----->	1.110
$0.000	A	2		-1	1.012				
$0.000	A	3			-1	1.012			
$408.097	B	3			-1	<---->	1.035		
$0.000	A	4				-1	1.012		
$114.921	C	4				-1	<------	----->	1.058
$0.000	A	5					-1	1.012	
$172.381	B	5					-1	<---->	1.035
$0.000	A	6						-1	1.012
	Surplus Funds:			($0)	$250	($0)	$250	$0	$300
	Required Payments:			$0	$250	$0	$250	$0	$300

Initial Investment $744.463

Investment Data

Ready

Figure 3.40: Optimal solution to Taco-Viva's construction fund problem

ANALYZING THE SOLUTION

The value of the target cell (J2) in Figure 3.40 indicates that a total of $744,463 must be invested to meet the payments on Taco-Viva's construction project. Cells I6 and I7 indicate that approximately $635,843 should be placed in investment B at the beginning of month 1 ($B_1 = 635.843$) and approximately $108,621 should be placed in investment C ($C_1 = 108.621$).

At the beginning of month 3, the first $250,000 payment is due. At that time, the funds placed in investment B at the beginning of month 1 will mature and be worth $658,097 ($1.035*635,843 = 658,097$). Thus, after making the payment of $250,000 at the beginning of month 3, a total of $408,097 will be left to reinvest at the beginning of month 3. Cell I11 in our solution indicates that this amount should be reinvested in investment B at the beginning of month 3 ($B_3 = 408.097$).

At the beginning of month 4, the funds placed in investment C at the beginning of month 1 will mature and be worth $114,921. Our solution indicates that this amount should be reinvested investment C ($C_4 = 114.921$).

If you trace through the cash flows for the remaining months, you will discover that our model is doing exactly what it was designed to do. The amount of money scheduled to mature at the beginning of each month is exactly equal to the amount of money scheduled to be reinvested after required payments are made. Thus, out of an infinite number of possible investment schedules, our LP model found the one schedule that requires the least amount of money up front.

SUMMARY

This chapter described how to formulate an LP problem algebraically, implement it in a spreadsheet, and solve it using Solver. The decision variables in the algebraic formulation of a model correspond to the changing cells in the spreadsheet. The LHS formulas for each constraint in an LP model must be implemented in different cells in the spreadsheet. Also, a cell in the spreadsheet must represent the objective function in the LP model. Thus, there is a direct relationship between the various components of an algebraic formulation of an LP problem and its implementation in a spreadsheet.

There are many ways a given LP problem can be implemented in a spreadsheet. The process of building spreadsheet models is more an art than a science. A good spreadsheet implementation represents the problem in a way that clearly communicates its purpose and results.

REFERENCES

Hilal, S., and W. Erickson. "Matching Supplies to Save Lives: Linear Programming the Production of Heart Valves." *Interfaces*, vol. 11, no. 6, 1981.

Lanzenauer, C., et al. "RRSP Flood: LP to the Rescue." *Interfaces*, vol. 17, no. 4, 1987.

McKay, A. "Linear Programming Applications on Microcomputers." *Journal of the Operational Research Society*, vol. 36, July 1985.

Roush, W., et al. "Using Chance-Constrained Programming for Animal Feed Formulation at Agway." *Interfaces*, vol. 24, no. 2, 1994.

Shogan, A. *Management Science*. Englewood Cliffs, NJ: Prentice Hall, 1988.

Williams, H. *Model Building in Mathematical Programming*. New York: Wiley, 1985.

Spreadsheets, LP Solvers Create New Applications for Linear Programming

Source: Bulkely, William M., "The Right Mix: New Software Makes the Choice Much Easier," *The Wall Street Journal*, March 27, 1987, p. 17.

EXCEL'S SOLVER PROVIDES one of the most effective ways to handle LP models in a spreadsheet, but it was not the first. Spreadsheet solvers such as What's Best! and LP88 were being used increasingly at the time that the most popular spreadsheet programs began to bundle a solver with their new releases. LP88 can be used as a standalone program or with a spreadsheet. What's Best! was designed initially as an add-in to Lotus 1-2-3, but current releases also work with Microsoft Excel and Quattro Pro.

The Wall Street Journal reported in March, 1987 that the availability of solvers for personal computers allowed many businesses to transfer LP models from mainframe computers. Newfoundland Energy Ltd., for example, evaluated its mix of crude oils to purchase with LP on a mainframe for 25 years. Since it began using a personal computer for this application, the company has saved thousands of dollars per year in mainframe access time charges.

The expansion of access to LP also spawned new applications. Therese Fitzpatrick, a nursing administrator at Grant Hospital in Chicago, used What's Best! to create a staff scheduling model that was projected to save the hospital $80,000 per month in overtime and temporary hiring costs. The task of scheduling 300 nurses so that those with appropriate skills were in the right place at the right time had required 20 hours per month. The LP model enabled Therese to do the job in four hours, even with such complicating factors as leaves, vacations, and variations in staffing requirements at different times and days of the week.

Hawley Fuel Corp., a New York wholesaler of coal, found that it could minimize its cost of purchases while still meeting customers' requirements for sulfur and ash content by optimizing a spreadsheet LP model. Charles Howard of Victoria, British Columbia, developed an LP model to increase electricity generation from a dam just by opening and closing the outlet valves at the right time.

Questions and Problems

1. In creating the spreadsheet models for the problems in this chapter, cells in the spreadsheets had to be reserved to represent each of the decision variables in the algebraic models. We reserved these cells in the spreadsheets by entering values of zero in them. Why didn't we place some other value or formula in these cells? Would doing so have made any difference?

2. Refer to question 13 at the end of chapter 2. Implement a spreadsheet model for this problem and solve it using Solver.

3. Refer to question 16 at the end of chapter 2. Implement a spreadsheet model for this problem and solve it using Solver.

4. Refer to question 17 at the end of chapter 2. Implement a spreadsheet model for this problem and solve it using Solver.

5. Refer to question 19 at the end of chapter 2. Implement a spreadsheet model for this problem and solve it using Solver.

6. Refer to question 20 at the end of chapter 2. Implement a spreadsheet model for this problem and solve it using Solver.

7. The Weedwacker Company manufactures two types of lawn trimmers: an electric model and a gas model. The company has contracted to supply a national discount retail chain with a total of 30,000 electric trimmers and 15,000 gas trimmers during the next three months. However, Weedwacker's production capability is limited in three departments: production, assembly, and packaging. The following table summarizes the hours of processing time available and the processing time required by each department, for both types of trimmers:

	Hours Required per Trimmer		
	Electric	Gas	Hours Available
Production	0.20	0.40	10,000
Assembly	0.30	0.50	15,000
Packaging	0.10	0.10	5,000

The company makes its electric trimmer in-house for $55 and its gas trimmer for $85. Alternatively, it can buy electric and gas trimmers from another source for $67 and $95, respectively. How many gas and electric trimmers should Weedwacker make and how many should it buy from its competitor in order to fulfill its contract in the least costly manner?

a. Formulate an LP model for this problem.

b. Create a spreadsheet model for this problem and solve it using Solver.

c. What is the optimal solution?

8. A manufacturer of prefabricated homes has decided to subcontract four components of the homes. Several companies are interested in receiving this business, but none can handle more than one subcontract. The bids made by the companies for the various subcontracts are summarized in the following table.

Bids by Companies (in $1,000s) for Various Subcontracts

Component	Company			
	A	B	C	D
1	185	225	193	207
2	200	190	175	225
3	330	320	315	300
4	375	389	425	445

Assuming all the companies can perform each of the subcontract equally well, to which company should each subcontract be assigned if the home manufacturer wants to minimize payments to the subcontractors?

a. Formulate an LP model for this problem.

b. Create a spreadsheet model for this problem and solve it using Solver.

c. What is the optimal solution?

9. Tarmac Chemical Corporation produces a special chemical compound—called CHEMIX—that is used extensively in high school chemistry classes. This compound must contain at least 30% sulfur, at least 40% iron oxide, and at least 30% but no more than 45% potassium. Tarmac's marketing department has estimated that it will need at least 600 pounds of this compound to meet the expected demand during the coming school session. Tarmac can buy three compounds to mix together to produce CHEMIX. The makeup of these compounds is given below.

Compound	Sulfur	Iron Oxide	Potassium
1	20%	60%	20%
2	40%	30%	30%
3	10%	40%	50%

Compounds 1, 2, and 3 cost $5.00, $5.25, and $5.50 per pound, respectively. Tarmac wants to use an LP model to determine the least costly way of producing enough CHEMIX to meet the demand expected for the coming year.

a. Formulate an LP model for this problem.

b. Create a spreadsheet model for this problem and solve it using Solver.

c. What is the optimal solution?

10. Maintenance at a major theme park in central Florida is an on-going process that occurs 24 hours a day. Because it is a long drive from most residential areas to the park, employees do not like to work shifts of fewer than eight hours. These 8-hour shifts start every four hours throughout the day. The number of maintenance workers needed at different times throughout the day varies. The following table summarizes the minimum number of employees needed in each 4-hour time period.

Time Period	Minimum Employees Needed
12 a.m. to 4 a.m.	90
4 a.m. to 8 a.m.	215
8 a.m. to 12 p.m.	250
12 p.m. to 4 p.m.	165
4 p.m. to 8 p.m.	300
8 p.m. to 12 a.m.	125

The maintenance supervisor wants to determine the minimum number of employees to schedule that meets the minimum staffing requirements.

a. Formulate an LP model for this problem.

b. Create a spreadsheet model for this problem and solve it using Solver.

c. What is the optimal solution?

11. Radmore Memorial Hospital has a problem in its fluids analysis lab. The lab has available two machines, that analyze various fluid samples. Recently, the demand for analyzing blood samples has increased so much that the lab director is having difficulty getting all the samples analyzed quickly enough and still completing the other fluid work that comes into the lab. The lab works with three types of blood specimens. Either machine can be used to process any of the specimens. However, the amount of time required by the machines varies depending on the type of specimen being analyzed. These times are summarized in the following table.

Required Specimen Processing Time in Hours

Machine	Specimen Type		
	1	2	3
A	2	4	3
B	5	3	2

Both machines can be used a total of 16 hours a day, 7 days a week. During an average week, the lab receives 40 type 1 specimens, 30 type 2 specimens, and 15 type 3 specimens. The lab director wants to know how many of the three specimens should be analyzed on each machine in order to minimize the total time the machines are devoted to analyzing blood samples.

a. Formulate an LP model for this problem.

b. Create a spreadsheet model for this problem and solve it using Solver.

c. What is the optimal solution?

d. Will there be any difficulty in implementing this solution?

12. Virginia Tech has its own power generating plant that burns up to 30 tons of coal per hour. The electricity generated by this plant supplies power to the university and to local businesses and residences in the Blacksburg area. The plant burns three types of coal, which produce steam that drives the turbines that generate the electricity. The Environmental Protection Agency (EPA) requires that emissions from the coal furnace smoke stacks contain no more than 2800 parts per million (ppm) of sulfur and emit no more than 17 kilograms per hour (kph) of coal dust. The following table summarizes the amounts of sulfur, coal dust, and steam that result from burning each type of coal.

Coal	Sulfur (in ppm)	Coal Dust (in kph)	Pounds of Steam Produced per Hour
1	1100	1.7	24,000
2	2700	3.2	28,000
3	3500	2.4	36,000

The three types of coal can be mixed and burned in any combination. The resulting emission of sulfur or coal dust and the pounds of steam produced by any mixture are given as the weighted average of the values shown in the table for each type of coal. For example, if the coals are mixed to produce a blend that consisted of 20% of coal 1, 45% of coal 2, and 35% of coal 3, the resulting sulfur emission of this blend is:

0.2*1100 + 0.45*2700 + 0.35*3500 = 2660

The manager of this facility wants to determine the blend of coal that will produce the maximum pounds of steam per hour without violating the EPA requirements.

a. Formulate an LP model for this problem.

b. Create a spreadsheet model for this problem and solve it using Solver.

c. What is the optimal solution?

13. A real estate developer is planning to build an apartment building specifically for graduate students on a parcel of land adjacent to a major university. Three types of apartments can be included in the building: efficiencies, and one-, two-, or three-bedroom units. Each efficiency requires 500 square

feet; each one-bedroom apartment requires 700 square feet; each two-bedroom apartment requires 800 square feet; and each three-bedroom unit requires 1,000 square feet.

The developer believes that the building should include no more than 15 one-bedroom units, 22 two-bedroom units, and 10 three-bedroom units. Local zoning ordinances do not allow the developer to build more than 40 units in this particular building location, and restrict the building to a maximum of 40,000 square feet. The developer has already agreed to lease 5 one-bedroom units and 8 two-bedroom units to a local rental agency that is a "silent partner" in this endeavor. Market studies indicate that efficiencies can be rented for $350 per month, one-bedrooms for $450 per month, two-bedrooms for $550 per month, and three-bedrooms for $750 per month. How many rental units of each type should the developer include in the building plans in order to maximize the potential rental income from the building?

a. Formulate an LP model for this problem.

b. Create a spreadsheet model for this problem and solve it using Solver.

c. What is the optimal solution?

d. Which constraint in this model limits the builder's potential rental income from increasing any further?

14. Kentwood Electronics manufactures three components for stereo systems: CD players, tape decks, and stereo tuners. The wholesale price and manufacturing cost of each item are given below.

Component	Wholesale Price	Manufacturing Cost
CD Player	$150	$75
Tape Deck	$85	$35
Stereo Tuner	$70	$30

Each CD player produced requires 3 hours of assembly; each tape deck requires 2 hours of assembly; and each tuner requires 1 hour of assembly. The marketing department has indicated that it can sell no more than 150,000 CD players, 100,000 tape decks, and 90,000 stereo tuners. However, the demand is expected to be at least 50,000 units of each item, and Kentwood wants to meet this demand. If Kentwood has 400,000 hours of assembly time available, how many CD players, tape decks, and stereo tuners should it produce in order to maximize profits while meeting the minimum demand figures?

a. Formulate an LP model for this problem.

b. Create a spreadsheet model for this problem and solve it using Solver.

c. What is the optimal solution?

15. The Rent-A-Dent car rental company allows its customers to pick up a rental car at one location and return it to *any* of its locations. Currently, two locations (1 and 2) have 15 and 18 surplus cars, respectively, and four locations (3, 4, 5, and 6) each need 10 cars. The costs of getting the surplus cars from locations 1 and 2 to the other locations are summarized below.

Costs of Transporting Cars Between Locations

	Location 3	Location 4	Location 5	Location 6
Location 1	$54	$17	$23	$30
Location 2	$24	$18	$19	$31

Because 33 surplus cars are available at locations 1 and 2, and 40 cars are needed at locations 3, 4, 5, and 6, some locations will not receive as many cars as they need. However, management wants to make sure that all the surplus cars are sent where they are needed, and that each location needing cars receives at least five.

a. Formulate an LP model for this problem.

b. Create a spreadsheet model for this problem and solve it using Solver.

c. What is the optimal solution?

16. A winery has the following capacity to produce an exclusive dinner wine at either of its two vineyards at the indicated costs:

Vineyard	Capacity	Cost per Bottle
1	3,500 bottles	$23
2	3,100 bottles	$25

Four Italian restaurants around the country are interested in purchasing this wine. Because the wine is exclusive, they all want to buy as much as they need but will take whatever they can get. The maximum amounts required by the restaurants and the prices they are willing to pay are summarized below.

Restaurant	Maximum Demand	Price
1	1,800 bottles	$69
2	2,300 bottles	$67
3	1,250 bottles	$70
4	1,750 bottles	$66

The costs of shipping a bottle from the vineyards to the restaurants are summarized below.

| | Restaurant | | | |
Vineyard	1	2	3	4
1	$7	$8	$13	$9
2	$12	$6	$8	$7

The winery needs to determine the production and shipping plan that allows it to maximize its profits on this wine.

a. Formulate an LP model for this problem.

b. Create a spreadsheet model for this problem and solve it using Solver.

c. What is the optimal solution?

17. Howie's Carpet World has just received an order for carpets for a new office building. The order is for 4,000 yards of carpet 4-feet wide, 20,000 yards of carpet 9-feet wide, and 9,000 yards of carpet 12-feet wide. Howie can order two kinds of carpet rolls, which he will then have to cut to fill this order. One type of roll is 14-feet wide, 100-yards long, and costs $1,000 per roll; the other is 18-feet wide, 100-yards long, and costs $1,400 per roll. Howie needs to determine how many of the two types of carpet rolls to order and how they should be cut. He wants to do this in the least costly way possible.

a. Formulate an LP model for this problem.

b. Create a spreadsheet model for this problem and solve it using Solver.

c. What is the optimal solution?

18. The Pitts Barbeque Company makes three kinds of barbeque sauce: Extra Hot, Hot, and Mild. Pitts's vice president of marketing estimates that the company can sell 8,000 cases of its Extra Hot sauce plus 10 extra cases for every dollar it spends promoting this sauce; 10,000 cases of Hot sauce plus 8 extra cases for every dollar spent promoting this sauce; and 12,000 cases of its Mild sauce plus 5 extra cases for every dollar spent promoting this sauce. Although each barbeque sauce sells for $10 per case, the cost of producing the different types of sauce varies. It costs the company $6 to produce a case of Extra Hot sauce, $5.50 to produce a case of Hot sauce, and $5.25 to produce a case of Mild sauce. The president of the company wants to make sure the company manufactures at least the minimum amounts of each sauce that the marketing vice president thinks the company can sell. A budget of $25,000 total has been approved for promoting these items. How many cases of each type of sauce should be made and how do you suggest that the company allocate the promotional budget if it wants to maximize profits?

a. Formulate an LP model for this problem.

b. Create a spreadsheet model for this problem and solve it using Solver.

c. What is the optimal solution?

19. Acme Manufacturing makes a variety of household appliances at a single manufacturing facility. The expected demand for one of these appliances during the next four months is shown in the following table along with the expected production costs and the expected capacity for producing these items.

	Month			
	1	2	3	4
Demand	420	580	310	540
Production Cost	$42.60	$45.00	$46.00	$49.70
Production Capacity	500	520	450	550

Acme estimates it costs $1.50 per month for each unit of this appliance carried in inventory. Currently, Acme has no inventory on hand for this product. Acme wants to determine how many of each appliance to manufacture during each of the next four months to meet the expected demand at the lowest possible total cost.

a. Formulate an LP model for this problem.

b. Create a spreadsheet model for this problem and solve it using Solver.

c. What is the optimal solution?

20. A furniture manufacturer produces two types of tables (country and contemporary) using three types of machines. The time required to produce the tables on each machine is given in the following table.

Machine	Country	Contemporary	Total Machine Time Available per Week
Router	1.5	2.0	1,000
Sander	3.0	4.5	2,000
Polisher	2.5	1.5	1,500

Country tables sell for $350 and contemporary tables sell for $450. Management has determined that at least 20% of the tables made should be country and at least 30% should be contemporary. How many of each type of table should the company produce if it wants to maximize its revenue?

a. Formulate an LP model for this problem.

b. Create a spreadsheet model for this problem and solve it using Solver.

c. What is the optimal solution?

d. How will your spreadsheet model differ if there are 25 types of tables and 15 machine processes involved in manufacturing them?

21. Carter Enterprises is involved in the soybean business in South Carolina, Alabama, and Georgia. The president of the company, Earl Carter, goes to a commodity sale once a month where he buys and sells soybeans in bulk. Carter uses a local warehouse for storing his soybean inventory. This warehouse charges $10 per ton of soybeans stored per month. The warehouse guarantees Carter the capacity to store up to 400 tons of soybeans. Carter has estimated what he believes the price per ton of soybeans will be during each of the next six months. These prices are summarized in the table below.

Month	Price per Ton
1	$135
2	$110
3	$150
4	$175
5	$130
6	$145

Assume Carter currently has 70 tons of soybeans stored in the warehouse and does not want to have any soybeans left at the end of the six-month period. How many tons of soybeans should Carter buy and sell during each of the next six months to maximize his profit trading soybeans?

a. Formulate an LP model for this problem.

b. Create a spreadsheet model for this problem and solve it using Solver.

c. What is the optimal solution?

22. Jack Potts recently won $1,000,000 in Las Vegas and is trying to determine how to invest his winnings. He has narrowed his decision down to five investments, which are summarized in the following table.

	Summary of Cash Inflows and Outflows (at beginning of year)				
	A	B	C	D	E
1994	−1.00	0.00	−1.00	0.00	−1.00
1995	+0.45	−1.00	0.00	0.00	0.00
1996	+1.05	0.00	0.00	−1.00	1.25
1997	0.00	+1.30	+1.65	1.30	0.00

If Jack invests $1 in investment A at the beginning of 1994, he will receive $0.45 at the beginning of 1995 and another $1.05 at the beginning of 1996. Alternatively, he can invest $1 in investment B at the beginning of 1995 and receive $1.30 at the beginning of 1997. Entries of 0.00 in the table indicate times when no cash inflows or outflows can occur. At the beginning of any year, Jack can place any or all of his money in a savings account that is expected to yield 5% per year. Jack does not want to have more than half of his money invested in any single investment (besides the savings account) at the beginning of any year. How do you suggest Jack invest his winnings if he wants to maximize the amount of money he'll have at the beginning of 1997?

a. Formulate an LP model for this problem.

b. Create a spreadsheet model for this problem and solve it using Solver.

c. What is the optimal solution?

CHAPTER 4

Sensitivity Analysis and the Simplex Method

IN CHAPTERS 2 AND 3 we studied how to formulate and solve LP models for a variety of decision problems. However, formulating and solving an LP model does not necessarily mean that the original decision problem has been solved. After solving a model, a number of questions often arise about the optimal solution to the LP model. In particular, we might be interested in how sensitive the optimal solution is to changes in various coefficients of the LP model.

Businesses rarely know with certainty what costs will be incurred or the exact amount of resources that will be consumed or available in a given situation or time period. Thus, optimal solutions obtained using models that assume all relevant factors are known with certainty might be viewed with skepticism by management. Sensitivity analysis can help overcome this skepticism and provide a better picture of how the solution to a problem will change if different factors in the model change. Sensitivity analysis also can help answer a number of practical managerial questions that might arise about the solution to an LP problem.

THE PURPOSE OF SENSITIVITY ANALYSIS

As noted in chapter 2, any problem that can be stated in the following form is an LP problem:

$$\text{MAX (or MIN)}: \quad c_1X_1 + c_2X_2 + \ldots + c_nX_n$$
$$\text{Subject to}: \quad a_{11}X_1 + a_{12}X_2 + \ldots + a_{1n}X_n \leq b_1$$
$$\vdots$$
$$a_{k1}X_1 + a_{k2}X_2 + \ldots + a_{kn}X_n \geq b_k$$
$$\vdots$$
$$a_{m1}X_1 + a_{m2}X_2 + \ldots + a_{mn}X_n = b_m$$

All the coefficients in this model (the c_j, a_{ij}, and b_i) represent numeric constants. So, when we formulate and solve an LP problem, we implicitly assume that we can specify the exact values for these coefficients. However, in the real world these coefficients might change from day to day or minute to minute. For example, the price a company charges for its products can change on a daily, weekly, or monthly basis. Similarly, if a skilled machinist calls in sick, a manufacturer might have less capacity to produce items on a given machine than was originally planned.

Realizing that such uncertainties exist, a manager should consider how sensitive an LP model's solution is to changes or estimation errors that might occur in: (1) the objective function coefficients (the c_j), (2) the constraint coefficients (the a_{ij}), and (3) the RHS values for the constraints (the b_i). A manager also might ask a number of "What if?" questions about these values. For example, What if the cost of a product increases by 7%? What if a reduction in setup time allows for additional capacity on a given machine? What if a worker's suggestion results in a product requiring only two hours of labor rather than three? Sensitivity analysis addresses these issues by revealing the sensitivity of the solution to uncertainty or errors in the model coefficients, as well as the sensitivity to changes in these coefficients that might occur because of human intervention.

APPROACHES TO SENSITIVITY ANALYSIS

You can perform sensitivity analysis on an LP model in a number of ways. If you want to determine the effect of some change in the model, the most direct approach is to simply change the model and re-solve it. This approach is suitable if the model does not take an excessive amount of time to change or solve. If you are interested in studying the consequences of *simultaneously* changing several coefficients in the model, this might be the only practical approach to sensitivity analysis.

Solver also provides some sensitivity information after solving an LP problem. As mentioned in chapter 3, one of the benefits of using the simplex method to solve LP problems is its speed—it is considerably faster than the other optimization techniques offered by Solver. However, another advantage of using the simplex method is that it provides more sensitivity analysis information than the other techniques. In particular, the simplex method provides us with information about:

- the range of values the objective function coefficients can assume without changing the optimal solution
- the impact on the optimal objective function value of increases or decreases in the availability of various constrained resources

- the impact on the optimal objective function value of forcing changes in the values of certain decision variables away from their optimal values
- the impact that changes in constraint coefficients will have on the optimal solution to the problem

AN EXAMPLE PROBLEM

We will again use the Blue Ridge Hot Tubs problem to illustrate the types of sensitivity analysis information available using Solver. The LP formulation of the problem is repeated below, where X_1 represents the number of Aqua-Spas and X_2 represents the number of Hydro-Luxes to be produced:

$$\text{MAX}: \quad 350X_1 + 300X_2 \qquad \} \text{ profit}$$

$$\text{Subject to}: \quad 1X_1 + 1X_2 \leq 200 \qquad \} \text{ pump constraint}$$

$$9X_1 + 6X_2 \leq 1{,}566 \qquad \} \text{ labor constraint}$$

$$12X_1 + 16X_2 \leq 2{,}880 \qquad \} \text{ tubing constraint}$$

$$1X_1 \geq 0$$

$$1X_2 \geq 0 \qquad \Big\} \text{ nonnegativity conditions}$$

This model is implemented in the spreadsheet shown in Figure 4.1. (See chapter 3 for details on the procedure used to create and solve this spreadsheet model.)

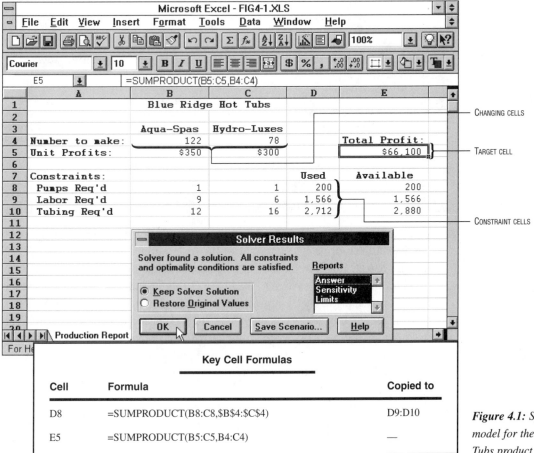

Figure 4.1: Spreadsheet model for the Blue Ridge Hot Tubs product mix problem

After solving the LP model, Solver displays the Solver Results dialog box, shown in Figure 4.1. This dialog box provides three report options: Answer, Sensitivity, and Limits. You can select any of these reports after a model has been solved. To select all three reports, highlight the reports, then click OK. To access each report, click the appropriate tab at the bottom of the screen.

THE ANSWER REPORT

Figure 4.2 shows the Answer Report for the Blue Ridge Hot Tubs problem. This report summarizes the solution to the problem, and is fairly self-explanatory. The first section of the report summarizes the original and final (optimal) value of the target cell. The next section summarizes the original and final (optimal) values of the adjustable (or changing) cells representing the decision variables.

Figure 4.2: Answer Report for the hot tub problem

The final section of this report provides information about the constraints. In particular, the Cell Value column shows the final (optimal) value assumed by each constraint cell. Note that these values correspond to the final value assumed by the LHS formula of each constraint. The Formula column indicates the upper or lower bounds that apply to each constraint cell. The Status column indicates which constraints are binding and which are nonbinding. A constraint is **binding** if it is satisfied as a strict equality in the optimal solution; otherwise, it is **nonbinding**. Notice that the constraints for the number of pumps and amount of labor used are both binding, meaning that *all* the available pumps and labor hours will be used if this solution is implemented. Therefore, these constraints are preventing Blue Ridge Hot Tubs from achieving a higher level of profit.

Finally, the values in the Slack column indicate the difference between the LHS and RHS of each constraint. By definition, binding constraints have zero slack and nonbinding constraints have some positive level of slack. The values in the Slack column indicate that if this solution is implemented, all the available pumps and labor hours will be used, but 168 feet of tubing will be left over. The slack values for the nonnegativity conditions indicate the amounts by which the decision variables exceed their respective lowers bounds of zero.

The Answer Report does not provide any information that could not be derived from the solution shown in the spreadsheet model. However, the format of this report gives a convenient summary of the solution that can be incorporated easily into a word processing document as part of a written report to management.

Report Headings

When creating the reports described in this chapter, Solver will try to use various text entries from the original spreadsheet to generate meaningful headings and labels in the reports. Given the various ways in which a model can be implemented, Solver might not always produce meaningful headings. However, you can change any text entry to make the report more meaningful or descriptive.

THE SENSITIVITY REPORT

Figure 4.3 shows the Sensitivity Report for the Blue Ridge Hot Tubs problem. This report summarizes information about the changing cells and constraints for our model. This information is useful in evaluating how sensitive the optimal solution is to changes in various coefficients in the model.

Figure 4.3: Sensitivity Report for the hot tub problem

CHANGES IN THE OBJECTIVE FUNCTION COEFFICIENTS

Chapter 2 introduced the level curve approach to solving a graphical LP problem and showed how to use this approach to solve the Blue Ridge Hot Tubs problem. This graphical solution is repeated in Figure 4.4.

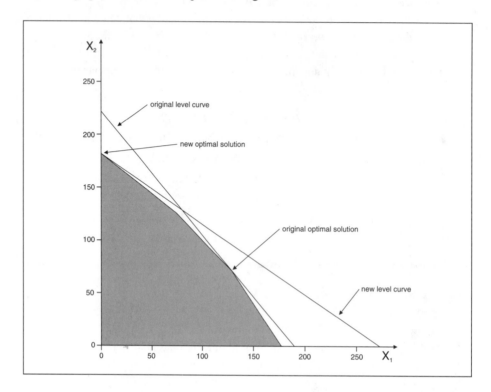

Figure 4.4: How changes in the objective function coefficients can change the slope of the level curve and the optimal solution

The slope of the original level curve in Figure 4.4 is determined by the coefficients in the objective function of the model (the values 350 and 300). In Figure 4.4, we can see that if the slope of the level curve were different, the corner point represented by $X_1 = 0$, $X_2 = 180$ would be the optimal solution. Of course, the only way to change the level curve for the objective function is to change the coefficients in the objective function. So if the objective function coefficients are at all uncertain, we might be interested in determining how much these values could change before the optimal solution would change.

For example, if the owner of Blue Ridge Hot Tubs does not have complete control over the costs of producing hot tubs (which is likely because he purchases the fiberglass hot tub shells from another company), the profit figures in the objective function of our LP model might not be the exact profits earned on hot tubs produced in the future. So before the manager decides to produce 122 Aqua-Spas and 78 Hydro-Luxes, he might want to determine how sensitive this solution is to the profit figures in the objective. That is, the manager might want to determine how much the profit figures could change before the optimal solution of $X_1 = 122$, $X_2 = 78$ would change. This information is provided in the Sensitivity Report shown in Figure 4.3.

The original objective function coefficients associated with the changing cells are listed in the Objective Coefficient column in Figure 4.3. The next two columns show the allowable increases and decreases in these values. For example, the objective function value associated with Aqua-Spas (or variable X_1) can increase by as much as $100 or decrease by as much as $50 without changing the optimal solution, assuming all other coefficients remain constant. (You can verify this by changing the profit coefficient for Aqua-Spas to any value in the range from $300 to $450 and re-solving the model.) Similarly, the objective function value associated with Hydro-Luxes (or variable X_2) can increase by $50 or decrease by approximately $66.67 without changing the optimal values of the decision variables, assuming all other coefficients remain constant. (Again, you can verify this by re-solving the model with different profit values for Hydro-Luxes.)

A NOTE ABOUT SENSITIVITY

The phrase "assuming all other coefficients remain constant" in the previous paragraph underscores the fact that the allowable increases and decreases shown in the Sensitivity Report apply only if *all* the other coefficients in the LP model do not change. The objective coefficient for Aqua-Spas can assume any value from $300 to $450 without changing the optimal solution—*but this is guaranteed to be true only if all the other coefficients in the model remain constant (including the objective function coefficient for X_2).* Similarly, the objective function coefficient for X_2 can assume any value between $233.33 and $350 without changing the optimal solution—*but this is guaranteed to be true only if all the other coefficients in the model remain constant (including the objective function coefficient for X_1).* Later in this chapter, you will see how to determine whether the current solution remains optimal if changes are made in two or more objective coefficients at the same time.

CHANGES IN THE RHS VALUES

As noted earlier, constraints that have zero slack in the optimal solution to an LP problem are called binding constraints. Binding constraints prevent us from further improving (that is, maximizing or minimizing) the objective function. For example, the Answer Report in Figure 4.2 indicates that the constraints for the number of pumps and hours of labor available are binding, whereas the constraint on the amount of tubing available is nonbinding. This is also evident in Figure 4.3 by comparing the Final Value column with the Constraint R.H. Side column. The values in the Final Value column represent the LHS values of each constraint at the optimal solution. A constraint is binding if its Final Value is equal to its Constraint R.H. Side value.

After solving an LP problem you might want to determine how much better or worse the solution would be if we had more or less of a given resource. For example, Howie Jones might wonder how much more profit could be earned if additional pumps or labor hours were available. The Shadow Price column in Figure 4.3 provides the answers to such questions.

The **shadow price** for a constraint indicates the amount by which the objective function value changes given a unit *increase* in the RHS value of the constraint, assuming all other coefficients remain constant. If a shadow price is positive, a unit increase in the RHS value of the associated constraint results in an increase in the optimal objective function value. If a shadow price is negative, a unit increase in the RHS of the associated constraint results in a decrease in the optimal objective function value. To analyze the effects of decreases in the RHS values, you reverse the sign on the shadow price. That is, the negated shadow price for a constraint indicates the amount by which the optimal objective function value changes given a unit *decrease* in the RHS value of the constraint, assuming all other coefficients remain constant. The shadow price values apply provided that the increase or decrease in the RHS value falls within the allowable increase or allowable decrease limits in the Sensitivity Report for each constraint.

For example, Figure 4.3 indicates that the shadow price for the labor constraint is 16.67. Therefore, if the number of available labor hours increased by any amount in the range from 0 to 234 hours, the optimal objective function value changes (increases) by $16.67 for each additional labor hour. If the number of available labor hours decreased by any amount in the range from 0 to 126 hours, the optimal objective function value changes (decreases) by –$16.67 for each lost labor hour. A similar interpretation holds for the shadow price for the constraint on the number of pumps. (It is coincidental that the shadow price for the pump constraint (200) is the same as that constraint's RHS and Final Values.)

SHADOW PRICES FOR NONBINDING CONSTRAINTS

Now let's consider the shadow price for the nonbinding tubing constraint. The tubing constraint has a shadow price of zero with an allowable increase of infinity and an allowable decrease of 168. Therefore, if the RHS value for the tubing constraint increases by *any* amount, the objective function value does not change (or changes by zero). This result is not surprising. Because the optimal solution to this problem leaves 168 feet of tubing unused, *additional* tubing will not produce a better solution. Furthermore, because the optimal solution includes 168 feet of unused tubing, we can reduce the RHS value of this constraint by 168 without affecting the optimal solution.

As this example illustrates, the shadow price of a nonbinding constraint is always zero. There is always some amount by which the RHS value of a nonbinding constraint can be changed without affecting the optimal solution.

A NOTE ABOUT SHADOW PRICES AND THEIR RANGES

One important point needs to be made concerning shadow prices. To illustrate this point, let's suppose that the RHS of the labor constraint for our example problem increase by 162 hours (from 1,566 to 1,728) due to the addition of new workers. Because this increase is within the allowable increase listed for the shadow price for the labor constraint, you might expect that the optimal objective function value would increase by $16.67*162 = $2,700. That is, the new optimal objective function value would be approximately $68,800 ($66,100 + $16.67*162 = $68,800). Figure 4.5 shows the re-solved model after increasing the RHS value for the labor constraint by 162 labor hours to 1,728.

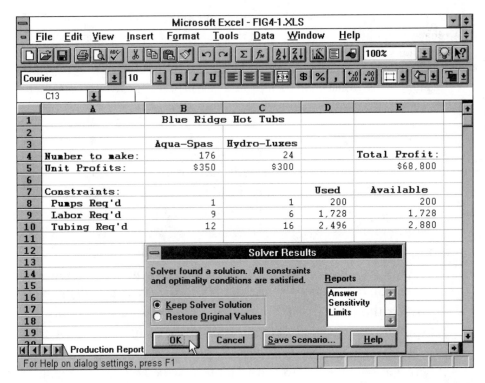

Figure 4.5: Solution to the revised hot tub problem with 162 additional labor hours

In Figure 4.5, the new optimal objective function value is $68,800, as expected. But this solution involves producing 176 Aqua-Spas and 24 Hydro-Luxes. That is, the optimal solution to the revised problem is *different* from the solution to the original problem shown in Figure 4.1. This is not surprising because changing the RHS of a constraint also changes the feasible region for the problem. The effect of increasing the RHS of the labor constraint is summarized graphically in Figure 4.6.

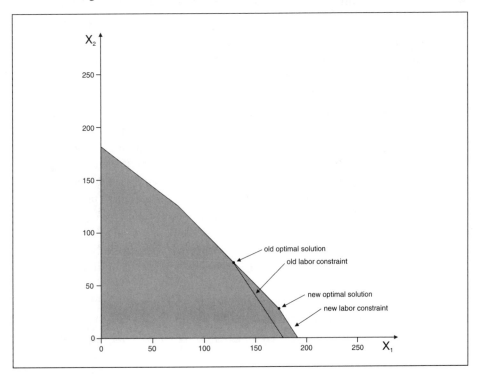

Figure 4.6: How changes in the RHS value of a constraint can change the feasible region and optimal solution

So, although shadow prices indicate how the objective function value changes if a given RHS value changes, they *do not* tell you which values the decision variables need to assume in order to achieve this new objective function value. Determining the new optimal values for the decision variables requires that you make the appropriate changes in the RHS value and re-solve the model.

Another Interpretation of Shadow Prices

Unfortunately, there is no one universally accepted way of reporting shadow prices for constraints. In some software packages, the signs of the shadow prices do not conform to the convention used by Solver. Regardless of which software package you use, there is another way to look at shadow prices that should always lead to a proper interpretation. The absolute value of the shadow price always indicates the amount by which the objective function will be *improved* if the corresponding constraint is *loosened*. A less than or equal to constraint is loosened by *increasing* its RHS value, whereas a greater than or equal to constraint is loosened by *decreasing* its RHS value. (The absolute value of the shadow price can also be interpreted as the amount by which the objective will be made *worse* if the corresponding constraint is *tightened*.)

SHADOW PRICES AND THE VALUE OF ADDITIONAL RESOURCES

In the previous example, an additional 162 hours of labor allowed us to increase profits by $2,700. A question might then arise as to how much we should be willing to pay to acquire these additional 162 hours of labor. The answer to this question is, "It depends. . . ."

If labor is a *variable cost* that was subtracted (along with other variable costs) from the selling price of the hot tubs to determine the marginal profits associated with each type of tub, we should be willing to pay up to $2,700 *above and beyond* what we would ordinarily pay to acquire 162 hours of labor. In this case, notice that both the original and revised profit figures of $66,100 and $68,800, respectively, represent the profit earned *after* the normal labor charge has been paid. Therefore, we could pay a premium of up to $2,700 to acquire the additional 162 hours of labor (or an extra $16.67 per additional labor hour) and still earn at least as much profit as we would have without the additional 162 hours of labor. Thus, if the normal labor rate is $12 per hour, we could pay up to $28.67 per hour to acquire each of the additional 162 hours of labor.

On the other hand, if labor is a *fixed* or sunk cost, which must be paid regardless of how many hot tubs are produced, it would not (or should not) have been subtracted from the selling price of the hot tubs in determining the marginal profit coefficients for each tub produced. In this case, we should be willing to pay a maximum of $16.67 per hour to acquire each of the additional 162 hours of labor.

OTHER USES OF SHADOW PRICES

Because shadow prices represent the marginal values of the resources in an LP problem, they can help us answer a number of other managerial questions that might arise. For example, suppose Blue Ridge Hot Tubs is considering introducing a new model of hot tub called the Typhoon-Lagoon. Suppose that each unit of this new model requires 1 pump, 8 hours of labor, and 13 feet of tubing, and can be sold to generate a marginal profit of $320. Would production of this new model be profitable?

Because Blue Ridge Hot Tubs has limited resources, the production of any Typhoon-Lagoons would consume some of the resources currently devoted to the production of Aqua-Spas and Hydro-Luxes. So, producing Typhoon-Lagoons will reduce the number of pumps, labor hours, and tubing available for producing the other types of hot tubs. The shadow prices in Figure 4.3 indicate that each pump taken away from production of the current products will reduce profits by $200. Similarly, each labor hour taken away from the production of the current products will reduce profits by $16.67. The shadow price for the tubing constraint indicates that the supply of tubing can be reduced without adversely affecting profits.

Because each Typhoon-Lagoon requires 1 pump, 8 hours of labor, and 13 feet of tubing, the diversion of resources required to produce one unit of this new model would cause a reduction in profit of $200*1 + $16.67*8 + $0*13 = $333.33. This reduction would be partially offset by the $320 increase in profit generated by each Typhoon-Lagoon. The net effect of producing each Typhoon-Lagoon would be a $13.33 reduction in profit ($320 − $333.33 = −$13.33). Therefore, the production of Typhoon-Lagoons would not be profitable (although the company might choose to produce a small number of Typhoon-Lagoons to enhance its product line for marketing purposes).

Another way to determine whether or not Typhoon-Lagoons should be produced is to add this alternative to our model and solve the resulting LP problem. The LP model for this revised problem is represented as follows, where X_1, X_2, and X_3 represent the number of Aqua-Spas, Hydro-Luxes, and Typhoon-Lagoons to be produced, respectively:

$$\text{MAX:} \quad 350X_1 + 300X_2 + 320X_3 \qquad \text{\} profit}$$

$$\text{Subject to:} \quad 1X_1 + 1X_2 + 1X_3 \leq 200 \qquad \text{\} pump constraint}$$

$$9X_1 + 6X_2 + 8X_3 \leq 1{,}566 \qquad \text{\} labor constraint}$$

$$12X_1 + 16X_2 + 13X_3 \leq 2{,}880 \qquad \text{\} tubing constraint}$$

$$X_1, X_2, X_3 \geq 0 \qquad \text{\} nonnegativity conditions}$$

This model is implemented and solved in the spreadsheet, as shown in Figure 4.7. Notice that the optimal solution to this problem involves producing 122 Aqua-Spas ($X_1 = 122$), 78 Hydro-Luxes ($X_2 = 78$), and no Typhoon-Lagoons ($X_3 = 0$). So, as expected, the optimal solution does not involve producing Typhoon-Lagoons. Figure 4.8 shows the Sensitivity Report for our revised model.

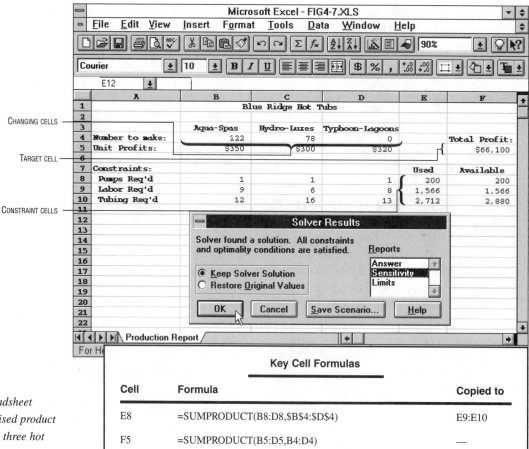

Figure 4.7: *Spreadsheet model for the revised product mix problem with three hot tub models*

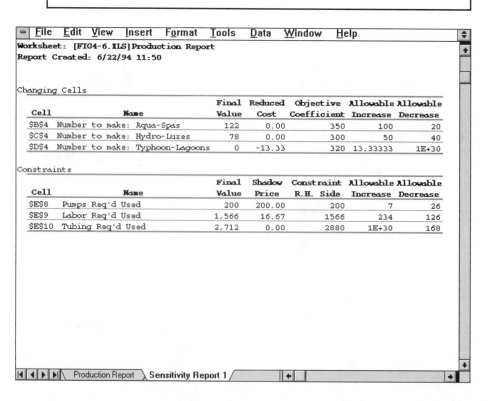

Figure 4.8: *Sensitivity Report for the revised product mix problem with three hot tub models*

THE MEANING OF THE REDUCED COSTS

The Sensitivity Report in Figure 4.8 for our revised model is identical to the sensitivity report for our original model *except* that it includes an additional row in the Changing Cells section. This row reports sensitivity information on the number of Typhoon-Lagoons to produce. Notice that the Reduced Cost column indicates that the reduced cost value for Typhoon-Lagoons is −13.33. This is the same number that we calculated in the previous section when determining whether or not it would be profitable to produce Typhoon-Lagoons.

The reduced cost for each variable is equal to the per-unit amount the product contributes to profits minus the per-unit value of the resources it consumes (where the consumed resources are priced at their shadow prices). For example, the reduced cost of each variable in this problem is calculated as:

Reduced cost of Aqua-Spas $= 350 - 200*1 - 16.67*9 - 0*12 = 0$

Reduced cost of Hydro-Luxes $= 300 - 200*1 - 16.67*6 - 0*16 = 0$

Reduced cost of Typhoon-Lagoons $= 320 - 200*1 - 16.67*8 - 0*13 = -13.33$

The allowable increase in the objective function coefficient for Typhoon-Lagoons equals 13.33. This means that the current solution will remain optimal provided that the marginal profit on Typhoon-Lagoons is less than or equal to $320 + $13.33 = 333.33 (because this would keep its reduced cost less than or equal to zero). However, if the marginal profit for Typhoon-Lagoons is more than $333.33, producing this product would be profitable and the optimal solution to the problem would change.

It is interesting to note that the shadow prices (marginal values) of the resources equate exactly with the marginal profits of the products that, at optimality, assume values between their simple lower and upper bounds. This will always be the case. In the optimal solution to an LP problem, the variables that assume values *between* their simple lower and upper bounds always have reduced cost values of zero. (In our example problem, all the variables have implicit simple upper bounds of positive infinity.) The variables with optimal values equal to their simple lower bounds have reduced cost values that are less than or equal to zero for maximization problems, or greater than or equal to zero for minimization problems. Variables with optimal values equal to their simple upper bounds have reduced cost values that are greater than or equal to zero for maximization problems, or less than or equal to zero for minimization problems. Figure 4.9 summarizes these relationships.

Type of Problem	Optimal Value of Decision Variable	Optimal Value of Reduced Cost
Maximization	at simple lower bound	≤ 0
	between lower and upper bounds	$= 0$
	at simple upper bound	≥ 0
Minimization	at simple lower bound	≥ 0
	between lower and upper bounds	$= 0$
	at simple upper bound	≤ 0

Figure 4.9: Summary of optimal reduced cost values

Generally, at optimality, a variable assumes its largest possible value (or is set equal to its simple upper bound) if this variable helps improve the objective function value. In a maximization problem, the variable's reduced cost must be nonnegative to indicate that if the variable's value increased, the objective value would increase (improve). In a minimization problem, the variable's reduced cost must be nonpositive to indicate that if the variable's value increased, the objective value would decrease (improve).

Similar arguments can be made for the optimal reduced costs of variables at their lower bounds. At optimality, a variable assumes its smallest (lower bound) value if it cannot be used to improve the objective value. In a maximization problem, the variable's reduced cost must be nonpositive to indicate that if the variable's value increased, the objective value would decrease (worsen). In a minimization problem, the variable's reduced cost must be nonnegative to indicate that if the variable's value increased, the objective value would increase (worsen).

Sometimes a variable that assumes a value equal to its simple lower or upper bound in the optimal solution also has a reduced cost of zero. If the solution is nondegenerate, this condition indicates that an alternate optimal solution exists because the value of this variable can change without affecting the optimal objective function value.

KEY POINTS

Our discussion of Solver's sensitivity report highlights some key points concerning shadow prices and their relationship to reduced costs. These key points are summarized as:

- The shadow prices of resources equate the marginal value of the resources consumed with the marginal benefit of the goods being produced.

- Resources in excess supply have a shadow price (or marginal value) of zero.

- The reduced cost of a product is the difference between its marginal profit and the marginal value of the resources it consumes.

- Products whose marginal profits are less than the marginal value of the goods required for their production will not be produced in an optimal solution.

ANALYZING CHANGES IN CONSTRAINT COEFFICIENTS

Given what we know about reduced costs and shadow prices, we can now analyze how changes in some constraint coefficients affect the optimal solution to an LP problem. For example, it is unprofitable for Blue Ridge Hot Tubs to manufacture Typhoon-Lagoons assuming that each unit requires 8 hours of labor. However, what would happen if the product could be produced in only 7 hours? The reduced cost value for Typhoon-Lagoons is calculated as:

$320 − $200*1 − $16.67*7 − $0*13 = $3.31

Because this new reduced cost value is positive, producing Typhoon-Lagoons would be profitable in this scenario and the solution shown in Figure 4.7 would no longer be optimal. We could also reach this conclusion by changing the labor requirement for Typhoon-Lagoons in our spreadsheet model and re-solving the problem. In fact, we have to do this to determine the new optimal solution if each Typhoon-Lagoon requires only 7 hours of labor.

As another example, suppose that we wanted to know the maximum amount of labor that is required to assemble a Typhoon-Lagoon while keeping its production economically justifiable. The production of Typhoon-Lagoons would be profitable provided that the reduced cost for the product is greater than or equal to zero. If L_3 represents the amount of labor required to produce a Typhoon-Lagoon, we want to find the maximum value of L_3 that keeps the reduced cost for Typhoon-Lagoons greater than or equal to zero. That is, we want to find the maximum value of L_3 that satisfies the inequality:

$$\$320 - \$200*1 - \$16.67*L_3 - \$0*13 \geq 0$$

If we solve this inequality for L_3 we obtain:

$$L_3 \leq \frac{120}{16.67} = 7.20$$

Thus, the production of Typhoon-Lagoons would be economically justified provided that the labor required to produce them does not exceed 7.20 hours per unit. Similar types of questions can be answered using knowledge of the basic relationships between reduced costs, shadow prices, and optimality conditions.

SIMULTANEOUS CHANGES IN OBJECTIVE FUNCTION COEFFICIENTS

Earlier, we noted that the values in the Allowable Increase and Allowable Decrease columns in the Sensitivity Report for the objective function coefficients indicate the maximum amounts by which each objective coefficient can change without altering the optimal solution—*assuming all other coefficients in the model remain constant*. A technique known as The 100% Rule determines whether the current solution remains optimal when more than one objective function coefficient changes. The following two situations could arise when applying this rule:

Case 1. All variables whose objective function coefficients change have non-zero reduced costs.

Case 2. At least one variable whose objective function coefficient changes has a reduced cost of zero.

In case 1, the current solution remains optimal provided that the objective function coefficient of each changed variable remains within the limits indicated in the Allowable Increase and Allowable Decrease columns of the Sensitivity Report.

Case 2 is a bit more tricky. In case 2 we must perform the following analysis where:

c_j = the original objective function coefficient for variable X_j

Δc_j = the planned change in c_j

I_j = the allowable increase in c_j given in the Sensitivity Report

D_j = the allowable decrease in c_j given in the Sensitivity Report

$$r_j = \begin{cases} \dfrac{\Delta c_j}{I_j}, & \text{if } \Delta c_j \geq 0 \\ \dfrac{-\Delta c_j}{D_j}, & \text{if } \Delta c_j < 0 \end{cases}$$

Notice that r_j measures the ratio of the planned change in c_j to the maximum allowable change for which the current solution remains optimal. If only one objective function coefficient changed, the current solution remains optimal provided that $r_j \leq 1$ (or, if r_j is expressed as a percentage, it must be less than or equal to 100%). Similarly, if more than one objective function coefficient changes, the current solution will remain optimal provided that $\sum r_j \leq 1$. (Note that if $\sum r_j > 1$, the current solution, might remain optimal, but this is not guaranteed.)

THE LIMITS REPORT

The Limits Report for the original Blue Ridge Hot Tubs problem is shown in Figure 4.10. This report lists the optimal value of the target cell. It then summarizes the optimal values for each changing cell and indicates what values the target cell assumes if each changing cell is set to its upper or lower limits. The values in the Lower Limits column indicate the smallest value each changing cell can assume while the values of all other changing cells remain constant and all the constraints are satisfied. The values in the Upper Limits column indicate the largest value each changing cell can assume while the values of all other changing cells remain constant and all the constraints are satisfied.

THE SIMPLEX METHOD

We have repeatedly mentioned that the simplex method is the preferred method for solving LP problems. This section provides an overview of the simplex method and shows how it relates to some of the items that appear on the Answer Report and the Sensitivity Report.

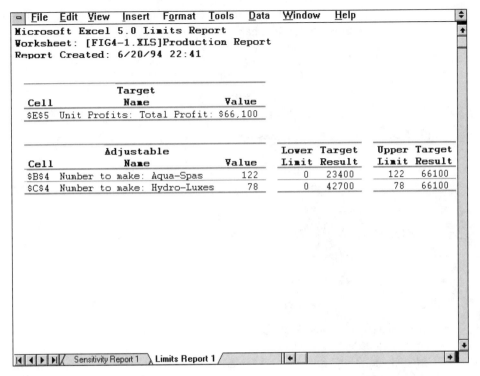

Figure 4.10: Limits Report for the original Blue Ridge Hot Tubs problem

CREATING EQUALITY CONSTRAINTS USING SLACK VARIABLES

Because our original formulation of the LP model for the Blue Ridge Hot Tubs problem has only *two* decision variables (X_1 and X_2) you might be surprised to learn that Solver actually used *five* variables to solve this problem. As you saw in chapter 2 when we plotted the boundary lines for the constraints in an LP problem, it is easier to work with equal to conditions rather than less than or equal to, or greater than or equal to conditions. Similarly, the simplex method requires that *all* constraints in an LP model be expressed as equalities.

To solve an LP problem using the simplex method, Solver temporarily turns all inequality constraints into equality constraints by adding one new variable to each less than or equal to constraint and subtracting one new variable from each greater than or equal to constraint. The new variables used to create equality constraints are called **slack variables**.

For example, consider the less than or equal to constraint:

$$a_{k1}X_1 + a_{k2}X_2 + \ldots + a_{kn}X_n \leq b_k$$

Solver can turn this constraint into an equal to constraint by adding the non-negative slack variable S_k to the LHS of the constraint:

$$a_{k1}X_1 + a_{k2}X_2 + \ldots + a_{kn}X_n + S_k = b_k$$

The variable S_k represents the amount by which $a_{k1}X_1 + a_{k2}X_2 + \ldots + a_{kn}X_n$ is less than b_k. Now consider the greater than or equal to constraint:

$$a_{k1}X_1 + a_{k2}X_2 + \ldots + a_{kn}X_n \geq b_k$$

Solver can turn this constraint into an equal to constraint by subtracting the non-negative slack variable S_k from the LHS of the constraint:

$$a_{k1}X_1 + a_{k2}X_2 + \ldots + a_{kn}X_n - S_k = b_k$$

In this case, the variable S_k represents the amount by which $a_{k1}X_1 + a_{k2}X_2 + \ldots + a_{kn}X_n$ exceeds b_k.

To solve the original Blue Ridge Hot Tubs problem using the simplex method, Solver actually solved the following modified problem involving *five* variables:

$$
\begin{array}{lllll}
\text{MAX:} & 350X_1 + 300X_2 & & & \}\ \text{profit} \\
\text{Subject to:} & 1X_1 + 1X_2 + S_1 & = & 200 & \}\ \text{pump constraint} \\
& 9X_1 + 6X_2 + S_2 & = & 1{,}566 & \}\ \text{labor constraint} \\
& 12X_1 + 16X_2 + S_3 & = & 2{,}880 & \}\ \text{tubing constraint} \\
& X_1, X_2, S_1, S_2, S_3 \geq & & 0 & \}\ \text{nonnegativity conditions}
\end{array}
$$

We will refer to X_1 and X_2 as the *structural variables* in the model to distinguish them from the slack variables.

Recall that we did not set up slack variables in the spreadsheet or include them in the formulas in the constraint cells. Solver automatically sets up the slack variables it needs to solve a particular problem. The only time Solver even mentions these variables is when it creates an Answer Report like the one shown in Figure 4.2. The values in the Slack column in the Answer Report correspond to the optimal values of the slack variables.

BASIC FEASIBLE SOLUTIONS

After all the inequality constraints in an LP problem have been converted into equalities (by adding or subtracting appropriate slack variables), the constraints in the LP model represent a system (or collection) of linear equations. If there are a total of *n* variables in a system of *m* equations, one strategy for finding a solution to the system of equations is to select any *m* variables and try to find values for them that solve the system, assuming all other variables are set equal to their lower bounds (which are usually zero). This strategy requires more variables than constraints in the system of equations—or that $n \geq m$.

The *m* variables selected to solve the system of equations in an LP model are sometimes called **basic variables**, while the remaining variables are called **nonbasic variables**. If a solution to the system of equations can be obtained using a given set of basic variables (while the nonbasic variables are all set equal to zero), that solution is called a **basic feasible solution**. Every basic feasible solution corresponds to one of the extreme points of the feasible region for the LP problem, and we know that the optimal solution to the LP problem also occurs at an extreme point. So the challenge in LP is to find the set of basic variables (and their optimal values) that produce the basic feasible solution corresponding to the optimal extreme point of the feasible region.

Because our modified problem involves three constraints and five variables, we could select three variables in ten different ways to form possible basic feasible solutions for the problem. Figure 4.11 summarizes the results for these ten options.

	Basic Variables	Nonbasic Variables	Solution	Objective Value
1	S_1, S_2, S_3	X_1, X_2	$X_1 = 0, X_2 = 0, S_1 = 200, S_2 = 1566, S_3 = 2880$	0
2	X_1, S_1, S_3	X_2, S_2	$X_1 = 174, X_2 = 0, S_1 = 26, S_2 = 0, S_3 = 792$	60,900
3	X_1, X_2, S_3	S_1, S_2	$X_1 = 122, X_2 = 78, S_1 = 0, S_2 = 0, S_3 = 168$	66,100
4	X_1, X_2, S_2	S_1, S_3	$X_1 = 80, X_2 = 120, S_1 = 0, S_2 = 126, S_3 = 0$	64,000
5	X_2, S_1, S_2	X_1, S_3	$X_1 = 0, X_2 = 180, S_1 = 20, S_2 = 486, S_3 = 0$	54,000
6*	X_1, X_2, S_1	S_2, S_3	$X_1 = 108, X_2 = 99, S_1 = -7, S_2 = 0, S_3 = 0$	67,500
7*	X_1, S_1, S_2	X_2, S_3	$X_1 = 240, X_2 = 0, S_1 = -40, S_2 = -594, S_3 = 0$	84,000
8*	X_1, S_2, S_3	X_2, S_1	$X_1 = 200, X_2 = 0, S_1 = 0, S_2 = -234, S_3 = 480$	70,000
9*	X_2, S_2, S_3	X_1, S_1	$X_1 = 0, X_2 = 200, S_1 = 0, S_2 = 366, S_3 = -320$	60,000
10*	X_2, S_1, S_3	X_1, S_2	$X_1 = 0, X_2 = 261, S_1 = -61, S_2 = 0, S_3 = -1296$	78,300

Note: * denotes infeasible solutions

Figure 4.11: Possible basic feasible solutions for the original Blue Ridge Hot Tubs problem

The first five solutions in Figure 4.11 are feasible and, therefore, represent basic feasible solutions to this problem. The remaining solutions are infeasible because they violate the nonnegativity conditions. The best feasible alternative shown in Figure 4.11 corresponds to the optimal solution to the problem. In particular, if X_1, X_2, and S_3 are selected as basic variables and S_1 and S_2 are nonbasic and assigned their lower bound values (zero), we try to find values for X_1, X_2, and S_3 that satisfy the following constraints:

$$1X_1 + 1X_2 = 200 \qquad \} \text{ pump constraint}$$
$$9X_1 + 6X_2 = 1,566 \qquad \} \text{ labor constraint}$$
$$12X_1 + 16X_2 + S_3 = 2,880 \qquad \} \text{ tubing constraint}$$

Notice that S_1 and S_2 in the modified equal to constraints are not included in the above constraint equations because we are assuming that the values of these nonbasic variables are equal to zero (their lower bounds). Using linear algebra, the simplex method determines that the values $X_1 = 122$, $X_2 = 78$, and $S_3 = 168$ satisfy the equations given above. So, a basic feasible solution to this problem is $X_1 = 122$, $X_2 = 78$, $S_1 = 0$, $S_2 = 0$, $S_3 = 168$. As indicated in Figure 4.11, this solution produces an objective function value of $66,100. Figure 4.12 shows the relationships between the basic feasible solutions listed in Figure 4.11 and the extreme points of the feasible region for this problem.

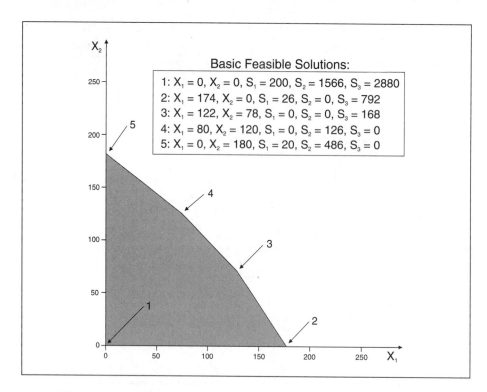

Figure 4.12: The relationship between basic feasible solutions and extreme points

FINDING THE BEST SOLUTION

The simplex method operates by first identifying *any* basic feasible solution (or extreme point) for an LP problem, then moving to an adjacent extreme point, if such a move improves the value of the objective function. When no adjacent extreme point has a better objective function value, the current extreme point is optimal and the simplex method terminates.

The process of moving from one extreme point to an adjacent one is accomplished by switching one of the basic variables with one of the nonbasic variables to create a new basic feasible solution that corresponds to the adjacent extreme point. For example, in Figure 4.12, moving from the first basic feasible solution (point 1) to the second basic feasible solution (point 2) involves making X_1 a basic variable and S_2 a nonbasic variable. Similarly, we can move from point 2 to point 3 and from point 3 to point 4 by switching basic variables with nonbasic variables. So starting at point 1 in Figure 4.6, the simplex method could move to point 2, then to the optimal solution at point 3. Alternatively, the simplex method could move from point 1 through points 5 and 4 to reach the optimal solution at point 3. Thus, although there is no guarantee that the simplex method will take the shortest route to the optimal solution of an LP problem, it will find the optimal solution eventually.

To determine whether or not switching a basic and nonbasic variable will result in a better solution, the simplex method calculates the reduced cost for each nonbasic variable to determine if the objective function could be improved if any of these variables are substituted for one of the basic variables. (Note that unbounded solutions are detected easily in the simplex method by the existence of a nonbasic variable that could improve the objective value by an infinite amount if it were made basic). This process continues until no further improvement in the objective function value is possible.

SUMMARY

This chapter described the methods for assessing how sensitive an LP model is to various changes that might occur in the model or its optimal solution. The impact of changes in an LP model can be analyzed easily by re-solving the model. Solver also provides a significant amount of sensitivity information automatically. For LP problems, the maximum amount of sensitivity information is obtained by solving the problem using the simplex method.

   The simplex method considers only the extreme points of the feasible region, and is an efficient way of solving LP problems. In this method, slack variables are first introduced to convert all constraints to equal to constraints. The simplex method systematically moves to better and better corner point solutions until no adjacent extreme point provides an improved objective function value.

REFERENCES

Bazaraa, M. and J. Jarvis. *Linear Programming and Network Flows*. New York: Wiley, 1990.

Shogan, A. *Management Science*. Englewood Cliffs, NJ: Prentice Hall, 1988.

Wagner, H. and D. Rubin. "Shadow Prices: Tips and Traps for Managers and Instructors." *Interfaces*, vol. 20, no. 4, 1990.

Winston, W. *Operations Research: Applications and Algorithms*. Belmont, CA: Duxbury Press, 1994.

Fuel Management and Allocation Model Helps National Airlines Adapt to Cost and Supply Changes

Source: Darnell, D. Wayne and Carolyn Loflin, "National Airlines Fuel Management and Allocation Model," *Interfaces*, vol. 7, no. 2, February 1977, pages 1–16.

FUEL IS A MAJOR COMPONENT in the cost structure of an airline. Price and availability of fuel can vary from one air terminal to the next, and it is sometimes advantageous for an aircraft to carry more than the necessary minimum for the next leg of its route. Fuel loaded for the purpose of taking advantage of price or availability at a specific location is said to be tankered. A disadvantage of tankering is that fuel consumption increases when an aircraft is carrying more weight.

The use of LP to determine when and where to fuel aircraft saved National Airlines several million dollars during the first two years of implementation. In particular, National Airlines saw its average fuel costs drop 11.75% during a period when the average fuel cost for all domestic trunk airlines increased by 2.87%.

The objective function in the Fuel Management and Allocation Model consists of fuel costs and increases in operating costs from tankering. The constraints in the model address availability, minimum reserves, and aircraft capacities.

A particularly useful feature of the Fuel Management and Allocation Model is a series of reports that assist management in modifying the fuel-loading plan when sudden changes occur in availability or price. Shadow prices, along with the associated range of applicability, provide information about supply changes. Information about changes in price per gallon comes from the allowable increase and decrease for objective function coefficients.

For example, the availability report might indicate that the optimal quantity to purchase at Los Angeles from Shell West is 2,718,013 gallons; but if its supply decreases and fuel must be purchased from the next most attractive vendor, total cost would increase at the rate of $0.0478 per gallon (the shadow price). This fuel would be replaced by a prior purchase of up to 159,293 gallons from Shell East at New Orleans, tankered to Los Angeles.

The price report shows, for example, that vendor substitutions should be made if the current price of Shell West at Los Angeles, $0.3074, increases to $0.32583 or decreases to $0.27036. The report also indicates what that substitution should be.

Questions and Problems

1. Howie Jones used the following information to calculate the profit coeffi-
    cients for Aqua-Spas and Hydro-Luxes: pumps cost $225 each, labor costs
    $12 per hour, tubing costs $2 per foot. In addition to pumps, labor, and tub-
    ing, the production of Aqua-Spas and Hydro-Luxes consumes, respectively,
    $243 and $246 per unit in other resources that are not in short supply.
    Using this information, Howie calculated the marginal profits on Aqua-
    Spas and Hydro-Luxes as:

	Aqua-Spas	Hydro-Luxes
Selling Price	$950	$875
Pump Cost	−$225	−$225
Labor Cost	−$108	−$72
Tubing Cost	−$24	−$32
Other Variable Costs	−$243	−$246
Marginal Profit	$350	$300

    Howie's accountant reviewed these calculations and thinks Howie made a
    mistake. For accounting purposes, factory overhead is assigned to products
    at a rate of $16 per labor hour. Howie's accountant argues that because
    Aqua-Spas require 9 labor hours, the profit margin on this product should
    be $144 less. Similarly, because Hydro-Luxes require 6 labor hours, the
    profit margin on this product should be $96 less. Who is right and why?

2. A variable that assumes an optimal value *between* its lower and upper
    bounds has a reduced cost value of zero. Why must this be true? (Hint:
    What if such a variable's reduced cost value is not zero? What does this
    imply about the value of the objective function?)

3. Implement the following LP problem in a spreadsheet. Use Solver to solve
    the problem and create a sensitivity report. Use this information to answer
    the following questions.

    $$\text{MAX}: \ 4X_1 + 2X_2$$

    $$\text{Subject to}: \ 2X_1 + 4X_2 \le 20$$

    $$3X_1 + 5X_2 \le 15$$

    $$X_1, X_2 \ge 0$$

    a. What range of values can the objective function coefficient for variable
        X_1 assume without changing the optimal solution?

    b. Is the optimal solution to this problem unique, or is there an alternate
        optimal solution?

c. How much does the objective function coefficient for variable X_2 have to increase before it enters the optimal solution at a strictly positive level?

d. What is the optimal objective function if X_2 equals 1?

e. What is the optimal objective function if the RHS value for the second constraint changes from 15 to 25?

f. Is the current solution still optimal if the coefficient for X_2 in the second constraint changes from 5 to 1? Explain.

4. Implement the following LP model in a spreadsheet. Use Solver to solve the problem and create a Sensitivity Report. Use this information to answer the following questions.

$$\text{MAX:} \quad 2X_1 + 4X_2$$
$$\text{Subject to:} \quad -X_1 + 2X_2 \leq 8$$
$$X_1 + 2X_2 \leq 12$$
$$X_1 + X_2 \geq 2$$
$$X_1, X_2 \geq 0$$

a. Which of the constraints are binding at the optimal solution?

b. Is the optimal solution to this problem unique, or is there an alternate optimal solution?

c. What is the optimal solution to this problem if the value of the objective function coefficient for variable X_1 is zero?

d. How much can the objective function coefficient for variable X_2 decrease before changing the optimal solution?

e. Given the objective in this problem, if management could increase the RHS value for any of the constraints for identical costs, which would you choose to increase and why?

5. Implement the following LP model in a spreadsheet. Use Solver to solve the problem and create a Sensitivity Report. Use this information to answer the following questions.

$$\text{MIN:} \quad 5X_1 + 3X_2 + 4X_3$$
$$\text{Subject to:} \quad X_1 + X_2 + 2X_3 \geq 2$$
$$5X_1 + 3X_2 + 2X_3 \geq 1$$
$$X_1, X_2, X_3 \geq 0$$

a. What is the smallest value the objective function coefficient for X_3 can assume without changing the optimal solution?

b. What is the optimal objective function value if the objective function coefficient for X_3 changes to -1? (Hint: The answer to this question is not given in the Sensitivity Report. Consider what the new objective function is relative to the constraints.)

c. What is the optimal objective function value if the RHS value of the first constraint increases to 7?

    d. What is the optimal objective function value if the RHS value of the first constraint decreases by 1?

    e. Will the current solution remain optimal if the objective function coefficients for X_1 and X_3 both decrease by 1?

6. Use Solver to create Answer and Sensitivity reports for question 13 at the end of chapter 2, and answer the following questions.

    a. How much excess wiring and testing capacity exists in the optimal solution?

    b. What is the company's total profit if it has 10 additional hours of wiring capacity?

    c. By how much does the profit on alternators need to increase before their production is justified?

    d. Does the optimal solution change if the marginal profit on generators decreases by $50 and the marginal profit on alternators increases by $75?

    e. Suppose the marginal profit on generators decreases by $25. What is the maximum profit that can be earned on alternators without changing the optimal solution?

    f. Suppose the amount of wiring required on alternators is reduced to 1.5 hours. Does this change the optimal solution? Why or why not?

7. Use Solver to create Answer and Sensitivity reports for question 19 at the end of chapter 2, and answer the following questions.

    a. How much can the price of watermelons drop before it is no longer optimal to plant only watermelons?

    b. How much does the price of cantaloupes have to increase before it is profitable to grow any?

    c. Suppose the price of watermelons drops by $60 per acre and the price of cantaloupes increases by $50 per acre. Is the current solution still optimal?

    d. Suppose the farmer can lease up to 20 acres of land from a neighboring farm to plant additional crops. How many acres should the farmer lease, what should he plant, and what is the maximum amount he should pay to lease each acre?

    e. Suppose the farmer discovers a hybrid cantaloupe that produces exactly the same marginal profit as the original cantaloupe but requires no watering. Is it profitable to plant this type of cantaloupe?

8. Use Solver to create a Sensitivity Report for question 9 at the end of chapter 3, and answer the following questions.

    a. Suppose the cost of the first two compounds increases by $1 per pound and the cost of the third compound increases by $0.50 per pound. Does the optimal solution change?

    b. How does the solution change if the maximum amount of potassium allowed decreases from 45% to 40%?

c. How much does the cost of the mix increase if the specifications for CHEMIX change to require at least 31% sulfur? (Hint: Remember that the shadow price indicates the impact on the objective function if the RHS value of the associated constraint increases by 1.)

9. Use Solver to create a Sensitivity Report for question 13 at the end of chapter 3, and answer the following questions.

   a. How many more three-bedroom units can be built in the development if the zoning board does not restrict the developer to 40 units?

   b. By how much does the developer's monthly rental income increase if the zoning board allows the developer to build five more units in the complex?

   c. If the developer built one efficiency unit, what effect does this have on the total rental income?

10. Use Solver to create a Sensitivity Report for question 14 at the end of chapter 3, and answer the following questions.

    a. What total profit level is realized if 100 extra hours of labor are available?

    b. Assume a marginal labor cost of $11 per hour in determining the unit profits of each of the three products. How much should management pay to acquire 100 additional labor hours?

    c. Interpret the reduced cost value for tuners. Why are more tuners not being produced?

11. Use Solver to create a Sensitivity Report for question 15 at the end of chapter 3, and answer the following questions.

    a. Is the optimal solution unique? How can you tell?

    b. Which location is receiving the fewest cars?

    c. Suppose a particular car at location 1 must be sent to location 3 in order to meet a customer request. How much does this increase costs for the company?

    d. Suppose location 6 must have at least 8 cars shipped to it. What impact does this have on the optimal objective function value?

12. Consider the following LP problem:

    $$\text{MAX:} \quad 4X_1 + 2X_2$$
    $$\text{Subject to:} \quad 2X_1 + 4X_2 \leq 20$$
    $$3X_1 + 5X_2 \leq 15$$
    $$X_1, X_2 \geq 0$$

    a. Use slack variables to rewrite this problem so that all its constraints are equal to constraints.

    b. Identify the different sets of basic variables that might be used to obtain a solution to the problem.

    c. Of the possible sets of basic variables, which lead to feasible solutions and what are the values for *all* the variables at each of these solutions?

    d. Graph the feasible region for this problem and indicate which basic feasible solution corresponds to each of the extreme points of the feasible region.

    e. What is the value of the objective function at each of the basic feasible solutions?

    f. What is the optimal solution to the problem?

    g. Which constraints are binding at the optimal solution?

13.   Consider the following LP problem:

$$\text{MAX}: \quad 2X_1 + 4X_2$$

$$\text{Subject to}: \quad -X_1 + 2X_2 \leq 8$$
$$X_1 + 2X_2 \leq 12$$
$$X_1 + X_2 \geq 2$$
$$X_1, X_2 \geq 0$$

    a. Use slack variables to rewrite this problem so that all its constraints are equal to constraints.

    b. Identify the different sets of basic variables that might be used to obtain a solution to the problem.

    c. Of the possible sets of basic variables, which lead to feasible solutions and what are the values for *all* the variables at each of these solutions?

    d. Graph the feasible region for this problem and indicate which basic feasible solution corresponds to each of the extreme points of the feasible region.

    e. What is the value of the objective function at each of the basic feasible solutions?

    f. What is the optimal solution to the problem?

    g. Which constraints are binding at the optimal solution?

14.   Consider the following LP problem:

$$\text{MIN}: \quad 5X_1 + 3X_2 + 4X_3$$

$$\text{Subject to}: \quad X_1 + X_2 + 2X_3 \geq 2$$
$$5X_1 + 3X_2 + 2X_3 \geq 1$$
$$X_1, X_2, X_3 \geq 0$$

    a. Use slack variables to rewrite this problem so that all its constraints are equal to constraints.

    b. Identify the different sets of basic variables that might be used to obtain a solution to the problem.

    c. Of the possible sets of basic variables, which lead to feasible solutions and what are the values for all the variables at each of these solutions?

    d. What is the value of the objective function at each of the basic feasible solutions?

    e. What is the optimal solution to the problem?

    f. Which constraints are binding at the optimal solution?

15.   Consider the following constraint, where S is a slack variable:

$$2X_1 + 4X_2 + S = 16$$

a. What was the original constraint before the slack variable was included?

b. What value of S is associated with each of the following points:

$X_1 = 2, X_2 = 2$

$X_1 = 8, X_2 = 0$

$X_1 = 1, X_2 = 3$

$X_1 = 4, X_2 = 1$

16.   Consider the following constraint, where S is a slack variable:

$$3X_1 + 4X_2 - S = 12$$

a. What was the original constraint before the slack variable was included?

b. What value of S is associated with each of the following points:

$X_1 = 5, X_2 = 0$

$X_1 = 2, X_2 = 2$

$X_1 = 7, X_2 = 1$

$X_1 = 4, X_2 = 0$

Parket Sisters

A Case in Linear

Programming

COMPUTERS and word processors notwithstanding, the art of writing by hand recently entered a boom era. People are buying fountain pens again, and mechanical pencils are becoming more popular than ever. Joe Script, the president and CEO of Parket Sisters, a small but growing pen and pencil manufacturer, wants to establish a better foothold in the market. The writing market is divided into two main sectors. One, dominated by Mont Blanc, Cross, Parker Brothers, Waterman, Schaffer, and a few others, caters to people who want writing instruments. The product lines from these companies consist of pens and pencils of elaborate design, lifetime warranty, and high price. At the other end of the market are manufacturers like BIC, Pentel, and many companies from the far east, offering good quality items, low price, few trims, and limited diversity. These pens and pencils are meant to be used for a limited time and disposed of when the ink in a ballpoint pen runs out, or when the lead in a mechanical pencil won't retract or extend. In short, these items are not meant for repair.

Joe thinks that there must be a middle ground, and that is where he wants to position his company. Parket Sisters makes high-quality items, with limited trim and diversity, but also offers lifetime warranties. Furthermore, its pens and pencils are ergonomically efficient. Joe knows that some people want the status of the Mont Blanc Meisterstuck pen, for example, but he has never met a person who said that writing with such a pen is enjoyable. The pen is too large and clumsy for smooth writing. Parket Sisters' products, on the other hand, have a reputation for working well, are easy to hold and use, and cause limited "writer's fatigue."

Parket Sisters makes only three items—a ballpoint pen, a mechanical pencil, and a fountain pen. All are available in just one color, black, and are sold mostly in specialty stores and from better catalog companies. The per-unit profit of the items is $3.00 for the ballpoint pen, $3.00 for the mechanical pencil, and $5.00 for the fountain pen. These values take into account labor, the cost of materials, packing, quality control, and so on.

The company is trying to plan its production mix for each week. Joe believes that the company can sell any number of pens and pencils it produces, but production is currently limited by the available resources. Because of a recent strike and certain cash-flow problems, the suppliers of

Contributed by Jack Yurkiewicz, Lubin School of Business, Pace University, New York.

these resources are selling them to Parket Sisters in limited amounts. In particular, Joe can count on getting at most 1000 ounces of plastic, 1200 ounces of chrome, and 2000 ounces of stainless steel each week from his suppliers, and these figures are not likely to change in the near future. Because of Joe's excellent reputation, the suppliers will sell Joe any amount (up to his limit) of the resources he needs when he requires them. That is, the suppliers do not require Joe to buy some fixed quantities of resources in advance of his production of pens and pencils; therefore, these resources can be considered variable costs rather than fixed costs for the pens and pencils.

Each ballpoint pen requires 1.2 ounces of plastic, 0.8 ounces of chrome, and 2 ounces of stainless steel. Each mechanical pencil requires 1.7 ounces of plastic, no chrome, and 3 ounces of stainless steel. Each fountain pen requires 1.2 ounces of plastic, 2.3 ounces of chrome, and 4.5 ounces of stainless steel. Joe believes LP could help him decide what his weekly product mix should consist of.

Getting his notes and notebooks, Joe grapples with the LP formulation. In addition to the constraints of the available resources, he recognizes that the model should include many other constraints (such as labor time availability and materials for packing). However, Joe wants to keep his model simple. He know that eventually he'll have to take other constraints into account, but as a first-pass model, he'll restrict the constraints to just the three resources: plastic, chrome, and stainless steel.

With only these three constraints, Joe can formulate the problem easily as:

$$\text{MAX: } 3.0x_1 + 3.0x_2 + 5.0x_3$$

$$\text{Subject to: } 1.2x_1 + 1.7x_2 + 1.2x_3 \leq 1000$$

$$0.8x_1 + 0x_2 + 2.3x_3 \leq 1200$$

$$2.0x_1 + 3.0x_2 + 4.5x_3 \leq 2000$$

where

x_1 = the number of ballpoint pens

x_2 = the number of mechanical pencils

x_3 = the number of fountain pens

Joe's knowledge of Excel and the Solver feature is limited so he asks you to enter and solve the problem for him, then answer the following questions. (Assume each question is independent unless otherwise stated.)

1. What should the weekly product mix consist of, and what is the weekly net profit?

2. Is the optimal solution from question 1 unique, or are there alternate answers to this question? Explain your response.

3. What is the marginal value of one more unit of chrome? Of plastic?

4. A local distributor has offered to sell Parket Sisters an additional 500 ounces of stainless steel for $0.60 per ounce more than it ordinarily pays. Should the company buy the steel at this price? Explain your response.

5. If Parket Sisters buys the additional 500 ounces of stainless steel noted in question 4, what is the new optimal product mix and what is the new optimal profit? Explain your response.

6. Suppose that the distributor offers to sell Parket Sisters some additional plastic at a price of only $1.00 over its usual cost of $5.00 per ounce. However, the distributor will sell the plastic only in lots of 500 ounces. Should Parket Sisters buy one such lot? Explain your response.

7. The distributor is willing to sell the plastic in lots of just 100 ounces instead of the usual 500-ounce lots, still at $1.00 over Parket Sisters' cost of $5.00 per ounce. How many lots (if any) should Parket Sisters buy? What is the optimal product mix if the company buys these lots, and what is the optimal profit?

8. Parket Sisters has an opportunity to sell some of its plastic for $6.50 per ounce to another company. The other company (which does not produce pens and pencils and, therefore, is not a competitor) wants to buy 300 ounces of plastic from Parket Sisters. Should Parket Sisters sell the plastic to the other company? What happens to Parket Sisters' product mix and overall profit if it does sell the plastic? Be as specific as possible.

9. The chrome supplier might have to fulfill an emergency order, and would be able to send only 1000 ounces of chrome this week instead of the usual 1200 ounces. If Parket Sisters receives only 1000 ounces of chrome, what is the optimal product mix and optimal profit? Be as specific as possible.

10. The R&D department at Parket Sisters has been redesigning the mechanical pencil to make it more profitable. The new design requires 1.1 ounces of plastic, 2.0 ounces of chrome, and 2.0 ounces of stainless steel. If the company can sell one of these pencils at a net profit of $3.00, should it approve the new design? Explain your response.

11. If the per-unit profit on ballpoint pens decreases to $2.50, what is the optimal product mix and what is the company's total profit?

12. The Marketing department suggested introducing a new felt tip pen that requires 1.8 ounces of plastic, 0.5 ounces of chrome, and 1.3 ounces of stainless steel. What profit must this product generate in order to make it worthwhile to produce?

13. What must the minimum per-unit profit of mechanical pencils be in order to make them worthwhile to produce?

14. Management believes that the company should produce at least 20 mechanical pencils per week to round out its product line. What effect would this have on overall profit? Give a numerical answer.

15. If the profit on a fountain pen is $6.75 instead of $5.00, what is the optimal product mix and optimal profit?

CHAPTER 5

Networks

A NUMBER OF PRACTICAL DECISION PROBLEMS in business fall into a category known as **network flow problems**. These problems share a common characteristic—they can be described or displayed in a graphical form known as a **network**. This chapter focuses on several types of network flow problems: transshipment problems, shortest path problems, maximal flow problems, and transportation/assignment problems. Although specialized solution procedures exist for solving network flow problems, we will consider how to formulate and solve these problems as LP problems. We will also consider a different type of network problem known as the minimum spanning tree problem.

TRANSSHIPMENT PROBLEMS

Let's begin our study of network flow problems by considering the transshipment problem. As you will see, the other types of network flow problems all can be viewed as special cases of the transshipment problem. So, once you understand how to formulate and solve transshipment problems, the other types of problems will be easy to solve. The following example illustrates the transshipment problem.

The Bavarian Motor Company (BMC) manufactures expensive luxury cars in Hamburg, Germany, and exports cars to sell in the United States. The exported cars are shipped from Hamburg to ports in Newark, New Jersey, and Jacksonville, Florida. From these ports, the cars are transported by rail or truck to distributors located in Boston, Massachusetts; Columbus, Ohio; Atlanta, Georgia; Richmond, Virginia; and Mobile, Alabama. Figure 5.1 shows the possible shipping routes available to the company along with the transportation cost for shipping each car along the indicated path.

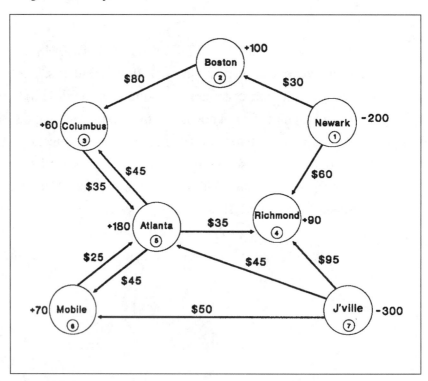

Figure 5.1: Network representation of the BMC transshipment problem

Currently, 200 cars are available at the port in Newark and 300 are available in Jacksonville. The numbers of cars needed by the distributors in Boston, Columbus, Atlanta, Richmond, and Mobile are 100, 60, 180, 90, and 70, respectively. BMC would like to determine the least costly way of transporting cars from the ports in Newark and Jacksonville to the cities where they are needed.

CHARACTERISTICS OF NETWORK FLOW PROBLEMS

Figure 5.1 illustrates a number of characteristics common to all network flow problems. All network flow problems can be represented as a collection of nodes connected by arcs. The larger circles in Figure 5.1 are called **nodes** in the terminology of network flow problems, and the lines connecting the nodes are called **arcs**. The arcs in a network indicate the valid paths, routes, or connections between the nodes in a network flow problem. When the lines connecting the nodes in a network are arrows that indicate a direction, the arcs in the network are called **directed arcs**. This chapter discusses directed arcs primarily but, for convenience, refers to them as arcs.

The notion of **supply nodes** (or sending nodes) and **demand nodes** (or receiving nodes) is another common element of network flow problems illustrated in Figure 5.1. The nodes representing the port cities of Newark and Jacksonville are both supply nodes because each has a supply of cars to send to other nodes in the network. Richmond represents a demand node because it demands to receive cars from the other nodes. All the other nodes in this network are transshipment nodes. **Transshipment nodes** can both send to and receive from other nodes in the network. For example, the node representing Atlanta in Figure 5.1 is a transshipment node because it can *receive* cars from Jacksonville, Mobile, and Columbus, and it can also *send* cars to Columbus, Mobile, and Richmond.

The net supply or demand for each node in the network is indicated by a positive or negative number next to each node. **Positive numbers** represent the *demand* at a given node, and **negative numbers** represent the *supply* available at a node. For example, the value +90 next to the node for Richmond indicates that the number of cars needs to increase by 90—or that Richmond has a *demand* for 90 cars. The value –200 next to the node for Newark indicates that the number of cars can be reduced by 200—or that Newark has a *supply* of 200 cars. A transshipment node can have either a net supply or demand, but not both. In this particular problem, all the transshipment nodes have demands. For example, the node representing Mobile in Figure 5.1 has a demand for 70 cars.

THE DECISION VARIABLES FOR NETWORK FLOW PROBLEMS

The goal in a network flow model is to determine how many items should be moved (or flow) across each of the arcs. In our example, BMC needs to determine the least costly method of transporting cars along the various arcs shown in Figure 5.1 to distribute cars where they are needed. Thus, each of the arcs in a network flow model represents a decision variable. Determining the optimal flow for each arc is the equivalent of determining the optimal value for the corresponding decision variable.

It is customary to use numbers to identify each node in a network flow problem. In Figure 5.1 the number 1 identifies the node for Newark, 2 identifies the node for Boston, and so on. You can assign numbers to the nodes in any manner, but it is best to use a series of consecutive integers. The node numbers provide a convenient way to identify the decision variables needed to formulate the LP model for the problem. For each arc in a network flow model, you need to define one decision variable as:

X_{ij} = the number of items shipped (or flowing) *from* node i *to* node j

The network in Figure 5.1 for our example problem contains 11 arcs. Therefore, the LP formulation of this model requires the following 11 decision variables:

X_{12} = the number of cars shipped *from* node 1 (Newark) *to* node 2 (Boston)

X_{14} = the number of cars shipped *from* node 1 (Newark) *to* node 4 (Richmond)

X_{23} = the number of cars shipped *from* node 2 (Boston) *to* node 3 (Columbus)

X_{35} = the number of cars shipped *from* node 3 (Columbus) *to* node 5 (Atlanta)

X_{53} = the number of cars shipped *from* node 5 (Atlanta) *to* node 3 (Columbus)

X_{54} = the number of cars shipped *from* node 5 (Atlanta) *to* node 4 (Richmond)

X_{56} = the number of cars shipped *from* node 5 (Atlanta) *to* node 6 (Mobile)

X_{65} = the number of cars shipped *from* node 6 (Mobile) *to* node 5 (Atlanta)

X_{74} = the number of cars shipped *from* node 7 (Jacksonville) *to* node 4 (Richmond)

X_{75} = the number of cars shipped *from* node 7 (Jacksonville) *to* node 5 (Atlanta)

X_{76} = the number of cars shipped *from* node 7 (Jacksonville) *to* node 6 (Mobile)

THE OBJECTIVE FUNCTION FOR NETWORK FLOW PROBLEMS

Each unit that flows from node i to node j in a network flow problem usually incurs some cost, c_{ij}. This cost might represent a monetary payment, a distance, or some other type of penalty. The objective in most network flow problems is to minimize the total cost, distance, or penalty that must be incurred to solve the problem.

In our example problem, different monetary costs must be paid for each car shipped across a given arc. For example, it costs $30 to ship each car from node 1 (Newark) to node 2 (Boston). Because X_{12} represents the number of cars shipped from Newark to Boston, the total cost incurred by cars shipped along this path is determined by $\$30X_{12}$. Similar calculations can be done for the other arcs in the network. Because BMC is interested in minimizing the total shipping costs, the objective function for this problem is expressed as:

$$\text{MIN:} \quad + 30X_{12} + 60X_{14} + 80X_{23} + 35X_{35} + 45X_{53} + 35X_{54}$$
$$+ 45X_{56} + 25X_{65} + 95X_{74} + 45X_{75} + 50X_{76}$$

THE CONSTRAINTS FOR NETWORK FLOW PROBLEMS

Just as the number of arcs in the network determines the number of variables in the LP formulation of a network flow problem, the number of nodes determines the number of constraints. In particular, there must be one constraint for each node. A simple rule, known as the *balance-of-flow rule*, applies to constructing the constraints for *any* network flow problem. This rule is stated as:

Balance-of-Flow Rule. For each node in a network flow problem where supplies are represented by negative numbers and demands are represented by positive numbers, the flow into a node minus the flow out of the node must be greater than or equal to the supply or demand at the node. That is, the following relationship exists at each node:

Inflow – Outflow ≥ Supply or Demand

(Note that if the total supply in the network equals the total demand, the balance-of-flow rule can also be stated for each node as an equality: Inflow – Outflow = Supply or Demand.)

If you follow the balance-of-flow rule, you can generate all the constraints for a network flow problem easily. In each case, you must create a simple linear function that sums the variables flowing into the node, subtracts the variables flowing out of the node, and restricts this quantity to be greater than or equal to the supply or demand for the node. For example, consider node 1 (Newark) in Figure 5.1. No arcs flow into this node but two arcs (represented by X_{12} and X_{14}) flow out of the node. According to the balance-of-flow rule, the constraint for this node is:

Constraint for node 1: $-X_{12} - X_{14} \geq -200$

Notice that the supply at this node is represented by –200 following the convention we established earlier. If we multiply both sides of this equation by –1, we see that it is equivalent to $+X_{12} + X_{14} \leq +200$. (Note that multiplying an inequality by –1 reverses the sign of the inequality.) Both of these constraints indicate that the total number of cars flowing out of Newark must not exceed 200. So if we include either of these constraints in the model, we can ensure that no more than 200 cars will be shipped from Newark.

Now consider the constraint for node 2 (Boston) in Figure 5.1. Because Boston has a demand for 100 cars, the balance-of-flow rule requires that the total number of cars coming into Boston from Newark (via X_{12}) minus the total number of cars being shipped out of Boston to Columbus (via X_{23}) must leave at least 100 cars in Boston. This condition is imposed by the constraint:

Constraint for node 2: $+X_{12} - X_{23} \geq +100$

Note that this constraint makes it possible to leave more than the required number of cars in Boston. However, our objective is to minimize costs, therefore, we can be sure that an excess number of cars will never be shipped to any city, because that would result in unnecessary costs being incurred.

Using the balance-of-flow rule, the constraints for each of the remaining nodes in our example problem are represented as:

Constraint for node 3: $+X_{23} + X_{53} - X_{35} \geq +60$

Constraint for node 4: $+X_{14} + X_{54} + X_{74} \geq +90$

Constraint for node 5: $+X_{35} + X_{65} + X_{75} - X_{53} - X_{54} - X_{56} \geq +180$

Constraint for node 6: $+X_{56} + X_{76} - X_{65} \geq +70$

Constraint for node 7: $-X_{74} - X_{75} - X_{76} \geq -300$

Each constraint indicates that the flow into a given node minus the flow out of that same node must be greater than or equal to the supply or demand at the node. So, if you draw a graph of a network flow problem like the one in Figure 5.1, it is easy to write out the constraints for the problem by following the balance-of-flow rule. Of course, we also need to specify the following nonnegativity condition for all the decision variables because negative flows should not occur on arcs:

$X_{ij} \geq 0$ for all ij

IMPLEMENTING THE MODEL IN A SPREADSHEET

As noted earlier in this book, there is often more than one way to implement an LP model. To illustrate this point, this section presents two approaches to implementing the model for the BMC problem. The first approach provides a simple, easy-to-understand presentation of the model and is probably the best approach to take for smaller network flow problems with relatively few nodes and arcs. The type of spreadsheet model used in this approach is shown in Figure 5.2 (and in the file FIG5-2.XLS on your data disk).

CHANGING CELLS ARE SHOWN IN WHITE

CONSTRAINT CELLS

TARGET CELL

	File	Edit	View	Insert	Format	Tools	Data	Window	Help	
	A	B	C	D	E	F	G	H	I	
1	Quantity Shipped:				Bavarian Motor Company					
2										
3	From:	To: Newark	Boston	Columbus	Richmond	Atlanta	Mobile	J'ville	Total Out	
4	Newark	0	0	0	0	0	0	0	0	
5	Boston	0	0	0	0	0	0	0	0	
6	Columbus	0	0	0	0	0	0	0	0	
7	Richmond	0	0	0	0	0	0	0	0	
8	Atlanta	0	0	0	0	0	0	0	0	
9	Mobile	0	0	0	0	0	0	0	0	
10	J'ville	0	0	0	0	0	0	0	0	
11	Total In	0	0	0	0	0	0	0		
12										
13	Tot. In - Tot. Out	0	0	0	0	0	0	0		
14	Supply/Demand	-200	100	60	90	180	70	-300		
15										
16	Unit Shipping Costs:							Total Cost:	$0	
17										
18	From:	To: Newark	Boston	Columbus	Richmond	Atlanta	Mobile	J'ville		
19	Newark	$0	$30	$0	$60	$0	$0	$0		
20	Boston	$0	$0	$80	$0	$0	$0	$0		
21	Columbus	$0	$0	$0	$0	$35	$0	$0		
22	Richmond	$0	$0	$0	$0	$0	$0	$0		
23	Atlanta	$0	$0	$45	$35	$0	$45	$0		
24	Mobile	$0	$0	$0	$0	$25	$0	$0		
25	J'ville	$0	$0	$0	$95	$45	$50	$0		
26										
27										

Shipping Report

Key Cell Formulas

Cell	Formula	Copied to
B11	=SUM(B4:B10)	C11:H11
B13	=B11–VLOOKUP(B3,$A$4:$I$10,9,0)	C13:H13
I4	=SUM(B4:H4)	I5:I10
I16	=SUMPRODUCT(B19:H25,B4:H10)	—

Figure 5.2: Spreadsheet implementation of the BMC transshipment problem

As shown at the top of Figure 5.2, one approach to modeling a transshipment problem is to create a matrix, or table, of decision variables in which each row corresponds to a source (or From) node and each column corresponds to a destination (or To) node. In the most general transshipment problem, every node could be a transshipment node (that is, a node that can both send and receive). Therefore, this table must represent each node by both a From row and a To column. The cells in this table correspond to all the arcs that are possible in a fully interconnected network. Because it is rare for networks to be fully interconnected, only a small subset of the entries in this table represent the actual decision variables for a given problem. The cells corresponding to the actual decision variables in our problem appear in white, while all other cells are shaded. For example, cell C4 in Figure 5.2 corresponds to the number of cars shipped from Newark to Boston (X_{12}), and cell E4 corresponds to the number of cars shipped from Newark to Richmond (X_{14}). The other white cells in the table correspond to the remaining decision variables in the problem. Later, we will use Solver to determine the optimal values for the white cells representing decision variables while leaving values of zero in all the shaded cells. That is, only the white cells will be listed as changing cells when we introduce Solver to this problem.

The column at the far right of the table, Total Out, provides row sums—or the total amount being shipped from each location listed in column A. To calculate these row sums, the following formula is entered in cell I4 and copied to cells I5 through I10:

Formula for cell I4:   =SUM(B4:H4)

(copy to I5 through I10)

The shaded cells will all remain equal to 0 provided that we do not allow Solver to change them. Thus, the row sum in cell I4 effectively represents the sum of cells C4 and E4. Similarly, the row sum in cell I8 represents the sum of cells D8, E8, and G8. Also, notice that the total amount being shipped from Richmond (cell I7) will always be 0 because there are no white cells in row 7. This reflects the fact that Richmond is a demand node and cannot supply cars to other locations.

The row at the bottom of the table, Total In, provides column sums—or the total amount being shipped to each location listed across the top of the table. The following formula is entered in cell B11 and copied to cells C11 through H11:

Formula for cell B11:   =SUM(B4:B10)

(copy to C11 through H11)

The total amounts shipped to Newark and Jacksonville will always be zero because these columns contain no white cells. This reflects the fact that Newark and Jacksonville are supply nodes and cannot receive cars from other locations.

The balance-of-flow rule indicates that for each node in the network, the total flow into the node minus the total flow out of the node must be greater than or equal to the supply or demand of the node. Thus, to implement the LHS formulas for each constraint in our problem, we need to calculate the difference between the values in the Total In row and the Total Out column for each city (Tot. In – Tot. Out). The following formula is entered in cell B13 and copied to cells C13 through H13:

Formula for cell B13:   =B11–VLOOKUP(B3,$A$4:$I$10,9,0)

(copy to C13 through H13)

The Supply/Demand row provides the RHS values for the constraints. (Note that the function VLOOKUP(B3,$A$4:$I$10,9,0) in the previous formula takes the entry in B3 (Newark) and looks it up in the first column in the range $A$4:$I$10 (column A), then returns the value on the same row and in the ninth column of the given range (the value in cell I4). The value 0 appearing as the last argument in this function indicates that the entries in the first column of the given range are *not* in alphabetical order.)

To implement the objective function for this model, we first make a copy of the matrix representing the quantities to be shipped and fill in the appropriate unit shipping costs, as shown at the bottom of Figure 5.2. The objective function for the model is then implemented in cell I16 as:

Formula for cell I16:   =SUMPRODUCT(B19:H25,B4:H10)

Figure 5.3 shows the Solver parameters and options required to solve this model. The changing cells shown in Figure 5.3 are selected individually and are separated by commas. The process of indicating the changing cells using this type of spreadsheet layout is a bit tedious and prone to error. Note that nonnegativity conditions are placed not only on the changing cells but also on the shaded (nonchanging) cells (all cells in the range B4:H10). This is done purely for convenience and does not affect the optimal solution. Solver allows common lower bounds to be placed on a contiguous range of cells, but not on a collection of noncontiguous cells. Thus, to place nonnegativity conditions only on the changing cells requires us to define separate nonnegativity constraints for each contiguous block of changing cells—a tedious and unnecessary task.

Figure 5.3: Solver parameters and options for the BMC transshipment problem

ANALYZING THE SOLUTION

Figure 5.4 shows the optimal solution for BMC's transshipment problem. The solution indicates that 110 cars should be shipped from Newark to Boston ($X_{12} = 110$), 90 cars from Newark to Richmond ($X_{14} = 90$), 10 cars from Boston to Columbus ($X_{23} = 10$), 50 cars from Atlanta to Columbus ($X_{53} = 50$), 230 cars from Jacksonville to Atlanta ($X_{75} = 230$), and 70 cars from Jacksonville to Mobile ($X_{76} = 70$). Cell I16 indicates that the total cost associated with this shipping plan is $25,600. The values of the constraint cells in B13 through H13 indicate that all the cars available at the supply nodes are being shipped and that exactly the right number of cars are remaining at each transshipment and demand node.

	File	Edit	View	Insert	Format	Tools	Data	Window	Help		
	A	B	C	D	E	F	G	H	I	
1	Quantity Shipped:			Bavarian Motor Company						
2										
3	From:	To: Newark	Boston	Columbus	Richmond	Atlanta	Mobile	J'ville	Total Out	
4	Newark	0	110	0	90	0	0	0	200	
5	Boston	0	0	10	0	0	0	0	10	
6	Columbus	0	0	0	0	0	0	0	0	
7	Richmond	0	0	0	0	0	0	0	0	
8	Atlanta	0	0	50	0	0	0	0	50	
9	Mobile	0	0	0	0	0	0	0	0	
10	J'ville	0	0	0	0	230	70	0	300	
11	Total In	0	110	60	90	230	70	0		
12										
13	Tot. In - Tot. Out	-200	100	60	90	180	70	-300		
14	Supply/Demand	-200	100	60	90	180	70	-300		
15										
16	Unit Shipping Costs:							Total Cost:	$25,600	
17										
18	From:	To: Newark	Boston	Columbus	Richmond	Atlanta	Mobile	J'ville		
19	Newark	$0	$30	$0	$60	$0	$0	$0		
20	Boston	$0	$0	$80	$0	$0	$0	$0		
21	Columbus	$0	$0	$0	$0	$35	$0	$0		
22	Richmond	$0	$0	$0	$0	$0	$0	$0		
23	Atlanta	$0	$0	$45	$35	$0	$45	$0		
24	Mobile	$0	$0	$0	$0	$25	$0	$0		
25	J'ville	$0	$0	$0	$95	$45	$50	$0		
26										
27										

Shipping Report

Figure 5.4: Optimal solution for the BMC transshipment problem

This solution is summarized graphically, as shown in Figure 5.5. The values in the boxes next to each arc indicate the optimal flows for the arcs. The optimal flow for all the other arcs in the problem, which are not shown in Figure 5.5, is 0. Notice that the amount flowing into each node minus the amount flowing out of each node is equal to the supply or demand at the node. For example, 230 cars are being shipped from Jacksonville to Atlanta. Atlanta will keep 180 of the cars (to satisfy the demand at this node) and send the extra 50 to Columbus.

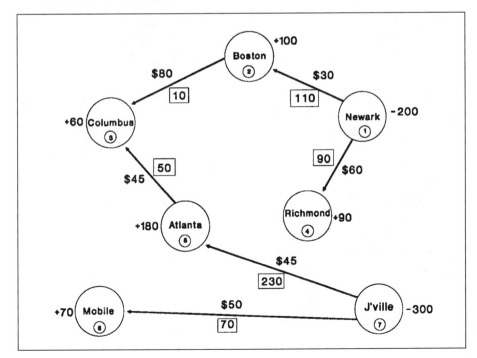

Figure 5.5: Network representation of the optimal solution for the BMC transshipment problem

ANOTHER APPROACH TO IMPLEMENTING THE MODEL

As mentioned earlier, selecting the changing cells individually when completing the Solver Parameters dialog box in Figure 5.3 is a tedious process. For network flow problems with a large number of nodes and arcs, the type of implementation shown in Figure 5.4 is extremely awkward and inefficient.

An alternate approach to implementing network flow problems provides a better way to solve larger problems. This alternate approach is understood best by writing out the LP formulation of the model in an organized manner as:

MIN:

$$+30X_{12} +60X_{14} +80X_{23} +35X_{35} +45X_{53} +35X_{54} +45X_{56} +25X_{65} +95X_{74} +45X_{75} +50X_{76}$$

Subject to:

$$
\begin{array}{llllllll}
-1X_{12} & -1X_{14} & & & & & & \geq -200 \\
+1X_{12} & & -1X_{23} & & & & & \geq +100 \\
& & +1X_{23} & -1X_{35} & +1X_{53} & & & \geq +60 \\
& +1X_{14} & & & & +1X_{54} & +1X_{74} & \geq +90 \\
& & & +1X_{35} & -1X_{53} & -1X_{54} & -1X_{56} & +1X_{65} & +1X_{75} & \geq +180 \\
& & & & & +1X_{56} & -1X_{65} & +1X_{76} & \geq +70 \\
& & & & & & -1X_{74} & -1X_{75} & -1X_{76} & \geq -300 \\
\end{array}
$$

$$X_{12}, X_{14}, X_{23}, X_{35}, X_{53}, X_{54}, X_{56}, X_{65}, X_{74}, X_{75}, X_{76} \geq 0$$

The constraints in this model are the same as the constraints we constructed previously using the balance-of-flow rule for each of the seven nodes in the network—here, however, the variables are lined up in columns. This reveals three properties that exist in the constraints of *all* network flow problems:

1. Each variable X_{ij} appears with a nonzero coefficient in the two constraints that correspond to its From node (i) and its To node (j).

2. Each variable's coefficient is -1 in the constraint corresponding to its From node (i).

3. Each variable's coefficient is $+1$ in the constraint corresponding to its To node (j).

Before we continue, let's make sure you understand these points. Notice that the seven constraints in the LP model correspond, respectively, to the balance-of-flow constraints needed for nodes 1, 2, 3, ..., 7 in Figure 5.1. Now consider variable X_{12}, which corresponds to the arc *from* node 1 (Newark) *to* node 2 (Boston). This variable has a coefficient of -1 in the constraint corresponding to node 1 (its From node) and a coefficient of $+1$ in the constraint corresponding to node 2 (its To node). Similarly, the variable X_{54} has a coefficient of -1 in the constraint corresponding to node 5 (its From node) and a coefficient of $+1$ in the constraint corresponding to node 4 (its To node). This property holds for *all* the variables in the model. You can take advantage of this property to simplify the process of setting up the spreadsheet model for large network flow problems.

THE NODE-ARC INCIDENCE MATRIX

As illustrated in the preceding discussion, if you had a list of the From and To nodes for each arc in a network flow problem, you could generate the necessary constraints for the problem easily. For example, consider the arcs shown in Figure 5.6 for the BMC problem. In this figure, a column has been established for each node in the network. The variable X_{12} (representing the arc from node 1 to node 2) has a coefficient of −1 in the column for node 1 and a coefficient of +1 in the column for node 2. This is reflected by the first row in Figure 5.6. Similarly, the variable X_{14} has a coefficient of −1 in the column for node 1 and a coefficient of +1 in the column for node 4. This is reflected by the second row in Figure 5.6. Examining Figure 5.6 reveals that each arc has a coefficient of −1 in the column corresponding to its From node and a coefficient of +1 in the column corresponding to its To node. This type of matrix is known as a **node-arc incidence matrix**.

Notice that the columns in Figure 5.6 for the nodes contain the same coefficients as the constraints in the LP model for the problem discussed earlier. Therefore, if we can construct a node-arc incidence matrix in a spreadsheet, we can implement the associated network flow problem easily.

Arcs		Nodes						
From	To	1	2	3	4	5	6	7
1	2	−1	+1	0	0	0	0	0
1	4	−1	0	0	+1	0	0	0
2	3	0	−1	+1	0	0	0	0
3	5	0	0	−1	0	+1	0	0
5	3	0	0	+1	0	−1	0	0
5	4	0	0	0	+1	−1	0	0
5	6	0	0	0	0	−1	+1	0
6	5	0	0	0	0	+1	−1	0
7	4	0	0	0	+1	0	0	−1
7	5	0	0	0	0	+1	0	−1
7	6	0	0	0	0	0	+1	−1

Figure 5.6: Node-arc incidence matrix for the BMC transshipment problem

IMPLEMENTING THE MODEL IN A SPREADSHEET

A node-arc incidence matrix like the one shown in Figure 5.6 is generated easily in a spreadsheet. The matrix for our example problem is shown in Figure 5.7 (and in the file FIG5-7.XLS on your data disk).

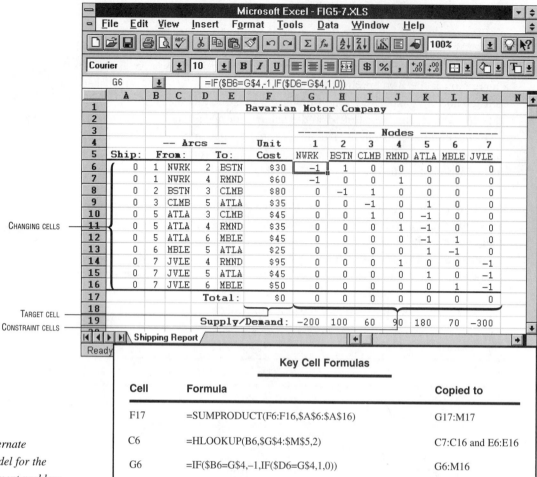

Figure 5.7: Alternate spreadsheet model for the BMC transshipment problem

In this spreadsheet, an abbreviation for each node is listed in cells G5 through M5. The From and To nodes for each arc are listed in columns B and D, respectively. (You can use the HLOOKUP( ) function to display the appropriate abbreviations for each arc's From and To node in columns C and E.) The node-arc incidence matrix is generated by placing the following formula in cell G6 and copying it to cells G6 through M16:

Formula for cell G6: =IF($B6=G$4,–1,IF($D6=G$4,1,0))
(copy to G6 through M16)

This formula first checks to see if the value in cell B6 equals the value in cell G4. If so, the value –1 is returned for cell G6; otherwise, the formula next checks to see if the value in cell D6 equals the value in cell G4. If so, the formula returns the value 1 for cell G6; otherwise, it returns the value 0 for G6. After this formula is copied, it returns the value –1 in the column corresponding to the From node of each arc, and returns the value +1 in the column corresponding to the To node of each arc. Using this type of spreadsheet layout, you can generate the node-arc incidence matrix for any network flow problem by entering this single formula and copying it throughout the appropriate range.

As indicated in Figure 5.7, cells A6 through A16 represent changing cells, or the variables X_{12}, X_{14}, X_{23}, ..., X_{76}. Column F shows the unit costs associated with each arc. The objective function for this problem is implemented in cell F17 using the formula:

Formula for cell F17:   =SUMPRODUCT(F6..F16,$A$6..$A$16)
(copy to G17 through M17)

The constraint cells for the model are implemented by copying this formula to cells G17 through M17. Cells G19 through M19 display the RHS values for the constraint cells.

Figure 5.8 shows the Solver parameters and options required to solve this model. Because the decision variables for this model are organized in a contiguous range of cells, it is much easier to define the changing cells using this model rather than the one discussed earlier. This type of layout also facilitates the inclusion of alternate objective functions and lower or upper bounds on the decision variables. Also, as the size of the problem increases this type of spreadsheet layout is more effective because no extraneous shaded cells clutter the spreadsheet. There are many advantages to using the node-arc incidence implementation of network flow problems. For this reason, the node-arc incidence implementation is used throughout the remainder of this chapter.

Figure 5.8: Solver parameters and options for the alternate spreadsheet model of the BMC transshipment problem

Figure 5.9 shows the optimal solution for this model. Not surprisingly, the optimal solution shown here is identical to the one obtained earlier and summarized graphically in Figure 5.5.

Microsoft Excel - FIG5-7.XLS

File   Edit   View   Insert   Format   Tools   Data   Window   Help

Courier   10   B I U

P1

	A	B	C	D	E	F	G	H	I	J	K	L	M	N
1						Bavarian Motor Company								
2														
3							———————— Nodes ————————							
4		— Arcs —				Unit	1	2	3	4	5	6	7	
5	Ship:	From:			To:	Cost	NWRK	BSTN	CLMB	RMND	ATLA	MBLE	JVLE	
6	110	1	NWRK	2	BSTN	$30	−1	1	0	0	0	0	0	
7	90	1	NWRK	4	RMND	$60	−1	0	0	1	0	0	0	
8	10	2	BSTN	3	CLMB	$80	0	−1	1	0	0	0	0	
9	0	3	CLMB	5	ATLA	$35	0	0	−1	0	1	0	0	
10	50	5	ATLA	3	CLMB	$45	0	0	1	0	−1	0	0	
11	0	5	ATLA	4	RMND	$35	0	0	0	1	−1	0	0	
12	0	5	ATLA	6	MBLE	$45	0	0	0	0	−1	1	0	
13	0	6	MBLE	5	ATLA	$25	0	0	0	0	1	−1	0	
14	0	7	JVLE	4	RMND	$95	0	0	0	1	0	0	−1	
15	230	7	JVLE	5	ATLA	$45	0	0	0	0	1	0	−1	
16	70	7	JVLE	6	MBLE	$50	0	0	0	0	0	1	−1	
17			Total:			$25,600	−200	100	60	90	180	70	−300	
18														
19			Supply/Demand:				−200	100	60	90	180	70	−300	

Shipping Report

Ready

Figure 5.9: Optimal solution to the BMC problem

THE CASE OF DEMAND EXCEEDING SUPPLY

The approach to solving the network flow problem for BMC can be used to solve virtually any network flow problem where the total supply in the network meets or exceeds the total demand. But what happens if you encounter a problem in which the total demand exceeds the total supply? An example of this type of problem is shown on the left in Figure 5.10.

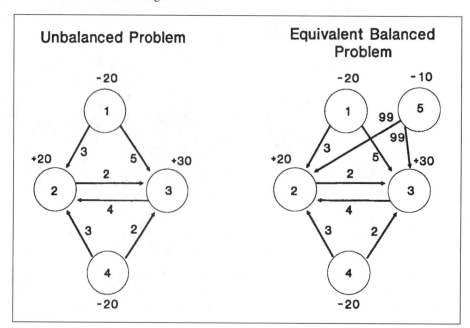

Figure 5.10: Example of balancing a network where demand exceeds supply

Because the total demand in the network on the left in Figure 5.10 is 50 and the total supply is only 40, it is impossible to satisfy the demand at each node. If you try to solve such a problem using the balance-of-flow rule to generate the constraints, Solver will indicate that the problem is infeasible. However, these types of problems are not uncommon. For example, numerous retail stores might demand more of an item than is available from a central warehouse facility. Rather than accepting that there is no feasible solution to the problem, you might want to determine the optimal method of distributing the supply that is available. The right side of Figure 5.10 gives a simple example of how this might be done.

As indicated in Figure 5.10, a network flow problem in which the total demand exceeds the total supply can be balanced so that the total supply equals total demand. This is accomplished by adding an artificial, or dummy, node to the problem and assigning it an artificial supply equal to the amount by which the total demand exceeds the total supply in the rest of the network. This dummy node is then connected directly to each demand node by arcs that have some arbitrarily large costs. The large costs on these arcs should make any flow on them highly undesirable from a cost minimization view. (If different costs are associated with not meeting demands at various nodes, such costs can be used in place of the arbitrary ones.) After adding the dummy supply node, the balance-of-flow rule can be used to formulate the constraints of the problem. The optimal solution to such a problem will have some flow going from the dummy node to one or more demand nodes. Such shipments simply represent unmet demand at the different nodes.

In solving such a problem, it is a good idea to calculate the total cost of flows over legitimate arcs in one cell, and the costs of flows over dummy arcs in a separate cell. A third Total Cost cell can sum these two sub-totals and can be used as the target (objective) cell. In this way, the true cost of the optimal solution (that is, the cost of actual flows over the legitimate arcs) is clear.

OTHER NETWORK FLOW PROBLEMS

As mentioned earlier, different types of network flow problems can be viewed as special cases of a transshipment problem. We will now discuss two such problems: the shortest path problem and the maximal flow problem.

Special algorithms enable you to solve these different types of network flow problems more efficiently than the simplex method. These algorithms are especially valuable in solving extremely large problems. However, as computers become faster and more powerful, the simplex method is fast enough for an increasing number of these problems. Here, we consider how to model these problems as network flow problems and how to formulate and solve them as LP problems.

SHORTEST PATH PROBLEMS

For many problems, you might be interested in determining the shortest (or least costly) route or path through a network from a starting node to an ending node. For example, many cities are developing computerized maps of city streets to help emergency vehicles identify the quickest route to a given location. Each street intersection on the map represents a node in a network, and the streets connecting the intersections represent arcs. Depending on the day of the week and the time of day, the time required to travel various streets can increase or decrease due to changes in traffic patterns. So the quickest route (or shortest path) for getting from one point in the city to another can change frequently. In emergency situations, lives or property can be lost or saved depending on how quickly emergency vehicles arrive where they are needed. The ability to quickly determine the shortest path to the location of an emergency situation is extremely useful in these situations. The following examples illustrate other applications of shortest path problems.

AN EXAMPLE OF A SHORTEST PATH PROBLEM

Gail Sanders owns West Coast Travel Company, a travel agency based in Petaluma, California. To help customers book airline reservations, her travel agency has computerized access to the flight schedules of all major airlines. When a customer calls or comes in to make airline reservations, Gail first determines where the person needs to go, the travel dates, and the approximate times of departure and arrival. With this information, Gail uses her computer to determine what flights are available, the average travel times between various airports, and the cost of the flight segments. She then helps the customer determine which flight schedule is best.

Gail has noticed that customers tend to fall into two categories. Some want to find the cheapest flight. These customers are usually willing to travel a somewhat circuitous route, change planes several times, and endure lengthy layovers provided that they pay the lowest possible price. Other customers are more interested in booking the flights that get them where they want to go as quickly as possible, regardless of price. Gail would like a system that takes all the possible flight schedules for a given customer's travel plans and automatically determines the schedule that, at her discretion, either minimizes the total cost of the trip or minimizes the expected travel time.

To see how Gail would benefit by solving shortest path problems, consider the simplified network shown in Figure 5.11 for a customer who wants to travel from San Francisco to Washington, DC. The nodes in this graph represent airports in the various cities shown. The arcs indicate the possible flight segments between the various cities. For each arc, Figure 5.11 lists both the dollar cost of the associated flight and the average travel time between the various airports. For example, the flight from San Francisco to Seattle costs $95 and takes an average of 3.5 hours between the time the passenger arrives at the airport in San Francisco and the time the passenger arrives in Seattle. Because flight times are often delayed by weather or mechanical failure, Gail believes that the average travel time between airports is a more reliable estimate of actual travel time than the scheduled departure and arrival times.

Solving this problem as a network flow model requires the various nodes to have some supply or demand. In Figure 5.11, node 1 (San Francisco) has a supply of 1, node 7 (Washington, DC) has a demand of 1, and all other nodes have a demand (or

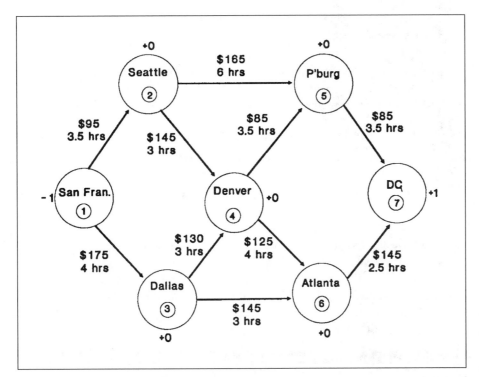

Figure 5.11: Network of possible routes for West Coast Travel's shortest path problem

supply) of 0. If we view this model as a transshipment problem, we want to find either the least costly way or the quickest way of shipping 1 unit (1 person) from node 1 to node 7. The route this unit of supply takes corresponds to either the least costly path or the shortest path through the network, depending on which objective is being pursued.

AN LP MODEL FOR THE EXAMPLE PROBLEM

Using the balance-of-flow rule, the LP model to minimize the travel cost in this problem is represented as:

MIN:

$$+95X_{12} +175X_{13} +145X_{24} +165X_{25} +130X_{34} +145X_{36} +85X_{45} + 125X_{46} +85X_{57} +145X_{67}$$

Subject to:

$$
\begin{aligned}
-X_{12} \quad -X_{13} \qquad\qquad\qquad\qquad\qquad\qquad &= -1 \\
+X_{12} \qquad\quad -X_{24} \quad -X_{25} \qquad\qquad\qquad &= 0 \\
+X_{13} \qquad\qquad\quad -X_{34} \quad -X_{36} \qquad &= 0 \\
+X_{24} \qquad +X_{34} \qquad -X_{45} \quad -X_{46} \qquad &= 0 \\
+X_{25} \qquad\qquad +X_{45} \qquad -X_{57} \quad &= 0 \\
+X_{36} \qquad +X_{46} \qquad -X_{67} &= 0 \\
+X_{57} \quad +X_{67} &= +1 \\
X_{12}, X_{13}, X_{24}, X_{25}, X_{34}, X_{36}, X_{45}, X_{46}, X_{57}, X_{67} &\geq 0
\end{aligned}
$$

Because the total supply equals the total demand in this problem, the constraint can be stated as equalities. The first constraint in this model ensures that the 1 unit of supply available at node 1 is shipped to node 2 or node 3. The next five constraints indicate that anything flowing to nodes 2, 3, 4, 5, and 6 must also flow out of these nodes because each has a demand of 0. For example, if the unit of supply leaves node 1 for node 2 (via X_{12}), the second constraint ensures that it will leave node 2 for node 4 or node 5 (via X_{24} or X_{25}). The last constraint indicates that the unit must ultimately flow to node 7. Thus, the solution to this problem indicates the least costly sequence of flights from node 1 (San Francisco) to node 7 (Washington, DC).

THE SPREADSHEET MODEL AND SOLUTION

A spreadsheet model of this problem is implemented as shown in Figure 5.12 (and in the file FIG5-12.XLS on your data disk). This model includes calculations of both the total cost (cell F16) and total expected travel time (cell G16) associated with any solution. Either of these cells can be chosen as the objective function according to the customer's demands. The optimal flight schedule shown in Figure 5.12 is obtained using the Solver parameters and options shown in Figure 5.13.

The optimal solution shown in Figure 5.12 indicates that the least costly travel plan involves flying from node 1 (San Francisco) to node 2 (Seattle), then from node 2 (Seattle) to node 5 (Pittsburgh), then from node 5 (Pittsburgh) to node 7 (Washington, DC). The total cost of this sequence of flights is $345 and the total travel time is 13 hours.

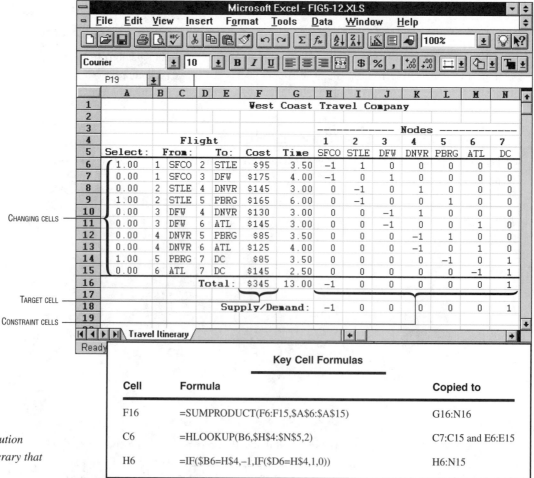

Figure 5.12: Solution showing the itinerary that minimizes cost

Figure 5.13: Solver
parameters and options for
the West Coast Travel's
shortest path problem

Using this spreadsheet, we can also determine the sequence of flights that minimizes the expected travel time by instructing Solver to minimize the value in cell G16. Figure 5.14 shows the optimal solution obtained in this case. Notice that this travel plan involves flying from San Francisco to Dallas, from Dallas to Atlanta, and from Atlanta to Washington, DC. This itinerary results in a minimum expected travel time of 9.5 hours and a cost of $465.

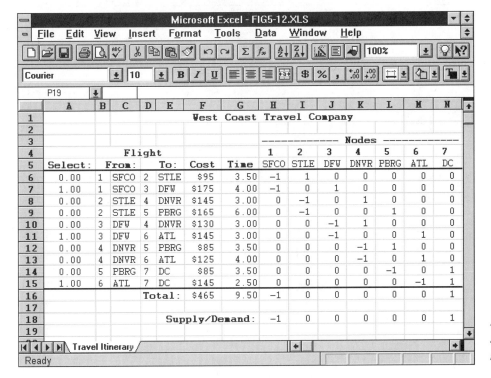

Figure 5.14: Solution
showing the itinerary that
minimizes travel time

NETWORK FLOW MODELS AND INTEGER SOLUTIONS

Up to this point, each of the network flow models solved generated integer solutions. If you use the simplex method to solve any network flow model having integer constraint RHS values, then the optimal solution automatically assumes integer values. This property is helpful because the items flowing through most network flow models represent discrete units (such as cars or people).

Sometimes it is tempting to place additional constraints (or side-constraints) on a network model. For example, in the West Coast Travel problem, suppose that the customer wants to get to Washington, DC as quickly as possible but has only $400 to spend. We can add a budget constraint to the model to keep the total cost value in cell F16 less than or equal to $400. If we then re-solve the model to minimize the expected travel time value in cell G16, we obtain the solution shown in Figure 5.15. Unfortunately, this solution is useless because it indicates that fractional numbers of flights should be taken. Thus, if we add side-constraints to network flow problems that do not obey the balance-of-flow rule, we can no longer ensure that the solution to the LP formulation of the problems will be integral. If integer solutions are needed for such problems, the integer programming techniques discussed in chapter 6 must be applied.

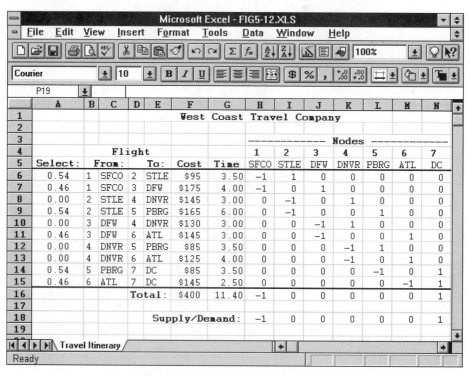

Figure 5.15: Example of a non-integer solution to a network problem with side constraints

THE EQUIPMENT REPLACEMENT PROBLEM

The equipment replacement problem is another common business problem that can be modeled as a shortest path problem. This type of problem involves determining the least costly schedule for replacing equipment over a specified length of time. Consider the following example.

Jose Maderos is the owner of Compu-Train, a small company that provides hands-on software education and training for businesses in and around Boulder, Colorado. Jose leases the computer equipment used in his business and he likes to keep the equipment up to date so that it will run the latest state-of-the-art software in an efficient manner.

Jose is negotiating a new lease arrangement with the equipment supplier. At the beginning of any of the next 5 years, Jose can trade in his old equipment and lease new equipment for the amounts indicated below:

Year	Lease Cost
1	$32,000
2	$32,500
3	$34,500
4	$35,000
5	$37,000

To make sure his equipment does not become outdated, Jose decides to replace his equipment at least every 2 years. The leasing company agreed to give him a 60% refund on the original lease price (listed above) if he turns in the equipment after 1 year, and a 20% refund on the original lease price if he turns in the equipment after 2 years.

Jose realizes that no matter what he does, he still has to pay $32,000 to obtain the equipment initially. However, he wants to determine when he should replace his equipment to minimize the remaining leasing costs over the next 5 years.

To see how Jose's equipment replacement problem can be modeled as a shortest path problem, consider the network representation of this problem shown in Figure 5.16. Each node corresponds to a point in time during the next 5 years when Jose can replace his equipment. Each arc in this network represents a choice available to Jose. For example, the arc from node 1 to node 2 indicates that Jose can keep his equipment for 1 year and then replace it for a net cost of $13,300 ($32,500 − 0.6*$32,000 = $13,300). Alternatively, the arc from node 1 to node 3 indicates that Jose can keep his equipment for 2 years and replace it at the beginning of year 3 for a net cost of $28,100 ($34,500 − 0.2*$32,000 = $28,100).

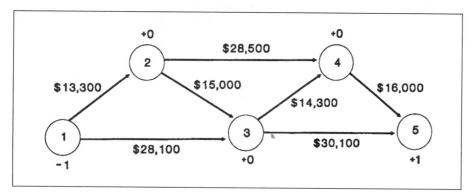

Figure 5.16: Network representation of Compu-Train's equipment replacement problem

The arc from node 2 to node 3 indicates that if Jose replaces his equipment at the beginning of year 2, he can keep the new equipment for 1 year and replace it at the beginning of year 3 at a net cost of $15,000 ($34,500 − 0.6*$32,500 = $15,000). The remaining arcs and costs in the network can be interpreted in the same way. Jose's decision problem is to determine the least costly (or shortest) way of getting from node 1 to node 5 in this network.

THE SPREADSHEET MODEL AND SOLUTION

The LP formulation of Jose's decision problem can be generated from the graph in Figure 5.16 using the balance-of-flow rule in the same manner as the previous network flow problems. The spreadsheet implementation of this problem in Figure 5.17 (and in the file FIG5-17.XLS on your data disk) shows the optimal solution that is obtained using the Solver parameters and options shown in Figure 5.18.

Figure 5.17: Spreadsheet model for Compu-Train's equipment replacement problem

Key Cell Formulas		
Cell	**Formula**	**Copied to**
D13	=SUMPRODUCT(D6:D12,$A$6:$A$12)	E13:I13
E6	=IF($B6=E$5,−1,IF($C6=E$5,1,0))	E6:I12

Figure 5.18: Solver parameters and options for Compu-Train's equipment replacement problem

The optimal solution to this problem indicates that if Jose replaces his equipment at the beginning of years 2, 4, and 5 his total leasing cost will be $57,800. This amount is in addition to the $32,000 he has to pay up front at the beginning of year 1.

SUMMARY OF SHORTEST PATH PROBLEMS

You can model any shortest path problem as a transshipment problem by assigning a supply of 1 to the starting node, a demand of 1 to the ending node, and a demand of 0 to all other nodes in the network. Because the examples presented here involved only a small number of paths through each of the networks, it might have been easier to solve these problems simply by enumerating the paths and calculating the total distance of each one. However, in a problem with many nodes and arcs, an automated LP model is preferable to a manual solution approach.

MAXIMAL FLOW PROBLEMS

The maximal flow problem (or max flow problem) is another type of network flow problem involving a single supply node and a single demand node. However, in a maximal flow problem, the amount of flow that can occur over each arc is limited by some capacity restriction. The goal in a max flow problem is to determine the maximum amount of flow that can occur in the network. This type of network is used to model the flow of oil in a pipeline (where the amount of oil that can flow through a pipe in a unit of time is limited by the diameter of the pipe). Traffic engineers also use this type of network to determine the maximum number of cars that can travel through a collection of streets with different capacities imposed by the number of lanes in the streets and speed limits. The following example illustrates a max flow problem.

AN EXAMPLE OF A MAXIMAL FLOW PROBLEM

The Northwest Petroleum Company operates an oil field and refinery in Alaska. The crude obtained from the oil field is pumped through the network of pumping substations shown in Figure 5.19 to the company's refinery located 500 miles from the oil field. The amount of oil that can flow through each of the pipelines, represented by the arcs in the network, varies due to differing pipe diameters. The numbers next to the arcs in the network indicate the maximum amount of oil that can flow through the various pipelines (measured in thousands of barrels per hour). The company wants to determine the maximum number of barrels per hour that can flow from the oil field to the refinery.

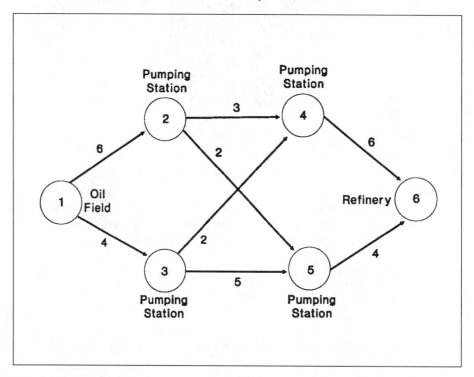

Figure 5.19: Network representation of Northwest Petroleum's oil refinery operation

The max flow problem appears to be very different from the network flow models described earlier because it does not include specific supplies or demands for the nodes. However, you can solve the max flow problem in the same way as a transshipment problem if you add a return arc from the ending node to the starting node, assign a demand of 0 to all the nodes in the network, and attempt to maximize the flow over the return arc. Figure 5.20 shows these modifications to the problem.

To understand the network in Figure 5.20, suppose that k units are shipped from node 6 to node 1 (where k represents some integer). Because node 6 has a supply of 0, it can send k units to node 1 only if these units can be returned through the network to node 6 (to balance the flow at node 6). The capacities on the arcs limit how many units can be returned to node 6. Therefore, the maximum flow through the network corresponds to the largest number of units that can be shipped from node 6 to node 1 and then returned through the network to node 6 (to balance the flow at this node). We can solve an LP model to determine the maximal flow by maximizing the flow from node 6 to node 1, given appropriate upper bounds on each arc and the usual balance-of-flow constraints. This model is represented as:

$$MAX: \quad X_{61}$$

$$Subject\ to: \quad +X_{61} - X_{12} - X_{13} = 0$$
$$+X_{12} - X_{24} - X_{25} = 0$$
$$+X_{13} - X_{34} - X_{35} = 0$$
$$+X_{24} + X_{34} - X_{46} = 0$$
$$+X_{25} + X_{35} - X_{56} = 0$$
$$+X_{46} + X_{56} - X_{61} = 0$$

with the following bounds on the decision variables:

$$0 \le X_{12} \le 6 \qquad 0 \le X_{25} \le 2 \qquad 0 \le X_{46} \le 6$$
$$0 \le X_{13} \le 4 \qquad 0 \le X_{34} \le 2 \qquad 0 \le X_{56} \le 4$$
$$0 \le X_{24} \le 3 \qquad 0 \le X_{35} \le 5 \qquad 0 \le X_{61} \le \infty$$

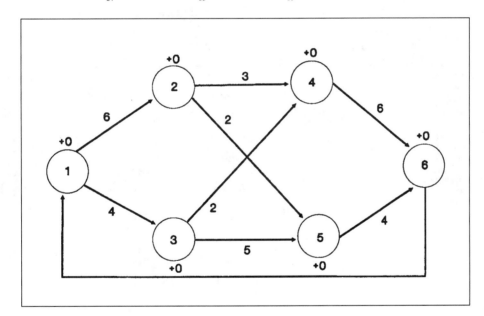

Figure 5.20: Network structure of Northwest Petroleum's max flow problem

THE SPREADSHEET MODEL AND SOLUTION

This model is implemented in the spreadsheet shown in Figure 5.21 (and in the file FIG5-21.XLS on your data disk). This spreadsheet model differs from the earlier network models in a few minor, but important, ways. First, column D in Figure 5.21 represents the upper bounds for each arc. Second, the objective function (or target cell) is represented by cell A14, which contains the formula:

Formula in cell A14:   =A13

Cell A14 represents the flow from node 6 to node 1 (or X_{61}). This cell corresponds to the variable we want to *maximize* in the objective function of the LP model. The Solver parameters and options shown in Figure 5.22 are used to obtain the optimal solution shown in Figure 5.21.

Because the arcs leading to node 6 (X_{46} and X_{56}) have a total capacity for 10 units of flow, it might be surprising to learn that only 9 units can flow through the network. However, the optimal solution shown in Figure 5.22 indicates that the maximal flow through the network is just 9 units.

The optimal flows identified in Figure 5.21 for each arc are shown in the boxes next to the capacities for each arc in Figure 5.23. In Figure 5.23, the arc from node 5 to node 6 is at its full capacity of 4 units, whereas the arc from node 4 to node 6 is 1 unit below its full capacity of 6 units. Although the arc from node 4 to node 6 can carry 1 additional unit of flow, it is prevented from doing so because all the arcs flowing to node 4 (X_{24} and X_{34}) are at full capacity.

Figure 5.21: *Spreadsheet model for Northwest Petroleum's max flow problem*

Figure 5.22: Solver parameters and options for Northwest Petroleum's max flow problem

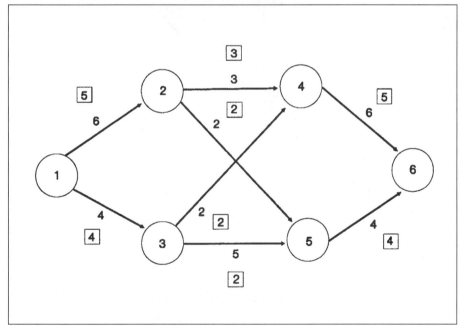

Figure 5.23: Network representation of the solution to Northwest Petroleum's max flow problem

A graph like Figure 5.23, which summarizes the optimal flows in a max flow problem, is helpful in identifying where increases in flow capacity would be most effective. For example, from this graph we can see that even though X_{24} and X_{34} are both at full capacity, increasing their capacity will not necessarily increase the flow through the network. Increasing the capacity of X_{24} would allow for an increased flow through the network because an additional unit could then flow from node 1 to node 2 to node 4 to node 6. However, increasing the capacity of X_{34} would not allow for an increase in the total flow because the arc from node 1 to node 3 is already at full capacity.

TRANSPORTATION/ASSIGNMENT PROBLEMS

Chapter 3 presented an example of another type of network flow problem known as the transportation/assignment problem. The example involved the Tropicsun Company—a grower and distributor of fresh citrus products. The company wanted to determine the least expensive way of transporting freshly picked fruit from three citrus groves to three processing plants. The network representation of the problem is repeated in Figure 5.24.

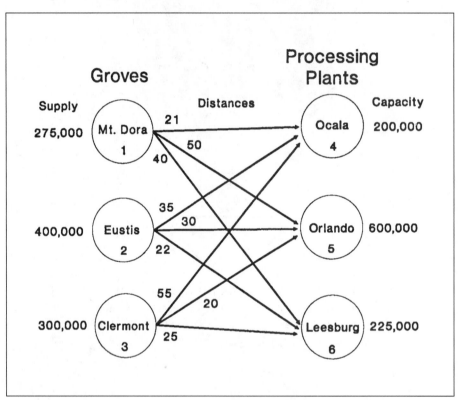

Figure 5.24: Network representation of Tropicsun's transportation/assignment problem

The network shown in Figure 5.24 differs from the earlier network flow problems in this chapter because it contains no transshipment nodes. Each node in Figure 5.24 is either a sending node or a receiving node. The lack of transshipment nodes is the key feature that distinguishes transportation/assignment problems from other types of network flow problems. As you saw in chapter 3, this property allows you to set up and solve transportation/assignment problems conveniently in a spreadsheet. Although it is possible to solve transportation/assignment problems in the same way in which we solved general network flow problems, it is much easier to implement and solve these problems using the approach described in chapter 3.

MINIMAL SPANNING TREE PROBLEMS

Another type of network problem is known as the minimal spanning tree problem. This type of problem cannot be solved as an LP problem, but is solved easily using a simple manual algorithm.

For a network with n nodes, a **spanning tree** is a set of $n - 1$ arcs that connects all the nodes and contains no loops. A minimum spanning tree problem involves determining the set of arcs that connects all the nodes in a network while minimizing the total length (or cost) of the selected arcs. Consider the following example.

Jon Fleming is responsible for setting up a local area network (LAN) in the design engineering department of Windstar Aerospace Company. A LAN consists of a number of individual computers connected to a centralized computer or file server. Each computer in the LAN can access information from the file server and communicate with the other computers in the LAN.

Installing a LAN involves connecting all the computers together with coaxial cables. Individual computers do not have to be connected directly to the file server, but there must be some link between each computer in the network. Figure 5.25 summarizes all the possible connections that Jon can make. Each node in this figure represents one of the computers to be included in the LAN. Each line connecting the nodes represents a possible connection between pairs of computers. The dollar amount on each line represents the cost of making the connection.

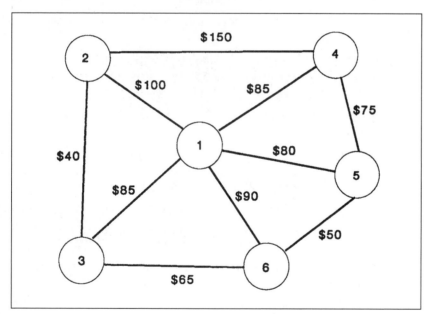

Figure 5.25: Network representation of Windstar Aerospace's minimal spanning tree problem

The arcs in Figure 5.25 have no specific directional orientation, indicating that information can move in either direction across the arcs. Also note that the communication links represented by the arcs do not exist yet. Jon's challenge is to determine which links to establish. Because the network involves $n = 6$ nodes, a spanning tree for this problem consists of $n - 1 = 5$ arcs that results in a path existing between any pair of nodes. The objective is to find the minimal (least costly) spanning tree for this problem.

AN ALGORITHM FOR THE MINIMAL SPANNING TREE PROBLEM

You can apply a simple algorithm to solve minimal spanning tree problems. The steps to this algorithm are:

1. Select any node. Call this the current subnetwork.

2. Add to the current subnetwork the cheapest arc that connects any node within the current subnetwork to any node not in the current subnetwork. (Ties for the cheapest arc can be broken arbitrarily.) Call this the current subnetwork.

3. If all the nodes are in the subnetwork, stop; this is the optimal solution. Otherwise, return to step 2.

SOLVING THE EXAMPLE PROBLEM

You can program this algorithm easily or, for simple problems, execute it manually. The following steps illustrate how to execute the algorithm manually for the example problem shown in Figure 5.25.

Step 1. If we select node 1 in Figure 5.25, then node 1 is the current subnetwork.

Step 2. The cheapest arc connecting the current subnetwork to a node not in the current subnetwork is the $80 arc connecting nodes 1 and 5. This arc and node 5 are added to the current subnetwork.

Step 3. Four nodes (nodes 2, 3, 4, and 6) remain unconnected—therefore, return to step 2.

Step 2. The cheapest arc connecting the current subnetwork to a node not in the current subnetwork is the $50 arc connecting nodes 5 and 6. This arc and node 6 are added to the current subnetwork.

Step 3. Three nodes (nodes 2, 3, and 4) remain unconnected—therefore, return to step 2.

Step 2. The cheapest arc connecting the current subnetwork to a node not in the current subnetwork is the $65 arc connecting nodes 6 and 3. This arc and node 3 are added to the current subnetwork.

Step 3. Two nodes (nodes 2 and 4) remain unconnected—therefore, return to step 2.

Step 2. The cheapest arc connecting the current subnetwork to a node not in the current subnetwork is the $40 arc connecting nodes 3 and 2. This arc and node 2 are added to the current subnetwork.

Step 3. One node (node 4) remains unconnected—therefore, return to step 2.

Step 2. The cheapest arc connecting the current subnetwork to a node not in the current subnetwork is the $75 arc connecting nodes 5 and 4. This arc and node 4 are added to the current subnetwork.

Step 3. All the nodes are now connected. Stop; the current subnetwork is optimal.

Figure 5.26 shows the optimal (minimal) spanning tree generated by this algorithm. The algorithm described here produces the optimal (minimal) spanning tree regardless of which node is selected initially in step 1. You can verify this by solving the example problem again starting with a different node in step 1.

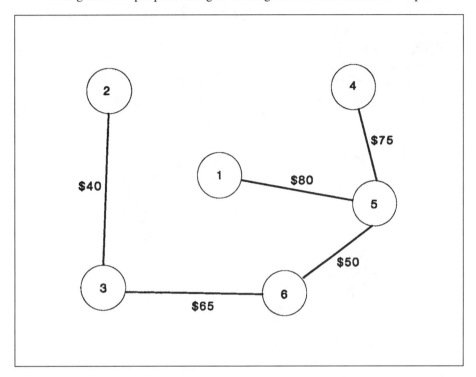

Figure 5.26: Optimal solution to Windstar Aerospace's minimal spanning tree problem

SUMMARY

This chapter presented several business problems modeled as network flow problems, including transshipment problems, shortest path problems, maximal flow problems, and transportation/assignment problems. It also introduced the minimal spanning tree problem and presented a simple algorithm for solving this type of problem manually.

Although special algorithms exist for solving network flow problems, you can also formulate and solve them as LP problems. The constraints in an LP formulation of a network flow problem have a special structure that enables you to implement and solve these models easily in a spreadsheet. Although there might be more efficient ways of solving network flow problems, the methods discussed in this chapter are probably the most practical. For extremely complex network flow problems, you might need to use a specialized algorithm. Unfortunately, you are unlikely to find this type of software at your local software store. However, various network optimization packages can be found in the technical/scientific directories on many major computer networks.

REFERENCES

Glover, F. and D. Klingman. "Network Applications in Industry and Government." *AIIE Transactions*, vol. 9, no. 4, 1977.

Glover, F., D. Klingman, and N. Phillips. *Network Models and Their Applications in Practice*. New York: Wiley, 1992.

Phillips, D. and A. Diaz. *Fundamentals of Network Analysis*. Englewood Cliffs, NJ: Prentice Hall, 1981.

Vemuganti, R., et al. "Network Models for Fleet Management." *Decision Sciences*, vol. 20, Winter 1989.

Yellow Freight System Boosts Profits and Quality with Network Optimization

Source: Braklow, John W., William W. Graham, Stephen M. Hassler, Ken E. Peck and Warren B. Powell, "Interactive Optimization Improves Service and Performance for Yellow Freight System," *Interfaces*, 22:1, January-February 1992, pages 147-172.

ONE OF THE LARGEST motor carriers in the United States, Yellow Freight System, Inc. of Overland Park, Kansas, uses network modeling and optimization to assist management in load planning, routing empty trucks, routing trailers, dropping or adding direct service routes, and strategic planning of terminal size and location. The system, called SYSNET, operates on a network of Sun workstations optimizing over a million network flow variables. The company also uses a tactical planning room equipped with graphical display tools that allow planning meetings to be conducted interactively with the system.

The company competes in the less-than-truckload (LTL) segment of the trucking market. That is, they contract for shipments of any size, regardless of whether the shipment fills the trailer. To operate efficiently, Yellow Freight must consolidate and transfer shipments at 23 break-bulk terminals located throughout the United States. At these terminals, shipments might be reloaded into different trailers depending on the final destination. Each break-bulk terminal serves several end-of-line terminals, in a hub-and-spoke network. Normally, shipments are sent by truck to the break-bulk dedicated to the origination point. Local managers occasionally try to save costs by loading direct, which means bypassing a break-bulk and sending a truckload of consolidated shipments directly to the final destination. Before SYSNET, these decisions were made in the field without accurate information on how they would affect costs and reliability in the entire system.

Since its implementation in 1989, SYSNET has scored high with upper management. Often, the first response to a new proposal is, "Has it been run through SYSNET?" The benefits attributed to the new system include:

- an increase of 11.6% in freight loaded directly, saving $4.7 million annually

- better routing of trailers, saving $1 million annually

- savings of $1.42 million annually by increasing the average number of pounds loaded per trailer

- reduction in claims for damaged merchandise

- a 27% reduction in the number of late deliveries

- tactical planning projects with SYSNET in 1990 that identified $10 million in annual savings

Equally important has been the effect on the management philosophy and culture at Yellow Freight. Management now has greater control over network operations; tradition, intuition, and "gut feel" have been replaced with formal analytical tools; and Yellow Freight is better able to act as a partner with customers in total quality management and just-in-time inventory systems.

Questions and Problems

1. This chapter followed the convention of using negative numbers to represent the supply at a node and positive numbers to represent the demand at a node. Another convention is just the opposite—using positive numbers to represent supply and negative numbers to represent demand. How does the balance-of-flow rule need to be changed to accommodate this alternate convention?

2. To use the balance-of-flow rule, constraints for supply nodes must have negative RHS values. Some LP software packages cannot solve problems in which the constraints have negative RHS values. How can the constraints for supply nodes be modified so that they can be solved by such packages?

3. Refer to the equipment replacement problem discussed in this chapter. In addition to the lease costs described for the problem, suppose that it costs Compu-Train $2,000 extra in labor costs whenever they replace their existing computers with new ones. What effect does this have on the formulation and solution of the problem?

4. Draw the network representation of the following network flow problem.

$$\text{MIN:} \quad + 7X_{12} + 6X_{14} + 3X_{23} + 4X_{24} + 5X_{32} + 9X_{43} + 8X_{52} + 5X_{54}$$

$$\text{Subject to:} \quad -X_{12} - X_{14} \qquad\qquad\qquad \geq -5$$

$$+ X_{12} + X_{52} + X_{32} - X_{23} - X_{24} \geq +4$$

$$- X_{32} + X_{23} + X_{43} \qquad\qquad \geq +8$$

$$+ X_{14} + X_{24} + X_{54} - X_{43} \qquad \geq +0$$

$$- X_{52} - X_{54} \qquad\qquad\qquad \geq -7$$

$$X_{ij} \geq 0 \text{ for all } i \text{ and } j$$

5. Draw the network representation of the following network flow problem. What kind of network flow problem is this?

$$\text{MIN:} \quad +2X_{13} + 6X_{14} + 5X_{15} + 4X_{23} + 3X_{24} + 7X_{25}$$

$$\text{Subject to:} \quad -X_{13} - X_{14} - X_{15} \geq -8$$

$$- X_{23} - X_{24} - X_{25} \geq -7$$

$$+ X_{13} + X_{23} \qquad\qquad \geq +5$$

$$+ X_{14} + X_{24} \qquad\qquad \geq +5$$

$$+ X_{15} + X_{25} \qquad\qquad \geq +5$$

$$X_{ij} \geq 0 \text{ for all } i \text{ and } j$$

6. Many problems can be formulated and solved as LP problems in various ways. Question 19 at the end of chapter 3 is such a problem. Show how this problem can be represented graphically as a network flow problem.

7. A construction company wants to determine the optimal replacement policy for the earth mover it owns. The company has a policy of not keeping an earth mover for more than 5 years, and has estimated the

annual operating costs and trade-in values for earth movers during each of the 5 years they might be kept as:

	Age in Years				
	0–1	1–2	2–3	3–4	4–5
Operating Cost	$8,000	$9,100	$10,700	$9,200	$11,000
Trade-in Value	$14,000	$9,000	$6,000	$3,500	$2,000

Assume that new earth movers cost $25,000 and that the company's current earth mover is 2 years old. The company wants to determine the least costly plan for replacing its earth movers during the next 5 years.

a. Draw the network representation of this problem.

b. Write out the LP formulation of this problem.

c. Solve the problem using Solver. Interpret your solution.

d. What other economic factors might you consider and build into this model to make it more realistic?

8. The Ortega Food Company needs to ship 100 cases of hot tamales from its warehouse in San Diego to a distributor in New York City at minimum cost. The costs associated with shipping between various cities are:

	To					
From	Los Angeles	Denver	St. Louis	Memphis	Chicago	New York
San Diego	5	13	—	45	—	105
Los Angeles	—	27	19	50	—	95
Denver	—	—	14	30	32	—
St. Louis	—	14	—	35	24	—
Memphis	—	—	35	—	18	25
Chicago	—	—	24	18	—	17

a. Draw the network representation of this problem.

b. Write out the LP formulation of this problem.

c. Solve the problem using Solver. Interpret your solution.

9. A furniture manufacturer has warehouses in cities represented by nodes 1, 2, and 3 in Figure 5.27. The values on the arcs indicate the per unit shipping costs required to transport living room suites between the various cities. The supply of living room suites at each warehouse is indicated by the negative number next to nodes 1, 2, and 3. The demand for living room suites is indicated by the positive number next to the remaining nodes.

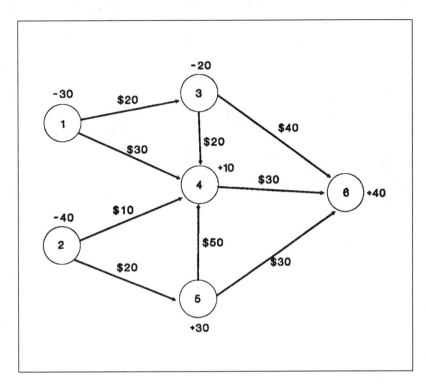

Figure 5.27: Network representation of the furniture manufacturer problem

a. Identify the supply, demand, and transshipment nodes in this problem.

b. Use Solver to determine the least costly shipping plan for this problem.

10. The graph in Figure 5.28 represents various flows that can occur through a sewage treatment plant with the numbers on the arcs representing the maximum flow (in tons of sewage per hour) that can be accommodated. Formulate an LP model to determine the maximum tons of sewage per hour that can be processed by this plant.

11. A company has 3 warehouses that supply 4 stores with a given product. Each warehouse has 30 units of the product. Stores 1, 2, 3, and 4 require 20, 25, 30, and 35 units of the product, respectively. The per unit shipping costs from each warehouse to each store are:

	Store			
Warehouse	1	2	3	4
1	5	4	6	5
2	3	6	4	4
3	4	3	3	2

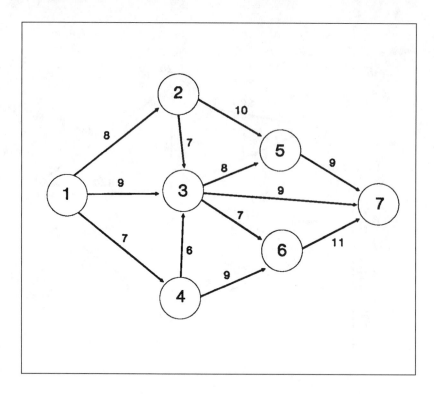

Figure 5.28: Network
representation of the sewage
treatment plant problem

a. Draw the network representation of this problem. What kind of problem is this?

b. Formulate an LP model to determine the least expensive shipping plan to fill the demands at the stores.

c. Solve the problem using Solver.

12.   Refer to question 11. Suppose that shipments are not allowed between warehouse 1 and store 2 or between warehouse 2 and store 3. What is the easiest way to modify the spreadsheet you created in question 11 so that you can solve this modified problem? What is the optimal solution to the modified problem?

13.   A used-car broker needs to transport his inventory of cars from locations 1 and 2 in Figure 5.29 to used-car auctions being held at locations 4 and 5. The costs of transporting cars along each of the routes are indicated on the arcs. The trucks used to carry the cars can hold a maximum of 10 cars. Therefore, the maximum number of cars that can flow over any arc is 10.

a. Formulate an LP model to determine the least costly method of distributing the cars from locations 1 and 2 so that 20 cars will be available for sale at location 4, and 10 cars will be available for sale at location 5.

b. Use Solver to find the optimal solution to this problem.

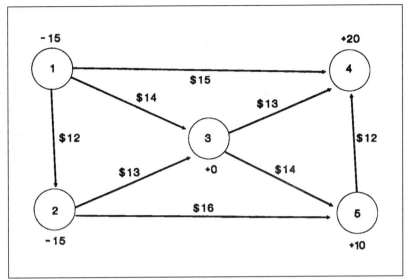

Figure 5.29: Network representation of the used-car problem

14. A new airport being built will have three terminals and two baggage pickup areas. An automated baggage delivery system has been designed to transport the baggage from each terminal to the two baggage pickup areas. This system is depicted graphically in Figure 5.30, where nodes 1, 2, and 3 represent the terminals, and nodes 7 and 8 represent the baggage pickup areas. The maximum number of bags per minute that can be handled by each part of the system is indicated by the value on each arc in the network.

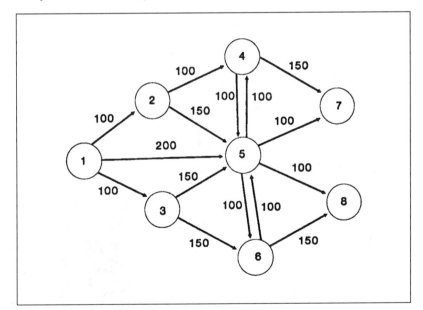

Figure 5.30: Network representation of the airport terminal problem

a. Formulate an LP model to determine the maximum number of bags per minute that can be delivered by this system.

b. Use Solver to find the optimal solution to this problem.

15. Bull Dog Express runs a small airline that offers commuter flights between several cities in Georgia. The airline flies into and out of small airports only. These airports have limits on the number of flights Bull Dog Express can make each day. The airline can make 5 round-trip flights daily between Savannah and Macon, 4 round-trip flights daily between Macon and Albany, 2 round-trip flights daily between Macon and Atlanta, 2 round-trip flights daily between Macon and Athens, 2 round-trip flights daily between Athens and Atlanta, and 2 round-trip flights daily from Albany to Atlanta. The airline wants to determine the maximum number of times connecting flights from Savannah to Atlanta can be offered in a single day.

a. Draw the network representation of this problem.

b. Formulate an LP model for this problem. What kind of problem is this?

c. Use Solver to determine the optimal solution to this problem.

16. The U.S. Department of Transportation (DOT) is planning to build a new interstate to run from Detroit, Michigan, to Charleston, South Carolina. A number of different routes have been proposed and are summarized in Figure 5.31, where node 1 represents Detroit and node 12 represents Charleston. The numbers on the arcs indicate the estimated construction costs of the various links (in millions of dollars). It is estimated that all of the routes will require approximately the same total driving time to make the trip from Detroit to Charleston. Thus, the DOT is interested in identifying the least costly alternative.

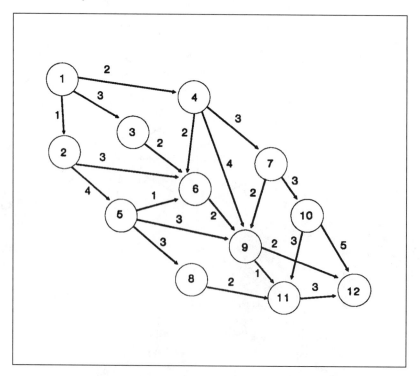

Figure 5.31: *Network representation of the DOT problem*

a. Formulate an LP model to determine the least costly construction plan.

b. Use Solver to determine the optimal solution to this problem.

17. A building contractor is designing the ductwork for the heating and air conditioning system in a new, single-story medical building. Figure 5.32 summarizes the possible connections between the primary air handling unit (node 1) and the various air outlets to be placed in the building (nodes 2 through 9). The arcs in the network represent possible ductwork connections, and the values on the arcs represent the feet of ductwork required.

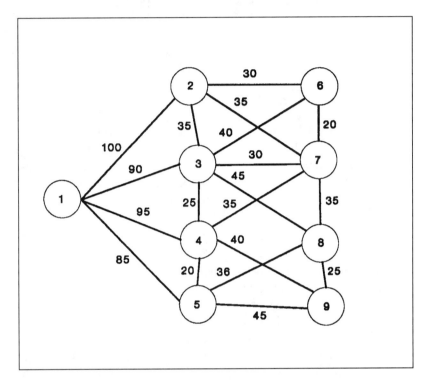

Figure 5.32: Network representation of the ductwork problem

Starting at node 1, use the minimal spanning tree algorithm to determine how much ductwork should be installed to provide air access to each vent while requiring the least amount of ductwork.

Maneuvers in the
Senate
A Case in Network
Modeling

SHERILL Wiley, the only reporter from Channel Four covering United States congressional proceedings, knows that the public's perception of partisan politics in the Senate is not entirely correct. Although republicans and democrats are often at loggerheads over many national issues—such as the crime bill, health care reform, and others—members of the two parties frequently vote together on bills that are considered beneficial to both. Sherill was surprised at the level of cooperation between the parties when passing legislation that benefits a particular region. For example, if a democratic senator from the west is sponsoring a bill that would provide funding to divert water from a river so that part of his sun-drenched state would eventually receive it, quite a few republican senators would vote for such a bill. The republican senators know that when they need votes for a project that would be advantageous for their states, the democratic senators would return the favor and vote for that bill.

Richard Kennely, the leading republican in the Senate and a strong conservative from a midwest state, has little if any direct interaction with Robin Doll.

Doll, a senator from a New England state, is the Senate's most liberal democrat. The two senators have never served on a committee together or participated in a joint task force. Yet the two often rely on each other and their respective parties when voting on many fiscal issues.

Senator Doll recently added an amendment to a finance bill that would provide funding for research on the effects of using a mouse when working on a computer. Several universities from Doll's state submitted grant proposals to do this research, citing the widespread use of the mouse and the growing number of people who complain of wrist and arm fatigue as a result. If the bill and the attached amendment pass, the universities in Doll's state would be the main beneficiaries of the funding. Sherill knows that Senator Kennely, who was recently on national television railing against what he referred to as "excessive spending for trivial research," would be the main opponent to the bill. Senator Doll cannot directly influence Senator Kennely's position or vote. But she can contact other senators with whom she has influence, pleading her case and hoping that they, in turn,

Contributed by Jack Yurkiewicz, Lubin School of Business, Pace University, New York.

will influence others who might eventually influence Senator Kennely to vote in favor of the bill.

After many years as a reporter in Washington, Sherill has developed a sense of the amount of influence one senator has on another, based on party affiliation, school ties, past favors, mutual interests, and so on. She even developed a numerical system, on a scale from 0 to 10 that quantifies the amount of influence one senator has on another. A 10 means that a particular senator is almost guaranteed to secure the vote of another senator, and a 0 means that there is no interaction at all between two senators. Sherill created a table that shows the senators' names and the amount of influence each has on the other.

Sherill saw Senators Abbott, Bartle, Crumb, Dodge, and Fernandez leave

Senator Doll's office one morning last week. Looking at her influence table, she notes that Doll's influence on Abbott rates a 7, on Bartle a 6, a 9 for Crumb, only a 3 for Dodge, and a 4 for Fernandez. Later that week, Senator Abbott called in Senators Bartle and Dodge for a strategy meeting. Abbott's influence on Bartle is a 7 and on Dodge a 5.

Bartle next met with Senators Dodge, Evans, and Fernandez. Bartle's influence rating on these senators is a 4 on Dodge and on Evans, and a 5 on Fernandez. The senators continued to hold meetings with each other and with Senators Gene and Harris.

Sherill summarized the influence rating of all the senators in the following table:

From–To	Abbott	Bartle	Crumb	Dodge	Evans	Fernandez	Gene	Harris	Kennely
Doll	7	6	9	3	4				
Abbott		7		5					
Bartle				4	4	5			
Crumb		5			3				
Dodge					6		5		6
Evans					6		8		7
Fernandez					8			2	5
Gene									8
Harris									2

Sherill believes that if all the senators (other than Doll) bear at least 20 total units of influence on Senator Kennely, he would not be able to resist and he would have to vote for Senator Doll's bill. With Kennely's support, the bill would definitely pass because the rest of the republicans and democrats will follow their leaders.

Considering the amount of networking that takes place between the senators, Sherill thinks she can build and solve a network model to predict if the bill will pass or not.

Formulate a network model for Sherill and solve it. Will the bill pass? (Hint: Make a node for each senator.)

The Alpha Beta Chi Sorority

A Case in Network Analysis

FALL semester has always been Kim Harrison's favorite time of year on campus. The cooler temperatures, changing leaves, and football games are always a lot of fun. But as a senior, Kim is a lot busier than ever before. In addition to her class work, she is interviewing for jobs and serving as the pledge coordinator for her sorority, Alpha Beta Chi (ABC).

ABC is a fairly new sorority on campus and has just 15 members. But after fall rush, 5 new pledges are going to join the sorority. One of Kim's responsibilities is to assign each pledge a "big sister" from among the existing members of ABC. Over the years, many feelings have been hurt during the process of assigning big sisters.

Often, more than one pledge (or "little sister") wants to be assigned to the same big sister; but each member of ABC can serve as a big sister to only one pledge. Kim wants to determine a way to match up little sisters with big sisters as fairly as possible so that everyone will be happy.

As a first step in making the assignments, Kim asks each pledge to identify five existing members of ABC whom she would most like to have as a big sister. Kim then asks the pledges to rank order these potential big sisters from 5 down to 1, where 5 represents the person they most want as a big sister, 4 represents their next choice, and so on. These rankings are summarized in the following table:

Pledges	Big Sisters														
	1	2	3	4	5	6	7	8	9	10	11	12	13	14	15
1			5		3			1			2				4
2		5		2		1		4		3					
3	2		3			4		5				1			
4		5	4				1		2						3
5		3			5					2			4	1	

After much consideration, Kim decides that this problem is similar to some of the problems she encountered in a management science class she took during her sophomore year. She knows that every pledge must be assigned a big sister, and each potential big sister can be assigned no more than one pledge. Ideally, Kim wants to assign each pledge to the big sister to whom she gave a ranking of 5. The sum of the rankings for such an assignment is 25 because each of the 5 pledges would be assigned to the big sister they ranked as number 5. But in the above table, that would involve assigning pledges 2 and 4 to the same big sister, which is not allowable. Kim figures that the next best strategy is to determine the assignment that maximizes the sum of the rankings.

1. Create a spreadsheet model for Kim's problem and solve it. Which pledges should be assigned to which big sisters?

2. Can you think of another objective that Kim might use to solve her problem?

Integer Linear Programming

WHEN SOME OR ALL of the decision variables in an LP problem are restricted to assuming only integer values, the resulting problem is referred to as an **integer linear programming** (ILP) problem. Many practical business problems need integer solutions. For example, chapter 3 presented an employee scheduling problem for the Air-Express company in which we determined the optimal number of employees to assign to each shift. When we formulated this problem as an LP problem, its optimal solution involved allocating fractional numbers of workers (for example, 7.33 workers) to different shifts; this is not an integer feasible solution. Similarly, if an airline is trying to decide how many 757s, 747s, and 737s to purchase, it must obtain an integer solution because the airline cannot buy fractions of planes.

This chapter discusses how to solve optimization problems in which certain decision variables must assume only integer values. This chapter also shows how the use of integer variables allows us to build more accurate models for a number of business problems.

INTEGRALITY CONDITIONS

To illustrate some of the issues involved in an ILP problem, let's consider again the decision problem faced by Howie Jones, the owner of Blue Ridge Hot Tubs, described in chapters 2 and 3. This company sells two models of hot tubs, the Aqua-Spa and the Hydro-Lux, which it produces by purchasing prefabricated fiberglass hot tub shells and installing a common water pump and an appropriate amount of tubing. Each Aqua-Spa produced requires 1 pump, 9 hours of labor, and 12 feet of tubing, and contributes $350 to profits. Each Hydro-Lux produced requires 1 pump, 6 hours of labor, and 16 feet of tubing, and contributes $300 to profits. Assuming the company has 200 pumps, 1,566 labor hours, and 2,880 feet of tubing available, we created the following LP formulation for this problem where X_1 and X_2 represent the number of Aqua-Spas and Hydro-Luxes to produce:

$$\text{MAX:} \quad 350X_1 + 300X_2 \qquad \} \text{ profit}$$
$$\text{Subject to:} \quad 1X_1 + 1X_2 \leq 200 \quad \} \text{ pump constraint}$$
$$9X_1 + 6X_2 \leq 1{,}566 \quad \} \text{ labor constraint}$$
$$12X_1 + 16X_2 \leq 2{,}880 \quad \} \text{ tubing constraint}$$
$$X_1, X_2 \geq 0 \quad \} \text{ nonnegativity conditions}$$

Blue Ridge Hot Tubs is undoubtedly interested in obtaining the best possible *integer solution* to this problem because hot tubs can be sold only as discrete units. Thus, we can be sure the company wants to find the *optimal integer solution* to this problem. So, in addition to the constraints stated above, we add the following integrality condition to the formulation of the problem:

X_1 and X_2 must be integers

An **integrality condition** indicates that some (or all) of the variables in the formulation must assume only integer values. We refer to such variables as the **integer variables** in a problem. In contrast, variables that are not required to assume strictly integer values are referred to as **continuous variables**. Although it is easy to state integrality conditions for a problem, such conditions often make a problem more difficult (and sometimes impossible) to solve.

RELAXATION

One approach to finding the optimal integer solution to a problem is to relax, or ignore, the integrality conditions and solve the problem as if it were a standard LP problem where all the variables are assumed to be continuous. This model is sometimes referred to as the **LP relaxation** of the original ILP problem. Consider the following ILP problem:

$$\text{MAX:} \quad 2X_1 + 3X_2$$
$$\text{Subject to:} \quad X_1 + 3X_2 \leq 8.25$$
$$2.5X_1 + X_2 \leq 8.75$$
$$X_1, X_2 \geq 0$$
$$X_1, X_2 \text{ must be integers}$$

The LP relaxation for this problem is represented by:

$$\text{MAX:} \quad 2X_1 + 3X_2$$

$$\text{Subject to:} \quad X_1 + 3X_2 \leq 8.25$$

$$2.5X_1 + X_2 \leq 8.75$$

$$X_1, X_2 \geq 0$$

The only difference between the ILP and its LP relaxation is that all integrality conditions imposed by the ILP are dropped in the relaxation. However, as illustrated in Figure 6.1, this change has a significant impact on the feasible regions for the two problems.

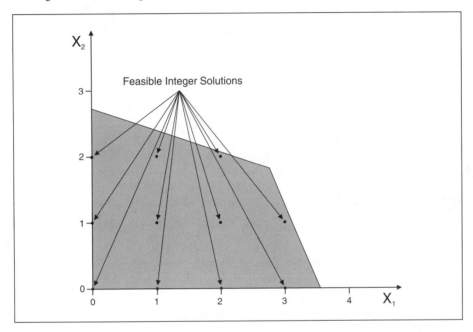

Figure 6.1: *Integer feasible region vs. LP feasible region*

As shown in Figure 6.1, the feasible region for the ILP consists of only 11 discrete points. On the other hand, the feasible region for its LP relaxation consists of an infinite number of points represented by the shaded area. This figure illustrates an important point about the relationship between the feasible region of an ILP and its LP relaxation. The feasible region of the LP relaxation of an ILP problem *always* encompasses *all* the feasible integer solutions to the original ILP problem. Although the relaxed feasible region might include additional noninteger solutions, it will *not* include any integer solutions that are not feasible solutions to the original ILP.

SOLVING THE RELAXED PROBLEM

The LP relaxation of an ILP problem is often easy to solve using the simplex method. As explained in chapter 2, an optimal solution to an LP problem occurs at one of the corner points of its feasible region (assuming that the problem has a bounded optimal solution). Thus, if we are extremely lucky, the optimal solution to the LP relaxation of an ILP problem might occur at an integer corner point of the relaxed feasible region. In this case, we find the optimal integer solution to the ILP problem simply by solving its LP relaxation. This is exactly what happened in chapters 2 and 3 when we originally solved the relaxed LP model for the hot tub problem. Figure 6.2 (and the file FIG6-2.XLS on your data disk) shows the solution to this problem.

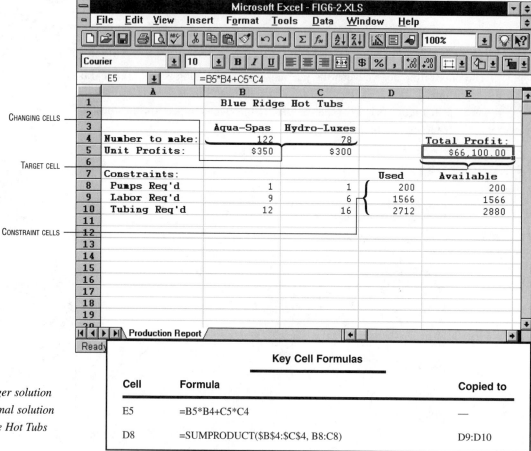

Figure 6.2: *Integer solution obtained as optimal solution to the Blue Ridge Hot Tubs LP problem*

Key Cell Formulas

Cell	Formula	Copied to
E5	=B5*B4+C5*C4	—
D8	=SUMPRODUCT($B$4:$C$4, B8:C8)	D9:D10

The optimal solution to the relaxed LP formulation of the hot tub problem assigns integer values to the decision variables ($X_1 = 122$ and $X_2 = 78$). So in this case, the relaxed LP problem happens to have an integer-valued optimal solution. However, as you might expect, this will not always be the case.

Suppose, for example, that Blue Ridge Hot Tubs has only 1,520 hours of labor and 2,650 feet of tubing available during their next production cycle. The company might be interested in solving the following ILP problem:

$$\text{MAX:} \quad 350X_1 + 300X_2 \qquad \} \text{ profit}$$

$$\text{Subject to:} \quad 1X_1 + 1X_2 \le 200 \qquad \} \text{ pump constraint}$$

$$9X_1 + 6X_2 \le 1{,}520 \qquad \} \text{ labor constraint}$$

$$12X_1 + 16X_2 \le 2{,}650 \qquad \} \text{ tubing constraint}$$

$$X_1, X_2 \ge 0 \qquad \} \text{ nonnegativity conditions}$$

$$X_1, X_2 \text{ must be integers} \quad \} \text{ integrality conditions}$$

If we relax the integrality conditions and solve the resulting LP problem, we obtain the solution shown in Figure 6.3. This solution indicates that producing 116.9444 Aqua-Spas and 77.91666 Hydro-Luxes will generate a maximum profit of $64,306. But this solution violates the integrality conditions stated in the original problem. As a general rule, the optimal solution to the LP relaxation of an ILP problem is not guaranteed to produce an integer solution. In such cases, other techniques must be applied to find the optimal integer solution for the problem being solved. (There are some exceptions to this rule. In particular, the network flow problems discussed in chapter 5 often can be viewed as ILP problems. For reasons that go beyond the scope of this text, the LP relaxation of these network problems will always have integer solutions if the supplies and/or demands at each node are integers and the problem is solved using the simplex method.)

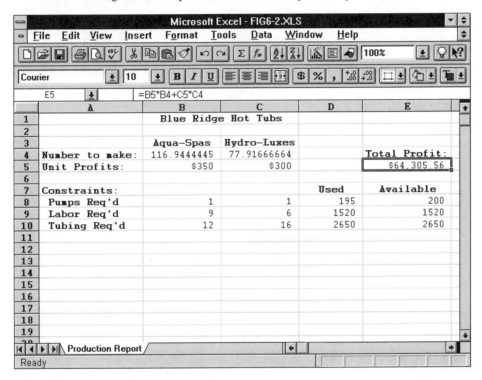

Figure 6.3: Noninteger solution obtained as optimal solution to the revised Blue Ridge Hot Tubs LP problem

BOUNDS

Before discussing how to solve ILP problems, an important point must be made about the relationship between the optimal solution to an ILP problem and the optimal solution to its LP relaxation: *The objective function value for the optimal solution to the ILP problem can never be better than the objective function value for the optimal solution to its LP relaxation.*

For example, the solution shown in Figure 6.3 indicates that if the company could produce (and sell) fractional numbers of hot tubs, it could make a maximum profit of $64,306 by producing 116.9444 Aqua-Spas and 77.91666 Hydro-Luxes. No other feasible solution (integer or otherwise) could result in a better value of the objective function. If a better feasible solution existed, the optimization procedure would have identified this better solution as optimal because our aim was to maximize the value of the objective function.

Although solving the LP relaxation of the revised hot tub problem might not provide the optimal integer solution to our original ILP problem, it does indicate that the objective function value of the optimal integer solution cannot possibly be greater than $64,306. This information can be important in helping us evaluate the quality of integer solutions we might discover during our search for the optimal solution.

Key Concept

For *maximization* problems, the objective function value at the optimal solution to the LP relaxation represents an *upper bound* on the optimal objective function value of the original ILP problem. For *minimization* problems, the objective function value at the optimal solution to the LP relaxation represents a *lower bound* on the optimal objective function value of the original ILP problem.

ROUNDING

As mentioned earlier, the solution to the LP relaxation of an ILP problem might satisfy the ILP problem's integrality conditions and, therefore, represent the optimal integer solution to the problem. But what should we do if this is not the case (as usually happens)? One technique that frequently is applied involves rounding the relaxed LP solution.

When the solution to the LP relaxation of an ILP problem does not result in an integer solution, it is tempting to think that simply rounding this solution will generate the optimal integer solution. Unfortunately, this is not the case. For example, if the values for the decision variables shown in Figure 6.3 are manually rounded up to their closest integer values, as shown in Figure 6.4, the resulting solution is infeasible. The company cannot manufacture 117 Aqua-Spas and 78 Hydro-Luxes because this would involve using more labor and tubing than are available.

```
Microsoft Excel - FIG6-2.XLS
File   Edit   View   Insert   Format   Tools   Data   Window   Help

Courier      10     B  I  U
E5              =B5*B4+C5*C4
```

	A	B	C	D	E
1		Blue Ridge Hot Tubs			
2					
3		Aqua-Spas	Hydro-Luxes		
4	Number to make:	117	78		Total Profit:
5	Unit Profits:	$350	$300		$64,350.00
6					
7	Constraints:			Used	Available
8	Pumps Req'd	1	1	195	200
9	Labor Req'd	9	6	1521	1520
10	Tubing Req'd	12	16	2652	2650
11					
12					
13					
14					
15					
16					
17					
18					
19					

Production Report

Ready

Figure 6.4: Infeasible integer solution obtained by rounding up

Because rounding up does not always work, perhaps we should round down, or truncate, the values for the decision variables identified in the LP relaxation. As shown in Figure 6.5, this results in a feasible solution where 116 Aqua-Spas and 77 Hydro-Luxes are manufactured for a total profit of $63,700. However, this approach presents two possible problems. First, rounding down could also result in an infeasible solution, as shown in Figure 6.6.

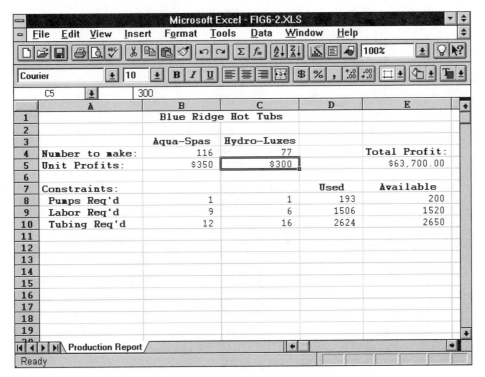

Figure 6.5: Feasible integer solution obtained by rounding down

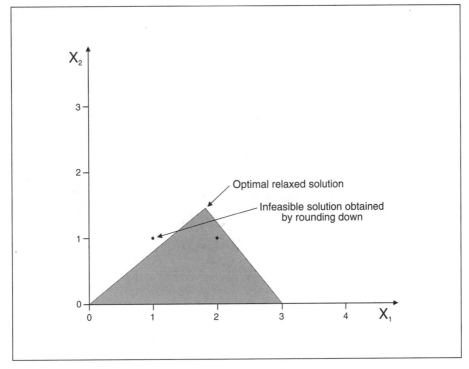

Figure 6.6: How rounding down can result in an infeasible integer solution

Another problem with rounding down is that even if it results in a feasible integer solution to the problem, there is no guarantee that it is the *optimal* integer solution. For example, the integer solution obtained by rounding down shown in Figure 6.5 produced a total profit of $63,700. However, as shown in Figure 6.7, a better integer solution exists for this problem. If the company produces 118 Aqua-Spas and 76 Hydro-Luxes, it can achieve a total profit of $64,100 (which is the optimal integer solution to this problem). Simply rounding the solution to the LP relaxation of an ILP problem is not guaranteed to provide the optimal integer solution. Although the integer solution obtained in this problem by rounding is very close to the optimal integer solution, rounding does not always work this well.

As we have seen, the solution to the LP relaxation of an ILP is not guaranteed to produce an integer solution, and rounding the solution to the LP relaxation is not guaranteed to produce the optimal integer solution. Therefore, we need another way to find the optimal integer solution to an ILP problem. Various procedures have been developed for this purpose. The most effective and widely used of these procedures is the branch-and-bound (B&B) algorithm. The **B&B algorithm** theoretically allows us to solve *any* ILP problem by solving a series of LP problems called candidate problems. A complete discussion of how the B&B algorithm works is given at the end of this chapter.

Figure 6.7: Optimal integer solution to the revised Blue Ridge Hot Tubs problem

STOPPING RULES

Finding the optimal solution for simple ILP problems can sometimes require the evaluation of hundreds of candidate problems. More complex problems can require the evaluation of thousands of candidate problems, which can be a very time-consuming task even for the fastest computers. For this reason, many ILP packages allow you to specify a suboptimality tolerance of X% (where X is some numeric value), which tells the B&B algorithm to stop when it finds an integer solution that is no more than X% worse than the optimal integer solution. This is another area where obtaining upper or lower bounds on the optimal integer solution can be helpful.

As noted earlier, if we relax all the integrality conditions in an ILP with a maximization objective and solve the resulting LP problem, the objective function value at the optimal solution to the relaxed problem provides an upper bound on the optimal integer solution. For example, when we relaxed the integrality conditions for the revised Blue Ridge Hot Tubs problem and solved it as an LP, we obtained the solution shown in Figure 6.3, which has an objective function value of $64,306. Thus, we know that the optimal integer solution to this problem cannot have an objective function value greater than $64,306. Now, suppose the owners of Blue Ridge Hot Tubs are willing to settle for *any* integer solution to their problem that is no more than 5% below the optimal integer solution. It is easy to determine that 95% of $64,306 is $61,090 (0.95*$64,306 = $61,090). Therefore, any integer solution with an objective function value of at least $61,090 can be no worse than 5% below the optimal integer solution.

Specifying suboptimality tolerances can be helpful if you are willing to settle for a good but suboptimal solution to a difficult ILP problem. However, most B&B packages employ some sort of default suboptimality tolerance and, therefore, might produce a suboptimal solution to the ILP problem without indicating that a better solution might exist. (We will look at an example where this occurs shortly.) It is important to be aware of suboptimality tolerances because they can determine whether or not the true optimal solution to an ILP problem is found.

SOLVING ILP PROBLEMS USING SOLVER

Now that you have some understanding of the effort required to solve ILP problems, you can appreciate how using Solver simplifies this process. This section shows how to use Solver with the revised Blue Ridge Hot Tubs problem.

Figure 6.8 (and the file FIG6-8.XLS on your data disk) shows the Solver parameters required to solve the revised Blue Ridge Hot Tubs problem as a standard LP problem. However, none of these parameters indicate that the cells representing the decision variables (cells B4 and C4) must assume integer values. To communicate this to Solver, we need to add constraints to the problem by clicking the Add button.

Figure 6.8: Solver parameters for the relaxed Blue Ridge Hot Tubs problem

Clicking this button displays the Add Constraint dialog box shown in Figure 6.9. In this dialog box, cells B4 through C4 are specified as the cell references for the additional constraints. Because we want these cells to assume only integer values, we need to select the int option from the drop-down menu, as shown in Figure 6.9.

Figure 6.9: Selecting integer constraints

After clicking the OK button, we return to the Solver Parameters dialog box shown in Figure 6.10. This dialog box now indicates that cells B4 and C4 are constrained to assume only integer values. We can now click the Solve button to determine the optimal solution to the problem, shown in Figure 6.11.

Figure 6.10: Solver parameters for the revised Blue Ridge Hot Tubs problem with integer constraints

Figure 6.11: Solution to the revised Blue Ridge Hot Tubs problem with integer constraints

The Solver Results dialog box in Figure 6.11 indicates that Solver found a solution that satisfies all constraints and optimality conditions. Thus, we might suspect that the optimal integer solution to this problem involves producing 117 Aqua-Spas and 77 Hydro-Luxes for a total profit of $64,050. However, if you refer back to Figure 6.7, you will recall that an even better integer solution to this problem can be obtained by producing 118 Aqua-Spas and 76 Hydro-Luxes for a total profit of $64,100. So why did Solver select an integer solution with a total profit of $64,050 when a better integer solution exists? The answer lies in Solver's suboptimality tolerance factor.

By default, Solver uses a suboptimality tolerance factor of 5%. So when Solver found the integer solution with the objective function value of $64,050 shown in Figure 6.11, it determined that this solution was within 5% of the optimal integer solution and, therefore, it abandoned its search. To ensure that Solver finds the best possible solution to an ILP problem, we must change its suboptimality tolerance factor by clicking the Options button in the Solver Parameters dialog box. Figure 6.12 shows the resulting Solver Options dialog box.

Figure 6.12: Changing the suboptimality tolerance factor

As shown in Figure 6.12, you can set a number of options to control Solver's operations. The Tolerance option represents Solver's suboptimality tolerance value. To make sure Solver finds the best possible solution to an ILP problem, we must change this setting from its default value of 5% to 0%. If we do this and re-solve the current problem, we obtain the solution shown in Figure 6.13. This solution is the best possible integer solution to the problem.

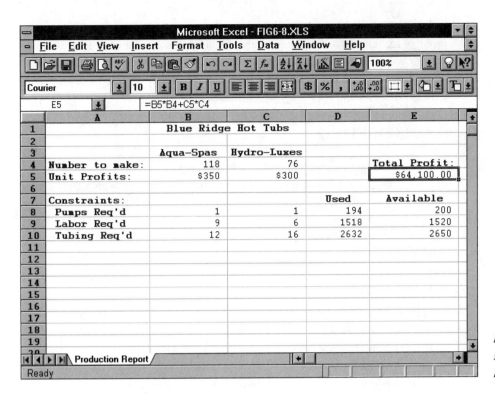

Figure 6.13: *Optimal integer solution to the revised Blue Ridge Hot Tubs problem*

OTHER ILP PROBLEMS

Many decision problems encountered in business can be modeled as ILPs. As we have seen from the Blue Ridge Hot Tubs example, some problems that are initially formulated as LP problems might turn into ILP formulations if they require integer solutions. However, the importance of ILP extends beyond simply allowing us to obtain integer solutions to LP problems.

The ability to constrain certain variables to assume only integer values enables us to model a number of important conditions more accurately. For example, up to this point we have not considered the impact of quantity discounts, setup or lump-sum costs, or batch size restrictions on a given decision problem. Without ILP techniques we could not model these decision issues. We now consider several examples that illustrate the expanded modeling capabilities available through the use of integer variables.

BINARY VARIABLES

As mentioned earlier, some LP problems naturally evolve into ILP problems when we realize that we need to obtain integer solutions. For example, in the Air-Express problem discussed in chapter 3, we needed to determine the number of workers to assign to each of seven shifts. Because workers are discrete units, it might be appropriate to impose integrality conditions on the decision variables in this model representing the number of workers scheduled for each shift. To do so, we would change the continuous variables in the model into **general integer variables**, or variables that could assume *any* integer value (provided that the constraints of the problem are not violated). In many other situations, we might want to use **binary integer variables** (or binary variables), which can assume *only two* integer values: 0 and 1. Binary variables can be useful in a number of practical modeling situations, as illustrated in the following examples.

CAPITAL BUDGETING

In a capital budgeting problem, a decision maker is presented with several potential projects or investment alternatives and must determine which projects or investments to choose. The projects or investments typically require different amounts of various resources (for example, money, equipment, personnel) and generate different cash flows to the company. The cash flows for each project or investment are converted to a net present value (NPV). The problem is to determine which set of projects or investments to select in order to achieve the maximum possible NPV. Consider the following example:

In his position as vice president of research and development (R&D) for CRT Technologies, Mark Schwartz is responsible for evaluating and choosing which R&D projects to support. The company received 18 R&D proposals from its scientists and engineers, and identified six projects as being consistent with the company's mission. However, the company does not have the funds available to undertake all six projects. Mark must determine which of the projects to select. The funding requirements for each project are summarized below along with the NPV the company expects each project to generate.

Project	Expected NPV (in $000s)	Capital (in $000s) Required in				
		Year 1	Year 2	Year 3	Year 4	Year 5
1	$141	$75	$25	$20	$15	$10
2	$187	$90	$35	$0	$0	$30
3	$121	$60	$15	$15	$15	$15
4	$83	$30	$20	$10	$5	$5
5	$265	$100	$25	$20	$20	$20
6	$127	$50	$20	$10	$30	$40

The company currently has $250,000 available to invest in new projects. It has budgeted $75,000 for continued support for these projects in year 2 and $50,000 per year for years 3, 4, and 5.

DEFINING THE DECISION VARIABLES

Mark must decide which of the six projects to select. Thus, we need six variables to represent the alternatives under consideration. We will let X_1, X_2, ..., X_6 represent the six decision variables for this problem and assume they operate as:

$$X_i = \begin{cases} 1, \text{ if project } i \text{ is selected} \\ 0, \text{ otherwise} \end{cases} \quad i = 1, 2, \ldots, 6$$

Each decision variable in this problem is a binary variable that assumes the value 1 if the associated project is selected, or the value 0 if the associated project is not selected. In essence, each variable acts like an "on/off switch" to indicate whether or not a given project has been selected. As we'll see, it takes some effort to ensure that these variables actually operate in this way. For now, just accept that this is possible.

DEFINING THE OBJECTIVE FUNCTION

The objective in this problem is to maximize the total NPV of the selected projects. This is stated mathematically as:

MAX: $141X_1 + 187X_2 + 121X_3 + 83X_4 + 265X_5 + 127X_6$

Notice that this objective function simply sums the NPV figures for the selected projects.

DEFINING THE CONSTRAINTS

Several sets of constraints apply to this problem. The most obvious constraints involve the amount of capital available in each year. We need one capital constraint for each year to ensure that the selected projects do not require more capital than is available. This set of constraints is represented by:

$$75X_1 + 90X_2 + 60X_3 + 30X_4 + 100X_5 + 50X_6 \leq 250 \quad \} \text{ year 1 capital constraint}$$

$$25X_1 + 35X_2 + 15X_3 + 20X_4 + 25X_5 + 20X_6 \leq 75 \quad \} \text{ year 2 capital constraint}$$

$$20X_1 + 0X_2 + 15X_3 + 10X_4 + 20X_5 + 10X_6 \leq 50 \quad \} \text{ year 3 capital constraint}$$

$$15X_1 + 0X_2 + 15X_3 + 5X_4 + 20X_5 + 30X_6 \leq 50 \quad \} \text{ year 4 capital constraint}$$

$$10X_1 + 30X_2 + 15X_3 + 5X_4 + 20X_5 + 40X_6 \leq 50 \quad \} \text{ year 5 capital constraint}$$

SETTING UP THE BINARY VARIABLES

In our formulation of this problem, we assume that each decision variable is a binary variable. We must include this assumption in the formal statement of our model by adding the constraints:

$X_i \leq 1$, $i = 1, 2, \ldots, 6$

$X_i \geq 0$, $i = 1, 2, \ldots, 6$

All X_i must be integers

The first set of constraints indicates that all the decision variables must be less than or equal to 1. The next set of constraints are the standard nonnegativity conditions, which indicate that all the decision variables must be greater than or equal to 0. Finally, the last constraint indicates that all the decision variables must assume integer values. Together, these three sets of constraints indicate that the decision variables can assume only integer values in the closed interval from 0 to 1. Therefore, these constraints ensure that the decision variables will operate as binary variables.

IMPLEMENTING THE MODEL

The ILP model for the CRT Technologies project selection problem is summarized as:

$$\text{MAX}: \quad 141X_1 + 187X_2 + 121X_3 + 83X_4 + 265X_5 + 127X_6$$

$$\text{Subject to}: \quad 75X_1 + 90X_2 + 60X_3 + 30X_4 + 100X_5 + 50X_6 \leq 250$$

$$25X_1 + 35X_2 + 15X_3 + 20X_4 + 25X_5 + 20X_6 \leq 75$$

$$20X_1 + 0X_2 + 15X_3 + 10X_4 + 20X_5 + 10X_6 \leq 50$$

$$15X_1 + 0X_2 + 15X_3 + 5X_4 + 20X_5 + 30X_6 \leq 50$$

$$10X_1 + 30X_2 + 15X_3 + 5X_4 + 20X_5 + 40X_6 \leq 50$$

$$X_i \leq 1, \quad i = 1, 2, \dots, 6$$

$$X_i \geq 0, \quad i = 1, 2, \dots, 6$$

$$\text{All } X_i \text{ must be integers}$$

This model is implemented in the spreadsheet shown in Figure 6.14 (and in the file FIG6-14.XLS on your data disk). In this spreadsheet, the data for each project are listed in a separate row. Cells B6 through B11 contain values of 0 to indicate that they are reserved for representing the six variables in our algebraic model. The LHS formula for the capital constraint is entered in cell D13 then copied to cells E13 through H13, as:

Formula for cell D13:   =SUMPRODUCT(D6:D11,$B$6:$B$11)
(copy to E13 through H13)

The RHS values for the constraints are listed in cells D14 through H14. Finally, the objective function of the model is implemented in cell D16 as:

Formula for cell D16:   =SUMPRODUCT(C6:C11,B6:B11)

SOLVING THE MODEL

To solve this model, we must tell Solver where we have implemented our objective function, decision variables, and constraints. When building the spreadsheet model for this problem, we did not specify that the decision variables must assume only integer values between 0 and 1 (as indicated by the last three constraint sets in our model). However, we can ensure that these conditions are satisfied by the way we describe the problem to Solver.

The Solver Parameters dialog box shown in Figure 6.15 indicates that the objective function is implemented in cell D16 and that the decision variables are represented by cells B6 through B11. Also, notice that four sets of constraints are specified for this problem.

The first three sets of constraints indicate that cells B6 through B11 must assume integer values no greater than 1 and no less than 0. Thus, these constraints ensure that cells B6 through B11 will operate as binary variables. Notice that we

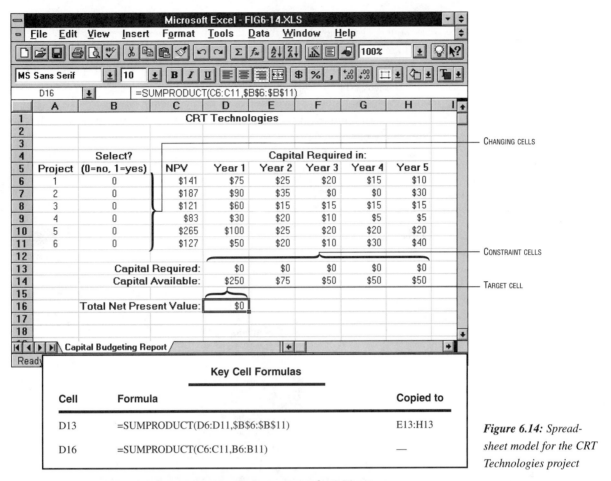

Figure 6.14: Spreadsheet model for the CRT Technologies project

Key Cell Formulas

Cell	Formula	Copied to
D13	=SUMPRODUCT(D6:D11,$B$6:$B$11)	E13:H13
D16	=SUMPRODUCT(C6:C11,B6:B11)	—

Figure 6.15: Solver parameters for the CRT Technologies project

implemented these constraints by referring to the cells in the spreadsheet that represent our decision variables—we do not have to set up separate cells in the spreadsheet to implement these constraints. The last set of constraints shown in the dialog box indicates that the values in cells D13 through H13 must be less than or equal to the values in cells D14 through H14 when the problem is solved. These conditions correspond to the capital constraints in the problem.

Because this model contains six decision variables and each variable can assume only one of two values, at most $2^6 = 64$ possible integer solutions exist for this problem. Some of these integer solutions will not fall in the feasible region, so we might suspect that this problem will not be too difficult to solve optimally. If we set the suboptimality tolerance factor to 0 (in the Solver Options dialog box) and solve the problem we obtain the solution shown in Figure 6.16.

Figure 6.16: Optimal integer solution to the CRT Technologies project selection problem

Project	Select? (0=no, 1=yes)	NPV	Year 1	Year 2	Year 3	Year 4	Year 5
1	1	$141	$75	$25	$20	$15	$10
2	0	$187	$90	$35	$0	$0	$30
3	0	$121	$60	$15	$15	$15	$15
4	1	$83	$30	$20	$10	$5	$5
5	1	$265	$100	$25	$20	$20	$20
6	0	$127	$50	$20	$10	$30	$40
	Capital Required:		$205	$70	$50	$40	$35
	Capital Available:		$250	$75	$50	$50	$50
	Total Net Present Value:		$489				

COMPARING THE OPTIMAL SOLUTION TO A HEURISTIC SOLUTION

The optimal solution shown in Figure 6.16 indicates that if CRT Technologies selects projects 1, 4, and 5, it can achieve a total NPV of $489,000. Although this solution does not use all of the capital available in each year, it is still the best possible integer solution to the problem.

Another approach to solving this problem is to create a ranked list of the projects in decreasing order by NPV and then select projects from this list, in order, until the capital is depleted. As shown in Figure 6.17, if we apply this heuristic to the current problem, we would select projects 5 and 2, but we could not select any more projects due to a lack of capital in year 5. This solution would generate a total NPV of $452,000. Again, we can see the potential benefit of optimization techniques over heuristic solution techniques.

```
┌─────────────────────────────────────────────────────────────────────┐
│ —              Microsoft Excel - FIG6-14.XLS              ▼ ◆         │
│ ▫  File  Edit  View  Insert  Format  Tools  Data  Window  Help   ◆   │
├─────────────────────────────────────────────────────────────────────┤
│ [toolbar icons]                                100%    ▼  ♀ ▶?        │
├─────────────────────────────────────────────────────────────────────┤
│ MS Sans Serif   ▼  10  ▼  B I U ≡ ≡ ≡ ⊞ $ % , ⁺⁰ ⁰⁰ ⊡ ▼ ◇ ▼ ▦ ▼    │
├─────────────────────────────────────────────────────────────────────┤
│ D16     ▼      =SUMPRODUCT(C6:C11,$B$6:$B$11)                         │
└─────────────────────────────────────────────────────────────────────┘
```

	A	B	C	D	E	F	G	H	I
1			CRT Technologies						
2									
3									
4		Select?			Capital Required in:				
5	Project	(0=no, 1=yes)	NPV	Year 1	Year 2	Year 3	Year 4	Year 5	
6	5	1	$265	$100	$25	$20	$20	$20	
7	2	1	$187	$90	$35	$0	$0	$30	
8	1	0	$141	$75	$25	$20	$15	$10	
9	6	0	$127	$50	$20	$10	$30	$40	
10	3	0	$121	$60	$15	$15	$15	$15	
11	4	0	$83	$30	$20	$10	$5	$5	
12									
13		Capital Required:		$190	$60	$20	$20	$50	
14		Capital Available:		$250	$75	$50	$50	$50	
15									
16		Total Net Present Value:		$452					
17									
18									

```
┌─────────────────────────────────────────────────────────────────────┐
│ ◄ ◄ ► ►│ \ Capital Budgeting Report /          ◄               ►     │
│ Ready                                              NUM                │
└─────────────────────────────────────────────────────────────────────┘
```

Figure 6.17: A suboptimal heuristic solution to the CRT Technologies project selection problem

BINARY VARIABLES AND LOGICAL CONDITIONS

Binary variables can be used to model a number of logical conditions that might apply in a variety of problems. For example, in the CRT Technologies problem, several of the projects under consideration (for example, projects 1, 3, and 6) might represent alternative approaches for producing a certain part for a product. The company might want to limit the solution to include *no more than one* of these three alternatives. The following type of constraint accomplishes this restriction:

$$X_1 + X_3 + X_6 \leq 1$$

Because X_1, X_3, and X_6 represent binary variables, no more than one of them can assume the value 1 and still satisfy the above constraint. If we want to ensure that the solution includes *exactly one* of these alternatives, we could include the following constraint in our model:

$$X_1 + X_3 + X_6 = 1$$

As an example of another type of logical condition, suppose that project 4 involves a microwave communications technology that will not be available to the company unless it undertakes project 5. In other words, the company cannot select project 4 unless it also selects project 5. This type of relationship can be imposed on the solution with the constraint:

$$X_4 - X_5 \leq 0$$

The four possible combinations of values for X_4 and X_5 and their relationships to the previous constraint are summarized as:

Value of			
X_4	X_5	Meaning	Feasible?
0	0	Do not select either project	yes
1	1	Select both projects	yes
0	1	Select 5, but not 4	yes
1	0	Select 4, but not 5	no

As indicated in this table, the previous constraint prohibits any solution in which project 4 is selected and project 5 is not selected.

As these examples illustrate, you can model certain logical conditions using binary variables. Several problems at the end of this chapter allow you to use binary variables (and your own creativity) to formulate models for decision problems that involve these types of logical conditions.

THE FIXED-CHARGE PROBLEM

In most of the LP problems discussed in earlier chapters, we formulated objective functions to maximize profits or minimize costs. In each of these cases we associated a per-unit cost or per-unit profit with each decision variable to create the objective function. However, in some situations the decision to produce a product results in a lump-sum, or fixed-charge, cost in addition to a per-unit cost or profit. These types of problems are known as **fixed-charge** or fixed-cost problems. The following are some examples of fixed-costs:

• the cost to lease, rent, or purchase a piece of equipment or a vehicle that will be required if a particular action is taken

• the setup cost required to prepare a machine or production line to produce a different type of product

• the cost to construct a new production line or facility that will be required if a particular decision is made

• the cost of hiring additional personnel that will be required if a particular decision is made

In each of these examples, the fixed costs are *new* costs that will be incurred if a particular action or decision is made. In this respect, fixed costs are different from **sunk costs**, which are costs that will be incurred regardless of what decision is made. Sunk costs are irrelevant for decision-making purposes because, by definition, decisions do not influence these costs. On the other hand, fixed costs are important factors in decision making because the decision determines whether or not these costs will be incurred. The following example illustrates the formulation and solution of a fixed-charge problem.

Remington Manufacturing is planning its next production cycle. The company can produce three products, each of which must undergo machining, grinding, and assembly operations. The table below summarizes the hours of machining, grinding, and assembly required by each unit of each product, and the total hours of capacity available for each operation.

Operation	Hours Required By			Total Hours Available
	Product 1	Product 2	Product 3	
Machining	2	3	6	600
Grinding	6	3	4	300
Assembly	5	6	2	400

The cost accounting department has estimated that each unit of product 1 manufactured and sold will contribute $48 to profit, and each unit of products 2 and 3 contributes $55 and $50, respectively. However, manufacturing a unit of product 1 requires a setup operation on the production line that costs $1,000. Similar setups are required for products 2 and 3 at costs of $800 and $900, respectively. The marketing department believes it can sell all the products produced. Therefore, the management of Remington wants to determine the most profitable mix of products to produce.

DEFINING THE DECISION VARIABLES

Although only three products are under consideration in this problem, we need six variables to formulate the problem accurately. We can define these variables as:

X_i = the amount of product i to be produced, $i = 1, 2, 3$

$$Y_i = \begin{cases} 1, \text{ if } X_i > 0 \\ 0, \text{ if } X_i = 0 \end{cases} \quad i = 1, 2, 3$$

We need three variables, X_1, X_2, and X_3, to correspond to the amount of products 1, 2, and 3 produced. Each of the X_i variable has a corresponding binary variable, Y_i, that will equal 1 if X_i assumes any positive value, or will equal 0 if X_i is 0. For now, do not be concerned about how this relationship between the X_i and Y_i is enforced. We will explore that soon.

DEFINING THE OBJECTIVE FUNCTION

Given our definition of the decision variables, the objective function for our model is stated as:

MAX: $48X_1 + 55X_2 + 50X_3 - 1000Y_1 - 800Y_2 - 900Y_3$

The first three terms in this function calculate the marginal profit generated by the number of products 1, 2, and 3 sold. The last three terms in this function subtract the fixed costs for the products produced. For example, if X_1 assumes a positive value, we know from our definition of the Y_1 variables that Y_1 should equal 1. And if $Y_1 = 1$, the value of the objective function will be reduced by $1,000 to reflect payment of the setup cost. On the other hand, if $X_1 = 0$ we know that $Y_1 = 0$. Therefore, if no units of X_1 are produced, the setup cost for product 1 will not be incurred in the objective. Similar relationships exist between X_2 and Y_2 and between X_3 and Y_3.

DEFINING THE CONSTRAINTS

Several sets of constraints apply to this problem. Capacity constraints are needed to ensure that the number of machining, grinding, and assembly hours used does not exceed the number of hours available for each of these resources. These constraints are stated as:

$2X_1 + 3X_2 + 6X_3 \le 600$ } machining constraint

$6X_1 + 3X_2 + 4X_3 \le 300$ } grinding constraint

$5X_1 + 6X_2 + 2X_3 \le 400$ } assembly constraint

We also need to include nonnegativity conditions on the X_i variables as:

$X_i \ge 0$, $i = 1, 2, 3$

Three sets of constraints on the Y_i variables are needed to ensure that they operate as binary variables. These constraints are represented by:

$Y_i \le 1$, $i = 1, 2, 3$

$Y_i \ge 0$, $i = 1, 2, 3$

All Y_i must be integers

As mentioned earlier, we must ensure that the required relationship between the X_i and Y_i variables is enforced. In particular, the value of the Y_i variables can be determined from the X_i variables. Therefore, we need constraints to establish this *link* between the value of the Y_i variables and the X_i variables. These linking constraints are represented by:

$X_1 \le M_1 Y_1$

$X_2 \le M_2 Y_2$

$X_3 \le M_3 Y_3$

In each of these constraints, the M_i is a numeric constraint that represents an upper bound on the optimal value of the X_i. Let's assume that all the M_i are arbitrarily large numbers; for example, $M_i = 10,000$. Then each constraint sets up a link between the value of the X_i and the Y_i. For example, if any X_i variables in the above constraints assume a value greater than 0, the corresponding Y_i variable must assume the value 1 or the constraint will be violated. On the other hand, if any of the X_i variables are equal to 0, the corresponding Y_i variables could equal 0 or 1 and still satisfy the constraint. However, if we consider the objective function to this problem, we know that when given a choice, Solver will always set the Y_i equal to 0 (rather than 1) because this results in a better objective function value. Therefore, we can conclude that if any X_i variables are equal to 0, Solver will set the corresponding Y_i variable equal to 0 because this is feasible and results in a better objective function value.

DETERMINING VALUES FOR "BIG M"

The M_i values used in the linking constraints are sometimes referred to as **Big M** values because they can be assigned arbitrarily large values. However, for reasons that go beyond the scope of this text, these types of problems are much easier to solve if the M_i values are kept as small as possible. As indicated earlier, the M_i values impose upper bounds on the values of the X_i. So, if a problem indicates that a company could manufacture and sell no more than 60 units of X_1, for example, we could let $M_1 = 60$. However, even if upper bounds for the X_i are not explicitly indicated, it is sometimes easy to derive implicit upper bounds for these variables.

Let's consider the variable X_1 in the Remington problem. What is the maximum number of units of X_1 that can be produced in this problem? Referring back to our capacity constraints, if the company produces 0 units of X_2 and X_3, it would run out of machining capacity after producing $600/2 = 300$ units of X_1. Similarly it would run out of grinding capacity after producing $300/6 = 50$ units of X_1, and it would run out of assembly capacity after producing $400/5 = 80$ units of X_1. Therefore, the maximum number of units of X_1 the company can produce is 50. Using similar logic we can determine that the maximum units of X_2 the company can produce is $MIN(600/3, 300/3, 400/6) = 66.67$, and the maximum units of X_3 is $MIN(600/6, 300/4, 400/2) = 75$. Thus, for this problem reasonable upper bounds for X_1, X_2, and X_3 are represented by $M_1 = 50$, $M_2 = 67$, and $M_3 = 75$, respectively. (Note that the method illustrated here for obtaining reasonable values for the M_i does not apply if any of the coefficients in the machining, grinding, or assembly constraints are negative. Why is this?) When possible, you should determine reasonable values for the M_i in this type of problem. However, if this is not possible, you can assign arbitrarily large values to the M_i.

IMPLEMENTING THE MODEL

Using the values for the M_i calculated earlier, our ILP formulation of Remington's production planning model is summarized as:

$$MAX: \quad 48X_1 + 55X_2 + 50X_3 - 1000Y_1 - 800Y_2 - 900Y_3$$

Subject to:
$$2X_1 + 3X_2 + 6X_3 \leq 600 \quad \} \text{ machining constraint}$$
$$6X_1 + 3X_2 + 4X_3 \leq 300 \quad \} \text{ grinding constraint}$$
$$5X_1 + 6X_2 + 2X_3 \leq 400 \quad \} \text{ assembly constraint}$$

$$X_1 - 50Y_1 \leq 0$$
$$X_2 - 67Y_2 \leq 0 \quad \left.\right\} \text{ linking constraints}$$
$$X_3 - 75Y_3 \leq 0$$

$$Y_i \leq 1, i = 1, 2, 3$$
$$Y_i \geq 0, i = 1, 2, 3 \quad \left.\right\} \text{ binary constraints}$$

All Y_i must be integers

$$X_i \geq 0, i = 1, 2, 3 \quad \} \text{ nonnegativity conditions}$$

This model expresses the linking constraints in a slightly different (but algebraically equivalent) manner in order to follow our convention of having all the variables on the LHS of the inequality and a constant on the RHS. This model is implemented in the spreadsheet shown in Figure 6.18 (and in the file FIG6-18.XLS on your data disk).

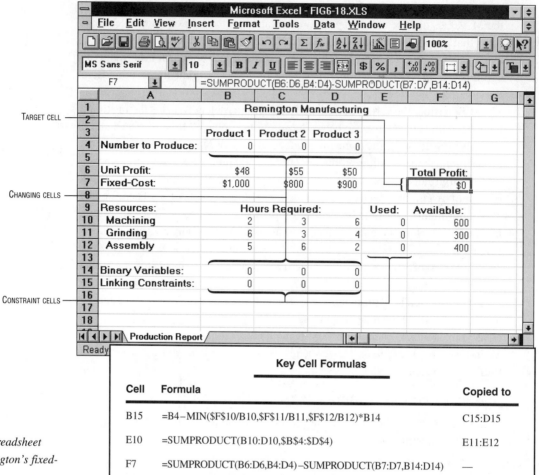

Figure 6.18: Spreadsheet model for Remington's fixed-charge problem

Key Cell Formulas

Cell	Formula	Copied to
B15	=B4−MIN($F$10/B10,$F$11/B11,$F$12/B12)*B14	C15:D15
E10	=SUMPRODUCT(B10:D10,$B$4:$D$4)	E11:E12
F7	=SUMPRODUCT(B6:D6,B4:D4)−SUMPRODUCT(B7:D7,B14:D14)	—

In the spreadsheet in Figure 6.18, cells B4, C4, and D4 represent the variables X_1, X_2, and X_3, and cells B14, C14, and D14 represent Y_1, Y_2, and Y_3. The coefficients for the objective function are in cells B6 through D7. The objective function is implemented in cell F7 with the formula:

Formula for cell F7: =SUMPRODUCT(B6:D6,B4:D4) − SUMPRODUCT(B7:D7,B14:D14)

Cells B10 through D12 contain the coefficients for the machining, grinding, and assembly constraints. The LHS formulas for these constraints are implemented in cells E10 through E12, and cells F10 through F12 contain the RHS values for these constraints.

Finally, the LHS formulas for the linking constraints are entered in cells B15 through D15 as:

Formula for cell B15: $= B4 - MIN(F10/B10, F11/B11, F12/B12)*B14$

Formula for cell C15: $= C4 - MIN(F10/C10, F11/C11, F12/C12)*C14$

Formula for cell D15: $= D4 - MIN(F10/D10, F11/D11, F12/D12)*D14$

Instead of entering the values for M_i in these constraints, we implemented formulas that would automatically calculate correct M_i values if the user of this spreadsheet changed any of the coefficients or RHS values in the capacity constraints.

Potential Pitfall

It is important to note that we are treating cells B14, C14, and D14, which represent the binary variables Y_1, Y_2, and Y_3, just like any other cells representing decision variables. We simply entered values of 0 into these cells to indicate that they represent decision variables. Ultimately, Solver will determine what values should be placed in these cells so that all the constraints are satisfied and the objective function is maximized. Some people try to make Solver's job "easier" by placing IF( ) functions in these cells to determine whether the values should be 0 or 1 depending on the values of cells B4, C4, and D4, which correspond to the variables X_1, X_2, and X_3. Although this approach seems to make sense, it can produce unwanted results. Using IF( ) functions in this way introduces *nonlinearities* in the spreadsheet model that can prevent Solver from finding the optimal solution to the problem. In chapter 8, Nonlinear Programming, we will see that nonlinear programming problems are very difficult to solve optimally. Thus, it is best to create a model so that it can be solved using linear optimization methods.

SOLVING THE MODEL

The Solver Parameters dialog box shown in Figure 6.19 indicates the settings required to solve this problem. Notice that the ranges B4 through D4 and B14 through D14, which correspond to the X_i and Y_i variables, are both listed as ranges of cells that can be changed. Also, notice that the necessary constraints have been imposed on cells B14 through D14 to ensure that they assume only binary values.

Figure 6.19: Solver parameters for Remington's fixed-charge problem

Because so few integer variables exist in this problem, we should be able to obtain an optimal integer solution easily. If we set the suboptimality tolerance to 0 in the Solver Options dialog box and instruct Solver to assume a linear model, we obtain the optimal solution to this problem, as shown in Figure 6.20.

Figure 6.20: Optimal mixed-integer solution to Remington's fixed-charge problem

ANALYZING THE SOLUTION

The solution shown in Figure 6.20 indicates that the company should produce 0 units of product 1, 55.55 units of product 2, and 33.33 units of product 3 ($X_1 = 0$, $X_2 = 55.55$, and $X_3 = 33.33$). Solver assigned values of 0, 1, and 1 to cells B14, C14, and D14 ($Y_1 = 0$, $Y_2 = 1$, and $Y_3 = 1$). Thus, Solver maintained the proper relationship between the X_i and Y_i because the linking constraints were specified for this problem. Although the values in cells B15, C15, and D15 cannot be interpreted readily, these constraints are vital in implementing the appropriate logical relationships between the X_i and the Y_i. We could hide these cells easily to avoid confusion.

Because our formulation of this model did not specify that the X_i be integers, we should not be surprised by the fractional values obtained for these variables in this solution. If we round the values of X_2 and X_3 down to 55 and 33, we obtain an integer feasible solution with an objective function value of $2,975. If we want to find the optimal all-integer solution, we can add the appropriate integrality condition for the X_i to the constraint set and then re-solve the problem. This optimal all-integer solution is shown in Figure 6.21.

Figure 6.21: Optimal all-integer solution to Remington's fixed-charge problem

Note that more computational effort is required to obtain the all-integer solution shown in Figure 6.21 (48 candidate problems) versus the effort required to obtain the mixed-integer solution shown in Figure 6.20 (4 candidate problems). All this additional work resulted in only a $5 improvement in the objective function over the all-integer solution we obtained from rounding down the solution in Figure 6.20. This highlights two important points. First, problems involving binary integer variables are often easier to solve than problems involving general integer variables. Second, good near-optimal solutions often can be obtained by rounding, so this approach is not necessarily ineffective—and could be the only practical solution available for large ILPs that are difficult to solve.

MINIMUM ORDER/PURCHASE SIZE

Many investment, production, and distribution problems have minimum purchase amounts or minimum production lot size requirements that must be met. For example, a particular investment opportunity might require a minimum investment of $25,000. Or, a supplier of a given part used in a production process might require a minimum order of 10 units. Similarly, many manufacturing companies have a policy of not producing any units of a given item unless a certain minimum lot size will be produced.

To see how these types of minimum order/purchase requirements can be modeled, suppose that in the previous problem Remington Manufacturing did not want to produce any units of product 3 (X_3) unless it produced at least 40 units of this product. This type of restriction is modeled as:

$$X_3 \leq M_3 Y_3$$

$$X_3 \geq 40 Y_3$$

The first constraint is the same type of linking constraint described earlier, in which M_3 represents an upper bound on X_3 (or an arbitrarily large number) and Y_3 represents a binary variable. If X_3 assumes any positive value, Y_3 must equal 1 (if $X_3 > 0$ then $Y_3 = 1$). However, according to the second constraint, if Y_3 equals 1, then X_3 must be greater than or equal to 40 (if $Y_3 = 1$ then $X_3 \geq 40$). On the other hand, if X_3 equals 0, Y_3 must also equal 0 in order to satisfy both constraints. Together, these two constraints ensure that if X_3 assumes any positive value, that value must be at least 40. This example illustrates how binary variables can be used to model a practical condition that is likely to occur in a variety of decision problems.

QUANTITY DISCOUNTS

In all of the LP problems considered to this point, we have assumed that the profit or cost coefficients in the objective function were constant. For example, consider our revised Blue Ridge Hot Tubs problem, which is represented by:

$$\text{MAX}: \quad 350X_1 + 300X_2 \qquad \} \text{ profit}$$

Subject to:
$$1X_1 + 1X_2 \leq 200 \qquad \} \text{ pump constraint}$$
$$9X_1 + 6X_2 \leq 1{,}520 \qquad \} \text{ labor constraint}$$
$$12X_1 + 16X_2 \leq 2{,}650 \qquad \} \text{ tubing constraint}$$
$$X_1, X_2 \geq 0 \qquad \} \text{ nonnegativity conditions}$$
$$X_1, X_2 \text{ must be integers} \qquad \} \text{ integrality conditions}$$

This model assumes that *every* additional Aqua-Spa (X_1) manufactured and sold results in a $350 increase in profit. It also assumes that every additional Hydro-Lux (X_2) manufactured and sold results in a $300 increase in profit. However, as the production of these products increases, quantity discounts might be obtained on component parts that would cause the profit margin on these items to increase.

For example, suppose that if the company produces more than 75 Aqua-Spas, it will be able to obtain quantity discounts and other economies of scale that would increase the profit margin to $375 per unit for each unit produced in excess of 75. Similarly, suppose that if the company produces more than 50 Hydro-Luxes, it will be able to increase its profit margin to $325 for each unit produced in excess of 50. That is, each of the first 75 units of X_1 and the first 50 units of X_2 would produce profits of $350 and $300 per unit, respectively, and each additional unit of X_1 and X_2 would produce profits of $375 and $325 per unit, respectively. How do we model this type of problem?

FORMULATING THE MODEL

In order to accommodate the different profit rates that can be generated by producing Aqua-Spas and Hydro-Luxes, we need to define new variables for the problem, where

X_{11} = the number of Aqua-Spas produced at $350 profit per unit

X_{12} = the number of Aqua-Spas produced at $375 profit per unit

X_{21} = the number of Hydro-Luxes produced at $300 profit per unit

X_{22} = the number of Hydro-Luxes produced at $325 profit per unit

Using these variables, we can begin to reformulate our problem as:

$$\text{MAX: } 350X_{11} + 375X_{12} + 300X_{21} + 325X_{22}$$

$$\begin{aligned}
\text{Subject to: } & 1X_{11} + 1X_{12} + 1X_{21} + 1X_{22} \leq 200 && \} \text{ pump constraint} \\
& 9X_{11} + 9X_{12} + 6X_{21} + 6X_{22} \leq 1{,}520 && \} \text{ labor constraint} \\
& 12X_{11} + 12X_{12} + 16X_{21} + 16X_{22} \leq 2{,}650 && \} \text{ tubing constraint} \\
& \text{All } X_{ij} \geq 0 && \} \text{ simple lower bounds} \\
& \text{All } X_{ij} \text{ must be integers} && \} \text{ integrality conditions}
\end{aligned}$$

This formulation is not complete. Notice that the variable X_{12} would always be preferred over X_{11} because X_{12} requires exactly the same resources as X_{11} and generates a larger per-unit profit. The same relationship holds between X_{22} and X_{21}. Thus, the optimal solution to the problem is $X_{11} = 0$, $X_{12} = 118$, $X_{21} = 0$, and $X_{22} = 76$. However, this solution is not allowable because we cannot produce any units of X_{12} until we have produced 75 units of X_{11}; and we cannot produce any units of X_{22} until we have produced 50 units of X_{21}. Therefore, we must identify some additional constraints to ensure that these conditions are met.

THE MISSING CONSTRAINTS

To ensure that the model does not allow any units of X_{12} to be produced unless we have produced 75 units of X_{11}, consider the constraints:

$$X_{12} \leq M_{12}Y_1$$

$$X_{11} \geq 75Y_1$$

In the first constraint, M_{12} represents some arbitrarily large numeric constant and Y_1 represents a binary variable. The first constraint requires that $Y_1 = 1$ if any units of X_{12} are produced (if $X_{12} > 0$ then $Y_1 = 1$). However, if $Y_1 = 1$ then the second constraint would require X_{11} to be at least 75. According to the second constraint, the only way that fewer than 75 units of X_{11} can be produced is if $Y_1 = 0$, which, by the first constraint, implies $X_{12} = 0$. These two constraints do not allow any units of X_{12} to be produced unless at least 75 units of X_{11} have been produced.

The following constraints ensure that the model does not allow any units of X_{22} to be produced unless we have produced 50 units of X_{21}:

$$X_{22} \leq M_{22}Y_2$$

$$X_{21} \geq 50Y_2$$

If we include these new constraints in our previous formulation (along with the constraints necessary to make Y_1 and Y_2 operate as binary variables), we would have an accurate formulation of the decision problem. The optimal solution to this problem is $X_{11} = 75$, $X_{12} = 43$, $X_{21} = 50$, $X_{22} = 26$.

A CONTRACT AWARD PROBLEM

Other conditions often arise in decision problems that can be modeled effectively using binary variables. The following example, which involves awarding contracts, illustrates some of these conditions.

> B&G Construction is a commercial building company located in Tampa, Florida. The company has recently signed contracts to construct four buildings in different locations throughout southern Florida. Each building project requires large amounts of cement to be delivered to the building sites. At B&G's request, three cement companies have submitted bids for supplying the cement for these jobs. The following table summarizes the prices the three companies charge per delivered ton of cement and the maximum amount of cement that each company can provide.

	Cost per Delivered Ton of Cement				
	Project 1	Project 2	Project 3	Project 4	Max. Supply
Company 1	$120	$115	$130	$125	525
Company 2	$100	$150	$110	$105	450
Company 3	$140	$95	$145	$165	550
Total Tons Needed	450	275	300	350	

For example, company 1 can supply a maximum of 525 tons of cement, and each ton delivered to projects 1, 2, 3, and 4 will cost $120, $115, $130, and $125, respectively. The costs vary primarily because of the different distances between the cement plants and the construction sites. The numbers in the last row of the table indicate the total amount of cement (in tons) required for each project.

In addition to the maximum supplies listed, each cement company placed special conditions on its bid. Specifically, company 1 indicated that it will not supply orders of less than 150 tons for any of the construction projects. Company 2 indicated that it can supply more than 200 tons to no more than one of the projects. Company 3 indicated that it will accept only orders that total 200 tons, 400 tons, or 550 tons.

B&G can contract with more than one supplier to meet the cement requirements for a given project. The problem is to determine what amounts to purchase from each supplier to meet the demands for each project at the least total cost.

This problem seems like a transportation problem in which we want to determine how much cement should be shipped from each cement company to each construction project in order to meet the demands of the projects at a minimum cost. However, the special conditions imposed by each supplier require side-constraints, which are not usually found in a standard transportation problem. First, we'll discuss the formulation of the objective function and the transportation constraints. Then, we'll consider how to implement the side-constraints required by the special conditions in the problem.

FORMULATING THE MODEL: THE OBJECTIVE FUNCTION AND TRANSPORTATION CONSTRAINTS

To begin formulating this problem, we need to define our decision variables as:

X_{ij} = tons of cement purchased from company i for construction project j

The objective function to minimize total cost is represented by:

$$\text{MIN:} \quad 120X_{11} + 115X_{12} + 130X_{13} + 125X_{14}$$
$$+100X_{21} + 150X_{22} + 110X_{23} + 105X_{24}$$
$$+140X_{31} + 95X_{32} + 145X_{33} + 165X_{34}$$

To ensure that the maximum supply of cement from each company is not exceeded, we need the following constraints:

$$X_{11} + X_{12} + X_{13} + X_{14} \leq 525 \quad \} \text{ supply from company 1}$$
$$X_{21} + X_{22} + X_{23} + X_{24} \leq 450 \quad \} \text{ supply from company 2}$$
$$X_{31} + X_{32} + X_{33} + X_{34} \leq 550 \quad \} \text{ supply from company 3}$$

To ensure that the requirement for cement at each construction project is met, we need the following constraints:

$$X_{11} + X_{21} + X_{31} = 450 \quad \} \text{ demand for cement at project 1}$$
$$X_{12} + X_{22} + X_{32} = 275 \quad \} \text{ demand for cement at project 2}$$
$$X_{13} + X_{23} + X_{33} = 300 \quad \} \text{ demand for cement at project 3}$$
$$X_{14} + X_{24} + X_{34} = 350 \quad \} \text{ demand for cement at project 4}$$

IMPLEMENTING THE TRANSPORTATION CONSTRAINTS

The objective function and the constraints of this problem are implemented in the spreadsheet model shown in Figure 6.22 (and in the file FIG6-22.XLS on your data disk).

In this spreadsheet, the costs per delivered ton of cement are shown in cells B5 through E7. Cells B11 through E13 represent the decision variables in the model. The objective function is entered in cell H15 as:

Formula for cell H15:   =SUMPRODUCT(B5:E7,B11:E13)

The LHS formulas of the supply constraints are entered in cells F11 through F13 as:

Formula for cell F11:   =SUM(B11:E11)
(copy to F12 through F13)

Cells G11 through G13 contain the RHS values for these constraints. The LHS formulas for the demand constraints are entered in cells B14 through E14 as:

Formula for cell B14:   =SUM(B11:B13)
(copy to C14 through E14)

Cells B15 through E15 contain the RHS values for these constraints.

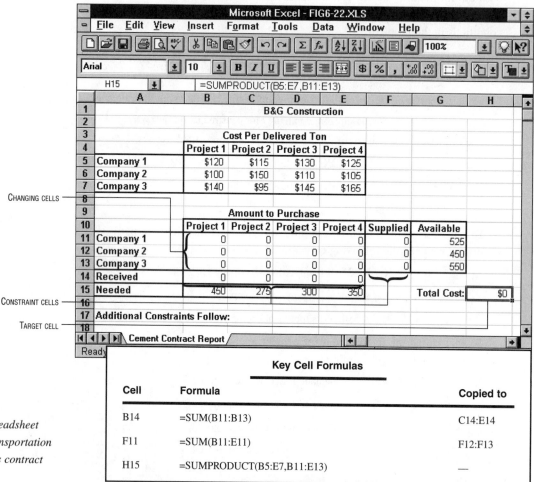

Key Cell Formulas		
Cell	Formula	Copied to
B14	=SUM(B11:B13)	C14:E14
F11	=SUM(B11:E11)	F12:F13
H15	=SUMPRODUCT(B5:E7,B11:E13)	—

Figure 6.22: Spreadsheet model for the transportation portion of B&G's contract award problem

FORMULATING THE MODEL: THE SIDE-CONSTRAINTS

Company 1 indicated that it will not accept orders for less than 150 tons for any of the construction projects. This minimum order-size restriction is modeled by the following eight constraints, where the Y_{ij} represent binary variables:

$X_{11} \leq 525Y_{11}$ (implement as $X_{11} - 525Y_{11} \leq 0$)

$X_{12} \leq 525Y_{12}$ (implement as $X_{12} - 525Y_{12} \leq 0$)

$X_{13} \leq 525Y_{13}$ (implement as $X_{13} - 525Y_{13} \leq 0$)

$X_{14} \leq 525Y_{14}$ (implement as $X_{14} - 525Y_{14} \leq 0$)

$X_{11} \geq 150Y_{11}$ (implement as $X_{11} - 150Y_{11} \geq 0$)

$X_{12} \geq 150Y_{12}$ (implement as $X_{12} - 150Y_{12} \geq 0$)

$X_{13} \geq 150Y_{13}$ (implement as $X_{13} - 150Y_{13} \geq 0$)

$X_{14} \geq 150Y_{14}$ (implement as $X_{14} - 150Y_{14} \geq 0$)

Each constraint has an algebraically equivalent constraint, which will ultimately be used in implementing the constraint in the spreadsheet. The first four constraints represent linking constraints that ensure if X_{11}, X_{12}, X_{13}, or X_{14} is greater than 0, then its associated binary variable (Y_{11}, Y_{12}, Y_{13}, or Y_{14}) must equal 1. (These constraints also indicate that 525 is the maximum value that can be assumed by X_{11}, X_{12}, X_{13}, and X_{14}.) The next four constraints ensure that if X_{11}, X_{12}, X_{13}, or X_{14} is greater than 0, it must be at least 150. We include these constraints in the formulation of this model to ensure that any order given to company 1 is for at least 150 tons of cement.

Company 2 indicated that it can supply more than 200 tons to no more than one of the projects. This type of restriction is represented by the following set of constraints where, again, the Y_{ij} represent binary variables:

$X_{21} \leq 200 + 250Y_{21}$ (implement as $X_{21} - 200 - 250Y_{21} \leq 0$)

$X_{22} \leq 200 + 250Y_{22}$ (implement as $X_{22} - 200 - 250Y_{22} \leq 0$)

$X_{23} \leq 200 + 250Y_{23}$ (implement as $X_{23} - 200 - 250Y_{23} \leq 0$)

$X_{24} \leq 200 + 250Y_{24}$ (implement as $X_{24} - 200 - 250Y_{24} \leq 0$)

$Y_{21} + Y_{22} + Y_{23} + Y_{24} \leq 1$ (implement as is)

The first constraint indicates that the amount supplied from company 2 for project 1 must be less than 200 if $Y_{21} = 0$, or less than 450 (the maximum supply from company 2) if $Y_{21} = 1$. The next three constraints have similar interpretations for the amount supplied from company 2 to projects 2, 3, and 4, respectively. The last constraint indicates that at most one of Y_{21}, Y_{22}, Y_{23}, and Y_{24} can equal 1. Therefore, only one of the projects can receive more than 200 tons of cement from company 2.

The final set of constraints for this problem addresses company 3's stipulation that it will accept only orders totaling 200, 400, or 550 tons. This type of condition is modeled using binary Y_{ij} variables as:

$X_{31} + X_{32} + X_{33} + X_{34} = 200Y_{31} + 400Y_{32} + 550Y_{33}$

    (implement as $X_{31} + X_{32} + X_{33} + X_{34} - 200Y_{31} - 400Y_{32} - 500Y_{33} = 0$)

$Y_{31} + Y_{32} + Y_{33} \leq 1$

    (implement as is)

These constraints allow for the total amount ordered from company 3 to assume four distinct values. If $Y_{31} = Y_{32} = Y_{33} = 0$ then no cement will be ordered from company 3. If $Y_{31} = 1$ then 200 tons must be ordered. If $Y_{32} = 1$ then 400 tons must be ordered. Finally, if $Y_{33} = 1$ then 550 tons must be ordered from company 3. These two constraints enforce the special condition imposed by company 3.

IMPLEMENTING THE SIDE-CONSTRAINTS

Although the side-constraints in this problem allow us to impose important restrictions on the feasible solutions that can be considered, these constraints serve a "mechanical" purpose—to make the model work—but are not of primary interest to management. Thus, it is often convenient to implement side-constraints in an out-of-the-way area of the spreadsheet so that they do not detract from the primary purpose of the spreadsheet, in this case, to determine how much cement to order from each potential supplier. Figure 6.23 shows how the side-constraints for the current problem can be implemented in a spreadsheet.

To implement the side-constraints for company 1, we enter the batch-size restriction of 150 in cell B19 and reserve cells B20 through E20 to represent the binary variables Y_{11}, Y_{12}, Y_{13}, and Y_{14}. The LHS formulas for the linking constraints for company 1 are implemented in cells B21 through E21 as:

Formula for cell B21:   =B11–$G$11*B20
(copy to C21 through E21)

Cell F21 contains a reminder for us to tell Solver that these cells must be less than or equal to 0. The LHS formulas for the batch-size constraints for company 1 are implemented in cells B22 through E22 as:

Formula for cell B22:   =B11–$B$19*B20
(copy to C22 through E22)

Cell F22 contains a reminder for us to tell Solver that these cells must be greater than or equal to 0.

To implement the side-constraints for company 2, we enter the maximum supply value of 200 in cell B24 and reserve cells B25 through E25 to represent the binary variables Y_{21}, Y_{22}, Y_{23}, and Y_{24}. The LHS formulas for the maximum supply constraints are implemented in cells B26 through E26 as:

Formula for cell B26:   =B12–$B$24–($G$12–$B$24)*B25
(copy to C26 through E26)

Cell F26 reminds us to tell Solver that these cells must be less than or equal to 0. As discussed earlier, to ensure that no more than one order from company 2 exceeds 200 tons, the sum of the binary variables for company 2 cannot exceed 1. The LHS formula for this constraint is entered in cell E27 as:

Formula for cell E27:   =SUM(B25:E25)

Cell F28 reminds us to tell Solver that this cell must be less than or equal to 1.

To implement the side-constraints for company 3, the three possible total order amounts are entered in cells B29 through D29. Cells B30 through D30 are reserved to represent the binary variables Y_{31}, Y_{32}, and Y_{33}. The LHS formula for company 3's total supply side-constraint is entered in cell D31 as:

Formula for cell D31:   =SUM(B13:E13)–SUMPRODUCT(B29:D29,B30:D30)

Cell E31 reminds us to tell Solver that cell D31 must equal 0. Finally, to ensure that no more than one of the binary variables for company 3 is set equal to 1 we enter the sum of these variables in cell D32 as:

Formula for cell D32:   =SUM(B30:D30)

Cell E32 reminds us to tell Solver that this cell must be less than or equal to 1.

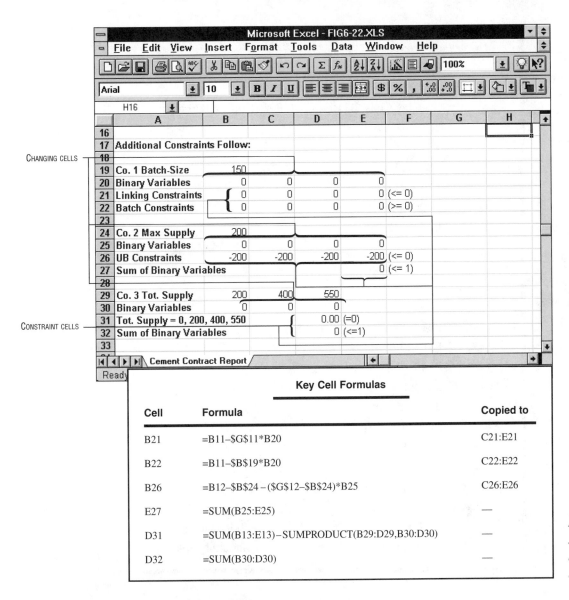

CHANGING CELLS

CONSTRAINT CELLS

Key Cell Formulas

Cell	Formula	Copied to
B21	=B11–$G$11*B20	C21:E21
B22	=B11–$B$19*B20	C22:E22
B26	=B12–$B$24 – ($G$12–$B$24)*B25	C26:E26
E27	=SUM(B25:E25)	—
D31	=SUM(B13:E13)–SUMPRODUCT(B29:D29,B30:D30)	—
D32	=SUM(B30:D30)	—

Figure 6.23: Spreadsheet model for the side-constraints in B&G's contract award problem

SOLVING THE MODEL

Due to the large number of variables and constraints in this problem, we summarized the Solver parameters and options required for this problem in Figure 6.24. Note that all of the cells representing binary variables must be identified as changing cells and must be constrained to assume only integer values between 0 and 1.

Solver parameters:

    Set Target Cell: H15

    Equal to: Min

    By Changing Cells: B11:E13,B20:E20,B25:E25,B30:D30

    Subject to the Constraints:

        $B11{:}E13 \geq 0$

        $B20{:}E20 \geq 0$

        $B20{:}E20 \leq 1$

        $B20{:}E20 = $ integer

        $B25{:}E25 \geq 0$

        $B25{:}E25 \leq 1$

        $B25{:}E25 = $ integer

        $B30{:}D30 \geq 0$

        $B30{:}D30 \leq 1$

        $B30{:}D30 = $ integer

        $F11{:}F13 \leq G11{:}G13$

        $B14{:}E14 = B15{:}E15$

        $B21{:}E21 \leq 0$

        $B22{:}E22 \geq 0$

        $B26{:}E26 \leq 0$

        $E27 \leq 1$

        $D31 = 0$

        $D32 \leq 1$

Solver options:

    Assume Linear Model   Tolerance = 0%

    Use Automatic Scaling   Iterations = 100

Figure 6.24: *Solver parameters and options for B&G's contract award problem*

ANALYZING THE SOLUTION

The optimal solution to this problem is shown in Figure 6.25. In this solution, the amounts of cement required by each construction project are met exactly. Also, each condition imposed by the side-constraints for each company is met. Specifically, the orders awarded to company 1 are for at least 150 tons; only one of the orders awarded to company 2 exceeds 200 tons; and the sum of the orders awarded to company 3 is exactly equal to 400 tons.

Figure 6.25: Optimal solution to B&G's contract award problem

BRANCH-AND-BOUND

As mentioned earlier, a special procedure, known as the branch-and-bound (B&B) algorithm is required to solve ILPs. Although we can easily indicate the presence of integer variables in a model, it usually requires quite a bit of effort on Solver's part to actually solve an ILP problem using the B&B algorithm. To better appreciate and understand what is involved in the B&B algorithm, let's consider how it works.

The B&B algorithm starts by relaxing all the integrality conditions in an ILP and solving the resulting LP problem. As noted earlier, if we are lucky, the optimal solution to the relaxed LP problem might happen to satisfy the original integrality conditions. If this occurs then we are done—the optimal solution to the LP relaxation is also the optimal solution to the ILP. However, it is more likely that the optimal solution to the LP will violate one or more of the original integrality conditions. For example, consider the following problem whose integer and relaxed feasible regions were shown in Figure 6.1 and are repeated in Figure 6.26:

$$\text{MAX:} \quad 2X_1 + 3X_2$$

$$\text{Subject to:} \quad X_1 + 3X_2 \leq 8.25$$

$$2.5X_1 + X_2 \leq 8.75$$

$$X_1, X_2 \geq 0$$

$$X_1, X_2 \text{ must be integers}$$

If we relax the integrality conditions in this problem and solve the resulting LP problem, we obtain the solution $X_1 = 2.769$, $X_2 = 1.826$ shown in Figure 6.26. This solution clearly violates the integrality conditions stated in the original problem. Part of the difficulty here is that none of the corner points of the relaxed feasible region are integer feasible (other than the origin). We know that the optimal solution to an LP problem will occur at a corner point of its feasible region but, in this case, none of those corner points (except the origin) correspond to integer solutions. Thus, we need to modify the problem so that the integer feasible solutions to the problem occur at corner points of the relaxed feasible region. This is accomplished by branching.

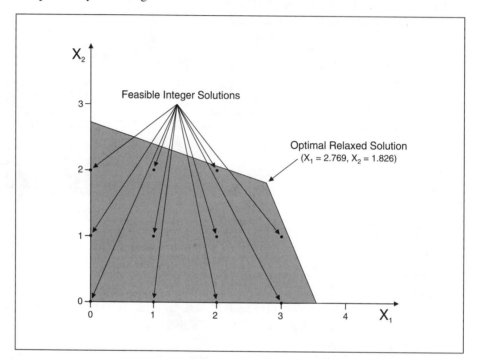

Figure 6.26: Solution to LP relaxation at noninteger corner point

BRANCHING

Any integer variable in an ILP that assumes a fractional value in the optimal solution to the relaxed problem can be designated as a **branching variable**. For example, the variables X_1 and X_2 in the previous problem should assume only integer values but were assigned the values $X_1 = 2.769$ and $X_2 = 1.826$ in the optimal solution to the LP relaxation of the problem. Either of these variables could be selected as branching variables.

Let's arbitrarily choose X_1 as our branching variable. Because the current value of X_1 is not integer feasible, we want to eliminate this solution from further consideration. Many other solutions in this same vicinity of the relaxed feasible region can be eliminated as well. That is, X_1 must assume a value less than or equal to 2 ($X_1 \leq 2$) or greater than or equal to 3 ($X_1 \geq 3$) in the optimal integer solution to the ILP. Therefore, all other possible solutions where X_1 assumes values between 2 and 3 (such as the current solution where $X_1 = 2.769$) can be eliminated from consideration. By branching on X_1, our original ILP problem can be subdivided into the following two candidate problems:

Problem I: MAX: $2X_1 + 3X_2$

Subject to: $X_1 + 3X_2 \leq 8.25$

$2.5X_1 + X_2 \leq 8.75$

$X_1 \leq 2$

$X_1, X_2 \geq 0$

X_1, X_2 must be integers

Problem II: MAX: $2X_1 + 3X_2$

Subject to: $X_1 + 3X_2 \leq 8.25$

$2.5X_1 + X_2 \leq 8.75$

$X_1 \geq 3$

$X_1, X_2 \geq 0$

X_1, X_2 must be integers

The integer and relaxed feasible regions for each candidate problem are shown in Figure 6.27. Notice that a portion of the relaxed feasible region shown in Figure 6.26 has been eliminated in Figure 6.27, but none of the feasible integer solutions shown in Figure 6.26 have been eliminated. This is a general property of the branching operation in the B&B algorithm. Also notice that several feasible integer solutions now occur on the boundary lines of the feasible regions shown in Figure 6.27. More importantly, one of these feasible integer solutions occurs at an extreme point of the relaxed feasible region for problem I (at the point $X_1 = 2$, $X_2 = 0$). If we relax the integrality conditions in problem I and solve the resulting LP, we could obtain an integer solution because one of the corner points of the relaxed feasible region corresponds to such a point. (However, this integer feasible extreme point still might not be the optimal solution to the relaxed LP problem.)

BOUNDING

The next step in the B&B algorithm is to select one of the existing candidate problems for further analysis. Let's arbitrarily select problem I. If we relax the integrality conditions in problem I and solve the resulting LP, we obtain the solution $X_1 = 2$, $X_2 = 2.083$ and an objective function value of 10.25. This value represents an *upper bound* on the best possible integer solution that can be obtained from problem I. That is, because the relaxed solution to problem I is not integer feasible, we have not yet found the best possible integer solution for this problem. However, we do know that the objective function value of the best possible integer solution that can be obtained from problem I can be no greater than 10.25. As we shall see, this information can be useful in reducing the amount of work required to locate the optimal integer solution to an ILP problem.

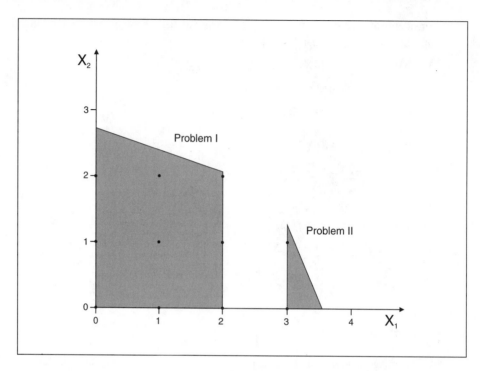

Figure 6.27: Feasible solutions to the candidate problems after the first branch

BRANCHING AGAIN

Because the relaxed solution to problem I is not entirely integer feasible, the B&B algorithm proceeds by selecting X_2 as a branching variable and creating two additional candidate problems from problem I. These problems are represented as:

Problem III: MAX: $2X_1 + 3X_2$

Subject to: $X_1 + 3X_2 \leq 8.25$

$2.5X_1 + X_2 \leq 8.75$

$X_1 \leq 2$

$X_2 \leq 2$

$X_1, X_2 \geq 0$

X_1, X_2 must be integers

Problem IV: MAX: $2X_1 + 3X_2$

Subject to: $X_1 + 3X_2 \leq 8.25$

$2.5X_1 + X_2 \leq 8.75$

$X_1 \leq 2$

$X_2 \geq 3$

$X_1, X_2 \geq 0$

X_1, X_2 must be integers

Problem III is created by adding the constraint $X_2 \leq 2$ to problem I. Problem IV is created by adding the constraint $X_2 \geq 3$ to problem I. Thus, our previous solution to problem I (where $X_2 = 2.083$) will be eliminated from consideration as a possible solution to the LP relaxations of problems III and IV.

Problem IV is infeasible because there are no feasible solutions where $X_2 \geq 3$. The integer and relaxed feasible regions for problems II and III are summarized in Figure 6.28.

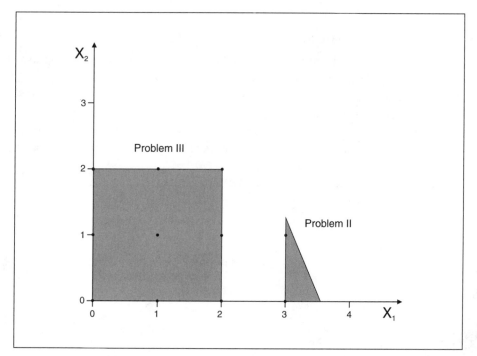

Figure 6.28: *Feasible solutions to the candidate problems after the second branch*

All of the corner points to the relaxed feasible region of problem III correspond to integer feasible solutions. Thus, if we relax the integrality conditions in problem III and solve the resulting LP problem, we must obtain an integer feasible solution. The solution to problem III is represented by $X_1 = 2$, $X_2 = 2$ and has an objective function value of 10.

BOUNDING AGAIN

Although we have obtained an integer feasible solution to our problem, we won't know if it is the *optimal* integer solution until we evaluate the remaining candidate problem (that is, problem II). If we relax the integrality conditions in problem II and solve the resulting LP problem, we obtain the solution $X_1 = 3$, $X_2 = 1.25$ with an objective function value of 9.75.

Because the solution to problem II is not integer feasible, we might be inclined to branch on X_2 in a further attempt to determine the best possible integer solution for problem II. However, this is not necessary. Earlier we noted that for *maximization* ILP problems, the objective function value at the optimal solution to the LP relaxation of the problem represents an *upper bound* on the optimal objective function value of the original ILP problem. This means that even though we do not yet know the optimal integer solution to problem II, we do know that its objective function value cannot be greater than 9.75. And because 9.75 is worse than the objective function value for the integer solution obtained from problem III, we cannot find a better integer solution by continuing to branch problem II. Therefore, problem II can be eliminated from further consideration. Because we have no more candidate problems to consider, we can conclude that the optimal integer solution to our problem is $X_1 = 2$, $X_2 = 2$ with an optimal objective function value of 10.

SUMMARY OF B&B EXAMPLE

The steps involved in the solution to our example problem can be represented graphically in the form of a *branch-and-bound tree,* as shown in Figure 6.29. Although Figure 6.26 indicates that 11 integer solutions exist for this problem, we do not have to locate all of them in order to prove that the integer solution we found is the optimal solution. The bounding operation of the B&B algorithm eliminated the need to explicitly enumerate all the integer feasible solutions and select the best of those as the optimal solution.

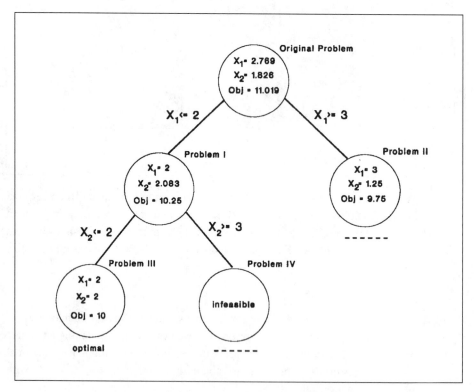

Figure 6.29: Branch-and-bound tree for the example problem

If the relaxed solution to problem II was greater than 10 (say 12.5), then the B&B algorithm would have continued branching from this problem in an attempt to find a better integer solution (an integer solution with an objective function value greater than 10). Similarly, if problem IV had a feasible noninteger solution, we would have needed to perform further branching from that problem if its relaxed objective value was better than that of the best known integer feasible solution. Thus, the first integer solution obtained using B&B will not always be the optimal integer solution. A more detailed description of the operations of the B&B algorithm is given in Figure 6.30.

THE BRANCH-AND-BOUND ALGORITHM

1. Relax all the integrality conditions in ILP and solve the resulting LP problem. If the optimal solution to the relaxed LP problem happens to satisfy the original integrality conditions, stop—this is the optimal integer solution. Otherwise, proceed to step 2.

2. If the problem being solved is a maximization problem let $Z_{best} = -\text{infinity}$. If it is a minimization problem, let $Z_{best} = +\text{infinity}$. (In general, Z_{best} represents the objective function value of the best known integer solution as the algorithm proceeds.)

3. Let X_j represent one of the variables that violated the integrality conditions in the solution to the problem that was solved most recently and let b_j represent its noninteger value. Let $\text{INT}(b_j)$ represent the largest integer that is less than b_j. Create two new candidate problems: one by appending the constraint $X_j \leq \text{INT}(b_j)$ to the most recently solved LP problem, and the other by appending the constraint $X_j \geq \text{INT}(b_j)+1$ to the most recently solved LP problem. Place both of these new LP problems in a list of candidate problems to be solved.

4. If the list of candidate problems is empty, proceed to step 9. Otherwise, remove a candidate problem from the list, relax any integrality conditions in the problem, and solve it.

5. If there is no solution to the current candidate problem (that is, it is infeasible), proceed to step 4. Otherwise, let Z_{cp} denote the optimal objective function value for the current candidate problem.

6. If Z_{cp} is not better than Z_{best} (for a maximization problem $Z_{cp} \leq Z_{best}$ or for a minimization problem $Z_{cp} \geq Z_{best}$), proceed to step 4.

7. If the solution to the current candidate problem *does not* satisfy the original integrality conditions, proceed to step 3.

8. If the solution to the current candidate problem *does* satisfy the original integrality conditions, a better integer solution has been found. Thus, let $Z_{best} = Z_{cp}$ and save the solution obtained for this candidate problem. Then go back to step 4.

9. Stop. The optimal solution has been found and has an objective function value given by the current value of Z_{best}.

Figure 6.30: Detailed description of the B&B algorithm for solving ILP problems

SUMMARY

This chapter discussed the issues involved in formulating and solving ILP problems. In some cases, acceptable integer solutions to ILP problems can be obtained by rounding the solution to the LP relaxation of the problem. However, this procedure can lead to suboptimal solutions, which might still be viable if you can show that the solution obtained by rounding is within an acceptable distance from the optimal integer solution. This approach might be the only practical way to obtain integer solutions for some ILP problems.

The B&B algorithm is a powerful technique for solving ILP problems. A great deal of skill and creativity are involved in formulating ILPs so that they can be solved efficiently using the B&B technique. Binary variables can be useful in overcoming a number of the simplifying assumptions often made in the formulation of LP models. Here again, quite a bit of creativity might be required on the part of the model builder to identify the constraints to implement various logical conditions in a given problem.

REFERENCES

Bean, J., et al. "Selecting Tenants in a Shopping Mall." *Interfaces*, vol. 18, no. 2, 1988.

Calloway, R., M. Cummins, and J. Freeland. "Solving Spreadsheet-Based Integer Programming Models: An Example From the Telecommunications Industry." *Decision Sciences*, vol. 21, 1990.

Nauss, R. and R. Markland. "Theory and Application of an Optimizing Procedure for the Lock Box Location Analysis." *Management Science*, vol. 27, no. 8, 1981.

Nemhauser, G. and L. Wolsey, *Integer and Combinatorial Optimization*. New York: Wiley, 1988.

Peiser, R. and S. Andrus. "Phasing of Income-Producing Real Estate." *Interfaces*, vol. 13, no. 1, 1983.

Stowe, J. "An Integer Programming Solution for the Optimal Credit Investigation/Credit Granting Sequence." *Financial Management*, vol. 14, Summer 1985.

Who Eats the Float?—Maryland National Improves Check Clearing Operations and Cuts Costs

Source: Markland, Robert E., and Robert M. Nauss, "Improving Transit Check Clearing Operations at Maryland National Bank," *Interfaces*, vol. 13, no. 1, February 1983, pages 1–9.

MARYLAND NATIONAL BANK (MNB) of Baltimore typically processes about 500,000 checks worth over $250,000,000 each day. Those checks not drawn on MNB or a local bank must be cleared via the Federal Reserve System, a private clearing bank, or a "direct send" by courier service to the bank on which they were drawn.

Because funds are not available until the check clears, banks try to maximize the availability of current funds by reducing the float—the time interval required for a check to clear. Banks publish an availability schedule listing the number of days before funds from a deposited check are available to the customer. If clearing time is longer than the schedule, the bank must "eat the float." If the check is cleared through the Federal Reserve and clearing takes longer than the Federal Reserve availability schedule, then the Federal Reserve "eats the float." If clearing time is actually less than the local bank's availability schedule, the customer "eats the float." The cost of float is related to the daily cost of capital.

MNB uses a system based on binary integer LP to decide the timing and method to be used for each bundle of checks of a certain type (called a cash letter). Total clearing costs (the objective function) include float costs, clearing charges from the Federal Reserve or private clearing banks, and transportation costs for direct sends. Constraints ensure that exactly one method is chosen for each check type and that a method can be used only at a time that method is available. Use of this system saves the bank about $100,000 annually.

Questions and Problems

1. As shown in Figure 6.1, the feasible region for an ILP consists of a relatively small, *finite* number of points, whereas the feasible region of its LP relaxation consists of an *infinite* number of points. Why, then, are ILPs so much harder to solve than LPs?

2. Identify reasonable values for M_{12} and M_{22} in the example on quantity discounts presented in this chapter.

3. The following questions refer to the CRT Technologies project selection example presented in this chapter. Formulate a constraint to implement the conditions described in each of the following statements.

   a. Out of projects 1, 2, 4, and 6, CRT's management wants to select exactly two projects.

   b. Project 2 can be selected only if project 3 is selected and vice-versa.

   c. Project 5 cannot be undertaken unless both projects 3 and 4 are also undertaken.

   d. If projects 2 and 4 are undertaken, then project 5 must also be undertaken.

4. The following questions refers to the Blue Ridge Hot Tubs example discussed in this chapter.

   a. Suppose Howie Jones has to purchase a single piece of equipment for $1,000 in order to produce any Aqua-Spas or Hydro-Luxes. How will this affect the formulation of the model of his decision problem?

   b. Suppose Howie must buy one piece of equipment that costs $900 in order to produce any Aqua-Spas and a different piece of equipment that costs $800 in order to produce any Hydro-Luxes. How will this affect the formulation of the model for his problem?

5. The following problem was solved as an LP problem in chapter 3. Now find its optimal integer solution.

   The manager of the Air-Express hub in Baltimore, MD, is concerned about labor costs at the hub and is interested in determining the most effective way to schedule workers. The hub operates seven days a week, and the number of packages it handles each day varies from day to day. Using historical data on the average number of packages received each day, the manager estimates the number of workers needed to handle the packages as:

Day of Week	Workers Required
Sunday	18
Monday	27
Tuesday	22
Wednesday	26
Thursday	25
Friday	21
Saturday	19

The package handlers working for Air-Express are unionized and are guaranteed a five-day work week with two consecutive days off. The base wage for the handlers is $655 per week. Because most workers prefer to have Saturday or Sunday off, the union has negotiated bonuses of $25 per day for its members who work on these days. The possible shifts and salaries for package handlers are:

Shift	Days Off	Wage
1	Sunday and Monday	$680
2	Monday and Tuesday	$705
3	Tuesday and Wednesday	$705
4	Wednesday and Thursday	$705
5	Thursday and Friday	$705
6	Friday and Saturday	$680
7	Saturday and Sunday	$655

How many package handlers should be assigned to each shift if the manager wants to have at least the required number of workers available each day at the least possible cost?

a. Formulate an ILP model for this problem.

b. Create a spreadsheet model for this problem and solve it.

c. What is the optimal solution?

6. Health Care Systems of Florida (HCSF) is planning to build a number of new emergency care clinics in central Florida. HCSF management has divided a map of the area into seven regions. They want to locate the emergency centers so that all seven regions will be conveniently served by at least one facility. Five possible sites are available for constructing the new facilities. The regions that can be served conveniently by each site are indicated by X in the following table:

	Possible Building Sites				
Region	Sanford	Altamonte	Apopka	Casselberry	Maitland
1	X		X		
2	X	X		X	X
3		X	X	X	
4		X	X		X
5	X	X		X	
6			X		X
7	X			X	
Cost ($000s)	$450	$650	$550	$500	$525

a. Formulate an ILP problem to determine which sites should be selected in order to provide convenient service to all locations in the least costly manner.

b. Implement your model in a spreadsheet and solve it.

c. What is the optimal solution?

7. Kentwood Electronics manufactures three components for stereo systems: CD players, tape decks, and stereo tuners. The wholesale price and manufacturing cost of each item are:

Component	Wholesale Price	Manufacturing Cost
CD Player	$150	75
Tape Deck	85	35
Stereo Tuner	70	30

Each CD player produced requires 3 hours of assembly; each tape deck requires 2 hours of assembly; and each tuner requires 1 hour of assembly. However, the company only manufactures these products in batches of 25—partial batches are not allowed. The marketing department believes it can sell no more than 150,000 CD players, 100,000 tape decks, and 90,000 stereo tuners. It expects a demand for at least 50,000 units of each item and wants to be able to meet this demand. If Kentwood has 400,000 hours of assembly time available, how many batches of CD players, tape decks, and stereo tuners should it produce in order to maximize profits while meeting the minimum demand figures supplied by marketing?

a. Formulate an ILP model for this problem. (Hint: Let your decision variables represent the number of batches of each item to produce.)

b. Create a spreadsheet model for this problem and solve it.

c. What is the optimal solution?

8. A developer of video game software has seven proposals for new games. Unfortunately, the company cannot develop all the proposals because its budget for new projects is limited to $950,000 and it has only 20 programmers to assign to new projects. The financial requirements, returns, and the number of programmers required by each project are summarized below. Projects 2 and 6 require specialized programming knowledge that only one of the programmers has. Both of these projects cannot be selected because the programmer with the necessary skills can be assigned to only one of the projects.

Project	Programmers Required	Capital Required	Estimated NPV
1	7	$250	$650
2	6	$175	$550
3	9	$300	$600
4	5	$150	$450
5	6	$145	$375
6	4	$160	$525
7	8	$325	$750

Note: All dollar amounts represent thousands.

a. Formulate an ILP model for this problem.

b. Create a spreadsheet model for this problem and solve it.

c. What is the optimal solution?

9. Tropicsun is a leading grower and distributor of fresh citrus products with three large citrus groves scattered around central Florida in the cities of Mt. Dora, Eustis, and Clermont. Tropicsun currently has 275,000 bushels of citrus at the grove in Mt. Dora, 400,000 bushels at the grove in Eustis, and 300,000 at the grove in Clermont. Tropicsun has citrus processing plants in Ocala, Orlando, and Leesburg with processing capacities to handle 200,000, 600,000, and 225,000 bushels, respectively. Tropicsun contracts with a local trucking company to transport its fruit from the groves to the processing plants. The trucking company charges a flat rate of $8 per mile regardless of how many bushels of fruit are transported. The following table summarizes the distances (in miles) between each grove and processing plant:

Distances (in Miles) Between Groves and Plants

Grove	Ocala	Orlando	Leesburg
Mt. Dora	21	50	40
Eustis	35	30	22
Clermont	55	20	25

Tropicsun wants to determine how many bushels to ship from each grove to each processing plant in order to minimize the total transportation cost.

a. Formulate an ILP model for this problem.

b. Create a spreadsheet model for this problem and solve it.

c. What is the optimal solution?

10.   A manufacturer is considering alternatives for building new plants in order to be located closer to three of its primary customers with whom it intends to develop long-term, sole-supplier relationships. The net cost of manufacturing and transporting each unit of the product to its customers will vary depending on where the plant is built and the production capacity of the plant. These costs are summarized in the table below:

Plant	Net Cost Per Unit To Supply Customer		
	X	Y	Z
1	35	30	45
2	45	40	50
3	70	65	50
4	20	45	25
5	65	45	45

The annual demand for products from customers X, Y, and Z is expected to be 40,000, 25,000, and 35,000 units, respectively. The annual production capacity and construction costs for each plant are:

Plant	Production Capacity	Construction Cost (in $000s)
1	40,000	$1,325
2	30,000	$1,100
3	50,000	$1,500
4	20,000	$1,200
5	40,000	$1,400

The company wants to determine which plant to build in order to satisfy customer demand at a minimum total cost.

a. Formulate an ILP model for this problem.

b. Create a spreadsheet model for this problem and solve it.

c. What is the optimal solution?

11.   Refer to question 10. Suppose plants 1 and 2 represent different building alternatives for the same site (that is, only one of these plants can be built). Similarly, suppose plants 4 and 5 represent different building alternatives for another site.

a. What additional constraints are required to model these new conditions?

b. Revise the spreadsheet for question 10 to reflect these additional constraints and solve the resulting problem.

c. What is the optimal solution?

12. Clampett Oil purchases crude oil products from suppliers in Texas (TX), Oklahoma (OK), Pennsylvania (PA), and Alabama (AL) from which it refines four end-products: gasoline, kerosene, heating oil, and asphalt. Because of differences in the quality and chemical characteristics of the oil from the different suppliers, the amount of each end-product that can be refined from a barrel of crude oil varies depending of the source of the crude. Additionally, the amount of crude available from each source varies, as does the cost of a barrel of crude from each supplier. These values are summarized below. For example, the first line of this table indicates that a barrel of crude from Texas can be refined into 2 barrels of gasoline, 2.8 barrels of kerosene, 1.7 barrels of heating oil, or 2.4 barrels of asphalt. Each supplier requires a minimum purchase of at least 500 barrels.

Raw Material Characteristics

Crude Oils	Barrels Available	Possible Production Per Barrel				Cost Per Barrel	Trucking Cost
		Gas	Kero.	Heat	Asphalt		
TX	1,500	2.00	2.80	1.70	2.40	$22	$1,500
OK	2,000	1.80	2.30	1.75	1.90	$21	$1,700
PA	1,500	2.30	2.20	1.60	2.60	$22	$1,500
AL	1,800	2.10	2.60	1.90	2.40	$23	$1,400

The company owns a tanker truck that picks up whatever crude oil it purchases. This truck can hold 2000 barrels of crude. The cost of sending the truck to pick up oil from the various locations is shown in the column labeled "Trucking Cost." The company's plans for its next production cycle specify 750 barrels of gasoline, 800 barrels of kerosene, 1000 barrels of heating oil, and 300 barrels of asphalt to be produced.

a. Formulate an ILP model that can be solved to determine the purchasing plan that will allow the company to implement its production plan at the least cost.

b. Implement this model in a spreadsheet and solve it.

c. What is the optimal solution?

13. Dan Boyd is a financial planner trying to determine how to invest $1,000,000 for one of his clients. The cash flows for the investments under consideration are summarized in the following table:

Summary of Cash In-Flows and Out-Flows (at beginning of year)

	A	B	C	D	E
1996	−1.00	0.00	−1.00	0.00	−1.00
1997	+0.45	−1.00	0.00	0.00	0.00
1998	+1.05	0.00	0.00	−1.00	1.25
1999	0.00	+1.30	+1.65	+1.30	0.00

For example, if Dan invests $1 in investment A at the beginning of 1996, he will receive $0.45 at the beginning of 1997 and another $1.05 at the beginning of 1998. Alternatively, he can invest $1 in investment B at the beginning of 1997 and receive $1.30 at the beginning of 1999. Entries of "0.00" in the above table indicate times when no cash in-flows or out-flows can occur. At the beginning of a year, Dan can place any or all of the available money in a savings account that is expected to yield 5% per year. The minimum required investments for each possible investment are:

Investment	Minimum Required Investment
A	$25,000
B	40,000
C	35,000
D	50,000
E	30,000
Savings Account	0

How should Dan plan his investments if he wants to maximize the amount of money available to his client in 1999?

a. Formulate an ILP model for this problem.

b. Create a spreadsheet model for this problem and solve it using Solver.

c. What is the optimal solution?

14. The Mega-Bucks Corporation is planning its production schedule for the next four weeks and is forecasting the following demand for compound X—a key raw material used in its production process:

	Compound X	
Week	Required	
1	400 lbs.	
2	150 lbs.	
3	200 lbs.	
4	350 lbs.	

The company currently has no compound X on hand. The supplier of this product only delivers in batch sizes that are multiples of 100 pounds (0, 100, 200, 300, and so on). The price of this material is $125 per 100 pounds. Deliveries can be arranged weekly, but there is a delivery charge of $50. Mega-Bucks estimates that it costs $15 for each 100 pounds of compound X held in inventory from one week to the next. Assuming Mega-Bucks does not want more than 50 pounds of compound X in inventory at the end of week 4, how much should it order each week so that the demand for this product will be met in the least costly manner?

a. Formulate an ILP model for this problem.

b. Create a spreadsheet model for this problem and solve it using Solver.

c. What is the optimal solution?

15. An automobile manufacturer is considering mechanical design changes in one of its top-selling cars to reduce the weight of the car by 400 pounds to improve its fuel efficiency. Design engineers have identified 10 changes that could be made in the car to make it lighter (for example, using composite body pieces rather than metal). The weight saved by each design change and the estimated costs of implementing each change are summarized below:

Design Change	Weight Saved	Cost
1	50 lbs.	$150,000
2	75 lbs.	350,000
3	25 lbs.	50,000
4	150 lbs.	450,000
5	60 lbs.	90,000
6	95 lbs.	35,000
7	200 lbs.	650,000
8	40 lbs.	75,000
9	80 lbs.	110,000
10	30 lbs.	30,000

Changes 4 and 7 represent alternate ways of modifying the engine block and, therefore, only one of these options could be selected. The company wants to determine which changes to make in order to reduce the total weight of the car by 400 lbs. in the least costly manner.

a. Formulate an ILP model for this problem.

b. Create a spreadsheet model for this problem and solve it.

c. What is the optimal solution?

16. The emergency services coordinator for Clarke County is interested in locating the county's two ambulances to maximize the number of residents that can be reached within 4 minutes in emergency situations. The county is divided into 5 regions, and the average times required to travel from one region to the next are summarized below:

	To Region				
From Region	1	2	3	4	5
1	0	4	6	3	2
2	4	0	2	3	6
3	6	2	0	5	3
4	3	3	5	0	7
5	2	6	3	7	0

The population in regions 1, 2, 3, 4, and 5 are estimated as 45,000, 65,000, 28,000, 52,000, and 43,000, respectively. In which two regions should the ambulances be placed?

a. Formulate an ILP model for this problem.

b. Implement your model in a spreadsheet and solve it.

c. What is the optimal solution?

17. A company manufactures three products: A, B, and C. The company currently has an order for three units of product A, 7 units of product B, and 4 units of product C. There is no inventory for any of these products. All three products require special processing that can be done on one of two machines. The cost of producing each product on each machine is summarized below:

	Cost of Producing a Unit of Product		
Machine	A	B	C
1	$13	$9	$10
2	$11	$12	$8

The time required to produce each product on each machine is summarized below:

	Time (Hours) Needed To Produce a Unit of Product		
Machine	A	B	C
1	0.4	1.1	0.9
2	0.5	1.2	1.3

Assume machine 1 can be used for 8 hours and machine 2 can be used for 6 hours. Each machine must undergo a special setup operation to prepare it to produce each product. After completing this setup for a product, any number of that product type can be produced. The setup costs for producing each product on each machine are summarized below.

	Setup Costs for Producing		
Machine	A	B	C
1	$55	$93	$60
2	$65	$58	$75

   a. Formulate an ILP model to determine how many units of each product to produce on each machine in order to meet demand at a minimum cost.

   b. Implement your model in a spreadsheet and solve it.

   c. What is the optimal solution?

18. Solve the following problem manually using the B&B algorithm. You can use the computer to solve the individual problems generated. Create a branch-and-bound tree to display the steps you complete.

$$\text{MAX:} \quad 6X_1 + 8X_2$$
$$\text{Subject to:} \quad 6X_1 + 3X_2 \leq 18$$
$$2X_1 + 3X_2 \leq 9$$
$$X_1, X_2 \geq 0$$
$$X_1, X_2 \text{ must be integers}$$

19. During the execution of the B&B algorithm, many candidate problems are likely to be generated and awaiting further analysis. In the B&B example in this chapter, we chose the next candidate problem to analyze in a rather arbitrary way. What other, more structured ways might we use to select the next candidate problem? What are the pros and cons of these techniques?

New York City Tour

A Case in Integer Programming

JOHN Peters kept humming the score from *On the Town*, his favorite Broadway show and movie musical, over and over. *On the Town* is a whimsical lark written by Leonard Bernstein in the 1940s that tells the story of three sailors on a 24-hour shore leave in New York City. The sailors want to see as many sights as possible in the short time they have. John remembers seeing the movie version of the musical for the first time and being awed by the sights of the city, particularly the Statue of Liberty, Rockefeller Center, and the many museums. Since seeing the movie, John's great wish has been to visit New York City.

Now John has an opportunity to fulfill his wish. John works as an accountant for a firm in Idaho and is being sent by his company on a business trip to Europe. He must stop in New York City to get his connecting flight, and with some juggling of the airline schedules, John managed to arrange a two-day stopover in New York City. In those two days, John wants to see as much of the city as he can.

What should John see? He has about 20 hours total in which to visit some of the many attractions that the city has to offer. These 20 hours take into account the travel time between sights, time for food and rest, times when the attractions are closed, and so on. There are literally hundreds of places to visit, so

John knows that he has to narrow down his choices. He decides to consult the Michelin Guide, which is know for its reliable and accurate assessments of the various sights in both foreign and domestic cities. The attractions are rated by stars. A three-star attraction is very highly recommended, a two-star attraction is recommended, a one-star rating indicates the attraction is interesting, and a no-star rating indicates that the attraction is worth seeing only if time allows. Because of the limited time John has, he feels that he should visit only three- and two-star attractions; anything less would not be worth his time on this trip.

The Michelin Guide indicates that New York City has almost two dozen three-star attractions and almost three dozen two-star attractions. Because almost all these attractions are on Manhattan Island (New York City), John will ignore sights in the other four boroughs. Based on his interests, John further decides to omit some three-star and two-star attractions, including the Bronx Zoo, Rockefeller Center, and The Cloisters. After reading more about each attraction, he came up with a list of 11 possible attractions he wants to visit. John knows that he cannot do justice to these 11 attractions in just 20 hours. The Michelin Guide gives recommendations for the number of hours that a visitor should spend at each attraction. John

Contributed by Jack Yurkiewicz, Lubin School of Business, Pace University, New York.

knows that these are rough time estimates. For example, he could easily spend the entire 20 hours at the Metropolitan Museum of Art, one of the world's great art galleries, instead of just the 5 hours recommended by the Michelin Guide. However, spending 1 hour there would not be enough either, and if he had to do that, perhaps he would just skip that sight entirely.

John decides that he will not spend more than 3 hours at any one attraction, no matter how much there is to see or do there. To keep matters simple, he decides to measure the time spent at an attraction in intervals of hours; that is, all visitation times are rounded to the nearest hour. Thus he could spend 1, 2, or 3 hours at a sight, or even 0 hours (which means he will not visit that sight at all). John is more interested in some attractions than others, and visiting these for longer times will be more enjoyable for him than visiting less desirable sights. Thus a 3-hour visit to the Frick Collection, described

by Michelin as "one of the most beautiful private museums in the world," housing everything from Old Masters to Louis XVI furniture, will give him less enjoyment than a 3-hour visit to the Metropolitan Museum of Art. This is not only because the Metropolitan offers more to see, but the Frick Collection requires less time to see everything than the Metropolitan. So a 1-hour visit to the Frick Collection will give him more enjoyment than a 1-hour visit to the Metropolitan. John must consider the number of sights to see at an attraction, how much time he has to spend there, and how desirable it is for him to visit the attraction.

John put all these factors in the following table. The table shows the attraction, its assigned number of Michelin stars, how much time the Michelin Guide recommends a visitor spend there, and how much enjoyment John will get from spending 1, 2, or 3 hours at the attraction. He measures enjoyment on an arbitrary scale of 0 to 100.

| Attraction | Stars | Michelin Guide's Recommended Visit Time | Actual Visit Time | | | |
| | | | 0 hrs | 1 hr | 2 hrs | 3 hrs |
			Enjoyment Rating			
Statue of Liberty	***	4	0	10	50	80
World Trade Center	***	2.5	0	50	90	95
Greenwich Village	**	2	0	30	40	60
Empire State Building	***	2	0	25	75	90
United Nations	***	3	0	40	50	75
Museum of Modern Art	***	2.5	0	35	50	75
Frick Collection	***	2.5	0	40	50	60
Whitney Museum	**	1.5	0	20	45	65
Metropolitan Museum of Art	***	5	0	40	60	100
Guggenheim Museum	**	1.5	0	20	30	65
Museum of Natural History	***	4	0	20	50	90

As a final consideration, John realizes that a visit to the top of the World Trade Center or to the top of the Empire State Building both offer spectacular views of the city. Thus, he decides that he will visit either one or the other (or perhaps neither if he can get more enjoyment from visiting some other sights), but not both.

The question is simple. What attractions should John visit and how much time should he spend at each in order to maximize his total enjoyment earned by his trip to New York City? Formulate and solve an integer programming model to solve John's problem.

Discount Software, Inc.
A Case in Integer
Programming

WHILE finishing his undergraduate studies at Indiana University, Don Conway became very interested in computer programming and, in his spare time, developed a number of simple software packages. His first package, Check-O-Matic, was designed to help pay bills and balance his checkbook each month. A number of his friends also started using this package and passed it on to their friends. Before he knew it, Don was getting requests for his package from people all across the country. Don's second product was a personal scheduling package called Date-O-Matic. It also proved to be quite popular. So when Don graduated, he decided to create his own business, Discount Software, Inc.

Discount Software, Inc. (DSI) manufactures, markets, and distributes a number of software products through direct mail advertising. Currently, DSI's catalog lists more than 500 individual software titles. Most of the programs are relatively simple shareware products that cost $30 or less and are packaged with no written documentation. Because of the low profit margins on these products, it is important for DSI to keep its operating costs as low as possible. The main cost incurred in the business (other than printing the catalogs) is the cost of the computer disks on which the software is distributed.

Don recently developed a spreadsheet package called Calc-O-Matic. This package consists of 10 program modules that are stored in separate files. To save disk space, each file is distributed in a compressed file format. The sizes (in bytes) of these compressed files are shown below in ascending order.

File	Size in Bytes
1	210,596
2	222,195
3	236,792
4	434,537
5	468,372
6	482,779
7	788,191
8	801,689
9	925,131
10	1,009,117

When a computer disk is formatted, the surface of the disk is divided into numerous storage locations known as clusters. Each disk that DSI uses contains 2,847 clusters, and each cluster has 512 bytes of storage capacity. More than one cluster on a disk can be assigned to a specific file, but no two files can be assigned to the same cluster. For example, the first file listed in the table occupies 412 clusters (because 210,596/512 = 411.32). This file does not fill up the last cluster assigned to it entirely (only 32% of the last cluster is used). However, the unused space in the last cluster cannot be allocated to another file—it simply remains vacant.

Don wants to determine how the 10 files should be grouped onto the disks in order to minimize the total number of disks required to ship a copy of Calc-O-Matic. A single file cannot be split between two or more disks. If a file will not fit on a given disk, it must be placed on another disk that can contain the entire file.

Create an integer programming model to determine the minimum number of disks required to ship all the files. Implement your model in Excel and solve it. Indicate which files should be stored on each disk.

CHAPTER 7

Goal Programming and Multiple Objective Optimization

CHAPTER 6 discussed the modeling techniques that apply to optimization problems that require integer solutions. This chapter presents two other modeling techniques that are sometimes helpful in solving optimization problems. The first technique—goal programming—involves solving problems containing not one specific objective function, but rather a collection of goals that we would like to achieve. As we'll see, a goal can be viewed as a constraint with a flexible, or soft, RHS value.

The second technique—multiple objective optimization—is closely related to goal programming and applies to problems containing more than one objective function. In business and government, different groups of people frequently pursue different objectives. Therefore, it is quite possible that a variety of objective functions can be proposed for the same optimization problem.

Both techniques require an *iterative solution procedure* in which the decision maker investigates a variety of solutions to find one that is most satisfactory. Thus, unlike the LP and ILP procedures presented earlier, we cannot formulate a multiple objective or goal programming problem and solve one optimization problem to identify the optimal solution. In these problems we might need to solve several variations of the problem before we find an acceptable solution.

We'll begin with the topic of goal programming. Then we'll investigate multiple objective optimization and see how the concepts and techniques of goal programming can be applied to these problems as well.

GOAL PROGRAMMING

The optimization techniques presented in the preceding chapters have always assumed that the constraints in the model are **hard constraints**, or constraints that *cannot* be violated. For example, labor constraints indicated that the amount of labor used to produce a variety of products could not exceed some fixed amount (such as 1,566 hours). As another example, monetary constraints indicated that the amount of money invested in a number of projects could not exceed some budgeted amount (such as $850,000).

Hard constraints are appropriate in many situations; however, these constraints might be too restrictive in others. For example, when you buy a new car you probably have in mind a maximum purchase price that you do not want to exceed. We might call this your goal. However, you will probably find a way to spend more than this amount if it is impossible to acquire the car you really want for your goal amount. So the goal you have in mind is *not* a hard constraint that cannot be violated. We might view it more accurately as a **soft constraint** representing a target you would like to achieve.

Numerous managerial decision-making problems can be modeled more accurately using goals rather than hard constraints. Often, such problems do not have one explicit objective function to be maximized or minimized over a constraint set but, instead, can be stated as a collection of goals that might also include hard constraints. These types of problems are known as **goal programming** (GP) problems.

AN EXAMPLE

The technique of linear programming can help a decision maker analyze and solve a GP problem. The following example illustrates the concepts and modeling techniques used in GP problems.

Davis McKeown is the owner of a resort hotel and convention center in Myrtle Beach, South Carolina. Although his business is profitable, it is also highly seasonal; the summer months are the most profitable time of year. In order to increase profits during the rest of the year, Davis wants to expand his convention business but, to do so, he needs to expand his conference facilities. Davis hired a marketing research firm to determine the number and sizes of conference rooms that would be required by the conventions he wants to attract. The results of this study indicated that Davis's facilities should include at least 5 small (400 square foot) conference rooms, 10 medium (750 square foot) conference rooms, and 15 large (1,050 square foot) conference rooms. Additionally, the marketing research firm indicated that if the expansion consisted of a total of 25,000 square feet, Davis would have the largest convention center among his competitors—which would be desirable for advertising purposes. While discussing his expansion plans with an architect, Davis learned that he can expect to pay $18,000 for each small conference room in the expansion, $33,000 for each medium conference room, and $45,150 for each large conference room. Davis wants to limit his expenditures on the convention center expansion to approximately $1,000,000.

DEFINING THE DECISION VARIABLES

In this problem, the fundamental decision facing the hotel owner is how many small, medium, and large conference rooms to include in the conference center expansion. These quantities are represented by X_1, X_2, and X_3, respectively.

DEFINING THE GOALS

This problem is somewhat different from the problems presented earlier in this book. Rather than one specific objective, this problem involves a number of goals, which are stated (in no particular order) as:

Goal 1: The expansion should include approximately 5 small conference rooms.

Goal 2: The expansion should include approximately 10 medium conference rooms.

Goal 3: The expansion should include approximately 15 large conference rooms.

Goal 4: The expansion should consist of approximately 25,000 square feet.

Goal 5: The expansion should cost approximately $1,000,000.

Notice that the word "approximately" appears in each goal. This word underscores the fact that these are soft goals rather than hard constraints. For example, if the first four goals could be achieved at a cost of $1,001,000, it is very likely that the hotel owner would not mind paying an extra $1,000 to achieve such a solution. However, we must determine if we can find a solution that exactly meets all of the goals in this problem and, if not, what trade-offs can be made among the goals to determine an acceptable solution. We can formulate an LP model for this GP problem to help us make this determination.

DEFINING THE GOAL CONSTRAINTS

The first step in formulating an LP model for a GP problem is to create a goal constraint for each goal in the problem. A **goal constraint** allows us to determine how close a given solution comes to achieving the goal. To understand how these constraints should be formulated, let's begin with the three goal constraints associated with the number of small, medium, and large conference rooms in the expansion.

If we wanted to make sure that *exactly* 5 small, 10 medium, and 15 large conference rooms were included in the planned expansion, we would include the following hard constraints in our GP model:

$X_1 = 5$

$X_2 = 10$

$X_3 = 15$

However, the goals stated that the expansion should include *approximately* 5 small conference rooms, *approximately* 10 medium conference rooms, and *approximately* 15 large conference rooms. If it is impossible to achieve all the goals, the hotel owner might consider a solution involving only 14 large conference rooms. The hard constraints would not allow for such a solution; they are too restrictive. However, we can modify them easily to allow for departures from the stated goals, as:

$$X_1 + d_1^- - d_1^+ = 5 \quad \} \text{ small rooms}$$

$$X_2 + d_2^- - d_2^+ = 10 \quad \} \text{ medium rooms}$$

$$X_3 + d_3^- - d_3^+ = 15 \quad \} \text{ large rooms}$$

where $d_i^-, d_i^+ \geq 0$ for all i

The RHS value of each goal constraint (the values 5, 10, and 15 in the previous constraints) is the **target value** for the goal because it represents the level of achievement that the decision maker wants to obtain for the goal. The variables d_i^- and d_i^+ are called **deviational variables** because they represent the amount by which each goal deviates from its target value. The d_i^- represent the amount by which each goal's target value is *underachieved,* and the d_i^+ represents the amount by which each goal's target value is *overachieved.*

To illustrate how deviational variables work, suppose that we have a solution where $X_1 = 3$, $X_2 = 13$, and $X_3 = 15$. In order to satisfy the first goal constraint listed above, its deviational variables would assume the values $d_1^- = 2$ and $d_1^+ = 0$ to reflect that the goal of having 5 small conference rooms is *underachieved* by 2. Similarly, in order to satisfy the second goal constraint, its deviational variables would assume the values $d_2^- = 0$ and $d_2^+ = 3$ to reflect that the goal of having 10 medium conference rooms is *overachieved* by 3. Finally, in order to satisfy the third goal constraint, its deviational variables would assume the values $d_3^- = 0$ and $d_3^+ = 0$ to reflect that the goal of having 15 medium conference rooms is *exactly* achieved.

We can formulate the goal constraints for the remaining goals in the problem in a similar manner. Because each small, medium, and large conference room requires 400, 750, and 1,050 square feet, respectively, and the hotel owner wants the total square footage of the expansion to be 25,000, the constraint representing this goal is:

$$400X_1 + 750X_2 + 1,050X_3 + d_4^- - d_4^+ = 25,000 \quad \} \text{ square footage}$$

Because each small, medium, and large conference room results in building costs of $18,000, $33,000, and $45,150, respectively, and the hotel owner wants to keep the cost of the expansion at approximately $1,000,000, the constraint representing this goal is:

$$18,000X_1 + 33,000X_2 + 45,150X_3 + d_5^- - d_5^+ = 1,000,000 \quad \} \text{ building cost}$$

The deviational variables in each of these goal constraints represent the amounts by which the actual values obtained for the goals deviate from their respective target values.

DEFINING THE HARD CONSTRAINTS

As noted earlier, not all of the constraints in a GP problem have to be goal constraints. A GP problem can also include one or more hard constraints typically found in LP problems. In our example, if $1,000,000 was the absolute maximum amount that the hotel owner was willing to spend on the expansion, this could be included in the model as a hard constraint. (As we'll see, it is also possible to change a soft constraint into a hard constraint during the analysis of a GP problem.)

GP OBJECTIVE FUNCTIONS

Although it is fairly easy to formulate the constraints for a GP problem, identifying an appropriate objective function can be quite tricky and usually requires some mental effort. Before formulating the objective function for our sample problem, let's consider some of the issues and options involved in this process.

The objective in a GP problem is to determine a solution that achieves all the goals as closely as possible. The *ideal* solution to any GP problem is one in which each goal is achieved exactly at the level specified by its target value. (In such an ideal solution all the deviational variables in all the goal constraints would equal 0.) Often, it is not possible to achieve the ideal solution because some goals might conflict with others. In such a case, we want to find a solution that deviates as little as possible from the ideal solution. One possible objective for our example GP problem is:

Minimize the sum of the deviations: MIN: $\sum_i (d_i^- + d_i^+)$

With this objective, we attempt to find a solution to the problem where all the deviational variables are 0—or where all the goals are met exactly. But if such a solution is not possible, will this objective always produce a desirable solution? The answer is "probably not."

The previous objective has a number of shortcomings. First, the deviational variables measure entirely different things. In our example problem, d_1^-, d_1^+, d_2^-, d_2^+, d_3^-, and d_3^+ all measure rooms of one size or another, whereas d_4^- and d_4^+ are measures of square footage, and d_5^- and d_5^+ are financial measures of building costs. One obvious criticism of the previous objective is that it is unclear how to interpret any numerical value the objective assumes (7 rooms + 1,500 dollars = 1,507 units of what?).

One solution to this problem is to modify the objective function so that it measures the sum of *percentage deviations* from the various goals. This is accomplished as follows, where t_i represents the target value for goal i:

Minimize the sum of the percentage deviations: MIN: $\sum_i \frac{1}{t_i}(d_i^- + d_i^+)$

In our example problem, if we arrive at a solution where the first goal is underachieved by 1 room ($d_1^- = 1$) and the fifth goal is overachieved by \$20,000 ($d_5^+ = 20,000$) and all other goals are achieved exactly (all other d_i^- and d_i^+ equal 0). Using the sum of percentage deviations objective, the optimal objective function value is:

$$\frac{1}{t_1}d_1^- + \frac{1}{t_5}d_5^+ = \frac{1}{5}*1 + \frac{1}{1,000,000}*20,000 \ = \ 20\% + 2\% \ = \ 22\%$$

Note that the percentage deviation objective can be used only if all the target values for all the goals are non-zero; otherwise a division by zero error will occur.

Another potential criticism of the previous objective functions concerns how they evaluate deviations. In the previous example, where the objective function value is 22%, the objective function implicitly assumes that having 4 small conference rooms (rather than 5) is 10 times worse than being \$20,000 over the desired building cost budget. That is, the budget overrun of \$20,000 would have to increase 10 times to \$200,000 before the percentage deviation on this goal equaled the 20% deviation caused by being 1 room below the goal of having 5 small conference rooms. Is having 1 fewer conference room really as undesirable as having to pay \$200,000 more than budgeted? Only the decision maker in this problem can answer this question. It would be nice to provide the decision maker a way to evaluate and change the implicit trade-offs among the goals if he or she wanted to do so.

Both of the previous objective functions view a deviation from any goal in any direction as being equally undesirable. For example, according to both of the previous objective functions, a solution resulting in a building cost of $900,000 (if $X_5 = 900,000$ and $d_5^- = 100,000$) is as undesirable as a solution with a building cost of $1,100,000 (if $X_5 = 1,100,000$ and $d_5^+ = 100,000$). But, the hotel owner probably would prefer to pay $900,000 for the expansion rather than $1,1000,000. So, while overachieving the building cost goal is an undesirable occurrence, underachieving this goal is probably desirable or at least neutral. On the other hand, underachieving the goal related to the number of small conference rooms might be viewed as undesirable, whereas overachieving this goal might be viewed as desirable or possibly neutral. Again, it would be nice to provide the decision maker a way to represent which deviations are desirable and undesirable in the objective function.

One solution to the previous criticisms is to allow the decision maker to assign weights to the deviational variables in the objective function of a GP problem to better reflect the importance and desirability of deviations from the various goals. So, a more useful type of objective function for a GP problem is:

Minimize the weighted sum of the deviations: MIN: $\displaystyle\sum_i (w_i^- d_i^- + w_i^+ d_i^+)$

or

Minimize the weighted sum of the percentage deviations: MIN: $\displaystyle\sum_i \frac{1}{t_i}(w_i^- d_i^- + w_i^+ d_i^+)$

In these weighted objective functions, the w_i^- and w_i^+ represent numeric constants that can be assigned values to weight the various deviational variables in the problem. A variable that represents a highly undesirable deviation from a particular goal is assigned a relatively large weight—making it highly undesirable for that variable to assume a value larger than 0. A variable that represents a neutral or desirable deviation from a particular goal is assigned a weight of 0 or some value lower than 0 to reflect that it is acceptable or even desirable for the variable to assume a value greater than 0.

Unfortunately, no standard procedure is available for assigning values to the w_i^- and w_i^+ in a way that guarantees you will find the most desirable solution to a GP problem. Rather, you need to follow an iterative procedure in which you try a particular set of weights, solve the problem, analyze the solution, and then refine the weights and solve the problem again. You might need to repeat this process many times to find a solution that is the most desirable to the decision maker.

Defining the Objective

In our example problem, assume that the decision maker considers it undesirable to underachieve any of the first three goals related to the number of small, medium, and large conference rooms, but is indifferent about overachieving these goals. Also assume that the decision maker considers it undesirable to underachieve the goal of adding 25,000 square feet, but equally undesirable to overachieve this goal. Finally, assume that the decision maker finds it undesirable to spend more than $1,000,000, but is indifferent about spending less than this amount. In this case, if we want to minimize the weighted percentage deviation for our example problem, we use the following objective:

$$\text{MIN: } \frac{w_1^-}{5}d_1^- + \frac{w_2^-}{10}d_2^- + \frac{w_3^-}{15}d_3^- + \frac{w_4^-}{25,000}d_4^- + \frac{w_4^+}{25,000}d_4^+ + \frac{w_5^+}{1,000,000}d_5^+$$

Notice that this objective omits (or assigns weights of 0 to) the deviational variables about which the decision maker is indifferent. Thus, this objective would not penalize a solution where, for example, 7 small conference rooms were selected (and therefore $d_1^+ = 2$) because we assume that the decision maker would not view this as an undesirable deviation from the goal of having 5 small conference rooms. On the other hand, this objective would penalize a solution where 3 small conference rooms were selected (and therefore $d_1^- = 2$) because this represents an undesirable deviation from the goal of having 5 small conference rooms. To begin our analysis of this problem we will assume that $w_1^- = w_2^- = w_3^- = w_4^- = w_4^+ = w_5^+ = 1$ and all other weights are 0.

IMPLEMENTING THE MODEL

To summarize, the LP model for our example GP problem is:

$$\text{MIN:} \quad \frac{w_1^-}{5} d_1^- + \frac{w_2^-}{10} d_2^- + \frac{w_3^-}{15} d_3^- + \frac{w_4^-}{25{,}000} d_4^- + \frac{w_4^+}{25{,}000} d_4^+ + \frac{w_5^+}{1{,}000{,}000} d_5^+$$

Subject to:

$$X_1 + \quad d_1^- - \quad d_1^+ \quad = \quad 5 \quad \} \text{ small rooms}$$

$$X_2 + \quad d_2^- - \quad d_2^+ \quad = \quad 10 \quad \} \text{ medium rooms}$$

$$X_3 + \quad d_3^- - \quad d_3^+ \quad = \quad 15 \quad \} \text{ large rooms}$$

$$400X_1 + \quad 750X_2 + \quad 1{,}050X_3 + d_4^- - d_4^+ = \quad 25{,}000 \quad \} \text{ square footage}$$

$$18{,}000X_1 + 33{,}000X_2 + 45{,}150X_3 + d_5^- - d_5^+ = 1{,}000{,}000 \quad \} \text{ building cost}$$

$d_i^-, d_i^+ \geq 0$ for all i

$X_i \geq 0$ for all i

X_i must be integers

Because this is an ILP model, it can be implemented in a spreadsheet in the usual way. One approach for doing this is shown in Figure 7.1 (and in the file FIG7-1.XLS on your data disk).

The first section of the spreadsheet lists basic data about the square footage and costs of the different conference rooms. The next section represents the decision variables, deviational variables, and goal constraints for the problem. Specifically, cells B6 through D6 correspond to X_1, X_2, and X_3—the number of small, medium, and large conference rooms to be included in the expansion. Cells E6 and F6 contain the following formulas, which calculate the total square footage and total building cost for any combination of small, medium, and large conference rooms:

Formula for cell E6:   = SUMPRODUCT(B2:D2,B6:D6)

Formula for cell F6:   = SUMPRODUCT(B3:D3,B6:D6)

Cells B7 through F8 correspond to the deviational variables in our algebraic model. These cells indicate the amount by which each goal is underachieved or overachieved. The LHS formulas for the goal constraints are implemented in cells B9 through F9. Specifically, in cell B9 we enter the following formula then copy it to cells C9 through F9:

Formula for cell B9:   =B6+B7–B8
(copy to C9 through F9)

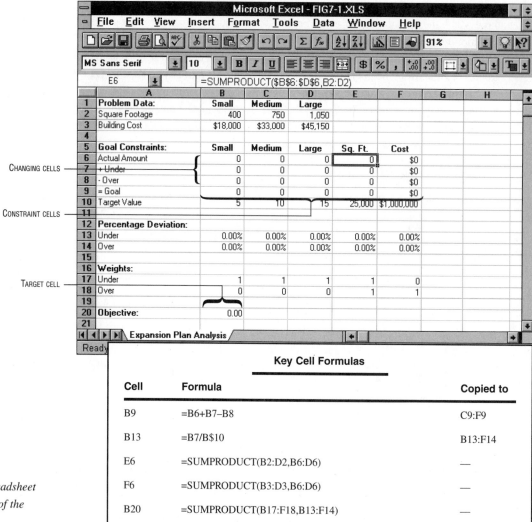

Figure 7.1: *Spreadsheet implementation of the GP model*

Key Cell Formulas

Cell	Formula	Copied to
B9	=B6+B7–B8	C9:F9
B13	=B7/B$10	B13:F14
E6	=SUMPRODUCT(B2:D2,B6:D6)	—
F6	=SUMPRODUCT(B3:D3,B6:D6)	—
B20	=SUMPRODUCT(B17:F18,B13:F14)	—

The target (or RHS) values for the goal constraints are listed in cells B10 through F10.

In order to implement the objective function, we first implemented formulas to convert the values of the deviational variables into percent format by dividing each deviational variable represented in cells B7 through F8 by the appropriate target value. This is done as follows:

Formula for cell B13:   =B7/B$10
(copy to B13 through F14)

Next, weights for each of the deviational variables are entered in cells B17 through F18. Because solving a GP problem is an iterative process in which you will probably need to change the weights for the objective, it is best to place the weights in a separate location on the spreadsheet.

Finally, cell B20 contains the following formula, which implements the objective function for the problem:

Formula for cell B20:   =SUMPRODUCT(B17:F18,B13:F14)

SOLVING THE MODEL

The model can be solved using the Solver parameters and options shown in Figure 7.2. The solution obtained using these settings is shown in Figure 7.3.

Figure 7.2: Solver parameters and options for the GP model

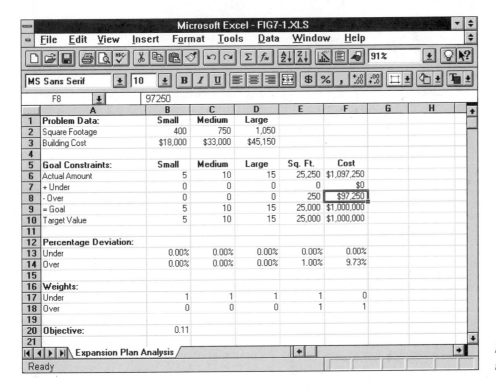

Figure 7.3: First solution to the GP model

ANALYZING THE SOLUTION

As shown in Figure 7.3, this solution includes exactly 5 small, 10 medium, and 15 large rooms in the expansion. Thus, there is no deviation at all from the target values for the first three goals, which would please the decision maker. However, considering the fourth and fifth goals, the current solution overachieves the targeted square footage level by 250 square feet (or 1%) and is over the building cost goal by $97,250 (or 9.73%).

REVISING THE MODEL

Although the decision maker might not mind being 1% over the square footage goal, exceeding the building cost goal by almost $100,000 most likely would be a concern. The decision maker might want to find another solution that comes closer to achieving the building cost goal. This can be done by adjusting the weights in the problem so that a larger penalty is assigned to overachieving the building cost goal. That is, we can increase the value in cell F18 representing w_5^+. Again, there is no way to tell exactly how much larger this value should be. As a rule-of-thumb, we might change its value by one order of magnitude, or from 1 to 10. If we make this change in the spreadsheet and re-solve the problem, we obtain the solution shown in Figure 7.4.

Figure 7.4: Second solution to the GP model

In Figure 7.4, notice that increasing the penalty for overachieving the building cost goal from 1 to 10 reduced the overachievement of this goal from $97,250 to $6,950. We are now within 1% of the target value for the building cost goal. However, in order to obtain this improved level of achievement on the building cost goal, we had to give up two large conference rooms, resulting in a 13.33% underachievement for this goal. If the decision maker considers this unacceptable, we can increase the penalty on this deviational variable from 1 to 10 and re-solve the problem. Figure 7.5 shows the resulting solution.

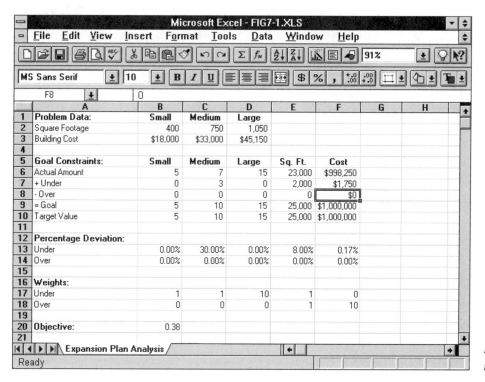

Figure 7.5: Third solution to the GP model

TRADE-OFFS: THE NATURE OF GP

In Figure 7.5, the target number of large conference rooms is met exactly, but the desired number of medium rooms is now underachieved by 3. Depending on the preferences of the decision maker, we could continue to fine-tune the weights in the problem until we reach a solution that is most satisfactory to the decision maker. The nature of GP involves making trade-offs among the various goals until a solution is found that gives the decision maker the greatest level of satisfaction. Thus, unlike the other applications of LP presented earlier, the use of LP in GP does not indicate immediately the best possible solution to the problem (unless the decision maker initially specifies an appropriately weighted objective function). Rather, it provides a method by which a decision maker can explore a variety of possible solutions and try to find the solution that comes closest to satisfying the goals under consideration.

SUMMARY OF GP

Figure 7.6 provides a summary of the steps involved in solving a GP problem.

Some additional points should be made before we leave the topic of GP. First, it is important to note that different GP solutions cannot be compared simply on the basis of their optimal objective function values. The user changes the weights in the objective functions from iteration to iteration; therefore, comparing their values is not appropriate because they measure different things. The objective function in a GP problem serves more of a mechanical purpose, allowing us to explore possible solutions. Thus, we should compare the solutions that are produced—not the objective function values.

SUMMARY OF GOAL PROGRAMMING

1. Identify the decision variables in the problem.

2. Identify any hard constraints in the problem and formulate them in the usual way.

3. State the goals of the problem along with their target values.

4. Create constraints using the decision variables that would achieve the goals exactly.

5. Transform the above constraints into goal constraints by including deviational variables.

6. Determine which deviational variables represent undesirable deviations from the goals.

7. Formulate an objective that penalizes the undesirable deviations.

8. Identify appropriate weights for the objective.

9. Solve the problem.

10. Inspect the solution to the problem. If the solution is unacceptable, return to step 8 and revise the weights as needed.

Figure 7.6: *Summary of the steps involved in formulating and solving a GP problem*

Second, in some GP problems, one or more goals might be viewed as being infinitely more important than the other goals. In this case, we could assign arbitrarily large weights to deviations from these goals to ensure that undesirable deviations from them never occur. This is sometimes referred to as *preemptive* GP because certain goals preempt others in order of importance. If the target values for these goals can be achieved, the use of preemptive weights effectively makes these goals hard constraints that should never be violated.

Third, we can place hard constraints on the amount by which we can deviate from a goal. For example, suppose that the owner of the hotel in our example problem wants to eliminate from consideration any solution that exceeds the target building cost by more than $50,000. We could easily build this requirement into our model with the hard constraint:

$$d_5^+ \leq 50,000$$

Fourth, the concept of deviational variables is not limited to GP. These types of variables can be used in other problems that are quite different from GP problems. So, understanding deviational variables can prove useful in other types of mathematical programming situations.

Finally, another type of objective function, called the **MINIMAX objective**, is sometimes helpful in GP when you want to minimize the maximum deviation from any goal. To implement the MINIMAX objective, we must create one additional constraint for each deviational variable as follows, where Q is the MINIMAX variable:

$$d_1^- \leq Q$$

$$d_1^+ \leq Q$$

$$d_2^- \leq Q$$

and so on . . .

The objective is to minimize the value of Q, stated as:

MIN: Q

Because the variable Q must be greater than or equal to the values of all the deviational variables, and because we are trying to minimize it, Q will always be set equal to the maximum value of the deviational variables. At the same time, this objective function tries to find a solution where the maximum deviational variable (and the value of Q) is as small as possible. Therefore, this technique allows us to minimize the maximum deviation from all the goals. As we'll see shortly, this type of objective is especially valuable if a GP problem involves hard constraints.

MULTIPLE OBJECTIVE OPTIMIZATION

We now consider how to solve LP problems involving multiple objective functions. These problems are called **multiple objective linear programming** (MOLP) problems.

Most of the LP and ILP problems discussed in previous chapters involved one objective function. These objective functions typically sought to maximize profits or minimize costs. However, another objective function could be formulated for most of these problems. For example, if a production process creates a toxic pollutant that is dangerous to the environment, a company might want to minimize this toxic by-product. However, this objective is likely to be in direct conflict with the company's other objective of maximizing profits. Problems with multiple objectives require analyzing the trade-offs among the different objectives.

MOLP problems can be viewed as special types of GP problems where, as part of solving the problem, we must also determine target values for each goal or objective. Analyzing these problems effectively also requires that we use the MINIMAX objective described earlier.

AN EXAMPLE

The following example illustrates the issues involved in an MOLP problem. Although this example involves only two objectives, the concepts and techniques presented apply to problems involving more than two objectives.

Laura Kelley recently completed her MBA and was hired by a major bank to help manage the bank's investments. Her first assignment is to invest $100,000 of the bank's deposits in two stock mutual funds named Medallion and Miser. The bank assigns risk ratings on a scale from 0 to 1 to all investments it considers. A rating of 0 indicates the lowest possible risk and a rating of 1 indicates the highest possible risk. The Medallion fund was assigned a risk rating of 0.7 on this scale and the Miser fund was assigned a risk rating of 0.4. The expected rate of return on investments in the Medallion fund is 18% for the coming year and the Miser's expected return is 13%. Laura must invest at least $25,000 in each of the two mutual funds and can invest the remaining $50,000 in whatever way she thinks is most appropriate. Laura has identified two possible objectives for this problem. She could choose to invest the money in a way that maximizes the expected return. Or, she could invest the money in a way that minimizes risk.

DEFINING THE DECISION VARIABLES

In this problem, Laura has to determine the amount of money to invest in each of the two mutual funds. Thus, we can define the decision variables as:

X_1 = amount of money to invest in the Medallion fund

X_2 = amount of money to invest in the Miser fund

DEFINING THE OBJECTIVES

This problem is different from the other types of LP problems we have considered in that it involves two objectives. Laura could formulate an objective to maximize the weighted average expected return. In words, the weighted average expected return is calculated as:

$$\binom{\text{Weighted average}}{\text{expected return}} = .18 \times \binom{\text{proportion of money invested}}{\text{in the Medallion fund}} + .13 \times \binom{\text{proportion of money invested}}{\text{in the Miser fund}}$$

The weighted average expected return is represented mathematically in an objective function as:

$$\text{MAX:} \quad \frac{.18X_1}{100,000} + \frac{.13X_2}{100,000} \quad \} \text{ weighted average return}$$

Alternatively, Laura might want to minimize the weighted average risk of her investments. Thus, the following objective function also can apply to this problem:

$$\text{MIN:} \quad \frac{.7X_1}{100,000} + \frac{.4X_2}{100,000} \quad \} \text{ weighted average risk}$$

In an LP model, Laura would be forced to decide which of these two objectives is most important or most appropriate and use that single objective in the model. However, in an MOLP model she can consider how both of these objectives (and any others she might want to formulate) can be incorporated into the analysis and solution of the problem.

DEFINING THE CONSTRAINTS

The constraints for this problem are formulated in the same way as for any LP problem. The following three constraints ensure that the entire $100,000 is invested in the two funds and that at least $25,000 is placed in each fund:

$X_1 + X_2 = 100,000$ } total investment

$X_1 \geq 25,000$ } minimum investment for the Medallion fund

$X_2 \geq 25,000$ } minimum investment for the Miser fund

IMPLEMENTING THE MODEL

To summarize, the MOLP formulation of this problem is represented as:

$$\text{MAX:} \quad \frac{.18X_1}{100,000} + \frac{.13X_2}{100,000} \quad \} \text{ weighted average return}$$

$$\text{MIN:} \quad \frac{.7X_1}{100,000} + \frac{.4X_2}{100,000} \quad \} \text{ weighted average risk}$$

$$\text{Subject to:} \quad X_1 + X_2 = 100,000 \quad \} \text{ total investment}$$

$$X_1 \geq 25,000 \quad \} \text{ minimum investment for the Medallion fund}$$

$$X_2 \geq 25,000 \quad \} \text{ minimum investment for the Miser fund}$$

This model is implemented in a spreadsheet in the usual way except that two cells represent the two objective functions. One approach to implementing this model is shown in Figure 7.7 (and in the file FIG7-7.XLS on your data disk).

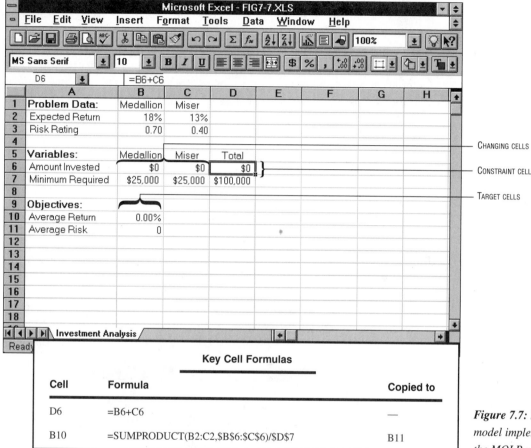

Key Cell Formulas		
Cell	Formula	Copied to
D6	=B6+C6	—
B10	=SUMPRODUCT(B2:C2,$B$6:$C$6)/$D$7	B11

Figure 7.7: Spreadsheet model implementation of the MOLP problem

In Figure 7.7, the first section of the spreadsheet displays the basic problem data. Cells B6 and C6 represent the decision variables X_1 and X_2, respectively. The lower bounds of $25,000 for these cells are listed in cells B7 and C7. The formula in cell D6 sums the values in B6 and C6 and will be constrained to equal the value in cell D7 ($100,000) when the problem is described to Solver. Finally, the two objectives for the problem are entered in cells B10 and B11 as:

Formula for cell B10:　　=SUMPRODUCT(B2:C2,$B$6:$C$6)/$D$7
(copy to B11)

DETERMINING TARGET VALUES FOR THE OBJECTIVES

An LP problem can have only one objective function, so how can we include two objectives in our spreadsheet model? If these objectives had target values, we could treat them the same way as the goals in our example earlier in this chapter. That is, the objectives in this problem can be stated as the following goals if we have appropriate values for t_1 and t_2:

Goal 1 : The weighted average expected return should be approximately t_1%.

Goal 2 : The weighted average level of risk should be approximately t_2.

This problem did not mention values for t_1 and t_2. However, because the first objective is to maximize the weighted average expected return, if we state this objective as a goal, a reasonable value for t_1 is the maximum possible weighted average expected return. Similarly, because the second objective is to minimize the weighted average level of risk, if we state this objective as a goal, a reasonable value for t_2 is the minimum possible weighted average risk. So, if we solve our model to find the solution that maximizes the first objective, the optimal value of this objective function would be a reasonable value to use as t_1 in the first goal. Similarly, if we solve the problem to find the solution that minimizes the second objective, the optimal value of this objective function would be a reasonable value to use as t_2 in the second goal. We could then view our MOLP problem in the format of a GP problem.

Figure 7.8 shows the Solver parameters and options required to determine the maximum weighted average expected return that could be realized in this problem. Note that this involves maximizing the value of cell B10. Figure 7.9 shows the optimal solution obtained by solving this LP problem. Notice that the best possible (maximum) weighted average return for this problem is 16.75% and this solution can be obtained by investing $75,000 in the Medallion fund and $25,000 in the Miser fund. Thus, a reasonable value for t_1 is 16.75%. It is impossible to obtain a solution to this problem with a weighted average expected return greater than this amount.

Figure 7.10 shows the Solver parameters and options required to determine the minimum weighted average risk that could be achieved in this problem. This involves minimizing the value of cell B11. Figure 7.11 shows the optimal solution obtained by solving this LP problem. Notice that the best possible (minimum) weighted average risk for this problem is 0.475 and this solution can be obtained

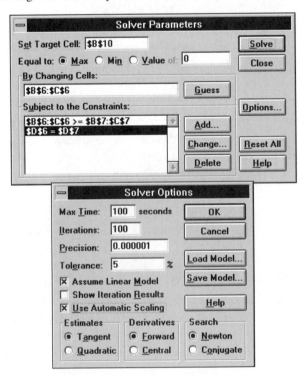

Figure 7.8: *Solver parameters and options to maximize expected returns*

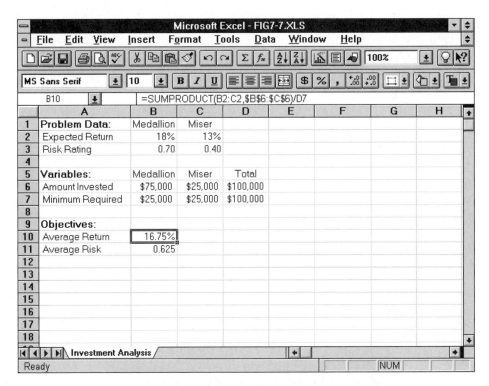

Figure 7.9: Optimal solution when maximizing expected return

Figure 7.10: Solver parameters and options to minimize risk

by investing $25,000 in the Medallion fund and $75,000 in the Miser fund. Thus, a reasonable value for t_2 is 0.475. It is impossible to obtain a solution to this problem with a weighted average risk level lower than this amount.

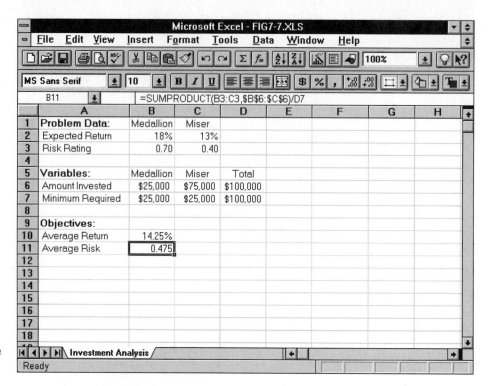

Figure 7.11: *Optimal solution when minimizing risk*

SUMMARIZING THE TARGET SOLUTIONS

Figure 7.12 indicates the location of the two solutions shown in Figures 7.9 and 7.11 in terms of the feasible region for this problem.

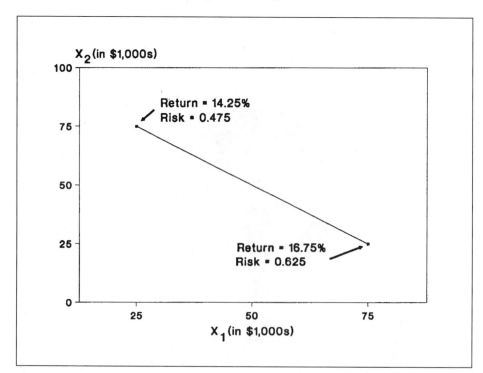

Figure 7.12: *Feasible region for the investment problem showing the solution that maximizes expected return versus the solution that minimizes risk*

Two important points should be observed here. First, this graph clearly shows that the two objectives in this problem conflict with one another. The solution with the highest expected return (16.75%) also has the highest risk level (0.625) and the solution with the lowest risk level (0.475) also has the lowest expected return (14.25%). This is not surprising, but does underscore the fact that this problem involves a trade-off between the two objectives. No single feasible point simultaneously optimizes both of the objective functions. In order to improve the value of one objective we must sacrifice the value of the other. This characteristic is common to most MOLP problems. Thus, the purpose of MOLP (and of GP) is to study the trade-offs among the objectives in order to find a solution that is the most desirable to the decision maker.

Second, the graph in Figure 7.12 shows only two corner points in the feasible region of this problem. Because we have already determined the levels of risk and return offered by the two solutions, if neither solution is acceptable to the decision maker, we will need to explore the *non-extreme* feasible solutions shown in Figure 7.12. As we'll see, this poses a tricky problem.

DETERMINING A GP OBJECTIVE

Now that we have target values for the two objectives in our problem, we can formulate a weighted GP objective to allow the decision maker to explore possible solutions. Earlier in this chapter we discussed several GP objectives and illustrated the use of an objective that minimized the weighted percentage deviation from the goals' target values. Let's consider how to formulate this same type of objective for the current problem.

We can restate the objectives of this problem as the goals:

Goal 1: The weighted average expected return should be approximately 16.75%.

Goal 2: The weighted average level of risk should be approximately 0.475.

The weighted average expected return can never exceed its target (optimum) value of 16.75%, so the percentage deviation from this goal is calculated as:

$$\frac{\text{target value} - \text{actual value}}{\text{target value}} = \frac{.1675 - \dfrac{(.18X_1 + .13X_2)}{100,000}}{.1675} = 1 - \frac{(.18X_1 + .13X_2)}{16,750}$$

Similarly, the weighted average risk level can never be less than its target (optimum) value of 0.475, so the percentage deviation from this goal is calculated as:

$$\frac{\text{actual value} - \text{target value}}{\text{target value}} = \frac{\dfrac{(.7X_1 + .4X_2)}{100,000} - 0.475}{0.475} = \frac{(.7X_1 + .4X_2)}{47,500} - 1$$

Both these percentage deviation calculations are linear functions of the decision variables. Thus, if we form an objective function as a weighted combination of these percentage deviation functions, we obtain the following linear objective function:

$$\text{MIN: } w_1 - \frac{w_1}{16,750}(.18X_1 + .13X_2) + \frac{w_2}{47,500}(.7X_1 + .4X_2) - w_2$$

Recall from chapter 2 that the optimal solution to an LP problem (that is, an optimization problem with linear constraints and a linear objective function) *always* occurs at an extreme point of the feasible region. So, if we use the preceding objective to solve our example problem as a GP problem we will *always* obtain one of the two extreme points shown in Figure 7.12 as the optimal solution to the problem, regardless of the weights assigned to w_1 and w_2. Thus, to explore the non-extreme feasible solutions to this GP problem (or any other GP problem with hard constraints), we need to use a different type of objective function.

THE MINIMAX OBJECTIVE

As it turns out, the MINIMAX objective, described earlier, can be used to explore the points on the edge of the feasible region—in addition to corner points. To illustrate this, let's attempt to minimize the maximum weighted percentage deviation from the target values for the goals in our example problem using the objective:

$$\text{MIN: the maximum of } (w_1 - \frac{w_1}{16,750}(.18X_1 + .13X_2)) \text{ and } (\frac{w_2}{47,500}(.7X_1 + .4X_2) - w_2)$$

We'll implement this objective by establishing a MINIMAX variable Q that we'll minimize with the objective:

$$\text{MIN: } Q$$

with the addition of the following constraints:

$$w_1 - \frac{w_1}{16,750}(.18X_1 + .13X_2) \leq Q$$

$$\frac{w_2}{47,500}(.7X_1 + .4X_2) - w_2 \leq Q$$

The first constraint indicates that the weighted percentage deviation from the ideal target expected return must be less than or equal to Q. The second constraint indicates that the weighted percentage deviation from the ideal target level of risk must also be less than or equal to Q. Thus, as we minimize Q, we are, in effect, also minimizing the percentage deviations from the targets for the goals. In this way, the maximum deviation from either goal is minimized—or we have MINImized the MAXimum deviation (hence the term MINIMAX).

IMPLEMENTING THE REVISED MODEL

The revised GP model of our investment problem is summarized as:

$$\text{MIN: } Q$$

Subject to:
$$X_1 + X_2 = 100,000 \qquad \} \text{ total investment}$$

$$X_1 \geq 25,000 \qquad \} \text{ minimum investment for the Medallion fund}$$

$$X_2 \geq 25,000 \qquad \} \text{ minimum investment for the Miser fund}$$

$$w_1 - \frac{w_1}{16,750}(.18X_1 + .13X_2) \leq Q \qquad \} \text{ goal 1 MINIMAX constraint}$$

$$\frac{w_2}{47,500}(.7X_1 + .4X_2) - w_2 \leq Q \qquad \} \text{ goal 2 MINIMAX constraint}$$

$$w_1, w_2 \text{ are positive constants}$$

The spreadsheet shown earlier in Figure 7.7 can be modified easily to implement this new model. The revised spreadsheet is shown in Figure 7.13 (and in the file FIG7-13.XLS on your data disk).

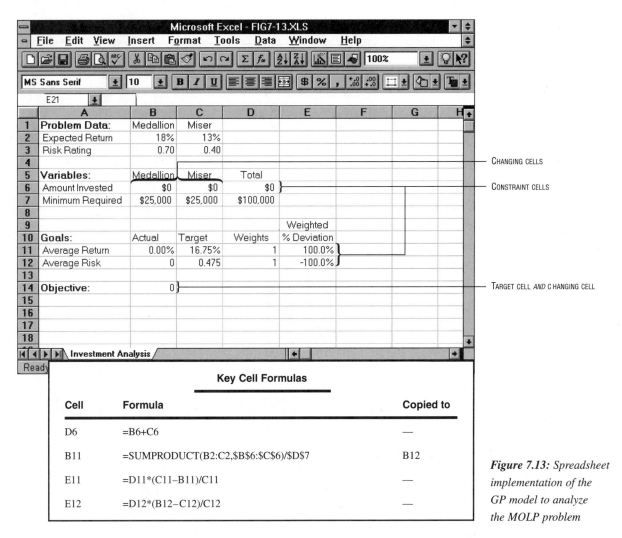

Figure 7.13: Spreadsheet implementation of the GP model to analyze the MOLP problem

In Figure 7.13, cells C11 and C12 contain the target values for the goals. Arbitrary weights for the deviations from the goals were entered in cells D11 and D12. Cells E11 and E12 contain the following formulas, which calculate the weighted percentage deviation from the goals:

Formula for cell E11: $= D11*(C11-B11)/C11$

Formula for cell E12: $= D12*(B12-C12)/C12$

The formulas in cells E11 and E12 are equivalent to the LHS formulas of the goal 1 and goal 2 MINIMAX constraints in our model. Finally, cell B14 is reserved to represent the MINIMAX variable Q.

SOLVING THE MODEL

The Solver parameters and options shown in Figure 7.14 were used to solve the model shown in Figure 7.13. The solution obtained for this model is shown in Figure 7.15.

Notice that the solution shown in Figure 7.15 ($X_1 = 41,407$, $X_2 = 58,953$) *does not* occur at an extreme point of the feasible region shown earlier in Figure 7.12. Also notice that this solution is within approximately 10% of achieving the target solution for each goal. Thus, the decision maker in this problem might find this solution more

Figure 7.14: Solver parameters and options for the GP implementation of the MOLP problem

Figure 7.15: Solution to the MOLP problem obtained through GP

appealing than the other solutions occurring at the extreme points of the feasible region. Using other weights would produce different solutions. Figure 7.16 shows a number of representative solutions indicated on the original feasible region for this problem.

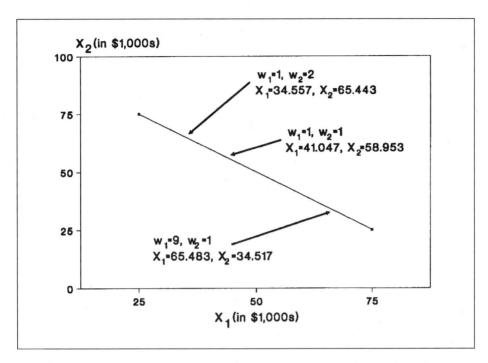

Figure 7.16: Graph of other solutions obtained using the MINIMAX objective

Figure 7.16 illustrates that as the relative weight on the first goal (w_1) increases, the solution is driven closer to achieving the target value for this goal (which occurs at the point X_1 = 75000, X_2 = 25000, as shown in Figure 7.12). As the relative weight on the second goal (w_2) increases, the solution is driven closer to achieving the target value for this goal (which occurs at the point X_1 = 25000, X_2 = 75000). Thus, with the MINIMAX objective the decision maker can explore all the points along this edge of the feasible region.

SUMMARY OF MOLP

Figure 7.17 provides a summary of the steps involved in solving an MOLP problem. Although the MOLP example in this chapter was somewhat simple, the same basic process applies in virtually any MOLP problem, regardless of the number of objectives or the complexity of the problem.

One advantage of using the MINIMAX objective to analyze MOLP problems is that the solutions generated are always *Pareto optimal*. That is, given any solution generated using this approach we can be certain that no other feasible solution allows an increase in any objective without decreasing at least one other objective. (There are one or two exceptions to this statement, but they go beyond the scope of this text.)

Although the MINIMAX objective is helpful in the analysis of MOLPs, its usefulness is not limited to these problems. Like deviational variables, the MINIMAX technique can prove useful in other types of mathematical programming situations.

SUMMARY

This chapter presented two separate but closely related issues in optimization—GP and MOLP. GP provides a way of analyzing potential solutions to a decision problem that involves soft constraints. Soft constraints can be stated as goals with target values. These goals can be translated into constraints through the use of

SUMMARY OF MULTIPLE OBJECTIVE OPTIMIZATION

1. Identify the decision variables in the problem.

2. Identify the objectives in the problem and formulate them in the usual way.

3. Identify the constraints in the problem and formulate them in the usual way.

4. Solve the problem once for each of the objectives identified in step 2 to determine the optimal value of each objective.

5. Restate the objectives as goals using the optimal objective values identified in step 4 as the target values.

6. For each goal, create a deviation function that measures the amount by which any given solution fails to meet the goal (either as an absolute or a percentage).

7. For each of the deviation functions identified in step 6, assign a weight to the deviation function and create a constraint that requires the value of the weighted deviation function to be less than the MINIMAX variable Q.

8. Solve the resulting problem with the objective of minimizing Q.

9. Inspect the solution to the problem. If the solution is unacceptable, adjust the weights in step 7 and return to step 8.

Figure 7.17: Summary of the steps involved in formulating and solving an MOLP problem

deviational variables, which measure the amount by which a given solution deviates from a particular goal. The objective in GP problems is to minimize some weighted function of the deviational variables. By adjusting the weights on the deviational variables, a variety of potential solutions can be analyzed.

MOLP provides a way to analyze LP problems involving multiple objectives that conflict with one another. Although an MOLP problem is somewhat different from a standard GP problem, the objectives can be restated as goals after identifying appropriate target values for the objectives. The MINIMAX objective is helpful in analyzing the possible solutions to an MOLP problem.

Solving a GP or MOLP problem is not as simple as solving a single LP problem. Rather, a sequence of problems must be solved to allow the decision maker to analyze the trade-offs among the various goals and objectives at different possible solutions. Thus, both of these procedures are highly iterative and interactive.

REFERENCES

Gass, S. "A Process for Determining Priorities and Weights for Large-Scale Linear Goal Programs." *Journal of the Operational Research Society*, vol. 37, August 1986.

Ignizio, J. "A Review of Goal Programming: A Tool for Multiobjective Analysis." *Journal of the Operational Research Society*, vol. 29, no. 11, 1978.

Steuer, R. *Multiple Criteria Optimization: Theory, Computation, and Application.* New York: Wiley, 1986.

Taylor, B. and A. Keown. "A Goal Programming Application of Capital Project Selection in the Production Area." *AIIE Transactions*, vol. 10, no. 1, 1978.

Truck Transport Corporation Controls Costs and Disruptions While Relocating a Terminal

Source: Schneiderjans, Marc J., N. K. Kwak and Mark C. Helmer, "An Application of Goal Programming to Resolve a Site Location Problem," *Interfaces*, vol. 12, no. 3, June 1982, pages 65–70.

THE TRUCK TRANSPORT CORPORATION, having decided to move its East St. Louis terminal, knew that relationships with customers and suppliers (independent truckers) were critical factors for continued profitable operations. Therefore, evaluating five potential new sites, management considered driver and customer preferences as well as costs in making its final selection.

At Truck Transport Corporation, the traditional approach to evaluating a new site is to include the candidate site in a transportation LP model with the four other terminals and 12 major customers, and find the solution that minimizes total transportation costs. This minimum cost solution is then compared with those for the other candidates to choose the most efficient site. An assignment problem is solved to assign independent truckers to terminals to minimize travel costs from the truckers' homes.

Some of the drivers, however, have strong preferences not to be assigned to particular terminals, usually on the basis of personal relationships with terminal managers. Some customers also have similar preferences. In a competitive market, failure to consider these preferences might cause the drivers or customers to do business elsewhere.

The linear goal programming model used to evaluate the sites combined the transportation problem and the trucker assignment problem. The constraints defined the following deviational variables, in declining order of priority: shortages in number of trips to major customers, shortages in number of trips assigned to each driver, number of driver preferences violated, number of customer preferences violated, increase in transportation costs from drivers' homes, and increase in transportation costs to the customers.

The model was validated by evaluating the East St. Louis site and comparing results to historical costs. The site ultimately selected fully satisfied the requirements for number of shipments and preferences. Total transportation costs for all drivers were projected to increase only $3,200, and customer transportation costs were projected to increase $1,400. The East St. Louis terminal was moved with no changes in the usual patterns of driver turnover or business with customers, and no complaints from drivers about decreased profitability because of the new site.

Questions and Problems

1. What is the difference between an objective function and a goal?

2. Is there an optimal solution to a GP or MOLP problem? Explain.

3. Suppose that the first goal in a GP problem is to make $2X_1 + 5X_2$ approximately equal to 25.

    a. Using the deviational variables d_1^- and d_1^+, what constraint can be used to express this goal?

    b. If we obtain a solution where $X_1 = 4$ and $X_2 = 3$, what values do the deviational variables assume?

    c. Consider a solution where $X_1 = 4$, $X_2 = 3$, $d_1^- = 6$, and $d_1^+ = 4$. Can this solution ever be optimal? Why or why not?

4. Consider the following MOLP:

    $$MAX: \quad 4X_1 + 2X_2$$
    $$MIN: \quad X_1 + 3X_2$$
    $$Subject\ to: \quad 2X_1 + X_2 \le 18$$
    $$X_1 + 4X_2 \le 12$$
    $$X_1 + X_2 \ge 4$$
    $$X_1, X_2 \ge 0$$

    a. Graph the feasible region for this problem.

    b. Calculate the value of each objective at each extreme point.

    c. What feasible points in this problem are Pareto optimal?

5. It has been suggested that one way to solve MOLP problems is to create a composite objective function as a linear combination of all the objectives in the problem. For example, in the previous problem we might weight the first objective by 0.75 and the second by 0.25 to obtain the composite objective, MAX: $3.25X_1 + 2.25X_2$. We then use this as the objective in an LP model to generate possible solutions. What problem, if any, do you see with this approach?

6. The owner of the Weiner-Meyer meat processing plant wants to determine the best blend of meats to use in the next production run of hamburgers. Three sources of meat can be used. The following table summarizes relevant characteristics of these meats:

	Meat 1	Meat 2	Meat 3
Cost per pound	$0.75	$0.87	$0.98
% Fat	15%	10%	5%
% Protein	70%	75%	80%
% Water	12%	10%	8%
% Filler	3%	5%	7%

A local elementary school has ordered 500 pounds of meat for $1.10 per pound. The only requirement is that the meat consist of at least 75% protein. Ordinarily, the owner would produce the blend of meats that achieved this objective in the least costly manner. However, with the concern of too much fat in school lunches, the owner also wants to produce a blend that minimizes the fat content of the meat produced.

a. Formulate an MOLP for this problem.

b. Implement your formulation in a spreadsheet and individually optimize the two objectives under consideration.

c. How much profit must be forfeited in order to fill this order using the mix that minimizes the fat content?

d. Solve this problem with the objective of minimizing the maximum percentage deviation from the target values of the goals. What solution do you obtain?

e. Assume the owner considers minimizing the fat content twice as important as maximizing profit. What solution does this imply?

7. A new Italian restaurant called the Olive Grove is opening in a number of locations in the Memphis area. The marketing manager for these stores has a budget of $150,000 to use in advertising and promotions for the new stores. The manager can run magazine ads at a cost of $2,000 each that result in 250,000 exposures each. TV ads result in approximately 1,200,000 exposures each, but cost $12,000 each. The manager wants to run at least 5 TV ads and 10 magazine ads, while maximizing the number of exposures generated by the advertising campaign. But the manager also wants to spend no more than $120,000 on magazine and TV advertising so that the remaining $30,000 could be used for other promotional purposes. However, the manager would spend more than $120,000 on advertising if it resulted in a substantial increase in advertising coverage.

a. Formulate a GP model for this problem assuming the marketing manager has the following goals:

Goal 1: Exposures should be maximized.

Goal 2: No more than $120,000 should be spent on advertising.

(Note that you will have to determine an appropriate target value for the first goal.) Assume the marketing manager wants to minimize the maximum percentage deviation from either goal.

b. Implement your model in a spreadsheet and solve it.

c. What is the solution you obtain?

d. What changes do you make to your model if the manager wants to spend less on advertising than your solution suggests?

8. The Chick'n-Pick'n fast-food chain is considering how to expand its operations. Three types of retail outlets are possible: a lunch counter operation designed for office buildings in downtown areas, an eat-in operation designed for shopping malls, and a standalone building with drive-through and sit-down facilities. The following table summarizes the number of jobs, startup costs, and annual returns associated with each type of operation:

	Lunch Counter	Mall	Standalone
Jobs	9	17	35
Costs	$150,000	$275,000	$450,000
Returns	$85,000	$125,000	$175,000

The company has $2,000,000 available to pay startup costs for new operations in the coming year. Additionally, there are 5 possible sites for lunch counter operations, 7 possible mall locations, and 3 possible standalone locations. The company wants to plan its expansion in a way that maximizes annual returns *and* the number of jobs created.

a. Formulate an MOLP for this problem.

b. Determine the best possible value for each objective in the problem.

c. Implement your model in a spreadsheet and solve it to determine the solution that minimizes the maximum percentage deviation from the optimal objective function values. What solution do you obtain?

d. Suppose management considers maximizing returns three times as important as maximizing the number of jobs created. What solution does this suggest?

9. A private foundation has offered $3 million to allocate to cities to help fund programs that aid the homeless. Grant proposals were received from cities A, B, and C seeking assistance of $750,000, $1.2 million, and $2.5 million, respectively. In the grant proposals, cities were requested to quantify the number of assistance units that would be provided using the funds (an assistance unit is a night on a bed in a shelter or a free meal). Cities A, B, and C reported they could provide 485,000, 850,000, and 1.5 million assistance units, respectively, with the funds requested during the coming year. The directors of the foundation have two objectives. They want to maximize the number of assistance units obtained with the $3 million. However, they also want to help each of the cities by funding as much of their individual requests as possible (this might be done by maximizing the minimum percentage of funding received by any city).

a. Formulate an MOLP for this problem.

b. Determine the best possible value for each objective in the problem.

c. Implement your model in a spreadsheet and solve it to determine the solution that minimizes the maximum percentage deviation from the optimal objective function values. What solution do you obtain?

10. The marketing manager for Glissen Paint is working on the weekly sales and marketing plan for the firm's industrial and contractor sales staff. Glissen's sales representatives contact two types of customers: existing customers and new customers. Each contact with an existing customer normally takes 3 hours of the salesperson's time (including travel time) and results in an average sale of $425. Contacts with new customers generally take a bit longer, on average 4 hours, and result in an average sale of $350. The company's

salespeople are required to work 40 hours a week, but often work more to achieve their sales quotas (on which their bonuses are based). The company has a policy limiting the number of hours a salesperson can work to 50 hours per week. The sales manager wants to set customer contact quotas for the salespeople that will achieve the following goals (listed in order of importance):

Goal 1: Each salesperson should achieve an average weekly sales level of $6,000.

Goal 2: Each salesperson should contact at least 10 existing customers per week.

Goal 3: Each salesperson should contact at least 5 new customers per week.

Goal 4: Each salesperson should limit overtime to no more than 5 hours per week.

a. Formulate this problem as a GP with an objective of minimizing the sum of the weighted undesirable percentage deviation from the goals.

b. Implement your model in a spreadsheet and solve it assuming equal weights on each goal. What solution do you obtain?

11. A major city in the northeast wants to establish a central transportation station from which visitors can ride busses to 4 historic landmarks. The city is arranged in a grid, or block, structure with equally spaced streets running north and south and equally spaced avenues running east and west. The coordinates of any corner of any block in the city can be identified by the street and avenue numbers intersecting at that particular corner. The following table gives the coordinates for the 4 historic landmarks:

Landmark	Street	Avenue
1	7	3
2	3	1
3	1	6
4	6	9

The transportation planners want to build the transportation station at the location in the city that minimizes the total travel distance (measured rectangularly) to each landmark. For example, if they built the station at 6th Street and 2nd Avenue, the total distance to each landmark will be:

Landmark	Distance
1	$|7 - 6| + |3 - 2| = 1 + 1 = 2$
2	$|3 - 6| + |1 - 2| = 3 + 1 = 4$
3	$|1 - 6| + |6 - 2| = 5 + 4 = 9$
4	$|6 - 6| + |9 - 2| = 0 + 7 = 7$

Total Distance = 22

a. Plot the locations of the various historical landmarks on a graph where the X-axis represents avenue numbers (starting at 0) and the Y-axis represents street numbers (starting at 0).

b. Formulate an LP model to determine the corner at which the central transportation station should be located. (Hint: Let the decision variables represent the street location (X_1) and avenue location (X_2) of the station and use deviational variables to measure the absolute street distance and absolute avenue distance from each landmark to X_1 and X_2. Minimize the sum of the deviational variables.)

12. A car dealer specializing in late model used cars collected the following data on the selling price and mileage of five cars of the same make and model year at an auto auction:

Mileage	Price
43,890	$12,500
35,750	$13,350
27,300	$14,600
15,500	$15,750
8,900	$17,500

Because there seems to be a strong relationship between mileage and price, the dealer wants to use this information to predict this type of car's market value on the basis of its mileage. The dealer thinks that the car's selling price can be predicted as:

Estimated price = A+B*mileage

A and B represent numeric constants (which might be positive or negative). Using the data collected at last week's auction, the dealer wants to determine appropriate values for A and B that minimize the following quantity:

$$\text{MIN}: |A+B*43890-12500|+|A+B*35750-13350|+|A+B*27300-14600|$$
$$+|A+B*15500-15750|+|A+B*8900-17500|$$

Notice that this objective seeks to find values of A and B that minimize the sum of the absolute value of the deviations between the actual prices of the cars and the estimated prices.

a. Create an LP model using deviational variables whose solution provides the best values for A and B using the stated criteria. That is, what values of A and B minimize the sum of the absolute deviations between the actual and estimated selling prices?

b. Implement your model in a spreadsheet and solve it.

c. Using the values of A and B determined by your solution, what should the estimated selling price be for each car?

13. Refer to question 12; suppose that the car dealer wanted to find values for A and B that minimized the maximum absolute deviation between the actual and estimated selling price for each car. What values of A and B achieve this objective?

14. A job in a machine shop must undergo five operations—A, B, C, D, and E. Each operation can be performed on either of two machines. The following table summarizes the time required for each machine to perform each operation:

	A	B	C	D	E
Machine 1	7	8	4	4	9
Machine 2	5	3	9	6	8

Formulate a model that can be solved to determine the job routing that minimizes the maximum amount of time used on either machine. That is, if t_i is the total time used on machine i, find the solution that minimizes the maximum of t_1 and t_2.

Nonlinear Programming

UP TO THIS POINT in our study of optimization, we have considered only mathematical programming models in which the objective function and constraints are *linear* functions of the decision variables. In many decision problems, the use of such linear functions is appropriate. Other types of optimization problems involve objective functions and constraints that *cannot* be modeled adequately using linear functions of the decision variables. These types of problems are called **nonlinear programming** (NLP) problems.

Formulating an NLP problem is virtually the same as formulating an LP problem. In each case you must identify the appropriate decision variables and formulate an appropriate objective function and constraints using these variables. As you'll see, the process of implementing and solving NLP problems in a spreadsheet is also similar to that for LP problems. However, the mechanics (that is, mathematical procedures) involved in solving NLP problems are very different. Although optimization software such as Solver makes this difference somewhat transparent to the user of such systems, it is important to understand these differences so you can understand the difficulties you might encounter when solving an NLP problem. This chapter discusses some of the unique features and challenges involved in solving NLP problems, and presents several examples of managerial decision-making problems that can be modeled as NLP problems.

THE NATURE OF NLP PROBLEMS

The main difference between an LP and NLP problem is that NLPs can have a nonlinear objective function and/or one or more nonlinear constraints. To understand the differences and difficulties nonlinearities introduce to an optimization problem, consider the various hypothetical NLP problems shown in Figure 8.1.

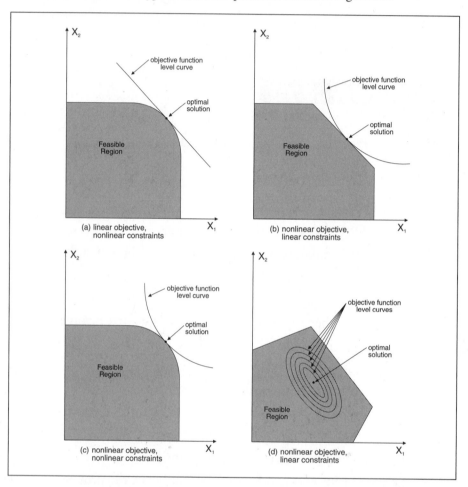

Figure 8.1: Examples of NLP problems with optimal solutions not *at a corner point of the feasible region*

The first graph in Figure 8.1, labeled (a), illustrates a problem with a linear objective function and a *nonlinear* feasible region. Note that the boundary lines of the feasible region for this problem are not all straight lines. At least one of the constraints in this problem must be nonlinear to cause the curve in the boundary line of the feasible region. This curve causes the unique optimal solution to this problem to occur at a solution that is not a corner point of the feasible region.

The second graph in Figure 8.1, labeled (b), shows a problem with a *nonlinear* objective function and a linear constraint set. As indicated in this graph, if an NLP problem has a nonlinear objective function, the level curves associated with the objective are also nonlinear. So from this graph we observe that a nonlinear objective can cause the optimal solution to the NLP problem to occur at a solution that is not a corner point of the feasible region—even if all the constraints are linear.

The third graph in Figure 8.1, labeled (c), shows a problem with a *nonlinear* objective and a *nonlinear* constraint set. Here again, we see that the optimal solution to this NLP problem occurs at a solution that is not a corner point of the feasible region.

Finally, the fourth graph in Figure 8.1, labeled (d), shows another problem with a *nonlinear* objective and a *linear* constraint set. The optimal solution to this problem occurs at a point in the interior of the feasible region.

These graphs illustrate the major difference between LP and NLP problems—an optimal solution to an LP problem always occurs at a corner point of its feasible region, but this is not true of NLP problems. The optimal solution to some NLP problems might not occur on the boundary of the feasible region at all, but at some point in the interior of the feasible region. Therefore, the strategy of searching the corner points of the feasible region employed by the simplex method to solve LP problems will not work with NLP problems. We need another strategy to solve NLP problems.

A SOLUTION STRATEGY FOR NLP PROBLEMS

The solution strategy most often used to solve NLP problems is called the **best feasible gradient search** (BFGS) algorithm. The mathematics involved in this procedure are very complex and go beyond the scope and purpose of this text. However, the basic idea behind this algorithm is fairly simple.

The BFGS algorithm first attempts to find any feasible solution to the NLP problem. This initial feasible solution is called the **starting point**. The BFGS algorithm then attempts to move from the starting point in a direction through the feasible region that results in the most rapid improvement in the objective function value. Movement in this direction continues until a boundary of the feasible region is encountered or the objective function value no longer improves. This results in a new, and better, feasible solution to the problem. The BFGS algorithm next attempts to identify another feasible direction in which to move to obtain further improvements in the objective function value. If such a direction exists, the algorithm moves in that direction until it encounters a boundary line of the feasible region or the objective function no longer improves. Again, this results in a new, and better, feasible solution to the problem. This process continues until the algorithm reaches a point where there is no feasible direction in which to move that results in an improvement in the objective function. When no further possibility for improvement exists (or the potential for further improvement becomes arbitrarily small), the BFGS algorithm terminates.

Figure 8.2 shows a graphical example of the BFGS algorithm. In this graph, an initial feasible solution occurs at the origin (point A). The fastest improvement in the objective function valve occurs by moving from point A in the direction that is perpendicular to the level curves of the objective function. Feasible movement in this direction is possible from point A to point B where a boundary of the feasible region is encountered. From point B, moving along the edge of the feasible region to point C further improves the objective function value. At point C the boundary of the feasible region begins to curve; therefore, continued movement in the direction from point B to point C is no longer feasible. From point C, a new direction through the interior of the feasible region allows movement to point D. This process continues from point D until the solution becomes arbitrarily close (or converges) to point E—the optimal solution.

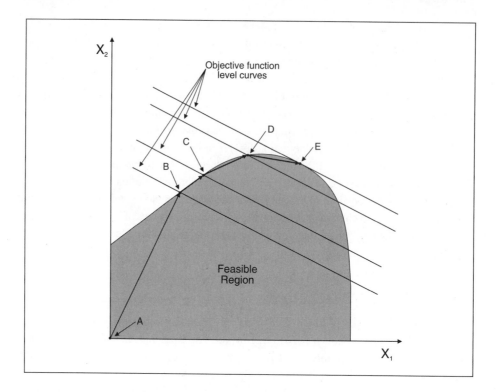

Figure 8.2: *The BFGS algorithm*

LOCAL VS. GLOBAL OPTIMAL SOLUTIONS

The BFGS algorithm terminates whenever it detects that no feasible direction exists in which it can move to produce a better objective function value (or when the amount of potential improvement becomes arbitrarily small). In such a situation, the current solution is a **local optimal solution**—a solution that is better than any other feasible solution in its immediate, or local, vicinity. However, a given local optimal solution might not be the best possible, or **global optimal**, solution to a problem. Another local optimal solution in some other area of the feasible region could be the best possible solution to the problem. This type of anomaly is illustrated in Figure 8.3.

If the BFGS algorithm starts at point A in Figure 8.3, it could move immediately to point B and then along the feasible direction from B to C. Because no feasible point in the vicinity of C produces a better objective function value, point C is a local optimal solution and the BFGS algorithm terminates at this point. However, this is clearly *not* the best possible solution to this problem. If the BFGS algorithm starts at point D in Figure 8.3, it could move immediately to point E, and then follow the feasible direction from E to F and from F to G. Note that point G is both a local and global optimal solution to this problem.

Figure 8.3 highlights two important points about NLP problems:

- The BFGS algorithm can terminate at a local optimal solution that might not be the global optimal solution to the problem.

- The local optimal solution at which the BFGS algorithm terminates depends on the initial starting point.

The possibility of terminating at a local optimal solution is an undesirable property of the BFGS algorithm—but we have encountered this type of difficulty before. In our study of integer programming, we noted that suboptimal solutions to ILPs might be acceptable if they are within some allowable tolerance of the global optimal solution. Unfortunately, with NLP problems we cannot determine easily how much worse a given local optimal solution is than the global optimal solution because there is no general way of obtaining bounds on the optimal objective function values for these problems. However, many NLP problems have a single local optimal solution that, by definition, must also be the global optimal solution. So in many problems, the BFGS algorithm will locate the global optimal solution. But, as a general rule, we will not know whether the solution obtained for an NLP problem is the global optimal solution. If this uncertainty presents a major concern, we can always try starting the BFGS algorithm from different points to determine if the problem has different local optimal solutions. This procedure often reveals the global optimal solution. (Two questions at the end of this chapter illustrate this process.)

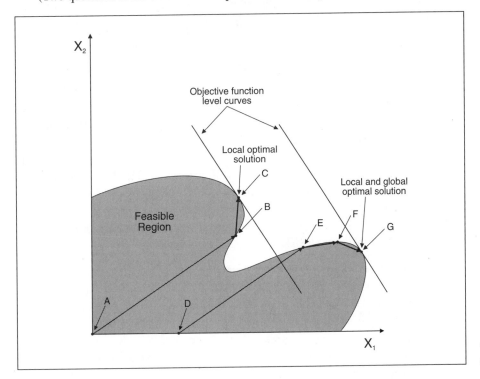

Figure 8.3: Local vs. global optimal solutions

A Note About "Optimal" Solutions

When Solver successfully solves an NLP problem, it displays the following message:

"Solver found a solution. All constraints and optimality conditions are satisfied."

Although this message might give us confidence in the solution obtained, it is important to remember that the solution might be a local optimal solution and is not necessarily the global optimal solution. If you think Solver might have stopped at a local optimal solution, it is advisable to re-solve the model using a different initial starting point.

> # A Note About Starting Points
>
> For reasons that go beyond the scope of this text, Solver sometimes has trouble solving an NLP problem if it starts at the null starting point, where all the decision variables are set equal to 0—even if this solution is feasible. Therefore, when solving an NLP problem, it is best to specify a non-null starting solution whenever possible.

We'll now consider several examples of NLP problems. These examples illustrate some of the differences between LP and NLP problems and provide insight into the broad range of problems that cannot be modeled adequately using LP.

PRICING PROBLEMS

One of the most fundamental problems faced by a business is to establish the prices for its products and services. In many of the LP examples considered earlier in this book, we assumed that the profit margins were known and the decision problem was to determine what mix of products to produce and sell in order to maximize profits. In many cases such an approach is appropriate. However, other situations exist where profit margin is a decision variable. That is, in some problems a decision maker must determine not only what to make but how much to charge for what is made. This type of problem is illustrated in the following extension of the Blue Ridge Hot Tubs example discussed in earlier chapters.

> Howie Jones, owner of Blue Ridge Hot Tubs, is facing a new problem. Although sales of the two hot tubs manufactured by his company (Aqua-Spas and Hydro-Luxes) have been brisk, the company is not earning the level of profits that Howie would like to achieve. Having established a reputation for high quality and reliability, Howie believes he can increase profits by increasing the prices of the hot tubs. However, he is concerned that a price increase might have a detrimental effect on demand, so Howie has engaged a marketing research firm to estimate the level of demand for Aqua-Spas and Hydro-Luxes at various prices. The marketing research firm used the technique of regression analysis (discussed in chapter 9) to develop a model of the relationship between the prices and demand for the hot tubs. After analyzing the situation, the marketing research firm concluded that a reasonable price range for the hot tubs would be between $1,000 and $1,500, and that within this range Howie could expect the demand for hot tubs in the next quarter to vary with price in approximately the following way:
>
> Demand for Aqua-Spas $= 300 - 0.175 * \text{price of Aqua-Spas}$
>
> Demand for Hydro-Luxes $= 325 - 0.15 * \text{price of Hydro-Luxes}$

Howie determined that the costs of manufacturing Aqua-Spas and Hydro-Luxes are $850 and $700 per unit, respectively. Ideally, he wants to produce enough hot tubs to meet demand exactly and carry no inventory. Each Aqua-Spa requires 1 pump, 9 hours of labor, and 12 feet of tubing; each Hydro-Lux requires 1 pump, 6 hours of labor, and 16 feet of tubing. Howie's suppliers have committed to supplying him with 200 pumps and 2800 feet of tubing. Also, 1,566 hours of labor are available for production. Howie wants to determine how much to charge for each type of hot tub and how many of each type to produce.

DEFINING THE DECISION VARIABLES

The basic decision to make in this problem is to determine the prices to charge for Aqua-Spas and Hydro-Luxes. We'll use the variables P_1 and P_2 to represent these prices. After we assign values to the price variables, we can determine the number of Aqua-Spas (X_1) and Hydro-Luxes (X_2) needed to meet the expected demand as:

$$X_1 = \text{Demand for Aqua-Spas} = 300 - 0.175 * P_1$$

$$X_2 = \text{Demand for Hydro-Luxes} = 325 - 0.15 * P_2$$

In this problem, X_1 and X_2 are *not* decision variables because no decision about their value is required after the values of P_1 and P_2 are set. We can determine the values of X_1 and X_2 directly from the values of P_1 and P_2.

DEFINING THE OBJECTIVE FUNCTION

The objective in this problem is to maximize profit. To calculate the total profit associated with any solution, we multiply the unit profits (unit price minus manufacturing cost) for each type of hot tub by the number of units sold, then sum the results. Therefore, the objective function for this problem is:

$$\text{MAX: } (P_1 - 850)X_1 + (P_2 - 700)X_2$$

The preceding objective looks like a standard objective for an LP problem. However, in this problem P_1 and P_2 are the decision variables, and the values of X_1 and X_2 depend on the values of P_1 and P_2, respectively. So this objective function is not a linear combination of the decision variables. This becomes apparent if we substitute the definitions of X_1 and X_2, given earlier, into the objective to obtain the algebraically equivalent objective function represented by:

$$\text{MAX: } (P_1 - 850)(300 - 0.175P_1) + (P_2 - 700)(325 - 0.15P_2)$$

After some simple algebra, this reduces to:

$$\text{MAX: } -0.175P_1^2 + 448.75P_1 - 0.15P_2^2 + 430P_2 - 482,500$$

The preceding objective function is not a simple linear combination of the decision variables P_1 and P_2 because these terms appear in squared form in this formula. Figure 8.4 illustrates this nonlinear relationship between total profit and P_1 and P_2. In each case, as the price of the hot tubs increases, profits also increase up to a maximum point and then begin to decrease as further price increases are more than offset by decreases in demand.

Figure 8.4: Nonlinear relationship between price of products and profits

DEFINING THE CONSTRAINTS

Because limited numbers of pumps, labor hours, and tubing are available, the following constraints are required for the problem:

$1X_1 + 1X_2 \leq 200$ } pump constraint

$9X_1 + 6X_2 \leq 1{,}566$ } labor constraint

$12X_1 + 16X_2 \leq 2{,}880$ } tubing constraint

where

$X_1 = 300 - 0.175P_1$

$X_2 = 325 - 0.150P_2$

and

$1{,}000 \leq P_1, P_2 \leq 1{,}500$

For convenience, the constraints are expressed in terms of the familiar symbols X_1 and X_2 corresponding to the number of Aqua-Spas and Hydro-Luxes produced. However, it is important to remember that X_1 and X_2 are directly dependent on the decision variables P_1 and P_2. Therefore, the equivalent representations of these constraints, expressed in terms of P_1 and P_2, are:

$300 - 0.175P_1 + 325 - 0.15P_2 \leq 200$ } pump constraint

$9(300 - 0.175P_1) + 6(325 - 0.15P_2) \leq 1{,}566$ } labor constraint

$12(300 - 0.175P_1) + 16(325 - 0.15P_2) \leq 2{,}880$ } tubing constraint

$1{,}000 \leq P_1, P_2 \leq 1{,}500$

The LHS of each constraint is a linear function of the decision variables. So, although this problem has a nonlinear objective function, it still has linear constraints.

Implementing the Model

In summary, the algebraic formulation of the model for this problem is represented by:

$$\text{MAX: } (P_1 - 850)X_1 + (P_2 - 700)X_2$$

Subject to:

$$1X_1 + 1X_2 \leq 200 \qquad \} \text{ pump constraint}$$
$$9X_1 + 6X_2 \leq 1,566 \qquad \} \text{ labor constraint}$$
$$12X_1 + 16X_2 \leq 2,880 \qquad \} \text{ tubing constraint}$$

where

$$X_1 = 300 - 0.175P_1$$
$$X_2 = 325 - 0.150P_2$$

and

$$1,000 \leq P_1, P_2 \leq 1,500$$

One approach to implementing this model in a spreadsheet is shown in Figure 8.5 (and in the file FIG8-5.XLS on your data disk). In this spreadsheet, cells B3 and C3 correspond, respectively, to the price of Aqua-Spas (P_1) and the price of Hydro-Luxes (P_2). Initially we can place any values in these cells. However, as discussed earlier, the final solution obtained for an NLP problem using the BFGS algorithm can be influenced by the initial starting point. So if we know good initial starting values for the decision variables or can determine them easily, it is a good idea to place these values in the appropriate cells in the spreadsheet. In this case we can see from Figure 8.4 that good starting values for P_1 and P_2 are approximately $1,300 and $1,400, respectively. These values are listed in cells B3 and C3.

Cells B4 and C4 contain the unit marginal cost for each type of hot tub. The profit margins for the products are calculated in cells B5 and C5 by subtracting the unit marginal costs in cells B4 and C4 from the unit prices in cells B3 and C3, respectively.

As indicated in our algebraic model, the number of units of Aqua-Spas (X_1) and Hydro-Luxes (X_2) demanded (and, therefore, the number to produce) can be determined directly from their respective prices. Cells B7 and C7 contain the following formulas, which determine X_1 and X_2:

Formula for cell B7:   =300−0.175*B3

Formula for cell C7:   =325−0.150*C3

The objective function for our algebraic model is implemented in cell B9 as:

Formula for cell B9:   =B5*B7+C5*C7

The functional portions of the constraints for the problem are implemented in cells D12 through D14 as:

Formula for cell D12:   =B12*$B$7+C12*$C$7
(copy to D13 through D14)

These formulas calculate the number of pumps, hours of labor, and feet of tubing required at any level of demand that results from any set of prices. The availability of these resources is shown in cells E12 through E14.

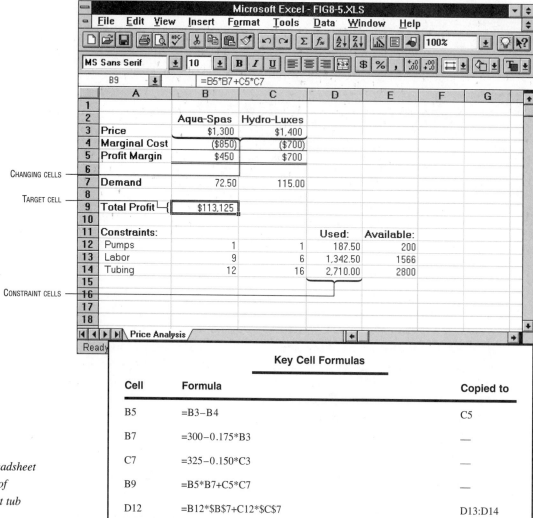

Figure 8.5: *Spreadsheet implementation of the nonlinear hot tub pricing problem*

SOLVING THE MODEL

As with any optimization problem, we must indicate to Solver where we have implemented the decision variables, objective function, and constraints for this model. Figure 8.6 shows the Solver parameters and options used to solve this problem, and Figure 8.7 shows the optimal solution.

ANALYZING THE SOLUTION

The optimal solution shown in Figure 8.7 indicates that a maximum profit of $113,347 can be achieved by charging $1,282 for Aqua-Spas and $1,433 for Hydro-Luxes. These optimal values are very close to the initial starting values inferred from Figure 8.4. There is probably some degree of uncertainty or imprecision in the functions used to estimate the relationship between demand for the hot tubs and the price of the hot tubs. For example, it is unlikely that *exactly* 110 Hydro-Luxes will be demanded at a price of $1,433. So Howie might prefer to use the original estimated prices of $1,300 and $1,400 shown in Figure 8.5 because these prices will likely produce a comparable level of profit and are easier to remember.

Figure 8.6: Solver parameters and options for the nonlinear hot tub pricing problem

Figure 8.7: Optimal solution to the nonlinear hot tub pricing problem

The solution shown in Figure 8.7 also illustrates that none of the resources are fully employed. That is, in the optimal solution to this problem none of the resources (constraints) are preventing the company from achieving greater levels of profit. This indicates that the optimal solution occurs at some point in the *interior* of the feasible region. The graph in Figure 8.8 illustrates this problem and its optimal solution. Notice that the level curves for this problem are not straight lines but instead form ellipses around the optimal solution. Thus, the optimal solution to this problem ($P_1 = 1{,}282$, $P_2 = 1{,}433$) occurs in the interior of the feasible region.

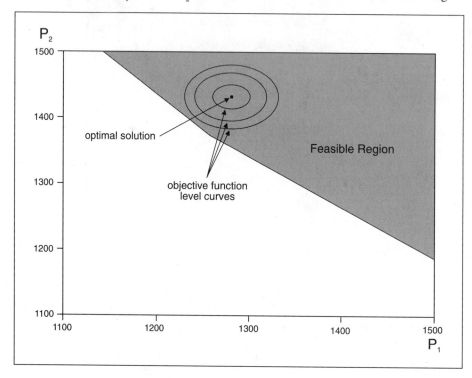

Figure 8.8: Graph of the nonlinear hot tub pricing

A Note About the Assume Linear Model Option

When solving an NLP problem, it is important *not* to select the Assume Linear Model option because this option causes Solver to attempt to apply the simplex method to the problem. When this option is selected, Solver conducts a number of internal tests to verify that the model is truly linear in the objective and constraints. If this option is selected and Solver's tests indicate that the model is *not* linear, a dialog box appears indicating that the conditions for linearity are not satisfied.

PORTFOLIO SELECTION PROBLEMS

One famous application of NLP involves determining the optimal mix of investments to hold in a portfolio in order to minimize the risk of the portfolio while achieving a desired level of return. One way to measure the risk inherent in an individual investment is the variance (or, alternatively, the standard deviation) of the returns it has generated over a period of time. One of the key objectives in portfolio selection is to smooth out the variation in the return on a portfolio by choosing investments whose returns tend to vary in opposite directions. That is, we'd like to choose investments that have a negative covariance or negative correlation so that when one investment generates a lower than average return another investment in our portfolio offsets this with a higher than average return. This tends to make the variance of the return of the portfolio smaller than that of any individual investment. The following example illustrates a portfolio selection problem.

Ray Dodson in an independent financial advisor. He recently met with a new client, Paula Ribben, who wanted Ray's advice on how best to diversify a portion of her investments. Paula has invested a good portion of her retirement savings in the stock of International Business Corporation (IBC). During the past 12 years, this stock has produced an average annual return of 7.64% with a variance of approximately 0.0026. Paula would like to earn more on her investments, but is very cautious and doesn't like to take risks. Paula has asked Ray to recommend a portfolio of investments that would provide at least a 12% average return with as little additional risk as possible. After some research Ray identified two additional stocks, from the National Motor Corporation (NMC) and the National Broadcasting System (NBS), that he believes could help meet Paula's investment objectives. Ray's initial research is summarized in Figure 8.9 (and in the file FIG8-9.XLS on your data disk).

Figure 8.9: Data for the portfolio selection problem

As indicated in Figure 8.9, shares of NMC have produced an average rate of return of 13.43% over the past 12 years, while those of NBS have generated an average return of 14.93%. Ray used the COVAR( ) function in Excel to create the covariance matrix in this spreadsheet. The numbers along the main diagonal in this matrix correspond to the variances of the returns for each stock. For example, the covariance matrix indicates that the variances in the annual returns for IBC, NMC, and NBS are 0.0026, 0.0028, and 0.0368, respectively. The entries off the main diagonal represent covariances between different pairs of stocks. For example, the covariance between IBC and NMC is approximately –0.00025, the covariance between IBC and NBS is approximately 0.00440, and the covaiance between NMC and NBS is approx-imately –0.00542.

Ray wants to determine what percentage of Paula's funds should be allocated to each of the stocks in order to achieve an overall expected return of 12% while minimizing the variance of the total return on the portfolio.

DEFINING THE DECISION VARIABLES

In this problem we must determine what percentage of the total funds invested should go toward the purchase of each of the three stocks. Thus, to formulate the model for this problem we need the following three decision variables:

p_1 = proportion of total funds invested in IBC

p_2 = proportion of total funds invested in NMC

p_3 = proportion of total funds invested in NBS

Because these variables represent proportions, we also need to ensure that they assume values no less than 0, and that they sum to 1 (or 100%). We will handle these conditions when we identify the constraints for the problem.

DEFINING THE OBJECTIVE

The objective in this problem is to minimize the risk of the portfolio as measured by its variance. In general, the variance of a portfolio consisting of n investments is defined in most finance texts as:

$$\text{Portfolio variance} = \sum_{i=1}^{n} \sigma_i^2 p_i^2 + 2 \sum_{i=1}^{n-1} \sum_{j=i+1}^{n} \sigma_{ij} p_i p_j$$

where

p_i = the percentage of the portfolio invested in investment i

σ_i^2 = the variance of investment i

$\sigma_{ij} = \sigma_{ji}$ = the covariance between investments i and j

If you are familiar with matrix multiplication, you might be interested to know that the portfolio variance can also be expressed in matrix terms as:

Portfolio variance = $\mathbf{p}^T \mathbf{C} \mathbf{p}$

where

$\mathbf{p}^T = (p_1, p_2, \dots, p_n)$

$\mathbf{C}$ = the $n \times n$ covariance matrix

Notice that if 100% of the funds available are placed in a single investment i, then the portfolio variance reduces to σ_i^2 — the variance for that single investment.

In our example problem we have:

$\sigma_1^2 = 0.00258, \quad \sigma_2^2 = 0.00276, \quad \sigma_3^2 = 0.03677$

$\sigma_{12} = -0.00025, \quad \sigma_{13} = 0.00440, \quad \sigma_{23} = -0.00542$

So, using the preceding formula the objective for our problem is stated as:

MIN:

$$0.00258p_1^2 + 0.00276p_2^2 + 0.03677p_3^2 + 2\left(-0.00025*p_1p_2 + 0.0044*p_1p_3 - 0.00542p_2p_3\right)$$

This objective function is *not* a linear combination of the decision variables, so we must solve this problem as an NLP.

DEFINING THE CONSTRAINTS

Only two main constraints apply to this problem. As mentioned earlier, because only three investments are under consideration for this portfolio, and our decision variables represent the percentage of funds invested in each of these investments, we must ensure that our decision variables sum to 100%. This can be accomplished easily as:

$p_1 + p_2 + p_3 = 1$

We also need a constraint to ensure that the expected return of the entire portfolio achieves or exceeds the desired return of 12%. This condition is expressed as:

$0.0764p_1 + 0.1343p_2 + 0.1493p_3 \geq 0.12$

The LHS of this constraint represents a weighted average of the expected returns from the individual investments. This constraint indicates that the weighted average expected return on the portfolio must be at least 12%.

Finally, because the decision variables must represent proportions, we should also include the following upper and lower bounds:

$p_1, p_2, p_3 \geq 0$

$p_1, p_2, p_3 \leq 1$

The last condition, requiring each of the p_i to be less than or equal to 1, is mathematically redundant because the p_i are also constrained to sum to 1. However, we will include this restriction for completeness.

IMPLEMENTING THE MODEL

In summary, the algebraic model for this problem is stated as:

MIN:

$$0.00258p_1^2 + 0.00276p_2^2 + 0.03677p_3^2 + 2\left(-0.00025*p_1p_2 + 0.0044*p_1p_3 - 0.00542p_2p_3\right)$$

Subject to:
$$p_1 + p_2 + p_3 = 1$$
$$0.0764p_1 + 0.1343p_2 + 0.1493p_3 \geq 0.12$$
$$p_1, p_2, p_3 \geq 0$$
$$p_1, p_2, p_3 \leq 1$$

One approach to implementing this model in a spreadsheet is shown in Figure 8.10 (and in the file FIG8-10.XLS on your data disk). In this spreadsheet, cells G9, H9, and I9 represent the decision variables p_1, p_2, and p_3, respectively. The initial values in these cells reflect the investor's current portfolio, which consists entirely of stock in IBC.

We can implement the objective function for this problem in a number of ways. The standard approach is to implement a formula that corresponds exactly to the algebraic form of the objective function. This is represented by:

Formula for cell H14:　　=G4*G9^2+H5*H9^2+I6*I9^2

　　　　　　　　　　　+2*(H4*G9*H9+I4*G9*I9+H6*H9*I9)

Figure 8.10: Spreadsheet implementation of the portfolio selection problem

Entering this formula is tedious and prone to error, and would be even more so if this example involved more than three stocks. The following is an alternative, and easier, way of expressing this objective:

Alternative formula for cell H14:   =SUMPRODUCT(MMULT(G9:I9,G4:I6),G9:I9)

This alternative formula uses matrix multiplication (the MMULT( ) function) to compute the portfolio variance. Although both formulas generate the same result, the second formula is much easier to enter and can accommodate any number of investments. Notice that the value 0.00258 in cell H14 in Figure 8.10 indicates that when 100% of the funds are invested in IBC stock, the variance of the portfolio is the same as the variance of the IBC stock.

The LHS formulas of the two main constraints are implemented in cells J9 and H11 as:

Formula for cell J9:   = SUM(G9:I9)

Formula for cell H11:   = SUMPRODUCT(B17:D17,G9:I9)

Figure 8.11 shows the Solver parameters and options used to solve this problem, and Figure 8.12 shows the optimal solution.

Figure 8.11: Solver parameters and options for the
portfolio selection problem

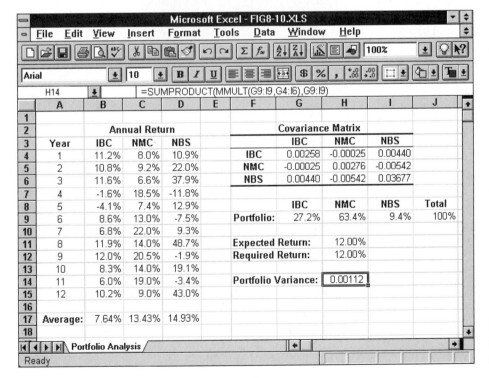

Figure 8.12: Optimal
solution to the portfolio
selection problem

ANALYZING THE SOLUTION

In contrast to the original solution shown in Figure 8.10, the optimal solution shown in Figure 8.12 indicates that a better solution would result by placing 27.2% of the investor's money in IBC, 63.4% in NMC, and 9.4% in NBS. Cell H11 indicates that this mix of investments would achieve the desired 12% expected rate of return, and cell H14 indicates that the variance for this portfolio would be only 0.00112.

The solution to this problem indicates that a portfolio exists that produces a *higher* expected return for Paula with *less* risk than was involved in her original portfolio. Paula's original investment would be called inefficient in the terms of portfolio theory. Portfolio theory stipulates that for each possible level of investment return, there is a portfolio that minimizes risk—and accepting any greater level of risk at that level of return is inefficient. The optimal trade-off between risk and return for a given portfolio problem can be summarized by a graph of the **efficient frontier**, which plots the minimal portfolio risk associated with each possible level of return. Figure 8.13 shows a graph of the efficient frontier for our example problem. This graph is helpful not only in identifying the maximum level of risk that should be accepted for each possible level of return, but also in identifying where further increases in expected returns incur much greater amounts of risk.

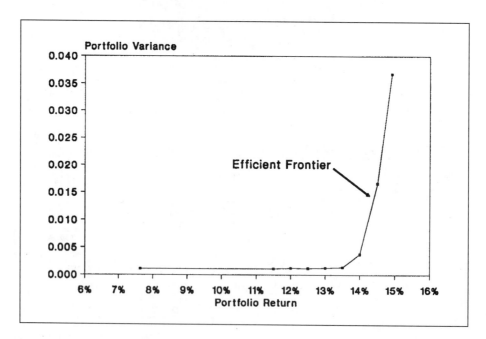

Figure 8.13: Efficient frontier for the portfolio selection problem

LOCATION PROBLEMS

A number of decision problems involve determining the location of a facility or service center. Examples might include determining the optimal location of warehouses, fire stations, or ambulance centers. The objective in these types of problems often is to determine a location that minimizes the distance between two or more service points. You might recall from basic algebra that the straight line (or Euclidian) distance between two points (X_1, Y_1) and (X_2, Y_2) on a standard X-Y graph is defined as:

$$\text{Distance} = \sqrt{(X_1 - X_2)^2 + (Y_1 - Y_2)^2}$$

This type of calculation is likely to be involved in any problem where the decision variables represent possible locations. The distance measure might occur in the objective function (for example, we might want to minimize the distance between two or more points) or it might occur in a constraint (for example, we might want to ensure that some minimum distance exists between two or more locations). Problems involving this type of distance measure are nonlinear. The following is an example of a location problem.

The Arctic Oil Company has recently drilled two new wells in a remote area of Alaska. The company is planning to install a pipeline to carry the oil from the two new wells to a transportation and refining (T&R) center, as illustrated in Figure 8.14.

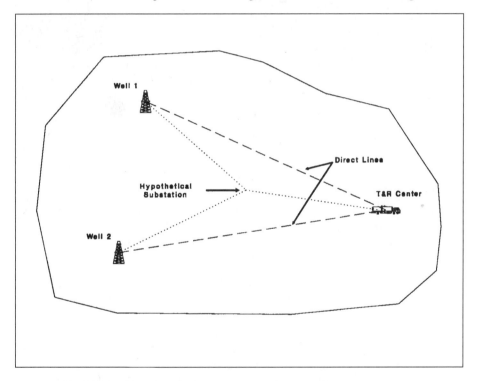

Figure 8.14: Map of Arctic Oil's pipeline location problem

Installing the pipeline is a very expensive undertaking, and the company wants to minimize the amount of pipeline required. Because the shortest distance between two points is a straight line, one of the analysts assigned to the project believes that a separate pipe should be run from each well to the T&R center. This alternative is indicated by the Direct Lines notation in Figure 8.14. Another alternative is to run separate pipes from each well to some intermediate substation where the two lines are joined into a single pipeline that continues on to the T&R center. This alternative is shown by the Hypothetical Substation notation in Figure 8.14. Arctic Oil's management wants to determine which alternative is best. Furthermore, if using the intermediate substation is best, management wants to determine where this station should be located.

DEFINING THE DECISION VARIABLES

In order to solve this problem, we first need to convert the map shown in Figure 8.14 into an X-Y graph. Figure 8.15 shows one approach for this conversion.

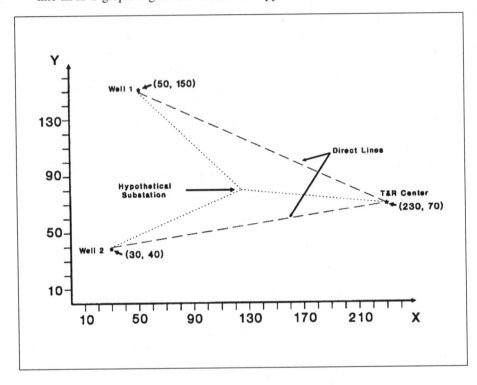

Figure 8.15: Coordinate locations of Oil Wells and T&R center

We can overlay the X- and Y-axes on this map in more than one way. The origin in Figure 8.15 could be located anywhere on the map without affecting the analysis. To establish the X-Y coordinates, we need an absolute reference point for the origin, but virtually any point on the map could be selected as the origin. Also we can express the scaling of the X-axis and Y-axis in a number of ways: meters, miles, inches, feet, and so on. For our purposes, we'll assume that each unit along the X- and Y-axes represents 10 miles.

In Figure 8.15, definite X-Y coordinates have been established to describe the locations of well 1, well 2, and the T&R center. These points are fixed and are not under the decision maker's control. However, the coordinates of the substation have not been firmly established. We could slide this point around on the graph in an attempt to minimize the amount of pipeline required to connect the two wells to the T&R center. Thus, the coordinates of the substation represent the decision variables in this problem, which are defined as:

X_1 = location of the substation with respect to the X-axis

Y_1 = location of the substation with respect to the Y-axis

If X_1 = 230 and Y_1 = 70, the substation would be located at the T&R center. In this case, separate pipelines would run directly from each well to the T&R center.

DEFINING THE OBJECTIVE

The objective in this problem is to minimize the total amount of pipeline needed. This is equivalent to minimizing the total distance from the wells to the substation plus the distance from the substation to the T&R center. Thus, the objective for this problem is stated as follows:

$$\text{MIN:} \sqrt{(50 - X_1)^2 + (150 - Y_1)^2} + \sqrt{(30 - X_1)^2 + (40 - Y_1)^2} + \sqrt{(230 - X_1)^2 + (70 - Y_1)^2}$$

The first term in the objective represents the distance from well 1, at location (50, 150), to the location of the substation, whose location is defined by the values X_1 and Y_1. The second term represents the distance from well 2, at location (30, 40), to the substation. The last term represents the distance from the T&R center, at location (230, 70), to the substation.

DEFINING THE CONSTRAINTS

Unlike all the previous optimization problems considered in this book, this problem has *no constraints*. This problem is an example of an unconstrained optimization problem.

IMPLEMENTING THE MODEL

One approach to implementing the model for this problem in a spreadsheet is shown in Figure 8.16 (and in the file FIG8-16.XLS on your data disk).

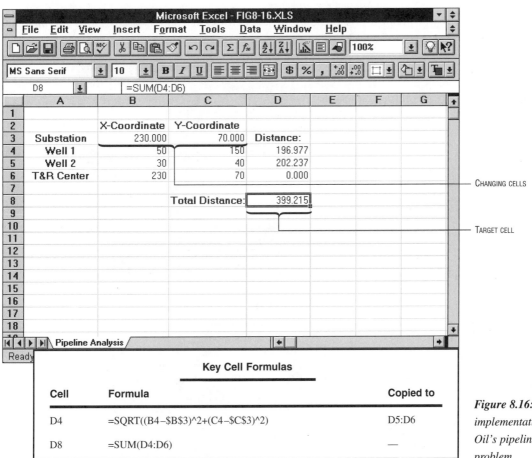

Figure 8.16: Spreadsheet implementation of Arctic Oil's pipeline location problem

In this spreadsheet, cells B3 and C3 represent the decision variables X_1 and Y_1, respectively. Starting values of 230 and 70 are entered manually for these cells. The locations of the oil wells and the T&R center are listed in terms of their X-Y coordinates in rows 4 through 6 of columns B and C. Column D calculates the distance from each well and from the T&R center to the substation. Specifically, cell D4 contains the following formula, which is copied to cells D5 and D6:

Formula for cell D4:   =SQRT((B4−$B$3)^2+(C4−$C$3)^2)
(copy to D5 and D6)

Cells D4 through D6 correspond to the three distances in the objective described earlier. Thus, the objective function for this problem is implemented easily in cell D8 with the formula:

Formula for cell D8:   =SUM(D4:D6)

The initial coordinates for the substation shown in Figure 8.16 place it at the same location as the T&R center. This causes the value in cell D6 to be 0, indicating no distance between the T&R center and the substation. The value in cell D4 indicates that the straight-line distance between well 1 and the T&R center is 196.98 miles. Similarly, the value in cell D5 indicates that the straight-line distance between well 2 and the T&R center is 202.24 miles. Thus, if separate pipelines are run from each oil well to the T&R center, a total of 399.215 miles of pipeline will be needed. The solution to this model should indicate whether establishing a substation can reduce this distance.

Figure 8.17 shows the Solver parameters and options used to solve this problem, and Figure 8.18 shows the optimal solution.

Figure 8.17: Solver parameters and options for Arctic Oil's pipeline location problem

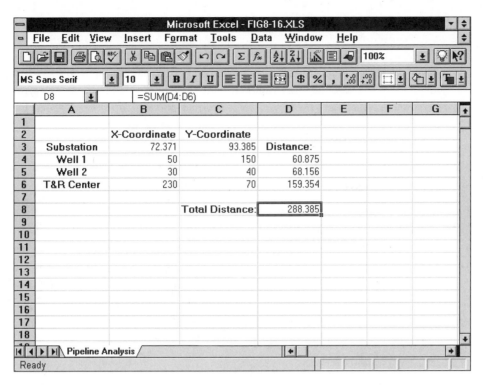

Figure 8.18: Optimal solution to Arctic Oil's pipeline location problem

The optimal solution in Figure 8.18 indicates that if a substation is located at the coordinates X = 72.371 and Y = 93.385, the total amount of pipeline needed is reduced from 399.2 miles to 288.385 miles. Figure 8.19 shows the optimal location of the substation.

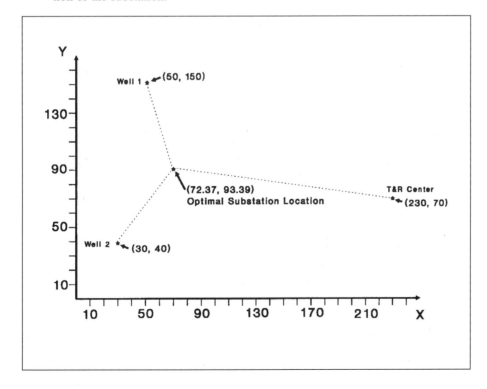

Figure 8.19: Graph of the optimal solution to Arctic Oil's pipeline location problem

ECONOMIC ORDER QUANTITY MODELS

The economic order quantity (EOQ) problem is a common business problem in which a decision maker must determine the optimal number of units of a product to purchase whenever an order is placed. Three costs must be considered in calculating the total annual cost of stocking a product: the actual purchase cost of the product, the fixed cost of placing orders, and the cost of holding (or carrying) the product in inventory:

Total annual cost = purchase cost + fixed ordering cost + holding cost

The basic model for an EOQ problem makes the following assumptions:

1. Demand for (or use of) the product is fairly constant throughout the year.

2. Each new order is delivered in full when the inventory level reaches 0.

Figure 8.20 illustrates the type of inventory patterns observed for a product when the preceding conditions are met. In each graph, the inventory levels are depleted at a constant rate, representing constant demand. Also, the inventory levels are replenished instantly whenever the inventory levels reach 0.

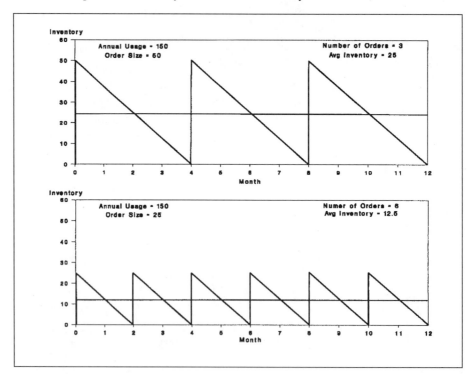

Figure 8.20: Inventory profiles of products for which the EOQ model assumptions are met

The key issue in an EOQ problem is to determine the optimal quantity to order whenever an order is placed for an item. The trade-offs in this decision are evident in Figure 8.20. The graphs indicate two ways of obtaining 150 units of a product during the year. In the first graph, an order for 50 units is received whenever the inventory level drops to 0. This requires that 3 purchase orders be issued during the year and results in an average inventory level of 25 units. In the second graph, an order for 25 units is received whenever the inventory level drops to 0. This requires that 6 purchase orders be issued throughout the year and results in an average inventory level of 12.5 units. Thus, the first ordering strategy results in fewer purchase orders (and lower ordering costs) but higher inventory levels (and higher carrying costs). The second ordering strategy results in more purchase orders (and higher ordering costs) but lower levels of inventory (and lower carrying costs).

Figure 8.21 shows the relationship between order quantity, carrying cost, ordering cost, and total cost. Notice that as the order quantity increases, ordering costs decrease and carrying costs increase. The goal in this type of problem is to find the EOQ that minimizes the total cost.

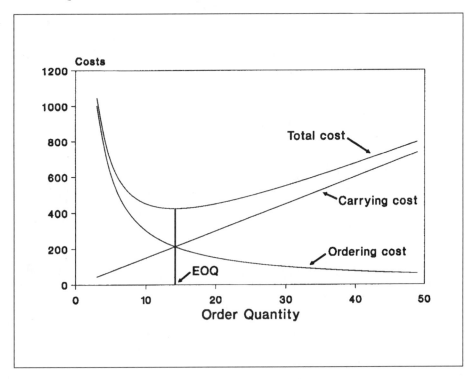

Figure 8.21: *Relationship between order quantity, carrying cost, ordering cost, and total cost*

The total annual cost of acquiring products that meet the stated assumptions is represented by:

$$\text{Total annual cost} = DC + \frac{D}{Q}S + \frac{Q}{2}Ci$$

where:

    D = annual demand for the item

    C = unit purchase cost for the item

    S = fixed cost of placing an order

    i = cost of holding one unit in inventory for a year (expressed as a

        percentage of C)

    Q = order quantity, or quantity ordered each time an order is placed

The first term in this formula (DC) represents the cost of purchasing a year's worth of the product. The second term ($\frac{D}{Q}S$) represents the annual ordering costs. Specifically, $\frac{D}{Q}$ represents the number of orders placed during a year. Multiplying this quantity by S represents the cost of placing these orders. The third term ($\frac{Q}{2}Ci$) represents the annual cost of holding inventory. On average, $\frac{Q}{2}$ units are held in inventory throughout the year (see Figure 8.20). Multiplying this term by Ci represents the cost of holding these units. The following example illustrates the use of an EOQ model.

Alan Wang is responsible for purchasing the paper used in all the copy machines and laser printers at the corporate headquarters of MetroBank. Alan projects that in the coming year he will need to purchase a total of 24,000 boxes of paper, which will be used at a fairly steady rate throughout the year. Each box of paper costs $35. Alan estimates that it costs $50 each time an order is placed (this includes the cost of placing the order plus the related costs in shipping and receiving). MetroBank assigns a cost of 18% to funds allocated to supplies and inventories because such funds are the lifeline of the bank and could be lent out to credit card customers who are willing to pay this rate on money borrowed from the bank. Alan has been placing paper orders once a month, but he wants to determine if another ordering pattern would be better. He wants to determine the most economical order quantity to use in purchasing the paper.

IMPLEMENTING THE MODEL

To solve this problem, we first need to create a spreadsheet model of the total cost formula described earlier, substituting the data for Alan's problem for the parameters D, C, S, and i. This spreadsheet implementation is shown in Figure 8.22 (and in the file FIG8-22.XLS on your data disk).

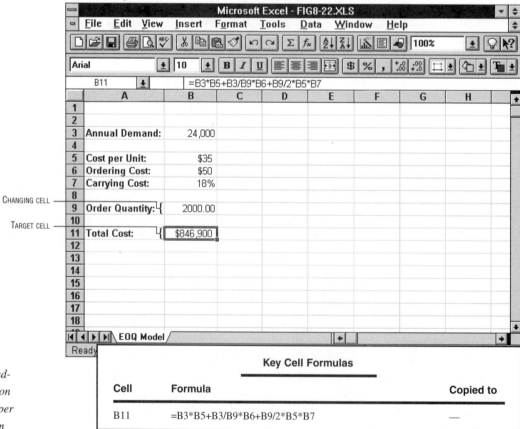

Figure 8.22: Spreadsheet implementation of MetroBank's paper purchasing problem

Cell	Formula	Copied to
B11	=B3*B5+B3/B9*B6+B9/2*B5*B7	—

In Figure 8.22, cell B3 represents the annual demand (D), cell B5 represents the per-unit cost (C), cell B6 represents the ordering cost (S), cell B7 represents the carrying cost (*i*), and cell B9 represents the order quantity (Q). The data corresponding to Alan's decision problem have been entered into the appropriate cells in this model. Because Alan places orders once a month (or 12 times a year), the order quantity in cell B9 is set at 24,000 ÷ 12 = 2,000.

SOLVING THE MODEL

The goal in this problem is to determine the order quantity (the value of Q) that minimizes the total cost. That is, we want Solver to determine the value for cell B9 that minimizes the value in cell B11. Figure 8.23 shows the Solver parameters and options required to solve this problem. Note that a constraint has been placed on cell B9 to prevent the order quantity from becoming 0 or negative. This constraint requires that at least one order must be placed during the year.

Figure 8.23: Solver parameters and options for MetroBank's paper purchasing problem

ANALYZING THE SOLUTION

The optimal solution to this problem is shown in Figure 8.24. This solution indicates that the optimal number of boxes for Alan to order at any time is approximately 617. Using this order quantity, costs are reduced by approximately $3,000 from the earlier level shown in Figure 8.22 when an order quantity of 2000 was used.

If Alan orders 617 boxes, he needs to place approximately 39 orders during the year (24,000 ÷ 617 = 38.89), or 1.333 orders per week (52 ÷ 39 = 1.333). As a practical matter, it might be easier for Alan to arrange for weekly deliveries of approximately 461 boxes. This would increase the total cost by only $167 to $844,055 but probably would be easier to manage.

Figure 8.24: *Optimal solution to MetroBank's paper purhcasing problem*

COMMENTS ON THE EOQ MODEL

There is another way to determine the optimal order quantity using the simple EOQ model. Using calculus, it can be shown that the optimal value of Q is represented by:

$$Q^* = \sqrt{\frac{2DS}{Ci}}$$

If we apply this formula to our example problem, we obtain:

$$Q^* = \sqrt{\frac{2 * 24,000 * 50}{35 * 0.18}} = \sqrt{\frac{2,400,000}{6.3}} = 617.214$$

The value obtained using calculus is almost the same value obtained using Solver (see cell B9 in Figure 8.24). The slight difference in the results might be due to rounding, or to Solver stopping just short of converging on the exact solution.

The simple EOQ model can be modified to account for such factors as quantity discounts and order backlogging. A complete discussion of the proper use and role of EOQ models in inventory control is beyond the scope of this text, but can be found in other texts devoted to production and operations management.

OPTIMIZATION OF EXISTING SPREADSHEETS

So far in our discussion of optimization we have always constructed an algebraic model of a decision problem and then implemented this model in a spreadsheet for solution and analysis. However, we can apply optimization techniques to virtually any existing spreadsheet model. Many existing spreadsheets involve financial calculations that are inherently nonlinear. The following is an example of how optimization can be applied to an existing spreadsheet.

Thom Pearman's life is changing dramatically. He and his wife recently bought a new home and are expecting their first child in a few months. These new responsibilities have prompted Thom to think about some serious issues, including life insurance. Ten years ago Thom purchased an insurance policy that provides a death benefit of $40,000. This policy is paid for in full and will remain in force for the rest of Thom's life. Alternatively, Thom can surrender this policy and receive an immediate pay-off of approximately $6,000 from the insurance company.

Ten years ago, the $40,000 death benefit provided by the insurance policy seemed more than adequate. However, Thom now feels that he needs more coverage to care for his wife and child adequately in the event of his untimely death. Thom is investigating a different kind of insurance that would provide a death benefit of $350,000 but also would require on-going annual payments to keep the coverage in force. He received the following estimates of the annual premiums for this new policy in each of the next 10 years:

Year	Premium
1	$423
2	$457
3	$489
4	$516
5	$530
6	$558
7	$595
8	$618
9	$660
10	$716

In order to pay the premiums for this new policy, one alternative Thom is considering involves surrendering his existing policy and investing the $6,000 he would receive to generate the after-tax income needed to pay the premiums on his new policy. However, to see if this is possible, he wants to determine the minimum rate of return he would have to earn on his investment to generate after-tax investment earnings that would cover the premium payments for the new policy. Thom likes the idea of keeping the $6,000 in case of an emergency and does not want to use it to pay premiums. Thom's marginal tax rate is 28%.

IMPLEMENTING THE MODEL

A spreadsheet model for Thom's decision problem is shown in Figure 8.25 (and in the file FIG8-25.XLS on your data disk). The strategy in this spreadsheet is to determine how much money would be invested at the beginning of each year, how much money would be earned during the year after taxes, and how much would be left at the end of the year after paying taxes and the insurance premium due for that year.

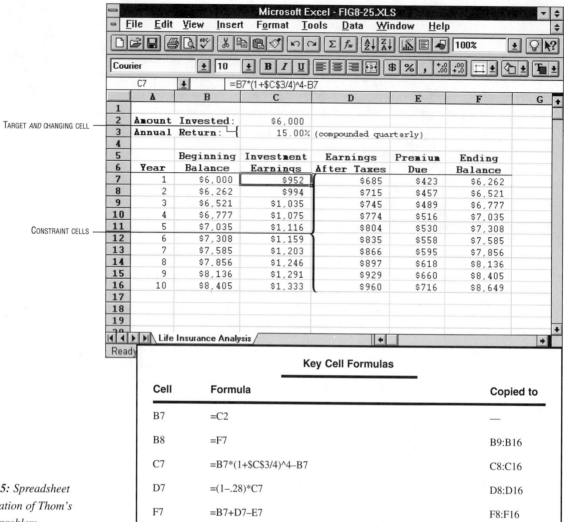

Figure 8.25: Spreadsheet implementation of Thom's insurance problem

As shown in Figure 8.25, cells C2 and C3 contain the assumptions about the initial amount invested and the expected annual return. The annual return of 15% was entered in C3 simply for planning purposes. This is the value that we'll attempt to minimize when we optimize the spreadsheet.

The beginning balance for the first year (cell B7) is equal to the initial amount of money invested. The beginning balance for each of the following years is the ending balance from the previous year. The formula shown for cell C7 at the top of the spreadsheet calculates the amount earned for the year given the interest rate in cell C3, which is assumed to be compounded quarterly. This same formula applies to cells C8 through C16.

Because Thom pays 28% in taxes, the values in the Earnings After Taxes column are 72% of the investment earnings listed in column C (100% − 28% = 72%). The values in the Ending Balance column are the beginning balances plus the earnings after taxes minus the premium due for the year.

OPTIMIZING THE SPREADSHEET MODEL

Three elements are involved in any optimization problem: one or more decision variables, an objective function, and constraints. The objective in the current problem is to determine the minimum annual return that will generate after-tax earnings to pay the premiums each year. Thus, the decision variable in this model is the interest rate in cell C3. The value in cell C3 also represents the objective in the problem because we want to minimize its value. For constraints, the after-tax earnings each year should be greater than or equal to the premium due for the year. Thus, we require that the values in cells D7 through D16 be greater than or equal to the values in cells E7 through E16. Figure 8.26 shows the Solver parameters and options required to solve this problem, and Figure 8.27 shows the optimal solution.

Figure 8.26: Solver parameters and options for Thom's insurance problem

ANALYZING THE SOLUTION

The solution shown in Figure 8.27 indicates that Thom needs to obtain an annual return of at least 13.29% in order for the after-tax earnings from his investment of $6,000 to pay the premiums on his new policy for the next 10 years. This rate of return causes his after-tax earnings in year 10 to equal exactly the premium payment of $716 due that year. Thus, in order for Thom's plan to succeed, he needs to identify an investment that is capable of producing at least a 13.29% annual return each year for the next 10 years.

Figure 8.27: Optimal solution to Thom's insurance problem

COMMENTS ON OPTIMIZING EXISTING SPREADSHEETS

One difficulty in optimizing an existing spreadsheet model is determining whether the underlying algebraic model is linear or nonlinear. This is important in determining whether a global optimal solution to the problem has been obtained. As mentioned earlier, if we instruct Solver to assume that the model is linear, it conducts a series of numerical tests to determine whether this assumption is appropriate. If Solver detects that the model is not linear, a message is displayed to that effect and we need to re-solve the model as an NLP. So when applying optimization techniques to an existing spreadsheet model, it is a good idea to instruct Solver to assume that the model is linear. If Solver can find a solution under this assumption, we can be confident that it is the global optimal solution. If Solver detects that the model is nonlinear, we must be aware that any solution obtained might represent a local optimal solution as opposed to the global optimal solution. In this case, we might re-solve the model several times from different starting points to see if better local optimal solutions exist for the problem. (Note that if a problem is poorly scaled, Solver's linearity tests will sometimes indicate that the model is not linear when, in fact it is.)

As you develop your skills and intuition about spreadsheet optimization, you might be inclined to skip the step of writing out algebraic formulations of your models. For straightforward problems this might be appropriate. However, in more complex problems this can lead to undesirable results. For example, in chapter 6, Integer Linear Programming, we noted how it can be tempting to implement the binary variables in a fixed-charge problem using an IF() function in a spreadsheet. Unfortunately, this causes Solver to view the problem as an NLP rather than as a mixed-integer LP problem. So how you implement the model for a problem can impact whether Solver finds the global optimal solution. As the model builder, you must understand what kind of model you have and implement it in the most appropriate way. Writing out the algebraic formulation of the model often helps to ensure that you thoroughly understand the model you are attempting to solve.

SENSITIVITY ANALYSIS

In chapter 4, we analyzed how sensitive the optimal solution to an LP model is to changes in various coefficients in the model. We noted that one advantage of using the simplex method to solve LP problems is that it provides expanded sensitivity information. A certain amount of sensitivity information is also available when using nonlinear optimization methods to solve linear or nonlinear problems.

To understand the sensitivity information available from nonlinear optimization, we'll compare it to what we learned in chapter 4 about the sensitivity information that results from using the simplex method. In chapter 4, we solved the following modified version of the Blue Ridge Hot Tubs problem where a third type of hot tub—the Typhoon-Lagoon—was included in the model:

$$\text{MAX}: \quad 350X_1 + 300X_2 + 320X_3 \qquad \} \text{ profit}$$

$$\text{Subject to}: \quad 1X_1 + 1X_2 + 1X_3 \leq 200 \qquad \} \text{ pump constraint}$$

$$9X_1 + 6X_2 + 8X_3 \leq 1{,}566 \qquad \} \text{ labor constraint}$$

$$12X_1 + 16X_2 + 13X_3 \leq 2{,}880 \qquad \} \text{ tubing constraint}$$

$$X_1, X_2, X_3 \geq 0 \qquad \} \text{ nonnegativity conditions}$$

The spreadsheet implementation of this problem is shown in Figure 8.28 (and in the file FIG8-28.XLS on your data disk). Figure 8.29 shows the Sensitivity Report generated for this problem after solving it using the simplex method. Figure 8.30 shows the Sensitivity Report for this problem after solving it using Solver's nonlinear optimizer.

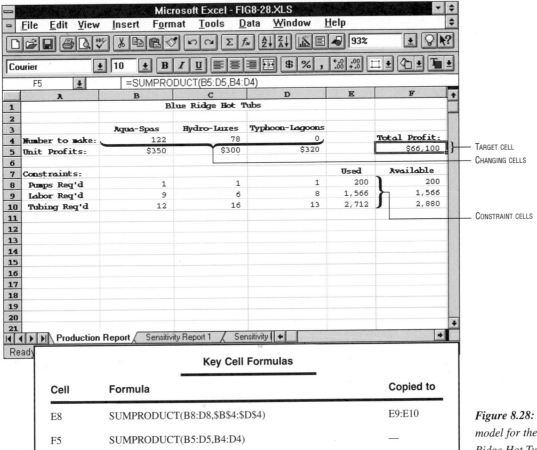

Figure 8.28: Spreadsheet model for the revised Blue Ridge Hot Tubs problem

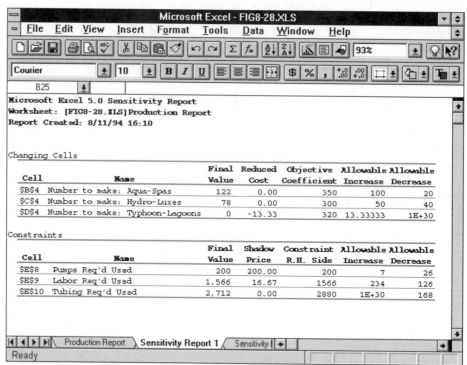

Figure 8.29: Sensitivity Report obtained after solving the model using the simplex method

Figure 8.30: Sensitivity Report obtained after solving the model using Solver's nonlinear optimizer

In comparing Figures 8.29 and 8.30, notice that the same optimal solution is obtained regardless of whether the problem is solved using the simplex method or the nonlinear optimizer. Both reports indicate that 122 Aqua-Spas, 78 Hydro-Luxes, and 0 Typhoon-Lagoons should be produced. Both reports also indicate that this solution requires 200 pumps, 1,566 labor hours, and 2,712 feet of tubing. The fact that the two optimization techniques found the same optimal solution is not surprising because this problem is known to have a unique optimal solution. However, if an LP problem has alternative optimal solutions, the simplex method and the nonlinear optimizer will not necessarily identify the same optimal solution.

Another similarity between the two Sensitivity reports is apparent if we compare the values in the Reduced Cost and Shadow Price columns in Figure 8.29 with the values in the Reduced Gradient and Lagrange Multiplier columns in Figure 8.30. The reduced cost for each variable in Figure 8.29 is the same as the reduced gradient for each variable in Figure 8.30. Similarly, the shadow price for each constraint in Figure 8.29 is the same as the Lagrange multiplier for each constraint in Figure 8.30. This is *not* simply a coincidence.

LAGRANGE MULTIPLIERS

In chapter 4, we saw that the shadow price of a constraint represents the marginal value of an additional unit of the resource represented by the constraint—or the amount by which the objective function would improve if the RHS of the constraint is loosened by one unit. This same interpretation applies in a more approximate sense to Lagrange multipliers. The main difference between shadow prices and Lagrange multipliers involves the range of RHS values over which the shadow price or Lagrange multiplier remains valid.

As discussed in chapter 4 (and shown in Figure 8.29), after solving an LP problem using the simplex method we can identify the allowable increase and decrease in a constraint's RHS value over which the shadow price of the constraint remains valid. We can do this because the objective function and constraints in an LP problem are all linear, making the impact of changes in a constraint's RHS value on the objective function value relatively easy to compute. However, in NLP problems we have no general way to determine such ranges for the RHS values of the constraints. So when using Solver's nonlinear optimizer to solve an optimization problem, we cannot determine easily the range of RHS values over which a constraint's Lagrange multiplier will remain valid. The Lagrange multipliers can be used only to estimate the approximate impact on the objective function of changing a constraint's RHS value by small amounts.

REDUCED GRADIENTS

In chapter 4 we saw that the reduced cost of a variable that assumes its simple lower (or upper) bound in the optimal solution generally represents the amount by which the objective function would be reduced (or improved) if this variable were allowed to increase by one unit. Again, this same interpretation applies in a more approximate sense to reduced gradient values. In particular, non-zero reduced gradient values indicate the approximate impact on the objective function value of very small changes in the value of a given variable. For example, in chapter 4 we saw that forcing the production of one Typhoon-Lagoon resulted in a $13.33 reduction in total profit for the problem shown in Figure 8.28. This is reflected by the reduced cost value for Typhoon-Lagoons in Figure 8.29 and the reduced gradient value for Typhoon-Lagoons in Figure 8.30.

Although we used an LP model to discuss the meaning of reduced gradients and Lagrange multipliers, their interpretation is the same for nonlinear problems. As stated earlier, an LP problem can be viewed as a special type of nonlinear programming problem where the objective function and constraints are linear.

SOLVER OPTIONS FOR SOLVING NLPs

Although we can represent an LP problem by a highly structured, and relatively simple, objective function and set of constraints, the objective function and constraints in an NLP problem can be virtually *any* mathematical function. Thus, it is not uncommon to encounter difficulties while trying to solve NLP problems.

Solver provides several options for controlling how it solves NLPs. These options—Estimates, Derivatives, and Search—are located at the bottom of the Solver Options dialog box, as shown in Figure 8.31. The default settings for these options work well for many problems. However, if you have difficulty solving an NLP, you might try changing these options to force Solver to use a different search strategy. A complete description of these options would require an in-depth understanding of calculus, which is not assumed in this book. The following descriptions provide a non-technical overview of these options.

SOLVER OPTIONS FOR NONLINEAR PROBLEMS

Figure 8.31: Solver options for NLP problems

The Estimates option determines how Solver estimates the values of the decision variables while searching for improved solutions. The default setting, Tangent, estimates values using a linear extrapolation technique, whereas the alternate setting, Quadratic, uses a nonlinear extrapolation technique.

The Derivatives option determines how Solver estimates derivatives. When using the default setting, Forward, Solver obtains estimates of first derivatives at a point by perturbing the point once in a forward direction and computing the rise over the run. With the Central setting, Solver obtains estimates of first derivatives by perturbing away from a point in both a backward and forward direction and computes the rise over the run between the two points. The Central setting requires twice as many recalculations as the Forward option but can improve the estimates of the derivatives, yielding better search directions and often fewer iterations. However, the difference in accuracy is usually not worth the extra effort, hence the default is Forward.

The Search option determines how Solver chooses a search direction along which to seek a feasible point with an improved objective value. The default setting, Newton, employs the BFGS method which, although effective, sometimes moves to the optimal solution in very small increments (and very slowly). The Conjugate setting requires more memory but generally identifies search directions that move toward the optimal solution more quickly.

As mentioned earlier, scaling problems often affect how easily Solver can solve a problem. Thus, selecting the Use Automatic Scaling option is also a possible remedy to try if Solver encounters difficulty in solving an NLP.

SUMMARY

This chapter introduced some of the basic concepts involved in nonlinear programming and discussed several applications. The steps involved in formulating and solving an NLP problem are not very different from those required to solve an LP problem—the decision variables are identified and an objective function and any constraints are stated in terms of the decision variables. Because the objective function and constraints in an NLP problem might be nonlinear, the calculations involved in solving NLP problems are different from those included in the simplex method, which is used most often to solve LP problems. NLP problems sometimes involve several local optimal solutions. Thus, finding the global optimal solution to a difficult NLP problem might require re-solving the model several times using different initial starting points.

REFERENCES

Bazaraa, M. and C. Shetty. *Nonlinear Programming: Theory and Algorithms.* New York: Wiley, 1993.

DeWitt, et al. "OMEGA: An Improved Gasoline Blending System for Texaco." *Interfaces*, vol. 19, no. 1, 1985.

Kolesar, P. and E. Blum. "Square Roots Law for Fire Engine Response Distances." *Management Science*, vol. 19, 1973.

Markowitz, H. *Portfolio Selection, Efficient Diversification of Investments.* New York: Wiley, 1959.

Taylor, B., L. Moore, and E. Clayton. "R&D Project Selection and Manpower Allocation with Integer Nonlinear Programming." *Management Science*, vol. 28, no. 10, 1982.

Vollman, T., W. Berry, and C. Whybark. *Manufacturing Planning and Control Systems.* Homewood, IL: Irwin, 1987.

Water Spilled Is Energy Lost: Pacific Gas and Electric Uses Nonlinear Optimization to Manage Power Generation

Source: Ikura, Yoshiro, George Gross and Gene Sand Hall, "PG&E's State-of-the-Art Scheduling Tool for Hydro Systems," *Interfaces*, vol. 16, no. 1, January–February 1986, pages 65–82.

THE POWER PRODUCED by a hydroelectric generator is a nonlinear function of the flow rate of water through the turbine and the pressure. Pressure, or head, is determined by the difference in water level upstream from the generator.

Pacific Gas and Electric Company (PG&E), the world's largest privately held utility, generates power from fossil fuels, nuclear energy, wind, solar energy, and geothermal steam, as well as hydropower. Its Sierra Nevada Hydro System is a complex network of 15 river basins, 143 reservoirs, and 67 power plants. Streamflow peaks markedly in the spring from snow melting in the mountains, whereas demand for electric power peaks in the summer.

Water spilled from a dam cannot be used to generate power at that dam, although it can increase the head at a dam downstream and contribute to power generation there. If the water spills at a time when all of the downstream reservoirs are full, it will spill from all the dams, and its energy will be lost forever. Hydrologists at PG&E attempt to maximize the useful generation of electricity by strategically timing controlled spills to manage the levels of all reservoirs in the system and minimize wasted flow. If done effectively, this reduces the company's reliance on fossil fuel and reduces the cost of electricity to its customers.

This problem was modeled as a nonlinear program with a nonlinear objective function and linear constraints. Because many of the constraints are network flow constraints, using a network flow algorithm along with the linear terms of the objective function produced a good starting point for the nonlinear programming algorithm. A good starting point can be a critical factor in the successful use of nonlinear programming.

PG&E management confirms that the optimization system saves between $10 and $45 million annually compared to manual systems, and the California Public Utilities Commission has recommended its use to others.

Questions and Problems

1. Can the BFGS algorithm be used to solve LP problems? If so, will it always identify a corner point of the feasible region as the optimal solution?

2. Consider an optimization problem with two variables and the constraints $X_1 \leq 5$, $X_2 \leq 5$ where both X_1 and X_2 are nonnegative.

   a. Sketch the feasible region for this problem.

   b. Sketch level curves of a nonlinear objective for this problem that would have exactly one local optimal solution that is also the global optimal solution.

   c. Redraw the feasible region and sketch level curves of a nonlinear objective for this problem that would have a local optimal solution that is not the global optimal solution.

3. Consider the following function:

   $$Y = -0.865 + 8.454X - 1.696X^2 + 0.132X^3 - 0.00331X^4$$

   a. Plot this function on an X-Y graph for positive values of X from 1 to 20.

   b. How many local maximum solutions are there?

   c. How many local minimum solutions are there?

   d. Use Solver to find the maximum value of Y using a starting value of $X = 2$. What value of Y do you obtain?

   e. Use Solver to find the maximum value of Y using a starting value of $X = 14$. What value of Y do you obtain?

4. Consider the following function:

   $$Y = 37.684 - 15.315X + 3.095X^2 - 0.218X^3 + 0.005X^4$$

   a. Plot this function on an X-Y graph for positive values of X from 1 to 20.

   b. How many local maximum solutions are there?

   c. How many local minimum solutions are there?

   d. Use Solver to find the minimum value of Y using a starting value of $X = 3$. What value of Y do you obtain?

   e. Use Solver to find the minimum value of Y using a starting value of $X = 18$. What value of Y do you obtain?

5. Refer to the pricing problem faced by Blue Ridge Hot Tubs discussed in this chapter. The optimal solution to this problem is shown in Figure 8.8. Because the optimal solution occurs at a point in the interior of the feasible region, there are no binding constraints. What values would you expect the Lagrange multipliers for this problem to be at the optimal solution? Create a Sensitivity Report for this problem to verify your answer.

6. Refer to the insurance problem faced by Thom Pearman discussed in this chapter. Let b_i represent the balance in his investment at the beginning of year i and let r represent the annual interest rate.

   a. What is the objective function for this problem? Is it linear or nonlinear?

   b. Write out the first two constraints for this problem algebraically. Are they linear or nonlinear?

7. In the insurance problem, suppose that Thom is confident that he can invest his money to earn a 15% annual rate of return compounded quarterly. Assuming a fixed 15% return, suppose he would now like to determine the minimum amount of money he must invest in order for his after-tax earnings to cover the planned premium payments.

    a. Make whatever changes are necessary to the spreadsheet and answer Thom's question.

    b. Is the model you solved linear or nonlinear?

8. Carnival Confections, Inc. produces two popular southern food items, pork-rinds and fried peanuts, which it sells at a local recreation area on weekends. The owners of the business have estimated their marginal profit function on these items to be:

    $$0.6p - 0.002p^2 + 0.5f - 0.0009f^2 - 0.001pf$$

    Note that p is the number of packages of pork-rinds produced and f is the number of packages of fried peanuts produced. Both of these items require deep frying. The company's fryer has the capacity to produce a total of 600 packages of pork-rinds and/or fried peanuts. One minute of labor is required to dry and package the pork-rinds, and 30 seconds are required to dry and package the peanuts. The company devotes a total of 16 hours of labor to producing these products each week.

    a. Formulate an NLP model for this problem.

    b. Implement your model in a spreadsheet.

    c. What is the optimal solution?

9. An air-ambulance service in Colorado is interested in keeping its helicopter in a central location that would minimize the flight distance to four major ski resorts. An X-Y grid was laid over a map of the area to determine the following latitude and longitude coordinates for the four resorts:

Resort	Longitude	Latitude
Bumpyride	35	57
Keyrock	46	48
Asprin	37	93
Goldenrod	22	67

    a. Formulate an NLP model to determine where the ambulance service should be located in order to minimize the total distance to each resort.

    b. Implement your model in a spreadsheet and solve it. Where should the ambulance service be located?

    c. What other factors might affect the decision and how might you incorporate them in your model? (Consider, for example, differences in the average number of skiers (and accidents) at the different resorts and the topography of the area.)

10. Suppose a company buys an item for \$0.50 per unit and has an annual demand for 15,000 units of this item. Assume it costs \$10 to place an order and the carrying cost is 25%. In what quantity should the item be ordered if the company wants to minimize the total cost of procuring this item?

11. The Heat-Aire Company has two plants that produce identical home heating units. However, production costs at the two differ due to the technology and labor used at each plant. The total costs of production at the plants depends on the quantity produced, and are described as:

    Total cost at plant 1: $2X_1^2 - 1X_1 + 15$

    Total cost at plant 2: $X_2^2 + 0.3X_2 + 10$

    Note that X_1 is the number of heaters produced at plant 1 and X_2 is the number of heaters produced at plant 2. Neither plant can make more than 5,000 heaters. How many heaters should be produced at each plant if management wants to produce 7,000 heaters at the lowest total cost?

    a. Formulate an NLP model for this problem.

    b. Implement your model in a spreadsheet and solve it.

    c. What is the optimal solution?

12. An investor wants to determine the safest way to structure a portfolio to achieve a 12% return from several investments. Investment A produces an average annual return of 15% with a variance of 0.0001. Investment B produces an average rate of return of 9% with a variance of 0.0001. Investment C produces an average rate of return of 21% with a variance of 0.0025. Investments A and B have a covariance of 0.00028, and investments A and C have a covariance of 0.0006. Investments B and C have a covariance of -0.000125.

    a. Formulate an NLP model to determine the portfolio that meets the investor's goals.

    b. Implement your model in a spreadsheet and solve it.

    c. What is the optimal solution?

13. The XYZ company produces two products. The total profit achieved from these products is described by the following equation:

    Total profit $= -0.2X_1^2 - 0.4X_2^2 + 8X_1 + 12X_2 + 1500$

    where $X_1 = $ thousands of units of product 1

    $X_2 = $ thousands of units of product 2

    Every 1,000 units of X_1 require 1 hour of time in the shipping department, and every 1,000 units of X_2 require 30 minutes in the shipping department. Each unit of each product requires 2 pounds of a special ingredient of which 64,000 pounds will be available in the next production period. Additionally, 80 hours of shipping labor will be available in the next production period. Demand for X_1 and X_2 is unlimited.

    a. Formulate an NLP model for this problem.

    b. Implement your model in a spreadsheet and solve it.

    c. What is the optimal solution?

14. A new mother wants to save and invest $75 a month over the next 18 years to establish a college education fund for her child. If she wants this fund to be worth $100,000 in 18 years, what is the minimum rate of return she would need to earn on her investment? Assume monthly compounding. (Hint: Consider using the future value function FV( ) in your spreadsheet.)

15. Refer to question 14. Suppose the mother knows of an investment that will guarantee a 12% annual return compounded monthly. What is the minimum amount she should invest each month to achieve her goal of having $100,000 saved 18 years from now?

Where to Put the Money
A Case in Nonlinear
Programming

BARBARA Roberts has $30,000 to invest for one year. She received this money as a small inheritance from a distant relative. Barbara wants to buy a notebook computer next year when she enters graduate school. Notebook computer prices are falling steadily, and by next September, one year from now, Barbara believes she can buy a lightweight notebook computer with a passive-matrix color screen for about $900. But Barbara does not want to use any of her $3,000 inheritance to buy the computer because she already earmarked that money to help pay the tuition for the first term. She wants to invest the money wisely so she will

have enough money from the interest earned to buy the computer.

Barbara's Uncle Louis, an investment manager, knows of three potential stocks in which she should invest. Barbara agrees with her uncle that the stock market is currently the best place to invest her inheritance. The banks are paying little in dividends and although the stock market is riskier, the returns are greater. The three stocks in Louis's portfolio are Amalgamated Industries, Babbage Computers, and Consolidated Foods. Louis gives Barbara the following chart, which shows these stocks and their returns, in percentages, over the last 10 years.

Year	Amalgamated Industries	Babbage Computers	Consolidated Foods
1985	−3.3	5.92	−2.4
1986	−4.7	−3.8	28.1
1987	11.9	−7	−7.2
1988	9.7	6.6	−2.3
1989	8.6	−4.2	20.4
1990	9.4	11.2	17.4
1991	5.3	3.2	−11.8
1992	−4.9	16.1	−6.6
1993	8.5	10.8	−13.4
1994	−8.3	−8.3	10.9

Contributed by Jack Yurkiewicz, Lubin School of Business, Pace University, New York.

Barbara wants to maximize the expected return in dollars for the next year. She also wants to minimize her risk. She and Louis agree that the standard measure of risk, the variance of the return of the portfolio, can be used in this situation. That is, Barbara wants to minimize the total variance (which also involves the covariance between the various pairs of stock) of the portfolio. Also, based on her uncle's recommendation, Barbara will diversify her potential holdings, by investing at least $500, but no more than $2,000, in any one stock.

Barbara wants to know if she will have enough money to buy a notebook computer next year, in addition to having the $3,000 for tuition. Formulate and solve a nonlinear programming model to determine how much money Barbara should invest in each stock in order to meet her financial goals.

CHAPTER 9

Regression Analysis

REGRESSION ANALYSIS is a modeling technique for analyzing the relationship between a *continuous* (real-valued) dependent variable Y and one or more independent variables X_1, X_2, ..., X_k. The goal in regression analysis is to identify a function that describes, as closely as possible, the relationship between these variables so that we can predict what value the dependent variable will assume given specific values for the independent variables. This chapter shows how to estimate these functions and how to use them to make predictions in a business environment.

AN EXAMPLE

As a simple example, consider the relationship between sales for a company and the amount of money it spends on advertising. Few would question that the level of sales for a company will depend on or be influenced by advertising. Thus, we could view sales as the dependent variable Y and advertising as the independent variable X_1. Although some relationship exists between sales and advertising, we might not know the exact functional form of this relationship. Indeed, there probably is not an exact functional relationship between these variables.

We expect that sales for a company depend to some degree on the amount of money the company spends on advertising. But many other factors might also affect a company's sales, such as general economic conditions, the level of competition in the marketplace, product quality, and so on. Nevertheless, we might be interested in studying the relationship between the dependent variable sales (Y) and the independent variable advertising (X_1) and predicting the average level of sales expected for a given level of advertising. Regression analysis provides the tool for making such predictions.

In order to identify a function that describes the relationship between advertising and sales for a company, we first need to collect sample data to analyze. Suppose that we obtain the data shown in Figure 9.1 (and in the file FIG9-1.XLS on your data disk) for a company on the level of sales observed for various levels of advertising expenditures in 10 different test markets around the country. We will assume that the different test markets are similar in terms of size and other demographic and economic characteristics. The main difference in each market is the level of advertising expenditure.

The data from Figure 9.1 are displayed graphically in Figure 9.2. This graph suggests a strong linear relationship between advertising expenditures and sales. Note that as advertising expenditures increase, sales increase proportionately. However, the relationship between advertising and sales is not perfect. For example, advertising expenditures of $70,000 were used in three different test markets and resulted in three different levels of sales. Thus, the level of sales that occurs for a given level of advertising is subject to random fluctuation.

The random fluctuation, or scattering, of the points in Figure 9.2 suggests that some of the variation in sales is not accounted for by advertising expenditures. Because of the scattering of points, this type of graph is called a **scatter diagram** or **scatter plot**. So although there is not a perfect *functional* relationship between sales and advertising (where each level of advertising yields one unique level of sales), there does seem to be a *statistical* relationship between these variables (where each level of sales is associated with a range or distribution of possible sales values).

Figure 9.1: Sample data for advertising expenditures and observed sales

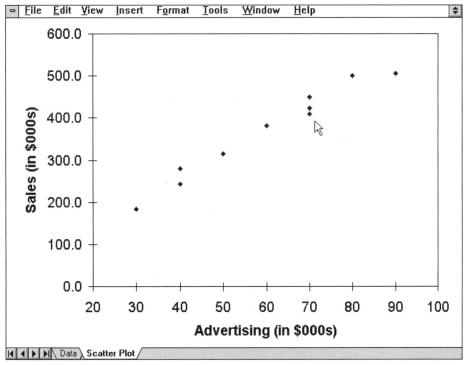

Figure 9.2: Scatter diagram of sales and advertising data

> ### *Creating a Scatter Plot*
> To create a scatter plot like the one shown in Figure 9.2:
> 1. Select cells B4 through C13 shown in Figure 9.1.
> 2. Click the Insert menu.
> 3. Click Chart.
> 4. Click As New Sheet.
>
> Excel's ChartWizard then prompts you to make a number of selections concerning the type of chart you want and how it should be labeled and formatted. After Excel creates a basic chart, you can customize it in many ways. Double-click a chart element to display a dialog box with options for modifying the appearance of the element.

REGRESSION MODELS

We will formalize the somewhat imprecise nature of a statistical relationship by adding an *error term* to what is otherwise a functional relationship. That is, in regression analysis we consider models of the form:

$$Y = f(X_1, X_2, ..., X_k) + \varepsilon \qquad\qquad \textbf{9.1}$$

where ε represents a random disturbance, or error, term. Equation 9.1 is a **regression model**. The number of independent variables in a regression model differs from one application to another. Similarly, the form of $f(\cdot)$ varies from simplelinear functions to more complex polynomial and nonlinear forms. In any case, the model in equation 9.1 conveys the two essential elements of a statistical relationship:

- A tendency for the dependent variable Y to vary with the independent variable(s) in a systematic way, as expressed by $f(X_1, X_2, ..., X_k)$ in equation 9.1

- An element of *unsystematic* or random variation in the dependent variable, as expressed by ε in equation 9.1.

The regression model in equation 9.1 indicates that for any values assumed by the independent variables $X_1, ..., X_k$ there is a probability distribution that describes the possible values that can be assumed by the dependent variable Y. This is portrayed graphically in Figure 9.3 for the case of a single independent variable. The curve drawn in Figure 9.3 represents the regression line (or regression function). It denotes the *systematic* variation between the dependent and independent variables (represented by $f(X_1, X_2, ..., X_k)$ in equation 9.1). The probability distributions in Figure 9.3 denote the *unsystematic* variation in the dependent variable Y at different levels of the independent variable. This represents random variation in the dependent variable (represented by ε in equation 9.1) that cannot be accounted for by the independent variable.

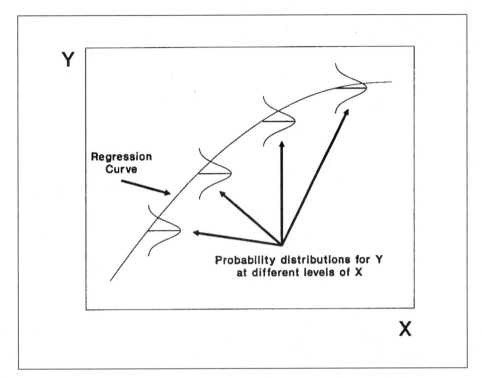

Figure 9.3: Diagram of the distribution of Y values at various levels of X

Notice that the regression function in Figure 9.3 passes through the mean, or average, value for each probability distribution. Therefore, the regression function indicates what value, on average, the dependent variable is expected to assume at various levels of the independent variable. If we want to predict what value the dependent variable Y would assume at some level of the independent variable, the best estimate we could make is given by the regression function. That is, our best estimate of the value Y will assume at a certain level of the independent variable X_1 is the mean (or average) of the distribution of values for Y at that level of X_1.

The actual value assumed by the dependent variable is likely to be somewhat different from our estimate because there is some random, unsystematic variation in the dependent variable that cannot be accounted for by our regression function. If we could repeatedly sample and observe actual values of Y at a given level of X_1, sometimes the actual value of Y would be higher than our estimated (mean) value and sometimes it would be lower. So the difference between the actual value of Y and our predicted value of Y would, on average, tend toward 0. For this reason, we can assume that the error term ε in equation 9.1 has an average, or expected, value of 0 if the probability distributions for the dependent variable Y at the various levels of the independent variable are normally distributed (bell-shaped) as shown in Figure 9.3.

SIMPLE LINEAR REGRESSION ANALYSIS

As mentioned earlier, the function $f(\cdot)$ in equation 9.1 can assume many forms. However, the scatter plot in Figure 9.2 suggests that a strong linear relationship exists between the independent variable in our example (advertising expenditures)

and the dependent variable (sales). That is, we could draw a straight line through the data in Figure 9.2 that would fit the data fairly well. So the formula of a straight line might account for the systematic variation between advertising and sales. Therefore, the following simple linear regression model might be an appropriate choice for describing the relationship between advertising and sales:

$$Y_i = \beta_0 + \beta_1 X_{1_i} + \varepsilon_i \tag{9.2}$$

In equation 9.2, Y_i denotes the *actual* sales value for the ith observation, X_{1_i} denotes the advertising expenditures associated with Y_i, and ε_i is an error term indicating that when X_{1_i} dollars are spent on advertising, sales might not always equal $\beta_0 + \beta_1 X_{1_i}$. The parameter β_0 represents a constant value (sometimes referred to as the y-intercept because it represents the point where the line goes through the Y-axis) and β_1 represents the slope of the line (that is, the amount by which the line rises or falls per unit increase in X_1). Assuming that a straight line accounts for the systematic variation between Y and X_1, the error terms ε_i represent the amounts by which the actual levels of sales are scattered around the regression line. Again, if the errors are scattered randomly around the regression line, they should average out to 0 or have an expected value of 0.

The model in equation 9.2 is a simple model because it contains only one independent variable. It is linear because none of the parameters (β_0 and β_1) appear as an exponent in the model or are multiplied or divided by one another.

Conceptually, it is important to understand that we are assuming that a large population of Y values occurs at each level of X_1. The parameters β_0 and β_1 represent, respectively, the intercept and slope of the *true* regression line relating these populations. For this reason, β_0 and β_1 are sometimes referred to as **population parameters**. We usually never know the exact numeric values for the population parameters in a given regression problem (we know that these values exist, but we don't know what they are). In order to determine the numeric values of the population parameters, we would have to look at the entire population of Y at each level of X_1—usually an impossible task. However, by taking a sample of Y values at selected levels of X_1 we can *estimate* the values of the population parameters. We will identify the estimated values of β_0 and β_1 as b_0 and b_1, respectively. The remaining problem is to determine the best values of b_0 and b_1 from our sample data.

DEFINING "BEST FIT"

An infinite number of values could be assigned to b_0 and b_1. So searching for the exact values for b_0 and b_1 to produce the line that best fits our sample data might seem like searching for a needle in a haystack—and it is certainly not something we want to do manually. To have the computer estimate the values for b_0 and b_1 that produce the line that best fits our data, we must give it some guidance and define what we mean by the best fit.

We will use the symbol $\hat{Y}_i$ to denote our estimated, or fitted, value of Y_i, which is defined as:

$$\hat{Y}_i = b_0 + b_1 X_{1_i} \tag{9.3}$$

We want to the find values for b_0 and b_1 that make all the *estimated* sales values ($\hat{Y}_i$) as close as possible to the *actual* sales values (Y_i). For example, the data in Figure 9.1 indicate that we spent $30,000 on advertising ($X_{1_1} = 30$) and observed sales of $184,400 ($Y_1 = 184.4$). So in equation 9.3, if we let $X_1 = 30$ we want $\hat{Y}$ to assume a value that is as close as possible to 184.4. Similarly, in the three instances in Figure 9.1 where $70,000 was spent on advertising ($X_{1_6} = X_{1_7} = X_{1_8} = 70$), we observed sales of $450,200, $423,600, and $410,200 ($Y_6 = 450.2$, $Y_7 = 423.6$, $Y_8 = 410.2$). So in equation 9.3, if we let $X_1 = 70$ we want $\hat{Y}$ to assume a value that is as close as possible to 450.2, 423.6, and 410.2.

If we could find values for b_0 and b_1 so that all the estimated sales values were exactly the same as all the actual sales values ($\hat{Y}_i = Y_i$ for all observations i), we would have the equation of the straight line that passes through each data point—in other words, the line would fit our data perfectly. This is impossible for the data in Figure 9.2 because a straight line could not be drawn to pass through each data point in the graph. In most regression problems it is impossible to find a function that fits the data perfectly because most data sets contain some amount of unsystematic variation.

Although we are unlikely to find values for b_0 and b_1 that will allow us to fit our data perfectly, we will try to find values that make the differences between the estimated values for the dependent variable and the actual values for the dependent variable ($Y_i - \hat{Y}_i$) as small as possible. We refer to the difference $Y_i - \hat{Y}_i$ as the **estimation error** for observation i because it measures how far away the estimated value $\hat{Y}_i$ is from the actual value Y_i. The estimation errors in a regression problem are also referred to as **residuals**.

Although different criteria can be used to determine the best values for b_0 and b_1, the most widely used method determines the values that minimize the sum of squared estimation errors—or error sum of squares (ESS) for short. That is, we will attempt to find values for b_0 and b_1 that minimize:

$$ESS = \sum_{i=1}^{n}(Y_i - \hat{Y}_i)^2 = \sum_{i=1}^{n}(Y_i - (b_0 + b_1 X_{1_i}))^2 \qquad \textbf{9.4}$$

Several observations should be made concerning ESS. Because each estimation error is squared, the value of ESS will always be nonnegative and, therefore, the smallest value ESS can assume is 0. The only way for ESS to equal 0 is for all the individual estimation errors to be 0 ($Y_i - \hat{Y}_i = 0$ for all observations), in which case the estimated regression line would fit our data perfectly. Thus, minimizing ESS seems to be a good objective to use in searching for the best values of b_0 and b_1. Because regression analysis finds the values of the parameter estimates that minimize the sum of squared estimation errors, it is sometimes referred to as the **method of least squares**.

SOLVING THE PROBLEM USING SOLVER

We can calculate the optimal parameter estimates for a linear regression model in a number of ways. As in earlier chapters, we can use Solver to find the values for b_0 and b_1 that minimize the ESS quantity in equation 9.4.

The problem of finding the optimal values for b_0 and b_1 in equation 9.4 is an unconstrained nonlinear optimization problem. Consider the spreadsheet in Figure 9.4.

Key Cell Formulas

Cell	Formula	Copied to
D4	=$I$2+$I$3*B4	D5:D13
E4	=C4−D4	E5:E13
F4	=E4^2	F5:F13
F15	=SUM(F4:F13)	—

Figure 9.4: Using Solver to solve the regression problem

In Figure 9.4, cells I2 and I3 represent the values for b_0 and b_1, respectively. These cells are labeled Intercept and Slope because b_0 represents the intercept in equation 9.3 and b_1 represents the slope. Values of 70 and 5 were entered for these cells as rough guesses of their optimal values.

To use Solver to calculate the optimal values of b_0 and b_1, we need to implement a formula in the spreadsheet that corresponds to the ESS calculation in equation 9.4. This formula represents the objective function to be minimized. To calculate the ESS, we first need to calculate the sales values estimated by the regression function in equation 9.3 for each observation in our sample. These estimated sales values ($\hat{Y}_i$) were created in column D as:

Formula for cell D4:   =$I$2+$I$3*B4

(copy to D5 through D13)

The estimation errors ($Y_i - \hat{Y}_i$) were calculated in column E as:

Formula for cell E4:   =C4−D4

(copy to E5 through E13)

The squared estimation errors ($(Y_i - \hat{Y}_i)^2$) were calculated in column F as:

Formula for cell F4:   =E4^2
(copy to F5 through F13)

Finally, the sum of the squared estimation errors (ESS) was calculated in cell F15 as:

Formula for cell F15:   =SUM(F4:F13)

Note that the formula in cell F15 corresponds exactly to equation 9.4.

The graph at the bottom of Figure 9.4 plots the line connecting the estimated sales values against the actual sales values. The intercept and slope of this line are determined by the values in I2 and I3. Although this line seems to fit our data fairly well, we do not know if this is the line that minimizes the ESS value. However, we can use the Solver parameters and options shown in Figure 9.5 to determine the values for I2 and I3 that minimize the ESS value in F15.

Figure 9.5: *Solver parameters and options for the regression problem*

Figure 9.6 shows the optimal solution to this problem. In this spreadsheet the intercept and slope of the line that best fits our data are $b_0 = 36.3424$ and $b_1 = 5.55029$, respectively. The ESS value of 3,336.24 associated with these optimal parameter estimates is better (or smaller) than the ESS value for the parameter estimates shown in Figure 9.4. No other values for b_0 and b_1 would result in an ESS value smaller than the one shown in Figure 9.6. Thus, the equation of the straight line that best fits our data according to the least squares criterion is represented by:

$$\hat{Y}_i = 36.3424 + 5.55029X_{1_i}$$

9.5

File	Edit	View	Insert	Format	Tools	Data	Window	Help			
	A	B	C	D	E	F	G	H	I	J	
1											
2		Advertising	Actual Sales	Est. Sales		Squared		Intercept	36.3424		
3	Obs	(in $000s)	(in $000s)	(in $000s)	Error	Error		Slope	5.55029		
4	1	30	184.4	202.9	-18.45	340.45					
5	2	40	279.1	258.4	20.75	430.39					
6	3	40	244.0	258.4	-14.35	206.04					
7	4	50	314.2	313.9	0.34	0.12					
8	5	60	382.2	369.4	12.84	164.87					
9	6	70	450.2	424.9	25.34	641.97					
10	7	70	423.6	424.9	-1.26	1.60					
11	8	70	410.2	424.9	-14.66	215.00					
12	9	80	500.4	480.4	20.03	401.37					
13	10	90	505.3	535.9	-30.57	934.45					
14											
15					ESS=	3336.24					

Figure 9.6: *Optimal solution to the regression problem*

SOLVING THE PROBLEM USING THE REGRESSION TOOL

In addition to Solver, Excel provides another tool for solving regression problems that is easier to use and provides more information about a regression problem. We'll demonstrate the use of this regression tool by referring back to the original data for the current problem, shown in Figure 9.1. Before you can use the regression tool in Excel, you need to make sure that the Analysis ToolPak add-in is available. You can do this by completing the following steps:

1. Click the Tools menu.

2. Click Add-Ins.

3. Click Analysis ToolPak. (If Analysis ToolPak is not listed among your available add-ins, exit Excel, double-click the MS Excel Setup icon, click Add/Remove, double-click Add-Ins, and select Analysis ToolPak. Then restart Excel and repeat the above instructions.)

After ensuring that the Analysis ToolPak is available, you can access the regression tool by completing the following steps:

1. Click the Tools menu.

2. Click Data Analysis.

3. Click Regression.

After you choose the Regression command, the Regression dialog box appears, as shown in Figure 9.7. This dialog box presents many options and selections; at this point we will focus on only three options: the Y-Range, the X-Range, and the Output-Range. The Y-Range corresponds to the range in the spreadsheet containing the sample observations for the *dependent* variable (C4 through C13 for the example in Figure 9.1). The X-Range corresponds to the range in the spreadsheet containing the sample observations for the *independent* variable (B4 through B13 for the current example). We also need to specify the output range where we want the regression results to be reported. In Figure 9.7, we selected the New Worksheet Ply option to indicate that we want the regression results placed on a new sheet named "Results." With the dialog box selections complete, we can click the OK button and Excel will calculate the least squares values for b_0 and b_1 (along with other summary statistics).

Figure 9.7: Regression dialog box

Figure 9.8 shows the Results sheet for our example. For now, we will focus on only a few values in Figure 9.8. Note that the value labeled "Intercept" in cell B17 represents the optimal value for b_0 ($b_0 = 36.342$). The value representing the coefficient for "X Variable 1" in cell B18 represents the optimal value for b_1 ($b_1 = 5.550$). Thus, the estimated regression function is represented by:

$$\hat{Y}_i = b_0 + b_1 X_{1_i} = 36.342 + 5.550 X_{1_i} \qquad 9.6$$

Equation 9.6 is essentially the same result we obtained earlier using Solver (see equation 9.5). Thus, we can calculate the parameter estimates for a regression function using either Solver or the regression tool shown in Figure 9.7. The advantage of the regression tool is that it does not require us to set up any special formulas or cells in the spreadsheet, and it produces additional statistical results about the problem under study.

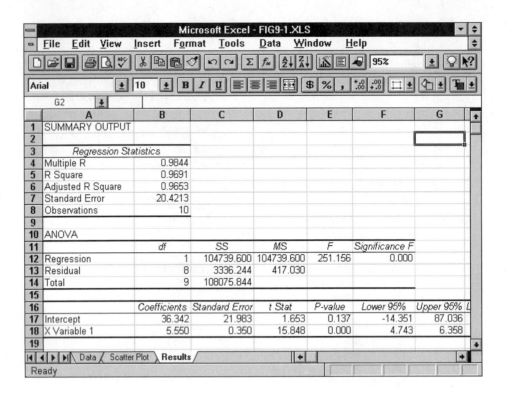

Figure 9.8: Results of the regression calculations

EVALUATING THE FIT

Our goal in the example problem is to identify the equation of a straight line that fits our data well. Having calculated the estimated regression line (using either Solver or the regression tool), we might be interested in determining how well the line fits our data. Using equation 9.6 we can compute the estimated or expected level of sales ($\hat{Y}_i$) for each observation in our sample. The $\hat{Y}_i$ values are calculated in column D of Figure 9.9 as:

Formula for cell D4: $= 36.342 + 5.550 * B4$
(copy to D5 through D13)

Figure 9.10 shows a graph of the estimated regression function along with the actual sales data. This function represents the expected amount of sales that would occur for each value of the independent variable (that is each value in column D of Figure 9.9 falls on this line). From this graph we see that the regression function seems to fit the data reasonably well in this example. In particular, it seems that the actual sales values fluctuate around this line in a fairly unsystematic, or random, pattern. Thus, it appears that we have achieved our goal of identifying a function that accounts for most, if not all, of the systematic variation between the dependent and independent variables.

	Key Cell Formulas	
Cell	**Formula**	**Copied to**
D4	=36.342+5.55*B4	D5:D13

Figure 9.9: Estimated sales values at each level of advertising

Figure 9.10: Graph of the regression line through the actual sales data

THE R² STATISTIC

In Figure 9.8, the value labeled "R Square" in cell B5 provides a goodness-of-fit measure. This value represents the **R² statistic** (also referred to as the **coefficient of determination**). This statistic ranges in value from 0 to 1 ($0 \leq R^2 \leq 1$) and indicates the proportion of the total variation in the dependent variable Y around its mean (average) that is accounted for by the independent variable(s) in the estimated regression function.

The total variation in the dependent variable Y around its mean is described by a measure known as the total sum of squares (TSS), which is defined as:

$$TSS = \sum_{i=1}^{n} (Y_i - \bar{Y})^2 \qquad\qquad 9.7$$

The TSS equals the sum of the squared differences between each observation Y_i in the sample and the average value of Y, denoted in equation 9.7 by $\bar{Y}$. The difference between each observed value of Y_i and the average value $\bar{Y}$ can be decomposed into two parts as:

$$Y_i - \bar{Y} = (Y_i - \hat{Y}_i) + (\hat{Y}_i - \bar{Y}) \qquad\qquad 9.8$$

Figure 9.11 illustrates this decomposition for a hypothetical data point. The value $Y_i - \hat{Y}_i$ in equation 9.8 represents the estimation error, or the amount of the total deviation between Y_i and $\bar{Y}$ that is not accounted for by the regression function. The value $\hat{Y}_i - \bar{Y}$ in equation 9.8 represents the amount of the total deviation in Y_i from $\bar{Y}$ that is accounted for by the regression function.

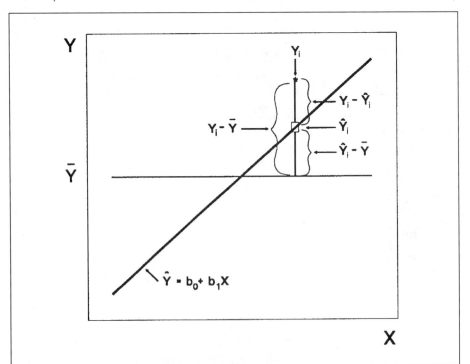

Figure 9.11: Decomposition of the total deviation into error and regression components

The decomposition of the individual deviation in equation 9.8 also applies to the TSS in equation 9.7. That is, the *total sum of squares* (TSS) can be decomposed into the following two parts:

$$\underbrace{\sum_{i=1}^{n}(Y_i - \overline{Y})^2}_{TSS} = \underbrace{\sum_{i=1}^{n}(Y_i - \hat{Y}_i)^2}_{ESS} + \underbrace{\sum_{i=1}^{n}(\hat{Y}_i - \overline{Y})^2}_{RSS}$$ 9.9

ESS is the quantity that is minimized in least squares regression. ESS represents the amount of variation in Y around its mean that the regression function cannot account for, or the amount of variation in the dependent variable that is unexplained by the regression function. Therefore, the regression sum of squares (RSS) represents the amount of variation in Y around its mean that the regression function can account for, or the amount of variation in the dependent variable that is explained by the regression function. In Figure 9.8, cells C12, C13, and C14 contain the values for RSS, ESS, and TSS, respectively.

Now consider the following definitions of the R^2 statistic:

$$R^2 = \frac{RSS}{TSS} = 1 - \frac{ESS}{TSS}$$ 9.10

From the previous definition of TSS in equation 9.9, we can see that if ESS = 0 (which can occur only if the regression function fits the data perfectly), then TSS = RSS and, therefore, $R^2 = 1$. On the other hand, if RSS = 0 (which means that the regression function was unable to explain any of the variation in the behavior of the dependent variable Y), then TSS = ESS and $R^2 = 0$. So, the closer the R^2 statistic is to the value 1, the better the estimated regression function fits the data.

From cell B5 in Figure 9.8 we observe that the value of the R^2 statistic is approximately 0.969. This indicates that approximately 96.9% of the total variation in our dependent variable around its mean has been accounted for by the independent variable in our estimated regression function. Because this value is fairly close to the maximum possible R^2 value (1), this statistic indicates that the regression function we have estimated fits our data well. This is confirmed by the graph in Figure 9.10.

THE MULTIPLE R STATISTIC

The multiple R statistic shown in the regression output in Figure 9.8 represents the strength of the linear relationship between actual and estimated values for the dependent variable. As with the R^2 statistic, the multiple R statistic varies between 0 and 1 with values near 1 indicating a good fit. When a regression model includes only one independent variable, the multiple R statistic is equivalent to the square root of the R^2 statistic. We'll focus on the R^2 statistic because its interpretation is more apparent than that of the multiple R statistic.

MAKING PREDICTIONS

Using the estimated regression in equation 9.6, we can make predictions about the level of sales expected for different levels of advertising expenditures. For example, suppose the company wants to estimate the level of sales that would occur if $65,000 were spent on advertising in a given market. Assuming the market in question is similar to those used in estimating the regression function, the expected sales level is estimated as:

$$\text{Estimated Sales (in \$000s)} = b_0 + b_1 \times 65 = 36.342 + 5.550 \times 65 = 397.092$$

So if the company spends $65,000 on advertising (in a market similar to those used to estimate the regression function), we would expect to observe sales of approximately $397,092. The *actual* level of sales is likely to differ somewhat from this value due to other random factors influencing sales.

THE STANDARD ERROR

A measure of the accuracy of the prediction obtained from a regression model is given by the standard deviation of the estimation errors—also known as the standard error, S_e. If we let n denote the number of observations in the data set, and k denote the number of independent variables in the regression model, the formula for the standard error is represented by:

$$S_e = \sqrt{\frac{\sum_{i=1}^{n}(Y_i - \hat{Y}_i)^2}{n-k-1}} \qquad \textbf{9.11}$$

The **standard error** measures the amount of scatter, or variation, in the actual data around the fitted regression function. Cell B7 in Figure 9.8 indicates that the standard error for our example problem is $S_e = 20.421$.

The standard error is useful in evaluating the level of uncertainty in predictions we make with a regression model. As a *very* rough rule-of-thumb, there is approximately a 68% chance of the actual level of sales falling within ±1 standard error of the predicted value $\hat{Y}_i$. Alternatively, the chance of the actual level of sales falling within ±2 standard errors of the predicted value $\hat{Y}_i$ is approximately 95%. In our example, if the company spends $65,000 on advertising we could be roughly 95% confident that the actual level of sales observed would fall somewhere in the range from $356,250 to $437,934 ($\hat{Y}_i \pm 2S_e$).

PREDICTION INTERVALS FOR NEW VALUES OF Y

To calculate a more accurate confidence interval for a prediction, or **prediction interval**, of a new value of Y when $X_1 = X_{1_h}$, we first calculate the estimated value $\hat{Y}_h$ as:

$$\hat{Y}_h = b_0 + b_1 X_{1_h} \qquad \textbf{9.12}$$

A $(1 - \alpha)\%$ prediction interval for a new value of Y when $X_1 = X_{1_h}$ is represented by:

$$\hat{Y}_h \pm t_{(1-\alpha/2;\, n-2)} S_p \qquad \textbf{9.13}$$

where $t_{(1-\alpha/2;\, n-2)}$ represents the $1 - \alpha/2$ percentile of a *t*-distribution with $n - 2$ degrees of freedom, and S_p represents the standard prediction error defined by:

$$S_p = S_e \sqrt{1 + \frac{1}{n} + \frac{(X_{1_h} - \overline{X})^2}{\sum_{i=1}^{n}(X_{1_i} - \overline{X})^2}} \qquad \textbf{9.14}$$

The rule-of-thumb presented earlier is a generalization of equation 9.13. Notice that S_p is always larger than S_e because the term under the square root symbol is always greater than 1. Also notice that the magnitude of the difference between S_p and S_e increases as the difference between X_{1_h} and $\overline{X}$ increases. Thus, the prediction intervals generated by the rule-of-thumb tend to underestimate the true amount of uncertainty involved in making predictions. This is illustrated in Figure 9.12.

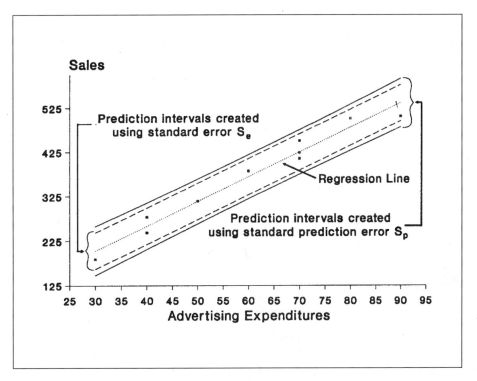

Figure 9.12: Comparison of prediction intervals obtained using the rule-of-thumb and the more accurate statistical calculation

As shown in Figure 9.12, for this example problem there is not a lot of difference between the prediction intervals created using the rule-of-thumb and the more accurate prediction interval given in equation 9.13. In a situation requiring a precise prediction interval, the various quantities needed to construct the prediction interval in equation 9.13 can be computed easily in Excel. Figure 9.13 provides an example of a 95% prediction interval for a new value of sales when $65,000 is spent on advertising.

To create this prediction interval, we must first use equation 9.12 to calculate the estimated sales level ($\hat{Y}_h$) when advertising equals $65,000 ($X_{1_h} = 65$). The value 65 is entered in cell B17 to represent X_{1_h} and the estimated sales level ($\hat{Y}_h$) is calculated in cell D17 as:

Formula for cell D17:   =36.342+5.550*B17

The expected level of sales when $65,000 is spent on advertising is approximately $397,100. The standard error (S_e) shown in cell B19 is extracted from the Results sheet shown in Figure 9.8 as:

Formula for cell B19:   =Results!B7

The standard prediction error (S_p) is calculated in cell B20 as:

Formula for cell B20:   =B19*SQRT(1+1/10+(B17–AVERAGE(B4:B13))^2/
                          (10*VARP(B4:B13)))

	File	Edit	View	Insert	Format	Tools	Data	Window	Help		
	A	B	C	D	E	F	G	H	

	A	B	C	D	E	F	G	H
1								
2		Advertising	Actual Sales	Est. Sales				
3	Obs	(in $000s)	(in $000s)	(in $000s)				
4	1	30	184.4	202.8				
5	2	40	279.1	258.3				
6	3	40	244.0	258.3				
7	4	50	314.2	313.8				
8	5	60	382.2	369.3				
9	6	70	450.2	424.8				
10	7	70	423.6	424.8				
11	8	70	410.2	424.8				
12	9	80	500.4	480.3				
13	10	90	505.3	535.8				
14								
15					95% Prediction Interval			
16					Lower limit	Upper limit		
17	Prediction	65	?	397.1	347.537	446.647		
18								
19	Se	20.4213237						
20	Sp	21.4895302						
21	t	2.30600563						
22								
23								
24								
25								

Data / Scatter Plot / Results / Regression Line /

Key Cell Formulas

Cell	Formula	Copied to
D17	=36.342+5.55*B17	—
B19	=Results!B7	—
B20	=B19*SQRT(1+1/10+(B17–AVERAGE(B4:B13))^2/ (10*VARP(B4:B13)))	—
B21	=TINV(1–0.95,8)	—
E17	=D17–B21*B20	—
F17	=D17+B21*B20	—

Figure 9.13: Example of calculating a prediction interval

The value 10 appearing in the preceding formula corresponds to the sample size n in equation 9.14. The appropriate t-value for a 95% confidence (or prediction) interval is calculated in cell B21 as:

Formula for cell B21:   =TINV(1–0.95,8)

The first argument in the preceding formula corresponds to 1 minus the desired confidence level (or $\alpha = 0.05$). The second argument corresponds to $n - 2$ ($10 - 2 = 8$). Cells E17 and E18 calculate the lower and upper limits of the prediction interval as:

Formula for cell E17:   =D17–B21*B20

Formula for cell E18:   =D17+B21*B20

The results indicate that when $65,000 is spent on advertising we expect to observe sales of approximately $397,100, but realize that the actual sales level is likely to deviate somewhat from this value. However, we can be 95% confident that the actual sales value observed will fall somewhere in the range from $347,537 to $446,647. (Notice that this prediction interval is somewhat wider than the range from $356,250 to $437,934 generated earlier using the rule-of-thumb.)

CONFIDENCE INTERVALS FOR MEAN VALUES OF Y

At times you might want to construct a confidence interval for the average, or mean, value of Y when $X_1 = X_{1_h}$. This involves a slightly different procedure from constructing a prediction interval for a *new individual* value of Y when $X_1 = X_{1_h}$. A $(1 - \alpha)\%$ confidence interval for the average value of Y when $X_1 = X_{1_h}$ is represented by:

$$\hat{Y}_h \pm t_{(1 - \alpha/2; \, n - 2)} S_a \qquad\qquad 9.15$$

where $\hat{Y}_h$ is defined by equation 9.12, $t_{(1 - \alpha/2; \, n - 2)}$ represents the $1 - \alpha/2$ percentile of a *t*-distribution with $n - 2$ degrees of freedom, and S_a is represented by:

$$S_a = S_e \sqrt{\frac{1}{n} + \frac{(X_{1_h} - \overline{X})^2}{\sum_{i=1}^{n}(X_{1_i} - \overline{X})^2}} \qquad\qquad 9.16$$

Comparing the definition of S_a in equation 9.16 with that of S_p in equation 9.14 reveals that S_a will always be smaller than S_p. Therefore, the confidence interval for the average value of Y when $X_1 = X_{1_h}$ will be tighter (or cover a smaller range) than the prediction interval for a new value of Y when $X_1 = X_{1_h}$. This type of confidence interval can be implemented in a similar way to that described earlier for prediction intervals.

A NOTE ABOUT EXTRAPOLATION

Predictions made using an estimated regression function might have little or no validity for values of the independent variable that are substantially different from those represented in the sample. For example, the advertising expenditures represented in the sample in Figure 9.1 range from $30,000 to $90,000. Thus, we cannot assume that our model will give accurate estimates of sales levels at advertising expenditures significantly above or below this range of values, because the relationship between sales and advertising might be quite different outside this range.

STATISTICAL TESTS FOR POPULATION PARAMETERS

Recall that the parameter β_1 in equation 9.2 represents the slope of the *true* regression line (or the amount by which the dependent variable Y is expected to change given a unit change in X_1). If no linear relationship exists between the dependent and independent variables, the true value of β_1 for the model in equation 9.2 should be 0. As mentioned earlier, we cannot calculate or observe the true value of β_1 but instead must estimate its value using the sample statistic b_1. However, because the value of b_1 is based on a sample rather than on the entire population of possible values, its value is probably not exactly equal to the true (but unknown) value of β_1. Thus, we might want to determine how different the true value of β_1 is from its estimated value b_1. The regression results in Figure 9.8 provide a variety of information addressing this issue.

Cell B18 in Figure 9.8 indicates that the estimated value of β_1 is $b_1 = 5.550$. Cells F18 and G18 give the lower and upper limits of a 95% confidence interval for the true value of β_1. That is, we can be 95% confident that $4.74 \leq \beta_1 \leq 6.35$. This indicates that for every \$1,000 increase in advertising we would expect to see an increase in sales of approximately \$4,740 to \$6,350. Notice that this confidence interval does not include the value 0. Thus we can be at least 95% confident that a linear relationship exists between advertising and sales ($\beta_1 \neq 0$). (If we want an interval other than a 95% confidence interval we can use the Confidence Level option in the Regression dialog box, shown in Figure 9.7, to specify a different interval.)

The t-statistic and p-value listed in cells D18 and E18 in Figure 9.8 provide another way of testing whether $\beta_1 = 0$. According to statistical theory, if $\beta_1 = 0$ then the ratio of b_1 to its standard error should follow a t-distribution with $n - 2$ degrees of freedom. Thus, the t-statistic for testing if $\beta_1 = 0$ in cell D18 is:

$$t\text{-statistic in cell D18} = \frac{b_1}{\text{standard error of } b_1} = \frac{5.550}{0.35022} = 15.84789$$

The p-value in cell E18 indicates the probability of obtaining an outcome that is more extreme than the observed test statistic value if $\beta_1 = 0$. In this case, the p-value is 0, indicating that there is virtually no chance that we will obtain an outcome as large as the observed value for b_1 if the true value of β_1 is 0. Therefore, we conclude that the true value of β_1 is not equal to 0. This is the same conclusion implied earlier by the confidence interval for β_1.

The t-statistic, p-value, and confidence interval for the intercept β_0 are listed in Figure 9.8 in row 17, and would be interpreted in the same way as demonstrated for β_1. Notice that the confidence interval for β_0 straddles the value 0 and, therefore, we cannot be certain that the intercept is significantly different from 0. The p-value for β_0 indicates that we have a 13.689% chance of obtaining an outcome more extreme than the observed value of b_0 if the true value of β_0 is 0. Both of these results indicate a fair chance that $\beta_0 = 0$.

ANALYSIS OF VARIANCE

The analysis of variance (ANOVA) results, shown in Figure 9.8, provide another way of testing whether or not $\beta_1 = 0$. The values in the MS column in the ANOVA table represent values known as the mean squared regression (MSR) and mean squared error (MSE), respectively. These values are computed by dividing the RSS and ESS values in C12 and C13 by the corresponding degrees of freedom values in cells B12 and B13.

If $\beta_1 = 0$ then the ratio of MSR to MSE follows an F-distribution. The statistic labeled "F" in cell E12 is:

$$F\text{-statistic in cell E12} = \frac{\text{MSR}}{\text{MSE}} = \frac{104739.600}{417.030} = 251.156$$

The value in F12 labeled "Significance F" is similar to the p-values described earlier, and indicates the probability of obtaining a value in excess of the observed value for the F-statistic if $\beta_1 = 0$. In this case, the significance of F is 0, indicating that there is virtually no chance that we would have obtained the observed value for b_1 if the true value of β_1 is 0. Therefore, we conclude that the true value of β_1 is not equal to 0. This is the same conclusion implied earlier by our previous analysis.

The F-statistic might seem a bit redundant, given that we can use the t-statistic to test whether or not $\beta_1 = 0$. However, the F-statistic serves a different purpose, which becomes apparent in multiple regression models with more than one independent variable. The F-statistic tests whether or not *all* of the β_i for *all* of the independent variables in a regression model are *all* simultaneously equal to 0. A simple linear regression model contains only one independent variable. In this case, the tests involving the F-statistic and the t-statistic are equivalent.

ASSUMPTIONS FOR THE STATISTICAL TESTS

The methods for constructing confidence intervals are based on important assumptions concerning the simple linear regression model presented in equation 9.2. Throughout this discussion, we assumed that the error terms ε_i are independent, normally distributed random variables with expected (or mean) values of 0 and constant variances. Thus, the statistical procedures for constructing intervals and performing t-tests apply only when these assumptions are true for a given set of data. As long as these assumptions are not seriously violated, the procedures described offer good approximations of the desired confidence intervals and t-tests. Various diagnostic checks can be performed on the residuals $(Y_i - \hat{Y}_i)$ to see whether or not our assumptions concerning the properties of the error terms are valid. These diagnostics are discussed in-depth in most statistics books, but are not repeated in this text. Excel also provides basic diagnostics that can be helpful in determining whether assumptions about the error terms are violated.

The Regression dialog box (shown in Figure 9.7) provides two options for producing graphs that highlight serious violations of the error term assumptions. These options are Residual Plots and Normal Probability Plots. Figure 9.14 shows the graphs produced by these two options for our example problem.

The first graph in Figure 9.14 results from the Residual Plots option. This graph plots the residuals (or estimation errors) versus each independent variable in the regression model. Our example problem involves one independent variable—therefore, we have one residual plot. If the assumptions underlying the regression model are met, the residuals should fall within a horizontal band centered around 0 and should display no systematic tendency to be positive or negative. The residual plot in Figure 9.14 indicates that the residuals for our example problem fall randomly within a range from –30 to +30. Thus, no serious problems are indicated by this graph.

The second graph in Figure 9.14 results from the Normal Probability Plot option. If the error terms in equation 9.2 are normally distributed random variables, the dependent variable in equation 9.2 is a normally distributed random variable prior to sampling. Thus, one way to evaluate whether we can assume that the error terms are normally distributed is to determine if we can assume that the dependent variable is normally distributed. The normal probability plot provides an easy way to evaluate whether the sample values on the dependent variable are consistent with the normality assumption. A plot that is approximately linear (such as the one in Figure 9.14) supports the assumption of normality.

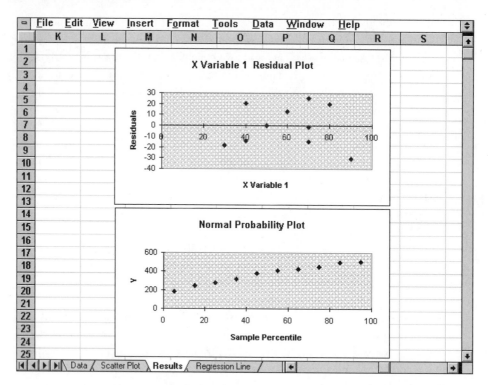

Figure 9.14: Residual plot and normal probability plot for the example problem

If the residual plot shows a systematic tendency for the residuals to be positive or negative, this indicates that the function chosen to model the systematic variation between the dependent and independent variables is inadequate and that another functional form would be more appropriate. An example of this type of residual plot is given in the first graph in Figure 9.15.

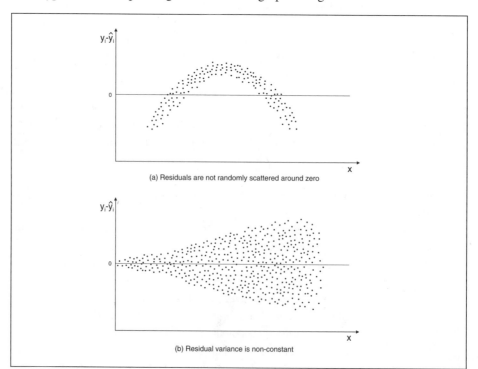

Figure 9.15: Residual plots indicating that the fitted regression model is not adequate

If the residual plot indicates that the magnitude of the residuals is increasing (or decreasing) as the value of the independent variable increases, we would question the validity of the assumption of constant error variances. An example of this type of residual plot is given in the second graph in Figure 9.15. (Note that checking for increasing or decreasing magnitude in the residuals requires multiple observations on Y at the same value of X and at various levels of X.) In some cases, a simple transformation of the dependent variable can correct the problem of nonconstant error variances. Such transformations are discussed in more advanced texts on regression analysis.

A NOTE ABOUT STATISTICAL TESTS

Regardless of the form of the distribution of the error terms, least squares regression can always be used to fit regression curves to data in order to predict the value the dependent variable will assume for a given level of the independent variables. Many decision makers never bother to look at residual plots or to construct confidence intervals for parameters in the regression models for the predictions they make. However, the accuracy of predictions made using regression models depends on how well the regression function fits the data. At the very least, we should always check to see how well a regression function fits a given data set. We can do so using residual plots, graphs of the actual data versus the estimated values, and the R^2 statistic.

INTRODUCTION TO MULTIPLE REGRESSION

We have seen that regression analysis involves identifying a function that relates the *systematic* changes in a continuous dependent variable to the values of one or more independent variables. That is, our goal in regression analysis is to identify an appropriate representation of the function $f(\cdot)$ in:

$$Y = f(X_1, X_2, ..., X_k) + \varepsilon \qquad \textbf{9.17}$$

The previous sections in this chapter introduced some of the basic concepts of regression analysis by considering a special case of equation 9.17 that involves a *single* independent variable. Although such a model might be appropriate in some situations, a business person is far more likely to encounter situations involving more than one (or multiple) independent variables. We'll now consider how *multiple* regression analysis can be applied to these situations.

MULTIPLE LINEAR REGRESSION

For the most part, multiple regression analysis is a direct extension of simple linear regression analysis. Although volumes have been written on this topic, we'll focus our attention on the multiple linear regression function represented by:

$$\hat{Y}_i = b_0 + b_1 X_{1_i} + b_2 X_{2_i} + ... + b_k X_{k_i} \qquad \textbf{9.18}$$

The regression function in equation 9.18 is similar to the simple linear regression function except that it allows for more than one (or "k") independent variables. Here again, $\hat{Y}_i$ represents the estimated value for the ith observation in our sample whose actual value is Y_i. The symbols $X_{1_i}, X_{2_i}, ..., X_{k_i}$ represent the observed values of the independent variables associated with observation i.

Assuming that each of these variables vary in a linear fashion with the dependent variable Y, the function in equation 9.18 might be applied appropriately to a variety of problems.

We can easily visualize the equation of a straight line in our earlier discussion of regression analysis. In multiple regression analysis, the concepts are similar but the results are more difficult to visualize. Figure 9.16 shows an example of the type of regression surface we might fit using equation 9.18 if the regression function involves only two independent variables. With two independent variables, we fit a *plane* to our data. With three or more independent variables we fit a *hyperplane* to our data. It is difficult to visualize or draw graphs in more than three dimensions, so we cannot actually see what a hyperplane looks like. However, just as a **plane** is a generalization of a straight line into three dimensions, a **hyperplane** is a generalization of a plane into more than three dimensions.

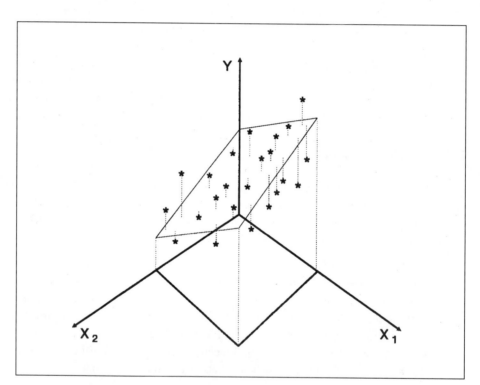

Figure 9.16: Example of a regression surface for two independent variables

Regardless of the number of independent variables, the goal in multiple regression analysis is the same as the goal in a problem with a single independent variable. That is, we want to find the values for b_0, b_1, ..., b_k in equation 9.18 that minimize the sum of squared estimation errors represented by:

$$ESS = \sum_{i=1}^{n} (Y_i - \hat{Y}_i)^2$$

We can use the method of least squares to determine the values for b_0, b_1, ..., b_k that minimize ESS. This should allow us to identify the regression function that best fits our data.

AN EXAMPLE

The following example illustrates how to perform multiple linear regression.

A real estate appraiser is interested in developing a regression model to help predict the fair market value of houses in a particular town. She visited the county courthouse and collected the data shown in Figure 9.17 (and in the file FIG9-17.XLS on your data disk). The appraiser wants to determine if the selling price of the houses can be accounted for by the total square footage of living area, the size of the garage (as measured by the number of cars that can fit in the garage) and the number of bedrooms in each house. (Note that a garage size of 0 indicates that the house has no garage.)

Figure 9.17: *Data for the real estate appraisal example*

In this example, the dependent variable Y represents the selling price of a house, and the independent variables X_1, X_2, and X_3 represent the total square footage, the size of the garage, and the number of bedrooms, respectively. To determine if the multiple linear regression function in equation 9.18 is appropriate for these data, we should first construct scatter plots between the dependent variable (selling price) and each independent variable, as shown in Figure 9.18. These graphs seem to indicate a linear relationship between each independent variable and the dependent variable. Thus, we have reason to believe that a multiple linear regression function would be appropriate for these data.

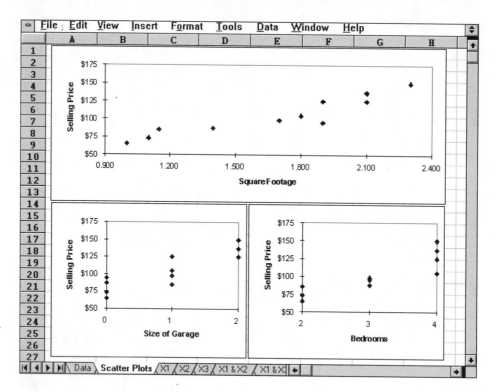

Figure 9.18: *Scatter plots of the real estate appraisal example*

SELECTING THE MODEL

In our discussion of modeling and problem solving in chapter 1, we noted that the best model is often the simplest model that accurately reflects the relevant characteristics of the problem being studied. This is particularly true in multiple regression models. The fact that a particular problem might involve numerous independent variables does not necessarily mean that all of the variables should be included in the regression function. We want to find the *simplest* regression function that adequately accounts for the behavior of the dependent variable we are studying.

MODELS WITH ONE INDEPENDENT VARIABLE

With this idea of simplicity in mind, the real estate appraiser in our example problem might begin her analysis by trying to estimate the selling prices of the houses in the sample using a simple regression function with only one independent variable. The appraiser might first try to fit each of the following three simple linear regression functions to the data:

$$\hat{Y}_i = b_0 + b_1 X_{1_i} \qquad\qquad \textbf{9.19}$$

$$\hat{Y}_i = b_0 + b_2 X_{2_i} \qquad\qquad \textbf{9.20}$$

$$\hat{Y}_i = b_0 + b_3 X_{3_i} \qquad\qquad \textbf{9.21}$$

In equations 9.19 through 9.21, $\hat{Y}_i$ represents the estimated or fitted selling price for the *i*th observation in the sample, and X_{1_i}, X_{2_i}, and X_{3_i} represent the total square footage, size of garage, and number of bedrooms for this same observation *i*, respectively.

To obtain the optimal values for the b_i in each regression function, the appraiser must perform three separate regressions. She would do so in the same way as described earlier in our example involving the prediction of sales from advertising expenditures. Figure 9.19 summarizes the results of these three regression functions.

Independent Variable in the Model	R^2	Adjusted-R^2	S_e	Parameter Estimates
X_1	0.870	0.855	10.299	$b_0 = 9.503$, $b_1 = 56.394$
X_2	0.759	0.731	14.030	$b_0 = 78.290$, $b_2 = 28.382$
X_3	0.793	0.770	12.982	$b_0 = 16.250$, $b_3 = 27.607$

Figure 9.19: Regression results for the three simple linear regression models

The values of the R^2 statistic in Figure 9.19 indicate the proportion of the total variation in the dependent variable around its mean accounted for by each of the three simple linear regression functions. (We will comment on the adjusted-R^2 and S_e values shortly.) The model that uses X_1 (square footage) as the independent variable accounts for 87% of the variation in Y (selling price). The model using X_2 (garage size) accounts for roughly 76% of the variation in Y, and the model that uses X_3 (number of bedrooms) as the independent variable accounts for about 79% of the variation in the selling price.

If the appraiser wants to use only one of the available independent variables in a simple linear regression model to predict the selling price of a house, it seems that X_1 would be the best choice because, according to the R^2 statistics, it accounts for more of the variation in selling price than either of the other two variables. In particular, X_1 accounts for about 87% of the variation in the dependent variable. This leaves approximately 13% of the variation in Y unaccounted for. Thus, the best linear regression function with one independent variable is represented by:

$$\hat{Y}_i = b_0 + b_1 X_{1_i} = 9.503 + 56.394 X_{1_i} \tag{9.22}$$

MODELS WITH TWO INDEPENDENT VARIABLES

Next, the appraiser might want to determine if one of the other two variables could be combined with X_1 in a *multiple* regression model to account for a significant portion of the remaining 13% variation in Y that was not accounted for by X_1. To do this, the appraiser could fit each of the following multiple regression functions to the data:

$$\hat{Y}_i = b_0 + b_1 X_{1_i} + b_2 X_{2_i} \tag{9.23}$$

$$\hat{Y}_i = b_0 + b_1 X_{1_i} + b_3 X_{3_i} \tag{9.24}$$

To determine the optimal values for the b_i in the regression model in equation 9.23, we would use the settings shown in the Regression dialog box in Figure 9.20. The Input X Range in this dialog box is the range in Figure 9.17 that corresponds to the values for X_1 (total square footage) and X_2 (garage size). After we click the OK button, Excel performs the appropriate calculations and displays the regression results shown in Figure 9.21.

Figure 9.21 lists *three* numbers in the Coefficients column. These numbers correspond to the parameter estimates b_0, b_1, and b_2. Note that the value listed for X Variable 1 is the coefficient for the first variable in the X Range (which, in some cases, might be X_2 or X_3 depending on how the data are arranged in the spreadsheet). The value for X Variable 2 corresponds to the second variable in the X Range (which might be X_3 or X_1 depending on the arrangement of the data).

Figure 9.20: Regression dialog box settings for the multiple regression model using square footage and garage size as independent variables

Figure 9.21: Results of the multiple regression model using square footage and garage size as independent variables

From the regression results in Figure 9.21, we know that when using X_1 (square footage) and X_2 (garage size) as independent variables the estimated regression function is:

$$\hat{Y}_i = b_0 + b_1 X_{1_i} + b_2 X_{2_i} = 27.684 + 38.576 X_{1_i} + 12.875 X_{2_i} \qquad \textbf{9.25}$$

Notice that adding the second independent variable caused the values of b_0 and b_1 to change from their earlier values shown in equation 9.22. Thus, the values assumed by the parameters in a regression model might vary depending on the number (and combination) of variables in the model.

SELECTING THE MODEL • 357

We could obtain the values for the parameters in the second multiple regression model (in equation 9.24) in the same way. Note, however, that before issuing the Regression command again we would need to rearrange the data in the spreadsheet so that the values for X_1 (total square footage) and X_3 (number of bedrooms) are located next to each other in one contiguous block. The regression tool in Excel (and in most other spreadsheet software packages) requires that the X Range be represented by one contiguous block of cells.

Important Software Note

When using the regression tool, the values for the independent variables *must* be listed in *adjacent* columns in the spreadsheet and cannot be separated by any intervening columns. That is, the Input X Range option in the Regression dialog box must always specify a contiguous block of numbers.

Figure 9.22 compares the regression results for the model in equation 9.24 and the results for the model in equation 9.23 versus the earlier results of the best simple linear regression model in equation 9.22, where X_1 was the only independent variable in the model.

Independent Variables in the Model	R^2	Adjusted-R^2	S_e	Parameter Estimates
X_1	0.870	0.855	10.299	$b_0 = 9{,}503$, $b_1 = 56.394$
X_1 and X_2	0.939	0.924	7.471	$b_0 = 27.684$, $b_1 = 38.576$, $b_2 = 12.875$
X_1 and X_3	0.877	0.847	10.609	$b_0 = 8.311$, $b_1 = 44.313$, $b_3 = 6.743$

Figure 9.22: Comparison of regression results for models with two independent variables versus the best model with one independent variable

These results indicate that when using X_1 (square footage) and X_3 (number of bedrooms) as independent variables, the estimated regression function is:

$$\hat{Y}_i = b_0 + b_1 X_{1_i} + b_3 X_{3_i} = 8.311 + 44.313 X_{1_i} + 6.743 X_{3_i} \qquad \textbf{9.26}$$

The appraiser was hoping that the inclusion of a second independent variable in the models in equation 9.23 and equation 9.24 might help to explain a significant portion of the remaining 13% of the variation in the dependent that was not accounted for by the simple linear regression function in equation 9.22. How can we tell if this happened?

INFLATING R^2

Figure 9.22 indicates that adding either X_2 or X_3 to the simple linear regression model caused the R^2 statistic to increase. This should not be surprising. As it turns out, the value of R^2 can never decrease as a result of adding an independent variable to a regression function. The reason for this is easy to see. Recall that $R^2 = 1 - ESS/TSS$. Thus, the only way R^2 could decrease as the result of adding an independent variable (X_n) to the model would be if ESS *increased*. However, because the method of least squares attempts to minimize ESS, a new independent variable cannot cause ESS to increase because this variable could simply be ignored by setting $b_n = 0$. In other words, if adding the new independent variable does not help to reduce ESS, least squares regression would simply ignore the new variable.

When you add *any* independent variable to a regression function, the value of the R^2 statistic can never decrease and will usually increase at least a little. Therefore, we can make the R^2 statistic arbitrarily large simply by including enough independent variables in the regression function—regardless of whether or not the new independent variables are related at all to the dependent variable. For example, the real estate appraiser could probably increase the value R^2 to some degree by including another independent variable in the model that represents the height of the mailbox at each house—which probably has little to do with the selling price of a house.

THE ADJUSTED-R^2 STATISTIC

The value of the R^2 statistic can be inflated artificially by including independent variables in a regression function that have little or no logical connection with the dependent variable. Thus, another goodness-of-fit measure, known as the **adjusted-R^2 statistic** (denoted by R_a^2), has been suggested which accounts for the number of independent variables included in a regression model. The adjusted-R^2 statistic is defined as:

$$R_a^2 = 1 - \left(\frac{ESS}{TSS}\right)\left(\frac{n-1}{n-k-1}\right)$$

9.27

where n represents the number of observations in the sample, and k represents the number of independent variables in the model. As variables are added to a regression model, the ratio of ESS to TSS in equation 9.27 will decrease (because ESS decreases and TSS remains constant), but the ratio of $n-1$ to $n-k-1$ will increase (because $n-1$ remains constant and $n-k-1$ decreases). Thus, if we add a variable to the model that does not reduce ESS enough to compensate for the increase in k, the adjusted-R^2 value will decrease.

The adjusted-R^2 value can be used as a "rule-of-thumb" to help us decide if an additional independent variable enhances the predictive ability of a model or if it simply inflates the R^2 statistic artificially. However, using the adjusted-R^2 statistic in this way is not foolproof and requires a good bit of judgment on the part of the person performing the analysis.

THE BEST MODEL WITH TWO INDEPENDENT VARIABLES

As shown in Figure 9.22, when X_2 (garage size) is introduced to the model the adjusted-R^2 *increases* from 0.855 to 0.924. We can conclude from this increase that the addition of X_2 to the regression model helps to account for a significant portion of the remaining variation in Y that was not accounted for by X_1. On the other hand, when X_3 is introduced as an independent variable in the regression model, the adjusted-R^2 statistic in Figure 9.22 *decreases* (from 0.855 to 0.847). This indicates that adding this variable to the model does not help account for a significant portion of the remaining variation in Y if X_1 is already in the model. The best model with two independent variables is given in equation 9.25, which uses X_1 (total square footage) and X_2 (garage size) as predictors of selling price. According to the R^2 statistic in Figure 9.22, this model accounts for about 94% of the total variation in Y around its mean. This model leaves roughly 6% of the variation in Y unaccounted for.

MULTICOLLINEARITY

We should not be too surprised that no significant improvement was observed when X_3 (number of bedrooms) was added to the model containing X_1 (total square footage), because both of these variables represent similar factors. That is, the number of bedrooms in a house is closely related (or correlated) to the total square footage in the house. Thus, if we have already used total square footage to help explain variations in the selling prices of houses (as in the first regression function), adding information about the number of bedrooms would be somewhat redundant. Our analysis confirms this.

The term **multicollinearity** is used to describe the situation when the independent variables in a regression model are correlated among themselves. Multicollinearity tends to increase the uncertainty associated with the parameters estimates (b_i) in a regression model and should be avoided whenever possible. Specialized procedures for detecting and correcting multicollinearity can be found in advanced texts on regression analysis.

THE MODEL WITH THREE INDEPENDENT VARIABLES

As a final test, the appraiser might want to see if X_3 (number of bedrooms) helps to explain a significant portion of the remaining 6% variation in Y that was not accounted for by the model using X_1 and X_2 as independent variables. This involves fitting the following multiple regression function to the data:

$$\hat{Y}_i = b_0 + b_1 X_{1_i} + b_2 X_{2_i} + b_3 X_{3_i}$$ 9.28

Figure 9.23 shows the regression results for this model. The results of this model are also summarized for comparison purposes in Figure 9.24, along with the earlier results for the best model with one independent variable and the best model with two independent variables.

Figure 9.23: Results of regression model using all three independent variables

Figure 9.24: Comparison of regression results for the model with three independent variables versus the best models with one and two independent variables

Independent Variables in the Model	R^2	Adjusted-R^2	S_e	Parameter Estimates
X_1	0.870	0.855	10.299	$b_0 = 9.503$, $b_1 = 56.394$
X_1 and X_2	0.939	0.924	7.471	$b_0 = 27.684$, $b_1 = 38.576$, $b_2 = 12.875$
X_1, X_2, and X_3	0.943	0.918	7.762	$b_0 = 26.440$, $b_1 = 30.803$, $b_2 = 12.567$ $b_3 = 4.576$

Figure 9.24 indicates that when X_3 is added to the model that contains X_1 and X_2, the R^2 statistic increases slightly (from 0.939 to 0.943). However, the adjusted-R^2 drops from 0.924 to 0.918. Thus, it does not appear that adding information about X_3 (number of bedrooms) helps to explain selling prices in any significant way when X_1 (total square footage) and X_2 (size of garage) are already in the model.

It is also interesting to note that the best model with two independent variables also has the smallest standard error S_e. This means that the confidence intervals around any predictions made with this model will be narrower (or more precise) than those of the other models. It can be shown that the model with the highest adjusted-R^2 always has the smallest standard error. For this reason, the adjusted-R^2 statistic is sometimes the sole criterion used to select which multiple regression model to use in a given problem. However, other procedures for selecting regression models exist and are discussed in advanced texts on regression analysis.

MAKING PREDICTIONS

On the basis of this analysis, the appraiser most likely would choose to use the estimated regression model in equation 9.25, which includes X_1 (total square footage) and X_2 (garage size) as independent variables. For a house with X_{1_i} total square feet and space for X_{2_i} cars in its garage, the estimated selling price $\hat{Y}_i$ is:

$$\hat{Y}_i = 27.684 + 38.576X_{1_i} + 12.875X_{2_i}$$

For example, the expected selling price (or average market value) of a house with 2,100 square feet and a two-car garage is estimated as:

$$\hat{Y} = 27.684 + 38.576 \times 2.1 + 12.875 \times 2 = 134.444$$

or approximately $134,444. Note that in making this prediction we expressed the square footage of the house in the same units in which X_1 (total square footage variable) was expressed in the sample used to estimate the model. This should be done for all independent variables when making predictions.

The standard error of the estimation errors for this model is 7.471. Therefore, we should not be surprised to see prices for houses with 2,100 square feet and two-car garages varying within roughly ±2 standard errors (or ±$14,942) of our estimate. That is, we expect prices on this type of house to be as low as $116,00 or as high as $143,000 depending on other factors not included in our analysis (such as age or condition of the roof, presence of a swimming pool, and so on).

As demonstrated earlier in the case of simple linear regression models, more accurate techniques exist for constructing prediction intervals using multiple regression models. In the case of a multiple regression model, the techniques used to construct prediction intervals require a basic knowledge of matrix algebra, which is not assumed in this text. The interested reader should consult advanced texts on multiple regression analysis for a description of how to construct more accurate prediction intervals using multiple regression models. Keep in mind that the simple rule-of-thumb described earlier gives an underestimated (narrower) approximation of the more accurate prediction interval.

BINARY INDEPENDENT VARIABLES

As just mentioned, the appraiser might want to include other independent variables in her analysis. Some of these, such as age of the roof, could be measured numerically and be included as an independent variable. But how would we create variables to represent the presence of a swimming pool or the condition of the roof?

The presence of a swimming pool can be included in the analysis with a binary independent variable coded as:

$$X_{p_i} = \begin{cases} 1, \text{ if house } i \text{ has a pool} \\ 0, \text{ otherwise} \end{cases}$$

The condition of the roof could also be modeled with binary variables. Here, however, we might need more than one binary variable to model all the possible conditions. If some qualitative variable can assume p possible values, we need $p - 1$ binary variables to model the possible outcomes. For example, suppose that the condition of the roof could be rated as good, average, or poor. There are three possible values for the variable representing the condition of the roof; therefore, we need two binary variables to model these outcomes. These binary variables are coded as:

$$X_{r_i} = \begin{cases} 1, \text{ if the roof of house } i \text{ is in good condition} \\ 0, \text{ otherwise} \end{cases}$$

$$X_{r+1_i} = \begin{cases} 1, \text{ if the roof of house } i \text{ is in average condition} \\ 0, \text{ otherwise} \end{cases}$$

It might appear that we left out a coding for a roof in poor condition. However, note that this condition is implied when $X_{r_i} = 0$ and $X_{r+1_i} = 0$. That is, if the roof is *not* in good condition (as implied by $X_{r_i} = 0$) *and* the roof is *not* in average condition (as implied by $X_{r+1_i} = 0$) then the roof must be in poor condition. Thus, we need only two binary variables to represent three possible roof conditions. For reasons that go beyond the scope of this text, the computer could not perform the least squares calculations if we included a third binary variable to indicate houses with roofs in poor condition. Also, it would be inappropriate to model the condition of the roof with a single variable coded as 1 for good, 2 for average, and 3 for poor because this implies that the average condition is twice as bad as the good condition, and that the poor condition is three times as bad as the good condition and 1.5 times as bad as the average condition.

As this example illustrates, we can use binary variables as independent variables in regression analysis to model a variety of conditions that are likely to occur. In each case, the binary variables would be placed in the X Range of the spreadsheet and appropriate b_i values would be calculated by the regression tool.

STATISTICAL TESTS FOR THE POPULATION PARAMETERS

Statistical tests for the population parameters in a multiple regression model are performed in much the same way as for the simple regression model. As described earlier, the F-statistic tests whether or not *all* of the β_i for *all* of the independent variables are *all* simultaneously equal to 0 ($\beta_1 = \beta_2 = ... = \beta_k = 0$). The value in the regression results labeled Significance of F indicates the probability of this condition being true for the data under consideration.

In the case of a multiple regression model, the *t*-statistics for each independent variable require a slightly different interpretation due to the possible presence of multicollinearity. Each *t*-statistic can be used to test whether or not the associated population parameter $\beta_i = 0$ *given all the other independent variables in the model*. For example, consider the *t*-statistics and p-values associated with the variable X_1 shown in Figures 9.21 and 9.23. The p-value for X_1 in cell E18 of Figure 9.21 indicates only a 0.01% chance that $\beta_1 = 0$ when X_2 is the only other independent variable in the model. The p-value for X_1 in cell E18 of Figure 9.23 indicates a 7.4% chance that $\beta_1 = 0$ when X_2 *and* X_3 are also in the model. This illustrates one of the potential problems caused by multicollinearity. Because X_1 and X_3 are highly correlated, it is less certain that X_1 plays a significant (non-zero) role in accounting for the behavior of the dependent variable Y when X_3 is also in the model.

In Figure 9.23 the p-value associated with X_3 indicates a 54.2% chance that $\beta_3 = 0$ given the other variables in the model. Thus, if we had started our analysis by including all three independent variables in the model, the p-value for X_3 in Figure 9.23 suggests that it might be wise to drop X_3 from the model because there is a fairly good chance that it contributes 0 ($\beta_3 = 0$) to explaining the behavior of the dependent variable, given the other variables in the model. In this case, if we drop X_3 from the model, we end up with the same model selected using the adjusted-R^2 criterion.

The statistical tests considered here are valid only when the underlying errors around the regression function are normally distributed random variables with constant means and variances. The graphical diagnostics described earlier apply equally to the case of multiple regression. However, the various statistics presented give reasonably accurate results if the assumptions about the distribution of the error terms are not violated too seriously. Furthermore, the R^2 and adjusted-R^2 statistics are purely descriptive in nature, and do not depend in any way on the assumptions about the distribution of the error terms.

POLYNOMIAL REGRESSION

When introducing the multiple linear regression function in equation 9.18, we noted that this type of model might be appropriate when the independent variables vary in a linear fashion with the dependent variable. Business problems exist where there is *not* a linear relationship between the dependent and independent variables. For example, suppose that the real estate appraiser in our earlier example had collected the data in Figure 9.25 (and in the file FIG9-25.XLS on your data disk) showing the total square footage and selling price for a number of houses. Figure 9.26 shows a scatter plot of these data.

Figure 9.25: Data for
nonlinear regression example

Figure 9.26: Scatter plot
of data showing nonlinear
relationship between total
square footage and
selling price

Figure 9.26 indicates a very strong relationship between total square footage and
the selling price of the houses in this sample. However, this relationship is *not* linear. Rather, more of a *curvilinear* relationship exists between these variables. Does
this mean that linear regression analysis cannot be used with these data? Not at all.

The data in Figure 9.25 (plotted in Figure 9.26) indicate a *quadratic* relationship between square footage and selling price. So, to account adequately for the variation in the selling price of houses, we need to use the following type of regression function:

$$\hat{Y}_i = b_0 + b_1 X_{1_i} + b_2 X_{1_i}^2 \qquad\qquad 9.29$$

where $\hat{Y}_i$ represents the estimated selling price of the *i*th house in our sample, and X_{1_i} represents the total square footage in the house. Notice that the second independent variable in equation 9.29 is the first independent variable squared (X_1^2).

EXPRESSING NONLINEAR RELATIONSHIPS USING LINEAR MODELS

Equation 9.29 is not a linear function because it contains the nonlinear variable X_1^2. It *is* linear with respect to the parameters the computer must estimate—namely, b_0, b_1, and b_2. That is, none of the parameters in the regression function appear as an exponent or are multiplied together. Thus, we can use least squares regression to estimate the optimal values for b_0, b_1, and b_2. Note that if we define a new independent variable as $X_{2_i} = X_{1_i}^2$ then the regression function in equation 9.29 is equivalent to:

$$\hat{Y}_i = b_0 + b_1 X_{1_i} + b_2 X_{2_i} \qquad\qquad 9.30$$

Equation 9.30 is equivalent to the multiple linear regression function in equation 9.29. As long as a regression function is linear with respect to its parameters, we can use Excel's regression analysis tool use to find the least squares estimates for the parameters.

To fit the regression function in equation 9.30 to our data, we must create a second independent variable to represent the values of X_{2_i}, as shown in Figure 9.27.

Figure 9.27: Modification of data to include squared independent variable

Because the X Range for the Regression command must be represented as one contiguous block, we inserted a new column between the square footage and selling price columns and placed the values of X_{2_i} in this column. Note that $X_{2_i} = X_{1_i}^2$ in column C in Figure 9.27:

Formula for cell C3:   =B3^2

(copy to C4 through C13)

The regression results are generated with a Y Range of D3:D13 and an X Range of B3:C13. Figure 9.28 shows the regression results.

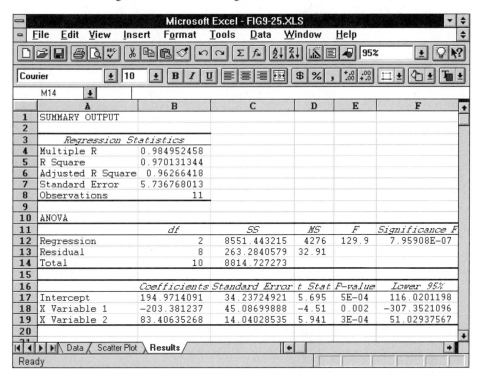

Figure 9.28: Regression results for nonlinear example problem

In Figure 9.28 the estimated regression function is represented by:

$$\hat{Y}_i = b_0 + b_1 X_{1_i} + b_2 X_{1_i}^2 = 194.9714 - 203.3812 X_{1_i} + 83.4063 X_{2_i} \qquad \textbf{9.31}$$

According to the R^2 statistic, this function accounts for 97.0% of the total variation in selling prices, so we expect that this function fits our data well. We can verify this by plotting the prices that would be estimated by the regression function in equation 9.31 for each observation in our sample against the actual selling prices.

To calculate the estimated selling prices, we applied the formula in equation 9.31 to each observation in the sample, as shown in Figure 9.29 where the following formula was entered in cell E3, then copied to cells E4 through E20:

Formula for cell E3:   =194.9714–203.3812*B3+83.4063*C3

(copy to E4 through E13)

The actual and estimated prices in columns D and E of Figure 9.29 are plotted against square footage in Figure 9.30. This graph indicates that our regression model accounts for the nonlinear, quadratic relationship between the square footage and selling price of a house in a reasonably accurate manner.

	A	B	C	D	E	F	G
		Sq. Feet	(Sq. Feet)^2	Price	Estimated		
1							
2	Obs	(in 000s)	(in 000,000s)	(in $000s)	Price		
3	1	1.000	1.000	$69	$75.0		
4	2	1.100	1.210	$73	$72.2		
5	3	1.200	1.440	$76	$71.0		
6	4	1.400	1.960	$78	$73.7		
7	5	1.600	2.560	$86	$83.1		
8	8	1.800	3.240	$97	$99.1		
9	6	1.900	3.610	$103	$109.6		
10	9	1.900	3.610	$108	$109.6		
11	7	2.100	4.410	$129	$135.7		
12	10	2.100	4.410	$137	$135.7		
13	11	2.200	4.840	$160	$151.2		

E3 =194.9714−203.3812*B3+83.4063*C3

Key Cell Formulas

Cell	Formula	Copied to
C3	=B3^2	C4:C13
E3	=194.9714−203.2812*B3+83.4063*C3	E4:E13

Figure 9.29: Estimated selling prices using the nonlinear regression model

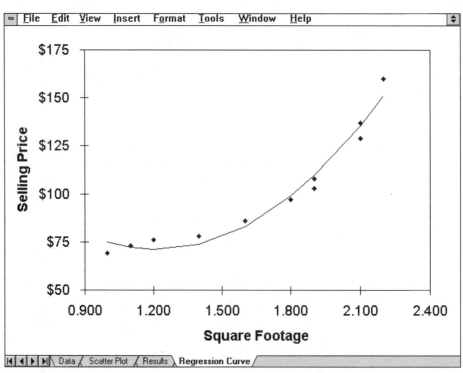

Figure 9.30: Plot of estimated regression function versus actual data

Summary of Nonlinear Regression

This brief example of a polynomial regression problem highlights the fact that regression analysis can be used not only in fitting straight lines or hyperplanes to linear data, but also in fitting other types of curved surfaces to nonlinear data. An in-depth discussion of nonlinear regression is beyond the intended scope of this book, but a wealth of information is available on this topic in numerous texts devoted solely to regression analysis.

This example should help you appreciate the importance of preparing scatter plots of each independent variable against the dependent variable in a regression problem to see if the relationship between the variables is linear or nonlinear. Relatively simple nonlinear relationships, such as the one described in the previous example, can often be accounted for by including squared or cubed terms in the model. In more complicated cases, sophisticated transformations of the dependent or independent variables might be required.

SUMMARY

This chapter presented an overview of some key issues involved in performing regression analysis. Regression analysis is a statistical technique that can be used to identify and analyze the relationship between one or more independent variables and a continuous dependent variable. The goal in regression analysis is to identify a function of the independent variables that adequately accounts for the behavior of the dependent variable. The method of least squares provides a way to determine the best values for the parameters in a regression model for a given sample of data. After identifying such a function, it can be used to predict what value the dependent variable will assume given specific values for the independent variables. Various statistical techniques are available for evaluating how well a given regression function fits a data set and for determining which independent variables are most helpful in explaining the behavior of the dependent variable. Although regression functions can assume a variety of forms, this chapter focused on linear regression models where a linear combination of the independent variables is used to model the dependent variable. Simple transformations of the independent variables can allow this type of model to fit both linear and nonlinear data sets.

REFERENCES

Montgomery D. and E. Peck. *Introduction to Linear Regression Analysis*. New York: Wiley, 1991.

Neter, J., W. Wasserman and M. Kutner. *Applied Linear Statistical Models*. Homewood, IL: Irwin, 1990.

Younger, M. *A First Course in Linear Regression*. Boston: Duxbury Press, 1985.

Better Predictions Create Cost Savings for Ohio National Bank

Source: Krajewski, L. J. and L. P. Ritzman, "Shift Scheduling in Banking Operations: A Case Application," *Interfaces*, vol. 10, no. 2, April 1980, pages 1–6.

THE OHIO NATIONAL BANK IN COLUMBUS must process checks for clearing in a timely manner in order to minimize float. This had been difficult because of wide and seemingly unpredictable variations in the volume of checks received.

As checks pass through the processing center, they are encoded with the dollar amount in magnetic ink at the bottom of the check. This operation requires a staff of clerks, whose work schedules must be planned so that staffing is adequate during peak times. Because the bank couldn't accurately predict these peaks, deadlines often were missed and the clerks often were required to work overtime.

The variations in check volume seemed to be caused by changes in business activity brought about by the calendar—that is, volume was influenced by certain months, days of the week, days of the month, and proximity to certain holidays. A linear regression model was developed to predict staffing needs using a set of binary (dummy) independent variables representing these calendar effects. The regression study was very successful. The resulting model had a coefficient of determination (R^2) of 0.94 and a mean absolute percentage error of 6%.

The bank then used these predictions as input to an LP shift-scheduling model that minimized the number of clerks needed to cover the predicted check volumes.

The planning process required data on check volumes and productivity estimates from the line supervisors in the encoding department. Initial reluctance of the supervisors to supply this information presented an obstacle to the implementation of the system. Eventually this was overcome by taking time to explain the reasons for the data collection to the supervisors.

The new system provides estimated savings of $700,000 in float costs and $300,000 in labor costs. The close-out time of 10 p.m. is now met 98% of the time; previously it was rarely met. Management has performed sensitivity analysis with the model to study the effects of productivity improvements associated with employing experienced full-time encoding clerks instead of part-time clerks.

Questions and Problems

1. Members of the Roanoke Health and Fitness Club pay an annual membership fee of $250 plus $3 each time they use the facility. Let X denote the number of times a person visits the club during the year. Let Y denote the total annual cost for membership in the club.

   a. What is the mathematical relationship between X and Y?

   b. Is this a functional or statistical relationship? Explain your answer.

2. In comparing two different regression models that were developed using the same data, we might say that the model with the higher R^2 value will provide the most accurate predictions. Is this true? Why or why not?

3. Show how R_a^2 and S_e are related algebraically (identify the function $f(\cdot)$ such that $R_a^2 = f(S_e)$).

4. Least squares regression finds the estimated values for the parameters in a regression model to minimize $ESS = \sum_{i=1}^{n}(Y_i - \hat{Y}_i)^2$. Why is it necessary to square the estimation errors? What problem might be encountered if we attempt to minimize just the sum of the estimation errors?

5. An accounting firm that specializes in auditing mining companies collected the following data on the long-term assets and long-term debt of 12 clients:

Long-Term Assets	Long-Term Debt
26	16
39	20
45	24
47	26
47	30
48	36
54	38
56	43
60	46
62	42
64	38
69	48

Note: All figures are in $1,000,000s

a. Prepare a scatter plot of the data. Does there appear to be a linear relationship between these variables?

b. Develop a simple linear regression model that can be used to predict long-term debt from long-term assets. What is the estimated regression equation?

c. Interpret the value of R^2.

d. Suppose that the accounting firm has a client with total assets of $50,000,000. Construct an approximate 95% confidence interval for the amount of long-term debt the firm expects this client to have.

6. The IRS wants to develop a method for detecting whether or not individuals have overstated their deductions for charitable contributions on their tax returns. To assist in this effort, the IRS supplied the following data listing the adjusted gross income (AGI) and charitable contributions for 11 taxpayers whose returns were audited and found to be correct.

AGI (in $1,000s)	Charitable Contributions
$55	$4,200
$58	$4,800
$63	$6,329
$67	$8,017
$74	$7,400
$78	$8,600
$83	$12,290
$88	$10,406
$92	$11,820
$98	$12,090
$105	$14,675

a. Prepare a scatter plot of the data. Does there appear to be a linear relationship between these variables?

b. Develop a simple linear regression model that can be used to predict the level of charitable contributions from a return's AGI. What is the estimated regression equation?

c. Interpret the value of R^2.

d. How might the IRS use the regression results to identify returns with unusually high charitable contributions?

7. Roger Gallagher owns a used car lot that deals solely in used Corvettes. He would like to develop a regression model to help predict the price he can expect to receive for the cars he owns. He collected the following data concerning a number of cars he has sold in recent months.

Mileage (in 1,000s)	Model Year	T-Top	Price
115	1968	y	$13,875
95	1970	n	$11,000
125	1972	n	$8,000
85	1974	y	$14,950
77	1976	y	$15,625
105	1978	n	$11,300
88	1979	n	$13,250
73	1981	y	$16,500
55	1983	n	$16,500
65	1987	y	$19,500
45	1988	n	$22,300
15	1988	n	$25,500
23	1991	y	$31,900

Let Y = selling price, X_1 = mileage, X_2 = model year, and X_3 = whether or not the car had a t-top.

a. If Roger wants to use a simple linear regression function to estimate the selling price of a car, which X variable do you recommend he use?

b. Determine the parameter estimates for the regression function represented by:

$$\hat{Y}_i = b_0 + b_1 X_{1_i} + b_2 X_{2_i}$$

What is the estimated regression function? Does X_2 help to explain the selling price of the cars if X_1 is also in the model? What might be the reason for this?

c. Set up a binary variable (X_{3_i}) to indicate whether or not each car in the sample has a t-top. Determine the parameter estimates for the regression function represented by:

$$\hat{Y}_i = b_0 + b_1 X_{1_i} + b_3 X_{3_i}$$

Does X_3 help to explain the selling price of the cars if X_1 is also in the model? Explain.

d. According to the previous model, on average, how much does a t-top add to the value of a car?

e. Determine the parameter estimates for the regression function represented by:

$$\hat{Y}_i = b_0 + b_1 X_{1_i} + b_2 X_{2_i} + b_3 X_{3_i}$$

What is the estimated regression function?

f. Of all the regression functions considered here, which do you recommend Roger use?

8. Refer to question 7. Prepare scatter plots of the values of X_1 and X_2 against Y.

a. Do these relationships seem to be linear or nonlinear?

b. Determine the parameter estimates for the regression function represented by:

$$\hat{Y}_i = b_0 + b_1 X_{1_i} + b_2 X_{2_i} + b_3 X_{3_i} + b_4 X_{4_i}$$

where $X_{4_i} = X_{2_i}^2$. What is the estimated regression function?

c. Consider the p-values for each β_i in this model. Do these values indicate that any of the independent variables should be dropped from the model?

9. The O-rings in the booster rockets on the space shuttle are designed to expand when heated to seal different chambers of the rocket so that solid rocket fuel is not ignited prematurely. According to engineering specifications, the O-rings expand by some amount, say at least 5%, in order to ensure a safe launch. Hypothetical data on the amount of O-ring expansion and the atmospheric temperature in Fahrenheit at the time of several different launches are given below:

Temperature	% O-ring Expansion
93	22.3
88	21.0
87	20.6
81	19.7
73	18.7
72	19.0
68	17.3
64	16.2
55	15.5

a. Prepare a scatter plot of the data. Does there appear to be a linear relationship between these variables?

b. Obtain a simple linear regression model to estimate the amount of O-ring expansion as a function of atmospheric temperature. What is the estimated regression function?

c. Interpret the R^2 statistic for the model you obtained.

d. Suppose that NASA officials are considering launching a space shuttle when the temperature is 29 degrees. What amount of O-ring expansion should they expect at this temperature according to your model?

e. On the basis of your analysis of these data, would you recommend that the shuttle be launched if the temperature is 29 degrees? Why or why not.

10. An analyst for Phidelity Investments wants to develop a regression model to predict the annual rate of return for a stock based on the price-earnings ratio of the stock and a measure of the stock's risk. The following data were collected for a random sample of stocks:

PE Ratio	Risk	Return
7.4	1.0	7.6
11.1	1.3	13.0
8.7	1.1	8.9
11.2	1.2	10.9
11.6	1.7	12.1
12.2	1.3	12.8
12.5	1.2	11.3
12.5	1.3	14.1
13.0	1.6	14.8
13.4	1.4	16.7

a. Prepare scatter plots for each independent variable versus the dependent variable. What type of model do these scatter plots suggest might be appropriate for the data?

b. Let Y = Return, X_1 = PE Ratio, and X_2 = Risk. Obtain the regression results for the following regression model:

$\hat{Y}_i = b_0 + b_1 X_{1_i} + b_2 X_{2_i}$

Interpret the value of R^2 for this model.

c. Obtain the regression results for the following regression model:

$\hat{Y}_i = b_0 + b_1 X_{1_i} + b_2 X_{2_i} + b_3 X_{3_i} + b_4 X_{4_i}$

where $X_{3_i} = X_{1_i}^2$ and $X_{4_i} = X_{2_i}^2$. Interpret the value of R^2 for this model.

d. Which of the previous two models would you recommend that the analyst use?

11. AutoReports is a consumer magazine that reports on the cost of maintaining various types of automobiles. The magazine collected the following data on the annual maintenance cost of a certain type of luxury imported automobile along with the age of the car:

Age	Maintenance Cost
1	$100
2	$375
2	$325
3	$455
3	$520
4	$485
4	$530
5	$595
5	$515
6	$700
6	$800
7	$1000
7	$950

a. Prepare a scatter plot of these data.

b. Fit the following regression model to the data:

$$\hat{Y}_i = b_0 + b_1 X_{1_i}$$

Plot the maintenance costs that are estimated by this model along with the actual costs in the sample. How well does this model fit the data?

c. Fit the following regression model to the data:

$$\hat{Y}_i = b_0 + b_1 X_{1_i} + b_2 X_{2_i}$$

where $X_{2_i} = X_{1_i}^2$. Plot the maintenance costs that are estimated by this model along with the actual costs in the sample. How well does this model fit the data?

d. Fit the following regression model to this data:

$$\hat{Y}_i = b_0 + b_1 X_{1_i} + b_2 X_{2_i} + b_3 X_{3_i}$$

where $X_{2_i} = X_{1_i}^2$ and $X_{3_i} = X_{1_i}^3$. Plot the maintenance costs that are estimated by this model along with the actual costs in the sample. How well does this model fit the data?

12. Throughout our discussion of regression analysis, we used the Regression command to obtain the parameter estimates that minimize the sum of squared estimation errors. Suppose that we want to obtain parameter estimates that minimize the sum of the absolute value of the estimation errors, or:

$$\text{MIN} : \sum_{i=1}^{n} \left| Y_i - \hat{Y}_i \right|$$

a. Use Solver to obtain the parameter estimates for a simple linear regression function that minimizes the sum of the absolute value of the estimation errors for the data in question 9.

b. What advantages, if any, do you see in using this alternate objective to solve a regression problem?

c. What disadvantages, if any, do you see in using this alternate objective to solve a regression problem?

13.   Throughout our discussion of regression analysis, we used the Regression command to obtain the parameter estimates that minimize the sum of squared estimation errors. Suppose that we want to obtain parameter estimates that minimize the absolute value of the maximum estimation error or:

$$\text{MIN: MAX} \left(|Y_1 - \hat{Y}_1|, |Y_2 - \hat{Y}_2|, ..., |Y_n - \hat{Y}_n| \right)$$

a. Use Solver to obtain the parameter estimates for a simple linear regression function that minimizes the absolute value of the maximum estimation error for the data in question 9.

b. What advantages, if any, do you see in using this alternate objective to solve a regression problem?

c. What disadvantages, if any, do you see in using this alternate objective to solve a regression problem?

The Georgia Public Service Commission A Case in Regression Analysis

NOLAN Banks is an auditor for the Public Service Commission for the state of Georgia. The Public Service Commission is a government agency responsible for ensuring that utility companies throughout the state manage their operations efficiently so that they can provide quality services to the public at fair prices.

Georgia is the largest state east of the Mississippi river, and various communities and regions throughout the state have different companies that provide water, power, and phone service. These companies have a monopoly in the areas they serve and, therefore, could take unfair advantage of the public. One of Nolan's jobs is to visit the companies and audit their financial records to detect whether or not any abuse is occurring.

A major problem Nolan faces in his job is determining whether or not the expenses reported by the utility companies are reasonable. For example, when he reviews a financial report for a phone company, he might see line maintenance costs of $1,345,948, and he needs to determine if this amount is reasonable. This determination is complicated by the fact that the companies differ in size—so he cannot compare the costs of one company directly to another. Similarly, he cannot come up with a simple ratio to determine costs (such as 2% for the ratio of line maintenance costs to total revenue) because a single ratio might not be appropriate for companies of different sizes.

To help solve this problem, Nolan wants you to build a regression model to estimate what level of line maintenance expense would be expected for companies of different sizes. One measure of size for a phone company is the number of customers it has. Nolan collected the following data on the number of customers and line maintenance expenses of 12 companies he audited in the past year and determined were being run in a reasonably efficient manner.

Customers (in 000s)	Line Maintenance Expense (in $000s)
25.3	484.6
36.4	672.3
37.9	839.4
45.9	694.9
53.4	836.4
66.8	681.9
78.4	1,037.0
82.6	1,095.6
93.8	1,563.1
97.5	1,377.9
105.7	1,711.7
124.3	2,138.6

1. Enter the data in a spreadsheet.
2. Create a scatter diagram of these data.
3. Use regression to estimate the parameters for the following linear equation for the data:

   $$\hat{Y} = b_0 + b_1 X_1$$

   What is the estimated regression equation?
4. Interpret the value for R^2 obtained using the equation from question 3.
5. According to the equation in question 3, what level of line maintenance expense would be expected for a phone company with 75,000 customers? Show how you arrive at this value.
6. Suppose that a phone company with 75,000 customers reports a line maintenance expense of $1,500,000. Based on the results of the linear model, should Nolan view this amount as reasonable or excessive?

7. In your spreadsheet, calculate the estimated line maintenance expense that would be predicted by the regression function for each company in the sample. Plot the predicted values you calculate on your graph (connected with a line) along with the original data. Does it appear that a linear regression model is appropriate?
8. Use regression to estimate the parameters for the following quadratic equation for the data:

   $$\hat{Y} = b_0 + b_1 X_1 + b_2 X_1^2$$

   To do this you must insert a new column in your spreadsheet next to the original X values. In this new column, calculate the values X_1^2. What is the new estimated regression equation for this model?
9. Interpret the value for R^2 obtained using the equation in question 8.

10. What is the value for the adjusted-R^2 statistic? What does this statistic tell you?

11. What level of line maintenance expense would be expected for a phone company with 75,000 customers according to this new estimated regression function? Show how you arrive at this value.

12. In your spreadsheet, calculate the estimated line maintenance expense that would be predicted by the quadratic regression function for each company in the sample. Plot these values on your graph (connected with a line) along with the original data and the original regression line.

13. Suppose that a phone company with 75,000 customers reports a line maintenance expense of $1,500,000. Based on the results of the quadratic model, should Nolan view this amount as reasonable or excessive?

14. Which of the two regression functions would you suggest Nolan use for prediction purposes?

CHAPTER 10

Discriminant Analysis

DISCRIMINANT ANALYSIS (DA) is a statistical technique that uses the information available in a set of independent variables to predict the value of a *discrete*, or *categorical*, dependent variable. Typically, the dependent variable in a DA problem is coded as a series of integer values representing various groups to which the observations in a sample belong. The goal of DA is to develop a rule for predicting to what group a *new* observation is most likely to belong based on the values the independent variables assume. To gain an understanding of the purpose and value of DA, consider the following business situations where DA could be useful.

Credit Scoring. The credit manager of a mortgage company classifies the loans it has made into two groups: those resulting in default and those that are current. For each loan, the manager has data describing the income, assets, liabilities, credit history, and employment history of the person who received the loan. The manager wants to use this information to develop a rule for predicting whether or not a new loan applicant will default if granted a loan.

Insurance Rating. An automotive insurance company uses claims data from the past five years to classify its current policyholders into three categories: high risk, moderate risk, and low risk. The company has data describing each policyholder's age, marital status, number of children, educational level, employment record, and number of traffic citations received during the past five years. The company wants to analyze how the three groups differ with regard to these characteristics, and use this information to predict into which risk category a new insurance applicant is likely to fall.

DA differs from most other predictive statistical methods (for example, regression analysis) because the dependent variable is *discrete,* or *categorical*, rather than *continuous*. For instance, in the first example given above, the credit manager wants to predict whether a loan applicant will: (1) default or (2) repay the loan. Similarly, in the second example, the company wants to predict into which risk category a new client is most likely to fall: (1) high risk, (2) moderate risk, or (3) low risk. In each example we can arbitrarily assign a number (1, 2, 3, …) to each group represented in the problem, and our goal is to predict to which group (1, 2, 3, …) a new observation is most likely to belong.

It might seem that we could handle these types of problems with least squares regression by using the independent variables to predict the value of a discrete dependent variable coded to indicate the group membership (1, 2, 3, …) of each observation in the sample. This is true for problems involving only two groups, such as the credit scoring example given earlier. However, the regression approach does not work in problems involving more than two groups, such as the insurance rating example. Because many DA problems involve the analysis of only two groups, we'll split our discussion of DA into two parts. The first introduces the concepts of DA and covers the regression approach to the two-group problem. The second presents the more general k-group problem in DA (where $k \geq 2$).

THE TWO-GROUP DA PROBLEM

The following personnel selection example illustrates the regression approach to two-group DA. Later, we'll extend this example to illustrate the more general k-group approach to DA.

> In her role as personnel director for ACME Manufacturing, Marie Becker is responsible for interviewing and hiring new hourly employees for the factory. As part of the pre-employment screening process, each prospective hourly employee is required to take an exam that measures mechanical and verbal aptitudes. Marie has access to historical data on the test scores received by all of ACME's current employees. As part of an annual performance evaluation, each factory employee is rated as performing at either a satisfactory or unsatisfactory level. Marie also has access to these data. Marie wants to analyze the data about current employees to see if there are differences between the pre-employment test scores for the satisfactory and unsatisfactory workers. If so, she wants to use this information to develop a rule for predicting whether or not a new potential employee will be a satisfactory or unsatisfactory worker on the basis of the test scores.

This example is somewhat over-simplified because it involves only two independent, or explanatory, variables—the mechanical and verbal aptitude test scores. The personnel director probably has access to many more variables that are likely to be important determinants of satisfactory and unsatisfactory job performance. However, this example is restricted to two independent variables for convenience in illustrating how DA works. The approach to DA described here can be applied to problems involving any number of independent variables.

The two groups of interest in this example—satisfactory and unsatisfactory employees—will be labeled group 1 and group 2, respectively. The mechanical and verbal aptitude test scores for the current ACME employees are listed in Figure 10.1

(and in the file FIG10-1.XLS on your data disk) in the Mechanical and Verbal columns. We will refer to this group of observations as the "analysis sample" because we will analyze this data set to develop a rule for classifying new job applicants. The Group column in the spreadsheet contains the value 1 for observations representing satisfactory employees, and the value 2 for unsatisfactory employees.

□	File	Edit	View	Insert	Format	Tools	Data	Window	Help			↕
		A	**B**	**C**	**D**	**E**	**F**	**G**			
1											
2				-- Test	Scores --						
3		Obs.	Group	Mechanical	Verbal						
4		1	1	44.7	36.1						
5		2	1	43.2	42.0						
6		3	1	42.5	30.8						
7		4	1	40.2	42.6						
8		5	1	41.9	37.1						
9		6	1	39.3	33.8						
10		7	1	38.6	40.3						
11		8	1	38.1	28.5						
12		9	1	37.9	44.7						
13		10	1	36.8	42.6						
14		11	1	35.8	35.2						
15		12	2	39.0	33.1						
16		13	2	37.5	36.4						
17		14	2	36.1	30.8						
18		15	2	35.6	27.2						
19		16	2	34.4	39.0						
20		17	2	32.8	35.2						
21		18	2	31.4	29.4						
22		19	2	29.5	37.9						
23		20	2	30.1	33.9						
24		Group	1	39.9	37.6						
25		Averages	2	34.0	33.6						
26											
27											

CENTROID COORDINATES

Key Cell Formulas

Cell	Formula	Copied to
C24	=AVERAGE(C4:C14)	D24
C25	=AVERAGE(C15:C23)	D25

Figure 10.1: Data for current ACME employees

GROUP LOCATIONS AND CENTROIDS

Because this data set includes only two independent variables, it is easy to display these data graphically, as shown in Figure 10.2. The points in Figure 10.2 labeled "c_1" and "c_2" represent the centroids for group 1 and group 2, respectively. A group's **centroid** is the set of averages for the independent variables for the group. The centroid indicates where a group is centered, or located. The coordinates of the group centroids are calculated in Figure 10.1 in the rows labeled "Group Averages" as:

Formula for cell C24: = AVERAGE(C4 : C14)
(copy to D24)

Formula for cell C25: = AVERAGE(C15 : C23)
(copy to D25)

The centroid for group 1 is (39.9, 37.6) and the centroid for group 2 is (34.0, 33.6).

Figure 10.2: *Graph of data for current employees*

We might expect that the more the centroids for the groups in a DA problem differ, the easier it is to distinguish between the groups. In general, this is true. For example, because the group centroids in Figure 10.2 are well separated, it is easy to see that the unsatisfactory employees tend to have lower mechanical and verbal aptitudes than the satisfactory employees. However, if the two groups' centroids were both located at the same point, it would be difficult to tell which group an observation belonged to based on only its location, because all observations would be scattered around the same centroid point.

Although the groups in Figure 10.2 are well separated, the two groups overlap some. This overlapping area makes it difficult to establish a rule or boundary line for separating the satisfactory employees from the unsatisfactory ones. One such boundary line has been drawn arbitrarily in Figure 10.2. DA provides an objective means for determining the best straight line for separating or distinguishing between groups.

CALCULATING DISCRIMINANT SCORES

Viewing the data in Figure 10.1 from a regression perspective, we want to model the behavior of the Group variable using the mechanical and verbal aptitude test scores. In the following regression equation, the dependent variable $\hat{Y}$ represents the estimated value of the Group variable, and X_1 and X_2 correspond to values for the independent variables representing the Mechanical and Verbal test scores, respectively:

$$\hat{Y}_i = b_0 + b_1 X_{1_i} + b_2 X_{2_i} \qquad \textbf{10.1}$$

Note that we can expand equation 10.1 easily to include any number of independent variables. But regardless of the number of independent variables in a problem, the purpose of the regression equation is to combine the information available in the variables into a single-valued estimate of the Group variable.

This estimated value of the Group variable is referred to as a **discriminant score** and is denoted by $\hat{Y}$. But what are the values of b_0, b_1, and b_2 that will result in the best discriminant scores for our data? We can use the regression tool in Excel to estimate these values.

The Regression dialog box in Figure 10.3 shows the settings required for the current problem. Notice that the Input Y-Range entry corresponds to the Group values shown in Figure 10.1, and the Input X-Range entry corresponds to the values of the mechanical and verbal aptitude test scores. Figure 10.4 shows the regression results.

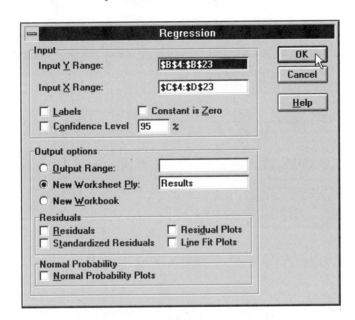

Figure 10.3: Regression dialog box for the personnel selection example

Figure 10.4: Regression results for the personnel selection example

The estimated value for b_0 is represented by the Intercept value in cell B17 of Figure 10.4, and the estimated values for b_1 and b_2 are shown in cells B18 and B19, respectively. Thus, our estimated regression function is:

$$\hat{Y}_i = 5.37734 - 0.079064X_{1_i} - 0.027380X_{2_i} \qquad \textbf{10.2}$$

(Note that because the dependent variable in a two-group DA problem assumes only two possible values, it cannot be a normally distributed variable. Thus, virtually all of the statistical results in the regression output for a two-group DA problem are not subject to their usual interpretation. Even the R^2 statistic is not a particularly meaning-ful goodness-of-fit measure for these types of problems. Later, we'll discuss another way to assess how well a given regression function performs on a DA problem.)

Equation 10.2 is applied to the data in our example to generate the discriminant score values for each observation. These values are listed in the Discrim. Score col-umn in Figure 10.5 (and in the file FIG10-5.XLS on your data disk).

File Edit View Insert Format Tools Data Window Help							
	A	B	C	D	E	F	G
1							
2			-- Test Scores --		Discrim.	Pred.	
3	Obs.	Group	Mechanical	Verbal	Score	Group	
4	1	1	44.7	36.1	0.856	1	
5	2	1	43.2	42.0	0.812	1	
6	3	1	42.5	30.8	1.174	1	
7	4	1	40.2	42.6	1.033	1	
8	5	1	41.9	37.1	1.050	1	
9	6	1	39.3	33.8	1.349	1	
10	7	1	38.6	40.3	1.222	1	
11	8	1	38.1	28.5	1.583	2	**
12	9	1	37.9	44.7	1.158	1	
13	10	1	36.8	42.6	1.302	1	
14	11	1	35.8	35.2	1.583	2	**
15	12	2	39.0	33.1	1.388	1	**
16	13	2	37.5	36.4	1.417	1	**
17	14	2	36.1	30.8	1.678	2	
18	15	2	35.6	27.2	1.816	2	
19	16	2	34.4	39.0	1.592	2	
20	17	2	32.8	35.2	1.820	2	
21	18	2	31.4	29.4	2.091	2	
22	19	2	29.5	37.9	2.006	2	
23	20	2	30.1	33.9	2.070	2	
24	Group	1	39.9	37.6	1.193		
25	Averages	2	34.0	33.6	1.764		
26			Cut-off Value:		1.479		
27							

Key Cell Formulas

Cell	Formula	Copied to
E4	=5.37734-0.079064*C4-0.027380*D4	E5:E23
E24	=AVERAGE(E4:E14)	—
E25	=AVERAGE(E15:E23)	—
E26	=(E24+E25)/2	—
F4	=IF(E4<=$E$26,1,2)	F5:F23
G4	=IF(F4<>B4,"**"," ")	G5:G23

Figure 10.5: *Discriminant scores for the personnel selection example*

For example, the discriminant score for the first observation is calculated in cell E4 as:

Formula for cell E4:   =5.37734–0.079064*C4–0.027380*D4   **10.3**

(copy to E5 through E23)

Equation 10.3 is copied to cells E5 through E23 to calculate the discriminant scores for each of the remaining observations. Cells E24 and E25 calculate the average discriminant score for each group using the following formulas:

Formula for cell E24:   =AVERAGE(E4:E14)

Formula for cell E25:   =AVERAGE(E15:E23)

We will refer to these average discriminant scores for groups 1 and 2 as $\hat{\bar{Y}}_1$ and $\hat{\bar{Y}}_2$, respectively.

THE CLASSIFICATION RULE

Because the discriminant scores are not equal to our group values of 1 and 2, we need a method for translating these scores into group membership predictions. The following classification rule can be used for this purpose.

Classification Rule. If an observation's discriminant score is less than or equal to some cut-off value, then assign it to group 1; otherwise, assign it to group 2.

The remaining problem is to determine an appropriate cut-off value. We can do so in a number of ways. One possibility is to select the cut-off value that minimizes the *number* of misclassifications in the analysis sample. However, this approach might not be best if our goal is to classify *new* observations correctly. Consider the situation that would occur if the independent variables were normally distributed with equal variances and covariances equal to 0. The resulting distributions of discriminant scores would be similar to those shown in Figure 10.6.

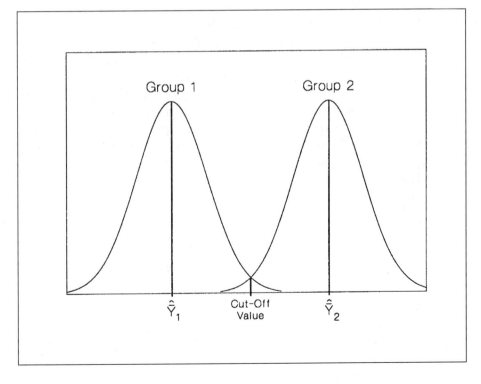

Figure 10.6: Possible distributions of discriminant scores

Notice that the distributions of discriminant scores for group 1 and group 2 are centered at $\hat{\bar{Y}}_1$ and $\hat{\bar{Y}}_2$, respectively. The area in Figure 10.6 where the tails of the distributions overlap corresponds to observations that are most likely to be classified incorrectly. Generally, DA attempts to minimize this area of overlap. With these data conditions it is easy to see that the mid-point between the average discriminant score for each group is likely to be the best choice for a cut-off value because this point minimizes the *probability* of misclassification for future observations. Even if the independent variables violate the normality assumption, this mid-point value often provides good classification results for new observations. The cut-off value listed in cell E26 of Figure 10.5 is the average of the estimates of $\hat{\bar{Y}}_1$ and $\hat{\bar{Y}}_2$:

$$\text{Cut-off value} = \frac{\hat{\bar{Y}}_1 + \hat{\bar{Y}}_2}{2} + \frac{1.193 + 1.764}{2} = 1.479 \qquad \textbf{10.4}$$

Note, however, that the mid-point cut-off value is not always optimal and, in some cases, might lead to poor classification results.

REFINING THE CUT-OFF VALUE

Because the tails of the distributions in Figure 10.6 overlap, we can be fairly certain that some observations will be classified incorrectly using the classification rule stated earlier. For example, our classification rule might predict that certain job applicants will be satisfactory employees when, in fact, they will be unsatisfactory. Hiring such employees could be a costly mistake. Alternatively, our classification rule might predict incorrectly that certain applicants will be unsatisfactory when, in fact, they would be very good employees. Not hiring these applicants would represent a lost opportunity (or opportunity cost) for the company. However, these *costs of misclassification* are not taken into account by the mid-point cut-off value in equation 10.4.

To illustrate another potential problem with the mid-point cut-off value, suppose that the personnel director knows from experience that the majority of applicants to the company are unqualified and would be unsatisfactory workers. In this case, the population of unqualified (potentially unsatisfactory) applicants is larger than the population of qualified (potentially satisfactory) applicants. Thus, a higher probability exists that a given applicant will be an unsatisfactory worker rather than a satisfactory worker. It would be helpful if we could incorporate these pre-existing, or prior, probabilities in our classification rule. However, the mid-point cut-off value in equation 10.4 assumes that new observations are equally likely to come from either group.

We can use an alternative method for specifying what cut-off value to use in our classification rule. This method considers the costs of misclassification and prior probabilities. Suppose that we define the costs of misclassification and prior probabilities as:

$C(1\,|\,2)$ = the cost of classifying an observation into group 1 when it belongs to group 2

$C(2\,|\,1)$ = the cost of classifying an observation into group 2 when it belongs to group 1

p_1 = the prior probability that a new observation belongs to group 1

p_2 = the prior probability that a new observation belongs to group 2

A general method for determining the cut-off value for the classification rule is represented by:

$$\text{Cut-off value} = \frac{\hat{\bar{Y}}_1 + \hat{\bar{Y}}_2}{2} + \frac{S^2_{\hat{Y}_P}}{\hat{\bar{Y}}_1 - \hat{\bar{Y}}_2} \times \text{LN}\left(\frac{p_2 C(1\,|\,2)}{p_1 C(2\,|\,1)}\right) \qquad \textbf{10.5}$$

where LN(·) represents the natural logarithm, and

$$S^2_{\hat{Y}_p} = \frac{(n_1 - 1)S^2_{\hat{Y}_1} + (n_2 - 1)S^2_{\hat{Y}_2}}{n_1 + n_2 - 2}$$

where n_i represents the number of observations in group i and $S^2_{\hat{Y}_i}$ represents the sample variance of the discriminant scores for group i. Notice that if the costs of misclassification are equal (C(1|2) = C(2|1)) and the prior probabilities are equal ($p_1 = p_2$), the cut-off value in equation 10.5 reduces to the mid-point cut-off value in equation 10.4 because LN(1) = 0.

To illustrate this refined cut-off value, suppose that the personnel director in our example believes there is a 40% chance that a given applicant would be a satisfactory employee ($p_1 = 0.40$) and a 60% chance that given applicant would be an unsatisfactory employee ($p_2 = 0.60$). Furthermore, suppose that the company considers it twice as costly to hire a person who turns out to be an unsatisfactory worker as it is to not hire a person who would have been a satisfactory worker. This implies that C(1|2) = 2*C(2|1).

To calculate the refined cut-off value obtained using equation 10.5, we first calculate $S^2_{\hat{Y}_1}$ and $S^2_{\hat{Y}_2}$ using Excel's VAR() function to obtain:

$$S^2_{\hat{Y}_1} = \text{VAR(E4 : E14)} = 0.0648$$

$$S^2_{\hat{Y}_2} = \text{VAR(E15 : E23)} = 0.0705$$

Because $n_1 = 11$ and $n_2 = 9$, $S^2_{\hat{Y}_p}$ is computed as:

$$S^2_{\hat{Y}_p} = \frac{(11-1)(0.0648)+(9-1)(0.0705)}{(11+9-2)} = 0.06733$$

We can then use equation 10.5 to compute the refined cut-off value as:

$$\text{Refined cut-off value} = \frac{1.193+1.764}{2} + \frac{0.06733}{1.193-1.764}\text{LN}\left(\frac{2(0.6)}{(0.4)}\right) = 1.349$$

This refined cut-off value reduces the chance of an observation from group 2 being misclassified into group 1 (which is the more costly mistake) and increases the chance of an observation from group 1 being misclassified into group 2 (which is the less costly mistake).

CLASSIFICATION ACCURACY

Our ultimate goal in DA is to predict to which group a *new* observation (or job applicant) belongs. Because we already know which group each observation in our analysis sample belongs to, it might seem pointless to try to classify these observations. Yet, by doing so we can get some idea of how accurate our classification rule is likely to be with other new observations whose true group memberships are unknown. For our example, if we use the mid-point cut-off value technique our classification rule is:

Classification Rule. If an observation's discriminant score is less than or equal to 1.479, then assign it to group 1; otherwise, assign it to group 2.

The Pred. Group column in Figure 10.5 contains the results of applying this classification rule. This rule is implemented by placing the following formula in cell F4 and copying it to cells F5 through F23:

Formula for cell F4:   =IF(E4<=1.479,1,2)
(copy to F5 through F23)

Comparing the values in the Pred. Group column to the values in the Group column indicates that a number of observations in the analysis sample were misclassified using the preceding classification rule. Misclassified observations can be identified easily by implementing the following formula in cell G4 and copying it to cells G5 through G23:

Formula for cell G4:   =IF(F4<>B4,"**"," ")
(copy to G5 through G23)

This marks the misclassified observations with asterisks (**) in Figure 10.5. Figure 10.7 summarizes these classification results.

Figure 10.7: Summary of classification results on the analysis sample for the two groups

		Predicted Group		
		1	2	Total
Actual Group	1	9	2	11
	2	2	7	9
	Total	11	9	20

Figure 10.7 shows that 9 of the 11 observations (81.8%) that belong to group 1 were classified correctly in this group, and the other 2 observations (18.2%) belonging to group 1 were misclassified into group 2. Similarly, 7 of the 9 observations (77.8%) that belong to group 2 were classified correctly in this group, and the other 2 observations (22.2%) belonging to group 2 were misclassified into group 1. Overall, 16 out of 20 observations (80.0%) in our analysis sample were classified correctly, and a total of 4 observations (20.0%) were misclassified.

From these results, we might expect that our classification rule will provide correct classifications approximately 80% of the time if we use it to predict the group membership of new applicants. Actually, the figure of 80% is probably somewhat favorably biased. That is, the observations in our analysis sample influenced the development of the classification rule; therefore, we expect that this rule might be successful in classifying these same observations. However, we should not expect the procedure to duplicate this level of accuracy when classifying new observations that did not influence the development of the classification rule.

CLASSIFYING NEW EMPLOYEES

As mentioned previously, the ultimate goal in DA is to predict into which group a new observation (or potential employee) is most likely to fall. In our example, this involves predicting whether or not a new job applicant will be a satisfactory or unsatisfactory employee. Figure 10.8 shows a new worksheet named Classification Sample. This worksheet is similar to the one in Figure 10.1, but here all the observations represent new job applicants being considered for employment. Because we do not know whether these applicants will be satisfactory or unsatisfactory employees, question marks (?) have been entered in the Group column. The values in the Mechanical and Verbal columns represent the applicants' scores on the two aptitude tests.

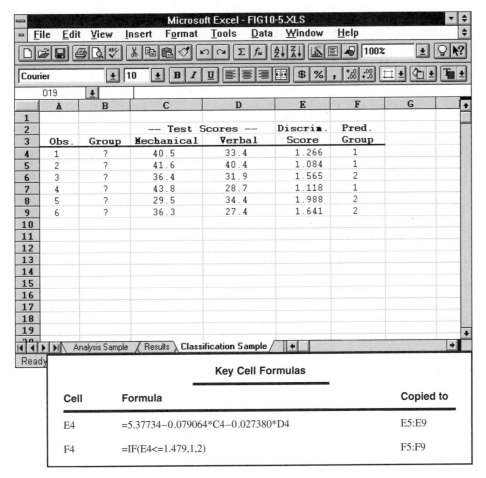

Figure 10.8: Predicted group memberships of new job applicants

We can use the regression results and classification rule developed for our analysis sample to calculate discriminant scores and predict whether each new observation (or applicant) would fall into group 1 or group 2. To calculate these scores, the following formula is implemented in cell E4 and copied to cells E5 through E9:

Formula for cell E4:   =5.37734−0.079064*C4−0.027380*D4
(copy to E5 through E9)

The classification rule is implemented by entering the following formula in cell F4 and copying it to cells F5 through F9:

Formula for cell F4:   =IF(E4<=1.479,1,2)
(copy to F5 through F9)

The Pred. Group column shows an *estimate*, or *forecast*, of which group each new job applicant would fall into if hired. For example, we are predicting that the applicants listed as observations 1, 2, and 4 in Figure 10.8 would be satisfactory employees (belonging to group 1) and the other applicants would be unsatisfactory (belonging to group 2).

Only time will tell how accurate these predictions are for the applicants hired, and we will never know if the predictions are correct for applicants that are not hired. But the DA technique has provided the personnel director with an objective way of incorporating the mechanical and verbal aptitude test scores in the hiring decision. As with any statistical tool, these results should be used in conjunction with other information available and with the decision maker's professional judgment of each applicant's potential value to the company.

THE *k*-GROUP DA PROBLEM

It might seem as if the regression approach for two-group DA could be extended easily to problems with more than two groups. For example, suppose that we have a problem with three groups (labeled A, B, and C) and one independent variable X. We could set up a dependent variable Y and assign it a value of 1, 2, or 3 to indicate observations belonging to group A, B, or C, respectively. We might attempt to model the behavior of this dependent variable as:

$$\hat{Y}_i = b_0 + b_1 X_i \qquad \qquad \textbf{10.6}$$

We could then apply regression analysis to estimate values for b_0 and b_1 so that we could calculate the discriminant scores $\hat{Y}_i$. Figure 10.9 displays hypothetical data for such a problem.

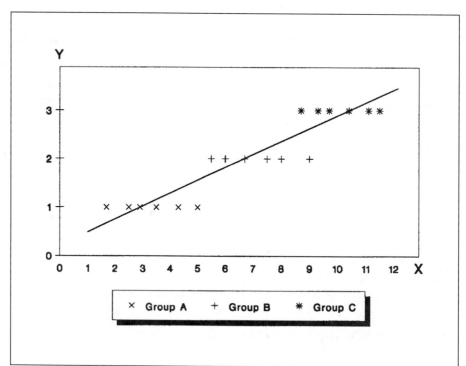

Figure 10.9: *Graph of three-group example with one independent variable showing a linear relationship*

Having obtained the discriminant scores, we might use the following rule to classify observations:

If the discriminant score is	Assign observation to group
$\hat{Y} < 1.5$	A
$1.5 \leq \hat{Y} \leq 2.5$	B
$\hat{Y} > 2.5$	C

Although such an approach might seem reasonable, it has a major flaw. Note that the linear relationship between the dependent and independent variables in Figure 10.9 is due solely to the manner in which the dependent variable numbers were assigned to the groups. That is, if we assign the number 2 to group A and the number 1 to group B, the linear relationship between the variables is destroyed, as illustrated in Figure 10.10.

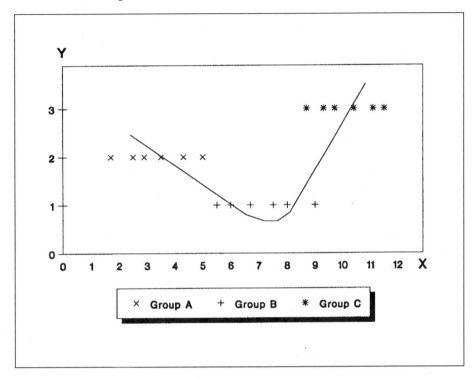

Figure 10.10: Graph of three-group example with one independent variable showing a nonlinear relationship

In general, the regression function in equation 10.6 cannot be used for DA problems with more than two groups because the relationship between the dependent and independent variables might not be linear. Even if we could make the relationship linear with some appropriate coding for the dependent variable, it can be very difficult to discern what this coding should be if the problem involves more than one independent variable. In this section we will discuss another approach to DA that can be used when the problem involves more than two groups.

MULTIPLE DISCRIMINANT ANALYSIS

To distinguish this approach from the two-group regression approach, we refer to it as **multiple discriminant analysis** (MDA). The following modified personnel selection example illustrates the MDA approach.

Suppose that instead of being rated as either satisfactory or unsatisfactory in their annual performance reviews, the employees for ACME Manufacturing are rated as performing in either a superior, average, or inferior manner. Marie wants to analyze the differences in pre-employment screening test scores for these three groups of employees and develop a rule for predicting to which group a new potential employee would belong. Her plan is to hire any applicant classified in the superior group and reject applicants in the inferior group. Applicants in the average group will be screened more closely with additional interviews and references checking before Marie makes a hiring decision.

In this example, the personnel director is interested in discriminating among *three* groups: (1) superior employees, (2) average employees, and (3) inferior employees. We cannot apply the regression-based technique described earlier to this example because it involves more than two groups. We are using three groups in this example for convenience in illustrating the MDA approach. This approach can be applied to problems involving any number of groups. The MDA approach also can accommodate more than two independent variables.

The data for this example are displayed in Figure 10.11 (and in the file FIG10-11.XLS on your data disk). The Analysis Sample worksheet contains data for the company's current employees, whom the personnel director has classified into one of the three groups: (1) superior, (2) average, and (3) inferior. These group assignments are indicated by the numbers in the Group column. Each employee's mechanical and verbal scores on the aptitude test are displayed in the adjacent columns.

	File	Edit	View	Insert	Format	Tools	Data	Window	Help			
		A	B	C	D	E	F	G	H		
1											
2				-- Test Scores --							
3		Obs.	Group	Mechanical	Verbal						
4		1	1	44.7	36.1						
5		2	1	43.2	42.0						
6		3	1	42.5	30.8						
7		4	1	40.2	42.6						
8		5	1	41.9	37.1						
9		6	1	39.3	33.8						
10		7	1	38.6	40.3						
11		8	2	38.1	28.5						
12		9	2	37.9	44.7						
13		10	2	36.8	42.6						
14		11	2	35.8	35.2						
15		12	2	39.0	33.1						
16		13	2	37.5	36.4						
17		14	3	36.1	30.8						
18		15	3	35.6	27.2						
19		16	3	34.4	39.0						
20		17	3	32.8	35.2						
21		18	3	31.4	29.4						
22		19	3	29.5	37.9						
23		20	3	30.1	33.9						
24		Group	1	41.5	37.5						
25		Averages	2	37.5	36.7						
26			3	32.8	33.3						
27											

CENTROID COORDINATES → (rows 24–26)

Key Cell Formulas

Cell	Formula	Copied to
C24	=AVERAGE(C4:C10)	D24
C25	=AVERAGE(C11:C16)	D25
C26	=AVERAGE(C17:C23)	D26

Figure 10.11: *Data for current employees classified into three groups*

Although the MDA approach is different from the regression technique described earlier for the two-group example, the basic idea is the same. Figure 10.12 shows the plot of all the scores on the aptitude tests for each group along with the centroids. Note that most of the observations in each group cluster around the group's centroid. If we don't already know to which group an observation belongs, we could classify the observation based on its proximity to the centroids. That is, to determine to which group a new observation belongs, we could plot it on this graph and visually judge the distance between it and each of the centroids. A logical classification rule is to assign observations to the group represented by the closest centroid. This is the approach taken in MDA, although at a somewhat more sophisticated level.

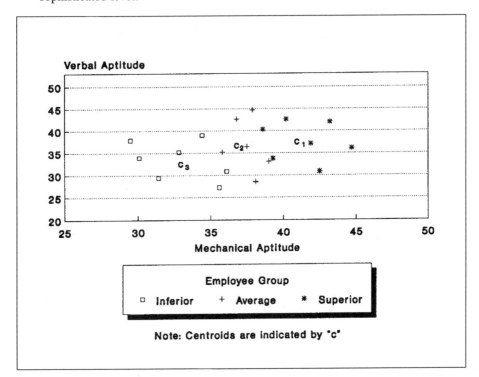

Figure 10.12: Graph of data for the three-group example

DISTANCE MEASURES

The problem with the visual approach is that some observations might be "too close to call," appearing to be equally close to several centroids. For example, in Figure 10.12 several points fall midway between two of the centroids and might be difficult to classify visually. Also, if the problem involves more than two independent variables, the graph displaying the data must be drawn in three or more dimensions, making a visual inspection of the data difficult or impossible. Rather than just "eyeballing" it, we need a more formal measure of the distance between each observation and each centroid.

You might recall from high school algebra that the Euclidean (straight-line) distance between two points (A_1, B_1) and (A_2, B_2) in two dimensions can be measured by:

$$\text{Distance} = \sqrt{(A_1 - A_2)^2 + (B_1 - B_2)^2} \qquad \textbf{10.7}$$

For example, the distance between two arbitrary points (3, 7) and (9, 5) is:

$$\sqrt{(3-9)^2 + (7-5)^2} = \sqrt{40} = 6.324$$

This distance formula generalizes easily to any number of dimensions. We can use this formula in MDA to measure the distance from a given observation to the centroid of each group, and then assign the observation to the group it is closest to.

From a statistical viewpoint, this distance measure in equation 10.7 is somewhat weak because it ignores the variances of the independent variables. To see this, suppose that X_1 represents one of the independent variables and X_2 the other. If X_2 has a much larger variance than X_1, the effects of *small but important* differences in X_1 could be masked or dwarfed in equation 10.7 by *large but unimportant* differences in X_2. Figure 10.13 illustrates this problem, where the ellipses represent regions containing 99% of the values belonging to each group.

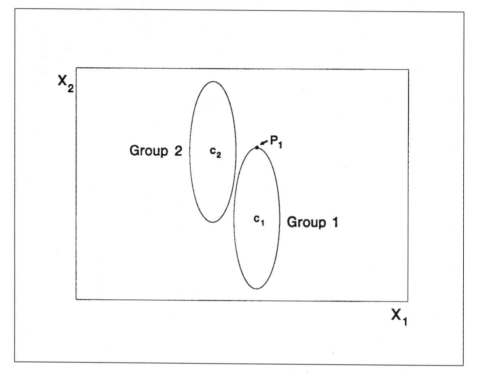

Figure 10.13: Regions containing 99% of the observations in each group

Consider the observation labeled P_1 in Figure 10.13. This observation appears to be closest to c_2 and, indeed, if we used the standard distance measure in equation 10.7, we would assign it to group 2 because its distance from c_1 with respect to the X_2-axis is relatively large. However, it is extremely unlikely that this observation belongs to group 2 because its location with respect to the X_1-axis far exceeds the typical values for group 2. Thus, it would be helpful to refine our distance measure in equation 10.7 to account for possible differences in the variances of the independent variables.

If we let D_{ij} represent the distance from observation i to the centroid for group j, we can define this distance as:

$$D_{ij} = \sqrt{\sum_k \frac{(x_{ik} - \bar{x}_{jk})^2}{s_{jk}^2}} \qquad \textbf{10.8}$$

where x_{ik} represents the value of observation i on the kth independent variable, $\bar{x}_{jk}$ represents the average value of group j on the kth independent variable, and s_{jk}^2 represents the sample variance of group j on the kth independent variable. (Don't be intimidated by how complex this formula looks; the idea behind it is quite simple.)

There are numerous variations on the distance measure in equation 10.8. One of the most popular variations—known as the **Mahalanobis distance measure**—refines the calculation in equation 10.8 to account for differences in the covariances between the independent variables. A discussion of these more sophisticated distance measures is beyond the scope of this book. But this discussion should give you a good understanding of how MDA works, regardless of the distance measure used.

MDA CLASSIFICATION

In MDA, we calculate the distance from an observation to the centroid for each of the possible groups. Then we assign the observation to the group that it is closest to based on these measurements.

To use the distance measure in equation 10.8, we need to calculate several values. First, we need to calculate the $\bar{x}_{jk}$ values—that is, the average value for group j on the kth independent variable. In other words, we need to calculate the centroid for each group. In Figure 10.14 (and in the file FIG10-14.XLS on your data disk) the $\bar{x}_{jk}$ values are calculated in cells C24 through D26 using the AVERAGE() function in a similar way as in the earlier two-group example. Similarly, s_{jk}^2 represents the variance for group j on the kth independent variable. These values are calculated in cells C27 through D29 using the VAR() function.

Columns E, F, and G in Figure 10.14 calculate the distance from each observation in the analysis sample to each centroid using the distance measure in equation 10.8. For observation 1, these calculations are summarized as:

$$\text{Distance from observation 1 to centroid of group 1} = \sqrt{\frac{(44.7-41.5)^2}{4.9} + \frac{(36.1-37.5)^2}{19.2}} = 1.49$$

$$\text{Distance from observation 1 to centroid of group 2} = \sqrt{\frac{(44.7-37.5)^2}{1.2} + \frac{(36.1-36.7)^2}{36.3}} = 6.47$$

$$\text{Distance from observation 1 to centroid of group 3} = \sqrt{\frac{(44.7-32.8)^2}{7.0} + \frac{(36.1-33.3)^2}{19.4}} = 4.54$$

Based on this analysis, MDA predicts that observation 1 belongs to group 1 because 1.49 is the smallest of the three distances. These, distances are calculated in cells E4, F4, and G4, using the following formulas:

Formula for cell E4:   = SQRT((C4 – $C$24)^2/$C$27 + (D4 – $D$24)^2/$D$27)
(copy to E5 through E23)

Formula for cell F4:   = SQRT((C4 – $C$25)^2/$C$28 + (D4 – $D$25)^2/$D$28)
(copy to F5 through F23)

Formula for cell G4:   = SQRT((C4 – $C$26)^2/$C$29 + (D4 – $D$26)^2/$D$29)
(copy to G5 through G23)

To complete the distance calculations for all the observations in Figure 10.14, the preceding formulas are copied down their respective columns.

The group assignments in the Pred. Group column are implemented using a nested IF() function. Cell H4 contains the formula:

Formula for cell H4:   = IF(E4 = MIN(E4:G4),1,IF(F4 = MIN(E4:G4),2,3))
(copy to H5 through H23)

This formula is copied to cells H5 through H23 to complete the group predictions for the analysis sample. Misclassified observations are identified by asterisks in column I as:

Formula for cell I4:   =IF(H4<>B4,"**"," ")
(copy to I5 through I23)

	A	B	C	D	E	F	G	H	I	J
	File	Edit	View	Insert	Format	Tools	Data	Window	Help	
1										
2			-- Test Scores --		Distance to Group:			Predicted		
3	Obs.	Group	Mechanical	Verbal	1	2	3	Group		
4	1	1	44.7	36.1	1.49	6.47	4.54	1		
5	2	1	43.2	42.0	1.28	5.19	4.39	1		
6	3	1	42.5	30.8	1.61	4.60	3.71	1		
7	4	1	40.2	42.6	1.29	2.61	3.49	1		
8	5	1	41.9	37.1	0.20	3.93	3.53	1		
9	6	1	39.3	33.8	1.32	1.64	2.43	1		
10	7	1	38.6	40.3	1.44	1.14	2.70	2	**	
11	8	2	38.1	28.5	2.56	1.47	2.29	2		
12	9	2	37.9	44.7	2.31	1.36	3.21	2		
13	10	2	36.8	42.6	2.40	1.16	2.58	2		
14	11	2	35.8	35.2	2.62	1.57	1.20	3	**	
15	12	2	39.0	33.1	1.51	1.47	2.34	2		
16	13	2	37.5	36.4	1.81	0.06	1.89	2		
17	14	3	36.1	30.8	2.86	1.60	1.37	3		
18	15	3	35.6	27.2	3.54	2.32	1.75	3		
19	16	3	34.4	39.0	3.22	2.86	1.41	3		
20	17	3	32.8	35.2	3.95	4.26	0.42	3		
21	18	3	31.4	29.4	4.92	5.66	1.05	3		
22	19	3	29.5	37.9	5.41	7.23	1.64	3		
23	20	3	30.1	33.9	5.20	6.70	1.05	3		
24	Group	1	41.5	37.5						
25	Averages	2	37.5	36.7						
26		3	32.8	33.3						
27	Group	1	4.9	19.2						
28	Variances	2	1.2	36.3						
29		3	7.0	19.4						
30										

Key Cell Formulas

Cell	Formula	Copied to
C24	=AVERAGE(C4:C10)	D24
C25	=AVERAGE(C11:C16)	D25
C26	=AVERAGE(C17:C23)	D26
C27	=VAR(C4:C10)	D27
C28	=VAR(C11:C16)	D28
C29	=VAR(C17:C23)	D29
E4	=SQRT((C4−$C$24)^2/$C$27+(D4−$D$24)^2/$D$27)	E5:E23
F4	=SQRT((C4−$C$25)^2/$C$28+(D4−$D$25)^2/$D$28)	F5:F23
G4	=SQRT((C4−$C$26)^2/$C$29+(D4−$D$26)^2/$D$29)	G5:G23
H4	=IF(E4=MIN(E4:G4),1,IF(F4=MIN(E4:G4)2,3))	H5:H23
I4	=IF(H4<>B4,"**"," ")	I5:I23

Figure 10.14: Distance calculations for the three-group example

The classification results for the analysis sample are summarized in Figure 10.15. Note that MDA misclassified one observation from group 1 and one observation from group 2. Thus, MDA was able to correctly classify 18 out of 20 (or 90%) of the observations in the analysis sample. Again, this accuracy rate is likely to be favorably biased and might overestimate how well MDA will perform on new observations not included in the analysis sample.

		Predicted Group			
		1	2	3	Total
	1	6	1	0	7
Actual Group	2	0	5	1	6
	3	0	0	7	7
	Total	6	6	8	20

Figure 10.15: Summary of classification results on the analysis sample for the three groups

Figure 10.16 presents the classification results for the same six *new* applicants that were classified using the two-group approach to DA in Figure 10.8. It is interesting to compare the results of these two figures.

Figure 10.16: Predicted group memberships of new applicants

Recall that the personnel director's plan is to classify applicants into three groups and hire any applicant in the superior group (group 1), reject any applicant in the inferior group (group 3), and conduct a follow-up interview and check the references on applicants in the average group (group 2). Note that applicants 1, 2, and 4, who were classified earlier as satisfactory, are now identified as superior candidates. Applicants 5 and 6, who were classified earlier as unsatisfactory, are now identified as inferior candidates. However, applicant 3, who was classified earlier as unsatisfactory, is now identified as average and requires additional screening by the personnel director before a hiring decision is made.

SOME FINAL COMMENTS ON DA

DA is a powerful technique with a deep and rich theoretical basis. Our discussion of DA has only scratched the surface, but it should give you a good understanding of the issues involved in DA and some of the methods for solving classification problems. Other techniques exist for performing DA and MDA and these might be more appropriate for a particular data set than the procedures described in this chapter. For example, the distance measure in equation 10.8 could be refined further to account for possible differences in the covariances of the independent variables. These more refined distance measures are available in most statistical packages (such as SAS and Minitab) that have DA options; but the underlying idea is the same as that presented in this chapter.

SUMMARY

DA is a statistical technique that can be used to develop a rule for predicting in which of two or more groups an observation belongs. DA is similar to regression analysis in that it uses a set of independent variables to predict the value of a dependent variable. However, in DA the dependent variable is coded in a discrete, or categorical, manner to represent the different groups under consideration.

This chapter presented two approaches to DA. When the problem involves only two groups, regression analysis can be used to develop a classification rule. However, when the problem involves more than two groups, the regression approach is no longer appropriate and the more general k-group approach to DA is required. The k-group DA approach can be used with problems involving two or more groups.

REFERENCES

Altman, E. I., R. B. Avery, R. A. Eisenbeis and J. F. Sinkey. *Application of Classification Techniques in Business, Banking and Finance.* Greenwich, CT: JAI Press, 1981.

Booth, D. E., A. Pervaiz, S. N. Ahkam and B. Osyk. "A Robust Multivariate Procedure for the Identification of Problem Savings and Loan Institutions." *Decision Sciences*, 1989, 20, 320-333.

Campbell, T. S. and J. K. Dietrich. "The Determinants of Default on Insured Conventional Residential Mortgage Loans." *Journal of Finance*, 38, 1983, 1569-1581.

Flury, B. and H. Riedwyl. *Multivariate Statistics: A Practical Approach.* New York: Chapman and Hall, 1988.

Hand, D. J. *Discrimination and Classification.* New York: Wiley, 1981.

Labe, R. "Database Marketing Increases Prospecting Effectiveness at Merrill Lynch." *Interfaces*, vol. 24, no. 5, 1994.

Morrison, D. F. *Multivariate Statistical Methods, Third Edition.* New York: McGraw-Hill, 1990.

Welker, R. B. "Discriminant and Classification Analysis as an Aid to Employee Selection." *Accounting Review*, 49, 1974, 514-523.

La Quinta Motor Inns Predicts Successful Sites with Discriminant Analysis

Source: Kimes, Sheryl E. and James A. Fitzsimmons, "Selecting Profitable Hotel Sites at La Quinta Motor Inns," *Interfaces*, vol. 20, no. 2, March–April 1990, pages 12–20.

MANAGEMENT AT LA QUINTA MOTOR INNS wanted a fast, reliable method for predicting whether potential sites for new inns would be successful. One of the first issues to be resolved in designing a regression model was to define a measure of success that would be useful in making predictions. After considering several alternatives, operating margin—defined as profit plus depreciation and interest expenses as a percentage of total revenue—was chosen. Total revenue and total profit were unsuitable measures because they are too highly correlated with the size of the inn. Occupancy was also considered unsuitable because it is too sensitive to the economic cycle.

Data were collected on all 151 existing inns operated by La Quinta at the time of the study. The regression model was developed using 57 inns, and the other 94 were set aside for validation. During the selection of independent variables, care was taken to measure collinearity and keep it under control. A coefficient of determination (R^2) of 0.51 was obtained for a model showing that operating margin is positively influenced by the price of the inn (a measure of the competitive room rate of the market area) and the location of nearby colleges. Negative influences were distance to the nearest La Quinta Inn (a reverse measure of market penetration) and median income in the market area (suggesting an industrial economic base). After careful analysis, one outlier was deleted from the data, substantially improving the model.

The regression model itself was not the tool that management had in mind, however. Management needed a criterion to use for either choosing or rejecting potential sites. After specifying an acceptable risk of choosing a bad site, classification tables were used to develop a decision rule for discriminating between "good" sites and "bad" sites. The cut-off value was a predicted operating margin of 35%.

The model was then tested on the 94 inns set aside for validation, and the error rates were as expected. Set up as a spreadsheet, the model is now used to screen potential sites for possible development, with the final decision made by the president of the company.

Questions and Problems

1. What is a centroid?

2. It can be argued that regression analysis and DA both use a set of independent variables to predict the value of a dependent variable. What, then, is the difference between regression analysis and DA?

3. In discussing the approach to DA using distance measures, we calculated the distance from an observation to the centroid of each group. We then assigned the observation to the group it was closest to based on the distance measures. Can you think of another way distance measures might be used to classify observations? What classification rule is used under this method? (Hint: Consider making classifications based on an observation's nearest neighbor.)

4. This chapter noted that the R^2 statistic cannot be relied upon as a goodness-of-fit measure in the regression approach to two-group DA. What was the value of the R^2 statistic for the two-group DA example in this chapter? How does it compare with the percentage of correctly classified observations in this same example?

5. The director of the MBA program at Salterdine University wants to use DA to determine which applicants to admit to the MBA program. The director believes that an applicant's undergraduate grade point average (GPA) and score on the GMAT exam are helpful in predicting which applicants will be good students. To assist in this endeavor, the director asked a committee of faculty members to classify 30 of the current students in the MBA program into two groups: (1) good students and (2) weak students. The following data summarize these ratings along with the GPA and GMAT scores for the 30 students.

   a. What are the coordinates of the centroids for the good students and the weak students?

   b. Use the regression approach to two-group DA to develop a classification rule for predicting to which group a new student will belong. State your classification rule.

   c. Create a table similar to Figure 10.7 that summarizes the accuracy of your classification rule on the current students. Overall, how accurate does your classification rule appear to be?

   d. Suppose that the MBA director receives applications for admission to the MBA program from the following individuals. According to DA, which of these individuals do you expect to be good students and which do you expect to be weak?

Student	Faculty Rating	GPA	GMAT
1	1	2.96	596
2	1	3.14	473
3	1	3.22	482
4	1	3.29	527
5	1	3.69	505
6	1	3.46	693
7	1	3.03	626
8	1	3.19	663
9	1	3.63	447
10	1	3.59	588
11	1	2.86	494
12	1	2.85	496
13	1	3.14	419
14	1	3.28	371
15	1	2.89	447
16	2	3.15	313
17	2	3.50	402
18	2	2.89	485
19	2	2.80	444
20	2	3.13	416
21	2	2.54	446
22	2	2.43	425
23	2	2.20	474
24	2	2.36	531
25	2	2.57	542
26	2	2.35	406
27	2	2.72	412
28	2	2.51	458
29	2	2.36	399
30	2	2.19	482

Name	GPA	GMAT
Mike Dimoupolous	3.02	450
Scott Frazier	2.97	587
Paula Curry	3.95	551
Terry Freeman	2.45	484
Dana Simmons	3.26	524

6. Refer to question 5. The MBA director could make two types of admission mistakes using DA. One mistake is to classify a student into the weak category (and, therefore, not admit the student) when, in fact, the student belongs in the good category. We will call this a type I error. The other type of error (which we will call a type II error) is to classify a student into the good category (and, therefore, admit the student) when, in fact, the student is a weak student. Suppose that the MBA director considers a type I error to be twice as costly as a type II error. How does the classification rule change to accommodate these unequal costs of misclassification? What is the new classification rule?

7. Refer to question 5 and answer the following questions.

   a. Use the distance measure approach to DA to classify each of the current students.

   b. Create a table similar to Figure 10.7 that summarizes the accuracy of the distance measure approach on the data for the current students. Overall, how accurate does the distance measure approach to DA appear to be on these data?

   c. Classify each of the five new applicants from question 5 using the distance measure approach. Whom do you expect to be good students and whom do you expect to be weak?

   d. If the two approaches to DA reach the same conclusion about a given applicant, what effect should this have on the MBA director's opinion of that applicant? What action might the director take if the two approaches to DA suggest conflicting classifications?

8. The manager of the commercial loan department for a bank wants to develop a rule to use in determining whether or not to approve various requests for loans. The manager believes that three key characteristics of a company's performance are important in making this decision: liquidity, profitability, and activity. The manager measures liquidity as the ratio of current assets to current liabilities. Profitability is measured as the ratio of net profit to sales. Activity is measured as the ratio of sales to fixed assets. The manager has collected the following data for a sample of 18 loans that the bank has made in the past five years. These loans have been classified into two groups: (1) those that were acceptable and (2) those that should have been rejected.

Observations	Category	Liquidity	Profitability	Activity
1	1	0.90	0.34	1.53
2	1	0.88	0.23	1.67
3	1	0.92	0.28	1.43
4	1	0.89	0.14	1.24
5	1	0.78	0.35	1.80
6	1	0.81	0.26	2.01
7	1	0.72	0.18	1.75
8	1	0.93	0.22	0.99
9	1	0.82	0.26	1.40
10	2	0.78	0.26	1.34
11	2	0.78	0.27	1.67
12	2	0.72	0.18	1.53
13	2	0.69	0.16	1.20
14	2	0.63	0.15	0.88
15	2	0.58	0.22	1.42
16	2	0.81	0.18	1.59
17	2	0.67	0.21	1.21
18	2	0.65	0.16	1.37

a. What are the coordinates of the centroids for the two groups?

b. Use the regression approach to two-group DA to develop a classification rule for predicting whether or not a given loan applicant will repay the loan, if approved. State your classification rule.

c. Create a table similar to Figure 10.7 that summarizes the accuracy of your classification rule on the data for the current loans. Overall, how accurate does your classification rule seem?

d. Suppose that the manager receives loan applications from companies with the following financial information. According to DA, which of these companies do you expect to be acceptable credit risks?

Company	Liquidity	Profitability	Activity
A	0.78	0.27	1.58
B	0.91	0.23	1.67
C	0.68	0.33	1.43
D	0.78	0.23	1.23
E	0.67	0.26	1.78

9. Refer to question 8. Suppose that the manager wants to classify loan applicants into one of three groups: (1) acceptable loan applications, (2) loan applications requiring further scrutiny, and (3) unacceptable loan applications. Assume that the first six observations given in question 8 correspond to group 1, the next six correspond to group 2, and the final six correspond to group 3.

   a. Use the distance measure approach to DA to classify each loan.

   b. Create a table similar to Figure 10.15 that summarizes the accuracy of the distance measure approach on the data for the current loans. Overall, how accurate does the distance measure approach to DA appear to be on these data?

   c. Classify each of the five new applicants from question 8 using the distance measure approach. Into which of the three groups do you expect each loan applicant to fall?

10. Consider the two-group personnel selection example discussed in this chapter. Some might argue that the best classification rule for this problem is the one that minimizes the number of misclassifications in the analysis sample. Formulate a mixed-integer programming model that could be solved to determine the linear classification rule that minimizes the number of misclassifications in the analysis sample. (Hint: Create one constraint for each observation. Include a unique binary variable in each constraint to indicate whether or not the observation is misclassified.)

Predicting Bank Failure
A Case in Discriminant
Analysis (DA)

THE number of bankruptcies in the banking industry recently reached an historic high unparalleled since the Great Depression. In 1984, fewer than 50 bankruptcy cases were filed with the Federal Deposit Insurance Corporation (FDIC), whereas in 1991, more than 400 were filed. To monitor the member banks and to assure their proper compliance with federal regulations, the FDIC commits substantial efforts to both on-site examinations and off-site surveillance activities. To facilitate this process, the FDIC is developing an early warning system that will alert the agency to banks that might be approaching or entering financial distress. Using the technique of DA, you'll help the FDIC develop such an early warning system.

Specifically, the FDIC wants to develop a procedure to help predict if a bank will enter financial distress in the coming year. The following financial ratios are helpful in making such predictions:

$$\text{Ratio 1} = \frac{\text{Total Capital}}{\text{Total Assets}}$$

$$\text{Ratio 2} = \frac{\text{Total Expenses}}{\text{Total Assets}}$$

$$\text{Ratio 3} = \frac{\text{Total Loans and Leases}}{\text{Total Deposits}}$$

The FDIC supplied you with data on these ratios collected one year ago for a sample of banks. It also indicated which banks are currently in financial distress. These data are summarized in the table (and in the file C10_CASE.XLS on your data disk).

1. Calculate the centroids for each group in the analysis sample. What do these values indicate?

2. Use the regression approach to 2-group DA to develop a rule for predicting whether or not a bank will enter financial distress. State the classification rule you identify.

3. Use the classification rule you identify in question 2 to classify each observation in the analysis sample. Develop a table (similar to Figure 10.7) summarizing the classification results. Overall, how accurate does this classification rule seem to be?

4. The FDIC also wants you to analyze the data using the distance measure approach discussed in this chapter. Complete this analysis and prepare another table summarizing the accuracy of this procedure on the analysis sample.

5. Which of the two methods would you recommend that the FDIC use?

		Analysis Sample		
Obs	Group	Ratio 1	Ratio 2	Ratio 3
1	1	8.1	0.13	0.64
2	1	6.6	0.10	1.04
3	1	5.8	0.11	0.66
4	1	12.3	0.09	0.80
5	1	4.5	0.11	0.69
6	1	9.1	0.14	0.74
7	1	1.1	0.12	0.63
8	1	8.9	0.12	0.75
9	1	0.7	0.16	0.56
10	1	9.8	0.12	0.65
11	2	7.3	0.10	0.55
12	2	14.0	0.08	0.46
13	2	9.6	0.08	0.72
14	2	12.4	0.08	0.43
15	2	18.4	0.07	0.52
16	2	8.0	0.08	0.54
17	2	12.6	0.09	0.30
18	2	9.8	0.07	0.67
19	2	8.3	0.09	0.51
20	2	20.6	0.13	0.79

Note: Group 1 = financially distressed banks

Group 2 = financially strong banks

6. Suppose that the FDIC also gave you the data below on six new banks. Based on the classification rule you developed using regression, which (if any) of the six new banks would you expect to enter financial distress?

Obs	Group	Ratio 1	Ratio 2	Ratio 3
1	?	3.3	0.13	0.63
2	?	9.2	0.08	0.26
3	?	9.3	0.09	0.59
4	?	3.2	0.16	0.57
5	?	11.4	0.09	0.69
6	?	8.1	0.14	0.72

Time-Series Analysis

A **TIME-SERIES** is a set of observations on a quantitative variable collected over time. For example, every night the evening news reports the closing value of the Dow Jones Industrial Average. These closing values represent a series of values for a quantitative variable over time—or a time-series. Most businesses keep track of a number of time-series variables. Examples might include daily, weekly, monthly, or quarterly figures on sales, costs, profits, inventory, back-orders, customer counts, and so on.

Businesses often are interested in forecasting future values of a time-series variable. For example, if we could accurately predict future closing values of the Dow Jones Industrial Average, we could become very wealthy investing in the stock market by "buying low and selling high." In constructing business plans, most companies make some attempt to forecast the expected levels of sales, costs, profits, inventory, back-orders, customer counts, and so on. These types of forecasts often are required inputs to the other types of modeling techniques discussed throughout this text.

In chapter 9, we investigated how to build and use regression models to predict the behavior of a dependent variable using one or more independent variables that are believed to be related to the dependent variable in a *causal* fashion. That is, when building a regression model, we often select independent variables that are believed to cause the observed behavior of the dependent variable. Although we can sometimes use this same approach to build a causal regression model for a time-series variable, we cannot always do so.

For example, we might not know which causal independent variables are influencing a particular time-series variable. And even if we do have some idea which causal variables are affecting a time-series, there might not be any data available for those variables. If data on the causal variables are available, the best regression function estimated from these data might not fit the data well. Finally, even if the estimated regression function fits the data well, we might have to forecast the values of the causal independent variables in order to estimate future values of the dependent (time-series) variable. Forecasting the causal independent variables might be more difficult than forecasting the original time-series variable.

TIME-SERIES METHODS

In some situations, it might be difficult, undesirable, or even impossible to forecast time-series data using a causal regression model. In these cases, the only alternative might be to use a time-series forecasting method in which we analyze the past behavior of the time-series variable in order to predict its future behavior. If we discover some sort of systematic behavior in the time-series variable, we might attempt to construct a model of this behavior to help us forecast its future behavior. For example, we might find a long-term upward (or downward) trend in the time-series that might be expected to continue in the future. Or, we might discover some predictable seasonal fluctuations in the data that could help us make estimates about the future.

This chapter presents a variety of methods for analyzing time-series data. We'll first discuss several techniques that are appropriate for *stationary* time-series, where there is no significant upward or downward trend in the data over time. Then, we'll discuss techniques for handling *non-stationary* time-series, where there is some upward or downward trend in the data over time. Finally, we'll discuss techniques for modeling seasonal patterns in time-series data.

MEASURING ACCURACY

Many methods are available for modeling time-series data. In most cases, it is impossible to know in advance which method will be the most effective for a given data set. Thus, a common approach to time-series analysis involves trying several modeling techniques on a given data set and evaluating how well they explain the past behavior of the time-series variable. We can evaluate these techniques by constructing line graphs that show the actual data versus the values predicted by the various modeling techniques. More formal quantitative measures of the accuracy of time-series modeling techniques also exist. Two common accuracy measures are the mean absolute deviation (MAD) and the mean square forecast error (MSE). These two quantities are defined as:

$$\text{MAD} = \sum_i \frac{\left|Y_i - \hat{Y}_i\right|}{n}$$

$$\text{MSE} = \sum_i \frac{\left(Y_i - \hat{Y}_i\right)^2}{n}$$

In each of these formulas, Y_i represents the *actual* value for the ith observation in the time-series and $\hat{Y}_i$ is the *forecasted* value for this observation. Both of these quantities measure the differences between the actual values in the time-series and the predicted, or fitted, values generated by the forecasting technique. The MSE measure is closely related to the sum of square estimation errors criterion introduced in our discussion of regression analysis. Although both the MAD and the MSE measures are commonly used in time-series modeling, we will focus on the MSE measure because it is somewhat easier to calculate.

EXTRAPOLATION MODELS

Extrapolation techniques for time-series analysis involve building models that account for the past behavior of a time-series variable in an effort to predict the future behavior of the variable. The general form of an extrapolation model is:

$$\hat{Y}_{t+1} = f(Y_t, Y_{t-1}, Y_{t-2}, \dots) \qquad \textbf{11.1}$$

where $\hat{Y}_{t+1}$ represents the predicted value for the time-series variable in time period $t + 1$, Y_t represents the value of the time-series variable in time period t, Y_{t-1} represents the value of the time-series variable in time period $t - 1$, and so on. The goal of an extrapolation model is to identify a function $f(\cdot)$ that produces accurate forecasts of future values of the time-series variable.

AN EXAMPLE

The following example demonstrates several of the most common extrapolation techniques used in time-series forecasting.

Electra-City is a retail store that sells audio and video equipment for the home and car. Each month the manager of the store must order merchandise from a distant warehouse. Currently, the manager is trying to estimate how many VCRs the store is likely to sell in the next month. To assist in this process, he has collected the data shown in Figure 11.1 (and in the file FIG11-1.XLS on your data disk) on the number of VCRs sold in each of the previous 24 months. He wants to use these data in making his prediction.

After collecting the data for a time-series variable, the next step in building a time-series model is to inspect the data plotted over time. Figure 11.1 includes a plot of the VCR data. Notice that this plot does not suggest a strong upward or downward trend in the data. This plot suggests that the number of VCRs sold each month fell somewhere between 30 and 40 units over the past two years with no apparent pattern or regularity from month to month. Thus, we expect that one of the extrapolation techniques discussed in the following sections would be an appropriate method for modeling these data.

Figure 11.1: Historical VCR
sales data for the Electra-
City forecasting problem

Creating a Line Graph

To create a scatter plot like the one shown in Figure 11.1:

1. Select cells A3 through B26.

2. Click the Insert menu.

3. Click Chart.

4. Click On This Sheet

5. Drag in the spreadsheet to indicate where you want the
   chart located.

Excel's ChartWizard then prompts you to make a number of
selections concerning the type of chart you want and how it
should be labeled and formatted. After Excel creates a basic
chart, you can customize it in many ways. Double-clicking a
chart element displays a dialog box with options for modifying
the appearance of the element.

MOVING AVERAGES

The **moving average** technique is probably the easiest extrapolation method to use
and understand. With this technique, the predicted value of the time-series in period
$t + 1$ (denoted by $\hat{Y}_{t+1}$) is simply the average of the k previous observations in the
series; that is:

$$\hat{Y}_{t+1} = \frac{Y_t + Y_{t-1} + \cdots + Y_{t-k+1}}{k} \qquad \text{11.2}$$

The value k in equation 11.2 determines how many previous observations will be included in the moving average. No general method exists for determining what value of k will be best for a particular time-series. Therefore, we must try several values of k to see which gives the best results. This is illustrated in Figure 11.2 (and in the file FIG11-2.XLS on your data disk) where the monthly number of VCRs sold for Electra-City is fit using moving average models with k values of 2 and 4.

	A	B	C	D	E	F	G	H	I
		Number of	2-Month	4-Month					
	Time Period	VCRs Sold	Moving Avg.	Moving Avg.					
3	1	33	--	--					
4	2	38	--	--					
5	3	31	35.50	--					
6	4	35	34.50	--					
7	5	30	33.00	34.25					
8	6	36	32.50	33.50					
9	7	34	33.00	33.00					
10	8	39	35.00	33.75					
11	9	39	36.50	34.75					
12	10	36	39.00	37.00					
13	11	40	37.50	37.00					
14	12	38	38.00	38.50					
15	13	37	39.00	38.25					
16	14	39	37.50	37.75					
17	15	32	38.00	38.50					
18	16	38	35.50	36.50					
19	17	37	35.00	36.50					
20	18	39	37.50	36.50					
21	19	37	38.00	36.50					
22	20	35	38.00	37.75					
23	21	37	36.00	37.00					
24	22	34	36.00	37.00					
25	23	35	35.50	35.75					
26	24	36	34.50	35.25					
27									
28		MSE:	6.93	7.66					

Key Cell Formulas

Cell	Formula	Copied to
C5	=AVERAGE(B3:B4)	C6:C26
C28	=SUMXMY2(B5:B26,C5:C26)/COUNT(C5:C26)	—
D7	=AVERAGE(B3:B6)	D8:D26
D28	=SUMXMY2(B7:B26,D7:D26)/COUNT(D7:D26)	—

Figure 11.2: Moving average forecasts for the VCR sales data

We generated the moving average forecasts in Figure 11.2 using the AVERAGE( ) function. For example, the 2-month moving average forecasts are generated by implementing the following formula in cell C5 and copying it to cells C6 through C26:

Formula for cell C5:   =AVERAGE(B3:B4)
(copy to C6 through C26)

The 4-month moving average forecasts are generated by implementing the following formula in cell D7 and copying it to cells D8 through D26:

Formula for cell D7:   =AVERAGE(B3:B6)
(copy to D8 through D26)

The actual VCR sales data are plotted in Figure 11.3 along with the predicted values from the two moving average models. This graph shows that the predicted values tend to be less volatile, or smoother, than the actual data. This should not be surprising because the moving average technique tends to average out the peaks and valleys occurring in the original data. Thus, the moving average technique is sometimes referred to as a *smoothing* method. The larger the value of k (or the more past data points are averaged together) the smoother the moving average prediction will be.

Figure 11.3: *Plot of moving average predictions versus actual VCR sales data*

We can evaluate the relative accuracy of the two moving average forecasting functions by comparing the MSE values for these two techniques shown in cells C28 and D28 in Figure 11.2. The following formulas calculate these MSE values:

Formula for cell C28:   =SUMXMY2(B5:B26,C5:C26)/COUNT(C5:C26)

Formula for cell D28:   =SUMXMY2(B7:B26,D7:D26)/COUNT(D7:D26)

(Note that the SUMXMY2( ) function calculates the sum of squared differences between corresponding values in two different ranges. The COUNT( ) function returns the number of values in a range.)

The MSE value describes the overall fit of the forecasting technique to the historical data. By comparing the MSE values for the two moving averages, we might conclude that the 2-month moving average (with an MSE of 6.93) provides more accurate forecasts than the 4-month moving average (with an MSE of 7.66). Note, however, that the MSE includes and weighs relatively old data with the same importance as the most recent data. Thus, selecting a forecast based on the total MSE of the forecasting functions might not be wise because a forecasting function might have achieved a lower total MSE by fitting older data points very well while being relatively inaccurate on more recent data.

Because we want to forecast *future* observations, we might be interested in how well the forecasting function performed on the most recent data. We can determine this by calculating other MSE values using only the most recent data. For example, if we calculate MSE values using only the two most recent time periods (periods 23 and 24), the 4-month moving average produces an MSE of 1.13 and the 2-month moving average produces an MSE of 2.50. (You should verify these figures on your own.) Thus, we might conclude that the 4-month moving average model should be used to predict the future because it produced the most accurate predictions of the actual values observed during the past two time periods.

FORECASTING WITH THE MOVING AVERAGE MODEL

Assuming that the manager of Electra-City is satisfied with the accuracy of the 2-month moving average model, the prediction of the number of VCRs to be sold in the next month (time period 25) is calculated as:

$$\hat{Y}_{25} = \frac{Y_{24} + Y_{23}}{2} = \frac{35 + 36}{2} = 35.5$$

To forecast *more* than one period into the future using the moving average technique, we must substitute forecasted values for unobserved actual values. For example, suppose that at the end of time period 24 we want to forecast the number of VCRs to be sold in time periods 25 *and* 26. Using a two-period moving average, the forecast for time period 26 is represented by:

$$\hat{Y}_{26} = \frac{Y_{25} + Y_{24}}{2}$$

However, at time period 24 we don't know the actual value for Y_{25}. We have to substitute $\hat{Y}_{25}$ for Y_{25} in the previous equation to generate the forecast for time period 26. Therefore, at time period 24 our estimate of the number of VCRs to be sold in time period 26 is:

$$\hat{Y}_{26} = \frac{\hat{Y}_{25} + Y_{24}}{2} = \frac{35.5 + 35}{2} = 35.25$$

WEIGHTED MOVING AVERAGES

One drawback of the moving average technique is that all the past data used in calculating the average are weighted equally. However, we can often obtain a more accurate forecast by assigning different weights to the data. The **weighted moving average** extrapolation technique is a simple variation on the moving average technique that allows for weights to be assigned to the data being averaged. In the weighted moving average technique, the forecasting function is represented by:

$$\hat{Y}_{t+1} = w_1 Y_t + w_2 Y_{t-1} + \dots + w_k Y_{t-k+1} \qquad \textbf{11.3}$$

where $0 \le w_i \le 1$ and $\sum_{i=1}^{k} w_i = 1$. Note that the simple moving average forecast in equation 11.2 is a special case of equation 11.3 where $w_1 = w_2 = \dots = w_k = \frac{1}{k}$.

Although the weighted moving average offers greater flexibility than the moving average, it is also a bit more complicated. In addition to determining a value for k, we must also determine values for the weights w_i in equation 11.3. However, for a given value of k, we can use Solver to determine the values for w_i that minimize the MSE (or MAD). The spreadsheet implementation of a 2-month weighted moving average model for the Electra-City example is shown in Figure 11.4 (and in the file FIG11-4.XLS on your data disk).

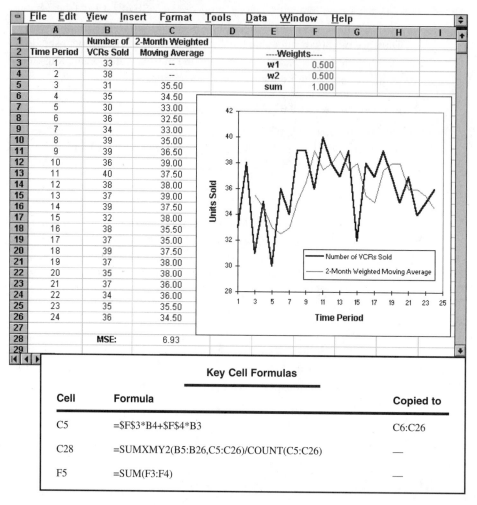

Figure 11.4: *Spreadsheet implementation of the weighted moving average model*

Key Cell Formulas		
Cell	Formula	Copied to
C5	=$F$3*B4+$F$4*B3	C6:C26
C28	=SUMXMY2(B5:B26,C5:C26)/COUNT(C5:C26)	—
F5	=SUM(F3:F4)	—

Cells F3 and F4 represent the weights w_1 and w_2, respectively. Cell F5 is the sum of cells F3 and F4. The weighted average forecasting function is implemented in cell C5 with the following formula, which is copied to cells C6 through C26:

Formula for cell C5:   =$F$3*B4+$F$4*B3
(copy to C6 through C26)

Notice that with $w_1 = w_2 = 0.5$ the weighted average predictions are identical to those of the simple moving average method shown in Figure 11.2. The formula for the MSE value in C28 is the same as the formula for the 2-month moving average described earlier.

We can use the Solver parameters and options shown in Figure 11.5 to identify the values for the weights in cells F3 and F4 that minimize the MSE. Notice that this is a nonlinear optimization problem because MSE represents a nonlinear objective function. Figure 11.6 shows the solution to this problem.

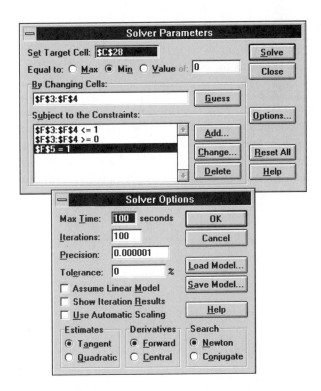

Figure 11.5: Solver parameters and options for the weighted moving average model

Figure 11.6: Optimal solution for the weighted moving average model

Notice that the optimal weights of $w_1 = 0.291$ and $w_2 = 0.709$ reduce the value of the MSE only slightly, from 6.93 to 6.29.

FORECASTING WITH THE WEIGHTED MOVING AVERAGE MODEL

Using the weighted moving average technique, the predicted number of VCRs to be sold at Electra-City in the next month (time period 25) is calculated as:

$$\hat{Y}_{25} = w_1 Y_{24} + w_2 Y_{23} = 0.291*36 + 0.709*35 = 35.3$$

We can also use the weighted moving average technique to forecast more than one time period into the future. However, as with the moving average technique, we must substitute forecasted values for unobserved actual values where needed. For example, suppose that at the end of time period 24 we want to forecast the number of VCRs to be sold in time periods 25 *and* 26. The weighted moving average forecast for time period 26 is represented by:

$$\hat{Y}_{26} = w_1 Y_{25} + w_2 Y_{24}$$

However, at time period 24 we don't know the actual value for Y_{25}. We have to substitute $\hat{Y}_{25}$ for Y_{25} in the previous equation to generate the forecast for time period 26. Therefore, at time period 24 our estimate of the number of VCRs to be sold in time period 26 is:

$$\hat{Y}_{26} = w_1 \hat{Y}_{25} + w_2 Y_{24} = 0.291*35.3 + 0.709*35 = 35.09$$

EXPONENTIAL SMOOTHING

Exponential smoothing is another averaging technique that allows weights to be assigned to past data. Exponential smoothing models assume the following form:

$$\hat{Y}_{t+1} = \hat{Y}_t + \alpha(Y_t - \hat{Y}_t) \qquad \textbf{11.4}$$

Equation 11.4 indicates that the predicted value for time period $t + 1$ ($\hat{Y}_{t+1}$) is equal to the predicted value for the previous period ($\hat{Y}_t$) plus an adjustment for the error made in predicting the previous period's value ($\alpha(Y_t - \hat{Y}_t)$). The parameter (alpha) in equation 11.4 can assume any value between 0 and 1 ($0 \leq \alpha \leq 1$).

It can be shown that the exponential smoothing formula in equation 11.4 is equivalent to:

$$\hat{Y}_{t+1} = \alpha Y_t + \alpha(1-\alpha)Y_{t-1} + (1-\alpha)^2 Y_{t-2} + \ldots + \alpha(1-\alpha)^n Y_{t-n} + \ldots$$

As shown in the previous equation, the forecast $\hat{Y}_{t+1}$ in exponential smoothing is a weighted combination of all previous values in the time-series where the most recent observation Y_t receives the heaviest weight (α), the next most recent observation Y_{t-1} receives the next heaviest weight ($\alpha(1-\alpha)$), and so on.

In an exponential smoothing model, small values of α tend to produce sluggish forecasts that do not react quickly to changes in the data. A value of α close to 1 produces a forecast that reacts more quickly to changes in the data. Figure 11.7 illustrates these relationships, showing the results of two exponential smoothing models for the VCR sales data with α-values of 0.1 and 0.9.

We can use Solver to determine the optimal value for α when building an exponential smoothing forecasting model for a particular data set. The spreadsheet implementation of the exponential smoothing forecasting model for the Electra-City example is shown in Figure 11.8 (and in the file FIG11-8.XLS on your data disk).

In Figure 11.8, cell F3 represents α. In an exponential smoothing forecasting model, it is customary to assume that $\hat{Y}_1 = Y_1$. Thus, in Figure 11.8, cell C3 contains the following formula:

Formula for cell C3:   =B3

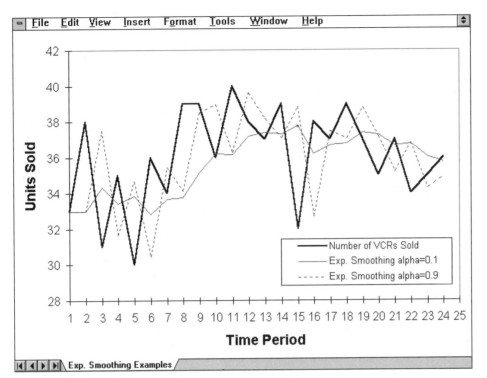

Figure 11.7: Two exponential smoothing models of the VCR sales data

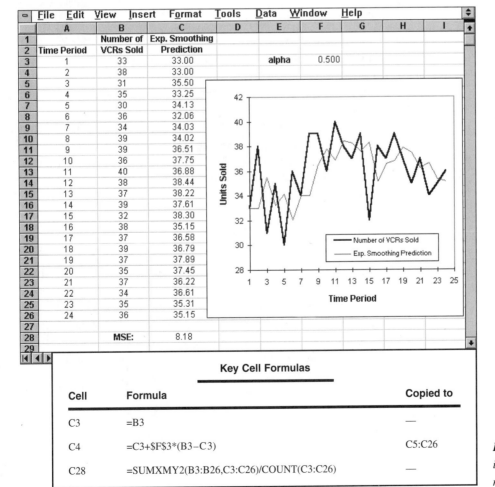

Figure 11.8: Spreadsheet implementation of the exponential smoothing model

Key Cell Formulas

Cell	Formula	Copied to
C3	=B3	—
C4	=C3+$F$3*(B3−C3)	C5:C26
C28	=SUMXMY2(B3:B26,C3:C26)/COUNT(C3:C26)	—

The forecasting function in equation 11.4 begins for time period $t = 2$ with the following formula, which is implemented in cell C4 and copied to cells C5 through C26:

Formula for cell C4:   =C3+$F$3*(B3−C3)
(copy to C5 through C26)

The formula in cell C28 calculates the MSE value as:

Formula for cell C28:   =SUMXMY2(B3:B26,C3:C26)/COUNT(C3:C26)

We can use the Solver parameters and options shown in Figure 11.9 to identify the value for α that minimizes the MSE. Again, this is a nonlinear optimization problem because the MSE represents a nonlinear objective function. Figure 11.10 shows the solution to this problem. Notice that the optimal value for α is given in cell F3 as 0.268.

FORECASTING WITH THE EXPONENTIAL SMOOTHING MODEL

Using the exponential smoothing model, the predicted number of VCRs to be sold at Electra-City in the next month (time period 25) is calculated as:

$$\hat{Y}_{25} = \hat{Y}_{24} + \alpha(Y_{24} - \hat{Y}_{24}) = 35.74 + 0.268*(36 - 35.74) = 35.81$$

An interesting property of the exponential smoothing technique becomes apparent when we try to use it to forecast more than one time period into the future. For example, suppose that at time period 24 we want to forecast the number of VCRs to be sold in time periods 25 *and* 26. The forecast for time period 26 is represented by:

$$\hat{Y}_{26} = \hat{Y}_{25} + \alpha(Y_{25} - \hat{Y}_{25})$$

Because Y_{25} is unknown at time period 24, we must substitute $\hat{Y}_{25}$ for Y_{25} in the previous equation. However, in that case we obtain $\hat{Y}_{26} = \hat{Y}_{25}$. In fact, the forecast for all future time periods would equal $\hat{Y}_{25}$. So when using exponential smoothing, the forecast for *all* future time periods equal the same value. This is consistent with the underlying idea of a stationary time-series. If a time-series is stationary (or has no trend), it is reasonable to assume that the forecast of the next time period and all future time periods should equal the same value. Thus, the exponential smoothing forecasting model for all future time periods ($t = 25, 26, 27, \ldots$) in the Electra-City example is represented by:

$$\hat{Y}_t = 35.81$$

TREND MODELS

The forecasting techniques presented so far are appropriate for stationary time-series data in which there is no significant trend in the data over time. However, it is not unusual for time-series data to exhibit some type of upward or downward trend over time. **Trend** is the long-term sweep or general direction of movement in a time-series. It reflects the net influence of long-term factors that affect the time-series in a fairly consistent and gradual way over time. In other words, the trend reflects changes in the data that occur with the passage of time.

Figure 11.9: Solver parameters and options for the exponential smoothing model

	A	B	C	D	E	F	G	H	I
1		Number of	Exp. Smoothing						
2	Time Period	VCRs Sold	Prediction						
3	1	33	33.00		alpha	0.268			
4	2	38	33.00						
5	3	31	34.34						
6	4	35	33.44						
7	5	30	33.86						
8	6	36	32.83						
9	7	34	33.68						
10	8	39	33.76						
11	9	39	35.17						
12	10	36	36.19						
13	11	40	36.14						
14	12	38	37.18						
15	13	37	37.40						
16	14	39	37.29						
17	15	32	37.75						
18	16	38	36.21						
19	17	37	36.69						
20	18	39	36.77						
21	19	37	37.37						
22	20	35	37.27						
23	21	37	36.66						
24	22	34	36.75						
25	23	35	36.01						
26	24	36	35.74						
27									
28		MSE:	7.49						
29									

Figure 11.10: Optimal solution for the exponential smoothing model

Because the moving average, weighted moving average, and exponential smoothing techniques involve some average of previous values to forecast future values, they consistently *underestimate* the actual values if there is an upward trend in the data. For example, consider the time-series data given by 2, 4, 6, 8, 10, 12, 14, 16, and 18. These data show a clear upward trend leading us to expect that the next value in the time-series should be 20. However, the forecasting techniques discussed up to this point would forecast that the next value in the series is less than or equal to 18 because no weighted average of the given data could exceed 18. Similarly, if there is a downward trend in the data over time, all of the methods discussed so far would produce predictions that *overestimate* the actual values in the time-series. In the following sections we'll consider several techniques that are appropriate for *non-stationary* time-series involving an upward or downward trend in the data over time.

AN EXAMPLE

The following example will be used to illustrate a variety of techniques for modeling trends in time-series data.

WaterCraft Inc. is a manufacturer of personal water crafts (also known as jet skis). Throughout its first five years of operation, the company has enjoyed a fairly steady growth in sales of its products. The officers of the company are preparing sales and manufacturing plans for the coming year. A critical input to these plans involves a forecast of the level of sales that the company expects to achieve. Quarterly sales data for the company during the past five years are given in Figure 11.11 (and in the file FIG11-11.XLS on your data disk).

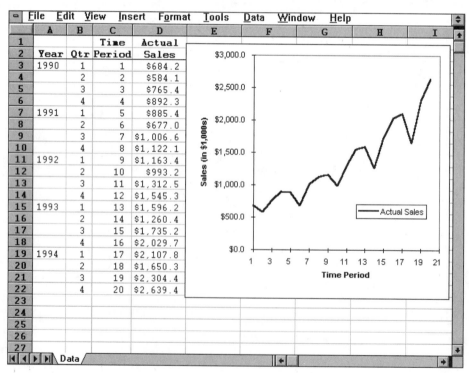

Figure 11.11: Historical sales data for the WaterCraft sales forecasting problem

The plot of the data in Figure 11.11 suggests a fairly strong upward trend in the data over time. Thus, to forecast the value of this time-series variable, we can use one of the forecasting techniques discussed in the following sections. These techniques account for a trend in the data.

HOLT'S METHOD

Holt's method is often an effective forecasting tool for time-series data that exhibit a linear trend. After observing the value of the time-series at period t (Y_t), Holt's method computes an estimate of the base, or expected, level of the time-series (E_t), and the expected rate of increase or decrease (trend) per period (T_t). The forecasting function in Holt's method is represented by:

$$\hat{Y}_{t+k} = E_t + kT_t \tag{11.5}$$

where

$$E_t = \alpha Y_t + (1 - \alpha)(E_{t-1} + T_{t-1}) \tag{11.6}$$

$$T_t = \beta(E_t - E_{t-1}) + (1 - \beta)T_{t-1} \tag{11.7}$$

We can use the forecasting function in equation 11.5 to obtain forecasts k time periods into the future where $k = 1, 2, 3$, and so on. The forecast for time period $t + k$ (or $\hat{Y}_{t+k}$) is the base level at time period t (given by E_t) plus the expected influence of the trend during the next k time periods (given by kT_t).

The smoothing parameters α and β (beta) in equations 11.6 and equation 11.7 can assume any value between 0 and 1 ($0 \le \alpha \le 1, 0 \le \beta \le 1$). If there is an upward trend in the data, E_t tends to be larger than E_{t-1}, making the quantity $E_t - E_{t-1}$ in equation 11.7 positive. This tends to increase the value of the trend adjustment factor T_t. Alternatively, if there is a downward trend in the data, E_t tends to be smaller than E_{t-1}, making the quantity $E_t - E_{t-1}$ in equation 11.7 negative. This tends to decrease the value of the trend adjustment factor T_t.

Although Holt's method might appear to be more complicated than the techniques discussed earlier, it is a simple three-step process:

1. Compute the base level E_t for time period t using equation 11.6.

2. Compute the expected trend value T_t for time period t using equation 11.7.

3. Compute the final forecast $\hat{Y}_{t+k}$ for time period $t + k$ using equation 11.5.

The spreadsheet implementation of Holt's method for the WaterCraft problem is shown in Figure 11.12 (and in the file FIG11-12.XLS on your data disk).

Cells J3 and J4 represent the values of α and β, respectively. Column E implements the base levels for each time period as required in step 1 (that is, this column contains the E_t values). Equation 11.6 assumes that for any time period t the base level for the previous time period (E_{t-1}) is known. It is customary to assume that $E_1 = Y_1$, as reflected by the formula in cell E3:

Formula for cell E3:   =D3

	A	B	C	D	E	F	G	H	I	J
1			Time	Actual	Base		Predicted			
2	Year	Qtr	Period	Sales	Level	Trend	Sales			
3	1990	1	1	$684.2	684.2	0.0	--		alpha	0.500
4		2	2	$584.1	634.2	-25.0	$684.2		beta	0.500
5		3	3	$765.4	687.3	14.0	$609.1			
6		4	4	$892.3	796.8	61.8	$701.3			
7	1991	1	5	$885.4	872.0	68.5	$858.6			
8		2	6	$677.0	808.7	2.6	$940.5			
9		3	7	$1,006.6	909.0	51.4	$811.4			
10		4	8	$1,122.1	1041.2	91.8	$960.4			
11	1992	1	9	$1,163.4	1148.2	99.4	$1,133.1			
12		2	10	$993.2	1120.4	35.8	$1,247.7			
13		3	11	$1,312.5	1234.3	74.9	$1,156.2			
14		4	12	$1,545.3	1427.3	133.9	$1,309.2			
15	1993	1	13	$1,596.2	1578.7	142.6	$1,561.1			
16		2	14	$1,260.4	1490.9	27.4	$1,721.3			
17		3	15	$1,735.2	1626.7	81.6	$1,518.3			
18		4	16	$2,029.7	1869.0	162.0	$1,708.4			
19	1994	1	17	$2,107.8	2069.4	181.2	$2,031.0			
20		2	18	$1,650.3	1950.4	31.1	$2,250.5			
21		3	19	$2,304.4	2143.0	111.8	$1,981.5			
22		4	20	$2,639.4	2447.1	208.0	$2,254.8			
23										
24						MSE	70179.3			
25										
26										
27										

Key Cell Formulas

Cell	Formula	Copied to
E3	=D3	—
E4	=$J$3*D4+(1–$J$3)*(E3+F3)	E5:E22
F3	=0	—
F4	=$J$4*(E4–E3)+(1–$J$4)*F3	F5:F22
G4	=SUM(E3:F3)	G5:G22
G24	=SUMXMY2(D4:D22,G4:G22)/COUNT(G4:G22)	—

Figure 11.12: Spreadsheet implementation of Holt's method

The remaining E_t values are calculated using equation 11.6 in cells E4 through E22 as:

Formula for cell E4:   =$J$3*D4+(1–$J$3)*(E3+F3)
(copy to E5 through E22)

Column F implements the expected trend values for each time period as required in step 2 (that is, this column contains the T_t values). Equation 11.7 assumes that for any time period t the expected trend value at the previous time period (T_{t-1}) is known. So we assume as an initial trend estimate that $T_t = 0$ (although any other initial trend estimate could be used), as reflected by the formula in cell F3:

Formula for cell F3:   =0

The remaining T_t values are calculated using equation 11.7 in cells F4 through F22 as:

Formula for cell F4:   =$J$4*(E4–E3)+(1–$J$4)*F3
(copy to F5 through F22)

According to equation 11.5, at any time period t the forecast for time period $t + 1$ is represented by:

$$\hat{Y}_{t+1} = E_t + 1*T_t$$

At time period $t = 1$ shown in Figure 11.12, the forecast for time period $t = 2$ (shown in cell G4) is obtained by summing the values in cells E3 and F3, which correspond to E_1 and T_1, respectively. Thus, the forecast for time period $t = 2$ is implemented in cell G4 as:

Formula for cell G4:   =E3+F3
(copy to G5 through G22)

This formula is copied to cells G5 through G22 to compute the predictions made using Holt's method for the remaining time periods.

Before making predictions using Holt's method, we want to identify optimal values for α and β. We can use Solver to determine the values for α and β that minimize the MSE (or the MAD). The MSE for the predicted values is calculated in cell G24 as:

Formula for cell G24:   =SUMXMY2(D4:D22,G4:G22)/COUNT(G4:G22)

We can use the Solver parameters and options shown in Figure 11.13 to identify the values for α and β that minimize the nonlinear MSE objective. Figure 11.14 shows the solution to this problem. The graph in Figure 11.14 indicates that the predictions obtained using Holt's method follow the trend in the data quite well.

Figure 11.13: Solver parameters and options for Holt's method

Figure 11.14: Optimal solution for Holt's method

FORECASTING WITH HOLT'S METHOD

We can use the results in Figure 11.14 to compute forecasts for any future time period. According to equation 11.5, at time period 20 the forecast for time period $20 + k$ is represented by:

$$\hat{Y}_{20+k} = E_{20} + kT_{20}$$

The values of E_{20} and T_{20} are given in Figure 11.14 in cells E22 and F22, respectively ($E_{20} = 2336.8$ and $T_{20} = 152.1$). So at time period 20, forecasts for time periods 21, 22, 23, and 24 are computed as:

$$\hat{Y}_{21} = E_{20} + 1{*}T_{20} = 2336.8 + 1{*}152.1 = 2{,}488.9$$

$$\hat{Y}_{22} = E_{20} + 2{*}T_{20} = 2336.8 + 2{*}152.1 = 2{,}641.0$$

$$\hat{Y}_{23} = E_{20} + 3{*}T_{20} = 2336.8 + 3{*}152.1 = 2{,}793.1$$

$$\hat{Y}_{24} = E_{20} + 4{*}T_{20} = 2336.8 + 4{*}152.1 = 2{,}945.2$$

Although we can use Holt's method to forecast a value for any future time period (or any value of $k \geq 1$), as the forecast horizon lengthens, our confidence in the accuracy of the forecast diminishes because there is no guarantee that the historical trends on which the model is based will continue indefinitely into the future.

MODELING TIME-SERIES TRENDS USING REGRESSION

We can build a regression model of a time-series if data are available for one or more independent variables that account for the systematic movements in the time-series. Even if no independent variables have a *causal* relationship with the time-series, some independent variables might have a *predictive* relationship with the time-series. A predictor variable does not have a cause-and-effect relationship with the time-series. Yet the behavior of a predictor variable might be correlated to that of the time-series in a way that helps us forecast future values of the time-series. In the following sections we'll consider how to use predictor variables as independent variables in regression models for time-series data.

As mentioned earlier, trend is the long-term sweep or general direction of movement in a time-series that reflects changes in the data over time. The mere passage of time does not *cause* the trend in the time-series. But like the consistent passage of time, the trend of a time-series reflects the steady upward or downward movement in the general direction of the series. Thus, time itself might represent a predictor variable that could be useful in accounting for the trend in a time-series.

LINEAR TREND MODEL

To see how we might use time as an independent variable, consider the following linear regression model:

$$Y_t = \beta_0 + \beta_1 X_{1_t} + \varepsilon_t \qquad \qquad \textbf{11.8}$$

where $X_{1_t} = t$. That is, the independent variable X_{1_t} represents the time period t ($X_{1_1} = 1$, $X_{1_2} = 2$, $X_{1_3} = 3$, and so on). The regression model in equation 11.8 assumes that the *systematic* variation in the time-series (Y_t) can be described by the regression function $\beta_0 + \beta_1 X_{1_t}$ (which is a linear function of time). The error term ε_t in equation 11.8 represents the *unsystematic*, or random, variation in the time-series not accounted for by our model. Because the values of Y_t are assumed to vary randomly around (above and below) the regression function $\beta_0 + \beta_1 X_{1_t}$, the average (or expected) value of ε_t is 0. Thus, if we use ordinary least squares to estimate the parameters in equation 11.8, our best estimate of Y_t for any time period t is:

$$\hat{Y}_t = b_0 + b_1 X_{1_t} \qquad \qquad \textbf{11.9}$$

In equation 11.9, the estimated value of the time-series at time period t ($\hat{Y}_t$) is a linear function of the independent variable, which is coded to represent time. Thus, equation 11.9 represents the equation of the line passing through the time-series that minimizes the sum of squared differences between the actual values (Y_t) and the estimated values $\hat{Y}_t$. We might interpret this line to represent the linear trend in the data.

An example of this technique is shown in Figure 11.15 (and in the file FIG11-15.XLS on your data disk) for the quarterly sales data for WaterCraft. We can use the Time Period values in column C as the values for the independent variable X_1 in our regression model. Thus, we can use the Regression command settings shown in Figure 11.16 to obtain the values for b_0 and b_1 required for the estimated regression function for these data.

Figure 11.17 shows the results of the Regression command, which indicate that the estimated regression function is:

$$\hat{Y}_t = 375.17 + 92.6255 X_{1_t} \qquad \qquad \textbf{11.10}$$

Figure 11.15 shows the predicted sales level for each time period in column E (labeled "Linear Trend") where the following formula is entered in cell E3 and copied to cells E4 through E22:

Formula for cell E3: =375.17+92.6255*C3
(copy to E4 through E22)

Figure 11.15: Spreadsheet implementation of the linear trend model

Key Cell Formulas

Cell	Formula	Copied to
E3	=375.17+92.6255*C3	E4:E22

Figure 11.16: Regression command settings for the linear trend model

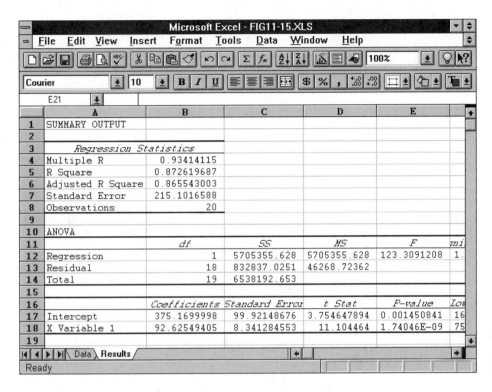

Figure 11.17: Regression results for the linear trend model

FORECASTING WITH THE LINEAR TREND MODEL

We can use equation 11.10 to generate forecasts of sales for any future time period t by setting $X_{1_t} = t$. For example, forecasts for time periods 21, 22, 23, and 24 are computed as:

$$\hat{Y}_{21} = 375.17 + 92.6255*21 = 2,320.3$$

$$\hat{Y}_{22} = 375.17 + 92.6255*22 = 2,412.9$$

$$\hat{Y}_{23} = 375.17 + 92.6255*23 = 2,505.6$$

$$\hat{Y}_{24} = 375.17 + 92.6255*24 = 2,598.2$$

Again, as the forecast horizon lengthens, our confidence in the accuracy of the forecasts diminishes because there is no guarantee that the historical trends on which the model is based will continue indefinitely into the future.

QUADRATIC TREND MODEL

Although the graph of the estimated linear regression function shown in Figure 11.15 accounts for the upward trend in the data, the actual values do not appear to be scattered randomly around the trend line, as was assumed by our regression model in equation 11.8. An observation is more likely to be substantially below the line or only slightly above the line. This suggests that the linear trend model might not be appropriate for this data.

As an alternative, we might try fitting a curved trend line to the data using the following quadratic model:

$$Y_t = \beta_0 + \beta_1 X_{1_t} + \beta_2 X_{2_t} + \varepsilon_t \qquad \text{11.11}$$

where $X_{1_t} = t$ and $X_{2_t} = t^2$. The resulting *estimated* regression function for this model is:

$$\hat{Y}_t = b_0 + b_1 X_{1_t} + b_2 X_{2_t} \qquad \textbf{11.12}$$

To estimate the quadratic trend function, we must add a column to the spreadsheet to represent the additional independent variable $X_{2_t} = t^2$. This can be accomplished as shown in Figure 11.18 (and in the file FIG11-18.XLS on your data disk) by inserting a new column D and placing the values t^2 in this column. Thus, the following formula is entered in cell D3 and copied to cells D4 through D22:

Formula for cell D3:   =C3^2

(copy to D4 through D22)

Figure 11.18: Spreadsheet implementation of the quadratic trend model

Key Cell Formulas

Cell	Formula	Copied to
D3	=C3^2	D4:D22
F3	=653.67+16.671*C3+3.617*D3	F4:F22

We can obtain the values of b_0, b_1, and b_2 required for the estimated regression function for these data using the Regression command settings shown in Figure 11.19.

Figure 11.20 shows the results of the Regression command, which indicate that the estimated regression function is:

$$\hat{Y}_t = 653.67 + 16.671\ X_{1_t} + 3.617\ X_{2_t} \qquad \textbf{11.13}$$

Figure 11.19: Regression command settings for the quadratic trend model

Figure 11.20: Regression results for the quadratic trend model

Figure 11.18 shows the estimated sales level for each time period in column F (labeled "Quadratic Trend") where the following formula is entered in cell F3 and copied to cells F4 through F22:

Formula for cell F3:   =653.67+16.671*C3+3.617*D3
(copy to F4 through F22)

Figure 11.18 also shows a graph of the sales levels predicted by the quadratic trend model versus the actual data. Notice that the quadratic trend curve fits the data better than the straight trend line shown in Figure 11.15. In particular, the deviations of the actual values above and below this curve are now more balanced.

FORECASTING WITH THE QUADRATIC TREND MODEL

We can use equation 11.13 to generate forecasts of sales for any future time period t by setting $X_{1_t} = t$ and $X_{2_t} = t^2$. For example, forecasts for time periods 21, 22, 23, and 24 are computed as:

$$\hat{Y}_{21} = 653.67 + 16.671*21 + 3.617*(21)^2 = 2,598.9$$

$$\hat{Y}_{22} = 653.67 + 16.671*22 + 3.617*(22)^2 = 2,771.1$$

$$\hat{Y}_{23} = 653.67 + 16.671*23 + 3.617*(23)^2 = 2,950.5$$

$$\hat{Y}_{24} = 653.67 + 16.671*24 + 3.617*(24)^2 = 3,137.2$$

As with earlier models, as the forecast horizon lengthens, our confidence in the accuracy of the forecasts diminishes because there is no guarantee that the historical trends on which the model is based will continue indefinitely into the future.

SEASONALITY

The goal of any forecasting procedure is to develop a model that accounts for as much of the systematic variation in the past behavior of a time-series as possible. The assumption is that a model that accurately explains what happened in the past will be useful in predicting what will happen in the future. Do the trend models shown in Figures 11.14, 11.15, and 11.18 adequately account for all the systematic variation in the time-series data?

All these graphs show a fairly regular pattern of fluctuation around the trend line. Notice that each point below the trend line is followed by three points at or above the trend line. This suggests some additional *systematic* (or predictable) variation in the time-series exists that is not accounted for by these models.

Although trend reflects the long-term direction or sweep in a time-series, a time-series can also include a strong seasonal component. This seasonal component, or **seasonality**, appears as a regular, repeating pattern in the data around the trend line. For example, in time-series data for monthly fuel oil sales, we would expect to see regular jumps in the data during the winter months each year. Similarly, monthly or quarterly sales data for suntan lotion would likely show consistent peaks during the summer and valleys during the winter.

Figures 11.14, 11.15, and 11.18 suggest that the data in the graphs include seasonal effects. In the second quarter of each year, sales drop well below the trend lines, whereas sales in the remaining quarters are at or above the trend line. Forecasts of future values for this time-series would be more accurate if they reflected these systematic seasonal effects. The following sections discuss several techniques for modeling seasonal effects in time-series data.

ADJUSTING TREND PREDICTIONS WITH SEASONAL INDICES

A simple and effective way of modeling seasonal effects in a time-series is to develop seasonal indices that reflect the average percentage by which observations in each season differ from their projected trend values. In the WaterCraft example, observations occurring in the second quarter fall below the values predicted using a trend model. Similarly, observations in the first, third, and fourth quarters are at or above the values predicted using a trend model. Thus, if we can determine seasonal indices representing the average amount by which the observations in a given quarter fall above or below the trend line, we could adjust our trend projections by these amounts and increase the accuracy of our forecasts.

We will demonstrate the calculation of seasonal indices for the quadratic trend model developed earlier. However, we could complete this process using any of the other trend models discussed in this chapter. In Figure 11.21 (and in the file FIG11-21.XLS on your data disk), columns A through F repeat the calculations for the quadratic trend model discussed earlier.

	File Edit View Insert Format Tools Data Window Help						
	A	B	C	D	E	F	G	H
1			Time		Actual	Quadratic	Actual as a	Seasonal
2	Year	Qtr	Period	Time^2	Sales	Trend	% of Trend	Forecast
3	1990	1	1	1	$684.2	$674.0	102%	$712.6
4		2	2	4	$584.1	$701.5	83%	$561.9
5		3	3	9	$765.4	$736.2	104%	$758.9
6		4	4	16	$892.3	$778.2	115%	$864.8
7	1991	1	5	25	$885.4	$827.5	107%	$874.9
8		2	6	36	$677.0	$883.9	77%	$708.0
9		3	7	49	$1,006.6	$947.6	106%	$976.8
10		4	8	64	$1,122.1	$1,018.5	110%	$1,131.8
11	1992	1	9	81	$1,163.4	$1,096.7	106%	$1,159.6
12		2	10	100	$993.2	$1,182.1	84%	$946.8
13		3	11	121	$1,312.5	$1,274.7	103%	$1,314.0
14		4	12	144	$1,545.3	$1,374.6	112%	$1,527.5
15	1993	1	13	169	$1,596.2	$1,481.7	108%	$1,566.6
16		2	14	196	$1,260.4	$1,596.0	79%	$1,278.4
17		3	15	225	$1,735.2	$1,717.6	101%	$1,770.5
18		4	16	256	$2,029.7	$1,846.4	110%	$2,051.7
19	1994	1	17	289	$2,107.8	$1,982.4	106%	$2,096.0
20		2	18	324	$1,650.3	$2,125.7	78%	$1,702.6
21		3	19	361	$2,304.4	$2,276.2	101%	$2,346.3
22		4	20	400	$2,639.4	$2,433.9	108%	$2,704.6
23								
24			Seasonal					
25		Qtr	Index					
26		1	105.7%					
27		2	80.1%					
28		3	103.1%					
29		4	111.1%					

Key Cell Formulas

Cell	Formula	Copied to
D3	=C3^2	D4:D22
F3	=653.67+16.671*C3+3.617*D3	F4:F22
G3	=E3/F3	G4:G22
C26	=SUMIF($B$3:$B$22,B26,$G$3:$G$22)/COUNTIF($B$3:$B$22,B26)	C27:C29
H3	=F3*VLOOKUP(B3,$B$26:$C$29,2)	H4:H22

Figure 11.21: Spreadsheet implementation to calculate seasonal indices and seasonal forecasts using the quadratic trend model

COMPUTING SEASONAL INDICES

The goal in developing seasonal indices is to determine the average percentage by which observations in each season differ from the values projected for them using the trend model. To accomplish this, in column G of Figure 11.21 we calculated the ratio of each actual value in column E to its corresponding projected trend value shown in column F, as:

Formula for cell G3: =E3/F3
(copy to G4 through G22)

The value in cell G3 indicates that the actual value in time period 1 was 102% of (or approximately 2% larger than) its estimated trend value. The value in cell G4 indicates that the actual value in time period 2 was 83% of (or approximately 17% smaller than) its estimated trend value. The remaining values in column G have similar interpretations.

We obtain the seasonal index for each quarter by computing the average of the values in column G on a quarter-by-quarter basis. For example, the seasonal index for quarter 1 equals the average of the values in cells G3, G7, G11, G15, and G19. The seasonal index for quarter 2 equals the average of the values in cells G4, G8, G12, G16, and G20. Similar computations are required to calculate seasonal indices for quarters 3 and 4. We can use separate AVERAGE() functions for each quarter to compute these averages. However, for large data sets, such an approach would be tedious and prone to error. Thus, the averages shown in cells C26 through C29 are calculated as:

Formula for cell C26: =SUMIF($B$3:$B$22,B26,$G$3:$G$22)/
(copy to C27 through C29) COUNTIF($B$3:$B$22,B26)

The SUMIF() and COUNTIF() functions perform conditional sums and counts. The SUMIF() function in the previous formula sums the values in cells G3 through G22 for which the corresponding value in cells B3 through B22 equals the value in cell B26. This corresponds to the sum of the values in column G that occur in quarter 1. The COUNTIF() function in the previous equation counts the number of elements in cells B3 through B22 that equal the value in cell B26—or the number of quarter 1 observations.

The seasonal index for quarter 1 shown in cell C26 indicates that, on average, the actual sales value in the first quarter of any given year will be 105.7% of (or 5.7% larger than) the estimated trend value for the same time period. Similarly, the seasonal index for quarter 2 shown in cell C27 indicates that, on average, the actual sales value in the second quarter of any given year will be 80.1% of (or approximately 20% less than) the estimated trend value for the same time period. The seasonal indices for the third and fourth quarters have similar interpretations.

We can use the calculated seasonal indices to refine or adjust the trend estimates. This is accomplished in column H of Figure 11.21 as:

Formula for cell H3: =F3*VLOOKUP(B3,$B$26:$C$29,2)
(copy to H4 through H22)

This formula takes the estimated trend value for each time period and multiplies it by the appropriate seasonal index for the quarter in which the time period occurs. The trend estimates for quarter 1 observations are multiplied by 105.7%, the trend estimates for quarter 2 observations are multiplied by 80.1%, and so on for quarters 3 and 4 observations.

Figure 11.22 shows a graph of the actual sales data versus the seasonal forecast calculated in column H of Figure 11.21. As this graph illustrates, the use of seasonal indices is very effective on this particular data set.

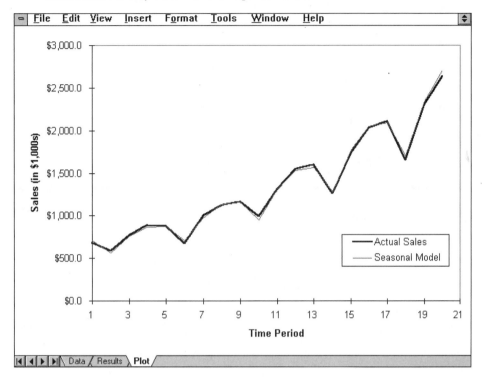

Figure 11.22: Plot of the predictions obtained using seasonal indices versus the actual WaterCraft sales data

FORECASTING WITH SEASONAL INDICES

We can use the seasonal indices to adjust trend projections of future time periods for the expected effects of seasonality. Earlier, we used the quadratic trend model to obtain the following forecasts of the expected level of sales in time periods 21, 22, 23, and 24:

$$\hat{Y}_{21} = 653.67 + 16.671*21 + 3.617*(21)^2 = 2,598.9$$

$$\hat{Y}_{22} = 653.67 + 16.671*22 + 3.617*(22)^2 = 2,771.1$$

$$\hat{Y}_{23} = 653.67 + 16.671*23 + 3.617*(23)^2 = 2,950.5$$

$$\hat{Y}_{24} = 653.67 + 16.671*24 + 3.617*(24)^2 = 3,137.2$$

To adjust these trend forecasts for the expected effects of seasonality, we multiply each of them by the appropriate seasonal index. Because time periods 21, 22, 23, and 24 occur in quarters 1, 2, 3, and 4, respectively, the seasonal forecasts are computed as:

Seasonal forecast for time period 21 = 2,598.9*105.7% = 2,747.03

Seasonal forecast for time period 22 = 2,771.1*80.1% = 2,219.65

Seasonal forecast for time period 23 = 2,950.5*103.1% = 3,041.97

Seasonal forecast for time period 24 = 3,137.2*111.1% = 3,485.43

Summary of the Calculation and Use of Seasonal Indices

1. Create a trend model and calculate the estimated value ($\hat{Y}_t$) for each observation in the sample.

2. For each observation, calculate the ratio of the actual value to the predicted trend value ($Y_t / \hat{Y}_t$).

3. For each season, compute the average of the ratios calculated in step 2. These are the seasonal indices.

4. Multiply any forecast produced by the trend model by the appropriate seasonal index calculated in step 3.

WINTER'S METHOD

Winter's method is another forecasting technique that we can apply to time-series exhibiting trend and seasonality. This method is similar to Holt's method (discussed earlier) but incorporates a number of adjustments for the possible effects of seasonality.

To demonstrate this method, we let p represent the number of seasons in the time-series (for quarterly data $p = 4$; for monthly data $p = 12$). The forecasting function in Winter's method is represented by:

$$\hat{Y}_{t+k} = \left(E_t + kT_t\right)S_{t+k-p} \qquad \text{11.14}$$

where

$$E_t = \alpha\frac{Y_t}{S_{t-p}} + \left(1 - \alpha\right)\left(E_{t-1} + T_{t-1}\right) \qquad \text{11.15}$$

$$T_t = \beta\left(E_t - E_{t-1}\right) + \left(1 - \beta\right)T_{t-1} \qquad \text{11.16}$$

$$S_t = \gamma\frac{Y_t}{E_t} + \left(1 - \gamma\right)S_{t-p} \qquad \text{11.17}$$

We can use the forecasting function in equation 11.14 to obtain forecasts k time periods into the future where $k = 1, 2, ..., p$. The forecast for time period $t + k$ ($\hat{Y}_{t+k}$) is obtained in equation 11.14 by multiplying the expected base level at time period $t + k$ (given by $E_t + kT_t$) by the most recent estimate of the seasonality associated with this time period (given by S_{t+k-p}). The smoothing parameters α, β, and γ (gamma) in equations 11.15, 11.16, and 11.17 can assume any value between 0 and 1 ($0 \le \alpha \le 1, 0 \le \beta \le 1, 0 \le \gamma \le 1$).

The expected base level of the time-series in time period t (E_t) is updated in equation 11.15, which takes a weighted average of the following two values:

- $E_{t-1} + T_{t-1}$, which represents the expected base level of the time-series at time period t before observing the actual value at time period t (given by Y_t)

- $\frac{Y_t}{S_{t-p}}$, which represents the deseasonalized estimate of the base level of the time-series at time period t after observing Y_t

The estimated per-period trend factor T_t is updated using equation 11.16, which is identical to the procedure in equation 11.7 used in Holt's method. The estimated seasonal adjustment factor for each time period is calculated using equation 11.17, which takes a weighted average of the following two quantities:

- S_{t-p}, which represents the most recent seasonal index for the season in which time period t occurs
- $\frac{Y_t}{E_t}$, which represents an estimate of the seasonality associated with time period t after observing Y_t

Winter's method is somewhat more complicated than the process of calculating seasonal indices described earlier, but it is basically a four-step process:

1. Compute the base level E_t for time period t using equation 11.15
2. Compute the estimated trend value T_t for time period t using equation 11.16
3. Compute the estimated seasonal index S_t for time period t using equation 11.17
4. Compute the final forecast $\hat{Y}_{t+k}$ for time period $t + k$ using equation 11.14

The spreadsheet implementation of Winter's method for the WaterCraft data is shown in Figure 11.23 (and in the file FIG11-23.XLS on your data disk). Cells D24, D25, and D26 represent the values of α, β, and γ, respectively.

Equations 11.15 and 11.17 assume that at time period t an estimate of the seasonal index from time period $t - p$ exists or that there is a value for S_{t-p}. Thus, our first task in implementing Winter's method is to estimate values for $S_1, S_2, ..., S_p$ (or, in this case, $S_1, S_2, S_3,$ and S_4). One easy way to make these initial estimates is to let:

$$S_t = \frac{Y_t}{\frac{1}{p}(Y_1 + Y_2 + \cdots + Y_p)}, t = 1, 2, ..., p \qquad \textbf{11.18}$$

Equation 11.18 indicates that the initial seasonal estimate S_t for each of the first p time periods is the ratio of the observed value in time period Y_t divided by the average value observed during the first p periods. In our example, the first four seasonal factors shown in column G in Figure 11.23 are calculated using equation 11.18 as:

Formula for cell G3:   =D3/AVERAGE($D$3:$D$6)

(copy to G4 through G6)

The first E_t value that can be computed using equation 11.15 occurs at time period $p + 1$ (in our example, time period 5) because this is the first time period for which S_{t-p} is known. However, to compute E_5 using equation 11.15, we also need to know E_4 (which cannot be computed using equation 11.15 because S_0 is undefined) and T_4 (which cannot be computed using equation 11.16 because E_4 and E_3 are undefined). Thus, we assume $E_4 = Y_4/S_4$ (so that $E_4*S_4 = Y_4$) and $T_4 = 0$, as reflected by placing the following formulas in cells E6 and F6:

Formula for cell E6:   =D6/G6

Formula for cell F6:   =0

We generated the remaining E_t values using equation 11.15, which is implemented in Figure 11.23 as:

Formula for cell E7:   = $D$24*D7/G3+(1–$D$24)*(E6+F6)

(copy to E8 through E22)

We generated the remaining T_t values using equation 11.16, which is implemented in Figure 11.23 as:

Formula for cell F7:   = $D$25*(E7–E6)+(1–$D$25)*F6

(copy to F8 through F22)

	A	B	C	D	E	F	G	H	I	J
1			Time	Actual	Base		Seasonal	Predicted		
2	Year	Qtr	Period	Sales	Level	Trend	Factor	Sales		
3	1990	1	1	$684.2	--	--	0.935	--		
4		2	2	$584.1	--	--	0.799	--		
5		3	3	$765.4	--	--	1.046	--		
6		4	4	$892.3	731.5	0.0	1.220	--		
7	1991	1	5	$885.4	839.0	53.8	0.995	$684.2		
8		2	6	$677.0	870.3	42.5	0.788	$712.9		
9		3	7	$1,006.6	937.5	54.8	1.060	$955.2		
10		4	8	$1,122.1	956.1	36.7	1.197	$1,210.4		
11	1992	1	9	$1,163.4	1080.8	80.7	1.036	$988.1		
12		2	10	$993.2	1210.8	105.4	0.804	$915.6		
13		3	11	$1,312.5	1277.2	85.8	1.044	$1,395.3		
14		4	12	$1,545.3	1327.2	67.9	1.181	$1,631.1		
15	1993	1	13	$1,596.2	1468.0	104.4	1.062	$1,445.1		
16		2	14	$1,260.4	1569.8	103.1	0.804	$1,264.6		
17		3	15	$1,735.2	1667.6	100.4	1.042	$1,746.3		
18		4	16	$2,029.7	1743.6	88.2	1.172	$2,087.2		
19	1994	1	17	$2,107.8	1908.7	126.7	1.083	$1,944.7		
20		2	18	$1,650.3	2044.5	131.2	0.805	$1,635.5		
21		3	19	$2,304.4	2193.5	140.1	1.046	$2,267.6		
22		4	20	$2,639.4	2292.5	119.6	1.162	$2,735.6		
23										
24			alpha	0.500			MSE	10431.4		
25			beta	0.500						
26			gamma	0.500						
27										

Key Cell Formulas

Cell	Formula	Copied to
G3	=D3/AVERAGE($D$3:$D$6)	G4:G6
E6	=D6/G6	—
E7	=$D$24*D7/G3+(1–$D$24)*(E6+F6)	E8:E22
F6	=0	—
F7	=$D$25*(E7–E6)+(1–$D$25)*F6	F8:F22
G7	=$D$26*D7/E7+(1–$D$26)*G3	G8:G22
H7	=SUM(E6:F6)*G3	H8:G22
H24	=SUMXMY2(D7:D22,H7:H22)/COUNT(H7:H22)	—

Figure 11.23: Spreadsheet implementation of Winter's method

We used equation 11.17 to generate the remaining S_t values in Figure 11.23 as:

Formula for cell G7: = $D$26*D7/E7+(1–$D$26)*G3
(copy to G8 through G22)

Finally, at time period 4, we can use the forecasting function in equation 11.14 to predict one period ahead for time period 5. This is implemented in Figure 11.23 as:

Formula for cell H7: =SUM(E6:F6)*G3
(copy to H8 through H22)

Before making predictions using Winter's method, we want to identify optimal values for α, β, and γ. We can use Solver to determine the values for α, β, and γ that minimize the MSE (or the MAD). The MSE for the predicted values is calculated in cell H24 as:

Formula for cell H24: =SUMXMY2(D7:D22,H7:H22)/COUNT(H7:H22)

We can use the Solver parameters and options shown in Figure 11.24 to identify the values for α, β, and γ that minimize the nonlinear MSE objective. Figure 11.25 shows the solution to this problem.

Figure 11.24: Solver parameters and options for Winter's method

	A	B	C	D	E	F	G	H	I	J
1			Time	Actual	Base		Seasonal	Predicted		
2	Year	Qtr	Period	Sales	Level	Trend	Factor	Sales		
3	1990	1	1	$684.2	--	--	0.935	--		
4		2	2	$584.1	--	--	0.799	--		
5		3	3	$765.4	--	--	1.046	--		
6		4	4	$892.3	731.5	0.0	1.220	--		
7	1991	1	5	$885.4	783.8	52.3	1.087	$684.2		
8		2	6	$677.0	838.9	55.1	0.805	$667.6		
9		3	7	$1,006.6	910.6	71.7	1.092	$935.5		
10		4	8	$1,122.1	967.1	56.5	1.173	$1,198.1		
11	1992	1	9	$1,163.4	1035.0	67.9	1.116	$1,112.5		
12		2	10	$993.2	1134.6	99.6	0.860	$888.0		
13		3	11	$1,312.5	1226.3	91.7	1.075	$1,348.4		
14		4	12	$1,545.3	1317.7	91.4	1.173	$1,546.4		
15	1993	1	13	$1,596.2	1414.3	96.6	1.126	$1,572.4		
16		2	14	$1,260.4	1499.9	85.6	0.845	$1,299.2		
17		3	15	$1,735.2	1592.4	92.5	1.086	$1,704.8		
18		4	16	$2,029.7	1696.0	103.6	1.191	$1,976.2		
19	1994	1	17	$2,107.8	1817.2	121.2	1.152	$2,026.0		
20		2	18	$1,650.3	1942.2	125.0	0.849	$1,637.3		
21		3	19	$2,304.4	2080.3	138.1	1.103	$2,245.9		
22		4	20	$2,639.4	2217.6	137.3	1.190	$2,643.1		
23										
24			alpha	0.243			MSE	5157.7		
25			beta	1.000						
26			gamma	0.780						
27										

Figure 11.25: Optimal solution for Winter's method

Figure 11.26 displays a graph of the predictions obtained using Winter's method against the actual data. This graph indicates that although Winter's method got off to a rocky start, it provides a forecasting function that fits the recent data in this problem reasonably well. The rocky start shown in the graph is common with Winter's method and can be attributed to the simple estimates we provided for the initial seasonal factors and for E_4 and T_4.

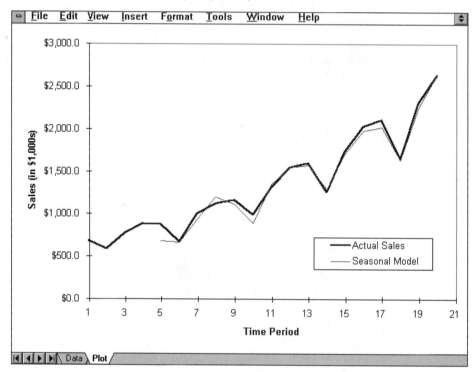

Figure 11.26: Plot of the predictions obtained using Winter's method versus the actual WaterCraft sales data

FORECASTING WITH WINTER'S METHOD

We can use the results in Figure 11.25 to compute forecasts for any future time period. According to equation 11.14, at time period 20 the forecast for time period $20 + k$ is represented by:

$$\hat{Y}_{20+k} = (E_{20} + kT_{20})S_{20+k-p}$$

Figure 11.25 shows the values of E_{20} and T_{20} in cells E22 and F22, respectively ($E_{20} = 2217.6$ and $T_{20} = 137.3$). At time period 20, forecasts for time periods 21, 22, 23, and 24 are computed as:

$$\hat{Y}_{21} = (E_{20} + 1*T_{20})S_{17} = (2217.6 + 1*137.3)1.152 = 2,712.8$$

$$\hat{Y}_{22} = (E_{20} + 2*T_{20})S_{18} = (2217.6 + 2*137.3)0.849 = 2,115.9$$

$$\hat{Y}_{23} = (E_{20} + 3*T_{20})S_{19} = (2217.6 + 3*137.3)1.103 = 2,900.3$$

$$\hat{Y}_{24} = (E_{20} + 4*T_{20})S_{20} = (2217.6 + 4*137.3)1.190 = 3,292.5$$

SEASONAL REGRESSION MODELS

As discussed in chapter 9, Regression Analysis, an indicator variable is a binary variable that assumes a value of 0 or 1 to indicate whether or not a certain condition is true. To model seasonality in a time-series, we might set up several indicator variables to indicate which season each observation represents. In general, if there are p seasons, we need $p - 1$ indicator variables in our model. For example, the WaterCraft sales data were collected on a quarterly basis. Because we have four seasons to model ($p = 4$), we need three indicator variables, which we define as:

$$X_{3_t} = \begin{cases} 1, & \text{if } Y_t \text{ is an observation from quarter 1} \\ 0, & \text{otherwise} \end{cases}$$

$$X_{4_t} = \begin{cases} 1, & \text{if } Y_t \text{ is an observation from quarter 2} \\ 0, & \text{otherwise} \end{cases}$$

$$X_{5_t} = \begin{cases} 1, & \text{if } Y_t \text{ is an observation from quarter 3} \\ 0, & \text{otherwise} \end{cases}$$

Notice that the definitions of X_{3_t}, X_{4_t}, and X_{5_t} assign a unique coding for the variables to each quarter in our data. These codings are summarized as:

Quarter	Value of X_{3_t}	X_{4_t}	X_{5_t}
1	1	0	0
2	0	1	0
3	0	0	1
4	0	0	0

Together, the values of X_{3_t}, X_{4_t}, and X_{5_t} indicate in which quarter observation Y_t occurs.

THE SEASONAL MODEL

We might expect that the following regression function would be appropriate for the time-series data in our example:

$$Y_t = \beta_0 + \beta_1 X_{1_t} + \beta_2 X_{2_t} + \beta_3 X_{3_t} + \beta_4 X_{4_t} + \beta_5 X_{5_t} + \varepsilon_t \qquad \textbf{11.19}$$

where, $X_{1_t} = t$ and $X_{2_t} = t^2$. This regression model combines the variables that account for a quadratic trend in the data with additional indicator variables discussed earlier to account for any systematic seasonal differences.

To better understand the effect of the indicator variables, notice that for observations occurring in the fourth quarter, the model in equation 11.19 reduces to:

$$Y_t = \beta_0 + \beta_1 X_{1_t} + \beta_2 X_{2_t} + \varepsilon_t \qquad \textbf{11.20}$$

because in the fourth quarter $X_{3_t} = X_{4_t} = X_{5_t} = 0$. For observations occurring in the first quarter, we can express equation 11.19 as:

$$Y_t = (\beta_0 + \beta_3) + \beta_1 X_{1_t} + \beta_2 X_{2_t} + \varepsilon_t \qquad \textbf{11.21}$$

because, by definition, in the first quarter $X_{3_t} = 1$ and $X_{4_t} = X_{5_t} = 0$. Similarly, for observations in the second and third quarters the model in equation 11.19 reduces to:

For the second quarter: $Y_t = (\beta_0 + \beta_4) + \beta_1 X_{1_t} + \beta_2 X_{2_t} + \varepsilon_t \qquad \textbf{11.22}$

For the third quarter: $Y_t = (\beta_0 + \beta_5) + \beta_1 X_{1_t} + \beta_2 X_{2_t} + \varepsilon_t \qquad \textbf{11.23}$

Equations 11.20 through 11.23 show that the values β_3, β_4, and β_5 in equation 11.19 indicate the average amounts by which the values of observations in the first, second, and third quarters are expected to differ from observations in the fourth quarter. That is, β_3, β_4, and β_5 indicate the expected effects of seasonality in the first, second, and third quarters, respectively, relative to the fourth quarter.

An example of the seasonal regression function in equation 11.19 is given in Figure 11.27 (and in the file FIG11-27.XLS on your data disk).

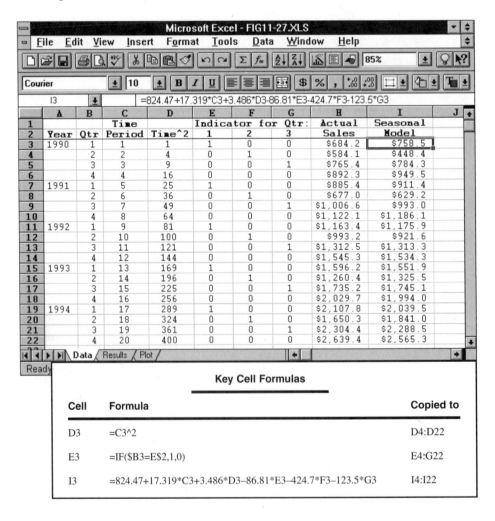

Figure 11.27: Spreadsheet implementation of the seasonal regression model

The major difference between Figures 11.18 and 11.27 is the addition of the data in columns E, F, and G in Figure 11.27. These columns represent the indicator values for the independent variables X_{3_t}, X_{4_t}, and X_{5_t}, respectively. We created these values by entering the following formula in cell E3 and copying it to E3 through G22:

Formula for cell E3:   =IF($B3=E$2,1,0)
(copy to E3 through G22)

We obtain the values of b_0, b_1, b_2, b_3, b_4, and b_5 required for the estimated regression function using the Regression command settings shown in Figure 11.28. Figure 11.29 shows the results of this command, which indicate that the estimated regression function is:

$$\hat{Y}_t = 824.472 + 17.319X_{1_t} + 3.485X_{2_t} - 86.805X_{3_t} - 424.736X_{4_t} - 123.453X_{5_t} \qquad \textbf{11.24}$$

In Figure 11.27, column I (labeled "Seasonal Model") shows the predicted sales level for each time period where the following formula is entered in cell I3 and copied to cells I4 through I22:

Formula for cell I3:   =824.472+17.319*C3+3.485*D3–86.805*E3–424.736*
(copy to I4 through I22)   F3–123.453*G3

The coefficients for the indicator variables are given by $b_3 = -86.805$, $b_4 = -424.736$, and $b_5 = -123.453$. Because X_{3_t} is the indicator variable for quarter 1 observations, the value of b_3 indicates that, on average, the sales level in quarter 1 of any year is expected to be approximately \$86,805 lower than the level expected for quarter 4. The value of b_4 indicates that the typical sales value in quarter 2 of any given year is expected to be approximately \$424,736 less than the level expected in quarter 4. Finally, the value of b_5 indicates that the typical sales value in quarter 3 is expected to be approximately \$123,453 less than the level expected in quarter 4.

Figure 11.28: Regression command settings for the seasonal regression model

In Figure 11.29 notice that $R^2 = 0.986$, suggesting that the estimated regression function fits the data very well. This is also evident from the graph in Figure 11.30, which shows the actual data versus the predictions of the seasonal forecasting model.

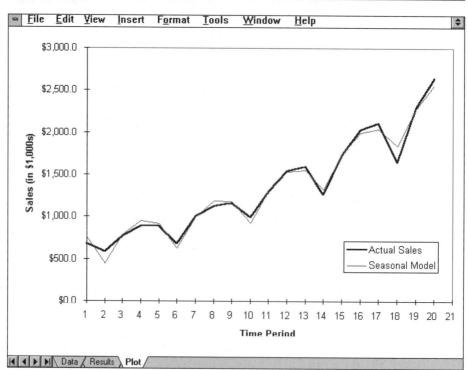

Figure 11.29: Regression results for the seasonal regression model

Figure 11.30: Plot of seasonal regression model predictions versus actual WaterCraft sales data

FORECASTING WITH THE SEASONAL REGRESSION MODEL

We can use the estimated regression function in equation 11.24 to forecast an expected level of sales for any future time period by assigning appropriate values to the independent variables. For example, forecasts of WaterCraft's sales in the next four quarters are represented by:

$$\hat{Y}_{21} = 824.472 + 17.319(21) + 3.485(21^2) - 86.805(1) - 424.736(0) - 123.453(0) = 2{,}638.7$$

$$\hat{Y}_{22} = 824.472 + 17.319(22) + 3.485(22^2) - 86.805(0) - 424.736(1) - 123.453(0) = 2{,}468.0$$

$$\hat{Y}_{23} = 824.472 + 17.319(23) + 3.485(23^2) - 86.805(0) - 424.736(0) - 123.453(1) = 2{,}943.4$$

$$\hat{Y}_{24} = 824.472 + 17.319(24) + 3.485(24^2) - 86.805(0) - 424.736(0) - 123.453(0) = 3{,}248.1$$

COMBINING FORECASTS

Given the number and variety of forecasting techniques available, it can be difficult to select a *single* method to use in predicting future values of a time-series variable. Indeed, the state-of-the-art research in time-series forecasting suggests that we should *not* use a single forecasting method. Rather, we can obtain more accurate forecasts by combining the forecasts from several methods into a composite forecast.

For example, suppose that we used three methods to build forecasting models of the same time-series variable. We denote the predicted value for time period t using each of these methods as F_{1_t}, F_{2_t}, and F_{3_t}, respectively. One simple approach to combining these forecasts into a composite forecast $\hat{Y}_t$ might involve taking a linear combination of the individual forecasts as:

$$\hat{Y}_t = b_0 + b_1 F_{1_t} + b_2 F_{2_t} + b_3 F_{3_t} \qquad \textbf{11.25}$$

We could determine the values for the b_i using Solver or least squares regression to minimize the MSE between the combined forecast $\hat{Y}_t$ and the actual data. The combined forecast $\hat{Y}_t$ in equation 11.25 will be at least as accurate as any of the individual forecasting techniques. To see this, suppose that F_{1_t} is the most accurate of the individual forecasting techniques. If $b_1 = 1$ and $b_0 = b_2 = b_3 = 0$, then our combined forecast would be $\hat{Y}_t = F_{1_t}$. Thus, b_0, b_2, and b_3 would be assigned non-zero values only if this helps to reduce the MSE and produce more accurate predictions.

In chapter 9, Regression Analysis, we noted that adding independent variables to a regression model can never decrease the value of the R^2 statistic. Therefore, it is important to ensure that each independent variable in a multiple regression model accounts for a significant portion of the variation in the dependent variable and does not simply inflate the value of R^2. Similarly, combining forecasts can never increase the value of the MSE. Thus, when combining forecasts, we must ensure that each forecasting technique plays a significant role in accounting for the behavior of the dependent time-series variable. Using the adjusted-R^2 statistic in building multiple regression models, as described in chapter 9, can also be applied to the problem of selecting forecasting techniques to combine in time-series analysis.

SUMMARY

This chapter presented several methods for forecasting future values of a time-series variable. The chapter discussed time-series methods for stationary data (without a strong upward or downward trend), non-stationary data (with a strong upward or downward linear or nonlinear trend), and data with repeating seasonal patterns. In each case, the goal is to fit models to the past behavior of a time-series and use the models to project future values.

Because time-series vary in nature (for example, with and without trend, with and without seasonality), it is helpful to be aware of the different forecasting techniques and the types of problems for which they are intended. There are many other time-series modeling techniques besides those discussed in this chapter. Descriptions of these other techniques can be found in texts devoted to time-series analysis.

In modeling time-series data, it is often useful to try several techniques and then compare them based on measures of forecast accuracy, including a graphical inspection of how well the model fits the historical data. If no one procedure is clearly better than the others, it might be wise to combine the forecasts from the different procedures using a weighted average or some other method.

REFERENCES

Clemen, R. T. "Combining Forecasts: A Review and Annotated Bibliography." *International Journal of Forecasting*, vol. 5, 1989.

Clements, D. and R. Reid. "Analytical MS/OR Tools Applied to a Plant Closure." *Interfaces*, vol. 24, no. 2, 1994.

Gardner, E. "Exponential Smoothing: The State of the Art," *Journal of Forecasting*, vol. 4, no. 1, 1985.

Georgoff, D. and R. Murdick. "Managers Guide to Forecasting." *Harvard Business Review*, vol. 64, no. 1, 1986.

Makridakis, S. and S. Wheelwright. *Forecasting: Methods and Applications*. New York: Wiley, 1986.

Pindyck, R. and D. Rubinfeld. *Econometric Models and Economic Forecasts*. New York: McGraw-Hill, 1989.

Check Processing Revisited—The Chemical Bank Experience

Source: Boyd, Kevin and Vincent A. Mabert, "A Two Stage Forecasting Approach at Chemical Bank of New York for Check Processing," *Journal of Bank Research*, vol. 8, no. 2, Summer 1977, pages 101-107.

CHEMICAL BANK OF NEW YORK employs more than 500 people to process checks averaging $2 billion per day. Scheduling shifts for these employees requires accurate predictions of check flows. This is done with a regression model that forecasts daily check volume using independent variables that represent calendar effects. The regression model used by Ohio National Bank (see "Better Predictions Create Cost Savings for Ohio National Bank" in chapter 9) is based on this Chemical Bank model.

The binary independent variables in the regression model represent months, days of the month, weekdays, and holidays. Of 54 possible variables, 29 were used in the model to yield a coefficient of determination (R^2) of 0.83 and a standard deviation of 142.6.

The forecast errors, or residuals, were examined for patterns that would suggest the possibility of improving the model. Analysts noticed a tendency for overpredictions to follow one another and underpredictions to follow one another, implying that check volumes could be predicted not only by calendar effects but also by the recent history of prediction errors.

An exponential smoothing model was used to forecast the residuals. The regression model combined with the exponential smoothing model then became the complete model for predicting check volumes. Fine-tuning was accomplished by investigating different values of the smoothing constant (α) from 0.05 to 0.50. A smoothing constant of 0.2 produced the best results, reducing the standard deviation from 142.6 to 131.8. Examination of the residuals for the complete model showed nothing but random variations, indicating that the exponential smoothing procedure was working as well as could be expected.

Although the complete model provides better forecasts on the average, it occasionally overreacts and increases the error for some periods. Nevertheless, the complete model is considered to be preferable to regression alone.

Questions and Problems

1. What is the result of using regression analysis to estimate a linear trend model for a stationary time-series?

2. A manufacturing company uses a certain type of steel rod in one of its products. The design specifications for this rod indicate that it must be between 0.353 to 0.357 inches in diameter. The machine that manufactures these rods is set up to produce them at 0.355 inches in diameter, but there is some variation in its output. Provided that the machine is producing rods within 0.353 to 0.357 inches in diameter, its output is considered acceptable or within control limits. Management uses a control chart to track the diameter of the rods being produced by the machine over time so that remedial measures can be taken if the machine begins to produce unacceptable rods. Figure 11.31 shows an example of this type of chart.

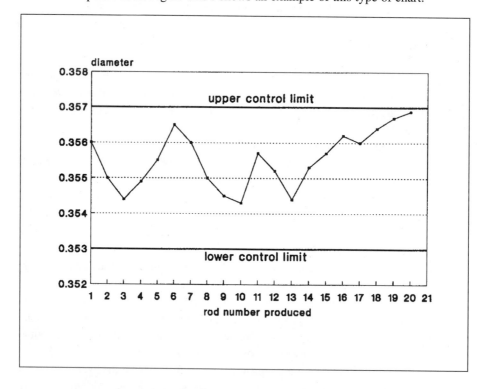

Figure 11.31: Graph for rod manufacturing problem

Unacceptable rods represent waste. Thus, management wants to develop a procedure to predict when the machine will start producing rods that are outside the control limits, so that appropriate actions can be taken to prevent the production of rods that must be scrapped. Of the time-series models discussed in this chapter, which is the most appropriate tool for this problem? Explain your answer.

3. Each month, Joe's Auto Parts uses exponential smoothing (with $\alpha = 0.25$) to predict the number of cans of brake fluid that will be sold during the next month. In June, Joe forecast that he would sell 37 cans of brake fluid during July. Joe actually sold 43 cans in July.

a. What is Joe's forecast for brake fluid sales in August and September?

b. Suppose that Joe sells 32 cans of brake fluid in August. What is the revised forecast for September?

Questions 4 through 9 refer to the following data set representing annual sales (in $1,000s) for a small business.

Year	Sales	Year	Sales
1975	283	1985	462
1976	288	1986	452
1977	336	1987	474
1978	388	1988	476
1979	406	1989	497
1980	412	1990	487
1981	416	1991	523
1982	435	1992	528
1983	428	1993	532
1984	435	1994	552

4. Prepare a line graph of these data. Do the data appear to be stationary or non-stationary?

5. Compute the 2-period and 4-period moving average predictions for the data set.

   a. Prepare a line graph comparing the moving average predictions against the original data.

   b. Do the moving averages tend to overestimate or underestimate the actual data? Why?

   c. Compute forecasts for 1995 and 1996 using the 2-period and 4-period moving average techniques.

6. Use Solver to determine the weights for a 3-period weighted moving average that minimizes the MSE for the data set.

   a. What are the optimal values for the weights?

   b. Prepare a line graph comparing the weighted moving average predictions against the original data.

   c. What are the forecasts for 1995 and 1996 using this technique?

7. Create an exponential smoothing model that minimizes the MSE for the data set. Use Solver to determine the optimal value of α.

   a. What is the optimal value of α?

   b. Prepare a line graph comparing the exponential smoothing predictions against the original data.

   c. What are the forecasts for 1995 and 1996 using this technique?

8. Use Holt's method to create a model that minimizes the MSE for the data set. Use Solver to determine the optimal values of α and β.

   a. What are the optimal values of α and β?

   b. Prepare a line graph comparing the predictions from Holt's method versus the original data.

   c. What are the forecasts for 1995 and 1996 using this technique?

9. Use regression analysis to fit a linear trend model to the data set.

   a. What is the estimated regression function?

   b. Interpret the R^2 value for your model.

   c. Prepare a line graph comparing the linear trend predictions against the original data.

   d. What are the forecasts for 1995 and 1996 using this technique?

   e. Fit a quadratic trend model to these data. What is the estimated regression function?

   f. Compare the adjusted-R^2 value for this model to that of the linear trend model. What is implied by this comparison?

   g. Prepare a line graph comparing the quadratic trend predictions against the original data.

   h. What are the forecasts for 1995 and 1996 using this technique?

   i. If you had to choose between the linear and quadratic trend models, which would you use? Why?

Questions 10 through 14 refer to the following data set representing the number of four-wheel drive utility vehicles sold by a local car dealer during the past three years.

Year	Quarter	Units Sold
1992	1	23
	2	25
	3	36
	4	31
1993	1	26
	2	28
	3	48
	4	36
1994	1	31
	2	42
	3	53
	4	43

10. Use regression analysis to fit a linear trend model to the data set.

   a. What is the estimated regression function?

   b. Interpret the R^2 value for your model.

   c. Prepare a line graph comparing the linear trend predictions against the original data.

   d. What are the forecasts for each quarter in 1995 using this technique?

   e. Calculate seasonal indices for each quarter using the results of the linear trend model.

   f. Use these seasonal indices to compute seasonal forecasts for each quarter in 1995.

11. Use regression analysis to fit a quadratic trend model to the data set.

   a. What is the estimated regression function?

   b. Compare the adjusted-R^2 value for this model to that of the linear trend model. What is implied by this comparison?

   c. Prepare a line graph comparing the quadratic trend predictions against the original data.

   d. What are the forecasts for each quarter in 1995 using this technique?

   e. Calculate seasonal indices for each quarter using the results of the quadratic trend model.

   f. Use these seasonal indices to compute seasonal forecasts for each quarter in 1995.

12. Use Holt's method to create a model that minimizes the MSE for the data set. Use Solver to determine the optimal values of α and β.

   a. What are the optimal values of α and β?

   b. Prepare a line graph comparing the predictions from Holt's method against the original data.

   c. What are the forecasts for each quarter in 1995 using this technique?

   d. Calculate seasonal indices for each quarter using the results of Holt's method.

   e. Use these seasonal indices to compute seasonal forecasts for each quarter in 1995.

13. Use Winter's method to create a seasonal model that minimizes the MSE for the data set. Use Solver to determine the optimal values of α, β, and γ.

   a. What are the optimal value of α, β, and γ?

   b. Prepare a line graph comparing the predictions from Winter's method against the original data.

   c. What are the forecasts for each quarter in 1995 using this technique?

14. Use regression analysis to fit a seasonal model with linear trend to the data set.

   a. What is the estimated regression function?

   b. Interpret the R^2 value for your model.

    c. Interpret the parameter estimates corresponding to the indicator variables in your model.

    d. Prepare a line graph comparing the linear trend predictions against the original data.

    e. What are the forecasts for each quarter in 1995 using this technique?

Questions 15 through 19 refer to the following data set representing the selling price of three-month old calves at a livestock auction during the past 22 weeks.

Week	Price	Week	Price
1	$176	12	$172
2	$172	13	$174
3	$174	14	$177
4	$177	15	$180
5	$173	16	$178
6	$171	17	$176
7	$172	18	$179
8	$173	19	$175
9	$174	20	$176
10	$173	21	$174
11	$171	22	$175

15. Prepare a line graph of these data. Do the data appear to be stationary or non-stationary?

16. Compute the 2-period and 4-period moving average predictions for the data set.

    a. Prepare a line graph comparing the moving average predictions against the original data.

    b. Compute the MSE for each of the two moving averages. Which appears to provide the best fit for this data set?

    c. Compute forecasts for the next two weeks using the 2-period and 4-period moving average techniques.

17. Use Solver to determine the weights for a 4-period weighted moving average on the data set that minimizes the MSE.

    a. What are the optimal values for the weights?

    b. Prepare a line graph comparing the weighted moving average predictions against the original data.

    c. What are the forecasts for weeks 23 and 24 using this technique?

18. Create an exponential smoothing model that minimizes the MSE for the data set. Use Solver to estimate the optimal value of α.

    a. What is the optimal value of α?

    b. Prepare a line graph comparing the exponential smoothing predictions against the original data.

    c. What are the forecasts for weeks 23 and 24 using this technique?

19. Use Holt's method to create a model that minimizes the MSE for the data set. Use Solver to estimate the optimal values of α and β.

    a. What are the optimal values of α and β?

    b. Are these values surprising? Why or why not?

Questions 20 through 23 refer to the following data set representing two years of monthly health insurance claims for a self-insured company.

Year	Month	Claims	Year	Month	Claims
1993	1	$10,159	1994	1	$12,300
1993	2	$11,175	1994	2	$13,224
1993	3	$12,310	1994	3	$13,606
1993	4	$12,446	1994	4	$13,659
1993	5	$13,213	1994	5	$16,442
1993	6	$16,412	1994	6	$17,334
1993	7	$17,405	1994	7	$19,605
1993	8	$14,233	1994	8	$18,997
1993	9	$14,606	1994	9	$15,971
1993	10	$12,969	1994	10	$15,740
1993	11	$13,980	1994	11	$16,919
1993	12	$14,755	1994	12	$18,931

20. Use regression analysis to fit a linear trend model to the data set.

    a. What is the estimated regression function?

    b. Interpret the R^2 value for your model.

    c. Prepare a line graph comparing the linear trend predictions against the original data.

    d. What are the forecasts for each of the first six months in 1995 using this technique?

    e. Calculate seasonal indices for each month using the results of the linear trend model.

    f. Use these seasonal indices to compute seasonal forecasts for the first six months in 1995.

21. Use regression analysis to fit a quadratic trend model to the data set.

    a. What is the estimated regression function?

    b. Compare the adjusted-R^2 value for this model to that of the linear trend model. What is implied by this comparison?

    c. Prepare a line graph comparing the quadratic trend predictions against the original data.

    d. What are the forecasts for each of the first six months in 1995 using this technique?

    e. Calculate seasonal indices for each month using the results of the quadratic trend model.

    f. Use these seasonal indices to compute seasonal forecasts for each of the first six months in 1995.

22. Use Holt's method to create a model that minimizes the MSE for the data set. Use Solver to determine the optimal values of α and β.

    a. What are the optimal values of α and β?

    b. Prepare a line graph comparing the predictions from Holt's method against the original data.

    c. What are the forecasts for each of the first six months in 1995 using this technique?

    d. Calculate seasonal indices for each month using the results of Holt's method.

    e. Use these seasonal indices to compute seasonal forecasts for each of the first six months in 1995.

23. Use Winter's method to create a seasonal model that minimizes the MSE for the data set. Use Solver to determine the optimal values of α, β, and γ.

    a. What are the optimal values of α, β, and γ?

    b. Prepare a line graph comparing the predictions from Winter's method against the original data.

    c. What are the forecasts for each of the first six months in 1995 using this technique?

Forecasting Boxoffice Returns: A Case in Time Series Analysis

FOR years, people in the motion picture industry—critics, film historians, and others—have eagerly awaited the second issue in January of *Variety*. Long considered the show business bible, *Variety* is a weekly trade newspaper that reports on all aspects of the entertainment industry: movies, television, recordings, concert tours, and so on. The second issue in January, called the Anniversary Edition, summarizes how the entertainment industry fared in the previous year, both artistically and commercially.

In this issue, *Variety* publishes its list of All Time Film Rental Champs. This list indicates, in descending order, motion pictures and the amount of money they returned to the studio. Because a movie theater rents a film from a studio for a limited time, the money paid for admission by ticket buyers is split between the studio and the theater owner. For example, if a ticket buyer pays $8.00 to see a particular movie, the theater owner keeps about $4.00 and the studio receives the other $4.00. The longer a movie plays in a theater, the greater the percentage of the admission price returned to the studio. A film playing for an entire summer could eventually return as much as 90% of the $8.00 to the studio. The theater owner also benefits from such a success because although the owner's percent-

age of the admission price is small, the sales of concessions (candy, soda, and so on) provide greater profits. Thus, both the studio and the theater owner win when a film continues to draw audiences for a long time. *Variety* lists the rental figures (the actual money amounts returned to the studios) that the films have accrued in their domestic releases (United States and Canada).

In addition, *Variety* provides a monthly Boxoffice Barometer of the film industry, which is a profile of the month's domestic boxoffice returns. This profile is not measured in dollars, but scaled according to some standard. By the late 1980s, for example, the scale was based on numbers around 100, with 100 representing the average boxoffice return of 1980. The figures from 1980 through 1989 are given in the table (and in the file C11CASE.XLS on your data disk).

All the figures are scaled around 1980's boxoffice returns, but instead of dollars, artificial numbers are used. Film executives can get a relative indication of boxoffice figures compared to the arbitrary 1980 scale. For example, in January 1980 the boxoffice returns to the film industry were 95% of the average that year, whereas in January 1981 the returns were 104% of the average of 1980 (or, they were 4% above the average of 1980's figure).

Contributed by Jack Yurkiewicz, Lubin School of Business, Pace University, New York.

Month	1980	1981	1982	1983	1984	1985	1986	1987	1988	1989
January	95	104	101	88	132	125	111	127	119	147
February	94	100	96	110	109	118	123	129	147	146
March	98	99	82	129	101	121	121	132	164	133
April	96	88	84	113	111	140	139	108	135	148
May	95	89	85	114	140	141	119	115	124	141
June	115	108	124	169	179	201	156	149	168	191
July	107	109	134	131	145	152	154	155	159	178
August	104	101	109	139	140	138	136	129	137	156
September	96	106	121	120	120	137	105	117	149	119
October	112	102	111	115	129	138	132	166	159	138
November	98	78	101	116	118	144	123	152	175	175
December	102	111	112	128	139	148	164	173	195	188

From the time series given in the table, you will make a forecast for the 12 months of the next year, 1990.

1. Produce a line graph of the data over time. From this graph, do you see a pattern? Can you detect any seasonality in the data?

2. Use exponential smoothing. Comment on the appropriateness of exponential smoothing on this data set. Use Solver to find the optimal (minimal MSE) smoothing constant. Plot the predictions from this model on the graph with the original data. How well does this technique fit the data? Make forecasts for the 12 months of 1990.

3. Use Holt's method. Comment on the appropriateness of Holt's method on this data set. Use Solver to find the optimal (minimal MSE) smoothing constants. Plot the predictions from this model on the graph with the original data. How well does this technique fit the data? What are your forecasts for the 12 months of 1990?

4. Use regression to build a linear trend model. Comment on the goodness-of-fit of this model to the

data. Plot the predictions from this model on the graph with the original data. How well does this technique fit the data?

5. Use Winter's method. Comment on the appropriateness of Winter's method on this data set. Use Solver to find the optimal (minimal MSE) smoothing constants. Plot the predictions from this model on the graph with the original data. How well does this technique fit the data? What are your forecasts for the 12 months of 1990?

6. Develop seasonal indices for the linear trend model developed in question 4. Use these indices to adjust predictions from the linear trend model for seasonal effects. Plot the predictions from this model on the graph with the original data. How well does this technique fit the data? Make forecasts for the 12 months of 1990 using this technique.

7. Using mean squared error as your criterion, in which forecasting method of those you tried do you have the most confidence for making accurate forecasts for 1990?

CHAPTER 12

Introduction to Simulation

CHAPTER 1 DISCUSSED how the calculations in a spreadsheet can be viewed as a mathematical model that defines a functional relationship between various input variables (or independent variables) and one or more bottom-line performance measures (or dependent variables). The following equation expresses this relationship:

$$Y = f(X_1, X_2, ..., X_k) \tag{12.1}$$

In many spreadsheets the values of various input cells are determined by the person using the spreadsheet. These input cells correspond to the independent variables X_1, X_2, ..., X_k in equation 12.1. Various formulas (represented by $f(\cdot)$ in equation 12.1) are entered in other cells of the spreadsheet to transform the values of the input cells into some bottom-line output (denoted by Y in equation 12.1). Simulation is a technique that is helpful in analyzing models where the value to be assumed by one or more independent variables is uncertain.

RANDOM VARIABLES AND RISK

In order to compute a value for the bottom-line performance measure of a spreadsheet model, each input cell must be assigned a specific value so that all the related calculations can be performed. However, some uncertainty often exists regarding the value that should be assumed by one or more independent variables (or input cells) in the spreadsheet. This is particularly true in spreadsheet models that represent future conditions. A **random variable** is any variable whose value cannot be predicted or set with certainty. Thus, many input variables in a spreadsheet model represent random variables whose actual values cannot be predicted with certainty.

For example, projections of the cost of raw materials, future interest rates, future numbers of employees, and expected product demand are random variables because their true values are unknown and will be determined in the future. If we cannot say with certainty what value one or more input variables in a model will assume, we also cannot say with certainty what value the dependent variable will assume. This uncertainty associated with the value of the dependent variable introduces an element of risk to the decision-making problem. Specifically, if the dependent variable represents some bottom-line performance measure that managers use to make decisions, and its value is uncertain, any decisions made on the basis of this value are based on uncertain (or incomplete) information. When such a decision is made, some chance exists that the decision will not produce the intended results. This chance, or uncertainty, represents an element of **risk** in the decision-making problem.

The term "risk" also implies the *potential* for loss. The fact that a decision's outcome is uncertain does not mean that the decision is particularly risky. For example, whenever we put money into a soft drink machine, there is a chance that the machine will take our money and not deliver the product. However, most of us would not consider this risk to be particularly great. From past experience, we know that the chance of not receiving the product is small. But even if the machine takes our money and does not deliver the product, most of us would not consider this to be a tremendous loss. Thus, the amount of risk involved in a given decision-making situation is a function of the uncertainty in the outcome of the decision and the magnitude of the potential loss. A proper assessment of the risk present in a decision-making situation should address both of these issues, as the examples in this chapter will demonstrate.

WHY ANALYZE RISK?

Many spreadsheets built by business people contain *estimated* values for the uncertain input variables in their models. If a manager cannot say with certainty what value a particular cell in a spreadsheet will assume, this cell most likely represents a random variable. Ordinarily, the manager will attempt to make an informed guess about the values such cells will assume. The manager hopes that inserting the expected, or most likely, values for all the uncertain cells in a spreadsheet will provide the most likely value for the cell containing the bottom-line performance measure (Y). The problem with this type of analysis is that it tells the decision maker nothing about the *variability* of the performance measure.

For example, in analyzing a particular investment opportunity, we might determine that the expected return on a $1,000 investment is $10,000 within two years. But how much variability exists in the possible outcomes? If all the potential outcomes are scattered closely around $10,000 (say from $9,000 to $11,000), then the investment opportunity might still be attractive. If, on the other hand, the potential outcomes are scattered widely around $10,000 (say from −$30,000 to +$50,000), then the investment opportunity might be unattractive. Although these two scenarios might have the same expected or average value, the risks involved are quite different. Thus, even if we can determine the expected outcome of a decision using a spreadsheet, it is just as important, if not more so, to consider the risk involved in the decision.

METHODS OF RISK ANALYSIS

Several techniques are available to help managers analyze risk. Three of the most common are best case/worst case analysis, what-if analysis, and simulation. Of these methods, simulation is the most powerful and, therefore, is the technique we will focus on in this chapter. Although the other techniques might not be effective in risk analysis, they are probably used more often than simulation by most managers in business today. This is largely due to the fact that most managers are unaware of the spreadsheet's ability to perform simulation and of the benefits provided by this technique. Before discussing simulation, let's first briefly look at the other methods of risk analysis to understand their strengths and weaknesses.

BEST CASE/WORST CASE ANALYSIS

If we don't know what value a particular cell in a spreadsheet will assume, we could enter a number that we think is the most likely value for the uncertain cell. If we enter such numbers for all the uncertain cells in the spreadsheet, we can easily calculate the most likely value of the bottom-line performance measure. (This is also called the **base case** scenario.) However, this scenario gives us no information about how far away the actual outcome might be from this expected or most likely value.

One simple solution to this problem is to calculate the value of the bottom-line performance measure using the **best case**, or most optimistic, and **worst case**, or most pessimistic, values for the uncertain input cells. These additional scenarios show the range of possible values that might be assumed by the bottom-line performance measure. As indicated in the earlier example about the $1,000 investment, knowing the range of possible outcomes is very helpful in assessing the risk involved in different alternatives. However, simply knowing the best case and worst case outcomes tells us nothing about the distribution of possible values within this range, nor does it tell us the probability of either scenario occurring.

Figure 12.1 displays several probability distributions that might be associated with the value of a bottom-line performance measure within a given range. Each of these distributions describe variables that have identical ranges and similar average values. But each distribution is very different in terms of the risk it represents to the decision maker. The appeal of best case/worst case analysis is that it is easy to do. Its weakness is that it tells us nothing about the shape of the distribution associated with the bottom-line performance measure. As we'll see later, knowing the shape of the distribution of the bottom-line performance measure can be critically important in helping us answer a number of managerial questions.

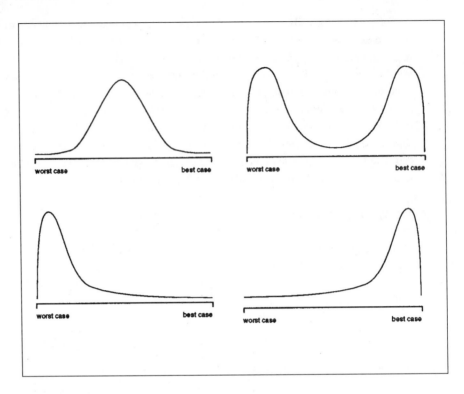

Figure 12.1: Possible distributions of performance measure values within a given range

WHAT-IF ANALYSIS

Prior to the introduction of electronic spreadsheets in the early 1980s, the use of best case/worst case analysis was often the only feasible way for a manager to analyze the risk associated with a decision. This process was extremely time consuming, error prone, and tedious, using only a piece of paper, pencil, and calculator to recalculate the performance measure of a model using different values for the uncertain inputs. The arrival of personal computers and electronic spreadsheets made it much easier for a manager to play out a large number of scenarios in addition to the best and worst cases—which is the essence of what-if analysis.

In **what-if analysis**, a manager changes the values of the uncertain input variables to see what happens to the bottom-line performance measure. By making a series of such changes, a manager can gain some insight into how sensitive the performance measure is to changes to the input variables. Although many managers perform this type of manual what-if analysis, it has three major flaws.

First, if the values selected for the independent variables are based on only the manager's judgment, the resulting sample values of the performance measure are likely to be biased. That is, if several uncertain variables can each assume some range of values, it would be difficult to ensure that the manager tests a fair, or representative, sample of all possible combinations of these values. To select values for the uncertain variables that correctly reflect their random variations, the values must be randomly selected from a distribution, or pool, of values that reflects the appropriate range of possible values as well as the appropriate relative frequencies of these variables.

Second, hundreds or thousands of what-if scenarios might be required to create a valid representation of the underlying variability in the bottom-line performance measure. No one would want to perform these scenarios manually nor would anyone be able to make sense of the stream of numbers that would flash on the screen.

The third problem with what-if analysis is that the insight the manager might gain from playing out various scenarios is of little value when recommending a decision to top management. What-if analysis simply does not supply the manager with the tangible evidence (facts and figures) needed to justify why a given decision was made or recommended. Additionally, what-if analysis does not address the problem identified in our earlier discussion of best case/worst case analysis—it does not allow us to estimate the distribution of the performance measure in a formal enough manner. Thus, what-if analysis is a step in the right direction, but it's not quite a large enough step to allow managers to analyze risk effectively in the decisions they face.

SIMULATION

Simulation is a technique that measures and describes various characteristics of the bottom-line performance measure of a model when one or more values for the independent variables are uncertain. If any independent variables in a model are random variables, the dependent variable (Y) also represents a random variable. The objective in simulation is to *describe* the distribution and characteristics of the possible values of the bottom-line performance measure Y, given the possible values and behavior of the independent variables X_1, X_2, ..., X_k.

The idea behind simulation is similar to the notion of playing out many what-if scenarios. The difference is that the process of assigning values to the cells in the spreadsheet that represent random variables is automated so that: (1) the values are assigned in a non-biased way, and (2) the spreadsheet user is relieved of the burden of determining these values. With simulation, we repeatedly and randomly generate sample values for each uncertain input variable (X_1, X_2, ..., X_k) in our model and then compute the resulting value of our bottom-line performance measure (Y). We can then use the sample values of Y to estimate the true distribution and other characteristics of the performance measure Y. For example, we can use the sample observations to construct a frequency distribution of the performance measure, to estimate the range of values over which the performance measure might vary, to estimate the performance measure mean and variance, and to estimate the probability that the actual value of the performance measure will be greater than (or less than) a particular value. All these measures provide greater insight into the risk associated with a given decision than a single value calculated based on the expected values for the uncertain independent variables.

A CORPORATE HEALTH INSURANCE EXAMPLE

The following example demonstrates the mechanics of preparing a spreadsheet model for risk analysis using simulation. The example presents a fairly simple model to illustrate the process and provide a sense of the amount of effort involved. However, the process for performing simulation is basically the same regardless of the size of the model.

Lisa Pon has just been hired as an analyst in the corporate planning department of Hungry Dawg Restaurants. Her first assignment is to determine how much money the company needs to accrue in the coming year to pay for its employees' health insurance claims. Hungry Dawg is a large, growing chain of restaurants that specializes in traditional southern foods. The company has become large enough that it no longer buys insurance from a private insurance company. The company is now self-insured, meaning that it pays health insurance claims with its own money (although it contracts with an outside company to handle the administrative details of processing claims and writing checks).

The money the company uses to pay claims comes from two sources: employee contributions (or premiums deducted from employees' paychecks), and company funds (the company must pay whatever costs are not covered by employee contributions). Each employee covered by the health plan contributes $125 per month. However, the number of employees covered by the plan changes from month to month as employees are hired and fired, quit, or simply add or drop health insurance coverage. A total of 18,533 employees were covered by the plan last month. The average monthly health claim per covered employee was $250 last month.

An example of how most analysts would model this problem is shown in Figure 12.2 (and in the file FIG12-2.XLS on your data disk). The spreadsheet begins with a listing of the initial conditions and assumptions for the problem. For example, cell D2 indicates that 18,533 employees are covered currently by the health plan, and cell D3 indicates that the average monthly claim per covered employee is $250. The average monthly contribution per employee is $125, as shown in cell D4. The values in cells D2 and D3 are unlikely to stay the same for the entire year. Thus, we need to make some assumptions about the rate at which these values are likely to increase during the year. For example, we might assume that the number of covered employees will increase by about 2% per month, and that the average claim per employee will increase at a rate of 1% per month. These assumptions are reflected in cells F2 and F3. The average contribution per employee is assumed to be constant over the coming year.

Microsoft Excel - FIG12-2.XLS

File   Edit   View   Insert   Format   Tools   Data   Window   Help

Courier   10   B I U $ %

I5

	A	B	C	D	E	F	G
1	Initial Conditions:				Assumptions:		
2		Number of Covered Employees		18,533	Increasing	2%	per month
3		Avg Claim per Employee		$250	Increasing	1%	per month
4		Amt Contrib. per Employee		$125	Constant		
5							
6		Number of	Employee	Avg Claim	Total		Company
7	Month	Employees	Contributions	per Emp.	Claims		Cost
8	1	18,904	$2,362,958	$252.50	$4,773,174		$2,410,217
9	2	19,282	$2,410,217	$255.03	$4,917,324		$2,507,107
10	3	19,667	$2,458,421	$257.58	$5,065,827		$2,607,406
11	4	20,061	$2,507,589	$260.15	$5,218,815		$2,711,226
12	5	20,462	$2,557,741	$262.75	$5,376,423		$2,818,682
13	6	20,871	$2,608,896	$265.38	$5,538,791		$2,929,895
14	7	21,289	$2,661,074	$268.03	$5,706,063		$3,044,989
15	8	21,714	$2,714,295	$270.71	$5,878,386		$3,164,091
16	9	22,149	$2,768,581	$273.42	$6,055,913		$3,287,332
17	10	22,592	$2,823,953	$276.16	$6,238,802		$3,414,849
18	11	23,043	$2,880,432	$278.92	$6,427,214		$3,546,782
19	12	23,504	$2,938,041	$281.71	$6,621,315		$3,683,275
20							$36,125,850
21							

Health Claims Projection

Ready

Figure 12.2: Original corporate health insurance model with expected values for uncertain variables

Using the assumed rate of increase in the number of covered employees (cell F2), we can create formulas for cells B8 through B19 that cause the number of covered employees to increase by the assumed amount each month. (The details of these formulas are covered later.) The expected monthly employee contributions shown in column C are calculated as $125 times the number of employees in each month. We can use the assumed rate of increase in average monthly claims (cell F3) to create formulas for cells D8 through D19 that cause the average claim per employee to increase at the assumed rate. The total claims for each month (shown in column E) are calculated as the average claim figures in column D times the number of employees for each month in column B. Because the company must pay for any claims that are not covered by the employee contributions, the company cost figures in column G are calculated as the total claims minus the employee contributions (column E minus column C). Finally, cell G20 sums the company cost figures listed in column G, and shows that the company can expect to contribute $36,125,850 of its revenues toward paying the health insurance claims of its employees in the coming year.

A Critique of the Base Case Model

Now let's consider the model we just described. The example model assumes that the number of covered employees will increase by *exactly* 2% each month and that the average claim per covered employee will increase by *exactly* 1% each month. Although these values might be reasonable approximations of what might happen, they are unlikely to reflect exactly what will happen. In fact, the number of employees covered by the health plan each month is likely to vary randomly around the average increase per month—that is, the number might decrease in some months and increase by more than 2% in others. Similarly, the average claim per covered employee might be lower than expected in certain months and higher than expected in others.

Both of these figures are likely to exhibit some uncertainty or random behavior, even if they do move in the general upward direction assumed throughout the year. So we cannot say with certainty that the total cost figure of $36,125,850 is exactly what the company will have to contribute toward health claims in the coming year. It is simply a prediction of what might happen. The actual outcome could be smaller or larger than this estimate. Using the original model, we have no idea how much larger or smaller the actual result could be—nor do we have any idea how the actual values are distributed around this estimate. We do not know if there is a 10%, 50%, or 90% chance of the actual total costs exceeding this estimate. To determine the variability or risk inherent in the bottom-line performance measure of total company costs, we'll apply the technique of simulation to our model.

RANDOM NUMBER GENERATORS

To perform simulation in an electronic spreadsheet, we must first place a **random number generator** (RNG) formula in each cell that represents a random, or uncertain, independent variable. Each RNG provides a sample observation from an appropriate distribution that represents the range and frequency of possible values for the variable. Once the RNGs are in place, new sample values are provided automatically by the RNGs each time the spreadsheet is recalculated. We can recalculate the spreadsheet n times, where n is the desired number of replications or scenarios, and the value of the bottom-line performance measure will be stored after each replication. We can analyze these stored observations to gain insight into the behavior and characteristics of the performance measure.

The process of simulation involves a lot of work, but, fortunately, the spreadsheet can do most of the work for us fairly easily. As mentioned earlier, the first step is to place an RNG formula in each cell that contains an uncertain value. Each formula will generate (or return) a number that represents a randomly selected value from a distribution, or pool, of values. The distributions from which these samples are taken should be representative of the underlying pool of values expected to occur in each uncertain cell.

THE RAND() FUNCTION

Excel, like most other spreadsheet packages, includes a built-in function called RAND() that provides the foundation for creating various RNGs. The **RAND() function** returns a uniformly distributed random number between 0.0 and 1.0 whenever the spreadsheet is recalculated (technically, $0 \leq \text{RAND}() \leq 0.99\overline{9}$). If you enter the RAND() formula in some cell in a spreadsheet, and press the recalculate key (function key [F9]) repeatedly, a series of random numbers between 0.0 and 1.0 appears in the cell.

The RAND() function enables us to do some interesting modeling. As a simple example, suppose that we want to simulate the toss of a fair coin in a spreadsheet. When tossing a fair coin there are two possible outcomes: heads or tails. If the coin is fair (that is, not weighted or biased toward one outcome over the other), we expect that each outcome has an equal probability of occurring each time we toss the coin. That is, the probability of heads is 0.5 and the probability of tails is 0.5 on any toss. However, before any given toss we cannot say with certainty whether the observed outcome will be heads or tails.

Using the RAND() function, we can create a formula that simulates the process of tossing the coin. Suppose that the value 1 represents the occurrence of heads and the value 0 represents the occurrence of tails. Now consider the following formula:

IF(RAND()<0.5,1,0)

Whenever the spreadsheet is recalculated, the RAND() function will return a random value between 0 and 1. If the value returned by RAND() is less than 0.5, the previous IF() function will return the value 1 (representing heads); otherwise, it will return the value 0 (representing tails). Because the RAND() function has a 0.5 probability of returning a value less than 0.5, there is a 50% chance that the IF() function will generate the heads value, and a 50% chance that it will generate the tails value each time the spreadsheet is recalculated.

As another example, suppose that we want to simulate rolling a fair, six-sided die using a spreadsheet. In this case, each roll of the die can produce one of six possible outcomes (the value 1, 2, 3, 4, 5, or 6). We need an RNG that randomly generates the integer numbers from 1 to 6 with each value having a 1/6 chance of occurring. Because RAND() generates uniformly distributed random numbers between 0.0 and 1.0, 6*RAND() would generate uniformly distributed random numbers between 0.0 and 6.0 (technically, $0 \leq 6*RAND() \leq 5.99\overline{9}$).

Now suppose that we took this interval from 0.0 to 6.0 and divided it into six equal pieces as follows:

	Lower Limit	Upper Limit
1	0.0	0.99$\overline{9}$
2	1.0	1.99$\overline{9}$
3	2.0	2.99$\overline{9}$
4	3.0	3.99$\overline{9}$
5	4.0	4.99$\overline{9}$
6	5.0	5.99$\overline{9}$

Because each of the six intervals is exactly the same size, the value of 6*RAND() is equally likely to fall in each of them. If the value generated by 6*RAND() falls between 0.0 and 0.99$\overline{9}$, we could associate this with the outcome of rolling a 1 on the die; if 6*RAND() falls between 1.0 and 1.99$\overline{9}$, we could associate this with rolling a 2 on the die, and so forth. This makes sense, but what mathematical function makes this association happen? Consider the following formula:

INT(6*RAND())+1

The INT() function returns the integer portion of the value inside its parentheses (for example, INT(4.85) = 4, INT(2.13) = 2). The following table summarizes the different outcomes generated using this formula:

If 6*RAND() falls in the interval	INT(6*RAND())+1 returns the value
0.0 to 0.99$\overline{9}$	1
1.0 to 1.99$\overline{9}$	2
2.0 to 2.99$\overline{9}$	3
3.0 to 3.99$\overline{9}$	4
4.0 to 4.99$\overline{9}$	5
5.0 to 5.99$\overline{9}$	6

Again, because each interval in the table is exactly the same size, the value of 6*RAND() is equally likely to fall in each interval. Therefore, each value generated by the formula INT(6*RAND())+1 also is equally likely to occur. Thus, the formula INT(6*RAND())+1 accurately simulates the act of rolling a fair, six-sided die.

GENERAL UNIFORM DISTRIBUTIONS

The previous examples illustrate how we can create formulas to simulate the occurrences of random events. RNG formulas are available to model events that follow several probability distributions. The two previous examples represent random variables that follow the **discrete uniform distribution**, which is appropriate for modeling random variables with n distinct possible outcomes, each outcome being equally likely (or having a $1/n$ probability of occurring). The following formula can be used to randomly generate the integers $a, a + 1, a + 2, ..., a + n - 1$ with equal probability of occurrence:

RNG for the discrete uniform distribution: INT(n*RAND())+a **12.2**

This formula is equivalent to the formula used in the die rolling example, where $a = 1$ and $n = 6$. Also, we could have used this same formula with $a = 0$ and $n = 2$ to simulate the toss of a fair coin.

Another commonly used RNG is for the **continuous uniform distribution**. This distribution is appropriate for modeling random variables that can assume any value (not just integer values) in the interval between the two points a and b (where $a < b$) and where all the values in this interval are equally likely to occur. A graph of the probability density function for this distribution is shown in the upper-left corner of Figure 12.3. The RNG formula for the continuous uniform distribution is:

RNG for the continuous uniform distribution: $a+(b - a)$*RAND()   **12.3**

This distribution is appropriate to use when only the upper and lower limits of the uncertain variable are known, and all values between these limits are equally likely to occur.

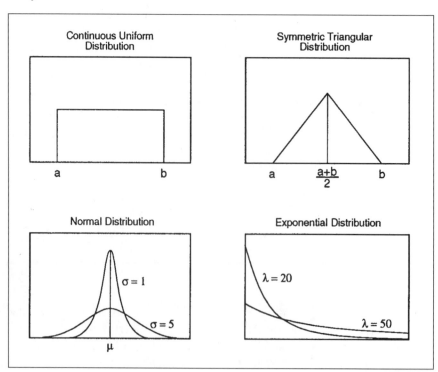

Figure 12.3: Graphs of common continuous probability distributions used in simulation

SYMMETRIC TRIANGULAR DISTRIBUTION

Sometimes a variable can assume any value between the two points a and b (where $a < b$), but all the values between these two points are not equally likely to occur (making the use of the continuous uniform distribution inappropriate). If the mid-point between the values a and b $((b + a)/2)$ is the most likely value for the variable, and a and b are the least likely values, it might be appropriate to model this variable using the symmetric triangular distribution, as shown in the upper-right corner of Figure 12.3. The RNG formula for the symmetric triangular distribution is:

RNG for the symmetric triangular distribution: $a+(b-a)*(RAND()+RAND())/2$ **12.4**

NORMAL DISTRIBUTION

The well-known, bell-shaped normal distribution is useful for modeling many random variables in the business world. This distribution has a location parameter μ, which represents the mean, or most likely, value. It also has a shape parameter σ (representing the standard deviation), which determines the width or spread of the distribution. Two representative normal distributions are shown in the lower-left corner of Figure 12.3. Note that these distributions have the same mean μ, but different standard deviations. With the normal distribution, approximately 68% of the observations are contained in the interval $\mu \pm \sigma$, approximately 95% of the observations fall in the range of values represented by $\mu \pm 2\sigma$, and more than 99% of the values fall in the interval $\mu \pm 3\sigma$. The RNG formula for a normally distributed random variable with mean μ and standard deviation σ is:

RNG for the normal distribution: $NORMINV(RAND(),\mu,\sigma)$ **12.5**

THE EXPONENTIAL DISTRIBUTION

The last RNG discussed here is for the exponential distribution. The shape of this distribution is determined by a single parameter λ. The value $1/\lambda$ represents both the mean and standard deviation of the distribution. As shown in the lower-right corner of Figure 12.3, the shape of this distribution is highly skewed to the right. Although most of the values tend to be less than or equal to the mean $1/\lambda$, unusually large values can occur. The RNG formula for the exponential distribution is:

RNG for the exponential distribution: $-1/\lambda*LN(RAND())$ **12.6**

The exponential distribution is useful for representing time between events, for example the times between the arrival of customers. We will use this distribution in chapter 14, Queuing Theory.

OTHER DISTRIBUTIONS

There are many other probability distributions for which RNGs have been created. Later in this chapter, we'll discuss other methods for generating random numbers from general discrete and binomial distributions. In chapter 13, we'll discuss a spreadsheet add-in package for simulation that offers a simple way to generate random numbers from many probability distributions. However, the RNGs presented here are sufficient for a large number of simulation tasks undertaken with spreadsheets.

DISCRETE VS. CONTINUOUS RANDOM VARIABLES

An important distinction exists between the random variables described earlier. In particular, the first three examples (coin flipping, die rolling, and the general discrete uniform distribution) involve RNGs that generate *discrete* outcomes, whereas the last four examples (continuous uniform, symmetric triangular, normal, and exponential) produce *continuous* outcomes. That is, the first three RNGs can return only a distinct set of individual values, whereas the other RNGs can return any of an infinite set of values. The distinction between discrete and continuous random variables is very important in simulation.

For example, the number of defective tires on a new car is a discrete random variable because it can assume only one of five distinct values: 0, 1, 2, 3, or 4. On the other hand, the amount of fuel in a new car is a continuous random variable because it can assume any value between 0 and the maximum capacity of the fuel tank. Thus, when selecting an RNG for an uncertain variable in a model, it is important to consider whether the variable can assume discrete or continuous values.

PREPARING THE MODEL FOR SIMULATION

To simulate the model for Hungry Dawg Restaurants described earlier, we must first select appropriate RNGs for the uncertain variables in the model. If available, historical data on the uncertain variables could be analyzed to determine appropriate RNGs for these variables. If past data are not available, or if we have reason to expect the future behavior of a variable to be significantly different from the past, then we must use judgment in selecting appropriate RNGs to model the random behavior of the uncertain variables.

For our example problem, let's assume that by analyzing historical data, we determined that the change in the number of covered employees from one month to the next is expected to vary uniformly between a 3% decrease and a 7% increase. (Note that this should cause the *average* change in the number of employees to be a 2% increase, because 0.02 is the mid-point between −0.03 and +0.07.) Further, assume that we can model the average monthly claim per covered employee as a normally distributed random variable with the mean (μ) increasing by 1% per month and a standard deviation (σ) of approximately 3%. (Note that this will cause the average increase in claims per covered employee from one month to the next to be approximately 1%.) These assumptions are reflected in cells F2 through H3 at the top of Figure 12.4 (and in the file FIG12-4.XLS on your data disk).

Important Note

If you retreive the spreadsheet in FIG12-4.XLS, many numbers on your screen will *not* match those shown in Figure 12.4 because these numbers are generated randomly.

To implement the formula to generate a random number of employees covered by the health plan, we'll use the RNG function in equation 12.3 for the continuous uniform distribution. This RNG generates random numbers between the values *a*

```
┌──────────────────────────────────────────────────────────────────────────┐
│ ▬                  Microsoft Excel - FIG12-4.XLS                    ▼ ▲   │
│ ▬  File   Edit   View   Insert   Format   Tools   Data   Window   Help  ▲ │
├──────────────────────────────────────────────────────────────────────────┤
│ [D][⌂][▤][⎙][▣][✓]  [✂][▦][▦][◇]  [↶][↷]  [Σ][ƒ]  [A/Z][Z/A]  [▦][▤][▦]  79%  [▼][♀][▶?] │
├──────────────────────────────────────────────────────────────────────────┤
│ Courier          ▼  10  ▼  [B][I][U]  [▤][▤][▤][▦]  [$][%][,][.0.0][.0.0]  [▦][▼][⬚][▼][▦][▼] │
└──────────────────────────────────────────────────────────────────────────┘
```

	A	B	C	D	E	F	G	H	I
1	Initial Conditions:				Assumptions:				
2	Number of Covered Employees			18,533	Max Decrease	3%	Max Increase	7%	Uniform
3	Avg Claim per Employee			$250	Mthly Increase	1%	Std Dev	3%	Normal
4	Amt Contrib. per Employee			$125	Constant				
5									
6		Number of	Employee	Avg Claim	Total		Company		
7	Month	Employees	Contributions	per Emp.	Claims		Cost		
8	1	18,380	$2,297,489	$252.50	$4,641,009		$2,343,520		
9	2	18,324	$2,290,522	$255.00	$4,672,588		$2,382,066		
10	3	19,047	$2,380,893	$257.61	$4,906,784		$2,525,891		
11	4	19,122	$2,390,255	$260.14	$4,974,420		$2,584,165		
12	5	19,816	$2,476,964	$262.74	$5,206,401		$2,729,438		
13	6	19,568	$2,446,042	$265.32	$5,191,793		$2,745,751		
14	7	19,922	$2,490,295	$268.06	$5,340,361		$2,850,066		
15	8	19,903	$2,487,854	$270.79	$5,389,445		$2,901,590		
16	9	19,835	$2,479,337	$273.46	$5,423,908		$2,944,571		
17	10	19,771	$2,471,314	$276.11	$5,458,911		$2,987,597		
18	11	20,637	$2,579,634	$278.91	$5,755,936		$3,176,302		
19	12	20,299	$2,537,379	$281.75	$5,719,289		$3,181,910		
20							$33,352,867		
21									
22									
23									
24									

```
┌──────────────────────────────────────────────────────────────────────────┐
│ |◀| |◀| |▶| |▶|  Health Claims Model /              |◆|                 |▶| │
│ Ready                                                                        │
└──────────────────────────────────────────────────────────────────────────┘
```

Key Cell Formulas

Cell	Formula	Copied to
B8	=$D$2*(1–$F$2+($F$2+$H$2)*RAND())	—
B9	=B8*(1–$F$2+($F$2+$H$2)*RAND())	B10:B19
C8	=$D$4*B8	C9:C19
D8	=NORMINV(RAND(),$D$3*(1+$F$3)^A8,$H$3)	D9:D19
E8	=D8*B8	E9:E19
G8	=E8–C8	G9:G19
G20	=SUM(G8:G19)	—

Figure 12.4: Modified corporate health insurance model with RNGs replacing expected values for uncertain variables

and *b*. Because the change in the number of employees from one month to the next can vary between a 3% decrease and a 7% increase, we'll let $a = -0.03$ and $b = 0.07$. If we enter these values for *a* and *b* into equation 12.3, we obtain:

$-0.03+(0.07-(-0.03))*RAND()$

which is equivalent to:

$-0.03+0.10*RAND()$

This formula generates random values between -0.03 and 0.07 (or $0.0699\overline{9}$).

The number of employees in any given month is equal to the number of employees in the previous month multiplied by the sum of 1 plus the random percentage change; that is:

$$\begin{array}{c}\text{Number of employees} \\ \text{in current month}\end{array} = \begin{array}{c}\text{Number of employees} \\ \text{in previous month}\end{array} * (1+(-0.03+0.10*RAND()))$$

which is equivalent to:

$$\begin{array}{c}\text{Number of employees} \\ \text{in current month}\end{array} = \begin{array}{c}\text{Number of employees} \\ \text{in previous month}\end{array} * (0.97+0.10*\text{RAND}()) \qquad \textbf{12.7}$$

If the RAND() function returns the value 0, this formula causes the number of employees in the current month to equal 97% of the number in the previous month (a 3% decrease). Alternatively, if the RAND() function returns the value 1, equation 12.7 causes the number of employees in the current month to equal 107% of the number in the previous month (a 7% increase). All the values between these two extremes (between 97% and 107%) are also possible and equally likely to occur.

The general relationship in equation 12.7 was used to create formulas that randomly generate the number of employees in each month. This was done in Figure 12.4 with the following formulas:

Formula for cell B8:   =$D$2*(1–$F$2+($F$2+$H$2)*RAND( ))

Formula for cell B9:   =B8*(1–$F$2+($F$2+$H$2)*RAND( ))
(copy to B10 through B19)

In these formulas, the terms "1–$F$2" and "$F$2+$H$2" generate the values 0.97 and 0.10, respectively, which are shown in equation 12.7.

To implement the formula to generate the average claims per covered employee in each month, we'll use the normal distribution RNG described in equation 12.5. This formula requires that we supply the value of the mean (μ) and standard deviation (σ) of the distribution from which we want to sample. The assumed 3% standard deviation (σ) for the average monthly claim, shown in cell H3 of Figure 12.4, is constant from month to month. Thus, the only remaining problem is to figure out the proper mean value (μ) for each month.

In this case, the mean for any given month should be 1% larger than the mean in the previous month. For example, the mean for month 1 is:

Mean in month 1 = (original mean)*1.01 $\qquad\qquad$ **12.8**

and the mean for month 2 is:

Mean in month 2 = (mean in month 1)*1.01 $\qquad\qquad$ **12.9**

If we substitute the RHS of equation 12.8 for "mean in month 1" in equation 12.9, we obtain the following equivalent definition for the mean in month 2:

Mean in month 2 = (original mean)*$(1.01)^2$

Similarly, the mean in month 3 is:

Mean in month 3 = (mean month 2)*1.01

which, after substitutions, is equivalent to:

Mean in month 3 = (original mean)*$(1.01)^3$

So, in general, the mean (μ) for month n is:

Mean in month n = (original mean)*$(1.01)^n$ $\qquad\qquad$ **12.10**

Thus, to generate the average claim per covered employee in each month, we'll use the following formula:

Formula for cell D8:   =NORMINV(RAND( ),$D$3*(1+$F$3)^A8,$H$3)
(copy to D9 through D19)

The term "\$D\$3*(1+\$F\$3)^A8" in this formula implements the general definition of the mean (μ) in month n given in equation 12.10.

At this point, the modifications to the model are complete. Each time the recalculate key (the function key [F9]) is pressed, the RNGs will automatically select new values for all the cells in the spreadsheet that represent uncertain (or random) variables. With each recalculation, a new value for the bottom-line performance measure (total company cost) will appear in cell G20. By pressing the recalculate key several times, we can observe representative values of the company's total cost for health claims.

REPLICATING THE MODEL

The next step in the simulation process involves recalculating the model several hundred times and recording the resulting values generated for the output cell, or bottom-line performance measure. Suppose that we want to perform 300 replications of the model and store the resulting observations of the dependent variable on a new worksheet named Simulation. To create and name this new worksheet:

1. Click the Insert menu.
2. Select Worksheet. Excel inserts a new worksheet in your workbook.
3. Click the Format menu.
4. Click Worksheet.
5. Click Rename.
6. Type Simulation.
7. Click OK.

Because we want to perform 300 replications of our model, we entered the numbers 1, 2, 3, ..., 300 starting in cell A3, as shown in Figure 12.5. This is done as follows:

1. Type the starting value (1) in cell A3 and press [Enter].
2. Click cell A3.
3. Click the Edit menu, click Fill, then click Series.
4. Select the Series in Columns option and enter a Stop value of 300.
5. Click OK.

Excel automatically fills the column below the selected cell (A3) with values increasing by 1 (the Step value) until it reaches the Stop value of 300. Because we want to track the company cost value in cell G20 of the Health Claims Model worksheet, we entered the following formula in cell B3:

Formula for cell B3:   ='Health Claims Model'!G20

Cell B2 contains the label Company Cost to identify the values that will ultimately appear in column B. (Column B was widened to display this value.)

We can now use the Data Table command to fill in the remainder of column B. Keep in mind that the Data Table command is designed for a purpose other than what we are using it for here. However, we can use this command to "trick" Excel into performing the replications needed in our simulation.

By using the Data Table command, we're instructing Excel to substitute each value in column A into some cell of the spreadsheet, recalculate the spreadsheet, and record in column B the associated value for the output cell (cell B3 in this case). Ordinarily, the values listed in the first column of a data table (column A) represent values that we want Excel to enter into some input cell of the spreadsheet. The resulting data table then shows what happens to the output cell given each of the input cell values. However, for our purposes we'll instruct Excel to enter each value in column A into an input cell that has no impact on the value of the output cell. For example, we might use cell A1 in Figure 12.5 as the input cell. In this way, we can "trick" Excel into recalculating the spreadsheet 300 times while storing the values of the output cell (cell G20 on the Health Claims Model worksheet) in column B.

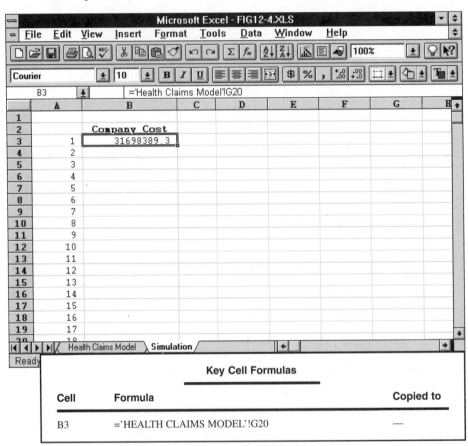

Figure 12.5: Worksheet prepared to simulate the corporate health insurance model

To execute the Data Table command:

1. Select the range A3 through B302.

2. Click the Data menu.

3. Click Table.

4. In the Table dialog box, enter cell A1 for the Column input cell.

5. Click OK.

Excel substitutes each value in the range A4 through A302 into cell A1, recalculates the workbook, and stores the resulting company cost figures in the adjacent cells in column B. Depending on your computer's speed, this recalculation might take 20 to 30 seconds, or possibly a couple of minutes.

After running the Data Table command, you should have a list of values in column B representing 300 possible company cost outcomes, similar to those shown in Figure 12.6. The numbers you generate on your computer will *not* match those in Figure 12.6. The procedure demonstrated here generates a *random* sample of 300 observations from an infinite number of possible values. Again, the random sample you generate will be different from the one shown in Figure 12.6, but the characteristics of your sample should be very similar to that shown in Figure 12.6.

Figure 12.6: Results of the Data Table command for the corporate health insurance problem

Each new entry Excel created, starting in cell B4, contains the array formula {=TABLE(,A1)}. This is how the Data Table command performs the repeated substitution and recalculation we just described. If we don't change the formulas in column B into values, every time the spreadsheet is recalculated we'll have to wait for this process to re-execute and we'll get a new sample of 300 replications. This wastes time and prevents us from focusing on the results of one batch of 300 observations in order to make decisions. To convert the formulas in column B to values:

1. Select the range B3 through B302.

2. Click the Edit menu.

3. Click Copy.

4. Click the Edit menu.

5. Click Paste Special.

6. Click Values.

7. Click OK.

8. Press [Enter].

The values in column B are now numeric constants that will not change even if the spreadsheet is recalculated.

Determining the Sample Size

You might wonder why we elected to perform 300 replications. Why not 200, or 800? Unfortunately, there is no easy answer to this question. Remember that the goal in simulation is to use a sample of observations on a bottom-line performance measure to estimate various characteristics about its behavior. For example, we might want to estimate the mean value of the performance measure and the shape of its probability distribution. However, we saw earlier that different values of the bottom-line performance measure occurred each time we manually recalculated the model in Figure 12.4. Thus, there is an infinite number of possibilities—or an **infinite population**—of total company cost values associated with this model.

We cannot analyze all of these infinite possibilities. But by taking a large enough sample from this infinite population, we can make reasonably accurate estimates about the characteristics of the underlying population of values. The larger the sample we take (that is, the more replications we do), the more accurate our final results will be. But performing many replications takes time and computer resources, so we must make a trade-off in terms of estimation accuracy versus convenience. There is no simple answer to the question of how many replications to perform, but as a minimum, you should always perform at least 100 replications, and more as time and resources permit or accuracy demands.

DATA ANALYSIS

As mentioned earlier, the objective of performing a simulation is to estimate various characteristics of the performance measure resulting from uncertainty in some or all of the input variables. After performing the replications, we must summarize and analyze the data in order to draw conclusions.

Most spreadsheet packages have built-in functions for performing statistical calculations. Excel also provides a data analysis tool we can use to generate numerous descriptive statistics automatically. To use the data analysis tool:

1. Click the Tools menu.
2. Click Data Analysis.
3. Click Descriptive Statistics.
4. Complete the Descriptive Statistics dialog box, as shown in Figure 12.7.
5. Click OK.

(If the Data Analysis option is not available on your Tools menu, select the Add-Ins option from the Tools menu, then select the Analysis ToolPak option. The Data Analysis option should then appear on your Tools menu. If Analysis ToolPak is not listed among your available add-ins, exit Excel, double-click the MS Excel Setup icon, click Add/Remove, double-click Add-Ins, then select Analysis ToolPak.)

Figure 12.8 shows the resulting descriptive summary statistics for our sample of company cost data. We could have generated these values using a variety of Excel's built-in statistical functions. For example, we could have calculated the mean value shown in cell E4 using the formula =AVERAGE(B3:B302). However, the Descriptive Statistics command simplifies this process. Note that we can edit the results produced by this command to delete any unnecessary information.

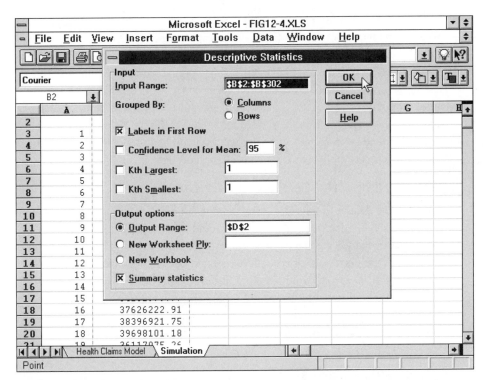

Figure 12.7: Descriptive
Statistics dialog box for
the corporate health
insurance problem

Figure 12.8: Statistical
results of the simulation data
for the corporate health
insurance model

THE BEST CASE AND THE WORST CASE

Decision makers usually want to know the best case and worst case scenarios to get
an idea of the range of possible outcomes they might face. This information is
available from the simulation results, as shown by the Minimum and Maximum

values listed in Figure 12.8. Although cell E4 indicates that the average value observed in this sample of 300 observations is approximately $35.9 million, cell E13 indicates that the smallest cost observed is about $30.3 million (representing the best case) and cell E14 indicates the largest cost is approximately $42.9 million (representing the worst case). (Note that if you generate your own sample of 300 observations, the statistics you calculate will *not* match those shown in Figure 12.8.) These figures should give the decision maker a good idea about the range of possible cost values that might occur. Note that these values might be difficult to determine manually in a complex model with many uncertain independent variables.

DETERMINING THE DISTRIBUTION OF OUTCOMES

Although the data in Figure 12.8 offer some insight into the best and worst possible outcomes of a decision, other factors should also be considered. The best and worst case scenarios are the most extreme outcomes, and might not be likely to occur. To determine the likelihood of these outcomes requires that we know something about the shape of the distribution of our bottom-line performance measure. Thus, we might also want to construct a frequency distribution and histogram for the 300 observations generated for our performance measure. To construct a frequency distribution and histogram:

1. Click the Tools menu.

2. Click Data Analysis.

3. Click Histogram.

4. Complete the Histogram dialog box, as shown in Figure 12.9.

5. Click OK.

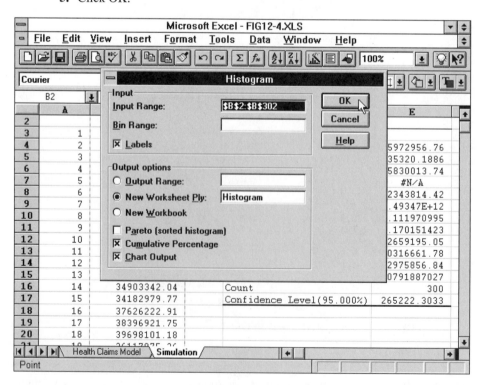

Figure 12.9: Histogram dialog box

The resulting new worksheet, named Histogram, contains a frequency distribution and histogram of our data which, after some simple formatting, appear as shown in Figure 12.10.

Figure 12.10: Frequency distribution and histogram for the corporate health insurance model

The Frequency column in Figure 12.10 indicates the number of observations from our simulation results that fall into the bins defined in column A. For example, the value in cell B2 indicates that 1 of the 300 replications resulted in a value that is less than or equal to $30,316,662. The value in cell B3 indicates that 5 of the 300 observations assumed values greater than $30,316,662 and less than or equal to $31,061,320. Similarly, cell C18 indicates that two observations have values between $41,486,540 and $42,231,198, and cell C19 indicates that one observation is greater than $42,231,198. In cell B10, we see that the most frequently occurring values are in the range $35,529,272 to $36,273,930. (Your results will *not* match those shown in Figure 12.10.)

The histogram in Figure 12.10 gives a visual representation of the frequency distribution values. This graph shows that the distribution of the total health claims the company must pay is somewhat bell-shaped.

THE CUMULATIVE DISTRIBUTION OF THE OUTPUT CELL

The Cumulative % column in Figure 12.10 shows the percentage of observations in the sample that are less than or equal to the values listed in column A. For example, cell C2 indicates that 0.33% of the 300 observations are less than $30,316,662; cell C3 indicates that 2% of the 300 observations are less than or equal to $31,061,320; and so on. These cumulative frequencies are also plotted on the graph shown in Figure 12.10.

Cumulative frequencies are helpful in answering a number of questions that might arise. For example, suppose that the chief financial officer (CFO) for Hungry Dawg Restaurants would rather accrue an excess of money to pay health claims than not accrue enough money. The CFO might want to know what amount the company should accrue so that there is only a 10% chance of coming up short of funds at the end of the year. The value in cell C14 of Figure 12.10 indicates that approximately 90% (or 91.67% to be exact) of the 300 observations are less than or equal to $39,252,564—or approximately 10% of the 300 sample observations are larger than $39,252,564. Thus, assuming that our sample is representative of the actual distribution of total health costs the company might incur, we could tell the CFO that if Hungry Dawg budgets $39,252,564 for health claims, there is roughly a 10% chance of the company not accruing enough funds.

Another way of answering the CFO's question is to sort the 300 observations in our sample in ascending order. (This can be done easily by selecting the range B3 through B302 in the Simulation worksheet and clicking the Ascending Sort button [A to Z] on the toolbar.) The 270th largest number represents the 90th percentile of the distribution because 90% of the values in the sample are less than this value (and only 10% are greater than this value). For the 300 values represented in Figure 12.10, the 270th largest number in the sample is $39,106,001, which is fairly close to the recommendation of $39,252,564 suggested by our previous analysis.

One final point underscores the value of simulation. How could we answer the CFO's question using best case/worst case analysis or what-if analysis? The fact is, we could not answer the question with any degree of accuracy without using simulation to obtain the cumulative frequencies shown in Figure 12.10.

THE UNCERTAINTY OF SAMPLING

To this point, we have used simulation to generate 300 observations on our bottom-line performance measure and then calculated various statistics to describe the characteristics and behavior of the performance measure. For example, Figure 12.8 indicates that the mean of our sample is approximately $35.9 million. Using the results in Figure 12.10, we estimate that approximately a 90% chance exists for the performance measure assuming a value less than $39.2 million. But what if we repeat this process and generate another 300 observations? Would the sample mean for the new 300 observations also be $35.9 million? Or would exactly 90% of the observations in the new sample be less than $39.2 million?

The answer to both of these questions is "probably not." The sample of 300 observations used in our analysis was taken from a population of values that is theoretically infinite in size. That is, if we had enough time and our computer had enough memory, we could generate an infinite number of values for our bottom-line performance measure. Theoretically, we could then analyze this infinite population of values to determine its true mean value, its true standard deviation, and the true probability of the performance measure being less than $39.2 million. Unfortunately, we do not have the time or computer resources to determine these true characteristics (or parameters) of the population. The best we can do is take a sample from this population and, based on our sample, make estimates about the true characteristics of the underlying population. Our estimates will differ depending on the sample we choose and the size of the sample.

The mean of the sample we take is probably not equal to the true mean we would observe if we could analyze the entire population of values for our performance measure. The sample mean we calculate is just an estimate of the true population mean. In our example problem, we estimated that a 90% chance exists for our output variable to assume a value less than $39.2 million. However, this most likely is not equal to the true probability we would calculate if we could analyze the entire population. Thus, there is some element of uncertainty surrounding the statistical estimates resulting from simulation because we are using a sample to make inferences about the population. Fortunately, there are ways of measuring and describing the amount of uncertainty present in some of the estimates we make about the population under study. This is typically done by constructing confidence intervals for the population parameters being estimated.

CONSTRUCTING A CONFIDENCE INTERVAL FOR THE TRUE POPULATION MEAN

Constructing a confidence interval for the true population mean is a simple process. If $\bar{y}$ and s represent, respectively, the mean and standard deviation of a sample size n from any population, then assuming n is sufficiently large ($n \geq 30$), the Central Limit Theorem tells us that the lower and upper limits of a 95% confidence interval for the true mean of the population are represented by:

$$95\% \text{ Lower Confidence Limit} = \bar{y} - 1.96 * \frac{s}{\sqrt{n}}$$

12.11

$$95\% \text{ Upper Confidence Limit} = \bar{y} + 1.96 * \frac{s}{\sqrt{n}}$$

Although we can be fairly certain that the sample mean $\bar{y}$ we calculate from our sample data is not equal to the true population mean, we can be 95% confident that the true mean of the population falls somewhere between the lower and upper limits in equation 12.11. If we want a 90% or 99% confidence interval, we must change the value 1.96 in equation 12.11 to 1.645 or 2.575, respectively. (The values 1.645 and 2.575 represent the 95 and 99.5 percentiles of the standard normal distribution, respectively.)

For our example, the lower and upper limits of a 95% confidence interval for the true mean of the population of total company cost values can be calculated easily, as shown in cells E20 and E21 in Figure 12.11. The formulas for these cells are:

Formula for cell E20:	=E4–1.96*E8/SQRT(E16)
Formula for cell E21:	=E4+1.96*E8/SQRT(E16)

	File	Edit	View	Insert	Format	Tools	Data	Window	Help		

	A	B	C	D	E
1					
2		Company Cost		*Company Cost*	
3	1	36078007.71			
4	2	38295654.84		Mean	35972956.76
5	3	35660471.43		Standard Error	135320.1886
6	4	39106001.67		Median	35830013.74
7	5	36519235.53		Mode	#N/A
8	6	35851519.67		Standard Deviation	2343814.42
9	7	36254870.2		Sample Variance	5.49347E+12
10	8	36279745.84		Kurtosis	-0.111970995
11	9	35623911.66		Skewness	0.170151423
12	10	34614220.06		Range	12659195.05
13	11	35905138.11		Minimum	30316661.78
14	12	31018989.85		Maximum	42975856.84
15	13	33772094.16		Sum	10791887027
16	14	34903342.04		Count	300
17	15	34182979.77		Confidence Level(95.000%)	265222.3033
18	16	37626222.91			
19	17	38396921.75			
20	18	39698101.18		95% Lower Confidence Limit:	$35,707,729
21	19	36117075.26		95% Upper Confidence Limit:	$36,238,184
22	20	37532159.66			
23	21	40061671.97		Target Proportion	0.90
24	22	39244089.2		95% Lower Confidence Limit:	0.866
25	23	35010396.82		95% Upper Confidence Limit:	0.934
26	24	35706679.51			
27	25	35919389.3			

Key Cell Formulas

Cell	Formula	Copied to
E20	=E4−1.96*E8/SQRT(E16)	—
E21	=E4+1.96*E8/SQRT(E16)	—
E24	=E23−1.96*SQRT((E23*(1−E23))/E16)	—
E25	=E23+1.96*SQRT((E23*(1−E23))/E16)	—

Figure 12.11: *Confidence intervals for population mean and population proportion*

Thus, we can be 95% confident that the true mean of the population of total company cost values falls somewhere in the interval from $35,707,729 to $36,238,184.

CONSTRUCTING A CONFIDENCE INTERVAL FOR A POPULATION PROPORTION

In our example we estimated that 90% of the population of total company cost values fall below $39.2 million based on our sample of 300 observations. However, if we could evaluate the entire population of total cost values, we might find that only 80% of these values fall below $39.2 million. Or we might find that 99% of the entire population falls below this mark. It would be helpful to determine how accurate the 90% value is. So, at times we might want to construct a confidence interval for the true proportion of a population that falls below (or above) some value, say Y_p.

To see how this is done, let $\bar{p}$ denote the proportion of observations in a sample of size n that falls below some value Y_p. Assuming that n is sufficiently large ($n \geq 30$), the Central Limit Theorem tells us that the lower and upper limits of a 95% confidence interval for the true proportion of the population falling below Y_p are represented by:

$$95\% \text{ Lower Confidence Limit} = \bar{p} - 1.96 * \sqrt{\frac{\bar{p}(1 - \bar{p})}{n}}$$

$$95\% \text{ Upper Confidence Limit} = \bar{p} + 1.96 * \sqrt{\frac{\bar{p}(1 - \bar{p})}{n}}$$

12.12

Although we can be fairly certain that the proportion of observations falling below Y_p in our sample is not equal to the true proportion of the population falling below Y_p, we can be 95% confident that the true proportion of the population falling below Y_p is contained within the lower and upper limits in equation 12.12. Again, if we want a 90% or 99% confidence interval, we must change the value 1.96 in equation 12.12 to 1.645 or 2.575, respectively.

Using these formulas, we can calculate the lower and upper limits of a 95% confidence interval for the true proportion of the population falling below $39.2 million. From our simulation results, we know that 90% of the observations in our sample are less than $39.2 million. Thus, our estimated value of $\bar{p}$ is 0.90. This value was entered into cell E23 in Figure 12.11. The upper and lower limits of a 95% confidence interval for the true proportion of the population falling below $39.2 million are calculated in cells E24 and E25 of Figure 12.11 using the following formulas:

Formula for cell E24:   =E23–1.96*SQRT(E23*(1–E23)/E16)

Formula for cell E25:   =E23+1.96*SQRT(E23*(1–E23)/E16)

We can be 95% confident that the true proportion of the population of total cost values falling below $39.2 million is between 0.866 and 0.934. Because this interval is fairly tight around the value 0.90, we can be reasonably certain that the $39.2 million figure quoted to the CFO has approximately a 10% chance of being exceeded.

SAMPLE SIZES AND CONFIDENCE INTERVAL WIDTHS

The formulas for the confidence intervals in equations 12.11 and 12.12 depend directly on the number of replications (n) in the simulation. As the number of replications (n) increases, the width of the confidence interval decreases (or becomes more precise). Thus, for a given level of confidence (for example, 95%), the only way to make the upper and lower limits of the interval closer together (or tighter) is to make n larger—that is, use a larger sample size. A larger sample should provide more information about the population and, therefore, allow us to be more accurate in estimating the true parameters of the population.

THE BENEFITS OF SIMULATION

What have we accomplished through simulation? Are we really better off than if we had just used the results of the original model proposed in Figure 12.2? The estimated value for the expected total cost to the company in Figure 12.2 is comparable to that obtained through simulation (although this will not always be the case). But remember that the goal of modeling is to give us greater insight into a problem to help us make more informed decisions.

The results of our simulation analysis do give us greater insight into the example problem. In particular, we now have some idea of the best and worst case total cost outcomes for the company. We have a better idea of the distribution and variability of the possible outcomes, and a more precise idea about where the mean of the distribution is located. We also now have a way of determining how likely it is for the actual outcome to fall above or below some value. Thus, in addition to our greater insight and understanding of the problem, we also have solid empirical evidence (the facts and figures) to support our recommendations.

ADDITIONAL USES OF SIMULATION

Earlier we indicated that simulation is a technique that *describes* the behavior or characteristics of a bottom-line performance measure. The next two examples show how describing the behavior of a performance measure gives a manager a useful tool in determining the optimal value for one or more controllable parameters in a decision problem. These examples reinforce the mechanics of using simulation and also demonstrate some additional simulation modeling techniques.

AN INVENTORY CONTROL EXAMPLE

According to the *Wall Street Journal* (7/18/94), U.S. businesses had a combined inventory worth $884.77 billion dollars as of the end of May 1994. Because so much money is tied up in inventories, businesses face many important decisions regarding the management of these assets. Frequently asked questions regarding inventory include:

- What's the best level of inventory for a business to maintain?
- When should goods be reordered (or manufactured)?
- How much safety stock should be held in inventory?

The study of inventory control principles is split into two distinct areas—one assumes that demand is known (or deterministic), and the other assumes that demand is random (or stochastic). If demand is known, various formulas can be derived that provide answers to the previous questions. (An example of one such formula is given in the discussion of the EOQ model in chapter 8.) However, when demand for a product is uncertain or random, answers to the previous questions cannot be expressed in terms of a simple formula. In these situations, the technique of simulation proves to be a useful tool, as illustrated in the following example.

Laura Tanner is the owner of Computers of Tomorrow (COT), a retail computer store in Austin, Texas. Competition in retail computer sales is fierce—both in terms of price and service. Laura is concerned about the number of stockouts occurring on a popular type of computer monitor. This monitor is priced competitively and generates a marginal profit of $45 per unit sold. Stockouts are very costly to the business because when customers cannot buy this item at COT, they simply buy it from a competing store and COT loses the sale (there are no backorders). Laura measures the effects of stockouts on her business in terms of **service level**, or the percentage of total demand that can be satisfied from inventory.

Laura has been following the policy of ordering 50 monitors whenever her daily ending inventory position (defined as ending inventory on hand plus outstanding orders) falls below her reorder point of 28 units. Laura places the order at the beginning of the next day. Orders are delivered at the beginning of the day and, therefore, can be used to satisfy demand on that day. For example, if the ending inventory position on day 2 is less than 28, Laura places the order at the beginning of day 3. If the actual time between order and delivery, or **lead time**, turns out to be 4 days, then the order arrives at the start of day 7. The current level of on-hand inventory is 50 units and no orders are pending.

COT sells an average of 6 monitors per day. However, the actual number sold on any given day can vary. By reviewing her sales records for the past several months, Laura determined that the daily demand for this monitor is a random variable that can be described by the following probability distribution:

Units Demanded:	0	1	2	3	4	5	6	7	8	9	10
Probability:	0.01	0.02	0.04	0.06	0.09	0.14	0.18	0.22	0.16	0.06	0.02

The manufacturer of this computer monitor is located in California. Although it takes an average of 4 days for COT to receive an order from this company, Laura has determined that the lead time of a shipment of monitors is also a random variable that can be described by the following probability distribution:

Lead Time (days):	3	4	5
Probability:	0.2	0.6	0.2

One way to guard against stockouts and improve the service level is to increase the reorder point for the item so that more inventory is on hand to meet the demand occurring during the lead time. Laura wants to determine the reorder point that results in an average service level of 99%.

CREATING THE RNGS

To solve this problem, we need to build a model to represent the inventory of computer monitors during an average month of 30 days. This model must account for the random daily demands that can occur and the random lead times encountered when orders are placed. First we'll consider how to create RNGs to model the daily demands and order lead times. Both variables are examples of *general, discrete* random variables because the possible outcomes they assume consist solely of integers, and the probabilities associated with each outcome are not equal (or not uniform).

To simulate the random order lead times, we need an RNG that returns the value 3 with probability 0.2, the value 4 with probability 0.6, and the value 5 with probability 0.2. Recall that RAND() returns a uniformly distributed random number between 0 and 1. If we subdivide the interval from 0 to 1 into three mutually exclusive and exhaustive pieces with widths corresponding to the probabilities associated with each possible lead time, we get:

Lower Limit	Upper Limit	Lead Time
0.0	0.19$\overline{9}$	3
0.2	0.79$\overline{9}$	4
0.8	0.99$\overline{9}$	5

The numbers generated by the RAND( ) function fall in the first interval (from 0 to 0.19$\overline{9}$) approximately 20% of the time, the second interval (from 0.2 to 0.79$\overline{9}$) approximately 60% of the time, and the third interval (from 0.8 to 0.99$\overline{9}$) approximately 20% of the time. The width of each of these intervals corresponds directly to the desired probability of each lead time value. So if we associate each interval with the indicated lead times, a lead time of 3 days has a 20% chance of occurring, a 4-day lead time has a 60% chance of occurring, and a 5-day lead time has a 20% chance of occurring.

We can use similar logic to break the interval from 0 to 1 into 11 mutually exclusive and exhaustive intervals to correspond to the different random demands that might occur. The intervals for both of the random variables in this problem are entered in Excel as shown in Figure 12.12 (and in the file FIG12-12.XLS on your data disk).

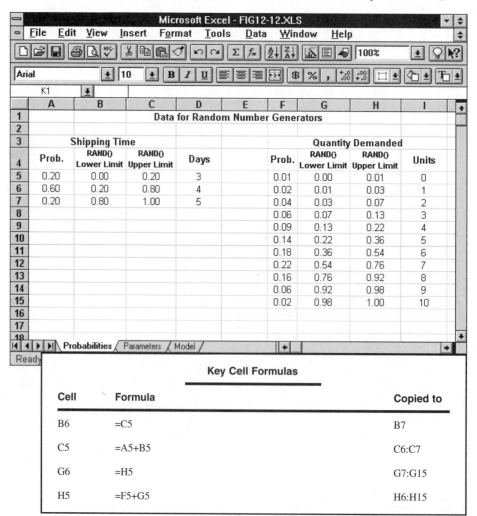

Figure 12.12: Probability distributions for shipping times and demand for COT's inventory problem

Given the data in Figure 12.12, we can use the following formulas to generate random order lead times and random daily demands that follow the appropriate probability distributions:

RNG for order lead time: =VLOOKUP(RAND(),$B$5:$D$7,3)

RNG for daily demand: =VLOOKUP(RAND(),$G$5:$I$15,3)

The RNG for order lead time generates a random number between 0 and 1 (using RAND()) then attempts to look up this value in column B, the first column in the range B5 through D7. If an exact match for the value generated by RAND() is not found, VLOOKUP selects the row in column B that contains the largest value that is *less than* the value generated by RAND(). The final argument in the VLOOKUP function (the value 3) causes the function to return the value in the third column (column D) of the selected row. For example, if the RAND() function returns the value 0.63, the VLOOKUP function would first match this with the value 0.2 in cell B6, because this is the largest value in column B that is less than 0.63. The function then returns the value 4 found in cell D6.

The VLOOKUP function for the RNG for daily demand operates in a similar manner. (Note that the two columns labeled "RAND() Upper Limit" in Figure 12.12 are not necessary but were included for clarity.) Implementing the RNGs in this way enables us to conveniently modify the probabilities associated with a random variable, and to easily implement an RNG for a general, discrete random variable that has numerous outcomes—such as the daily demand random variable in the current problem.

IMPLEMENTING THE MODEL

Now that we have a way of generating the random numbers needed in this problem, we can consider how the model should be built. As shown in Figure 12.13, we begin by creating a worksheet that lists the basic parameters for the model (or variables that are under the decision maker's control).

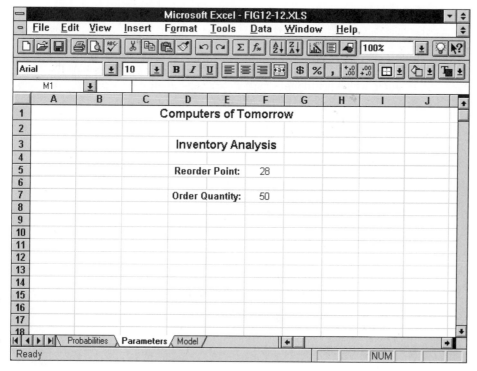

Figure 12.13: Parameters worksheet for COT's inventory problem

Laura wants to determine the reorder point that results in an average service level of 99%. Cell F5 in Figure 12.13 is used to represent the reorder point. The order quantity for the problem is given in cell F7 so that Laura could also use this model to investigate the impact of changes in order quantity.

Figure 12.14 shows the model representing 30 days of inventory activity. In this spreadsheet, column B represents the inventory on hand at the beginning of each day, which is simply the ending inventory from the previous day. The formulas in column B are:

Formula in cell B3:   =50

Formula in cell B4:   =F3

(copy to B5 through B32)

Column C represents the number of units scheduled to be received each day. We'll discuss the formulas in column C after we discuss columns H, I, and J, which relate to ordering and order lead times.

In column D, we use the technique described earlier to generate random daily demands, as:

Formula for cell D3:   =VLOOKUP(RAND(),Probabilities!$G$5:$I$15,3)

(copy to D4 through D32)

Because it is possible for demand to exceed the available supply, column E indicates how much of the daily demand can be met. If the beginning inventory (in column B) plus the ordered units received (in column C) is greater than or equal to the actual demand, then all the demand can be satisfied; otherwise, COT can sell only as many units as are available. This condition is modeled as:

Formula for cell E3:   =MIN(B3+C3,D3)

(copy to E4 through E32)

The values in column F represent the on-hand inventory at the end of each day, and are calculated as:

Formula for cell F3:   =B3+C3–E3

(copy to F4 through F32)

To determine whether or not to place an order, we first must calculate the inventory position, which was defined earlier as the ending inventory plus any outstanding orders. This is implemented in column G as follows:

Formula for cell G3:   =F3

Formula for cell G4:   =G3–E4+IF(H3=1,Parameters!$F$7,0)

(copy to G5 through G32)

Column H indicates if an order should be placed based on inventory position and the reorder point, as:

Formula for cell H3:   =IF(G3<Parameters!$F$5,1,0)

(copy to H4 through H32)

If an order is placed, we must generate the random lead time required to receive the order. This is done in column I as:

Formula for cell I3:   =IF(H3=0,0,VLOOKUP(RAND(),Probabilities!$B$5:$D$7,3))

(copy to I4 through I32)

	File	Edit	View	Insert	Format	Tools	Data	Window	Help		
	A	B	C	D	E	F	G	H	I	J	K	L
1			Units	Quantity	Demand		Inv.	Order?	Lead	Arrives		
2	Day	Beg. Inv.	Received	Demanded	Satisfied	End. Inv.	Pos.	(0=n,1=y)	Time	On Day		
3	1	50	0	9	9	41	41	0	0	0		
4	2	41	0	5	5	36	36	0	0	0		
5	3	36	0	5	5	31	31	0	0	0		
6	4	31	0	2	2	29	29	0	0	0		
7	5	29	0	8	8	21	21	1	5	11		
8	6	21	0	7	7	14	64	0	0	0		
9	7	14	0	9	9	5	55	0	0	0		
10	8	5	0	6	5	0	50	0	0	0		
11	9	0	0	9	0	0	50	0	0	0		
12	10	0	0	2	0	0	50	0	0	0		
13	11	0	50	1	1	49	49	0	0	0		
14	12	49	0	7	7	42	42	0	0	0		
15	13	42	0	8	8	34	34	0	0	0		
16	14	34	0	4	4	30	30	0	0	0		
17	15	30	0	7	7	23	23	1	3	19		
18	16	23	0	9	9	14	64	0	0	0		
19	17	14	0	7	7	7	57	0	0	0		
20	18	7	0	6	6	1	51	0	0	0		
21	19	1	50	7	7	44	44	0	0	0		
22	20	44	0	8	8	36	36	0	0	0		
23	21	36	0	5	5	31	31	0	0	0		
24	22	31	0	5	5	26	26	1	4	27		
25	23	26	0	9	9	17	67	0	0	0		
26	24	17	0	9	9	8	58	0	0	0		
27	25	8	0	6	6	2	52	0	0	0		
28	26	2	0	7	2	0	50	0	0	0		
29	27	0	50	3	3	47	47	0	0	0		
30	28	47	0	6	6	41	41	0	0	0		
31	29	41	0	9	9	32	32	0	0	0		
32	30	32	0	7	7	25	25	1	4	35		
33			Service Level:		91.15%							

Key Cell Formulas

Cell	Formula	Copied to
B4	=F3	B5:B32
C4	=COUNTIF($J$3:J3,A4)*Parameters!$F$7	C5:C32
D3	=VLOOKUP(RAND(),Probabilities!$G$5:$I$15,3)	D4:D32
E3	=MIN(D3,B3+C3)	E4:E32
E33	=SUM(E3:E32)/SUM(D3:D32)	—
F3	=B3+C3–E3	F4:F32
G3	=F3	—
G4	=G3–E4+IF(H3=1,Parameters!$F$7,0)	G5:G32
H3	=IF(G3<Parameters!$F$5,1,0)	H4:H32
I3	=IF(H3=0,0,VLOOKUP(RAND(),Probabilities!$B$5:$D$7,3))	I4:I32
J3	=IF(I3=0,0,A3+1+I3)	J4:J32

Figure 12.14: Spreadsheet representing a random month of inventory data

This formula returns the value 0 if no order was placed (if H3 = 0); otherwise, it returns a random lead time value (if H3 = 1).

If an order is placed, column J indicates the day on which the order will be received based on its random lead time in column I. This is done as:

Formula for cell J3:   =IF(H3=0,0,A3+1+I3))
(copy to I4 through I32)

The values in column C are coordinated with those in column J. The non-zero values in column J indicate the days on which orders will be received. For example, cell J7 indicates that an order will be received on day 11. The actual receipt of this order is reflected by the value of 50 in cell C13, which represents the receipt of an order at the beginning of day 11. The formula in cell C13 that achieves this is:

Formula for cell C13:   =COUNTIF($J$3:J12,A13)*Parameters!$F$7

This formula counts how many times the value in cell A13 (representing day 11) appears as a scheduled receipt day between days 1 through 10 in column J. This represents the number of orders scheduled to be received on day 11. We then multiply this by the order quantity (50), given in cell F7 on the Parameters worksheet, to determine the total units to be received on day 11. So the values in column C are generated as:

Formula for cell C3:   =0

Formula for cell C4:   =COUNTIF($J$3:J3,A4)*Parameters!$F$7
(copy to C5 through C32)

The service level for the model is calculated in cell E33 using the values in columns D and E as:

Formula for cell E33:   =SUM(E3:E32)/SUM(D3:D32)

Again, the service level represents the proportion of total demand that can be satisfied from inventory.

REPLICATING THE MODEL

The model in Figure 12.14 indicates one possible scenario that could occur if Laura uses a reorder point of 28 units for the computer monitor. In the scenario shown, the value in cell E33 indicates that 91.15% of the total demand is satisfied. By replicating this model over and over, Laura could keep track of the service level occurring in each replication and average these values to determine the expected service level obtained with a reorder point of 28.

Using the simulation techniques described earlier, Laura could repeat this process with reorder points of 30 units, 32 units, and so on, until she finds the reorder point that achieved her goal of an average service level of 99%. However, there is another, easier way that Laura can perform the replications, as shown in Figure 12.15.

We prepared the spreadsheet in Figure 12.15 to replicate our model using a two-input (or two-way) data table. In cell B11 we entered the value 1 and used the Edit, Fill, Series command to fill the remainder of this column with the values 2, 3, and so on, up to 200. Cells C10 through G10 contain the values 28, 30, 32, 34, and 36, respectively, to represent a variety of reorder points that Laura might want to investigate to determine which reorder point will produce the desired service level. To track the service level associated with each replication of the model, the following formula is entered in cell B10:

Formula in cell B10:   =Model!E33

Figure 12.15: Spreadsheet prepared to simulate the service level at various reorder points using a two-way data table

Important Software Note

When using a two-way data table, the formula whose value you want to track must be placed in the upper-left corner of the data table range.

We can now use the Data Table command to instruct Excel to substitute each value in the range C10 through G10 into cell F5 and recalculate the workbook 200 times, keeping track of the value that results in cell B10 for each replication. This is done as follows:

1. Select the range B10 through G210.

2. Click the Data menu.

3. Click Table.

4. In the Table dialog box, enter cell F5 for the Row input cell and enter cell A1 for the Column input cell.

5. Click OK.

Excel substitutes each value in the range C10 through G10 into cell F5. For each value substituted into cell F5, each value in the range B11 through B210 is substituted into cell A1 and the workbook is recalculated. The resulting value in cell B10 (representing the service level occurring in that replication) is then recorded in the appropriate cell in the data table. For each reorder point value entered into cell F5, the workbook is replicated 200 times and the service level observed in each replication is recorded in the appropriate column of the data table. This could take several seconds to several minutes depending on the speed of your computer. The results of this operation (after some simple formatting) are shown in Figure 12.16. (The random numbers you generate will *not* match those shown in Figure 12.16.)

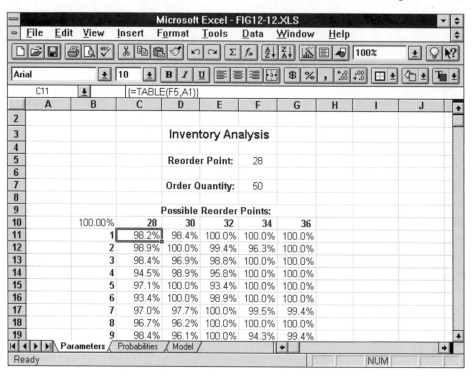

Figure 12.16: Results of the Data Table command for COT's inventory problem

Each new entry Excel created starting in cell C11 contains the array formula {=TABLE(F5,A1)}. This is how the Data Table command performs the repeated substitution and recalculation. If we don't change these formulas into values, every time the spreadsheet is recalculated we'll have to wait for this process to re-execute and we'll get a new sample of 200 replications for each reorder point listed at the top of the data table. To convert the contents of the data table into values:

1. Select the range C11 through G210.
2. Click the Edit menu.
3. Click Copy.
4. Click the Edit menu.
5. Click Paste Special.
6. Click Values.
7. Click OK.
8. Press [Enter].

The values in the data table are now numeric constants that will not change even if the spreadsheet is recalculated.

DATA ANALYSIS

The results of the simulation can be summarized easily using the Descriptive Statistics command described earlier. To do this:

1. Click the Tools menu.

2. Click Data Analysis.

3. Click Descriptive Statistics.

4. Complete the Descriptive Statistics dialog box, as shown in Figure 12.17.

5. Click OK. (This operation might take a minute or two if your computer is slow.)

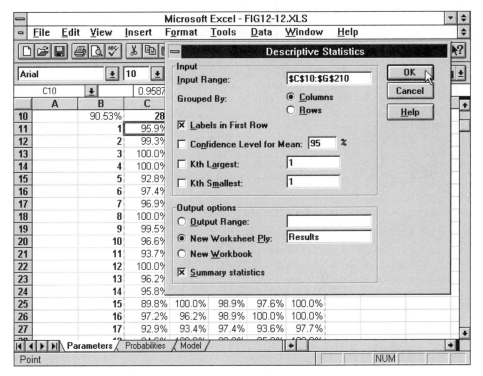

Figure 12.17: Descriptive Statistics dialog box for COT's inventory problem

The descriptive statistics about the sample data are placed on a new worksheet named Results. After deleting some of the extraneous information produced by the Descriptive Statistics command, and after some simple formatting, the results appear as shown in Figure 12.18.

Figure 12.18 indicates that COT's current reorder point of 28 units results in an average service level of approximately 96.24%. This implies that COT is unable to satisfy approximately 3.76% of the total demand using this reorder point. Cell C9 translates this into dollars as:

Formula for cell C9:   =(1–C4)*6*30*45
(copy to D9 through G9)

Because the average daily demand for the monitor is for 6 units, and each monitor sold generates a marginal profit of $45, cell C9 indicates that in an average month COT loses about $304.64 in profits due to stockouts on this item.

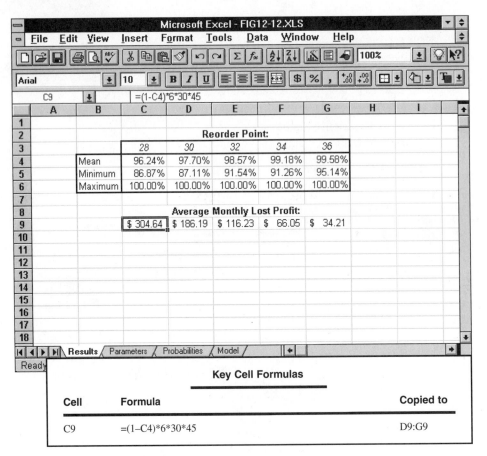

Figure 12.18: Simulation results for COT's inventory problem

However, our simulation results indicate that as the reorder point increases, the service level also increases and the percentage of lost sales decreases. Thus, if Laura increases the reorder point to 36, COT's average service level for the monitor would increase to 99.58% and the average monthly profit lost due to stockouts would decrease to approximately $34.21.

A FINAL COMMENT ON THE INVENTORY EXAMPLE

Although increasing the reorder point decreases the percentage of lost sales, it also increases the average level of inventory held and the number of orders that must be placed. Thus, another objective that might be considered in this problem involves weighing the costs of holding more inventory and placing more orders against the benefits of having fewer lost sales. We'll consider such an objective further in one of the problems at the end of this chapter.

AN OVERBOOKING EXAMPLE

Businesses that allow customers to make reservations for services (such as airlines, hotels, and car rental companies) know that some percentage of the reservations made will not be used for one reason or another, leaving these companies with a difficult decision problem. If they accept reservations for only the number of customers that can actually be served, then a portion of the company's assets will be underutilized when some customers with reservations fail to arrive. This results in an opportunity loss for the company. On the other hand, if they overbook (or accept more reservations than can be handled), then at times more customers will arrive than can actually be served. This typically results in additional financial costs to the company and often generates ill-will among those customers who cannot be served. The following example illustrates how simulation might be used to help a company determine the optimal number of reservations to accept.

Marty Ford is an operations analyst for Piedmont Commuter Airlines (PCA). Recently, Marty was asked to make a recommendation on how many reservations PCA should book on Flight 343—a flight in high demand from a small regional airport to a major hub airport. Historical data show that PCA frequently has seats left on Flight 343 if it accepts only 19 reservations (the plane's capacity). Industry statistics show that for every ticket sold for a commuter flight, a 0.10 probability exists that the ticket holder will not be on the flight. PCA sells nonrefundable tickets for Flight 343 for $85 per seat. Thus, every empty seat on this flight represents an opportunity cost—even if a no-show customer had purchased a ticket for the seat—because the seat could be filled by another passenger paying $85. On the other hand, if PCA overbooks this flight and more than 19 passengers show up, some of them will have to be bumped to a later flight. To compensate for the inconvenience of being bumped, PCA gives these passengers vouchers for a free meal, a free flight at a later date, and sometimes also pays for them to stay overnight in a hotel near the airport. PCA pays an average of $155 for each passenger who gets bumped. Marty wants to determine if PCA can increase profits by overbooking this flight and, if so, how many reservations should be accepted to produce the maximum average profit. Marty wants to set up a model that allows him to investigate the consequences of accepting up to 24 reservations.

IMPLEMENTING THE MODEL

A spreadsheet model for this problem is shown in Figure 12.19 (and in the file FIG12-19.XLS on your data disk).

This spreadsheet begins by listing the relevant data from the problem, including the number of seats available on the plane, the price PCA charges for each seat, the probability of a no-show (or a ticketed passenger not arriving in time for the flight), the cost of bumping passengers, and the number of reservations that will be accepted.

Cell G10 represents the random number of ticketed passengers who arrive for a flight. An RNG for this quantity is implemented in the worksheet named Passengers and will be described in detail shortly. The value produced by this RNG is returned in cell G10 using the following formula:

Formula for cell G10:   =Passengers!B28

Cell G12 represents the marginal profit that PCA earns by accepting a given number of reservations. The formula for this cell is:

Formula for cell G12:   =G5*G8–G5*MAX(0,G4–G10)–G7*MAX(0,G10–G4)

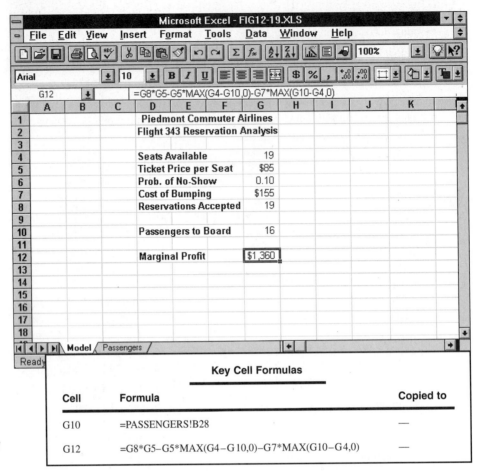

Figure 12.19: *Spreadsheet model for PCA's overbooking problem*

The first term in this formula (G5*G8) reflects the fact that PCA earns $85 for each reservation it accepts because its customers must pay for their tickets in advance, and tickets are nonrefundable. The next term (−G5*MAX(0,G4−G10)) indicates that PCA incurs an opportunity loss of $85 for each empty seat (or the amount by which G4 exceeds G10). The last term in this formula (−G7*MAX(0,G10−G4)) indicates that PCA incurs an average cost of $155 for each passenger that must be bumped when the number of passengers wanting to board exceeds the number of available seats (or the amount by which G10 exceeds G4).

CREATING THE RNGs

The uncertain, or random, element of this problem is the number of passengers arriving to board the plane, represented in cell G10 in Figure 12.19. We'll denote the number of passengers arriving to board the flight by R. If $n \geq R$ tickets are sold and each ticket holder has a $p = 0.1$ probability of not showing up (or $1 - p = 0.9$ probability of showing up), then R is a random variable that follows the binomial probability distribution—or a binomial random variable. Figure 12.20 shows one approach to creating an RNG for this binomial random variable.

	File	Edit	View	Insert	Format	Tools	Data	Window	Help

	A	B	C	D	E	F	G	H	I	J
1										
2	Passenger	Show up?								
3	Number	(0=n, 1=y)								
4	1	1								
5	2	1								
6	3	1								
7	4	1								
8	5	1								
9	6	1								
10	7	1								
11	8	1								
12	9	1								
13	10	1								
14	11	0								
15	12	1								
16	13	1								
17	14	0								
18	15	1								
19	16	1								
20	17	1								
21	18	1								
22	19	0								
23	20	0								
24	21	0								
25	22	0								
26	23	0								
27	24	0								
28	Sum	16								
29										

Key Cell Formulas

Cell	Formula	Copied to
B4	=IF(A4>MODEL!$G$8,0,IF(RAND()<MODEL!$G$6,0,1))	—
B28	=SUM(B4:B27)	—

Figure 12.20: Spreadsheet to calculate the number of passengers arriving to board

Because Marty wants to investigate the effects of accepting up to 24 reservations, up to 24 passengers could arrive to board a single flight. Each of these potential passengers is represented by one of the rows in Figure 12.20. However, the maximum number of passengers that can show up is determined by n, the number of reservations accepted (represented by cell G8 in Figure 12.19). Each passenger with a reservation has a probability p of not showing up (represented by cell G6 in Figure 12.19). The following formula determines whether each of the passengers listed has a reservation and, if so, whether or not each will be a no-show.

Formula for cell B4: =IF(A4>Model!$G$8,0,IF(RAND()<Model!$G$6,0,1))
(copy to B5 through B27)

The first IF statement determines whether the passenger number in column A is greater than the number of reservations accepted (given by cell G8 in the Model worksheet). If so, the value 0 is returned, indicating that the passenger will not show up because this passenger would not have been given a reservation in the first place. Otherwise, the passenger in column A has a reservation, and the second IF statement uses the RAND() function to generate a uniform random number between 0 and 1. If RAND() returns a value less than p (the probability of a no-show given in cell G6 in the Model worksheet), then the value 0 is returned, indicating that the passenger will be a no-show; otherwise the value 1 is returned, indicating that this passenger will show up. The formula in cell B28 sums the values in column B and represents the random number of passengers with reservations that will show up to board the flight.

Formula in cell B28: =SUM(B4:B27)

Note that this value is also reported in cell G10 in the Model worksheet shown in Figures 12.19 and 12.21.

REPLICATING THE MODEL

Marty wants to determine the number of reservations to accept that, on average, will result in the highest marginal profit. Figure 12.21 shows the spreadsheet in the format of a two-way data table.

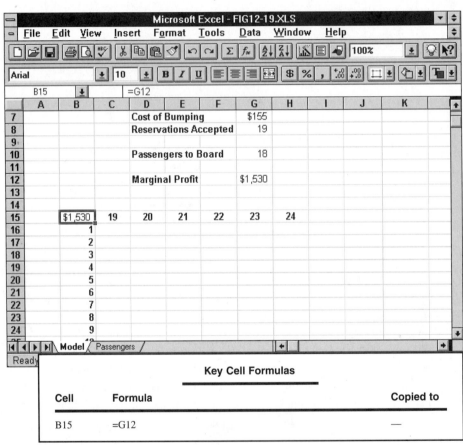

Figure 12.21: Spreadsheet prepared to simulate the average profit achieved by accepting different numbers of reservations using a two-way data table

In cell B16, we entered the value 1 and used the Edit, Fill, Series command to fill the remainder of this column with the values 2, 3, and so on, up to 200. Cells C15 through H15 contain the values 19, 20, 21, 22, 23, and 24, respectively, to represent different numbers of reservations that PCA might accept. The formula in cell B15 refers back to the marginal profit in cell G12 because this is the bottom-line performance measure we want to track in this model.

Formula for cell B15: =G12

We can now use the Data Table command to instruct Excel to substitute each value in the range C15 through H15 into cell G8 and recalculate the spreadsheet 200 times, keeping track of the value that results in cell B15 for each replication. This is done as follows:

1. Select the range B15 through H215.

2. Click the Data menu.

3. Click Table

4. In the Table dialog box, enter cell G8 for the Row input cell and enter cell A1 for the Column input cell.

5. Click OK.

Excel substitutes each value in the range C15 through H15 into cell G8. For each value substituted into cell G8, each value in the range B16 through B215 is substituted into cell A1 and the workbook is recalculated. The resulting value in cell B15 (representing the marginal profit earned in that replication) is then recorded in the appropriate cell in the data table. So for each possible number of reservations entered into cell G8, the spreadsheet is replicated 200 times and the marginal profit observed in each replication is recorded in the appropriate column of the data table. Again, this could take several seconds to several minutes depending on the speed of your computer.

When Excel is finished running the replications, we need to convert the formula entries in the data table into values by completing the following:

1. Select the range C16 through H215.

2. Click the Edit menu.

3. Click Copy.

4. Click the Edit menu.

5. Click Paste Special.

6. Click Values.

7. Click OK.

8. Press [Enter].

Figure 12.22 shows the results of the simulation and the average profit associated with each number of reservations accepted. (Your results will *not* match those shown in Figure 12.22.) These averages are calculated as:

Formula for cell C14:   =AVERAGE(C16:C215)
(copy to D14 through H14)

The averages in Figure 12.22 indicate that if PCA accepts only 19 reservations, its average marginal profit on this flight will be $1,451 (assuming vacant seats are counted as an opportunity cost at $85 per seat). As the number of reservations accepted increases, the average profit also increases and reaches a maximum of $1,675 at 22 reservations. Thus, it appears that the optimal number of reservations for PCA to accept is 22.

Figure 12.22: *Simulation results for PCA's over-booking problem*

A FINAL COMMENT ON THE OVERBOOKING EXAMPLE

This problem assumed that all the reservations available for Flight 343 would always be taken—or that there would never be unused reservations. However, if PCA accepts up to 22 reservations, there might be times when only 16 or 17 seats would be demanded. Thus, the demand for seats of this flight could be modeled more accurately as a random variable. We'll explore this issue more fully in one of the problems at the end of this chapter.

SUMMARY

This chapter introduced the concept of risk analysis and simulation. Many of the input cells in a spreadsheet represent random variables whose values cannot be determined with certainty. Any uncertainty in the input cells flows through the spreadsheet model to create a related uncertainty in the value of the output cell(s). Decisions made on the basis of these uncertain values involve some degree of risk.

Various methods of risk analysis are available, including best case/worst case analysis, what-if analysis, and simulation. Of these three methods, simulation is the only technique that provides hard evidence (facts and figures) that can be used objectively in making decisions. To simulate a model, RNGs are used to select representative values for each uncertain independent variable in the model. This process is repeated over and over to generate a sample of representative values for the dependent variable(s) in the model. The variability and distribution of the sample values for the dependent variable(s) can then be analyzed to gain insight into the possible outcomes that might occur. This technique can also be used to test different configurations of controllable parameters in the model in an attempt to determine the optimal values for these parameters.

REFERENCES

Banks, J. and J. Carson. *Discrete-Event Simulation*. Englewood Cliffs, NJ: Prentice Hall, 1984.

Hamzawi, S. "Management and Planning of Airport Gate Capacity: A Microcomputer-Based Gate Assignment Simulation Model." *Transportation Planning and Technology*, vol. 11, 1986.

Kaplan, A. and S. Frazza. "Empirical Inventory Simulation: A Case Study." *Decision Sciences*, vol. 14, January 1983.

Khoshnevis, B. *Discrete Systems Simulation*. New York: McGraw-Hill, 1994.

Law, A. and W. Kelton. *Simulation Modeling and Analysis*. New York: McGraw-Hill, 1990.

Marcus, A. "The Magellan Fund and Market Efficiency." *Journal of Portfolio Management*, Fall 1990.

Russell, R. and R. Hickle. "Simulation of a CD Portfolio." *Interfaces*, vol. 16, no. 3, 1986.

Vollman, T., W. Berry and C. Whybark. *Manufacturing Planning and Control Systems*. Homewood, IL: Irwin, 1987.

Watson, H. *Computer Simulation in Business*. New York: Wiley, 1981.

The U.S. Postal Service Moves to the Fast Lane

Source: Cebry, Michael E., Anura H. deSilva and Fred J. DiLisio, "Management Science in Automating Postal Operations: Facility and Equipment Planning in the United States Postal Service," *Interfaces*, vol. 22, no. 1, January-February 1992, pages 110-130.

MAIL FLOWS INTO THE U.S. POSTAL SERVICE at the rate of 500 million pieces per day, and it comes in many forms. There are standard-sized letters with 9-digit ZIP codes (with or without imprinted bar codes), 5-digit ZIP codes, typed addresses that can be read by optical character readers, handwritten addresses that are barely decipherable, Christmas cards in red envelopes addressed in red ink and so on. The enormous task of sorting all these pieces at the sending post office and at the destination has caused postal management to consider and adopt many new forms of technology. These include operator-assisted mechanized sorters, optical character readers (last-line and multiple-line), and bar code sorters. Implementation of new technology brings with it associated policy decisions, such as rate discounts for bar coding by the customer, finer sorting at the origin, and so on.

A simulation model called META (model for evaluating technology alternatives) assists management in evaluating new technologies, configurations, and operating plans. Using distributions based on experience or projections of the effects of new policies, META simulates a random stream of mail of different types, routes the mail through the system configuration being tested, and prints reports detailing total pieces handled, capacity utilization, work hours required, space requirements, and cost.

META has been used on several projects associated with the Postal Service corporate automation plan. These include facilities planning, benefits of alternate sorting plans, justification of efforts to enhance address readability, planning studies for reducing the time carriers spend sorting vs. delivering, and identification of mail types that offer the greatest potential for cost savings.

According to the Associate Postmaster General, " ... META became the vehicle to help steer our organization on an entirely new course at a speed we had never before experienced."

Questions and Problems

1. Under what condition(s) is it appropriate to use simulation to analyze a model? That is, what characteristics should a model possess in order for simulation to be used?

2. The graph of the probability distribution of a normally distributed random variable with a mean of 20 and standard deviation of 3 is shown in Figure 12.3.

    a. Use the RNG for the normal distribution discussed in the chapter to generate 100 sample values from this distribution.

    b. Produce a histogram of the 100 sample values you generated. Does your histogram look like the graph for this distribution in Figure 12.3?

    c. Repeat this experiment with the same RNG, only this time sample 1,000 values.

    d. Produce a histogram for the 1,000 sample values you generated. Does the histogram now more closely resemble the graph in Figure 12.3 for this distribution?

    e. Why does your second histogram look more "normal" than the first one?

3. The manager of Moore's Catalog Showroom is trying to predict how much revenue will be generated by each major department in the store during 1996. The manager has estimated the minimum and maximum growth rates possible for revenues in each department. The manager believes that any of the possible growth rates between the minimum and maximum values are equally likely to occur. These estimates are summarized in the following table:

Department	1995 Revenues	Growth Rates	
		Minimum	Maximum
Electronics	$6,342,213	2%	10%
Garden Supplies	$1,203,231	–4%	5%
Jewelry	$4,367,342	–2%	6%
Sporting Goods	$3,543,532	–1%	8%
Toys	$4,342,132	4%	15%

Create a spreadsheet to simulate the total revenues that could occur in the coming year. Run 500 replications of the model and do the following:

a. Construct a 95% confidence interval for the average level of revenues the manager could expect for 1996.

b. According to your model, what are the chances that total revenues in 1996 will be more than 5% larger than those in 1995?

4. Lynn Price recently completed her MBA and accepted a job with an electronics manufacturing company. Although she likes her job, she is also looking forward to retiring one day. To ensure that her retirement is comfortable, Lynn intends to invest $3,000 of her salary into a tax-sheltered retirement fund at the end of each year. Lynn is not certain what rate of return this investment will earn, but she expects the rate of return could be modeled appropriately as a normally distributed random variable with a mean of 12% and standard deviation of 2%.

   a. If Lynn is 30 years old, how much money should she expect to have in her retirement fund at age 60? (Use 500 replications.)

   b. What is the probability that Lynn will have more than $1 million in her retirement fund when she reaches age 60?

5. Acme Equipment Company is considering the development of a new machine that would be marketed to tire manufacturers. Research and development costs for the project are expected to be about $4 million but could vary between $2 and $6 million. The market life for the product is estimated to be 3 to 8 years with all intervening possibilities being equally likely. The company thinks it will sell 200 units per year, but acknowledges that this figure could be as low as 50 or as high as 350. The company will sell the machine for about $23,000. Finally, the cost of manufacturing the machine is expected to be about $14,000, but could vary from $13,000 to $15,000. The company's cost of capital is 15%.

   a. Use appropriate RNGs to create a spreadsheet to calculate the possible net present values (NPVs) that could result from taking on this project.

   b. Replicate the model 500 times. What is the expected NPV for this project?

   c. What is the probability of this project generating a positive NPV for the company?

6. Representatives from the American Heart Association are planning to go door-to-door throughout a community, soliciting contributions. From past experience they know that when someone answers the door, 80% of the time it is a female and 20% of the time it is a male. They also know that 70% of the females who answer the door make a donation, whereas only 40% of the males who answer the door make donations. The amount of money that females contribute follows a normal distribution with a mean of $20 and standard deviation of $3. The amount of money males contribute follows a normal distribution with a mean of $10 and standard deviation of $2.

   a. Create a spreadsheet model that simulates what might happen whenever a representative of the American Heart Association knocks on a door and someone answers.

   b. Replicate your model 500 times. What is the average contribution the Heart Association can expect to receive when someone answers the door?

   c. Suppose that the Heart Association plans to visit 300 homes on a given Saturday. If no one is home at 25% of the residences, what is the total amount that the Heart Association can expect to receive in donations?

7. After spending 10 years as an assistant manager for a large restaurant chain, Ray Clark has decided to become his own boss. The owner of a local submarine sandwich store wants to sell the store to Ray for $65,000 to be paid in installments of $13,000 in each of the next 5 years. According to the current owner, the store brings in revenue of about $100,000 per year and incurs operating costs of about 63% of sales. Thus, once the store is paid for, Ray should make about $35,000–$40,000 per year before taxes. Until the store is paid for, he will make substantially less—but he will be his own boss. Realizing that some uncertainty is involved in this decision, Ray wants to simulate what level of net income he can expect to earn during the next 5 years as he operates and pays for the store. In particular, he wants to see what could happen if sales are allowed to vary uniformly between $80,000 and $110,000, and if operating costs are allowed to vary uniformly between 60% and 65% of sales. Assume that Ray's payments for the store are deductible and that he is in the 28% tax bracket.

    a. Create a spreadsheet model to simulate the annual net income Ray would receive during each of the next 5 years if he decides to buy the store.

    b. Given the money he has in savings, Ray thinks he can get by for the next 5 years if he can make at least $12,000 from the store each year. Replicate the model 500 times and track the minimum amount of money Ray makes over the 5-year period represented by each replication. What is the probability that Ray will make at least $12,000 in each of the next 5 years?

8. Bob Davidson owns a newsstand outside the Waterstone office building complex in Atlanta, near Hartsfield International Airport. He buys his papers wholesale at $0.50 per paper and sells them for $0.75. Bob wonders what is the optimal number of papers to order each day. Based on history, he has found that demand (even though it is discrete) can be modeled by a normal distribution with a mean of 50 and standard deviation of 5. When he has more papers than customers, he can recycle all the extra papers the next day and receive $0.05 per paper. On the other hand, if he has more customers than papers, he loses some goodwill in addition to the lost profit on the potential sale of $0.25. Bob estimates the incremental lost goodwill costs five day's worth of business (that is, dissatisfied customers will go to a competitor the next week, but come back to him the week after that).

    a. Create a spreadsheet model to determine the optimal number of papers to order each day. Use 250 replications and round the demand values generated by the normal RNG to the closest integer value.

    b. Construct a 95% confidence interval for the expected payoff from the optimal decision.

9. Vinton Auto Insurance is trying to decide how much money to keep in liquid assets to cover insurance claims. In the past, the company held some of the premiums it received in interest-bearing checking accounts and put the rest into investments that are not quite as liquid, but tend to generate a higher investment return. The company wants to study cash flows to determine how much money it should keep in liquid assets to pay claims. After

reviewing historical data, the company determined that the average repair bill per claim is normally distributed with a mean of $1,700 and standard deviation of $400. It also determined that the number of repair claims filed each week is a random variable that follows the probability distribution given below:

Number of Repair Claims	Probability
1	0.05
2	0.06
3	0.10
4	0.17
5	0.28
6	0.14
7	0.08
8	0.07
9	0.05

In addition to repair claims, the company also receives claims for cars that have been "totaled" and cannot be repaired. A 20% chance of receiving this type of claim exists in any week. Typically these claims cost anywhere from $2,000 to $20,000, with $11,000 being the most common cost.

a. Create a spreadsheet model of the total claims cost incurred by the company in any week. (Hint: Using the VLOOKUP command in combination with RAND() is the easiest way to generate the random number of repair claims occurring each week. Use the symmetric triangular function to generate the costs of "totaled" cars.)

b. Replicate the model 500 times and create a histogram of the distribution of total cost values that were generated.

c. What is the average cost the company should expect to pay each week?

d. Suppose that the company decides to keep $20,000 cash on hand to pay claims. What is the probability that this amount would not be adequate to cover claims in any week?

10. The owner of a local car dealership has just received a call from a regional distributor stating that a $5,000 bonus will be awarded if the owner's dealership sells at least 10 new cars next Saturday. On an average Saturday, this dealership has 80 potential customers look at new cars, but there is no way to determine exactly how many customers will come this particular Saturday. The owner is fairly certain that the number would not be less than 40, but

also thinks it would be unrealistic to expect more than 120 (which is the largest number of customers to ever show up in one day). To generate the number of customers who arrive at the dealership next Saturday, we might use the following RNG:

=INT(40+(120−40)*(RAND()+RAND())/2)

The owner determined that, on average, about 1 out of 10 customers who look at cars at the dealership actually purchase a car—or, a 0.10 probability (or 10% chance) exists that any given customer will buy a new car.

a. Create a spreadsheet model for this problem and generate 100 random outcomes for the number of cars the dealership might sell next Saturday. (Hint: The number of cars sold next Saturday could be modeled by first using the RNG mentioned above to generate the number of customers arriving. For each arrival, if RAND()<0.1 then that customer will buy a car.)

b. What is the probability that the dealership will earn the $5,000 bonus?

c. If you were this dealer, what is the maximum amount of money you'd be willing to spend on sales incentives to try to earn this bonus?

11. Dr. Sarah Benson is an ophthalmologist who, in addition to prescribing glasses and contact lenses, performs optical laser surgery to correct near-sightedness. This surgery is fairly easy and inexpensive to perform. Thus, it represents a potential gold mine for her practice. To inform the public about this procedure, Dr. Benson advertises in the local paper and holds information sessions in her office one night a week at which she shows a videotape about the procedure and answers any questions potential patients might have. The room where these meetings are held can seat 10 people, and reservations are required. The number of people attending each session varies from week to week. Dr. Benson cancels the meeting if 2 or fewer people have made reservations. Using data from the previous year, Dr. Benson determined that the distribution of reservations is as follows:

Number of Reservations:	0	1	2	3	4	5	6	7	8	9	10
Probability:		0.02	0.05	0.08	0.16	0.26	0.18	0.11	0.07	0.05	0.01	0.01

Using data from the past year, Dr. Benson determined that about 25% of the people attending the information session elect to have the surgery performed. Of those who do not, most cite the cost of the procedure—$2,000—as their major concern.

a. On average, how much revenue does Dr. Benson's practice in laser surgery generate each week? (Use 500 replications.)

b. On average, how much revenue would the laser surgery generate each week if Dr. Benson did not cancel sessions with 2 or fewer reservations?

c. Dr. Benson believes that 35% of the people attending the information sessions would have the surgery if she reduced the price to $1,500. Under this scenario, how much revenue could Dr. Benson expect to realize per week from laser surgery?

12. One of the examples in this chapter dealt with determining the optimal reorder point for a computer monitor sold by Computers of Tomorrow (COT) in Austin, Texas. In this example we found that increasing the reorder point decreased the number of lost sales. However, this also increased the average amount of inventory carried. Suppose that it costs COT $0.30 per day in holding costs for each monitor in beginning inventory, and it costs $20 to place an order. Each monitor sold generates a profit of $45, and each lost sale results in an opportunity cost of $65 (including the lost profit of $45 and $20 in lost goodwill). Modify the spreadsheet given in the file FIG12-12.XLS on your data disk accordingly to determine the reorder point that maximizes the average monthly profit associated with this monitor.

13. One of the examples in this chapter dealt with determining the optimal number of reservations for Piedmont Commuter Airlines (PCA) to accept for one of its flights that uses a plane with 19 seats. The model discussed in the chapter assumes that all the reservations would be used, but some customers would not show up for the flight. It is probably more realistic to assume that the demand for these reservations is somewhat random. For example, suppose that the demand for reservations on this flight is given by the following probability distribution:

Reservations Demanded:	12	13	14	15	16	17	18	19	20	21	22	23	24
Probability:	0.01	0.03	0.04	0.07	0.09	0.11	0.15	0.18	0.14	0.08	0.05	0.03	0.02

The number of passengers receiving reservations depends on the number of reservations PCA accepts and the demand for these reservations. For each passenger receiving a reservation, a 0.10 probability exists that they will not arrive at the gate to board the plane. Modify the spreadsheet given in the file FIG12-19.XLS on your data disk accordingly to determine the number of reservations PCA should accept to maximize the average profit associated with this flight.

The Sound's Alive Company

A Case in Risk Analysis and Simulation

MARISSA Jones is the president and CEO of Sound's Alive, a company that manufactures and sells a line of speakers, CD players, receivers, high-definition televisions, and other items geared for the home entertainment market. Respected throughout the industry for bringing many high-quality, innovative products to market, Marissa is considering adding a speaker system to her product line.

The speaker market has changed dramatically during the last several years. Originally, high fidelity aficionados knew that to reproduce sound covering the fullest range of frequencies—from the lowest kettle drum to the highest violin—a speaker system had to be large and heavy. The speaker had various drivers: a woofer to reproduce the low notes, a tweeter for the high notes, and a mid-range driver for the broad spectrum of frequencies in between. Many speaker systems had a minimum of three drivers, but some had even more. The trouble was that such a system was too large for anything but the biggest rooms, and consumers were reluctant to spend thousands of dollars and give up valu-able wall space to get the excellent sound these speakers could reproduce.

The trend has changed during the past several years. Consumers still want good sound, but they want it from smaller boxes. Therefore, the satellite system became popular. Consisting of two small boxes that house either one driver (to cover the mid-range and high frequencies) or two (a mid-range and tweeter), a satellite system can easily be mounted on walls or shelves. To reproduce the low notes, a separate sub-woofer that is approximately the size of a cube 18 inches on a side is also needed. This sub-woofer can be placed anywhere in the room. Taking up less space than a typical large speaker system and sounding almost as good, yet costing hundreds of dollars less, these satellite systems are hot items in the high fidelity market.

Recently the separate wings of home entertainment—high fidelity (receivers, speakers, CD players, CDs, cassettes, and so on), television (large screen monitors, video cassette recorders, laser players), and computers (games with sounds, virtual reality software, and so on)—have merged into the home

Contributed by Jack Yurkiewicz, Lubin School of Business, Pace University, New York.

theater concept. To simulate the movie environment, a home theater system requires the traditional stereo speaker system plus additional speakers placed in the rear of the room so that viewers are literally surrounded with sound. Although the rear speakers do not have to match the high quality of the front speakers and, therefore, can be less expensive, most consumers choose a system in which the front and rear speakers are of equal quality, reproducing the full range of frequencies with equal fidelity.

It is this speaker market that Marissa wants to enter. She is considering having Sound's Alive manufacture and sell a home theater system that consists of seven speakers. Three small speakers—each with one dome tweeter that could reproduce the frequency range of 200 Hertz to 20,000 Hertz (upper-low frequencies to the highest frequencies)—would be placed in front, and three similar speakers would be placed strategically around the sides and back of the room. To reproduce the lowest frequencies (from 35 Hertz to 200 Hertz), a single sub-woofer would also be part of the system. This sub-woofer is revolutionary because it is smaller than the ordinary sub-woofer, only 10 inches per side, and it has a built-in amplifier to power it. Consumers and critics are thrilled with the music from early prototype systems, claiming that these speakers have the best balance of sound and size. Marissa is extremely encouraged by these early reviews, and although her company has never produced a product with its house label on it (having always sold systems from established high fidelity companies), she believes that

Sound's Alive should enter the home theater market with this product.

PHASE ONE: PROJECTING PROFITS

Marissa decides to create a spreadsheet that will project profits over the next several years. After consulting with economists, market analysts, employees in her own company, and employees from other companies that sell house brand components, Marissa is confident that the gross revenues for these speakers in 1995 would be around $6 million. She must also figure that a small percentage of speakers will be damaged in transit, or some will be returned by dissatisfied customers shortly after the sales. These returns and allowances (R&As) are usually calculated as 2% of the gross revenues. Hence, the net revenues are simply the gross revenues minus the R&As. Marissa believes that the 1995 labor costs for these speakers will be $995,100. The cost of materials (including boxes to ship the speakers) should be $915,350 for 1995. Finally, her overhead costs (rent, lighting, heating in winter, air conditioning in summer, security, and so on) for 1995 should be $1,536,120. Thus, the cost of goods sold is the sum of labor, material, and overhead costs. Marissa figures the gross profit as the difference between the gross revenues and the cost of goods sold. In addition, she must consider the selling, general, and administrative (SG&A) expenses. These expenses are more difficult to estimate, but the standard industry practice is to use 18% of the net revenues as the nominal percentage value for these expenses.

Therefore, Marissa's profit *before taxes* is the gross profit minus the SG&A value. To calculate taxes, Marissa multiplies her profits before taxes times the tax rate, currently 30%. If her company is operating at a loss, however, no taxes would have to be paid. Finally, Marissa's net (or after tax) profit is simply the difference between the profit before taxes and the actual taxes paid.

To determine the numbers for 1996 through 1998, Marissa assumes that gross revenues, labor costs, material costs, and overhead costs will increase over the years. Although the rates of increase for these items are difficult to estimate, Marissa figures that gross revenues will increase by 9% per year, labor costs will increase by 4% per year, material costs will increase by 6% per year, and overhead costs will increase by 3% per year. She figures that the tax rate will not change from the 30% mark, and she assumes that the SG&A value will remain at 18%.

The basic layout of the spreadsheet that Marissa creates is shown in the following figure (and in the file C12CASE.XLS on your data disk). (Ignore the Competition Assumptions section for now; we'll consider it later.) Construct the spreadsheet and determine the values for the years 1995 through 1998, then determine the totals for the four years.

Marissa not only wants to determine her net profits for 1995 through 1998, she also must justify her decisions to the company's Board of Trustees. Should she even consider entering this market, from a financial point of view? One way to answer this question is to find the net present value (NPV) of the net profits for 1995 through 1998. Use Excel's NPV capability to find the NPV, at the current interest rate of 5%, of the profits values for 1995 through 1998.

To avoid large values in the spreadsheet, enter all dollar calculations in thousands. For example, enter labor costs as 995.10 and overhead costs as 1536.12.

PHASE TWO: BRINGING COMPETITION INTO THE MODEL

With her spreadsheet complete, Marissa is confident that entering the home theater speaker market would be lucrative for Sound's Alive. However, she has not considered one factor in her calculations—competition. The current market leader and company she is most concerned about is the Bose Corporation. Bose pioneered the concept of a satellite speaker system, and its AMT series is very successful. Marissa is concerned that Bose will enter the home theater speaker market, cutting into her gross revenues. If Bose does enter the market, Marissa believes that Sound's Alive would still make money; however, she would have to revise her gross revenues estimate from $6 million to $4 million for 1995.

To account for the competition factor, Marissa revises her spreadsheet by adding a Competition Assumptions section. Cell F4 will contain either a 0 (no competition) or a 1 (if Bose enters the market). Cells F5 and F6 provide the gross revenue estimates (in thousands of dollars) for the two possibilities. Modify your spreadsheet to take these options into account. Use the IF() function for the gross revenues for 1995 (cell B12). If Bose does enter the market, not only would Marissa's gross revenues be lower, but the labor, materials, and overhead costs would

also be lower because Sound's Alive would be making and selling fewer speakers. Marissa thinks that if Bose enters the market, her 1995 labor costs would be $859,170, 1995 material costs would be $702,950, and 1995 overhead costs would be $1,288,750. She believes that her growth rate assumptions would stay the same whether or not Bose enters the market. Add these possible values to your spreadsheet using the IF() function in the appropriate cells.

Look at the net profits for 1995 through 1998. In particular, examine the NPV for the two scenarios: Bose does or does not enter the home theater speaker market.

PHASE THREE: BRINGING UNCERTAINTY INTO THE MODEL

Jim Allison, the chief of operations at Sound's Alive and a quantitative methods specialist, plays a key role in providing Marissa with estimates for the various revenues and costs. He is uneasy about the basic estimates for the growth rates. For example, although market research indicates that a 9% gross revenue increase per year is reasonable, Jim know that if this value is 7%, for example, the profit values and the NPV would be quite different. Even more troublesome is a potential tax increase, which would hit Sound's Alive hard. Jim believes that the tax rate could vary around the expected 30% figure. Finally, Jim is uncomfortable with the industry's standard estimate of 18% for the SG&A rate. Jim thinks that this value could be higher or even lower.

The Sound's Alive problem is too complicated for solving with what-if analysis because seven assumed values could change: the growth rates for gross revenues, labor, materials, overhead costs, tax rate, SG&A percent, and whether or not Bose enters the market. Jim believes that a Monte Carlo simulation would be a better approach. Jim thinks that the behavior of these variables can be modeled as:

Gross Revenues (%)

Normally distributed, mean = 9.9 std dev = 1.4

Labor Growth (%)

Normally distributed, mean = 3.45 std dev = 1.0

Materials (%)	Probability
4	0.10
5	0.15
6	0.15
7	0.25
8	0.25
9	0.10

Overhead (%)	Probability
2	0.20
3	0.35
4	0.25
5	0.20

Tax Rate (%)	Probability
30	0.15
32	0.30
34	0.30
36	0.25

SG&A (%)	Probability
15	0.05
16	0.10
17	0.20
18	0.25
19	0.20
20	0.20

Finally, Jim and Marissa agree that there is a 50/50 chance that Bose will enter the market.

Use simulation to analyze the Sound's Alive problem. Based on your results, what is the expected net profit for the years 1995 through 1998, and what is the expected NPV for this business venture?

The Board of Trustees told Marissa that the stockholders would feel comfortable with this business venture if its NPV is at least $5 million. What are the chances that Sound's Alive home theater venture will result in an NPV of $5 million or more?

CHAPTER 13

Add-In Assisted Simulation

CHAPTER 1 DISCUSSED how the calculations in a spreadsheet can be viewed as a mathematical model that defines a functional relationship between various input variables (or independent variables) and one or more bottom-line performance measures (or dependent variables). The following equation expresses this relationship:

$$Y = f(X_1, X_2, ..., X_k)$$ 13.1

In many spreadsheets the values of various input cells are determined by the person using the spreadsheet. These input cells correspond to the independent variables X_1, X_2, ..., X_k in equation 13.1. Various formulas (represented by $f(\cdot)$ in equation 13.1) are entered in other cells of the spreadsheet to transform the values of the input cells into some bottom-line output (denoted by Y in equation 13.1). Simulation is a technique that is helpful in analyzing models where the value to be assumed by one or more independent variables is uncertain.

Chapter 12 described how to perform simulation using the inherent capabilities of Excel. This chapter discusses how to perform simulation using a popular spreadsheet add-in called @RISK (pronounced "at risk").

RANDOM VARIABLES AND RISK

In order to compute a value for the bottom-line performance measure of a spreadsheet model, each input cell must be assigned a specific value so that all the related calculations can be performed. However, some uncertainty often exists regarding the value that should be assumed by one or more independent variables (or input cells) in the spreadsheet. This is particularly true in spreadsheet models that represent future conditions. A **random variable** is any variable whose value cannot be predicted or set with certainty. Thus, many input variables in a spreadsheet model represent random variables whose actual values cannot be predicted with certainty.

For example, projections of the cost of raw materials, future interest rates, future numbers of employees, and expected product demand are random variables because their true values are unknown and will be determined in the future. If we cannot say with certainty what value one or more input variables in a model will assume, we also cannot say with certainty what value the dependent variable will assume. This uncertainty associated with the value of the dependent variable introduces an element of risk to the decision-making problem. Specifically, if the dependent variable represents some bottom-line performance measure that managers use to make decisions, and its value is uncertain, any decisions made on the basis of this value are based on uncertain (or incomplete) information. When such a decision is made, some chance exists that the decision will not produce the intended results. This chance, or uncertainty, represents an element of **risk** in the decision-making problem.

The term "risk" also implies the *potential* for loss. The fact that a decision's outcome is uncertain does not mean that the decision is particularly risky. For example, whenever we put money into a soft drink machine, there is a chance that the machine will take our money and not deliver the product. However, most of us would not consider this risk to be particularly great. From past experience, we know that the chance of not receiving the product is small. But even if the machine takes our money and does not deliver the product, most of us would not consider this to be a tremendous loss. Thus, the amount of risk involved in a given decision-making situation is a function of the uncertainty in the outcome of the decision and the magnitude of the potential loss. A proper assessment of the risk present in a decision-making situation should address both of these issues, as the examples in this chapter will demonstrate.

WHY ANALYZE RISK?

Many spreadsheets built by business people contain *estimated* values for the uncertain input variables in their models. If a manager cannot say with certainty what value a particular cell in a spreadsheet will assume, this cell most likely represents a random variable. Ordinarily, the manager will attempt to make an informed guess about the values such cells will assume. The manager hopes that inserting the expected, or most likely, values for all the uncertain cells in a spreadsheet will provide the most likely value for the cell containing the bottom-line performance measure (Y). The problem with this type of analysis is that it tells the decision maker nothing about the variability of the performance measure.

For example, in analyzing a particular investment opportunity, we might determine that the expected return on a $1,000 investment is $10,000 within two years. But how much variability exists in the possible outcomes? If all the potential outcomes are scattered closely around $10,000 (say from $9,000 to $11,000), then the investment opportunity might still be attractive. If, on the other hand, the potential outcomes are scattered widely around $10,000 (say from –$30,000 up to +$50,000), then the investment opportunity might be unattractive. Although these two scenarios might have the same expected or average value, the risks involved are quite different. Thus, even if we can determine the expected outcome of a decision using a spreadsheet, it is just as important, if not more so, to consider the risk involved in the decision.

METHODS OF RISK ANALYSIS

Several techniques are available to help managers analyze risk. Three of the most common are best case/worst case analysis, what-if analysis, and simulation. Of these methods, simulation is the most powerful and, therefore, is the technique that we'll focus on in this chapter. Although the other techniques might not be completely effective in risk analysis, they are probably used more often than simulation by most managers in business today. This is largely due to the fact that most managers are unaware of the spreadsheet's ability to perform simulation and of the benefits provided by this technique. So before discussing simulation, let's first briefly look at the other methods of risk analysis to understand their strengths and weaknesses.

BEST CASE/WORST CASE ANALYSIS

If we don't know what value a particular cell in a spreadsheet will assume, we could enter a number that we think is the most likely value for the uncertain cell. If we enter such numbers for all the uncertain cells in the spreadsheet, we can easily calculate the most likely value of the bottom-line performance measure. This is also called the **base case** scenario. However, this scenario gives us no information about how far away the actual outcome might be from this expected, or most likely, value.

One simple solution to this problem is to calculate the value of the bottom-line performance measure using the **best case**, or most optimistic, and **worst case**, or most pessimistic, values for the uncertain input cells. These additional scenarios show the range of possible values that might be assumed by the bottom-line performance measure. As indicated in the earlier example about the $1,000 investment, knowing the range of possible outcomes is very helpful in assessing the risk involved in different alternatives. However, simply knowing the best case and worst case outcomes tells us nothing about the distribution of possible values within this range, nor does it tell us the probability of either scenario occurring.

Figure 13.1 displays several probability distributions that might be associated with the value of a bottom-line performance measure within a given range. Each of these distributions describes variables that have identical ranges and similar average values. But each distribution is very different in terms of the risk it represents to the decision maker. The appeal of best case/worst case analysis is that it is easy to do. Its weakness is that it tells us nothing about the shape of the distribution associated with the bottom-line performance measure. As we'll see later, knowing the shape of the distribution of the bottom-line performance measure can be critically important in helping us answer a number of managerial questions.

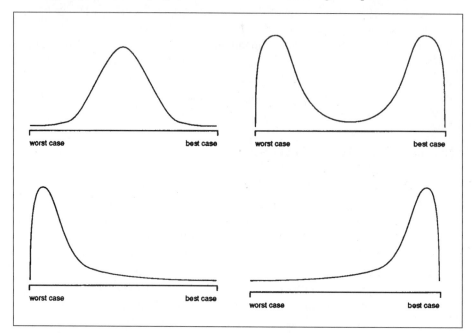

Figure 13.1: Possible distributions of performance measure values within a given range

WHAT-IF ANALYSIS

Prior to the introduction of electronic spreadsheets in the early 1980s, the use of best case/worst case analysis was often the only feasible way for a manager to analyze the risk associated with a decision. This process was extremely time consuming, error prone, and tedious, using only a piece of paper, pencil, and calculator to recalculate the performance measure of a model using different values for the uncertain inputs. The arrival of personal computers and electronic spreadsheets made it much easier for a manager to play out a large number of scenarios in addition to the best and worst cases—which is the essence of what-if analysis.

In **what-if analysis**, a manager changes the values of the uncertain input variables to see what happens to the bottom-line performance measure. By making a series of such changes, a manager can gain some insight into how sensitive the performance measure is to changes to the input variables. Although many managers perform this type of manual what-if analysis, it has three major flaws.

First, if the values selected for the independent variables are based only on the manager's judgment, the resulting sample values of the performance measure are likely to be biased. That is, if several uncertain variables can each assume some range of values, it would be difficult to ensure that the manager tests a fair, or representative, sample of all possible combinations of these values. To select values for the uncertain variables that correctly reflect their random variations, the values must be randomly selected from a distribution, or pool, of values that reflects the appropriate range of possible values, as well as the appropriate relative frequencies of these variables.

Second, hundreds or thousands of what-if scenarios might be required to create a valid representation of the underlying variability in the bottom-line performance measure. No one would want to perform these scenarios manually nor would anyone be able to make sense of the resulting stream of numbers that would flash on the screen.

The third problem with what-if analysis is that the insight the manager might gain from playing out various scenarios is of little value when recommending a decision to top management. What-if analysis simply does not supply the manager with the tangible evidence (facts and figures) needed to justify why a given decision was made or recommended. Additionally, what-if analysis does not address the problem identified in our earlier discussion of best case/worst case analysis—it does not allow us to estimate the distribution of the performance measure in a formal enough manner. Thus, what-if analysis is a step in the right direction, but it is not quite a large enough step to allow managers to analyze risk effectively in the decisions they face.

SIMULATION

Simulation is a technique that measures and describes various characteristics of the bottom-line performance measure of a model when one or more values for the independent variables are uncertain. If any independent variables in a model are random variables, the dependent variable (Y) also represents a random variable. The objective in simulation is to describe the distribution and characteristics of the possible values of the bottom-line performance measure Y, given the possible values and behavior of the independent variables X_1, X_2, ..., X_k.

The idea behind simulation is similar to the notion of playing out many what-if scenarios. The difference is that the process of assigning values to the cells in the spreadsheet that represent random variables is automated so that: (1) the values are assigned in a non-biased way, and (2) the spreadsheet user is relieved of the burden of determining these values. With simulation we repeatedly and randomly generate sample values for each uncertain input variable (X_1, X_2, ..., X_k) in our model and then compute the resulting value of our bottom-line performance measure (Y). We can then use the sample values of Y to estimate the true distribution and other characteristics of the performance measure Y. For example, we can use the sample observations to construct a frequency distribution of the performance measure, to estimate the range of values over which the performance measure might vary, to estimate its mean and variance, and to estimate the probability that the actual value of the performance measure will be greater than (or less than) a particular value. All these measures provide greater insight into the risk associated with a given decision than a single value calculated based on the expected values for the uncertain independent variables.

A CORPORATE HEALTH INSURANCE EXAMPLE

The following example demonstrates the mechanics of preparing a spreadsheet model for risk analysis using simulation. The example presents a fairly simple model to illustrate the process and give a sense of the amount of effort involved. However, the process for performing simulation is basically the same regardless of the size of the model.

Lisa Pon has just been hired as an analyst in the corporate planning department of Hungry Dawg Restaurants. Her first assignment is to determine how much money the company needs to accrue in the coming year to pay for its employees' health insurance claims. Hungry Dawg is a large, growing chain of restaurants that specializes in traditional southern foods. The company has become large enough that it no longer buys insurance from a private insurance company. The company is now self-insured, meaning that it pays health insurance claims with its own money (although it contracts with an outside company to handle the administrative details of processing claims and writing checks).

The money the company uses to pay claims comes from two sources: employee contributions (or premiums deducted from employees' paychecks), and company funds (the company must pay whatever costs are not covered by employee contributions). Each employee covered by the health plan contributes $125 per month. However, the number of employees covered by the plan changes from month to month as employees are hired and fired, quit, or simply add or drop health insurance coverage. A total of 18,533 employees were covered by the plan last month. The average monthly health claim per covered employee was $250 last month.

An example of how most analysts would model this problem is shown in Figure 13.2 (and in the file FIG13-2.XLS on your data disk). The spreadsheet begins with a listing of the initial conditions and assumptions for the problem. For example, cell D2 indicates that 18,533 employees are currently covered by the health plan, and cell D3 indicates that the average monthly claim per covered employee is $250. The average monthly contribution per employee is $125, as shown in cell D4. The values in cells D2 and D3 are unlikely to stay the same for the entire year. Thus, we need to make some assumptions about the rate at which these values are likely to increase during the year. For example, we might assume that the number of covered employees will increase by about 2% per month, and that the average claim per employee will increase at a rate of 1% per month. These assumptions are reflected in cells F2 and F3. The average contribution per employee is assumed to be constant over the coming year.

Using the assumed rate of increase in the number of covered employees (cell F2), we can create formulas for cells B8 through B19 that cause the number of covered employees to increase by the assumed amount each month. (The details of these formulas are covered later.) The expected monthly employee contributions shown in column C are calculated as $125 times the number of employees in each month. We can use the assumed rate of increase in average monthly claims (cell F3) to create formulas for cells D8 through D19 that cause the average claim per employee to increase at the assumed rate. The total claims for each month (shown in column E) are calculated as the average claim figures in column D times the number of employees for each month in column B. Because the company must pay for any claims that are not covered by the employee contributions, the company cost figures in column G are calculated as the total claims minus the employee contributions (column E minus column C). Finally, cell G20 sums the company cost figures listed in column G, and shows that the company can expect to contribute $36,125,850 of its revenues toward paying the health insurance claims of its employees in the coming year.

Figure 13.2: Original corporate health insurance model with expected values for uncertain variables

A CRITIQUE OF THE BASE CASE MODEL

Now let's consider the model we just described. The example model assumes that the number of covered employees will increase by *exactly* 2% each month and that the average claim per covered employee will increase by *exactly* 1% each month. Although these values might be reasonable approximations of what might happen, they are unlikely to reflect exactly what will happen. In fact, the number of employees covered by the health plan each month is likely to vary randomly around the average increase per month—that is, the number might decrease in some months and increase by more than 2% in others. Similarly, the average claim per covered employee might be lower than expected in certain months and higher than expected in others.

Both of these figures are likely to exhibit some uncertainty or random behavior, even if they do move in the general upward direction assumed throughout the year. So we cannot say with certainty that the total cost figure of $36,125,850 is exactly what the company will have to contribute toward health claims in the coming year. It is simply a prediction of what might happen. The actual outcome could be smaller or larger than this estimate. Using the original model, we have no idea how much larger or smaller the actual result could be—nor do we have any idea of how the actual values are distributed around this estimate. We do not know if there is a 10%, 50%, or 90% chance of the actual total costs exceeding this estimate. To determine the variability or risk inherent in the bottom-line performance measure of total company costs, we'll apply the technique of simulation to our model.

SPREADSHEET SIMULATION USING @RISK

To perform simulation in a spreadsheet, we must first place a **random number generator** (RNG) formula in each cell that represents a random, or uncertain, independent variable. Each RNG provides a sample observation from an appropriate distribution that represents the range and frequency of possible values for the variable. Once the RNGs are in place, new sample values are provided automatically each time the spreadsheet is recalculated. We can recalculate the spreadsheet n times, where n is the desired number of replications or scenarios, and the value of the bottom-line performance measure will be stored after each replication. We can analyze these stored observations to gain insights into the behavior and characteristics of the performance measure.

The process of simulation involves a lot of work but, fortunately, the spreadsheet can do most of the work for us fairly easily. In particular, the spreadsheet add-in package @RISK is designed specifically to make spreadsheet simulation a simple process. The @RISK software provides the following capabilities, which are not otherwise available while working in Excel: additional functions that are helpful in generating the random numbers needed in simulation; additional commands that are helpful in setting up and running the simulation; and graphical and statistical summaries of the simulation data. As we'll see, these capabilities make simulation a relatively easy technique to apply in spreadsheets.

INSTALLING @RISK

If you are running @RISK from a local area network, your instructor should give you directions on how to access this software. If you have your own copy of @RISK, you can install it as follows:

1. Insert the @RISK System disk (Disk 1 of 2) in drive A (or B).

2. Start Windows following your usual procedure.

3. From the Program Manager, click File, then click Run.

4. In the Command line, type A:\SETUP (or B:\SETUP), then click OK.

5. The rest of the installation is self-guided. Answer any questions according to your computer's specifications.

STARTING @RISK

You can access @RISK by double-clicking the @RISK icon in the @RISK for Excel program group in the Program Manager, as shown in Figure 13.3.

This loads the memory resident portion of @RISK and automatically takes you into Excel, where you see the @RISK toolbar shown in Figure 13.4. Shortly, we'll discuss the purpose of the buttons on this toolbar.

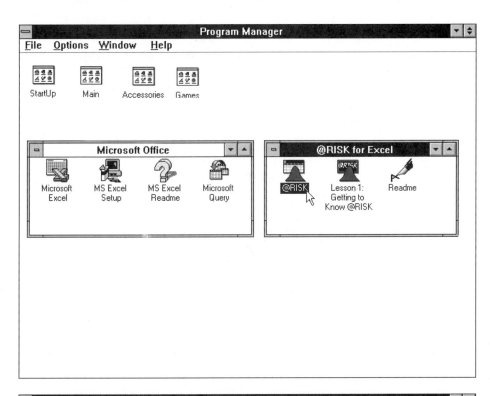

Figure 13.3: *@RISK icon in the @RISK for Excel program group*

RESULTS BUTTON (MAIN @RISK MENU)

SIMULATE BUTTON (RUN SIMULATION)

LIST BUTTON (LIST INPUTS BY OUTPUTS)
+OUTPUT BUTTON (ADD OUTPUT CELL)

SIMSETT BUTTON (SIMULATION SETTINGS)

SAVE BUTTON (SAVE SIMULATION RESULTS)
OPEN BUTTON (OPEN SIMULATION RESULTS)

Figure 13.4: *The @RISK toolbar in Excel*

RANDOM NUMBER GENERATORS

As mentioned earlier, the first step in spreadsheet simulation is to place an RNG formula in each cell that contains an uncertain value. Each of these formulas will generate (or return) a number that represents a randomly selected value from a distribution, or pool, of values. The distributions that these samples are taken from should be representative of the underlying pool of values expected to occur in each uncertain cell.

@RISK provides several functions that can be used to create the RNGs required for simulating a model. Figure 13.5 describes some of the RNGs that will be most useful to you.

Distribution	RNG	Description
Binomial	RiskBinomial(n,p)	Returns the number of "successes" in a sample of size n where each trial has a probability p of "success."
Discrete	RiskDiscrete($\{x_1, x_2, ..., x_n\},\{p_1, p_2, ..., p_n\}$)	Returns one of the n values represented by the x_i. The value x_i occurs with probability p_i.
Discrete	RiskDuniform ($\{x_1, x_2, ..., x_n\}$)	Returns one of the n values represented by the x_i. Each value x_i is equally likely to occur.
Poisson	RiskPoisson(λ)	Returns a random number of events occurring per some unit of measure (for example, arrivals per hour, defects per yard, and so on). The parameter λ represents the average number of events occurring per unit of measure.
Chi-square	RiskChisq(λ)	Returns a value from a chi-square distribution with mean λ.
Normal	RiskNormal(μ,σ)	Returns a value from a normal distribution with mean μ and standard deviation σ.
Truncated	RiskTnormal(μ,σ,min,max)	Same as RiskNormal except the distribution is truncated to the range specified by a minimum (*min*) and a maximum (*max*).
Triangular	RiskTriang(min,most likely,max)	Returns a value from a triangular distribution covering the range specified by a minimum (*min*) and a maximum (*max*). The shape of the distribution is then determined by the size of the most likely value relative to *min* and *max*.
Continuous	RiskUniform(min,max)	Returns a value in the range from a minimum (*min*) to a maximum (*max*). Each value in this range is equally likely to occur.

Figure 13.5: Commonly used RNGs supplied with @RISK

The functions listed in Figure 13.5 allow us to generate a variety of random numbers easily. For example, if we think that the behavior of an uncertain cell could be modeled as a normally distributed random variable with a mean of 125 and standard deviation of 10, then according to Figure 13.5 we could enter the formula =RiskNormal(125,10) in this cell. (The arguments in this function could also be formulas and could refer to other cells in the spreadsheet.) Using appropriate settings in @RISK (to be described shortly), we can instruct the spreadsheet to return a randomly selected value from a normal distribution with a mean of 125 and standard deviation of 10 for this cell whenever the spreadsheet is recalculated.

Similarly, a cell in our spreadsheet might have a 30% chance of assuming the value 10, a 50% chance of assuming the value 20, and a 20% chance of assuming the value 30. As noted in Figure 13.5, we could use the formula =RiskDiscrete({10,20,30},{0.3,0.5,0.2}) to model this random behavior. If we recalculated the spreadsheet many times, this formula would return the value 10 approximately 30% of the time, the value 20 approximately 50% of the time, and the value 30 approximately 20% of the time.

The arguments, or parameters, required by the RNG functions allow us to generate random numbers from distributions with a wide variety of shapes. Figures 13.6 and 13.7 illustrate some examples of the distributions. Additional information about these and other RNGs provided by @RISK is available in Appendix A of the @RISK manual and in the on-line Help facility in @RISK.

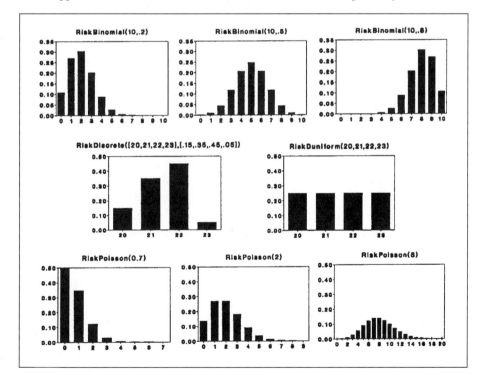

Figure 13.6: Examples of distributions associated with selected discrete RNGs

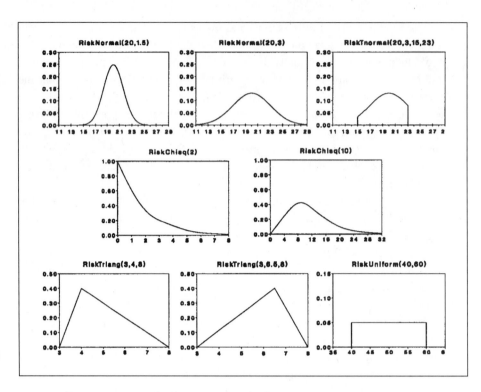

Figure 13.7: Examples of distributions associated with selected continuous RNGs

DISCRETE VS. CONTINUOUS RANDOM VARIABLES

An important distinction exists between the graphs in Figures 13.6 and 13.7. In particular, the RNGs depicted in Figure 13.6 generate *discrete* outcomes, whereas those represented in Figure 13.7 generate *continuous* outcomes. That is, the first four RNGs listed in Figure 13.5 can return only a distinct set of individual values, whereas the other RNGs can return any value from an infinite set of values. The distinction between discrete and continuous random variables is very important.

For example, the number of defective tires on a new car is a discrete random variable because it can assume only one of five distinct values: 0, 1, 2, 3, or 4. On the other hand, the amount of fuel in a new car is a continuous random variable because it can assume any value between 0 and the maximum capacity of the fuel tank. Thus, when selecting an RNG for an uncertain variable in a model, it is important to consider whether the variable can assume discrete or continuous values.

PREPARING THE MODEL FOR SIMULATION

To apply simulation to the model for Hungry Dawg Restaurants described earlier, we must first select appropriate RNGs for the uncertain variables in the model. If available, historical data on the uncertain variables could be analyzed to determine appropriate RNGs for these variables. If past data are not available, or if we have some reason to expect the future behavior of a variable to be significantly different from the past, then we must use judgment in selecting appropriate RNGs to model the random behavior of the uncertain variables.

For our example problem, let's assume that by analyzing historical data, we determined that the change in the number of covered employees from one month to the next is expected to vary uniformly between a 3% decrease and a 7% increase. (Note that this should cause the *average* change in the number of employees to be a 2% increase, because 0.02 is the mid-point between −0.03 and +0.07.) Further, assume that we can model the average monthly claim per covered employee as a normally distributed random variable with the mean (μ) increasing by 1% per month and a standard deviation (σ) of approximately 3%. (Note that this will cause the *average* increase in claims per covered employee from one month to the next to be approximately 1%.) These assumptions are reflected in cells F2 through H3 at the top of Figure 13.8 (and in the file FIG13-8.XLS on your data disk).

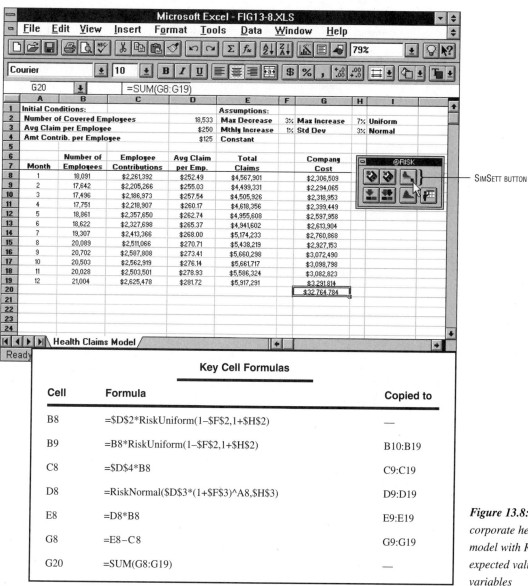

SIMSETT BUTTON

Key Cell Formulas

Cell	Formula	Copied to
B8	=$D$2*RiskUniform(1−$F$2,1+$H$2)	—
B9	=B8*RiskUniform(1−$F$2,1+$H$2)	B10:B19
C8	=$D$4*B8	C9:C19
D8	=RiskNormal($D$3*(1+$F$3)^A8,$H$3)	D9:D19
E8	=D8*B8	E9:E19
G8	=E8−C8	G9:G19
G20	=SUM(G8:G19)	—

Figure 13.8: Modified corporate health insurance model with RNGs replacing expected values for uncertain variables

To implement the formula to generate a random number of employees covered by the health plan, we'll use the RiskUniform() function described in Figure 13.5. Because the change in the number of employees from one month to the next can vary between a 3% decrease and a 7% increase, the number of employees in the current month is equal to the number of employees in the previous month multiplied by the sum of 1 plus the percentage change. Applying this logic, we obtain the following equation for the number of employees in a given month:

$$\frac{\text{Number of employees}}{\text{in current month}} = \frac{\text{Number of employees}}{\text{in previous month}} * \text{RiskUniform}(0.97, 1.07) \qquad \textbf{13.2}$$

If the RiskUniform() function returns the value 0.97, this formula causes the number of employees in the current month to equal 97% of the number in the previous month (a 3% decrease). Alternatively, if the RiskUniform() function returns the value 1.07, this formula causes the number of employees in the current month to equal 107% of the number in the previous month (a 7% increase). All the values between these two extremes (between 0.97 and 1.07) are also possible and equally likely to occur.

The general relationship in equation 13.2 was used to create formulas that randomly generate the number of employees in each month. This was done in Figure 13.8 with the following formulas:

Formula for cell B8:   =$D$2*RiskUniform(1–$F$2,1+$H$2)

Formula for cell B9:   =B8*RiskUniform(1–$F$2,1+$H$2)
(copy to B10 through B19)

In these formulas, the terms "1–$F$2" and "1+$H$2" generate the values 0.97 and 1.07, respectively, which are shown in equation 13.2.

To implement the formula to generate the average claims per covered employee in each month, we'll use the RiskNormal() function described in Figure 13.5. This formula requires that we supply the value of the mean (μ) and standard deviation (σ) of the distribution from which we want to sample. The assumed 3% standard deviation (σ) for the average monthly claim, shown in cell H3 in Figure 13.8, is constant from month to month. Thus, the only remaining problem is to figure out the proper mean value (μ) for each month.

In this case, the mean for any given month should be 1% larger than the mean in the previous month. For example, the mean for month 1 is:

Mean in month 1 = (original mean)*1.01   **13.3**

and the mean for month 2 is:

Mean in month 2 = (mean in month 1)*1.01   **13.4**

If we substitute the RHS of equation 13.3 for "mean in month 1" in equation 13.4, we obtain the following equivalent definition for the mean in month 2:

Mean in month 2 = (original mean)*$(1.01)^2$

Similarly, the mean in month 3 is:

Mean in month 3 = (mean in month 2)*1.01

which, after substitutions, is equivalent to:

Mean in month 3 = (original mean) * $(1.01)^3$

In general, the mean (μ) for month n is:

Mean in month n = (original mean)*$(1.01)^n$ **13.5**

Thus, to generate the average claim per covered employee in each month, we'll use the following formula:

Formula for cell D8:   =RiskNormal($D$3*(1+$F$3)^A8,$H$3)
(copy to D9 through D19)

The term "$D$3*(1+$F$3)^A8" in this formula implements the general definition of the mean (μ) in month *n* given in equation 13.5.

EXPECTED VALUES VS. SAMPLE VALUES

If we click the SimSett button on the @RISK toolbar shown in Figure 13.8, the Simulation Settings dialog box shown in Figure 13.9 appears.

SELECT THIS OPTION

Figure 13.9: The Simulation Settings dialog box

The Standard Recalc option in Figure 13.9 has three radio button selections: Expected Value, Monte Carlo, and True EV. This option determines whether the RNGs return random samples or expected values.

Every RNG has an average, or expected, value associated with its probability distribution. @RISK provides two options—Expected Value and True EV—that return the expected value of each RNG rather than random sample values. The only difference between these two options is that the Expected Value option (the default) rounds the expected value of a discrete RNG to its nearest integer value, whereas the True EV option does not. These options are helpful if we want to see what value the bottom-line performance measure would assume if all the uncertain cells in the spreadsheet assumed their expected values. However, to have the RNGs in our spreadsheet return random sample values, we must select the Monte Carlo option.

After selecting the Monte Carlo option, each time we press the recalculate key (the function key [F9]), the RNGs automatically select new values for all the cells in the spreadsheet that represent uncertain (or random) variables. Similarly, with each recalculation, a new value for the bottom-line performance measure (total company cost) appears in cell G20. Thus, by pressing the recalculate key several times, we can observe representative values of the company's total cost for health claims. This also helps to verify that we implemented the RNGs correctly and that they are generating appropriate values for each uncertain cell.

RUNNING THE SIMULATION

The next step in performing the simulation involves recalculating the spreadsheet several hundred or several thousand times and recording the resulting values generated for the output cell, or bottom-line performance measure. Fortunately, @RISK can do this for us if we indicate how many times we want it to recalculate (or replicate) the model and which cell(s) in the spreadsheet we want to track.

SELECTING THE OUTPUT CELLS TO TRACK

We can use the +Output button on the @RISK toolbar (see Figure 13.4) to indicate the output cell (or cells) that we want @RISK to track during the simulation. In the current example, cell G20 represents the output cell we want @RISK to track. To indicate this:

1. Click cell G20.

2. Click the +Output button on the @RISK toolbar.

In some simulations, we might want to analyze several performance measures. In such a case, we can follow the preceding procedure repeatedly to select additional output cells to track.

SELECTING THE NUMBER OF ITERATIONS

Figure 13.9 shows the Simulation Settings dialog box for @RISK. The # Iterations = option in this dialog box allows us to specify the number of iterations (or replications) to include in our simulation. Thus, to indicate that we want to perform 300 replications of our model:

1. Click the SimSett button to display the Simulation Settings dialog box.

2. Type 300 in the box labeled # Iterations =.

3. Click OK.

DETERMINING THE SAMPLE SIZE

You might wonder why we selected 300 replications. Why not 200, or 1000? Unfortunately, there is no easy answer to this question. Remember that the goal in simulation is to estimate various characteristics about the bottom-line performance measure(s) under consideration. For example, we might want to estimate the mean value of the performance measure and the shape of its probability distribution. However, a different value of the bottom-line performance measure occurs each time we manually recalculate the model in Figure 13.8. Thus, there is an infinite number of possibilities—or an **infinite population**—of total company cost values associated with this model.

We cannot analyze all of these infinite possibilities. But by taking a large enough sample from this infinite population, we can make reasonably accurate estimates about the characteristics of the underlying infinite population of values. The larger the sample we take (that is, the more replications we do), the more accurate our final results will be. But, performing many replications takes time, so we must make a trade-off in terms of estimation accuracy versus convenience. Thus, there is no simple answer to the question of how many replications to perform, but, as a bare minimum you should always perform at least 100 replications, and more as time permits or accuracy demands.

EXECUTING THE SIMULATION

Having identified the output cells to track and the number of replications to perform, we now need to instruct @RISK to perform the simulation by clicking the Simulate button on the @RISK toolbar (see Figure 13.4). @RISK then begins to perform the specified number of replications. Depending on the number of iterations selected, the size of the model, and the speed of your computer, it could take anywhere from several seconds to several minutes for these computations to be carried out.

For our example problem, @RISK performs 300 recalculations of the model, keeping track of the value in cell G20 for each replication. By default, @RISK updates the computer screen after each replication, which is very time-consuming. If you deselect the Update Display option shown in Figure 13.9, @RISK will not update the screen after each replication and will perform the replications much faster.

DATA ANALYSIS

As mentioned earlier, the objective of performing a simulation is to estimate various characteristics of the performance measure resulting from uncertainty in some or all of the input variables. After performing the replications, @RISK summarizes the output data, as shown in Figure 13.10.

Figure 13.10: Summary of results provided by @RISK for the corporate health insurance model

As shown in the Summary of Results area, the average (or mean) value for cell G20 is approximately $36.1 million. (Note that the Mean value of 3.611817E+07 shown in Figure 13.10 is in scientific notation. The "E+07" at the end of this notation indicates that the decimal point in the number should be shifted 7 places to the right to produce 36,118,170.) Additional information about the simulation results is available by clicking the Statistics button in the Results window, or by clicking the Graph button on the toolbar. (If you are working through this example on a computer, the graphs and statistics you generate will probably be somewhat different from the results shown here because you are working with a different sample of 300 observations.)

THE BEST CASE AND THE WORST CASE

Decision makers usually want to know the best case and worst case scenarios to get an idea of the range of possible outcomes they might face. This information is available from the simulation results, as shown by the Minimum and Maximum values listed in Figure 13.10.

Although the average total cost value observed in the 300 replications is $36.1 million, in one case the total cost is approximately $29.3 million (representing the best case) and in another case the total cost is approximately $42.5 million (representing the worst case). These figures should give the decision maker a good idea about the range of possible cost values that might occur. Note that these values might be difficult to determine manually in a complex model with many uncertain independent variables.

VIEWING THE DISTRIBUTION OF THE OUTPUT CELLS

The best and worst case scenarios are the most extreme outcomes, and might not be likely to occur. To determine the likelihood of these outcomes requires that we know something about the shape of the distribution of our bottom-line performance measure. To view a graph of the distribution of the results of the 300 replications generated for the output cell in our model:

1. In the Results window, select the row representing cell G20 in the Summary of Results area.
2. Click the Graph button on the toolbar (see Figure 13.10).

A histogram of the simulation data for cell G20 appears. This graph, shown in Figure 13.11, provides a visual summary of the approximate shape of the probability distribution associated with the output cell tracked by @RISK during the simulation.

We can use the Graph, Scaling options available on the Results menu to adjust the scale of the graph and change the minimum and maximum values displayed along the X- or Y-axis of the histogram.

As shown in Figure 13.11, the shape of the distribution associated with the total cost variable is somewhat bell-shaped, with a maximum value around $42 million and a minimum value around $29 million. Thus, we now have a clear idea of the shape of the distribution associated with our bottom-line performance measure—one of the goals in simulation.

If we tracked more than one output cell during the simulation, we could display histograms of the values occurring in these other cells by highlighting the appropriate cell in the Summary of Results area of the Results window, then clicking the Graph button. We could perform the same procedure to view the distributions of the input cells.

Figure 13.11: Histogram of costs for the corporate health insurance model

VIEWING THE CUMULATIVE DISTRIBUTION OF THE OUTPUT CELLS

At times we might want to view a graph of the cumulative probability distribution associated with one of the output cells tracked during a simulation. For example, suppose that the chief financial officer (CFO) for Hungry Dawg would rather accrue an excess of money to pay health claims than not accrue enough money. The CFO might want to know what amount the company should accrue so that there is only a 10% chance of coming up short of funds at the end of the year. So how much money would you recommend be accrued?

Figure 13.12 shows a graph of the cumulative probability distribution of the values that occurred in cell G20 during the simulation. This graph could help us answer the preceding question. To change the graph shown in Figure 13.11 to the cumulative distribution graph shown in Figure 13.12:

1. Click the Results menu.
2. Click Graph.
3. Click Type.
4. Click Cumulative Ascending.
5. Click Bar Graph.
6. Click OK.

This graph displays the probability of the selected output cell taking on a value smaller than each value on the X-axis. For example, this graph indicates that approximately a 10% chance exists of the output cell (Total Company Cost) assuming a value smaller than approximately $33 million. Similarly, this graph indicates that roughly an 80% chance exists of total costs being less than approximately $38 million (or a 20% chance of total costs exceeding approximately $38 million).

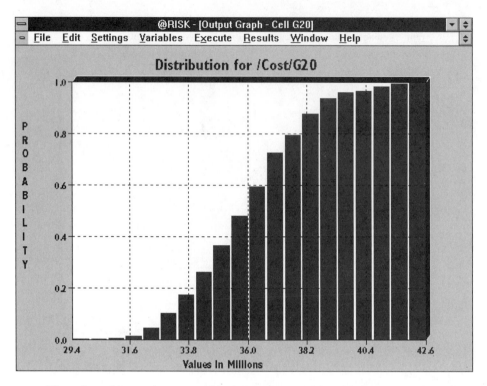

Figure 13.12: *Ascending cumulative frequency distribution of costs for the corporate health insurance model*

Thus, from this graph we would estimate that roughly a 10% chance exists of the company's costs exceeding approximately $39 million.

OBTAINING EXACT CUMULATIVE PROBABILITIES

We can obtain a more exact answer to the CFO's question from information in the Simulation Statistics window shown in Figure 13.10. The maximized version of this window is shown in Figure 13.13.

Scrolling down the Simulation Statistics window reveals a number of percentile values for the output cell G20. For example, the 10th percentile of the values generated for the output cell is $33,275,340. That is, 10% of the 300 values generated for cell G20 are less than or equal to $33,275,340. Similarly, the 90th percentile of the distribution of values is $38,850,620. That is, 90% of the 300 values generated for cell G20 are less than or equal to $38,850,620. Thus, based on these results, if the company accrues $38.9 million, we would expect that only a 10% chance exists of the actual company costs exceeding this amount.

In this case, the percentile value we want to find is given in the Simulation Statistics window. But what happens if we're interested in a percentile value that's not a multiple of 5? For example, what if we need to find the 88th percentile of the distribution? To do this:

1. Click Target #1 (Perc%)= in the /Cost Output G20 column shown in Figure 13.14.

2. Type 88 and then press [Enter]. The value 88% appears in the box.

The value for the 88th percentile (38,608,728) appears in the box labeled Target #1 (Value)= as shown in Figure 13.14.

@RISK - [Simulation Statistics]			
File Edit Settings Variables Execute Results Window Help			
Name	/Cost	Employees	per Emp.
Description	Output	Uniform(1-$F$2,1+$H$2)	Normal($D$3*(1+$F$3)^A8,$H$3)
Cell	G20	B8	D8
Percentile Values			
5% Perc =	3.271174E+07	.9749696	252.4501
10% Perc =	3.327534E+07	.9798481	252.4614
15% Perc =	3.368583E+07	.9849139	252.4686
20% Perc =	3.414086E+07	.989794	252.4745
25% Perc =	3.458672E+07	.9947392	252.4797
30% Perc =	3.481954E+07	.9997778	252.4842
35% Perc =	3.521061E+07	1.004709	252.4883
40% Perc =	3.553526E+07	1.009699	252.4923
45% Perc =	3.57986E+07	1.014929	252.496
50% Perc =	3.613591E+07	1.01975	252.4999
55% Perc =	3.638011E+07	1.024944	252.5036
60% Perc =	3.664338E+07	1.029871	252.5074
65% Perc =	3.688748E+07	1.034935	252.5113
70% Perc =	3.717914E+07	1.039709	252.5156
75% Perc =	3.750142E+07	1.044806	252.5201
80% Perc =	3.796689E+07	1.049683	252.5251
85% Perc =	3.835529E+07	1.05469	252.5309
90% Perc =	3.885062E+07	1.059895	252.538
95% Perc =	3.951677E+07	1.064987	252.5492
Filter Minimum =			
Filter Maximum =			
Type (1 or 2) =			

Figure 13.13: *Percentiles for the distribution of costs*

@RISK - [Simulation Statistics]			
File Edit Settings Variables Execute Results Window Help			
Name	/Cost	Employees	per Emp.
Description	Output	Uniform(1-$F$2,1+$H$2)	Normal($D$3*(1+$F$3)^A8,$H$3)
Cell	G20	B8	D8
85% Perc =	3.835529E+07	1.05469	252.5309
90% Perc =	3.885062E+07	1.059895	252.538
95% Perc =	3.951677E+07	1.064987	252.5492
Filter Minimum =			
Filter Maximum =			
Type (1 or 2) =			
# Values Filtered =			
Scenario #1 =	>75%		
Scenario #2 =	<25%		
Scenario #3 =	>90%		
Target #1 (Value)=	38608728		
Target #1 (Perc%)=	88%		
Target #2 (Value)=			
Target #2 (Perc%)=			
Target #3 (Value)=			
Target #3 (Perc%)=			
Target #4 (Value)=			
Target #4 (Perc%)=			
Target #5 (Value)=			
Target #5 (Perc%)=			
Target #6 (Value)=			
Target #6 (Perc%)=			
Target #7 (Value)=			

Figure 13.14: *Determining the 88th percentile*

This indicates that roughly a 12% chance exists of total costs exceeding $38.6 million. We can obtain other percentiles in a similar manner.

The ability to perform this type of analysis highlights the power and value of simulation and @RISK. For example, how could we have answered the CFO's question about how much money to accrue using best case/worst case analysis or what-if analysis? The fact is, we could not answer the question with any degree of accuracy without using simulation.

INCORPORATING GRAPHS AND STATISTICS INTO A SPREADSHEET

At times you will want to save some of the graphs or statistics created by @RISK. You can do so by selecting the Reports to Worksheet option from the Results menu. This option displays the Reports to Worksheet dialog box shown in Figure 13.15.

Figure 13.15: Reports to Worksheet dialog box

This dialog box provides options for saving different results to Excel. Excel automatically saves all the selected graphs and statistics in several worksheets of a new workbook.

SAVING GRAPHS TO SEPARATE FILES

Sometimes, you might want to save a particular graph in its own graph file (either bitmap or metafile) rather than saving it as a worksheet file. To do this:

1. With the graph displayed, click File, then click Save.

2. Click the type of file you want to save (either bitmap or metafile).

3. Enter a graph filename.

4. Click OK.

THE LIST BUTTON

The List button on the @RISK toolbar displays the Inputs By Output window shown in Figure 13.16.

Figure 13.16: Inputs By Output window

This window helps us to verify that our model is implemented correctly. The Outputs section shows information about all the cells selected for tracking as Outputs. The Delete Output button below this listing allows us to remove unwanted output cells so that @RISK will not track their values during the simulation runs. The Inputs section displays information about all the cells that contain RNGs (which @RISK refers to as Inputs). The buttons below this listing provide additional modeling features that are beyond the scope of this text.

THE OPEN AND SAVE BUTTONS

The Save button on the @RISK toolbar allows you to save the simulation results and graphs you create so that you can refer to them later without having to re-run the entire simulation. Then you can use the Open button on the @RISK toolbar to retrieve the saved simulation results. Whenever you quit @RISK, a dialog box appears asking if you want to save the current simulation data. If you click Yes, a summary file is created for the current simulation results. Later you can open this summary file in @RISK by clicking the Open button on the @RISK toolbar.

THE UNCERTAINTY OF SAMPLING

To this point, we have used simulation to generate 300 observations on our bottom-line performance measure and then calculated various statistics to describe the characteristics and behavior of the performance measure. For example, Figure 13.10 indicates that the mean company cost value in our sample is $36,118,170, and Figure 13.13 shows that a 90% chance exists of this performance measure assuming a value less than $38,850,620. But what if we repeat this process and generate another 300 observations? Would the sample mean for the new 300 observations also be exactly $36,118,170? Or would exactly 90% of the observations in the new sample be less than $38,850,620?

The answer to both these questions is "probably not." The sample of 300 observations used in our analysis was taken from a population of values that is theoretically infinite in size. That is, if we had enough time and our computer had enough memory, we could generate an infinite number of values for our bottom-line performance measure. Theoretically, we could then analyze this infinite population of values to determine its true mean value, its true standard deviation, and the true probability of the performance measure being less than $38,850,620. Unfortunately, we do not have the time or computer resources to determine these true characteristics (or parameters) of the population. The best we can do is take a sample from this population and, based on our sample, make estimates about the true characteristics of the underlying population. Our estimates will differ depending on the sample we choose and the size of the sample.

So, the mean of the sample we take is probably not equal to the true mean we would observe if we could analyze the entire population of values for our performance measure. The sample mean we calculate is just an estimate of the true population mean. In our example problem, we estimated that a 90% chance exists for our output variable to assume a value less than $38,850,620. However, this most likely is not equal to the true probability we would calculate if we could analyze the entire population. Thus, there is some element of uncertainty surrounding the statistical estimates resulting from simulation because we are using a sample to make inferences about the population. Fortunately, there are ways of measuring and describing the amount of uncertainty present in some of the estimates we make about the population under study. This is typically done by constructing confidence intervals for the population parameters being estimated.

CONSTRUCTING A CONFIDENCE INTERVAL FOR THE TRUE POPULATION MEAN

Constructing a confidence interval for the true population mean is a simple process. If $\bar{y}$ and s represent, respectively, the mean and standard deviation of a sample of size n from any population, then assuming n is sufficiently large ($n \geq 30$), the Central Limit Theorem tells us that the lower and upper limits of a 95% confidence interval for the true mean of the population are represented by:

$$95\% \text{ Lower Confidence Limit } = \bar{y} - 1.96 * \frac{s}{\sqrt{n}}$$

$$95\% \text{ Upper Confidence Limit } = \bar{y} + 1.96 * \frac{s}{\sqrt{n}}$$

13.6

Although we can be fairly certain that the sample mean we calculate from our sample data is not equal to the true population mean, we can be 95% confident that the true mean of the population falls somewhere between the lower and upper limits in equation 13.6. If we want a 90% or 99% confidence interval, we must change the value 1.96 in equation 13.6 to 1.645 or 2.575, respectively. The values 1.645 and 2.575 represent the 95 and 99.5 percentiles of the standard normal distribution, respectively.

For our example, the lower and upper limits of a 95% confidence interval for the true mean of the population of total company cost values can be calculated easily, as shown in cells B7 and B8 in Figure 13.17. (The sample mean and standard deviation shown in Figure 13.17 were obtained from Figure 13.10.) The formulas for these cells are:

Formula for cell B7:   =B4−1.96*B5/SQRT(B2)

Formula for cell B8:   =B4+1.96*B5/SQRT(B2)

Thus, we can be 95% confident that the true mean of the population of total company cost values falls somewhere in the interval from \$35,871,929 to \$36,364,411.

CONSTRUCTING A CONFIDENCE INTERVAL FOR A POPULATION PROPORTION

In our example we estimated that 90% of the population of total company cost values fall below \$38,850,620 based on our sample of 300 observations. However, if we could evaluate the entire population of total cost values, we might find that only 80% of these values fall below \$38,850,620. Or we might find that 99% of the entire population falls below this mark. It would be helpful to determine how accurate the 90% value is. So, at times we might want to construct a confidence interval for the true proportion of a population that falls below (or above) some value, say Y_p.

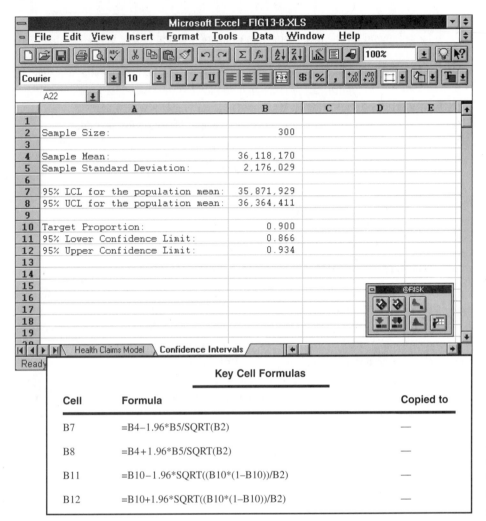

Figure 13.17: 95% confidence intervals for the corporate health insurance model

To see how this is done, let $\bar{p}$ denote the proportion of observations in a sample of size n that falls below some value Y_p. Assuming that n is sufficiently large ($n \geq 30$), the Central Limit Theorem tells us that the lower and upper limits of a 95% confidence interval for the true proportion of the population falling below Y_p are represented by:

$$\text{95\% Lower Confidence Limit} = \bar{p} - 1.96 * \sqrt{\frac{\bar{p}(1 - \bar{p})}{n}}$$

$$\text{95\% Upper Confidence Limit} = \bar{p} + 1.96 * \sqrt{\frac{\bar{p}(1 - \bar{p})}{n}}$$

13.7

Although we can be fairly certain that the proportion of observations falling below Y_p in our sample is not equal to the true proportion of the population falling below Y_p, we can be 95% confident that the true proportion of the population falling below Y_p is contained within the lower and upper limits in equation 13.7. Again, if we want a 90% or 99% confidence interval, we must change the value 1.96 in equation 13.7 to 1.645 or 2.575, respectively.

Using these formulas, we can calculate the lower and upper limits of a 95% confidence interval for the true proportion of the population falling below $38,850,620. From our simulation results we know that 90% of the observations in our sample are less than 38,850,620. Thus, our estimated value of $\bar{p}$ is 0.90. This value was entered into cell B10 in Figure 13.17. The upper and lower limits of a 95% confidence interval for the true proportion of the population falling below $38,850,620 are calculated in cells B11 and B12 of Figure 13.17 using the following formulas:

Formula for cell B11:   =B10–1.96*SQRT(B10*(1–B10)/B2)

Formula for cell B12:   =B10+1.96*SQRT(B10*(1–B10)/B2)

We can be 95% confident that the true proportion of the population of total cost values falling below $38,850,620 is between 0.866 and 0.934. Because this interval is fairly tight around the value 0.90, we can be reasonably certain that the $38,850,620 figure quoted to the CFO has approximately a 10% chance of being exceeded.

SAMPLE SIZES AND CONFIDENCE INTERVAL WIDTHS

The formulas for the confidence intervals in equations 13.6 and 13.7 depend directly on the number of replications (n) in the simulation. As the number of replications (n) increases, the width of the confidence interval decreases (or becomes more precise). Thus, for a given level of confidence (for example, 95%), the only way to make the upper and lower limits of the interval closer together (or tighter) is to make n larger—that is, use a larger sample size. A larger sample should provide more information about the population and, therefore, allow us to be more accurate in estimating the true parameters of the population.

THE BENEFITS OF SIMULATION

What have we accomplished through simulation? Are we really better off than if we had just used the results of the original model proposed in Figure 13.2? The estimated value for the expected total cost to the company in Figure 13.2 is comparable to that obtained through simulation (although this might not always be the case). But remember that the goal of modeling is to give us greater insight into a problem to help us make more informed decisions.

The results of our simulation analysis do give us greater insight into the example problem. In particular, we now have some idea of the best and worst case total cost outcomes for the company. We have a better idea of the distribution and variability of the possible outcomes, and a more precise idea about where the mean of the distribution is located. We also now have a way of determining how likely it is for the actual outcome to fall above or below some value. Thus, in addition to our greater insight and understanding of the problem, we also have solid empirical evidence (the facts and figures) to support our recommendations.

ADDITIONAL USES OF SIMULATION

Earlier we indicated that simulation is a technique that *describes* the behavior or characteristics of a bottom-line performance measure. The next two examples show how describing the behavior of a performance measure gives a manager a useful tool in determining the optimal value for one or more controllable parameters in a decision problem. These examples reinforce the mechanics of using simulation and also demonstrate some additional simulation modeling techniques.

AN INVENTORY CONTROL EXAMPLE

According to the *Wall Street Journal* (7/18/94), U.S. businesses had a combined inventory worth $884.77 billion dollars as of the end of May 1994. Because so much money is tied up in inventories, businesses face many important decisions regarding the management of these assets. Frequently asked questions regarding inventory include:

- What's the best level of inventory for a business to maintain?
- When should goods be reordered (or manufactured)?
- How much safety stock should be held in inventory?

The study of inventory control principles is split into two distinct areas—one assumes that demand is known (or deterministic), and the other assumes that demand is random (or stochastic). If demand is known, various formulas can be derived that provide answers to the previous questions (an example of one such formula is given in the discussion of the EOQ model in chapter 8.) However, when demand for a product is uncertain or random, answers to previous questions cannot be expressed in terms of a simple formula. In these situations, the technique of simulation proves to be a useful tool, as illustrated in the following example.

Laura Tanner is the owner of Computers of Tomorrow (COT), a retail computer store in Austin, Texas. Competition in retail computer sales is fierce—both in terms of price and service. Laura is concerned about the number of stockouts occurring on a popular type of computer monitor. This monitor is priced competitively and generates a marginal profit of $45 per unit sold. Stockouts are very costly to the business because when customers cannot buy this item at COT, they simply buy it from a competing store and COT loses the sale (there are no backorders). Laura measures the effects of stockouts on her business in terms of service level, or the percentage of total demand that can be satisfied from inventory.

Laura has been following the policy of ordering 50 monitors whenever her daily ending inventory position (defined as ending inventory on hand plus outstanding orders) falls below her reorder point of 28 units. Laura places the order at the beginning of the next day. Orders are delivered at the beginning of the day and, therefore, can be used to satisfy demand on that day. For example, if the ending inventory position on day 2 is less than 28, Laura places the order at the beginning of day 3. If the actual time between order and delivery, or **lead time**, turns out to be 4 days, then the order arrives at the start of day 7. The current level of on-hand inventory is 50 units and no orders are pending.

COT sells an average of 6 monitors per day. However, the actual number sold on any given day can vary. By reviewing her sales records for the past several months, Laura determined that the actual daily demand for this monitor is a random variable that can be described by the following probability distribution:

Units Demanded:	0	1	2	3	4	5	6	7	8	9	10
Probability:	0.01	0.02	0.04	0.06	0.09	0.14	0.18	0.22	0.16	0.06	0.02

The manufacturer of this computer monitor is located in California. Although it takes an average of 4 days for COT to receive an order from this company, Laura has determined that the lead time of a shipment of monitors is also a random variable that can be described by the following probability distribution:

Lead Time (days):	3	4	5
Probability:	0.2	0.6	0.2

One way to guard against stockouts and improve the service level is to increase the reorder point for the item so that more inventory is on hand to meet the demand occurring during the lead time. Laura wants to determine the reorder point that results in an average service level of 99%.

CREATING THE RNGs

To solve this problem, we need to build a model to represent the inventory of computer monitors during an average month of 30 days. This model must account for the random daily demands that can occur and the random lead times encountered when orders are placed. First we'll consider how to create RNGs to model the daily demands and order lead times. The data for these variables are entered in the spreadsheet as shown in Figure 13.18 (and in the file FIG13-18.XLS on your data disk).

Figure 13.18: RNG data for COT's inventory problem

The order lead time and daily demand variables are both examples of *general, discrete* random variables because the possible outcomes they assume consist solely of integers, and the probabilities associated with each outcome are not equal (or not uniform). Thus, using the RiskDiscrete() function described in Figure 13.5, the RNGs for each variable are:

RNG for order lead time: =RiskDiscrete(Data!$B$6:$B$8,Data!$C$6:$C$8)

RNG for daily demand: =RiskDiscrete(Data!$E$6:$E$16,Data!$F$6:$F$16)

IMPLEMENTING THE MODEL

Now that we have a way of generating the random numbers needed in this problem, we can consider how the model should be built. Figure 13.19 shows the model representing 30 days of inventory activity.

Because Laura wants to determine the reorder point that results in an average service level of 99%, cell D3 in Figure 13.19 is used to represent the reorder point. The order quantity is given in cell D4 so that Laura could also investigate the impact of changes in this value.

The inventory on hand at the beginning of each day is calculated in column B in Figure 13.19. The beginning inventory for each day is simply the ending inventory from the previous day. The formulas in column B are:

Formula for cell B8: =50

Formula for cell B9: =F8
(copy to B10 through B37)

Column C represents the number of units scheduled to be received each day. We'll discuss the formulas in column C after we discuss columns H, I, and J, which relate to ordering and order lead times.

In column D, we use the technique described earlier to generate random daily demands, as:

Formula for cell D8: =RiskDiscrete(Data!$E$6:$E$16,Data!$F$6:$F$16)
(copy to D9 through D37)

Because it is possible for demand to exceed the available supply, column E indicates how much of the daily demand can be met. If the beginning inventory (in column B) plus the ordered units received (in column C) is greater than or equal to the actual demand, then all the demand can be satisfied; otherwise, COT can sell only as many units as are available. This condition is modeled as:

Formula for cell E8: =MIN(B8+C8,D8)
(copy to E9 through E37)

The values in column F represent the on-hand inventory at the end of each day, and are calculated as:

Formula for cell F8: =B8+C8−E8
(copy to F9 through F37)

To determine whether or not to place an order, we first must calculate the inventory position, which was defined earlier as the ending inventory plus any outstanding orders. This is implemented in column G as:

Formula for cell G8: =F8

Formula for cell G9: =G8−E9+IF(H8=1,$D$4,0)
(copy to G10 through G37)

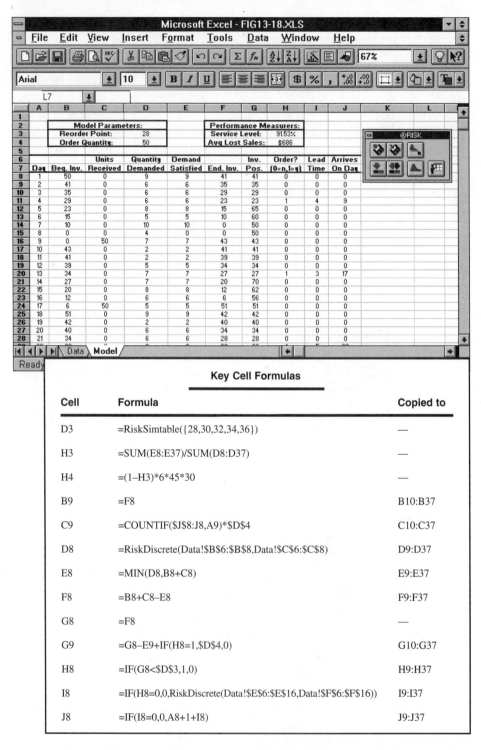

Figure 13.19: Spreadsheet model for COT's inventory problem

Column H indicates if an order should be placed based on inventory position and the reorder point, as:

Formula for cell H8:   =IF(G8<$D$3,1,0)
(copy to H9 through H37)

If an order is placed, then we must generate the random lead time required to receive the order. This is done in column I as:

Formula for cell I8:   =IF(H8=0,0,RiskDiscrete(Data!$B$6:$B$8,Data!$C$6:$C$8))
(copy to I9 through I37)

This formula returns the value 0 if no order was placed (if H8 = 0); otherwise, it returns a random lead time value (if H8 = 1).

If an order is placed, column J indicates the day on which the order will be received based on its random lead time in column I. This is done as:

Formula for cell J8:   =IF(H8=0,0,A8+1+I8)
(copy to J9 through J37)

The values in column C are coordinated with those in column J. The non-zero values in column J indicate the days on which orders will be received. For example, cell J11 indicates that an order will be received on day 9. The actual receipt of this order is reflected by the value of 50 in cell C16, which represents the receipt of an order at the beginning of day 9. The formula in cell C16 that achieves this is:

Formula for cell C16:   =COUNTIF($J$8:J15,A16)*$D$4

This formula counts how many times the value in cell A16 (representing day 9) appears as a scheduled receipt day between days 1 through 8 in column J. This represents the number of orders scheduled to be received on day 9. We then multiply this by the order quantity (50), given in cell D4 to determine the total units to be received on day 9. Thus, the values in column C are generated as:

Formula for cell C8:   =0

Formula for cell C9:   =COUNTIF($J$8:J8,A9)*$D$4
(copy to C10 through C37)

The service level for the model is calculated in cell H3 using the values in columns D and E as:

Formula for cell H3:   =SUM(E8:E37)/SUM(D8:D37)

Again, the service level represents the proportion of total demand that can be satisfied from inventory. The value in cell H3 indicates that in the scenario shown, 91.53% of the total demand is satisfied. Cell H4 translates this service level into dollars as:

Formula for cell H4:   =(1–H3)*6*45*30

Because the average daily demand for this monitor is for 6 units, and each monitor sold generates a marginal profit of $45, cell H4 indicates that in the scenario for this month, COT is losing about $686 in profits due to stockouts on this item.

REPLICATING THE MODEL

The model in Figure 13.19 indicates one possible scenario that could occur if Laura uses a reorder point of 28 units for the computer monitor. By replicating this model over and over, Laura could keep track of the service level occurring in each replication and average these values to determine the expected service level obtained with a reorder point of 28.

Using the simulation techniques described earlier, Laura could repeat this process with reorder points of 30 units, 32 units, and so on, until she finds the reorder point that achieves her goal of an average service level of 99%. However, there is another, easier way that Laura can perform the replications.

Suppose that we want to run five different simulations using reorder points of 28, 30, 32, 34, and 36, respectively. We can instruct @RISK to do this for us by entering the following formula in cell D3:

Formula for cell D3:   =RiskSimtable({28,30,32,34,36}).

In this case, @RISK sets the value of D3 to each number listed in the RiskSimtable() function. For each value, @RISK performs *n* replications of the model and summarizes the results. Before running the replications, we need to indicate the output cells we want to track by completing the following steps:

1. Click cell H3.
2. Click the +Output button on the @RISK toolbar.
3. Click cell H4.
4. Click the +Output button on the @RISK toolbar.

Suppose that we want to run 200 replications of the model for each possible reorder point value. To do this:

1. Click the SimSett button on the @RISK toolbar.
2. Enter 200 in the box labeled # Iterations =.
3. Enter 5 in the box labeled # Simulations = (because there are 5 values in the RiskSimtable() function in cell D3).
4. Click the Update Display option to deselect this option (to make the simulation run faster).
5. Click OK.
6. Click the Simulate button on the @RISK toolbar to start the simulation.

Completing the simulation could take several minutes depending on the speed of your computer. After performing the replications, @RISK summarizes the output data. Figure 13.20 shows the maximized Results window for the first simulation, which used a reorder point of 28.

DATA ANALYSIS

Figure 13.20 indicates that COT's current reorder point of 28 units results in an average service level of approximately 95.97%, with a minimum value of 85.22% and a maximum value of 100%. This implies that, on average, COT is unable to satisfy approximately 4.03% of the total demand using this reorder point. The results of tracking output cell H4 indicate that in an average month, COT loses about $326 in profits due to stockouts on the monitor.

By default, @RISK lists the results of one simulation at a time. To see the results of all five simulations at once, click the Merge Sim#'s button at the bottom of the Results window. Figure 13.21 shows the result of all five simulations.

By comparing the expected service levels of all five simulations shown in Figure 13.21, we see that as the reorder point increases, the service level also increases (or the percentage of lost sales decreases). So if Laura increases the

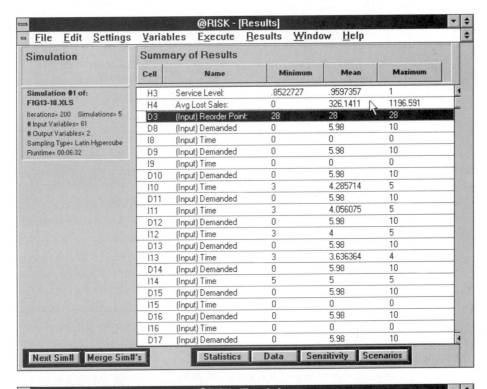

Figure 13.20: *Summary of results from first simulation of COT's inventory model*

Figure 13.21: *Summary of results from all five simulations of COT's inventory model*

reorder point to 36, COT's average service level for the monitor would increase to 99.57%, and the average monthly profit lost due to stockouts would decrease to approximately $34.62.

A FINAL COMMENT ON THE INVENTORY EXAMPLE

Although increasing the reorder point decreases the percentage of lost sales, it also increases the average level of inventory held and the number of orders that must be placed. Thus, another objective that might be considered in this problem involves weighing the costs of holding more inventory and placing more orders against the benefits of having fewer lost sales. We'll consider such an objective further in one of the problems at the end of this chapter.

AN OVERBOOKING EXAMPLE

Businesses that allow customers to make reservations for services (such as airlines, hotels, and car rental companies) know that some percentage of the reservations made will not be used for one reason or another, leaving these companies with a difficult decision problem. If they accept reservations for only the number of customers that can actually be served, then a portion of the company's assets will be underutilized when some customers with reservations fail to arrive. This results in an opportunity loss for the company. On the other hand, if they overbook (or accept more reservations than can be handled), then at times more customers will arrive than can actually be served. This typically results in additional financial costs to the company and often generates ill-will among those customers who cannot be served. The following example illustrates how simulation might be used to help a company determine the optimal number of reservations to accept.

Marty Ford is an operations analyst for Piedmont Commuter Airlines (PCA). Recently, Marty was asked to make a recommendation on how many reservations PCA should book on Flight 343—a flight in high demand from a small regional airport to a major hub airport. Historical data show that PCA frequently has seats left on Flight 343 if it accepts only 19 reservations (the plane's capacity). Industry statistics show that for every ticket sold for a commuter flight, a 0.10 probability exists that the ticket holder will not be on the flight. PCA sells nonrefundable tickets for Flight 343 for $85 per seat. Thus, every empty seat on this flight represents an opportunity cost—even if a no-show customer had purchased a ticket for the seat—because the seat could be filled by another passenger paying $85. On the other hand, if PCA overbooks this flight and more than 19 passengers show up, some of them will have to be bumped to a later flight.

To compensate for the inconvenience of being bumped, PCA gives these passengers vouchers for a free meal, a free flight at a later date, and sometimes also pays for them to stay overnight in a hotel near the airport. PCA pays an average of $155 for each passenger that gets bumped. Marty wants to determine if PCA can increase profits by overbooking this flight and, if so, how many reservations should be accepted to produce the maximum average profit. Marty wants to set up a model that allows him to investigate the consequences of accepting up to 24 reservations.

IMPLEMENTING THE MODEL

A spreadsheet model for this problem is shown in Figure 13.22 (and in the file FIG13-22.XLS on your data disk).

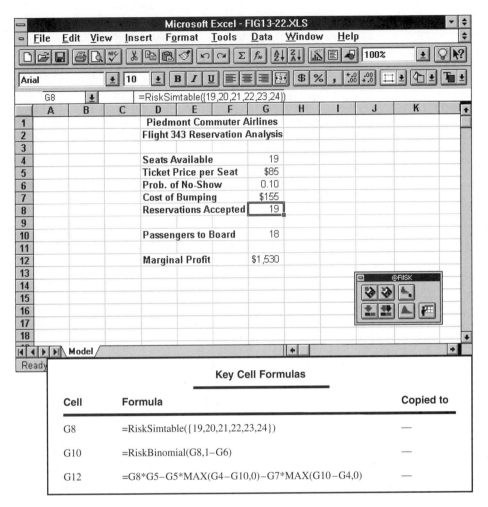

Figure 13.22: PCA model
with RNGs for uncertain
variables

The spreadsheet begins by listing the relevant data from the problem, including the number of seats available on the plane, the price PCA charges for each seat, the probability of a no-show (a ticketed passenger not arriving in time for the flight), the cost of bumping passengers, and the number of reservations that will be accepted.

The random element in this problem is the number of passengers arriving to board the plane, represented in cell G10 in Figure 13.22. Because each ticketed passenger has a 0.10 probability of being a no-show, a 0.9 probability exists that each ticketed passenger will arrive in time to board the flight. Thus, the RiskBinomial() function (described in Figure 13.5) is used in cell G10 to model the number of ticketed passengers that actually arrive for a flight:

Formula for cell G10: =RiskBinomial(G8,1–G6)

Cell G12 represents the marginal profit that PCA earns by accepting a given number of reservations. The formula for this cell is:

Formula for cell G12: =G5*G8–G5*MAX(0,G4–G10)–G7*MAX(0,G10–G4)

The first term in this formula (G5*G8) reflects the fact that PCA earns $85 for each reservation it accepts because its customers must pay for their tickets in advance, and tickets are nonrefundable. The next term (–G5*MAX(0,G4–G10)) indicates that PCA incurs an opportunity loss of $85 for each empty seat (or the amount by which G4 exceeds G10). The last term in this formula (–G7*MAX(0,G10–G4)) indicates that PCA incurs an average cost of $155 for each passenger that must be bumped when the number of passengers wanting to board exceeds the number of available seats (or the amount by which G10 exceeds G4).

REPLICATING THE MODEL

Marty wants to determine the number of reservations to accept that, on average, will result in the highest marginal profit. To do so, he needs to use the RiskSimtable( ) function to simulate what would happen if 19, 20, 21, 22, 23, and 24 reservations are accepted. Cell G8 contains the following formula:

Formula for cell G8:   =RiskSimtable({19,20,21,22,23,24})

This formula instructs @RISK to use six different values in cell G8 and simulate what will happen with each value.

Before starting the simulation, we must indicate the output cell(s) we want to track. To do so for our example problem:

1. Click cell G12.

2. Click the +Output button on the @RISK toolbar.

Next, we must indicate the number of simulations and the number of replications per simulation. To do so:

1. Click the SimSett button on the @RISK toolbar.

2. Enter 200 in the box labeled # Iterations = .

3. Enter 6 in the box labeled # Simulations = (because there are 6 values in the RiskSimtable() function in cell G8).

4. Click the Update Display option to deselect this option (to make the simulation run faster).

5. Click OK.

6. Click the Simulate button on the @RISK toolbar to start the simulation.

@RISK places the different values in cell G8, beginning with the value 19 and ending with the value 24, and runs a simulation consisting of 200 replications for each value. Depending on the speed of your computer, this could take several minutes.

After performing the replications, @RISK summarizes the output data. Figure 13.23 shows the maximized Results window for the first simulation, in which 19 reservations were accepted.

DATA ANALYSIS

Figure 13.23 indicates that PCA can, on average, expect to earn a marginal profit of approximately $1,453.84 when 19 reservations are accepted for Flight 343. The minimum and maximum marginal profit levels occurring in the 200 replications with 19 reservations are $1,020 and $1,615, respectively.

By default, @RISK lists the results of one simulation at a time. To see the results of all six simulations at once, click the Merge Sim#'s button at the bottom of the Results window. Figure 13.24 shows the results of all six simulations.

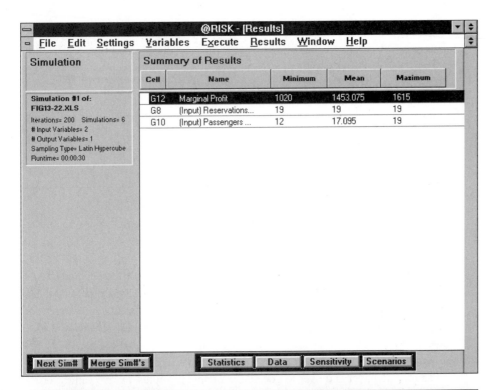

Figure 13.23: Summary of
results from first simulation
of the PCA model

Figure 13.24: Summary
of results from all six
simulations of the
PCA model

By comparing the expected profits of all six simulations, we see that they range
from a low of $1,453 (when 19 reservations are accepted) to a high of $1,683
(when 22 reservations are accepted). Thus, if PCA wants to maximize the expected
profit for Flight 343, it should accept 22 reservations for this flight.

A Final Comment on the Overbooking Example

This problem assumed that all the reservations available for Flight 343 would always be taken—or that there would never be unused reservations. However, if PCA accepts up to 22 reservations, there might be times when only 16 or 17 seats would be demanded. Thus, the demand for seats on this flight could be modeled more accurately as a random variable. We'll explore this issue more fully in one of the problems at the end of this chapter.

SUMMARY

This chapter introduced the concept of risk analysis and simulation. Many of the input cells in a spreadsheet represent random variables whose values cannot be determined with certainty. Any uncertainty in the input cells flows through the spreadsheet model to create a related uncertainty in the value of the output cell(s). Decisions made on the basis of these uncertain values involve some degree of risk.

Various methods of risk analysis are available, including best case/worst case analysis, what-if analysis, and simulation. Of these three methods, simulation is the only technique that provides hard evidence (facts and figures) that can be used objectively in making decisions. To simulate a model, RNGs are used to select representative values for each uncertain independent variable in the model. This process is repeated over and over to generate a sample of representative values for the dependent variable(s) in the model. The variability and distribution of the sample values for the dependent variable(s) can then be analyzed to gain insight into the possible outcomes that might occur. This chapter highlighted the use of the @RISK add-in to perform spreadsheet simulation.

REFERENCES

Banks, J. and J. Carson. *Discrete-Event Simulation.* Englewood Cliffs, NJ: Prentice Hall, 1984.

Hamzawi, S. "Management and Planning of Airport Gate Capacity: A Microcomputer-Based Gate Assignment Simulation Model." *Transportation Planning and Technology*, vol. 11, 1986.

Kaplan, A. and S. Frazza. "Empirical Inventory Simulation: A Case Study." *Decision Sciences*, vol. 14, January 1983.

Khoshnevis, B. *Discrete Systems Simulation.* New York: McGraw-Hill, 1994.

Law, A. and W. Kelton. *Simulation Modeling and Analysis.* New York: McGraw-Hill, 1990.

Marcus, A. "The Magellan Fund and Market Efficiency." *Journal of Portfolio Management*, Fall 1990.

Russell, R. and R. Hickle. "Simulation of a CD Portfolio." *Interfaces*, vol. 16, no. 3, 1986.

Vollman, T., W. Berry and C. Whybark. *Manufacturing Planning and Control Systems.* Homewood, IL: Irwin, 1987.

Watson, H. *Computer Simulation in Business.* New York: Wiley, 1981.

Spreadsheet Simulation Enables Big Rivers Electric to View Energy Forecasts as Probability Distributions

Source: Mumford, Lloyd G., David E. Schultz and Marvin D. Troutt, "Using Spreadsheet Simulation to Generate a Distribution of Forecasts for Electric Power Demand," *Journal of the Operational Research Society*, vol. 42, no. 11, November 1991, pages 931-939.

LIKE ANY BUSINESS that distributes a product, an electric utility company must begin its operations planning with a forecast of demand. Econometric forecasting methods are widely used to compute a point estimate of demand for electric power, and also a probability distribution of the forecast error.

Big Rivers Electric Corporation, a cooperative in western Kentucky, goes one step further. Using @RISK, it treats the input variables for the forecasting model as random variables and computes the point estimate of demand as a probability distribution rather than a single number. The company's model for the residential sector, for example, uses such independent variables as real per capita income and population (both modeled as triangular distributions using three independent forecasts), heating degree days and cooling degree days (both modeled as normally distributed with mean and standard deviations estimated from 17 years of data), and lagged average use. The latter is random because the forecast for the previous year is random.

A total of eight demand distributions are created because the cooperative has four members, and each forecasts both residential and small commercial and industrial sectors. These distributions are then imported into a spreadsheet that generates the total energy requirements forecast.

Questions and Problems

1. Under what condition(s) is it appropriate to use simulation to analyze a model? That is, what characteristics should a model possess in order for simulation to be used?

2. The graph of the probability distribution of a normally distributed random variable with a mean of 20 and standard deviation of 3 is shown in Figure 13.7.

    a. Use the RNG for the normal distribution discussed in the chapter to generate 100 sample values from this distribution.

    b. Produce a histogram of the 100 sample values you generated. Does your histogram look like the graph for this distribution in Figure 13.7?

    c. Repeat this experiment with the same RNG, only this time sample 1,000 values.

    d. Produce a histogram for the 1,000 sample values you generated. Does the histogram now more closely resemble the graph in Figure 13.7 for this distribution?

    e. Why does your second histogram look more "normal" than the first one?

3. The manager of Moore's Catalog Showroom is trying to predict how much revenue will be generated by each major department in the store during 1996. The manager has estimated the minimum and maximum growth rates possible for revenues in each department. The manager believes that any of the possible growth rates between the minimum and maximum values are equally likely to occur. These estimates are summarized in the following table:

Department	1995 Revenues	Growth Rates	
		Minimum	Maximum
Electronics	$6,342,213	2%	10%
Garden Supplies	$1,203,231	−4%	5%
Jewelry	$4,367,342	−2%	6%
Sporting Goods	$3,543,532	−1%	8%
Toys	$4,342,132	4%	15%

Create a spreadsheet to simulate the total revenues that could occur in the coming year. Run 500 replications of the model and do the following:

a. Construct a 95% confidence interval for the average level of revenues the manager could expect for 1996.

b. According to your model, what are the chances that total revenues in 1996 will be more than 5% larger than those in 1995?

4. Lynn Price recently completed her MBA and accepted a job with an electronics manufacturing company. Although she likes her job, she is also looking forward to retiring one day. To ensure that her retirement is comfortable, Lynn intends to invest $3,000 of her salary into a tax-sheltered retirement fund at the end of each year. Lynn is not certain what rate of return this investment will earn, but she expects that the rate could be modeled appropriately as a normally distributed random variable with a mean of 12% and standard deviation of 2%.

    a. If Lynn is 30 years old, how much money should she expect to have in her retirement fund at age 60? (Use 500 replications.)

    b. What is the probability that Lynn will have more than $1 million in her retirement fund when she reaches age 60?

5. Acme Equipment Company is considering the development of a new machine that would be marketed to tire manufacturers. Research and development costs for the project are expected to be about $4 million but could vary between $2 and $6 million. The market life for the product is estimated to be 3 to 8 years with all intervening possibilities being equally likely. The company thinks it will sell 200 units per year, but acknowledges that this figure could be as low as 50 or as high as 350. The company will sell the machine for about $23,000. Finally, the cost of manufacturing the machine is expected to be about $14,000, but could vary from $13,000 to $15,000. The company's cost of capital is 15%.

    a. Use appropriate RNGs to create a spreadsheet to calculate the possible net present values (NPVs) that could result from taking on this project.

    b. Replicate the model 500 times. What is the expected NPV for this project?

    c. What is the probability of this project generating a positive NPV for the company?

6. Representatives from the American Heart Association are planning to go door-to-door throughout a community, soliciting contributions. From past experience they know that when someone answers the door, 80% of the time it is a female and 20% of the time it is a male. They also know that 70% of the females who answer the door make a donation, whereas only 40% of the males who answer the door make donations. The amount of money that females contribute follows a normal distribution with a mean of $20 and standard deviation of $3. The amount of money males contribute follows a normal distribution with a mean of $10 and standard deviation of $2.

    a. Create a spreadsheet model that simulates what might happen whenever a representative of the American Heart Association knocks on a door and someone answers.

    b. Replicate your model 500 times. What is the average contribution the Heart Association can expect to receive when someone answers the door?

    c. Suppose that the Heart Association plans to visit 300 homes on a given Saturday. If no one is home at 25% of the residences, what is the total amount the Heart Association can expect to receive in donations?

7. After spending 10 years as an assistant manager for a large restaurant chain, Ray Clark has decided to become his own boss. The owner of a local submarine sandwich store wants to sell the store to Ray for $65,000 to be paid in installments of $13,000 in each of the next 5 years. According to the current owner, the store brings in revenue of about $100,000 per year and incurs operating costs of about 63% of sales. Thus, once the store is paid for, Ray should make about $35,000–$40,000 per year before taxes. Until the store is paid for, he will make substantially less—but he will be his own boss. Realizing that some uncertainty is involved in this decision, Ray wants to simulate what level of net income he can expect to earn during the next 5 years as he operates and pays for the store. In particular, he wants to see what could happen if sales are allowed to vary uniformly between $80,000 and $110,000 and if operating costs are allowed to vary uniformly between 60% and 65% of sales. Assume that Ray's payments for the store are deductible and that he is in the 28% tax bracket.

    a. Create a spreadsheet model to simulate the annual net income Ray would receive during each of the next 5 years if he decides to buy the store.

    b. Given the money he has in savings, Ray thinks he can get by for the next 5 years if he can make at least $12,000 from the store each year. Replicate the model 500 times and track the minimum amount of money Ray makes over the 5-year period represented by each replication. What is the probability that Ray will make at least $12,000 in each of the next 5 years?

8. Bob Davidson owns a newsstand outside the Waterstone office building complex in Atlanta, near Hartsfield International Airport. He buys his papers wholesale at $0.50 per paper and sells them for $0.75. Bob wonders what is the optimal number of papers to order each day. Based on history, he has found that demand (even though it is discrete) can be modeled by a normal distribution with a mean of 50 and standard deviation of 5. When he has more papers than customers, he can recycle all the extra papers the next day and receive $0.05 per paper. On the other hand, if he has more customers than papers, he loses some goodwill in addition to the lost profit on the potential sale of $0.25. Bob estimates the incremental lost goodwill costs five day's worth of business (that is, dissatisfied customers will go to a competitor the next week, but come back to him the week after that).

    a. Create a spreadsheet model to determine the optimal number of papers to order each day. Use 250 replications and round the demand values generated by the normal RNG to the closest integer value.

    b. Construct a 95% confidence interval for the expected payoff from the optimal decision.

9. Vinton Auto Insurance is trying to decide how much money to keep in liquid assets to cover insurance claims. In the past, the company held some of the premiums it received in interest-bearing checking accounts and put the rest into investments that are not quite as liquid, but tend to generate a higher investment return. The company wants to study cash flows to determine how much money it should keep in liquid assets to pay claims. After reviewing

historical data, the company determined that the average repair bill per claim is normally distributed with a mean of $1,700 and standard deviation of $400. It also determined that the number of repair claims filed each week is a random variable that follows the probability distribution given below:

Number of Repair Claims	Probability
1	0.05
2	0.06
3	0.10
4	0.17
5	0.28
6	0.14
7	0.08
8	0.07
9	0.05

In addition to repair claims, the company also receives claims for cars that have been "totaled" and cannot be repaired. A 20% chance of receiving this type of claim exists in any week. Typically these claims cost anywhere from $2,000 to $20,000, with $11,000 being the most common cost.

a. Create a spreadsheet model of the total claims cost incurred by the company in any week. (Hint: Use the RiskDiscrete( ) function to generate the random number of repair claims occurring each week. Use the RiskTriang( ) function to generate the costs of "totaled" cars.)

b. Replicate the model 500 times and create a histogram of the distribution of total cost values that were generated.

c. What is the average cost the company should expect to pay each week?

d. Suppose that the company decides to keep $20,000 cash on hand to pay claims. What is the probability that this amount would not be adequate to cover claims in any week?

10. The owner of a local car dealership has just received a call from a regional distributor stating that a $5,000 bonus will be awarded if the owner's dealership sells at least 10 new cars next Saturday. On an average Saturday, this dealership has 80 potential customers look at new cars, but there is no way to determine exactly how many customers will come this particular Saturday. The owner is fairly certain that the number would not be less than 40, but also thinks it would be unrealistic to expect more than 120 (which is the largest number of customers to ever show up in one day). To generate the number of customers who arrive at the dealership next Saturday, we might use the following RNG:

=RiskTriang(40,80,120)

The owner determined that, on average, about 1 out of 10 customers who look at cars at the dealership actually purchase a car—or, a 0.10 probability (or 10% chance) exists that any given customer will buy a new car.

a. Create a spreadsheet model for this problem and generate 100 random outcomes for the number of cars the dealership might sell next Saturday. (Hint: The number of cars sold is a binomial random variable where n = RiskTriang(40,80,120) and p = 0.1.)

b. What is the probability that the dealership will earn the $5,000 bonus?

c. If you were this dealer, what is the maximum amount of money you'd be willing to spend on sales incentives to try to earn this bonus?

11. Dr. Sarah Benson is an ophthalmologist who, in addition to prescribing glasses and contact lenses, performs optical laser surgery to correct nearsightedness. This surgery is fairly easy and inexpensive to perform. Thus, it represents a potential gold mine for her practice. To inform the public about this procedure, Dr. Benson advertises in the local paper and holds information sessions in her office one night a week at which she shows a videotape about the procedure and answers any questions potential patients might have. The room where these meetings are held can seat 10 people, and reservations are required. The number of people attending each session varies from week to week. Dr. Benson cancels the meeting if 2 or fewer people have made reservations. Using data from the previous year, Dr. Benson determined that the distribution of reservations is as follows:

Number of Reservations:	0	1	2	3	4	5	6	7	8	9	10
Probability:	0.02	0.05	0.08	0.16	0.26	0.18	0.11	0.07	0.05	0.01	0.01

Using data from the past year, Dr. Benson determined that about 25% of the people attending the information session elect to have the surgery performed. Of those who do not, most cite the cost of the procedure—$2,000—as their major concern.

a. On average, how much revenue does Dr. Benson's practice in laser surgery generate each week? (Use 500 replications.)

b. On average, how much revenue would the laser surgery generate each week if Dr. Benson did not cancel sessions with 2 or fewer reservations?

c. Dr. Benson believes that 35% of the people attending the information sessions would have the surgery if she reduced the price to $1,500. Under this scenario, how much revenue could Dr. Benson expect to realize per week from laser surgery?

12. One of the examples in this chapter dealt with determining the optimal reorder point for a computer monitor sold by Computers of Tomorrow (COT) in Austin, Texas. In this example we found that increasing the reorder point decreased the number of lost sales. However, this also increased the average amount of inventory carried.

Suppose that it costs COT $0.30 per day in holding costs for each monitor in beginning inventory, and it costs $20 to place an order. Each monitor sold generates a profit of $45, and each lost sale results in an opportunity cost of $65 (including the lost profit of $45 and $20 in lost goodwill). Modify the spreadsheet given in the file FIG13-18.XLS on your data disk accordingly to determine the reorder point that maximizes the average monthly profit associated with this monitor.

13. One of the examples in this chapter dealt with determining the optimal number of reservations for Piedmont Commuter Airlines (PCA) to accept for one of its flights that uses a plane with 19 seats. The model discussed in the chapter assumes that all the reservations would be used, but some customers would not show up for the flight. It is probably more realistic to assume that the demand for these reservations is somewhat random. For example, suppose that the demand for reservations on this flight is given by the following probability distribution:

Reservations Demanded:	12	13	14	15	16	17	18	19	20	21	22	23	24
Probability:	0.01	0.03	0.04	0.07	0.09	0.11	0.15	0.18	0.14	0.08	0.05	0.03	0.02

The number of passengers receiving reservations depends on the number of reservations PCA accepts and the demand for these reservations. For each passenger receiving a reservation, a 0.10 probability exists that they will not arrive at the gate to board the plane. Modify the spreadsheet given in the file FIG13-22.XLS on your data disk accordingly to determine the number of reservations PCA should accept to maximize the average profit associated with this flight.

The Sound's Alive Company
A Case in Risk Analysis and Simulation

MARISSA Jones is the president and CEO of Sound's Alive, a company that manufactures and sells a line of speakers, CD players, receivers, high-definition televisions, and other items geared for the home entertainment market. Respected throughout the industry for bringing many high-quality, innovative products to market, Marissa is considering adding a speaker system to her product line.

The speaker market has changed dramatically during the last several years. Originally, high fidelity aficionados knew that to reproduce sound covering the fullest range of frequencies—from the lowest kettle drum to the highest violin—a speaker system had to be large and heavy. The speaker had various drivers: a woofer to reproduce the low notes, a tweeter for the high notes, and a mid-range driver for the broad spectrum of frequencies in between. Many speaker systems had a minimum of three drivers, but some had even more. The trouble was that such a system was too large for anything but the biggest rooms, and consumers were reluctant to spend thousands of dollars and give up valuable wall space to get the excellent sound these speakers could reproduce.

The trend has changed during the past several years. Consumers still want good sound, but they want it from smaller boxes. Therefore, the satellite system became popular. Consisting of two small boxes that house either one driver (to cover the mid-range and high frequencies) or two (a mid-range and tweeter), a satellite system can easily be mounted on walls or shelves. To reproduce the low notes, a separate sub-woofer that is approximately the size of a cube 18 inches on a side is also needed. This sub-woofer can be placed anywhere in the room. Taking up less space than a typical large speaker system and sounding almost as good, yet costing hundreds of dollars less, these satellite systems are hot items in the high fidelity market.

Recently the separate wings of home entertainment—high fidelity (receivers, speakers, CD players, CDs, cassettes, and so on), television (large screen monitors, video cassette recorders, laser players), and computers (games with sounds, virtual reality software, and so on)—have merged into the home

Contributed by Jack Yurkiewicz, Lubin School of Business, Pace University, New York.

theater concept. To simulate the movie environment, a home theater system requires the traditional stereo speaker system plus additional speakers placed in the rear of the room so that viewers are literally surrounded with sound. Although the rear speakers do not have to match the high quality of the front speakers and, therefore, can be less expensive, most consumers choose a system in which the front and rear speakers are of equal quality, reproducing the full range of frequencies with equal fidelity.

It is this speaker market that Marissa wants to enter. She is considering having Sound's Alive manufacture and sell a home theater system that consists of seven speakers. Three small speakers—each with one dome tweeter that could reproduce the frequency range of 200 Hertz to 20,000 Hertz (upper-low frequencies to the highest frequencies)—would be placed in front, and three similar speakers would be placed strategically around the sides and back of the room. To reproduce the lowest frequencies (from 35 Hertz to 200 Hertz), a single sub-woofer would also be part of the system. This sub-woofer is revolutionary because it is smaller than the ordinary sub-woofer, only 10 inches per side, and it has a built-in amplifier to power it. Consumers and critics are thrilled with the music from early prototype systems, claiming that these speakers have the best balance of sound and size. Marissa is extremely encouraged by these early reviews, and although her company has never produced a product with its house label on it (having always sold systems from established high fidelity companies), she believes that Sound's Alive should enter the home theater market with this product.

PHASE ONE: PROJECTING PROFITS

Marissa decides to create a spreadsheet that will project profits over the next several years. After consulting with economists, market analysts, employees in her own company, and employees from other companies that sell house brand components, Marissa is confident that the gross revenues for these speakers in 1995 would be around $6 million. She must also figure that a small percentage of speakers will be damaged in transit, or some will be returned by dissatisfied customers shortly after the sales. These returns and allowances (R&As) are usually calculated as 2% of the gross revenues. Hence, the net revenues are simply the gross revenues minus the R&As. Marissa believes that the 1995 labor costs for these speakers will be $995,100. The cost of materials (including boxes to ship the speakers) should be $915,350 for 1995. Finally, her overhead costs (rent, lighting, heating in winter, air conditioning in summer, security, and so on) for 1995 should be $1,536,120. Thus, the cost of goods sold is the sum of labor, material, and overhead costs. Marissa figures the gross profit as the difference between the gross revenues and the cost of goods sold. In addition, she must consider the selling, general, and administrative (SG&A) expenses. These expenses are more difficult to estimate, but the standard industry practice is to use 18% of the net revenues as the nominal percentage value for these expenses. Therefore, Marissa's profit *before taxes* is the gross profit minus the SG&A value. To calculate taxes, Marissa multiplies her profits before taxes times the tax rate, currently 30%. If her company is operating at a loss, however, no taxes would have to be paid. Finally, Marissa's net (or after tax) profit is simply the difference between the profit before taxes and the actual taxes paid.

To determine the numbers for 1996 through 1998, Marissa assumes that gross revenues, labor costs, material costs, and overhead costs will increase over the years. Although the rates of increase for these items are difficult to estimate, Marissa figures that gross revenues will increase by 9% per year, labor costs will increase by 4% per year, material costs will increase by 6% per year, and overhead costs will increase by 3% per year. She figures that the tax rate will not change from the 30% mark, and she assumes that the SG&A value will remain at 18%.

The basic layout of the spreadsheet that Marissa creates is shown in the following figure (and in the file C12CASE.XLS on your data disk). (Ignore the Competition Assumptions section for now; we'll consider it later.) Construct the spreadsheet and determine the values for the years 1995 through 1998, then determine the totals for the four years.

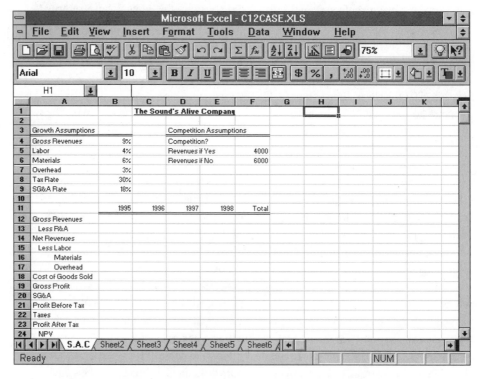

Marissa not only wants to determine her net profits for 1995 through 1998, she also must justify her decisions to the company's Board of Trustees. Should she even consider entering this market, from a financial point of view? One way to answer this question is to find the net present value (NPV) of the net profits for 1995 through 1998. Use your spreadsheet's NPV capability to find the NPV, at the current interest rate of 5%, of the profits values for 1995 through 1998.

To avoid large values in the spreadsheet, enter all dollar calculations in thousands. For example, enter labor costs as 995.10 and overhead costs as 1536.12.

PHASE TWO: BRINGING COMPETITION INTO THE MODEL

With her spreadsheet complete, Marissa is confident that entering the home theater speaker market would be lucrative for Sound's Alive. However, she has not considered one factor in her calculations—competition. The current market leader and company she is most concerned about is the Bose Corporation. Bose pioneered the concept of a satellite speaker system, and its AMT series is very successful. Marissa is concerned that Bose will enter the home theater speaker market, cutting into her gross revenues. If Bose does enter the market, Marissa believes that Sound's Alive would still make money; however, she would have to revise her gross revenues estimate from $6 million to $4 million for 1995.

To account for the competition factor, Marissa revises her spreadsheet by adding a Competition Assumptions section. Cell F4 will contain either a 0 (no competition) or a 1 (if Bose enters the market). Cells F5 and F6 provide the gross revenue estimates (in thousands of dollars) for the two possibilities. Modify your spreadsheet to take these options into account. Use the IF( ) function for the gross revenues for 1995 (cell B12). If Bose does enter the market, not only would Marissa's gross revenues be lower, but the labor, materials, and overhead costs would also be lower because Sound's Alive would be making and selling fewer speakers. Marissa thinks that if Bose enters the market, her 1995 labor costs would be $859,170, 1995 material costs would be $702,950, and 1995 overhead costs would be $1,288,750. She believes that her growth rate assumptions would stay the same whether or not Bose enters the market. Add these possible values to your spreadsheet using the IF( ) function in the appropriate cells.

Look at the net profits for 1995 through 1998. In particular, examine the NPV for the two scenarios: Bose does or does not enter the home theater speaker market.

PHASE THREE: BRINGING UNCERTAINTY INTO THE MODEL

Jim Allison, the chief of operations at Sound's Alive and a quantitative methods specialist, plays a key role in providing Marissa with estimates for the various revenues and costs. He is uneasy about the basic estimates for the growth rates. For example, although market research indicates that a 9% gross revenue increase per year is reasonable, Jim know that if this value is 7%, for example, the profit values and the NPV would be quite different. Even more troublesome is a potential tax increase, which would hit Sound's Alive hard. Jim believes that the tax rate could vary around the expected 30% figure. Finally, Jim is uncomfortable with the industry's standard estimate of 18% for the SG&A rate. Jim thinks that this value could be higher or even lower.

The Sound's Alive problem is too complicated for solving with what-if analysis because seven assumed values could change: the growth rates for gross revenues, labor, materials, overhead costs, tax rate, SG&A percent, and whether or not Bose enters the market. Jim believes that a Monte Carlo simulation would be a better approach. Jim thinks that the behavior of these variables can be modeled as:

Gross Revenues (%)

Normally distributed, mean = 9.9 std dev = 1.4

Labor Growth (%)

Normally distributed, mean = 3.45 std dev = 1.0

Materials (%)	Probability
4	0.10
5	0.15
6	0.15
7	0.25
8	0.25
9	0.10

Overhead (%)	Probability
2	0.20
3	0.35
4	0.25
5	0.20

Tax Rate (%)	Probability
30	0.15
32	0.30
34	0.30
36	0.25

SG&A (%)	Probability
15	0.05
16	0.10
17	0.20
18	0.25
19	0.20
20	0.20

Finally, Jim and Marissa agree that there is a 50/50 chance that Bose will enter the market.

Use simulation to analyze the Sound's Alive problem. Based on your results, what is the expected net profit for the years 1995 through 1998, and what is the expected NPV for this business venture?

The Board of Trustees told Marissa that the stockholders would feel comfortable with this business venture if its NPV is at least $5 million. What are the chances that Sound's Alive home theater venture will result in an NPV of $5 million or more?

CHAPTER 14

Queuing Theory

SOMETIMES IT SEEMS as if we spend most of our lives waiting in lines. We wait in lines at grocery stores, banks, airports, hotels, restaurants, theaters, theme parks, post offices, and traffic lights. At home we are likely to spend time waiting in an "electronic line" if we use the telephone to order merchandise from mail-order firms, or to call the customer service number of most computer hardware or software companies.

Some reports indicate that Americans spend *37 billion* hours a year waiting in lines. Much of this time represents a loss of a limited resource (time) that can never be recovered. Add the frustration and irritation many people experience while waiting in lines and it is easy to see why businesses should be interested in reducing or eliminating the amount of time their customers spend waiting in lines.

Waiting lines do not always contain people. In a manufacturing company, for example, subassemblies often wait in a line at machining centers to have the next operation performed on them. At a video rental store, returned videos often wait to be placed on shelves so they can be rented again. Electronic messages on the Internet sometimes wait at intermediate computing centers before they are sent to their final destinations. Costs could be reduced, or customer service improved, by reducing the amount of time that the subassemblies, videos, or electronic messages spend waiting in line.

In management science terminology, the term **queuing theory** represents the body of knowledge dealing with waiting lines. Queuing theory was conceived in the early 1900s when a Danish telephone engineer named A. K. Erlang began studying the congestion and waiting times occurring in the completion of telephone calls. Since then, a number of quantitative models have been developed to help business people understand waiting lines and make better decisions about how to manage them. This chapter introduces some of these models and discusses other issues involved in queuing theory.

THE PURPOSE OF QUEUING MODELS

Most queuing problems focus on determining the level of service that a company should provide. For example, grocery stores must determine how many cash registers to operate at a given time of day so that customers do not have to wait too long to check out. Banks must determine how many tellers to schedule at various times of day to maintain an acceptable level of service. Companies that lease copying machines must determine the number of technicians to employ so that repairs can be made in a timely manner.

In many queuing problems, management has some control over the level of service provided. In the examples just mentioned, customer waiting times could be kept to a minimum by employing a large number of servers (in the form of cashiers, tellers, and technicians). However, this can be expensive, or actually wasteful, if an excessive number of idle servers is maintained. On the other hand, employing a small number of servers keeps the cost of providing service low, but is likely to result in longer customer waiting times and greater customer dissatisfaction. Thus, a trade-off exists between the cost of providing service and the cost of having dissatisfied customers if service is lacking. The nature of this trade-off is illustrated in Figure 14.1.

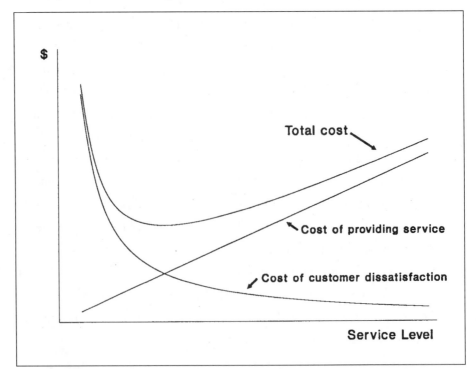

Figure 14.1: Trade-off between cost of providing service and customer satisfaction

Figure 14.1 indicates that as service levels increase, the cost of providing service also increases, but the cost of customer dissatisfaction decreases (as does the length of time customers must wait for service). As service levels decrease, the cost of providing service also decreases, but the cost of customer dissatisfaction increases. The objective in many queuing problems is to find the optimal service level that achieves an acceptable balance between the cost of providing service and customer satisfaction.

QUEUING SYSTEM CONFIGURATIONS

The queuing systems we encounter in everyday life are configured in a variety of ways. Three typical configurations are illustrated in Figure 14.2.

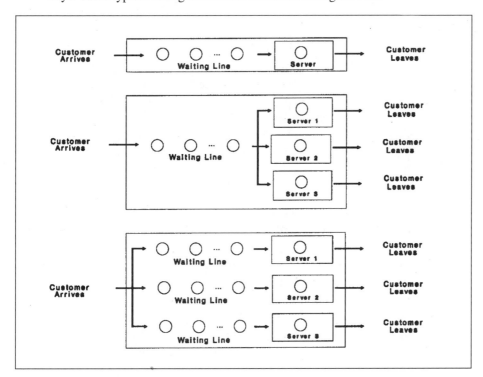

Figure 14.2: Examples of different queuing system configurations

The first configuration in Figure 14.2 represents a single-queue, single-server system. In this configuration, customers enter the system and wait in line on a first-in, first-out (FIFO) basis until they receive service, then they exit the system. This type of queuing system is employed at most Wendy's and Taco Bell restaurants. You might also encounter this type of queuing system at some automatic teller machines (ATMs).

The second configuration in Figure 14.2 represents a single-queue, multi-server system. Here again, customers enter the system and join a FIFO queue. Upon reaching the front of the line, a customer is serviced by the next available server. The example shows three servers, but there could be more or fewer servers depending on the problem at hand. This type of queuing system is found at most airport check-in counters, post offices, and banks.

The third configuration in Figure 14.2 represents a collection of single-queue, single-server systems. In this type of arrangement, when customers arrive they must choose one of the queues and then wait in that line to receive service. This type of system is found at most grocery stores and most Burger King and McDonalds restaurants.

This chapter discusses queuing models that can be used to analyze the first two types of configurations shown in Figure 14.2. In some cases, the individual queues in the third configuration in Figure 14.2 can be analyzed as independent, single-queue, single-server systems. Thus, the results presented for the first type of configuration can sometimes be generalized to analyze the third configuration also.

CHARACTERISTICS OF QUEUING SYSTEMS

To create and analyze mathematical models of the queuing configurations shown in Figure 14.2, we must make some assumptions about the way in which customers arrive to the system and the amount of time it takes for them to receive service.

ARRIVAL RATE

In most queuing systems, customers (or jobs in a manufacturing environment) arrive in a somewhat random fashion. That is, the number of arrivals that occurs in a given time period represents a random variable. It is often appropriate to model the arrival process in a queuing system as a Poisson random variable. To use the Poisson probability distribution, we must specify a value for the **arrival rate**, denoted as λ, representing the average number of arrivals per time period. The probability of x arrivals in a specific time period is represented by:

$$P(x) = \frac{\lambda^x e^{-\lambda}}{x!} \text{ for } x = 0, 1, 2, \ldots \qquad \textbf{14.1}$$

where e represents the base of the natural logarithm ($e = 2.71828$) and $x! = (x)(x-1)$ $(x-2) \ldots (2)(1)$. ($x!$ is referred to as x factorial and can be calculated using the FACT( ) function in Excel.)

For example, suppose that calls to the customer service hotline of a computer retailer occur at a rate of 5 per hour and follow a Poisson probability distribution ($\lambda = 5$). The probability distribution associated with the number of calls arriving in a given hour is illustrated in Figure 14.3 (and in the file FIG14-3.XLS on your data disk).

In Figure 14.3, the values in column B represent the probabilities associated with each value in column A. For example, the value in cell B5 indicates that a 0.0067 probability exists of 0 calls arriving in a given hour; cell B6 indicates that a 0.0337 probability exists of 1 call arriving, and so on. The histogram of the probability distribution indicates that, on average, we can expect approximately 5 calls to arrive in 1 hour. However, because the Poisson distribution is skewed to the right, a significantly larger number of calls (in this case, 13 or more) could arrive in some 1-hour time periods.

Figure 14.3 indicates that the probability of 6 calls occurring in a given hour is 0.1462. However, the 6 calls probably will not occur at the same time. Some random amount of time is likely to transpire between arriving calls. This time between arrivals is known as the **interarrival time**. If the number of arrivals in a given period of time follows a Poisson distribution with mean λ, it can be shown that the interarrival times follow an exponential probability distribution with mean $1/\lambda$.

For example, if calls to the computer retailer's hotline follow a Poisson distribution and occur at an average rate of $\lambda = 5$ per hour, the interarrival times follow an exponential distribution with an average interarrival time of $1/5 = 0.2$ hours. That is, calls occur once every 12 minutes, on average (because there are 60 minutes in an hour and 0.2*60 minutes = 12 minutes).

Key Cell Formulas

Cell	Formula	Copied to
B5	=($B$2^A5*EXP(–$B$2))/FACT(A5)	B6:B18

Figure 14.3: Example of a Poisson probability distribution with λ = 5

The exponential distribution plays a key role in queuing models. It is one of the few probability distributions that exhibit the memoryless (or lack of memory) property. An arrival process is **memoryless** if the time until the next arrival occurs does not depend on how much time has elapsed since the last arrival. The Russian mathematician Markov was the first to recognize the memoryless property of certain random variables. Therefore, the memoryless property is also sometimes referred to as the Markov or Markovian property.

All the queuing models presented in this chapter assume that arrivals follow a Poisson distribution (or, equivalently, that interarrival times follow an exponential distribution). To use these models, it is important to verify that this assumption is valid for the queuing system being modeled. One way to verify that arrivals can be approximated by the Poisson distribution is to collect data on the number of arrivals occurring per time period for several hours, days, or weeks. The average number of arrivals per time period can be calculated from these data and used as an estimate of λ. A histogram of the actual data can be constructed and compared to a histogram of the actual probabilities expected of a Poisson random variable with mean λ. If the histograms are similar, it is reasonable to assume that the arrival process is approximately Poisson. (Additional goodness-of-fit tests can be found in most texts on queuing and simulation.)

SERVICE RATE

A customer who arrives at a service facility spends some amount of time (possibly 0) waiting in line for service to begin. We refer to this time as **queue time**. **Service time** is the amount of time a customer spends at a service facility once the actual performance of service begins. (So service time *does not* include queue time.)

It is often appropriate to model the service times in a queuing system as an exponential random variable. To use the exponential probability distribution for this purpose, we must specify a value for the **service rate**, denoted by μ, representing the average number of customers (or jobs) that can be served per time period. The average service time per customer is 1/μ time periods. If the distribution of service times follows an exponential probability distribution, the probability that the time (*t*) required to service a given customer will be less than or equal to some specific value T is represented by:

$$P(t \leq T) = 1 - e^{-\mu T}, \text{ for } T \geq 0 \qquad \textbf{14.2}$$

Equation 14.2 represents the cumulative probability that an exponentially distributed service time will require less than or equal to T time periods. For example, suppose that the operator on the customer service hotline can service calls at a rate of 7 per hour, on average, and that the service times follow an exponential distribution (μ = 7). Figure 14.4 (and the file FIG14-4.XLS on your data disk) shows the probability that the service will be less than or equal to T hours, for various values of T.

Figure 14.4: Example of a cumulative exponential distribution with μ = 7

In Figure 14.4, the value in cell B6 indicates that a 0.3 probability exists that it will take less than or equal to 0.05 hours (or 3 minutes) to service any call. Similarly, the value in cell B9 indicates that a 0.75 probability exists that it will take less than or equal to 0.2 hours (or 12 minutes) to service any call.

With the exponential distribution, short service times are fairly common. The graph in Figure 14.4 rises fairly quickly and then slowly approaches the value 1.0. This results in a high probability of short service times. Long service times are also possible, but are far less likely. Thus, although it might be appropriate to model the service times for certain queuing systems using the exponential distribution, this distribution will not be appropriate in all applications.

One way to verify that the service rate can be modeled using the exponential distribution is to collect data on the service times occurring per time period for several hours, days, or weeks. The average number of customers serviced per time period can be calculated from these data and used as an estimate of the service rate μ. A cumulative frequency distribution of the actual data can be constructed and compared to the cumulative distribution of the actual probabilities expected of an exponential random variable with a service rate of μ. If the distributions are similar, it is reasonable to assume that the arrival process is approximately Poisson. (Again, additional goodness-of-fit tests can be found in most texts on queuing and simulation.)

KENDALL NOTATION

Given the variety of queuing models that exist, a system known as **Kendall notation** was developed to allow the key characteristics of a specific queuing model to be described in an efficient manner. With Kendall notation, simple queuing models can be described by three characteristics in the following general format:

1/2/3

The first characteristic identifies the nature of the arrival process using the following standard abbreviations:

M = Markovian interarrival times (following an exponential distribution)

D = deterministic interarrival times (not random)

The second characteristic identifies the nature of the service times using the following standard abbreviations:

M = Markovian service times (following an exponential distribution)

G = general service times (following a non-exponential distribution)

D = deterministic service times (not random)

Finally, the third characteristic indicates the number of servers available. So, using Kendall notation, an M/M/1 queue refers to a queuing model in which the time between arrivals follows an exponential distribution, the service times follow an exponential distribution, and there is 1 server. An M/G/3 queue refers to a model in which the interarrival times are assumed to be exponential, the service times follow some general distribution, and 3 servers are present.

An expanded version of Kendall notation involves specifying six (rather than three) queue characteristics. A more complete description of this notation can be found in advanced management science or queuing texts.

QUEUING MODELS

Numerous queuing models are available to evaluate different combinations of arrival distributions, service time distributions, and other queuing characteristics. This chapter discusses only a few of these models. Where possible, researchers have derived closed-form equations to calculate various operating characteristics of a particular queuing model. Typical operating characteristics of interest include:

Characteristic	Description
U	Utilization factor, or the percentage of time that all servers are busy
P_0	Probability that there are no units in the system
L_q	Average number of units in line waiting for service
L	Average number of units in the system (in line and being served)
W_q	Average time a unit spends in line waiting for service
W	Average time a unit spends in the system (in line and being served)
P_w	Probability that an arriving unit has to wait for service
P_n	Probability of n units in the system

Information about these operating characteristics can be helpful to managers who need to make decisions about the trade-offs between the costs of providing different levels of service and the associated impact on customers' experiences in the queuing system. This chapter does not show the derivation of the equations used to calculate operating characteristics. Rather, it simply states the equations for several common queuing models and shows how they can be used.

The equations for the queuing models we'll consider are implemented in spreadsheet templates in the file Q.XLS on your data disk. Figure 14.5 shows the introduction screen for these templates.

As Figure 14.5 indicates, the templates in this file can be used to analyze four types of queuing models: the M/M/s model, the M/M/s model with finite queue length, the M/M/s model with finite arrival population, and the M/G/1 model.

THE M/M/s MODEL

The M/M/s model is appropriate for analyzing queuing problems where the following assumptions are met:

- There are s servers, where s is a positive integer.
- Arrivals follow a Poisson distribution and occur at an average rate of λ per time period.
- Each server provides service at an average rate of μ per time period, and actual service times follow an exponential distribution.
- Arrivals wait in a single FIFO queue and are serviced by the first available server.
- $\lambda < s\mu$.

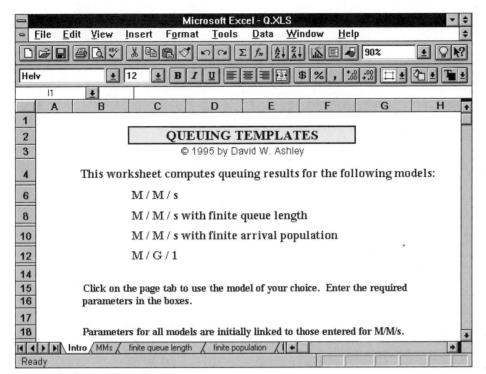

Figure 14.5: Introductory screen for queuing templates file Q.XLS

The final assumption indicates that the total service capacity of the system, $s\mu$, must be greater than the rate at which arrivals occur. If the arrival rate exceeds the system's total service capacity, the system would fill up over time and the queue would become infinitely long.

The formulas describing the operating characteristics of the M/M/s model are given in Figure 14.6. Although these formulas might seem somewhat daunting, they are easy to use when implemented in a spreadsheet template.

$$U = \lambda/(s\mu)$$

$$P_0 = \left(\sum_{n=0}^{s-1} \frac{(\lambda/\mu)^n}{n!} + \frac{(\lambda/\mu)^s}{s!} \left(\frac{s\mu}{s\mu - \lambda} \right) \right)^{-1}$$

$$L_q = \frac{P_0 (\lambda/\mu)^{s+1}}{(s-1)!(s-\lambda/\mu)^2}$$

$$L = L_q + \frac{\lambda}{\mu}$$

$$W_q = L_q/\lambda$$

$$W = W_q + \frac{1}{\mu}$$

$$P_w = \frac{1}{s!} \left(\frac{\lambda}{\mu} \right)^s \left(\frac{s\mu}{s\mu - \lambda} \right) P_0$$

$$P_n = \frac{(\lambda/\mu)^n}{n!} P_0, \quad \text{for } n \leq s$$

$$P_n = \frac{(\lambda/\mu)^n}{s! s^{(n-s)}} P_0, \quad \text{for } n > s$$

Figure 14.6: Formulas describing the operating characteristics of an M/M/s queue

The following example illustrates how the M/M/s model might be used.

The customer support hotline for Bitway Computers is currently staffed by a single technician. Calls arrive randomly at a rate of 5 per hour and follow a Poisson distribution. The technician can service calls at an average rate of 7 per hour, but the actual time required to handle a given call is an exponential random variable. The president of Bitway, Rod Taylor, has received numerous complaints from customers about the length of time they must wait "on hold" for service when calling the hotline. Rod wants to determine the average length of time customers currently wait before the technician answers their calls. If the average waiting time is more than 5 minutes, he wants to determine how many technicians would be required to reduce the average waiting time to 2 minutes or less.

THE CURRENT SITUATION

Because only one technician (or server) currently staffs Bitway's customer service hotline, we can calculate the operating characteristics for the hotline using an M/M/1 queuing model. Figure 14.7 shows the results of this model for Bitway's current configuration.

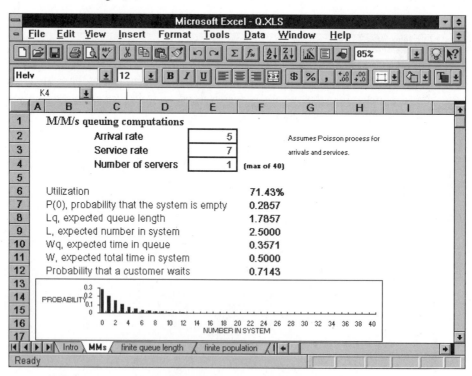

Figure 14.7: Results of the M/M/1 model for Bitway's customer service hotline

Cells E2, E3, and E4 contain the values for the arrival rate, service rate, and number of servers in our example problem, respectively. (Note that this template is designed to accommodate a maximum of 40 servers.) The various operating characteristics of this model are calculated automatically in column F.

The value in cell F12 indicates that a 0.7143 probability exists that callers to Bitway's customer service hotline must wait on hold before receiving service from the technician. The value in cell F10 indicates that the average length of this wait is 0.3571 hours (or approximately 21.42 minutes). The value in cell F11 indicates that, on average, a caller spends a total of 0.5 hours (or 30 minutes) waiting for service and being served under Bitway's current hotline configuration. Thus, it appears that the customer complaints to Bitway's president are justifiable.

ADDING A SERVER

To improve the level of service on the hotline, Bitway could investigate how the operating characteristics of the system would change if two technicians were assigned to answer calls. That is, incoming calls could be handled by either one of two equally capable technicians. We can calculate the operating characteristics for this configuration using an M/M/2 queuing model, as shown in Figure 14.8.

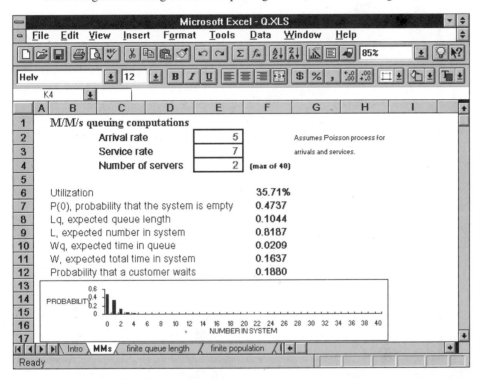

Figure 14.8: Results of the M/M/2 model for Bitway's customer service hotline

The value in cell F12 indicates that, with two servers, the probability that a caller must wait before receiving service drops significantly from 0.7143 to 0.1880. Similarly, cell F10 indicates that the average amount of time a caller must wait before service begins drops to 0.0209 hours (or approximately 1.25 minutes). Thus, it seems that adding a second technician to the customer service hotline would achieve the 2-minute average waiting time objective Rod wants.

Although the addition of a second server greatly reduces the average time hotline callers spend waiting for service to begin, it does not reduce the expected *service time*. For the M/M/1 model in Figure 14.7, which includes only one server, the expected total time in the system is 0.5 hours and the expected queue time is 0.3571 hours. This implies that the expected service time is $0.5 - 0.3571 = 0.1429$ hours. For the M/M/2 model in Figure 14.8, which includes two servers, the expected total time in the system is 0.1637 hours and the expected queue time is 0.0209 hours. This implies an expected service time of $0.1637 - 0.0209 = 0.1429$ hours (allowing for a slight rounding error). The M/M/2 model assumes that both servers can provide service at the same rate—in this case, an average of 7 calls per hour. Therefore, the average service time per call should be $1/7 = 0.1429$ hours, which is consistent with the observed results.

THE M/M/s MODEL WITH FINITE QUEUE LENGTH

The results for the M/M/s models in Figures 14.7 and 14.8 assume that the size or capacity of the waiting area is infinite, so that all arrivals to the system join the queue and wait for service. In some situations, however, the size or capacity of the waiting area might be restricted—in other words, there might be a finite queue length. The formulas describing the operating characteristics of an M/M/s queue with a finite queue length of K are summarized in Figure 14.9.

$$U = (L - L_q)/s$$

$$P_0 = \left(1 + \sum_{n=1}^{s} \frac{(\lambda/\mu)^n}{n!} + \frac{(\lambda/\mu)^s}{s!} \sum_{n=s+1}^{K} \left(\frac{\lambda}{s\mu}\right)^{n-s}\right)^{-1}$$

$$P_n = \frac{(\lambda/\mu)^n}{n!} P_0, \quad \text{for } n = 1, 2, ..., s$$

$$P_n = \frac{(\lambda/\mu)^n}{s!s^{n-s}} P_0, \quad \text{for } n = s+1, s+2, ..., K$$

$$P_n = 0, \text{ for } n > K$$

$$L_q = \frac{P_0(\lambda/\mu)^s\rho}{s!(1-\rho)^2}\left(1 - \rho^{K-s} - (K-s)\rho^{K-s}(1-\rho)\right), \quad \text{where } \rho = \lambda/(s\mu)$$

$$L = \sum_{n=0}^{s-1} nP_n + L_q + s\left(1 - \sum_{n=0}^{s-1} P_n\right)$$

$$W_q = \frac{L_q}{\lambda(1-P_K)}$$

$$W = \frac{L}{\lambda(1-P_K)}$$

Figure 14.9: Formulas describing the operating characteristics of an M/M/s queue with a finite queue length of K

To see how this queuing model might be used, suppose that Bitway's telephone system can keep a maximum of five calls on hold at any point in time. If a new call is made to the hotline when five calls are already in the queue, the new call receives a busy signal. One way to reduce the number of calls encountering busy signals is to increase the number of calls that can be put on hold. However, if a call is answered only to be put on hold for a long time, the caller might find this more annoying than receiving a busy signal. Thus, Rod might want to investigate what effect adding a second technician to answer hotline calls would have on the number of calls receiving busy signals and on the average time callers must wait before receiving service.

THE CURRENT SITUATION

Because only one technician (or server) currently staffs Bitway's customer service hotline, we can calculate the current operating characteristics for the hotline using an M/M/1 queuing model with a finite queue length of 5. Figure 14.10 shows the results of this model for Bitway's current configuration.

Cells E2, E3, and E4 contain the values for the arrival rate, service rate, and number of servers in our example problem, respectively. Cell E5 contains the maximum queue length of 5. Note that the template in Figure 14.10 is designed to accommodate a maximum of 40 servers and also requires that the sum of the values E4 and E5 not exceed 40.

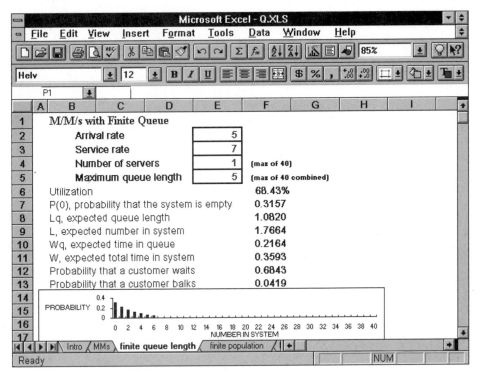

Figure 14.10: Results of the M/M/1 model with a finite queue length of 5 for Bitway's customer service hotline

The value in cell F13 indicates that a 0.0419 probability exists that callers to Bitway's customer service hotline will balk (or, in this case, receive a busy signal). A **balk** refers to an arrival that does not join the queue because the queue is full or too long. The value in cell F10 indicates that the average length of this wait is 0.2164 hours (or approximately 13 minutes). The value in cell F11 indicates that, on average, a caller spends a total of 0.3593 hours (or 21.55 minutes) either waiting for service or being served under Bitway's current hotline configuration.

ADDING A SERVER

To improve the level of service on the hotline, Bitway could investigate how the operating characteristics of the system would change if two technicians were assigned to answer calls. We can calculate the operating characteristics for this configuration using an M/M/2 queuing model with a finite queue length of 5, as shown in Figure 14.11.

The value in cell F13 indicates that, with two servers, the probability that a caller receives a busy signal drops to 0.0007. Similarly, cell F10 indicates that the average amount of time a caller must wait before service begins drops to 0.0204 hours (or approximately 1.22 minutes). Thus, it seems that adding a second technician to the customer service hotline would achieve the 2-minute average waiting time objective Rod wants and would virtually eliminate any chance of a customer receiving a busy signal.

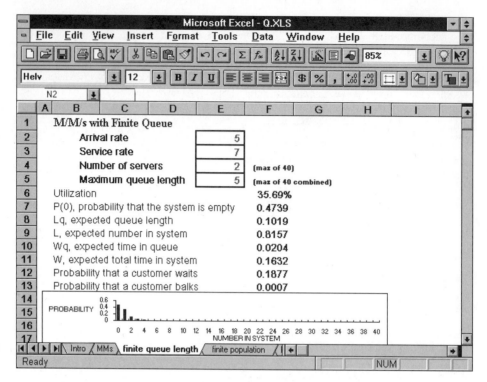

Figure 14.11: Results of the M/M/2 model with a finite queue length of 5 for Bitway's customer service hotline

THE M/M/s MODEL WITH FINITE POPULATION

The previous queuing models assume that the customers (or calls) arriving at the queuing system come from a population of potential customers that is infinite, or extremely large. Under this assumption, the mean arrival rate, λ, remains constant regardless of the number of calls in the system.

In some queuing problems, however, the possible number of arriving customers is finite. In other words, these queuing models have a finite arrival (or calling) population. In such a model, the average arrival rate for the system changes depending on the number of customers in the queue. The M/M/s model for finite arrival populations is appropriate for analyzing queuing problems where the following assumptions are met:

- There are s servers, where s is a positive integer.

- There are N potential customers in the arrival population.

- The arrival pattern of *each customer* follows a Poisson distribution with a mean arrival rate of λ per time period.

- Each server provides service at an average rate of μ per time period, and actual service times follow an exponential distribution.

- Arrivals wait in a single FIFO queue and are serviced by the first available server.

Note that the average arrival rate for this model (λ) is defined in terms of the rate at which *each customer* arrives. The formulas describing the operating characteristics for an M/M/s queue with a finite arrival population of size N are summarized in Figure 14.12.

$$P_0 = \left(\sum_{n=0}^{s-1} \frac{N!}{(N-n)!n!}\left(\frac{\lambda}{\mu}\right)^n + \sum_{n=s}^{N} \frac{N!}{(N-n)!s!s^{n-s}}\left(\frac{\lambda}{\mu}\right)^n \right)^{-1}$$

$$P_n = \frac{N!}{(N-n)!n!}\left(\frac{\lambda}{\mu}\right)^n P_0, \text{ if } 0 \leq n \leq s$$

$$P_n = \frac{N!}{(N-n)!s!s^{n-s}}\left(\frac{\lambda}{\mu}\right)^n P_0, \text{ if } s < n \leq N$$

$$P_n = 0, \text{ if } n > N$$

$$L_q = \sum_{n=s}^{N} (n-s)P_n$$

$$L = \sum_{n=0}^{s-1} nP_n + L_q + s\left(1 - \sum_{n=0}^{s-1} P_n\right)$$

$$W_q = \frac{L_q}{\lambda(N-L)}$$

$$W = \frac{L}{\lambda(N-L)}$$

Figure 14.12: Formulas describing the operating characteristics of an M/M/s queue with a finite arrival population of size N

One of the most common applications for the M/M/s model with a finite arrival population is the machine repair problem, as illustrated in the following example.

The Miller Manufacturing Company owns 10 identical machines that it uses in the production of colored nylon thread for the textile industry. Machine breakdowns occur following a Poisson distribution with an average of 0.01 breakdowns occurring per operating hour per machine. The company employs one technician to fix these machines when they break down. Service times to repair the machines are exponentially distributed with an average of 8 hours per repair. Thus, service is performed at a rate of 1/8 machines per hour. Management wants to analyze what impact adding another service technician would have on the average length of time required to fix a machine when it breaks down.

THE CURRENT SITUATION

The 10 machines in this problem represent a finite set of objects that can break down. Therefore, the M/M/s model for a finite calling operation is appropriate to use for analyzing this problem. The current operating characteristics for Miller Manufacturing's machine repair problem are summarized in Figure 14.13.

Because the individual machines break down at a rate of 0.01 per hour, this is the rate at which individual machines "arrive" for repair. Thus, cell E2 contains the value 0.01 to represent the arrival rate per customer (machine). The technician can service broken machines at an average rate of $1/8 = 0.125$ machines per hour, as indicated in cell E3. The number of servers (or technicians) is shown in cell E4. Because there are 10 machines that can break down, cell E5 contains a population size of 10. The spreadsheet calculates the overall arrival rate shown in cell H2. Because there are 10 machines, each with a 0.01 probability of breaking down each hour, the overall arrival rate of broken machines is 10*0.01 = 0.1, as indicated in cell H2.

The operating characteristics for this system are calculated in cells F6 through F12. According to cell F11, whenever a machine breaks down, it is out of operation for an average of 17.98 hours. Of this total down time, cell F10 indicates that the machine spends approximately 10 hours waiting for service to begin. Cell F9 indicates that approximately 1.5 machines are out of operation at any point in time.

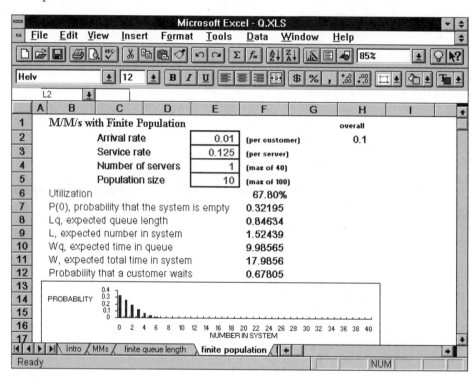

Figure 14.13: Results of the M/M/1 model with a finite population of 10 machines for Miller Manufacturing's machine repair problem

ADDING A SERVER

Figure 14.14 shows the expected operation of this system if Miller Manufacturing adds another repair technician.

Cell F10 indicates that when a machine breaks down, repairs start, on average, in only 0.82 hours (or approximately 49 minutes), in comparison to the 10-hour waiting time with only one technician. Similarly, cell F9 indicates that with two technicians, only 0.81 machines are out of operation at any point in time. Thus, by adding another repair technician, Miller Manufacturing can keep approximately one more machine in operation at all times. So if the marginal value of the output per hour for one machine exceeds the marginal cost per hour of employing another repair technician, the company should hire the additional technician.

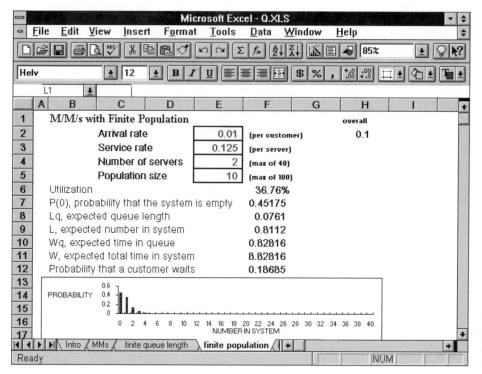

Figure 14.14: Results of the M/M/2 model with a finite population of 10 machines for Miller Manufacturing's machine repair problem

THE M/G/1 MODEL

All the models presented so far assume that service times follow an exponential distribution. As noted earlier in Figure 14.4, random service times from an exponential distribution can assume *any* positive value. However, in some situations this assumption is unrealistic. For example, consider the time required to change the oil in a car at an auto service center. This service probably requires *at least* 10 minutes and might require up to 30, 45, or even 60 minutes, depending on the service being performed. The M/G/1 queuing model enables us to solve queuing problems in which service times cannot be modeled accurately using an exponential distribution. The formulas describing the operating characteristics of an M/G/1 queue are summarized in Figure 14.15.

$$P_0 = 1 - \lambda/\mu$$

$$L_q = \frac{\lambda^2\sigma^2 + (\lambda/\mu)^2}{2(1 - \lambda/\mu)}$$

$$L = L_q + \lambda/\mu$$

$$W_q = L_q/\lambda$$

$$W = W_q + 1/\mu$$

$$P_w = \lambda/\mu$$

Figure 14.15: Formulas describing the operating characteristics of an M/G/1 queue

The M/G/1 queuing model is quite remarkable because it can be used to compute the operating characteristics for *any* 1-server queuing system where arrivals follow a Poisson distribution and the mean μ and standard deviation σ of the service times are known. That is, the formulas in Figure 14.15 do not require that service times follow one specific probability distribution. The following example illustrates the use of the M/G/1 queuing model.

> Cars arrive randomly at the Zippy-Lube oil change center following a Poisson distribution at an average rate of 3.5 cars per hour. After reviewing the historical data on operations at this business, the owner of Zippy-Lube, Olie Boe, has determined that the average service time per car is 15 minutes (or 0.25 hours) with a standard deviation of 2 minutes (or 0.0333 hours). Olie is concerned about the average number of cars waiting for service at his business. In particular, he worries that if a customer drives up and sees a long line of cars waiting, the customer will not be willing to wait for service and will simply go elsewhere for an oil change. Olie is considering expanding his business to include another service bay so that he would have two parallel service facilities with separate queues and separate servers. Olie wants to compare the operation of his current configuration with that of the a two-bay operation.

THE CURRENT SITUATION

We can model Olie's current service facility as an M/G/1 queue. The operating characteristics of this facility are shown in Figure 14.16.

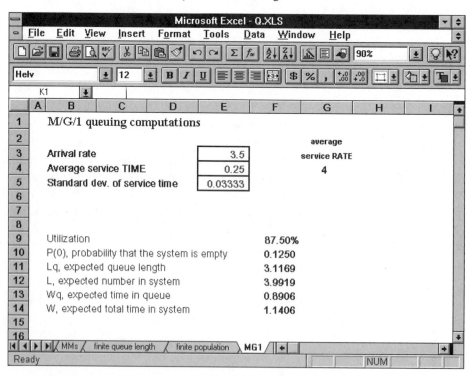

Figure 14.16: Results of the M/G/1 model with one service bay for Zippy-Lube

Cell E3 contains the average arrival rate of 3.5 cars per hour. The average service time per car (also in hours) is indicated in cell E4, and the standard deviation of the service time (in hours) is indicated in cell E5.

Cell F11 shows that an average of 3.11 cars wait for service at any given point in time. Cell F14 indicates that, on average, 1.14 hours (or about 68 minutes) elapse between the time a car arrives and leaves the system.

ADDING A SERVICE BAY

If Olie adds a parallel service bay to his operation and the arrival rate remains constant at 3.5 cars per hour, half these cars would be serviced by the existing facility and the other half would be serviced by the new bay. Thus, the arrival rate for each bay would be roughly half the current arrival rate, or 3.5/2 = 1.75 cars per hour. The operation of each individual bay is summarized by the results in Figure 14.17.

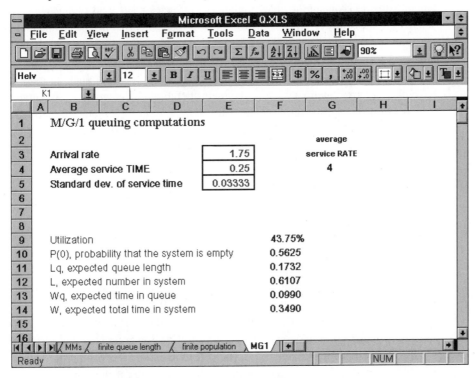

Figure 14.17: Results of the M/G/1 model with two service bays for Zippy-Lube

The value in cell F14 indicates that adding a second service bay dramatically reduces the total time a car spends in the system from 1.14 hours to 0.349 hours. Cell F11 indicates that the expected queue in front of each service bay consists of only 0.1732 cars, on average. Thus, the addition of a new service bay would significantly improve customer service and would likely result in an increase in the arrival rate because customers who previously balked when confronted with a lengthy queue would now consider stopping for service.

The M/D/1 MODEL

The M/G/1 model can be used when service times are random with known mean and standard deviation. However, service times might not be random in some queuing systems. For example, in a manufacturing environment it is not unusual to have a queue of material or subassemblies waiting to be serviced by a certain machine. The machine time required to perform the service might be predictable—such as exactly 10 seconds of machine time per piece. Similarly, an automatic car wash might spend exactly the same amount of time on each car it services. The M/D/1 model can be used in these types of situations where the service times are deterministic (not random).

The results for an M/D/1 model can be obtained using the M/G/1 model by setting the standard deviation of the service time to 0 ($\sigma = 0$). Setting $\sigma = 0$ indicates that no variability exits in the service times and, therefore, the service time for each unit is equal to the average service time μ.

SIMULATING QUEUES

Queuing theory is one of the oldest and most well-researched areas of management science. Discussions of other types of queuing models can be found in advanced texts on management science and in texts devoted solely to queuing theory. However, keep in mind that the technique of simulation can be used to analyze virtually any queuing problem you might encounter. Indeed, not all queuing models have closed-form equations to describe their operating characteristics. So simulation is often the only means available for analyzing complex queuing systems where customers balk (don't join a queue upon arrival), reneg (leave a queue before being served), or jockey (switch from one queue to another).

THE STEADY-STATE ASSUMPTION

The formulas used in this chapter describe the *steady-state* operations of the various queuing systems presented. At the beginning of each day, most queuing systems start in an "empty and idle" condition and go through a transient period as business activity gradually builds up to reach the normal, or **steady-state**, level of operation. The queuing models presented describe only the behavior of the system in its steady-state level of operation. A queuing system can have different levels of steady-state operations at different times throughout the day. For example, a restaurant might have one steady-state level of operation for breakfast, and different steady-state levels at lunch and dinner. So before using the models in this chapter, it is important to identify the arrival rate and service rate for the specific steady-state level of operation you want to study. If an analysis of the transient phase is needed or if you want to model the operation of the system across different steady-state levels, you should use simulation.

SUMMARY

Waiting lines, or queues, are a common occurrence in many types of businesses. The study of the operating characteristics of waiting lines is known as queuing theory. Numerous mathematical models are available to represent and study the behavior of different types of queues. These models have different assumptions about the nature of the arrival process to the queuing system, the allowable size and nature of the queuing discipline, and the service process within the system. For many models, closed-form equations have been developed to describe various operating characteristics of the system. When closed-form solutions are not possible, the technique of simulation must be used to analyze the behavior of the system.

REFERENCES

Gilliam, R. "An Application of Queueing Theory to Airport Passenger Security Screening." *Interfaces*, vol. 9, 1979.

Gross, D. and C. Harris. *Fundamentals of Queueing Theory*. New York: Wiley, 1985.

Hall, R. *Queueing Methods for Service and Manufacturing*. Englewood Cliffs, NJ: Prentice Hall, 1991.

Kolesar, P. "A Quick and Dirty Response to the Quick and Dirty Crowd: Particularly to Jack Byrd's 'The Value of Queueing Theory'." *Interfaces*, vol. 9, 1979.

Mann, L. "Queue Culture: The Waiting Line as a Social System." *American Journal of Sociology*, vol. 75, 1969.

"Wait Watchers" Try to Take Stress Out of Standing in Line

By Kathleen Doheny. Reprinted with permission from the *Los Angeles Times*, 7/15/91, V110 pB3 14 col in.

STANDING IN LINE—at the bank, the market, the movies—is the time-waster everyone loves to hate. Stand in just one 15-minute line a day, every day, and kiss goodby four days of idle time by year's end.

While we've been waiting and grumbling, researchers have been analyzing lines with an eye to making them, if not shorter, at least less stressful.

The field of line analysis—more scientifically known as queuing theory—began in the early 1900s when a Danish telephone engineer devised a mathematical approach to help design phone switches. Researchers found that the principles developed through that system, which helped process calls more efficiently, could be applied to help move people through lines more efficiently.

The concept has spread from the communications and computer industries to other fields, helping modern researchers predict such things as how long customers might wait for a restaurant lunch or how many customers might visit a bank ATM at noon on Saturday. Now, some researchers have gone beyond a mere mathematical analysis of lines, focusing as well on our psychological reactions.

In one recent study, Richard Larson, a professor of electrical engineering at the Massachusetts Institute of Technology, wanted to determine which of two approaches would be more tolerable to Bank of Boston customers. As Larson's researchers filmed the customers, one group watched an electronic news board while waiting in line; the other group was advised via an electric clock how long the wait would be before each one entered the line. About 300 customers, nearly a third of those filmed, were interviewed after they finished their transactions. The findings, published in the Sloan Management Review, an MIT publication circulated to corporate managers, showed that:

- Customers in both lines overestimated their waits by nearly a minute; those who watched the news board overestimated the most. On average, customers thought they waited 5.1 minutes to see a teller but actually waited 4.2 minutes.

- Watching the news board did not change customers' perceptions of their waiting time. But it did make the time spent more palatable, customers reported. (After the bank removed the news board, many customers asked that it be reinstalled.)

- The news board also seemed to make customers less fidgety. Without it, they touched their faces and played with their hair. With the news board in view they stood still with their arms at their sides.

- Customers who were advised of the length of the line via an electronic clock at the entry did not find the experience less stressful than those not told the expected waiting time, much to Larson's surprise. Nor were they more satisfied than the other group with the service. The electronic clock's display of waiting time may backfire, Larson speculates, by making respondents even more aware of time wasted standing in line.

- Customers in the lines with the clock tended to play "beat the clock." They felt they had "won" if they spent less time in line than predicted. The clock also seemed to make more customers balk at joining the line if the predicted delay was lengthy.

- In both lines, customers altered their definition of a "reasonable" wait depending on their time of arrival. They were willing to wait longer during lunch time than during other times of day.

Larson's recent findings bear out a formula published in 1984 by David Maister, a former Harvard Business School faculty member and now a business consultant. When it comes to lines, Maister said, satisfaction is tied to both perception and expectation.

"Nowhere in that [equation] does reality appear," Maister said with a laugh during a telephone interview. Giving a personal example of how perception influences reaction, he said he would wait "40 minutes for a performance by a world-class musician but less than 30 seconds for a hamburger."

Larson, a professional "wait watcher" for 20 years, puts it a bit differently: "When it comes to customer satisfaction, perception is reality."

If those concepts are true, taming customer unrest does not necessarily mean a business must beef up its staff to eliminate lines, Larson and Maister contend. It's much more a matter of "perception management," they say. "People in the service industries who think they have a line problem may be able virtually to erase customer dissatisfaction and customer complaints not by changing the statistic of the wait but by changing the environment of it," Larson said.

He points to a number of companies already actively wooing waiters. Some companies use a "queue delay guarantee," giving customers free dessert or money if the wait exceeds a preset time period.

Larson predicts customers can expect lines that segment them by personality type. Impatient souls may have the option of paying more to join an automated express line; "people watchers" could opt to wait for less expensive, friendlier human service.

Questions and Problems

1. Consider the three queuing configurations shown in Figure 14.2. For each configuration, describe a situation (besides the examples mentioned in the chapter) in which you have encountered or observed the same type of queuing system.

2. Of the queuing configurations shown in Figure 14.2, which would you prefer to wait in? Explain your response.

3. This chapter implies that customers find waiting in line to be an unpleasant experience. In addition to reducing the length of the wait itself, what other steps could a business take to reduce the frustration customers experience while waiting? Give specific examples.

4. Describe a situation in which a business might want customers to wait some amount of time before receiving service.

5. Tri-Cities Bank has a single drive-in teller window. On Friday mornings customers arrive at the drive-in window randomly, following a Poisson distribution at an average rate of 30 per hour.

    a. How many customers arrive per minute, on average?

    b. How many customers would you expect to arrive in a 10-minute interval?

    c. Use equation 14.1 to determine the probability of exactly 0, 1, 2, and 3 arrivals in a 10-minute interval. (You can verify your answers using the POISSON() function in Excel.)

    d. What is the probability of more than 3 arrivals occurring in a 10-minute interval?

6. Refer to question 5. Suppose that service at the drive-in window is provided at a rate of 40 customers per hour and follows an exponential distribution.

    a. What is the expected service time per customer?

    b. Use equation 14.2 to determine the probability that a customer's service time is 1 minute or less. (Verify your answer using the EXPONENTIAL() function in Excel.)

    c. What is the probability that the customer's wait time is 5 minutes or less, less than 1 minute, less than 3 minutes, and less than 5 minutes? (Verify your answers using the EXPONENTIAL() function in Excel.)

    d. What is the probability that a customer's service time is more than 3 minutes?

7. Refer to questions 5 and 6 and answer the following questions:

    a. What is the probability that the drive-in window is empty?

    b. What is the probability that a customer must wait for service?

    c. On average, how many cars wait for service?

    d. On average, what is the total length of time a customer spends in the system?

e. On average, what is the total length of time a customer spends in the queue?

f. What service rate would be required to reduce the average total time in the system to 2 minutes? (Hint: You can use Solver or simple what-if analysis to answer this question.)

8. The manager of the Radford Credit Union (RCU) wants to determine how many part-time tellers to employ to cover the peak demand time in its lobby from 11:00 a.m. to 2:00 p.m. RCU currently has three full-time tellers that handle the demand during the rest of the day, but during this peak demand time customers have been complaining that the wait time for service is too long. The manager at RCU has determined that customers arrive according to a Poisson distribution with an average of 60 arrivals per hour during the peak period. Each teller services customers at a rate of 24 per hour with service times following an exponential distribution.

a. On average, how long must customers wait in line before service begins?

b. Once service begins for a customer, how long does it take to complete the transaction, on average?

c. If one part-time teller is hired to work during the peak time period, what effect would this have on the average amount of time a customer spends waiting in the queue?

d. If one part-time teller is hired to work during the peak time period, what effect would this have on the average amount of time it takes to serve a customer?

9. The Orange Blossom Marathon takes place in Orlando, Florida, each December. The organizers of this race are trying to solve a problem that occurs at the finish line each year. Thousands of runners take part in this race. The fastest runners finish the 26-mile course in just over 2 hours, but the majority of the runners finish about 1 1/2 hours later. After runners enter the finish area, they go through one of four finish chutes where their times and places are recorded. (Each chute has its own queue.) During the time in which the majority of the runners finish the race, the chutes become backlogged and significant delays occur. The race organizers want to determine how many chutes should be added to eliminate this problem. At the time in question, runners arrive at the finish area at a rate of 50 per minute according to a Poisson distribution, and they randomly select one of the four chutes. The time required to record the necessary information for each finishing runner at any chute is an exponentially distributed random variable with a mean of 4 seconds.

a. On average, how many runners arrive at each chute per minute?

b. Under the current arrangement with 4 chutes, what is the expected length of the queue at each chute?

c. Under the current arrangement, what is the average length of time a runner waits before being processed?

d. How many chutes should be added if the race organizers want to reduce the queue time at each chute to an average of 5 seconds?

10. State University allows students and faculty to access its mainframe computer by modem. The university has 15 modem connections can be used. When all of the modem connections are in use, the phone system can keep up to 10 callers on hold waiting for a modem connection to become available. If all 15 modem connections are in use and 10 calls are already holding, a new caller receives a busy signal. Calls to the modem pool follow a Poisson distribution and occur at an average rate of 60 per hour. The length of each session with the mainframe is an exponential random variable with a mean of 15 minutes—therefore, each modem services an average of 4 callers per hour.

   a. On average, how many callers are on hold waiting for a modem connection?

   b. On average, how long is a caller kept on hold before receiving a modem connection?

   c. What is the probability that a caller receives a busy signal?

   d. How many modem connections would the university need to add to its modem pool in order for there to be no more than a 1% chance of a caller receiving a busy signal?

11. On Friday nights, patients arrive at the emergency room at Mercy Hospital following a Poisson distribution at an average rate of 7 per hour. Assume that an emergency room physician can treat an average of 3 patients per hour, and that the treatment times follow an exponential distribution. The board of directors for Mercy Hospital wants patients arriving at the emergency room to wait no more than 5 minutes before seeing a doctor. How many emergency room doctors should be scheduled on Friday nights to achieve this objective?

12. During tax season the IRS hires seasonal workers to help answer the questions of taxpayers who call a special 800 telephone number for tax information. Suppose that calls to this line occur at a rate of 60 per hour and follow a Poisson distribution. The IRS workers manning the phone lines can answer an average of 5 calls per hour with the actual service times following an exponential distribution. Assume that 10 IRS workers are available and, when they are all busy, the phone system can keep 5 additional callers on hold.

   a. What is the probability that a caller receives a busy signal?

   b. What is the probability that a caller is put on hold before receiving service?

   c. On average, how long must a caller wait before speaking with an IRS agent?

   d. How many additional workers would be required if the IRS wants no more than a 5% chance of a caller receiving a busy signal?

13. Several hundred personal computers (PCs) are in use at the corporate headquarters for National Insurance Corporation. The pattern of breakdowns for these PCs follows a Poisson distribution with an average rate of 4.5 breakdowns per 5-day work week. The company has a repair technician

on staff to repair the PCs. The average time required to repair a PC varies somewhat, but takes an average of 1 day with a standard deviation of 0.5 days.

a. What is the average service time in terms of a 5-day work week?

b. What is the standard deviation of the service times in terms of a 5-day work week?

c. On average, how many PCs are either being repaired or waiting to be repaired?

d. On average, how much time transpires from the time a PC breaks down to the time it is repaired?

14. Refer to question 13. Suppose that National Insurance estimates it loses $40 a day in productivity and efficiency for each PC that is out of service. How much should the company be willing to pay to increase service capacity to the point where an average of 7 PCs a week could be repaired?

15. A manufacturer of engine belts uses multi-purpose manufacturing equipment to produce a variety of products. A technician is employed to perform the setup operations needed to change the machines over from one product to the next. The amount of time required to set up the machines is a random variable that follows an exponential distribution with a mean of 20 minutes. The number of machines requiring a new setup is a Poisson random variable with an average of 2 machines per hour requiring setup. The technician is responsible for setups on five machines.

a. What percentage of time is the technician idle, or not involved in setting up a machine?

b. What should the technician do during this idle time?

c. On average, how long is a machine out of operation while waiting for the next setup to be completed?

d. If the company hires another, equally capable technician to perform setups on these machines, how long on average would a machine be out of operation while waiting for the next setup to be completed?

16. DeColores Paint Company owns 10 trucks that it uses to deliver paint and decorating supplies to builders. On average, each truck returns to the company's single loading dock at a rate of 3 times per 8-hour day (or at a rate of $3/8 = 0.375$ times per hour). The times between arrivals at the dock follow an exponential distribution. The loading dock can service an average of 4 trucks per hour with actual service times following an exponential distribution.

a. What is the probability that a truck must wait for service to begin?

b. On average, how many trucks wait for service to begin at any point in time?

c. On average, how long must a truck wait before service begins?

d. If the company builds and staffs another loading dock, how would your answers to parts a, b, and c change?

17. Suppose that arrivals to a queuing system with one server follow a Poisson distribution with an average of $\lambda = 5$ per time period, and that service times follow an exponential distribution with an average service rate of $\mu = 6$ per time period.

   a. Compute the operating characteristics for this system using the M/M/s model with s = 1.

   b. Compute the operating characteristics for this system using the M/G/1 model. (Note that the average service time for the exponential random variable is $1/\mu$ and the standard deviation of the service time is also $1/\mu$.)

   c. Compare the results obtained from the M/M/1 and M/G/1 models. (They should be the same.) Explain why they are the same.

CHAPTER 15

Project Management

AT SOME POINT, almost every manager assumes responsibility for the completion of some type of project. The project might be relatively simple—such as planning a company picnic or producing an employee newsletter—or it might be more complex—such as planning the launch of a space shuttle, designing and implementing a large computer information system, or constructing a multi-story office building. Successfully completing a project of any size requires a thorough analysis of the tasks involved, accurate estimates of the time and resources required, and a good understanding of the physical and logical interdependencies. Keeping track of all these details for even a relatively small project can be overwhelming.

This chapter presents two techniques that were developed to help managers plan, organize, and control projects: the Critical Path Method (CPM) and the Program Evaluation and Review Technique (PERT). Both techniques were developed concurrently but independently during the 1950s. CPM was developed by representatives of DuPont and Sperry-Rand to assist in the management of industrial projects where the time required to perform each activity in the project could be estimated with a high degree of accuracy. The focus of CPM is to determine when a project should be completed and to schedule when each activity in the project must begin in order to keep the project on schedule. PERT was developed jointly by representatives of the U.S. Navy, Lockheed, and the consulting firm of Booz, Allen and Hamilton working on the Polaris missile. Because many of the tasks required in the development of the Polaris had never been done before, the time required to complete the tasks was uncertain. Thus, PERT was designed for projects where the time required to perform each activity is essentially a random variable. PERT focuses on estimating the probability of completing a project by a given deadline.

Over the years, the two techniques have blended together, so that most practitioners today refer to them collectively as PERT/CPM or CPM/PERT. The fact that these techniques have stood the test of time and are still widely used is a tribute to their usefulness and simplicity. Indeed, the basic ideas behind PERT/CPM provide the underpinnings for a number of project management software tools that you can find at your local software store or advertised in any computer magazine. Although we'll explore the fundamental concepts of CPM and PERT using a spreadsheet, keep in mind that these project management software tools are more effective and efficient for managing a project of any significant size.

AN EXAMPLE

One of the key ideas in both CPM and PERT is that any project can be broken down into component activities that require different amounts of time and that must be accomplished in a specific order. The major difference between CPM and PERT involves how the time element of the activities is determined. However, both CPM and PERT require a detailed network of the project that clearly indicates each of the main activities in the project and their precedence relationships. The following example illustrates how to create such a project network.

> Tom Lightner is the owner of Lightner Construction, a general contracting company that specializes in the construction of single-family residences and small office buildings. Tom frequently has numerous construction projects going on at the same time and needs a formal procedure for planning, monitoring, and controlling each project. He is aware of various project scheduling techniques but has never used them. He wants to see how he might apply such techniques to one of the home-building projects he will be undertaking in the near future. Tom has identified each of the major activities required for this project and has estimated how much time each activity will require. Figure 15.1 summarizes this information along with the precedence relationships among the activities.

Activity	Description	Time Required (in days)	Immediate Predecessor Activity
A	excavate	3	—
B	lay foundation	4	A
C	rough plumbing	3	B
D	frame	10	B
E	finish exterior	8	D
F	install HVAC	4	D
G	rough electric	6	D
H	sheet rock	8	C, E, F, G
I	install cabinets	5	H
J	paint	5	H
K	final plumbing	4	I
L	final electric	2	J
M	install flooring	4	K, L

Figure 15.1: Activities for the Lightner Construction home-building project

CREATING THE PROJECT NETWORK

The activities in a project can be represented as a network in one of two ways. As noted in chapter 5, a network is a set of nodes that are connected in various ways by directed arcs. Thus, if we let the nodes in a network represent the activities in a project, we are employing the **Activity-On-Node** (AON) network design. Figure 15.2 shows this type of network for our example problem.

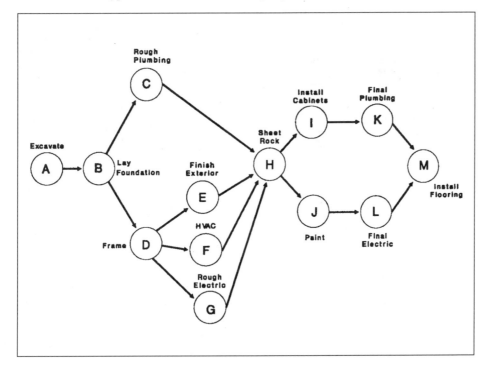

Figure 15.2: Activity-On-Node (AON) representation of the home-building project

The nodes in the network shown in Figure 15.2 correspond to each project activity in Figure 15.1. The arcs in this network indicate the precedence relationships between the activities (or nodes). For example, Figure 15.2 shows that we cannot start laying the foundation (activity B) until the excavation (activity A) is complete. Similarly, the arcs leading into node H indicate that the sheet rock cannot be installed until the activities represented by nodes C, E, F, and G are *all* complete.

In this type of network, activity A is called the **immediate predecessor** of activity B, and activities C and D are called the **immediate successors** of activity B. Throughout this chapter, we use the shortened terms *predecessor* and *successor* to mean immediate predecessor and immediate successor.

The second way to represent a project as a network is the **Activity-On-Arc** (AOA) design, in which the arcs represent the project's activities. Figure 15.3 shows an AOA network for our example problem.

The nodes in an AOA network represent the start and finish points (or milestones) for each activity. For example, in Figure 15.3 activity A starts at node 1 and ends at node 2. Activity B starts at node 2 and ends at node 3, and so on. Unfortunately, an AOA representation often produces a more complicated network when multiple activities start and end at common nodes. For example, because activity H (which begins at node 8) cannot begin until activities C, E, F, and G are complete, we might be inclined to draw the arcs for activities E, F, and G as starting at node 4 and finishing at node 8 (eliminating nodes 5, 6, and 7). However, an AOA network does not allow multiple arcs with common start and finish nodes. To get around this problem, we must include the "phantom" activities indicated by the dashed lines connecting nodes 5, 6, and 7 to node 8. AOA networks are mentioned here so that you will be aware of their existence (and shortcomings). In this chapter we'll use only the AON network representation, which many believe to be superior.

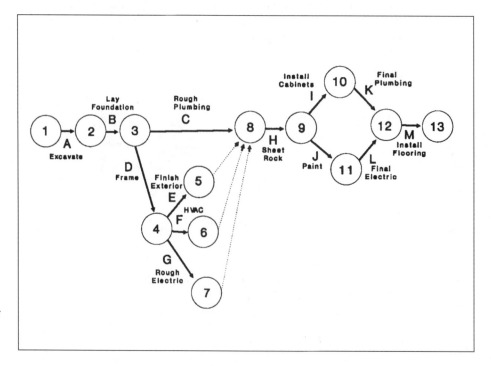

Figure 15.3: Activity-On-Arc (AOA) representation of the home-building project

A NOTE ON START AND FINISH POINTS

The techniques discussed in this chapter require that all projects have one unique start activity and one unique finish activity. This requirement is met by our example project shown in Figure 15.2 where activity A is the unique start point and activity M is the unique finish point. However, some projects involve multiple start and/or finish activities, as illustrated in Figure 15.4.

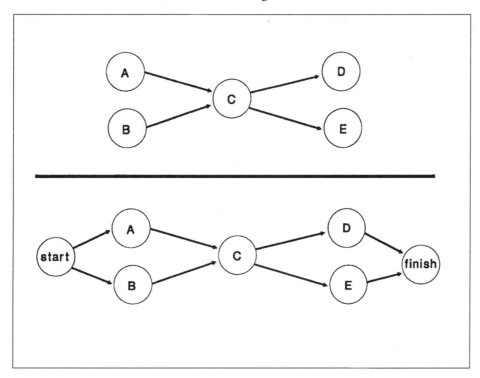

Figure 15.4: Using artificial start and finish activities to produce a network with unique start and finish points

The first network shown in Figure 15.4 represents a project with five activities: A, B, C, D, and E. However, this project does not have a unique start or finish activity. In such cases, it is necessary to create artificial start and/or finish activities, as shown by the second network in Figure 15.4. Here, we created an artificial start activity that precedes activities A and B. Similarly, we inserted an artificial finish activity that follows the completion of activities D and E. These activities are artificial because they require no time to complete and merely serve to give a project a unique start and finish point. Thus, by using artificial start and finish activities, we can ensure that the network for *any* project has a unique start and finish point.

CPM: AN OVERVIEW

After creating a network representation of a project, the next step in the CPM technique is to determine the earliest time that each activity in the network can start and finish. We determine these times by making what is called a **forward pass** through the network. Ultimately, this analysis determines the earliest time that the project itself can be completed. Next, we make a **backward pass** through the network to determine the latest time that each activity can start and finish without delaying the completion of the project.

One of the primary goals in CPM is to determine the critical path through the network. Figure 15.2 shows several paths that could be followed from the initial activity (node A) to the final activity (node M). For example, one path is given by the following set of activities: A→B→C→H→I→K→M. Another path through the network is given by: A→B→D→F→H→J→L→M. Figure 15.2 shows a total of eight paths through the network, each representing a set of activities that must be completed before the project is complete. Therefore, the earliest time that the project can be completed is the time required to complete the set of activities along the *longest* path through the network. The **critical path** is the longest path through a project network.

Any delays in the start or finish times of the activities on the critical path (also known as **critical activities**) delay the completion of the project. A project manager should always identify the critical activities in a project to focus attention on these activities and to avoid delays on these activities when possible.

In conducting the forward pass through the network, we will use the activity times to determine the earliest possible start time and the earliest possible finish time for each activity. The following notations represent these quantities:

t_i = amount of time required to perform activity i

EST_i = earliest start time for activity i

EFT_i = earliest finish time for activity i

During the backward pass, we'll determine the latest time that each activity can be started and finished without delaying the project. These quantities are represented as:

LST_i = latest start time for activity i

LFT_i = latest finish time for activity i

We'll record all the information about each project activity on the corresponding network node in the format shown in Figure 15.5.

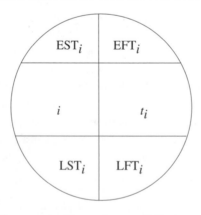

t_i = time required to perform activity i

EST_i = earliest possible start time for activity i

EFT_i = earliest possible finish time for activity i

LST_i = latest possible start time for activity i

LFT_i = latest possible finish time for activity i

Figure 15.5: Information recorded on the node for each project activity

THE FORWARD PASS

The first step in the CPM technique (after constructing the project network) is to determine the earliest time at which each activity in the network can start and finish. The term **time zero** identifies the time period at which the first project activity begins— just as the time on a stop watch starts from zero. Thus, in our example problem the earliest time at which activity A (excavation) can begin is time zero, or $EST_A = 0$.

In general, the earliest time at which an activity can finish is the earliest time at which it can start plus the expected time required to perform the activity. That is, for any activity i:

$$EFT_i = EST_i + t_i$$

For activity A, $EFT_A = EST_A + t_A = 0 + 3 = 3$. The project network in Figure 15.6 shows the earliest start and finish times for activity A.

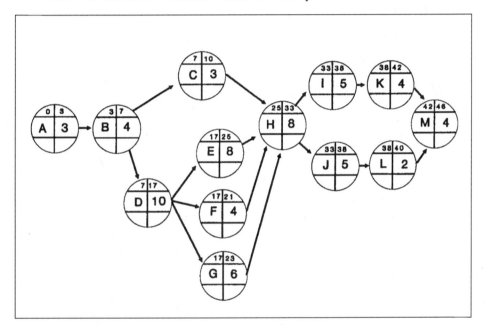

Figure 15.6: Results of forward pass calculation of earliest start and finish times

Now let's consider activity B. Because activity A must be completed before activity B can begin, the earliest start time for activity B equals the earliest finish time for activity A. That is, $EST_B = EFT_A = 3$. Activity B is expected to take 4 units of time; therefore, its earliest finish time is $EFT_B = EST_B + t_B = 3 + 4 = 7$.

Now let's consider activity C. Because activity B must be completed before activity C can begin, the earliest start time for activity C equals the earliest finish time for activity B. That is, $EST_C = EFT_B = 7$. Activity C is expected to take 3 units of time; therefore, its earliest finish time is $EFT_C = EST_C + t_C = 7 + 3 = 10$.

As you can see from these examples, calculating the earliest start and finish times for activities with a single predecessor activity is a simple process. We could apply this same logic to determine the earliest start and finish times for activities D, E, F, and G shown in Figure 15.6. You should verify the calculations for these activities on your own to make sure you understand the process. Figure 15.7 provides details of all the forward pass calculations for this example.

Earliest Start Times	Earliest Finish Times
$EST_A = 0$	$EFT_A = EST_A + t_A = 0 + 3 = 3$
$EST_B = EFT_A = 3$	$EFT_B = EST_B + t_B = 3 + 4 = 7$
$EST_C = EFT_B = 7$	$EFT_C = EST_C + t_C = 7 + 3 = 10$
$EST_D = EFT_B = 7$	$EFT_D = EST_D + t_D = 7 + 10 = 17$
$EST_E = EFT_D = 17$	$EFT_E = EST_E + t_E = 17 + 8 = 25$
$EST_F = EFT_D = 17$	$EFT_F = EST_F + t_F = 17 + 4 = 21$
$EST_G = EFT_D = 17$	$EFT_G = EST_G + t_G = 17 + 6 = 23$
$EST_H = MAX(EFT_C, EFT_E, EFT_F, EFT_G)$ $= MAX(10, 25, 21, 23) = 25$	$EFT_H = EST_H + t_H = 25 + 8 = 33$
$EST_I = EFT_H = 33$	$EFT_I = EST_I + t_I = 33 + 5 = 38$
$EST_J = EFT_H = 33$	$EFT_J = EST_J + t_J = 33 + 5 = 38$
$EST_K = EFT_I = 38$	$EFT_K = EST_K + t_K = 38 + 4 = 42$
$EST_L = EFT_J = 38$	$EFT_L = EST_L + t_L = 38 + 2 = 40$
$EST_M = MAX(EFT_K, EFT_L)$ $= MAX(42, 40) = 42$	$EFT_M = EST_M + t_M = 42 + 4 = 46$

Figure 15.7: Summary of forward pass calculations

Notice that the calculation of the earliest start time for activity H differs from the previous activities because it has *multiple* predecessors rather than a single predecessor. Activity H cannot begin until activities C, E, F, and G are *all* completed. Thus, if we consider the earliest finish times of activities C, E, F, and G, the latest of these times determines the earliest time at which activity H can start:

$$EST_H = MAX(EFT_C, EFT_E, EFT_F, EFT_G) = MAX(10, 25, 21, 23) = 25$$

The earliest start time of an activity is equal to the latest (or maximum) early finish time of the activities directly preceding it. This is true regardless of the number of predecessors an activity has.

The earliest start and finish times for the remaining activities are calculated using this same logic. Notice that the earliest start times for nodes I, J, K, and L are the earliest finish times of their respective predecessor activities. Because activity M has multiple predecessor activities, its earliest start time is the maximum of the earliest finish times of activities K and L.

KEY POINTS: The Forward Pass

- The earliest start time for the initial activity in a project is time zero.
- The earliest start time of an activity is equal to the latest (or maximum) early finish time of the activities directly preceding it.
- The earliest finish time of an activity is equal to its earliest start time plus the time required to perform the activity.

At the end of our forward pass, we have determined the earliest possible start and finish times of each activity in the network. Note that the last activity in the project, activity M, can be completed no earlier than 46 time units (in this case, days) from the beginning of the project. Thus, the earliest the project can be completed is 46 days.

THE BACKWARD PASS

After completing the forward pass, the next step in the CPM technique is to make a backward pass to determine the *latest* times at which the project activities can start and finish without delaying the project. This process identifies those activities that *must* start and finish at their earliest possible times in order to complete the project in the minimum possible time identified by the forward pass. These activities constitute the critical path through the network.

The logic behind the backward pass is similar to that of the forward pass. Here, however, we start at the final activity in the network and work backwards through the network to determine the latest time at which each activity could be finished without delaying the project. Consider activity M. If the project can be completed within 46 days, the latest finish time for activity M is 46, or $LFT_M = 46$.

In general, the latest time at which an activity can start without delaying a project is the latest time by which it must be finished minus the time required to perform the activity. That is, for any activity i:

$$LST_i = LFT_i - t_i$$

For activity M, $LST_M = LFT_M - t_M = 46 - 4 = 42$. Figure 15.8 shows the latest start and finish times for activity M.

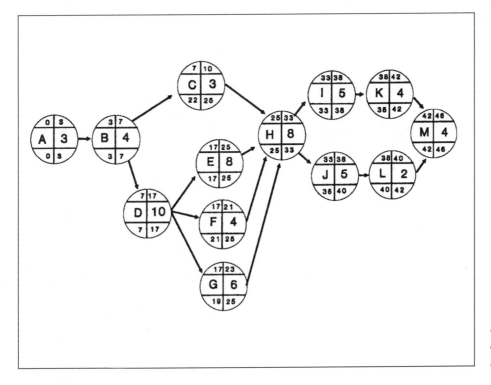

Figure 15.8: Results of backward pass calculation of latest start and finish times

Now let's consider activity L. Because activity L must be completed before activity M can begin, and activity M must begin no later than time period 42, activity L must be finished no later than time period 42. That is, $LFT_L = LST_M = 42$. Activity L is scheduled to take 2 units of time; therefore, the latest time at which this activity could start without delaying the project is $LST_L = LFT_L - t_L = 42 - 2 = 40$.

As another example, consider activity J. Because activity J must be completed before activity L can begin, and activity L must begin no later than time period 40, activity J must be finished no later than time period 40. That is, $LFT_J = LST_L = 40$. Activity J is scheduled to take 2 units of time; therefore, the latest time at which this activity could start without delaying the project is $LST_J = LFT_J - t_J = 40 - 5 = 35$.

Calculating the latest start and finish times for activities with a single successor activity is a simple process. We could apply this same logic to determine the earliest start and finish times for activities I and K, as shown in Figure 15.8. Again, you should verify the calculations for these activities on your own to make sure you understand the process. Figure 15.9 provides the details of the backward pass calculations for this example.

Latest Finish Times	Latest Start Times
$LFT_M = EFT_M = 46$	$LST_M = LFT_M - t_M = 46 - 4 = 42$
$LFT_L = LST_M = 42$	$LST_L = LFT_L - t_L = 42 - 2 = 40$
$LFT_K = LST_M = 42$	$LST_K = LFT_K - t_K = 42 - 4 = 38$
$LFT_J = LST_L = 40$	$LST_J = LFT_J - t_J = 40 - 5 = 35$
$LFT_I = LST_K = 38$	$LST_I = LFT_I - t_I = 38 - 5 = 33$
$LFT_H = MIN(LST_I, LST_J) = MIN(33, 35) = 33$	$LST_H = LFT_H - t_H = 33 - 8 = 25$
$LFT_G = LST_H = 25$	$LST_G = LFT_G - t_G = 25 - 6 = 19$
$LFT_F = LST_H = 25$	$LST_F = LFT_F - t_F = 25 - 4 = 21$
$LFT_E = LST_H = 25$	$LST_E = LFT_E - t_E = 25 - 8 = 17$
$LFT_D = MIN(LST_E, LST_F, LST_G)$ $= MIN(17, 21, 19) = 17$	$LST_D = LFT_D - t_D = 17 - 10 = 7$
$LFT_C = LST_H = 25$	$LST_C = LFT_C - t_C = 25 - 3 = 22$
$LFT_B = MIN(LST_C, LST_D) = MIN(22, 7) = 7$	$LST_B = LFT_B - t_B = 7 - 4 = 3$
$LFT_A = LST_B = 3$	$LST_A = LFT_A - t_A = 3 - 3 = 0$

Figure 15.9: Summary of backward pass calculations

Notice that the calculation of the latest finish time for activity H differs from the previous activities because it has *multiple* successors rather than a single successor. Activity H must be finished in time for activities I and J to begin by their latest start times. Thus, if we consider the latest start times for activities I and J, the earliest of these times determines the latest time by which activity H must be finished:

$$LFT_H = MIN(LST_I, LST_J) = MIN(33, 35) = 33$$

The latest finish time of an activity is equal to the earliest (or minimum) late start time of the activities directly following (or succeeding) it. This is true regardless of the number of successors an activity has.

The latest start and finish times for the remaining activities are calculated using this same logic. Notice that the latest finish times for nodes C, E, F, and G are the latest start times of their successor activities. Because activity D has multiple successor activities, its latest finish time is the minimum of the latest start times of activities E, F, and G. Similarly, because activity B has multiple successor activities, its latest finish time is the minimum of the latest start times of activities C and D. Finally, the latest finish time for activity A is the latest start time for activity B ($LFT_A = LST_B = 3$), and the latest start time for activity A is then determined by $LST_A = LFT_A - t_A = 0$.

KEY POINTS: *The Backward Pass*

- The latest finish time for the final activity in a project is equal to its earliest finish time as determined by the forward pass.
- The latest finish time for any other activity is equal to the earliest (or minimum) late start time of the activities directly following (or succeeding) it.
- The latest start time of an activity is equal to its latest finish time minus the time required to perform the activity.

DETERMINING THE CRITICAL PATH

As mentioned earlier, one of the key objectives of CPM is to determine the critical path through a project network. The critical path consists of the set of activities that, if delayed in any way, would cause a delay in the completion of the entire project. The activities on the critical path can be identified easily from the results of the forward pass and backward pass. Specifically, the activities whose latest start times equal their earliest start times make up the critical path (or, equivalently, whose latest finish times equal their earliest finish times). As shown by the heavier arcs in Figure 15.10, the critical path of activities in our example problem is: A→B→D→E→H→I→K→M. If any of the activities in this path do not start by their earliest start time, the overall time required to complete the project will increase (unless management intervenes in some way). (Note that it is possible for an activity network to have more than one critical path although this is not illustrated in our example.)

The non-critical activities in a project are distinguished by the presence of slack. **Slack** is the amount of time by which the start of an activity can be delayed without delaying the project. Critical activities have zero slack and non-critical activities have slack values that are strictly positive. The amount of slack for any activity i is defined as:

Slack for activity i = $LST_i - EST_i$

or, equivalently, as:

Slack for activity i = $LFT_i - EFT_i$

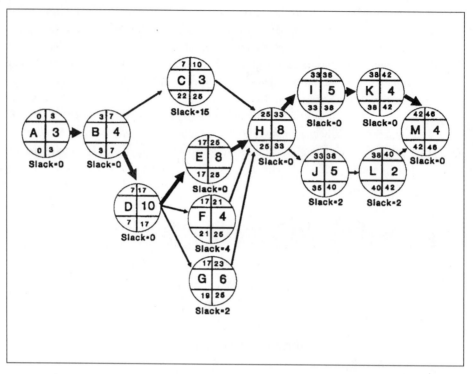

Figure 15.10: The critical path and slack conditions

In our example, activities C, F, G, J, and L are non-critical. Thus, we compute the slack for activity C as:

Slack for activity C = $LST_C − EST_C$ = 22 − 7 = 15

This indicates that activity C could be delayed up to 15 days beyond its earliest start time without delaying the project. The slack for activities F, G, J, and L are:

Slack for activity F = $LST_F − EST_F$ = 21 − 17 = 4

Slack for activity G = $LST_G − EST_G$ = 19 − 17 = 2

Slack for activity J = $LST_J − EST_J$ = 35 − 33 = 2

Slack for activity L = $LST_L − EST_L$ = 40 − 38 = 2

A NOTE ON SLACK

In Figure 15.10, note that activities J and L both appear to have 2 units of slack. Suppose that the start of activity J is delayed for 2 time periods and does not start until time period 35. Because it takes 5 units of time to perform activity J, this activity should be complete at time period 40. Thus, activity L cannot start any sooner than time period 40. So does activity L still have 2 units of slack? The answer is *no*.

If the start of activity J is delayed by 2 time units, the start of activity K is also delayed by 2 time units. Delaying the start of activity J by 2 time units depletes the slack available not only for activity J but also for activity L. So the amount of slack available at activity L depends on the amount of slack used at activity J.

You must be careful in interpreting how much slack is available for a given activity. To be precise, slack represents the amount of time by which the start of an activity can be delayed without delaying the entire project, *assuming that all predecessor activities start at their earliest start times.* If any activity on a non-critical path starts late, the slack available along the rest of the non-critical path is reduced. For this reason, it is safer to focus on the latest start times of each activity (rather than on slack) because if all activities start by their latest start times, the project should not be delayed.

KEY POINTS: *Determining the Critical Path*

- Critical activities have zero slack and cannot be delayed without delaying the completion of the project.
- Non-critical activities have some positive amount of slack that represents the amount of time by which the start times of these activities can be delayed without delaying the completion of the entire project, assuming that all predecessor activities start at their earliest start times.

PROJECT MANAGEMENT USING SPREADSHEETS

We can use a spreadsheet in a variety of ways to manage a project. As shown in Figure 15.11 (and in the file FIG15-11.XLS on your data disk), we can use a spreadsheet to perform all of the calculations required to determine the earliest and latest start and finish times for the project activities in our example problem, though this is a somewhat cumbersome process.

Microsoft Excel - FIG15-11.XLS

D9 = =MAX(E4,E6,E7,E8)

	A	B	C	D	E	F	G	H	I	J
1	Activity	Description	Time	EST	EFT	LST	LFT	Slack		
2	A	Excavate	3	0	3	0	3	0	**	
3	B	Foundation	4	3	7	3	7	0	**	
4	C	Rough Plumb.	3	7	10	22	25	15		
5	D	Frame	10	7	17	7	17	0	**	
6	E	Exterior	8	17	25	17	25	0	**	
7	F	HVAC	4	17	21	21	25	4		
8	G	Rough Elec.	6	17	23	19	25	2		
9	H	Sheet Rock	8	25	33	25	33	0	**	
10	I	Carpentry	5	33	38	33	38	0	**	
11	J	Paint	5	33	38	35	40	2		
12	K	Final Plumb.	4	38	42	38	42	0	**	
13	L	Final Elec.	2	38	40	40	42	2		
14	M	Flooring	4	42	46	42	46	0	**	
15										
16		Note: "**" denotes critical activities.								
17										
18										
19										

Start & Finish Times / Gantt Chart / Network /

Ready NUM

Figure 15.11: Spreadsheet calculations of start and finish times, slack, and critical activities

To create the spreadsheet in Figure 15.11, we first entered all the labels and the activity times. The earliest finish times in column E are calculated as the earliest start time for each activity plus the time required to perform the activity. The latest start times in column F are calculated as the latest finish time of each activity minus the time required to perform the activity. Unfortunately, no one formula can calculate the earliest start times shown in column D. Each cell in column D required an individual formula to implement the logic of the forward pass described earlier (and summarized in Figure 15.7). Similarly, each of the latest finish times in column G required a unique formula to implement the logic described earlier for the backward pass (summarized in Figure 15.9). The slack values in column H are calculated as the difference between the latest and earliest start times for each activity.

Although the spreadsheet approach is feasible for small projects, it would be tedious and impractical to build custom formulas to calculate the earliest start times and latest finish times for each activity in a large project. The next section describes another, more efficient, approach for calculating earliest and latest start and finish times for larger projects.

A **Gantt chart** is a popular technique for portraying the schedule of a project's activities over time. Figure 15.12 shows the earliest start and finish times for each activity in our example problem displayed in a Gantt chart. This type of chart is useful in helping a project manager see when activities can begin and end, and in keeping track of which activities are underway at any point in time.

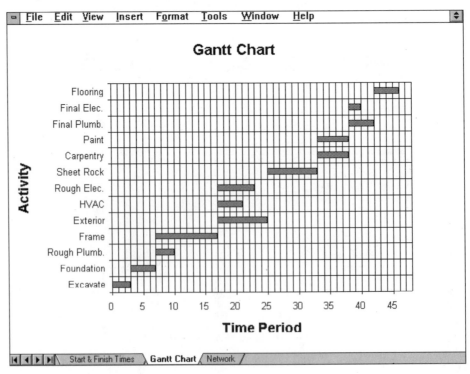

Figure 15.12: A Gantt chart for the example problem

Creating Gantt Charts in Excel

The Gantt chart in Figure 15.12 is a stacked horizontal bar chart that plots the EST and the time required to perform each activity. However, the bars for the EST for each activity are formatted so that they do not appear on the graph—giving the illusion that only the activity times are being graphed. To create a Gantt chart like the one shown in Figure 15.12:

1. Select the range B2 through D14 (shown in Figure 5.11).

2. Click the Insert menu.

3. Click Chart.

4. Click As New Sheet.

Excel's ChartWizard then prompts you to make a number of selections concerning the type of chart you want and how it should be formatted. Select the options to display a stacked horizontal bar chart. When finished with the ChartWizard, you need to reverse the order in which the bars are displayed on the graph. To do this:

1. Click the Format menu.

2. Click Bar Group.

3. Click Series Order.

4. Click Move Down (to reverse the order of the bars).

Finally, double-click any of the bars representing the EST of any activity, select the Patterns option and indicate that you want no border or area patterns. The basic Gantt chart is now complete. You can continue to customize the chart by clicking any element and specifying options in the resulting dialog boxes.

A weakness of both the Gantt chart and the table of start and finish times shown earlier in Figure 15.11 is that they do not show the precedence relationships between the activities in a project. For example, the Gantt chart shows that the painting and carpentry activities should both end at time period 38, and that the final electrical and final plumbing activities should begin at that point. But what happens if the painting activity is delayed? Would this prevent both the final electrical *and* final plumbing activities from starting on time? To answer this question we need to know if painting is a predecessor for both the final plumbing and final electrical activities. The Gantt chart does not provide this information. Thus, although the Gantt chart is a valuable monitoring tool, it does not tell the whole story about the precedence relationships among project activities.

As shown in Figure 15.13, we can display the network structure of a project in a spreadsheet. Here, we used the relationships in Figures 15.7 and 15.9 to calculate the earliest and latest start and finish times for each activity. Then we used Excel's drawing tool to draw arrows indicating the precedence relationships between activities. Again, this approach is feasible for small projects, but larger projects require specialized project management software tools.

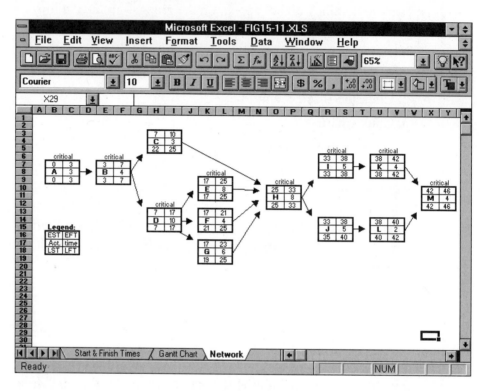

Figure 15.13: Project network implemented in a spreadsheet

DETERMINING EARLIEST AND LATEST START TIMES USING LP

As mentioned earlier, the process of creating spreadsheet formulas to calculate the earliest and latest start and finish times for project activities can be overwhelming for all but the smallest of projects. Fortunately, a simple LP approach exists for determining earliest and latest start times for projects of any size. If we know these start times, we can determine the earliest and latest finish times as:

$$EFT_i = EST_i + t_i$$

$$LFT_i = LST_i + t_i$$

AN LP MODEL FOR EARLIEST START TIMES

The logic behind the LP approach parallels that of the forward and backward passes described earlier. To explain this approach, we'll let T_i represent the time at which activity i begins, and let t_i represent the amount of time required to perform activity i. The LP model that determines the earliest start time for each activity in our example problem is:

$$\begin{aligned}
\text{MIN:} \quad & T_A + T_B + \ldots + T_M \\
\text{Subject to:} \quad & T_B \geq T_A + t_A \\
& T_C \geq T_B + t_B \\
& T_D \geq T_B + t_B \\
& T_E \geq T_D + t_D \\
& T_F \geq T_D + t_D \\
& T_G \geq T_D + t_D \\
& T_H \geq T_C + t_C \\
& T_H \geq T_E + t_E \\
& T_H \geq T_F + t_F \\
& T_H \geq T_G + t_G \\
& T_I \geq T_H + t_H \\
& T_J \geq T_H + t_H \\
& T_K \geq T_I + t_I \\
& T_L \geq T_J + t_J \\
& T_M \geq T_K + t_K \\
& T_M \geq T_L + t_L \\
& T_i \geq 0, \text{ for all } i
\end{aligned}$$

To understand the formulation of this model, consider the first constraint: $T_B \geq T_A + t_A$. This constraint indicates that the time at which activity B begins (T_B) must be greater than or equal to the time at which activity A begins (T_A) plus the time required to perform activity A (t_A). This follows logically from the project network shown in Figure 15.13 and our earlier discussion of the forward pass. Similarly, the second constraint indicates that the time at which activity C begins (T_C) must be greater than or equal to the time at which activity B begins (T_B) plus the time required to perform activity B (t_B).

If you compare this LP model with the project network in Figure 15.13, you will notice that each constraint in this model corresponds to one of the arcs representing the precedence relationships in the project network. Each arc in the network goes *from* one node *to* another node. In general, if an arc goes *from* activity *i to* activity *j*, the constraint takes the form:

$$T_j \geq T_i + t_i$$

This constraint indicates that the time at which activity *j* begins must be greater than or equal to the time at which activity *i* begins plus the time required to perform activity *i*. Because the objective function in this model seeks to minimize the sum of the start times of each activity, the solution to this model will provide the *earliest* possible start time for each activity in the project.

IMPLEMENTING THE MODEL IN A SPREADSHEET

Each constraint in our LP model takes the form:

$$T_j \geq T_i + t_i$$

or, equivalently:

$$T_j - T_i \geq t_i$$

where i represents the *from* node and j represents a *to* node of a particular arc in the network. The second form of the constraint indicates that the time between the start of activity j and activity i must be greater than or equal to the time required to perform activity i. We'll use the second form of the constraints to implement our model in the spreadsheet.

The type of spreadsheet layout needed to implement this model is shown in Figure 15.14 (and in the file FIG15-14.XLS on your data disk). To implement the constraints for this model, we need a list of the *from* and *to* nodes of all the arcs in the project network, and a list of the activities in the network and the time required to complete them (the t_i).

Figure 15.14: Spreadsheet model of the LP formulation of earliest start times

In Figure 15.14, cells D5 through D17 represent the T_i variables in our algebraic model (that is, D5 indicates the time at which activity A starts, D6 indicates the time at which activity B starts, and so on). The objective function is implemented in cell D18 as:

Formula for cell D18:   =SUM(D5:D17)

The LHS of the constraints are implemented in column H. Specifically, the LHS of the first constraint ($T_B - T_A$) is implemented in cell H5 then copied to cells H6 through H20 as:

Formula for cell H5: =VLOOKUP(G5,$B$5:$D$17,3) –
(copy to H6 through H20) VLOOKUP(F5,$B$5:$D$17,3)

The first VLOOKUP function in this formula corresponds to the value of T_B. The first VLOOKUP function takes the contents of cell G5 (the letter B) and looks for its match in the first column of the range $B$5:$D$17 (the match is in cell B6), then returns the value in the third column of the range—or the value in cell D6. Cell D6 corresponds to T_B. The second VLOOKUP function works in a similar way to return the appropriate value for T_A. The difference between the values of these two VLOOKUP functions represents the amount of time between the start of activities A and B.

The RHS values for each LHS formula in column H are implemented in column I as:

Formula for cell I5: =VLOOKUP(F5,$B$5:$C$17,2)
(copy to I6 through I20)

The formula in cell I5 returns the value t_A—or the amount of time required to perform activity A. Thus, after entering the data for the problem, we can use three simple formulas to implement the LP model regardless of the number of nodes and arcs in the project network.

SOLVING THE MODEL

Figure 15.15 shows the Solver parameters and options used to solve this problem. The optimal solution is shown in Figure 15.16. Notice that the earliest start times shown in Figure 15.16 correspond to those calculated earlier in Figure 15.13. In particular, the earliest start time for activity M is 42. Because it takes 4 units of time to perform this activity, its earliest finish time corresponds to time period 46.

Figure 15.15: Solver parameters and options for the earliest start times

Figure 15.16: Optimal solution for the earliest start times

AN LP MODEL FOR LATEST START TIMES

We can use the LP model for determining the earliest start times to also determine the latest start times if we make two simple modifications. First, we must change the objective from a minimization to a maximization. Second, we must include one additional constraint to ensure that the latest start time of the final project activity equals the earliest start time for this activity, identified from the solution to the previous model. Thus, the LP model for determining the latest start time for each activity in our example problem is:

$$\text{MAX}: \quad T_A + T_B + \ldots + T_M$$

$$\text{Subject to}: \quad T_B \geq T_A + t_A$$

$$T_C \geq T_B + t_B$$

$$T_D \geq T_B + t_B$$

$$T_E \geq T_D + t_D$$

$$T_F \geq T_D + t_D$$

$$T_G \geq T_D + t_D$$

$$T_H \geq T_C + t_C$$

$$T_H \geq T_E + t_E$$

$$T_H \geq T_F + t_F$$

$$T_H \geq T_G + t_G$$

$$T_I \geq T_H + t_H$$

$$T_J \geq T_H + t_H$$

$$T_K \geq T_I + t_I$$

$$T_L \geq T_J + t_J$$

$$T_M \geq T_K + t_K$$

$$T_M \geq T_L + t_L$$

$$T_M = 42$$

$$T_i \geq 0, \text{ for all } i$$

Because the objective function in this model seeks to maximize the sum of the activity start times, the solution will provide the *latest* possible start time for each activity, subject to the additional constraint that activity M starts no later than time period 42 ($T_M = 42$). Thus, the solution to this problem should reveal the latest time at which each activity can begin without delaying the earliest possible completion of the entire project.

IMPLEMENTING AND SOLVING THE MODEL IN A SPREADSHEET

We can implement the model to determine the latest start times in exactly the same way as described for the earliest start time model. Figure 15.19 illustrates the spreadsheet implementation of the latest start time model for our example problem.

Key Cell Formulas

Cell	Formula	Copied to
D18	=SUM(D5:D17)	—
H5	=VLOOKUP(G5,$B$5:$D$17,3)–VLOOKUP(F5,$B$5:$D$17,3)	H6:H20
I5	=VLOOKUP(F5,$B$5:$C$17,2)	I6:I20

Figure 15.17: Spreadsheet model of the LP formulation of the latest start times

Figure 15.18 shows the Solver parameters and options required to solve this problem. Notice that the maximization option (Max) is selected and an extra constraint is included to force the latest start time for activity M (represented by cell D17) to equal 42. The optimal solution to this problem is shown in Figure 15.19. The latest start times shown here correspond to those calculated earlier in Figure 15.13.

Figure 15.18: Solver parameters and options for the latest start times

Figure 15.19: Optimal solution for the latest start times

SUMMARIZING THE RESULTS

The results of our two LP models are summarized in the report shown in Figure 15.20. This summary sheet reads the earliest and latest start times from the sheets shown in Figures 15.16 and 15.19. These values are used to calculate the earliest and latest finish times for each activity. The slack time for each activity is calculated in the usual way, and critical activities are highlighted.

```
┌──────────────────────────────────────────────────────────────────────┐
│  Microsoft Excel - FIG15-14.XLS                                   ▼ ▲  │
│  File  Edit  View  Insert  Format  Tools  Data  Window  Help      ▼    │
│ ┌─────────────────────────────────────────────────────┐ 100% ▼  ⚙ ▶? │
│ Courier      ▼ 10 ▼  B I U  ▤▤▤▤ $ % , .0 .0 □ ▼ □ ▼    │
│        D2        ▼      ='Early Times'!D5                               │
```

	A	B	C	D	E	F	G	H	I	J	K
1	Activity	Description	Time	EST	EFT	LST	LFT	Slack			
2	A	Excavate	3	0	3	0	3	0	**		
3	B	Foundation	4	3	7	3	7	0	**		
4	C	Rough Plumb.	3	7	10	22	25	15			
5	D	Frame	10	7	17	7	17	0	**		
6	E	Exterior	8	17	25	17	25	0	**		
7	F	HVAC	4	17	21	21	25	4			
8	G	Rough Elec.	6	17	23	19	25	2			
9	H	Sheet Rock	8	25	33	25	33	0	**		
10	I	Carpentry	5	33	38	33	38	0	**		
11	J	Paint	5	33	38	35	40	2			
12	K	Final Plumb.	4	38	42	38	42	0	**		
13	L	Final Elec.	2	38	40	40	42	2			
14	M	Flooring	4	42	46	42	46	0	**		
15											
16		Note: "**" denotes critical activities									

```
│ ◄ ◄ ► ►│ Early Times / Late Times \ Summary /         │◄│           ► │
│ Ready                                                                  │
```

Key Cell Formulas

Cell	Formula	Copied to
D2	='Early Times'!D5	D3:D14
E2	=C2+D2	E3:E14
F2	='Late Times'!D5	F3:F14
G2	=C2+F2	G3:G14
H2	=F2–D2	H3:H14
I2	=IF(H2<=0.00001,"**"," ")	I3:I14

Figure 15.20: Summary of earliest and latest start and finish times

The LP approach to determining earliest and latest start and finish times is quite simple and can be applied to small, medium, or large projects. However, keep in mind that if any of the estimated activity times change, the LP model must be updated and re-solved to identify the impact of the change on the start and finish times throughout the project network.

PROJECT CRASHING

With the CPM technique, we can use the times required to perform each activity to determine the least amount of time required to complete the entire project. However, the time required to complete an activity can often be shortened, or crashed. For example, suppose that the amount of time it takes to paint a house is *normally* five days. But, by hiring more painters or asking the existing painters to work overtime, it might be possible to paint the same house in two days. Thus, activities can have normal times and crash times.

The **normal time** of an activity represents the ordinary amount of time required to complete the activity with the usual amount of resources and effort. The **crash time** of an activity represents the least amount of time in which an activity can be accomplished if extra effort and resources are applied to the activity. The extra effort and resources required to crash certain activities usually increase the cost of performing these activities.

In managing projects, we often need to evaluate the trade-offs between the cost of crashing certain activities and the benefit of accomplishing these activities in less than normal time. For example, in our problem we determined that it takes 46 working days to complete the construction of the house. But what if the buyer wants the house built in 35 days? We need some way to determine if this can be done and, if so, how much additional cost will be involved. Similarly, it is not unusual for some critical activities in a project to take more than their normal time. After all, projects are not immune to Murphy's Law, which states that if something *can* go wrong it *will* go wrong. When a critical activity is delayed, the completion of the project will be delayed unless management chooses to crash some of the remaining critical activities.

AN LP APPROACH TO CRASHING

We can use LP to help determine the least costly way of crashing a project to meet certain deadlines. To do this, we first must determine the normal time, normal cost, crash time, and crash cost for each project activity. Suppose that Tom asked his subcontractors to estimate crash times and costs for activities involved in our example problem. This information is summarized in Figure 15.21 (and in the file FIG15-21.XLS on your data disk) along with the normal times and normal costs that Tom originally estimated for each activity.

As shown in Figure 15.21, in his original plan Tom estimated that the framing activity (activity D) would take 10 days and cost $20,000. However, the subcontractor indicated that if this activity were crashed by the maximum amount, it could be completed in only 6 days but at a cost of $25,000. For planning purposes, Tom might assume that the time required to complete the framing activity can be reduced from its normal time of 10 days by no more than 4 days (10 − 6 = 4). This value is indicated in Figure 15.21 in the Allowable Crash Days column. Tom might also assume that each day this activity is crashed will increase the cost of the activity by approximately $1,250 (($25,000 − $20,000)/4 = $1,250). This value is shown for the framing activity in the Crash Cost Per Day column. The allowable number of crash days and crash costs per day for the remaining activities are determined in a similar way and are shown in Figure 15.21.

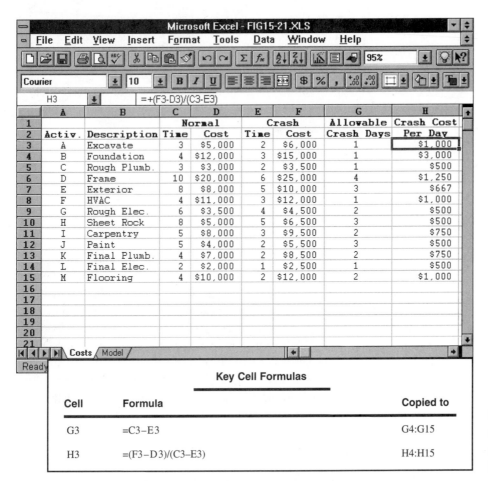

Figure 15.21: Summary of normal and crash times and costs for the home-building project

DETERMINING THE EARLIEST CRASH COMPLETION TIME

Tom might want to know the earliest possible date that the project could be completed and by what amount each activity would need to be crashed in order to achieve this date. An LP formulation of this problem is represented as:

$$\text{MIN:} \quad T_M + t_M - C_M$$

$$\text{Subject to:} \quad T_B - T_A \geq t_A - C_A$$

$$T_C - T_B \geq t_B - C_B$$

$$T_D - T_B \geq t_B - C_B$$

$$T_E - T_D \geq t_D - C_D$$

$$T_F - T_D \geq t_D - C_D$$

$$T_G - T_D \geq t_D - C_D$$

$$T_H - T_C \geq t_C - C_C$$

$$T_H - T_E \geq t_E - C_E$$

$$T_H - T_F \geq t_F - C_F$$

$$T_H - T_G \geq t_G - C_G$$

$$T_I - T_H \geq t_H - C_H$$

$$T_J - T_H \geq t_H - C_H$$

$$T_K - T_I \geq t_I - C_I$$

$$T_L - T_J \geq t_J - C_J$$

$$T_M - T_K \geq t_K - C_K$$

$$T_M - T_L \geq t_K - C_L$$

$C_i \leq$ allowable crash days for activity i

$T_i, C_i \geq 0$, for all i

where T_i = the time at which activity i begins

t_i = the normal activity time of activity i

C_i = amount of time by which activity i is crashed

This LP model is similar to the models discussed in the previous section except that this model allows for the project activities to be crashed. For example, the first time constraint indicates that the difference between the start times of activities A and B must be greater than or equal to the normal time for activity A minus the amount be which activity A is crashed. The rest of the time constraints can be interpreted in a similar way. Also note that this model places appropriate upper limits on the amount of time by which each activity can be crashed. Finally, the objective function in this problem attempts to minimize the final completion time of the project (which is equal to the start time for activity M, plus its normal activity time, minus the amount by which this activity is crashed). Thus, the solution to this model should indicate the earliest possible time at which the project can be completed if activities are crashed.

IMPLEMENTING THE MODEL

One approach to implementing this model in a spreadsheet is shown on the Model sheet in Figure 15.22. In this spreadsheet, the values in column D represent the start time of each activity (the T_i) and the values in column E correspond to the amount by which each activity is crashed (the C_i).

The LHS formulas for the time constraints are implemented in column I in the same manner as described in the previous section. Specifically, cell I5 contains the following formula, which is copied to cells I6 through I20:

Formula for cell I5:   =VLOOKUP(H5,$B$5:$D$17,3)–
(copy to I6 though I20)   VLOOKUP(G5,$B$5:$D$17,3)

This formula first finds the cell in column D that corresponds to the start time for activity B and then subtracts the cell in column D that represents the start time for activity A. The value returned by this formula represents the actual amount of time between the start of activity A and the start of activity B.

The RHS values of the time constraints are implemented in column J as:

Formula for cell J5:   =VLOOKUP(G5,$B$5:$C$17,2)–
(copy to H6 though H20)   VLOOKUP(G5,$B$5:$E$17,4)

Figure 15.22: Spreadsheet implementation of the crashing model to determine the earliest possible finish time

This formula first finds the cell in column C corresponding to the normal time for activity A then subtracts the cell in column E corresponding to the time by which activity A will be crashed.

The objective function for this problem is implemented in cell E20 with the following formula:

Formula for cell E20: =D17+C17−E17

This value represents the time at which the project will be completed. Finally, for informational purposes (and future reference), in cell E19 we implement the following formula to calculate the total cost associated with crashing the project:

Formula for cell E19: =SUMPRODUCT(Costs!H3:H15,Model!E5:E17)

This formula calculates the sum of products between the crash cost per day for each activity (calculated in cells H3 through H15 on the Costs sheet shown in Figure 15.21) and the amount by which each activity is crashed (represented by cells E5 through E17 on the Model sheet shown in Figure 15.22).

SOLVING THE MODEL

Figure 15.23 shows the Solver parameters and options used to solve this model. In defining the constraints for this problem, the values of cells E5 through E17 (the C_i) are required to be less than or equal to their maximum allowable values calculated earlier on the Costs sheet.

Figure 15.23: *Solver parameters and options for the earliest possible finish time*

The optimal solution for this problem, shown in Figure 15.24, indicates that by crashing various activities the project could be completed within 28 days rather than 46. However, the Total Crash Cost figure indicates this would raise the cost of the project by $19,000. (Note that in general, the total crash cost obtained when solving this type of model is not necessarily the minimum crash cost because the model minimizes completion time, not crash costs. Because other optimal solutions can occur, another crash schedule might also allow the project to be completed within 28 days but at a lower total crash cost. Thus, to verify that the minimum total crash cost is $19,000, we need to add a constraint to hold the finish time at 28 days and attempt to minimize the total crash cost. In this case, the solution shown in Figure 15.24 is optimal and the minimum total crash cost is, in fact, $19,000.)

Figure 15.24: Optimal solution for the earliest possible finish time

DETERMINING A LEAST COST CRASH SCHEDULE

Another use of a crashing model is to determine the least costly way to complete a project at some time earlier than would be possible using normal activity times. For example, if the homebuyer insists on the house being built within 35 days, we might want to determine the least costly way of crashing the schedule to meet this deadline.

We can solve this type of problem easily using the existing model. In this case, we would simply add a constraint to hold the project completion time at 35 days and attempt to minimize the total crash cost. The Solver parameters and options required to accomplish this are shown in Figure 15.25, and the optimal solution is shown in Figure 15.26.

The solution shown in Figure 15.26 indicates that it would cost an additional $8,500 to crash the project so that it could be completed within 35 days. The values in the Amount Crashed column indicate the amounts by which each activity must be crashed in order to implement this schedule.

Figure 15.25: *Solver parameters and options for the least cost crash schedule to complete the project by time period 35*

Figure 15.26: *Optimal solution for the least cost crash schedule to complete the project by time period 35*

CRASHING AS AN MOLP

As we have seen, two objectives can be pursued in our crashing model. On one hand, we might want to minimize the finish time of the project. On the other hand, we might want to minimize the cost of crashing the project. These two objectives are in conflict with one another because reducing the completion time of the project increases the crash costs. Thus, we could use the techniques for MOLPs described in chapter 7 if we want to study the cost/time trade-offs more formally in this type of problem.

Another way to study the cost/time trade-offs is to re-solve the problem several times to determine the minimum crash cost for each possible completion time. A graph showing the minimum crash cost for each possible completion time is useful in evaluating the trade-offs involved in crashing. Figure 15.27 shows such a graph for our example problem.

According to this graph, no crash costs will be incurred if the project is completed in its normal time of 46 days, but crash costs of $19,000 will be incurred if we complete the project in the least amount of time (28 days). Although it is relatively inexpensive to crash the project by a few days, the graph shows that it becomes increasingly expensive to crash the project by additional amounts. Note that a rather substantial increase in cost is incurred to complete the project in 28 days rather than 29. So this type of graph gives us a clear picture of the cost/time trade-offs involved in crashing a project.

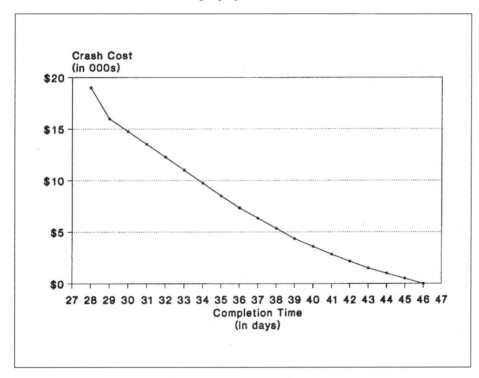

Figure 15.27: Graph of the relationship between crash cost and completion time

CERTAINTY VS. UNCERTAINTY

Throughout our discussion of CPM we assumed that the times required to complete project activities were known with certainty or could, at least, be estimated with a high degree of accuracy. This assumption does not hold for all projects. For example, consider the schedule of activities required to design and build the first space shuttle. Because no one had ever built a space shuttle before, no historical data were available for estimating how long it would take to perform many of the creative tasks required by this project. Even in projects where the same or similar tasks have been performed before, the amount of time required to perform them might be different. PERT was developed as an attempt to deal with uncertainty in activity times.

In recent years, a number of problems have surfaced regarding the PERT technique, causing many to question the wisdom of using this technique at all. The following discussion of PERT focuses on illuminating these weaknesses. We will then briefly consider how to overcome some of these problems using the technique of simulation.

PERT: AN OVERVIEW

PERT differs from CPM in that it assumes the times required to perform the project activities are *not* known with certainty. PERT assumes that the activity times are random variables that have some mean, or expected, value and some variance. However, rather than specifying a mean and variance for each activity, we must give three time estimates for each activity in the project. Specifically, for each activity PERT requires estimates of:

a_i = estimate of the duration of activity i assuming the most favorable conditions

b_i = estimate of the duration of activity i assuming the least favorable conditions

m_i = estimate of the most likely duration of activity i

We can think of a_i, b_i, and m_i as representing, respectively, the best case, worst case, and most likely times required to perform activity i. PERT uses these values to calculate the expected duration of each activity as:

$$t_i = \frac{a_i + 4m_i + b_i}{6}$$

and estimates the variance of each activity's duration as:

$$v_i = \frac{(b_i - a_i)^2}{36}$$

The preceding formulas are based on the assumption that the times required to perform each activity are random variables that follow the beta probability distribution. An in-depth understanding of the beta distribution is not necessary for our purposes. The beta distribution can be used to describe a wide variety of random variables, and is a reasonable choice for describing the behavior of most activity times when their true distributions are unknown.

After calculating the expected times for each activity, the next step in PERT is to identify the critical path for the project. In most project networks, a variety of paths can be followed to get from the start activity to the finish activity. Each path represents a sequence of activities that must be performed in order to complete the project. Because PERT assumes that the times required to perform the activities along a path are random variables, the time required to complete a given path is also a random variable with some mean and variance.

One of PERT's bolder assumptions is that the individual activity times in a project are independent of one another. This assumption allows us to calculate the expected time required to complete any path in the network as the sum of the expected times (the t_i) of the activities on the path. Similarly, the variance of the completion time for any path is the sum of the variances (the v_i) of the activities on the path. Because all the paths through a project network must be completed in order for the project to be completed, PERT views the path with the largest expected completion to be the most critical—the critical path.

The expected completion time and variance for the critical path are used in PERT to estimate the probability of completing the project by various dates and to assist in negotiating and setting deadlines for the project's completion. Many projects impose financial penalties for each day, week, or month a project is late; therefore, it is often important to identify a deadline for a project that management is confident will not be exceeded. Thus, in addition to identifying a critical path for management to scrutinize, PERT also claims to offer assistance in estimating and setting deadlines for a project.

THE PROBLEMS WITH PERT

The PERT technique presents a number of problems that should cause us to approach it with skepticism. First, as indicated above, PERT assumes that the time required to perform project activities are random variables that are independent of one another. Although this assumption makes it easy to complete the calculations in PERT, it is probably not a realistic assumption. For example, if one activity along the critical path (or any other path) runs a bit over its expected time, a diligent project manager will make sure that one or more of the subsequent activities run a bit under their expected times to catch up on the schedule. To the extent that these over- and under-runs offset one another, the expected completion time of the project should not be affected seriously. However, the variance of the completion times of the paths through the network will be reduced as a result.

The more serious problem in PERT involves the identification of the critical path. As described earlier, PERT identifies the critical path as the path with the longest expected completion time. Thus, an unsuspecting project manager might focus on the activities on the critical path, believing that they are the activities most likely to delay the completion of the project. In reality, activities *not* on the critical path can pose a greater risk of delaying the project. Consider the activity network shown in Figure 15.28.

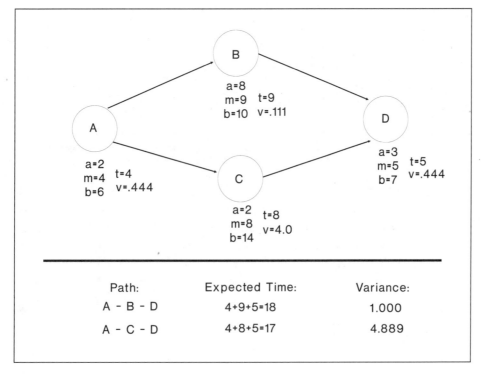

Path:	Expected Time:	Variance:
A - B - D	4+9+5=18	1.000
A - C - D	4+8+5=17	4.889

Figure 15.28: Example of a PERT network

The network in Figure 15.28 represents a simple project consisting of only four activities. The three time estimates (*a*, *b*, and *m*) required by PERT are given for each activity. The expected time and variance (*t* and *v*) are calculated for each activity. Only two paths run through this network: A to B to D, and A to C to D. The expected times and variances for each path are calculated as shown in Figure 15.28. The path consisting of A-B-D has an expected time of 18 and variance of 1.0. The path consisting of A-C-D has an expected time of 17 and variance of 4.889. Thus, PERT would identify A-B-D as the critical path and use its expected value and variance to make estimates about when the project will be completed.

Earlier, we indicated that the time to complete any path in a PERT network is a random variable. We can view the time to complete path A-B-D and the time to complete path A-C-D as two separate random variables whose probability distributions are similar to those shown in Figure 15.29. Notice that the distribution of the critical A-B-D path is centered at its expected value of 18 and has a relatively small variance. The distribution of the non-critical A-C-D path is centered at its expected value of 17 and has a much larger variance.

Figure 15.29: Graph of the distributions of completion times for each path through the PERT network

If we focus only on the distribution of the critical path shown in Figure 15.29, it appears that almost no chance exists that completing this path will take more than 21 time periods. Thus, if we apply the PERT technique to this project, we would conclude that the project can almost certainly be completed within 21 time units. However, the distribution of times for path A-C-D indicates a fairly significant probability that this non-critical path will take more than 21 days. So which path is really the critical path—the one with the longest expected completion time or the one with the smallest probability of completion by the desired deadline? And which activity in this project is really more critical—B or C? The fact that PERT causes us to ask such questions, and fails to answer them, should raise serious concerns about the wisdom of using this technique.

IMPLICATIONS

The preceding discussion makes it clear that activities *not* on PERT's critical path might, in fact, be more critical to the completion of a project than the activities PERT identifies as critical. Indeed, *every* activity in a project has some probability of being critical. For some activities, this probability might be near 0; for others it might be closer to 1. A project manager would want to focus on the activities with the highest probability of being critical—regardless of whether or not they fall on the critical path. Unfortunately, PERT does little to help us identify the project activities that are truly the most critical.

SIMULATING PROJECT NETWORKS

Although the PERT technique has serious drawbacks, it does highlight an important point—activity times in a project are likely to be somewhat random. Although CPM ignores this point entirely, by calculating the earliest and latest start times for each activity it at least shows which activities are likely to be critical if the actual activity times deviate from their expected values.

The best way to evaluate the impact of variability in activity times on the critical path and the completion time of a project involves the technique of simulation described in chapters 12 and 13. To simulate a project, we need to generate random times from appropriate probability distributions for each project activity. For the given set of random activity times, we can determine the critical path and the time required to complete the project. If we repeat this process many times, we can determine the frequency with which the project activities fall on the critical path. We could also analyze the resulting distribution project completion times to estimate more accurately the probability of completing the project within various time periods.

AN EXAMPLE

The following example, which is a modification of our earlier home-building example, illustrates the mechanics of simulating the duration of a project.

Tom has asked the subcontractors for each activity in the home-building process to supply a best case, most likely case, and worst case estimate of the amount of time required to complete each activity. Figure 15.30 shows these time estimates.

Tom wants to use these time estimates to conduct a simulation study of the project. In particular, he wants to determine how critical each activity is—that is, the probability of each activity falling on the critical path. He also wants to determine the number of days it will take to complete the entire project.

	Time Estimates		
Activity	a Best Case	m Most Likely Case	b Worst Case
A	2	3	5
B	3	4	6
C	2	3	7
D	8	10	14
E	6	8	10
F	3	4	5
G	4	6	8
H	7	8	10
I	4	5	7
J	3	5	9
K	3	4	6
L	1	2	4
M	3	4	6

Figure 15.30: Summary of time estimates for activities in the home-building project

GENERATING RANDOM ACTIVITY TIMES

To simulate the duration of this project, we first must identify probability distributions that describe the behavior of the random activity times. Because the three time estimates for each activity correspond to the best case, most likely case, and worst case scenarios for each activity, we might assume that the random behavior of the activity times can be approximated by a triangular probability distribution such as the one shown in Figure 15.31 for activity A. Notice that the shape of the triangular distribution varies depending on the parameters a, m, and b, which correspond (respectively) to the best case, most likely case, and worst case time estimates for a given activity.

The formula to generate a random number t from a triangular distribution with parameters $a \leq m \leq b$ is:

$$\text{If } r \leq \frac{m-a}{b-a}, \quad t = a + \sqrt{(b-a)(m-a)r}$$

$$\text{otherwise, } t = b - \sqrt{(b-a)(b-m)(1-r)}$$

where r is a continuous uniform random number between 0 and 1. Thus, to implement this random number generator, we first need to generate a continuous uniform random number r for each activity and then apply the preceding formula

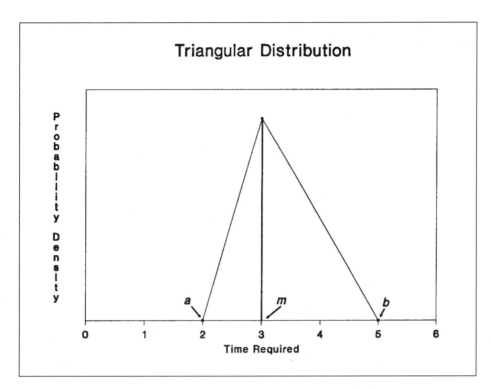

Figure 15.31: *Example of a triangular distribution of activity times*

to determine the random activity time *t*. (Most spreadsheet add-ins for simulation, such as @RISK and Crystal Ball, provide a TRIANG( ) function that simplifies the process of generating random numbers from a triangular distribution.)

IMPLEMENTING THE MODEL

A spreadsheet model for this problem is shown in Figure 15.32 (and in the file FIG15-32.XLS on your data disk).

The three times for each project activity are entered in columns B, C, and D. As described earlier, to implement the random number generator for each activity, a continuous uniform random number between 0 and 1 (representing *r*) first must be generated. This is done in the Random Number column E by entering the formula =RAND( ) in each cell in the column. The formula to generate the random values representing the time required for activity A is implemented in column F:

Formula for cell F3:　　=IF(E3<=(C3–B3)/(D3–B3),B3+SQRT((D3–B3)*
(copy to F4 through F15)　(C3–B3)*E3),D3–SQRT((D3–B3)*(D3–C3)*(1–E3)))

Using the randomly generated activity times, we can create formulas to calculate the earliest and latest start and finish times and the amount of slack available for each activity. We would accomplish this in the same manner as described earlier with respect to Figure 15.11. The activities on the critical path are indicated by slack values of 0.

Figure 15.32: *Spreadsheet model of the home-building project with random activity times*

Key Cell Formulas

Cell	Formula	Copied to
E3	=RAND()	E4:E15
F3	=IF(E3<=(C3–B3)/(D3–B3),B3+SQRT((D3–B3)*(C3–B3)*E3, D3–SQRT((D3–B3)*(D3–C3)*(1–E3)))	F4:F15
G3:K15	refer to spreadsheet file for details	—
L3	=IF(K3<=0.0001, "**"," ")	L4:L15

RUNNING THE SIMULATION

We can use the Data Table command (as described in chapter 12) to replicate this model repeatedly. To do so, we must identify the values in the model that we want to track. One objective in our problem is to determine how critical each activity is. Because critical activities are indicated by slack values of 0, we want to track the values in the Slack column for each activity in our model. However, because all paths go through activities A, B, H, and M, we know that these activities will always be critical, so there is no point in tracking their slack values. Thus, the slack value for activity C in the Model sheet in Figure 15.32 is repeated in cell B3 of the Simulation sheet shown in Figure 15.33 using the following formula:

Formula for cell B3:   =VLOOKUP(B2,Model!$A$3:$K$15,11)
(copy to C3 through J3)

This formula is copied to cells C3 through J3 to provide the slack values for activities D, E, F, G, I, J, K, and L, respectively.

	Microsoft Excel - FIG15-32.XLS									

B3 =VLOOKUP(B2,Model!$A$3:$K$15,11)

	A	B	C	D	E	F	G	H	I	J	K
1					A	C	T	I	V	I	T	Y	S	L	A	C	K		Finish
2		C	D	E	F	G	I	J	K	L	Time
3	1	15.89	0.00	0.00	5.66	4.24	0.00	1.40	0.00	1.40	49.14
4	2	18.25	0.00	0.00	5.49	2.78	0.00	0.80	0.00	0.80	49.06
5	3	13.36	0.00	0.00	4.17	0.20	0.00	2.73	0.00	2.73	49.83
6	4	14.85	0.00	0.00	3.69	2.61	0.00	0.08	0.00	0.08	49.44
7	5	12.12	0.00	0.00	4.13	2.88	0.94	0.00	0.94	0.00	49.35
8	6	16.86	0.00	0.00	3.65	1.78	0.00	3.35	0.00	3.35	51.38
9	7	12.30	0.00	0.00	4.39	1.49	1.10	0.00	1.10	0.00	49.32
10	8	12.06	0.00	0.00	4.01	2.46	0.00	2.58	0.00	2.58	47.69
11	9	13.89	0.00	0.00	3.72	2.05	0.00	2.44	0.00	2.44	48.56
12	10	14.99	0.00	0.00	3.14	0.74	0.00	2.11	0.00	2.11	47.32
13	11	14.87	0.00	0.00	3.33	1.24	0.57	0.00	0.57	0.00	47.23
14	12	11.69	0.00	0.00	4.25	2.01	0.00	2.25	0.00	2.25	47.79
15	13	17.13	0.00	0.00	3.93	1.24	0.00	1.14	0.00	1.14	48.50
16	14	12.99	0.00	0.00	2.32	0.48	0.79	0.00	0.79	0.00	48.57
17	15	15.68	0.00	0.00	4.01	3.85	0.00	4.08	0.00	4.08	51.38
18	16	12.24	0.00	0.00	4.55	0.93	0.00	3.79	0.00	3.79	48.76
19	17	14.16	0.00	0.00	2.49	1.14	0.00	4.03	0.00	4.03	49.41
20	18	18.56	0.00	0.00	4.94	4.37	0.00	0.11	0.00	0.11	51.70

Model / **Simulation** / Results

Key Cell Formulas

Cell	Formula	Copied to
B3	=VLOOKUP(B2,Model!$A$3:$K$15,11)	C3:J3
K3	=Model!J15	—

Figure 15.33: *Simulation sheet for the home-building project*

A second objective in our problem is to estimate the amount of time required to complete the project—or the finish time of activity M. This value is tracked in column K on the Simulation sheet shown in Figure 15.33 through the following formula in cell K3:

Formula for cell K3:   =Model!J15

The remainder of the spreadsheet shown in Figure 15.33 is completed using the Data Table command. Each row in this table represents the amount of slack for the activities and the project completion times that were observed in each replication of our project activity model. The simulation shown in Figure 15.33 consists of 100 such replications.

ANALYZING THE RESULTS

The Results sheet shown in Figure 15.34 provides the results of the simulation. In the top portion of this sheet, we used the AVERAGE() function to calculate the average amount of slack observed for each activity during the simulation. We also calculated the percentage of time each activity was critical during the 100 replications performed on the model. For example, this sheet indicates that activity D was on the critical path (or had 0 slack) in 100% of the replications, activity E was critical in 96% of the replications, and so on. Thus, this sheet clearly shows which activities are most likely to be critical and warrant the most attention.

	Microsoft Excel - FIG15-32.XLS	

File Edit View Insert Format Tools Data Window Help

B4 | =COUNTIF(Simulation!B3:B102,"<.0001")/100

	A	B	C	D	E	F	G	H	I	J	K
1			A	C	T	I	V	I	T	Y	S L A C K
2		C	D	E	F	G	I	J	K	L	
3	Average:	14.56	0.00	0.02	3.91	1.90	0.22	1.82	0.22	1.82	
4	% Critical:	0%	100%	96%	0%	4%	81%	19%	81%	19%	
5											
6											
7						F I N I S H	T I M E				
8						Average:	48.85				
9						Variance:	4.40				
10						Minimum:	43.16				
11						Maximum:	53.32				
12											
13						99% prob. of					
14						completion by:	53.73				
15											
16											
17											
18											
19											

Model / Simulation \ Results /

Ready

Key Cell Formulas

Cell	Formula	Copied to
B3	=AVERAGE(Simulation!B3:B102)	C3:J3
B4	=COUNTIF(Simulation!B3:B102,"<.001")/100	C4:J4
G8	=AVERAGE(Simulation!K3:K102)	—
G9	=VAR(Simulation!K3:K102)	—
G10	=MIN(Simulation!K3:K102)	—
G11	=MAX(Simulation!K3:K102)	—
G14	=NORMINV(0.99,G8,SQRT(G9))	—

Figure 15.34: *Results of the simulation*

The average and variance of the finish times observed during the simulation are shown in cells G8 and G9, respectively. Assuming that the finish times are normally distributed, roughly a 50% chance exists that the actual project completion time will exceed 48.85 time periods. Thus, we might want to determine the amount of time within which it is virtually certain that the project will be completed. That is, we might want to determine the 99th percentile of the distribution of project completion times. This is calculated in cell G12 as:

Formula in cell G14: =NORMINV(0.99,G8,SQRT(G9))

The result of this formula indicates a 99% chance exists that a normally distributed random variable with a mean of 48.85 and standard deviation of $\sqrt{4.40}$ will assume a value less than or equal to 53.73. Notice that this is consistent with the maximum finish time (shown in cell G11) observed during the simulation. Thus, we could be reasonably confident that the project can be completed within 54 time periods.

SUMMARY

This chapter presented a variety of techniques for managing projects by representing and analyzing a project in the form of a network. When the activity times in a project can be estimated with a reasonable amount of certainty, CPM can be applied to determine the earliest start and finish times for each activity and the earliest time for completing the entire project. CPM can also be used to determine the latest possible times that activities can start and finish without delaying the completion of the project. The slack in a project helps to distinguish between critical and non-critical activities. Various LP techniques can be used to analyze CPM networks and determine optimal crash schedules for projects that must be completed ahead of schedule.

When activity times cannot be estimated with certainty, they must be modeled as random variables. Although the PERT technique was designed to address these types of problems, it has some serious theoretical and practical shortcomings. However, simulation can be used to provide a more complete and accurate analysis of activity networks containing random activity times.

REFERENCES

Golenko, G. "On the Distribution of Activity Times in PERT." *Journal of the Operational Research Society*, vol. 39, August 1988.

Levy, F., A. Thompson and S. Weist. "The ABCs of the Critical Path Method." *Harvard Business Review*, vol. 41, September-October 1963.

Meredith, J. and S. Mantel. *Project Management: A Managerial Approach*. New York: Wiley, 1985.

Phillips, C. and E. Davis. *Project Management with CPM, PERT, and Precedence Diagramming*. New York: Van Nostrand Reinhold, 1983.

Ragsdale, C. "The Current State of Network Simulation in Project Management Theory and Practice." *OMEGA*, vol. 17, no. 1, 1989.

Schonberger, R. "Why Projects Are 'Always' Late: A Rationale Based on Manual Simulation of a PERT/CPM Network." *Interfaces*, vol. 11, no. 5, 1981.

Food and Drug Administration Uses PERT to Control the Timeliness of Research and Development Projects

Source: Kwak, N. K., and Lawrence Jones, "An Application of PERT to R&D Scheduling," *Information Processing and Management,* vol. 14, no. 2, 1978, pages 121-131

THE NATIONAL CENTER FOR DRUG ANALYSIS develops automated drug testing procedures for the U.S. Food and Drug Administration (FDA). The FDA uses these procedures to conduct production studies of drugs selected on the basis of therapeutic significance and how widely they are used.

To allocate personnel and facilities efficiently to drug testing studies, it is important to have a good estimate of when a new, automated testing procedure will be ready. If a method is not ready at the time samples are collected, either the samples must be analyzed manually or existing schedules must be reworked, causing serious disruptions.

The FDA chose PERT to manage methods of development projects because it treats activity completion times as random variables. This is appropriate for research and development activities, many of which are being done for the first time.

The PERT network for a development project consists of 24 nodes and 31 arcs. The network is updated weekly, giving management access to probabilities of completion times, activities on the critical path and second most critical path, slack times for non-critical activities, a list of completed activities, and so on. This information makes it easy to review and adjust personnel assignments and to control completion times. The PERT plans and reports are also useful to the individual chemists, providing a more comprehensive procedure for planning and organizing their work.

The director of the center successfully implemented the use of PERT by developing appropriate forms and computer programs, thoroughly training staff members in how to use PERT, and then incrementally introducing the procedure in a series of pilot tests. The pilot test results suggested some improvements, which were incorporated as the center proceeded with full implementation.

Questions and Problems

1. In this chapter, we stated that the longest path through an activity network is the critical path. Why isn't the completion time for a project defined by the shortest path through the network? Explain your answer.

2. Throughout this chapter, we assumed that a project manager identifies and organizes the activities in a project, estimates the time required for each activity, then determines how quickly the project can be completed. However, the deadlines for some projects are fixed before any planning begins. For example, consider the planning of a New Year's Eve celebration in the downtown area of a major city. Which, if any, of the techniques described in this chapter might be helpful in planning such an event?

3. In illustrating how to simulate an activity network, we used a triangular distribution based on three time estimates to generate random activity times. What problem might be encountered if we assume that activity times were normally distributed? (Hint: Consider the values that a normally distributed random variable with a mean of 5 and variance of 3 might assume.)

4. Consider the CPM network for the following set of activities:

Activity	Predecessor Activities
A	—
B	A
C	A, B

Is it necessary to draw an arc from the node for activity A to the node for activity C? Why or why not?

5. Consider the following set of activities:

Activity	Days Required	Predecessor Activities
A	3	—
B	2	A
C	5	A
D	8	B, C
E	4	B, C
F	2	D, E

a. Draw the CPM network for this problem.

b. Manually determine the earliest and latest start and finish times for each activity and the amount of slack for each activity.

c. What is the critical path?

d. How long should it take to complete the project?

6. Consider the following set of activities:

Activity	Days Required	Predecessor Activities
A	3	—
B	2	—
C	5	A, B
D	8	A, B
E	4	D

a. Draw the CPM network for this problem. (Remember that a CPM network requires unique start and finish nodes.)

b. Manually determine the earliest and latest start and finish times for each activity and the amount of slack for each activity.

c. What is the critical path?

d. How long should it take to complete the project?

7. Consider the following set of activities:

Activity	Time Required	Predecessor Activities
A	5	—
B	4	A
C	5	B
D	8	B
E	9	C
F	6	C, D
G	8	D
H	3	E, F, G

a. Draw the CPM network for this problem.

b. Identify each path through the network and its expected length.

c. What is the critical path?

8. Aerobatic, Inc. custom designs and manufactures light aircraft. The activities involved in this process are summarized below (where the time required is expressed in number of weeks).

Activity	Description	Time Required	Predecessor Activities
A	design	4	—
B	order and receive materials	5	A
C	construct frame	8	B
D	prepare engine	6	B
E	prepare avionics	5	B
F	cover frame	4	C
G	install engine	2	E, F
H	paint	2	F
I	install avionics	2	D, G, H
J	test	1	I

a. Draw the activity network for this problem.

b. Use LP to determine the earliest start time for each activity.

c. What is the earliest this project can be finished?

d. Use LP to determine the latest start time for each activity.

e. Create a spreadsheet to summarize the earliest and latest start and finish times, the slack for each activity, and the critical activities.

9. Linda Madison owns Creations, a business that provides hair and nail care services in a small college town. Recently, Linda has decided to expand her business to include tanning and massage services for her clients. In order to accommodate these new services and the additional clients they are expected to attract, Linda is relocating her business to a larger facility. However, the new location will require some renovation before she can relocate there. Linda has identified the following activities that must be performed before she can open at her new location.

Activity	Description	Days Required	Predecessor Activities
A	install new plumbing	10	—
B	order and receive furniture	20	—
C	order and receive flooring	15	—
D	construct partitions	5	—
E	paint and wallpaper	5	A, D
F	install furniture	3	E, B
G	install flooring	4	E, C
H	move inventory and records	2	F, G
I	clean old shop	2	H

a. Draw the activity network for this problem.

b. Use LP to determine the earliest start time for each activity.

c. What is the earliest this project can be finished?

d. Use LP to determine the latest start time for each activity.

e. Create a spreadsheet to summarize the earliest and latest start and finish times, the slack for each activity, and the critical activities.

10. Refer to question 9. Suppose that Linda's lease on her current facility expires in 20 days. The normal and crash times and costs for each activity in her moving project are summarized below. By what amount should each activity be crashed in order for her to complete the move within 20 days?

| Activity | Normal | | Crash | |
	Time	Cost	Time	Cost
A	10	$11,000	7	$15,000
B	20	5,000	18	6,000
C	15	3,000	12	3,500
D	5	1,500	3	2,000
E	5	750	2	1,200
F	3	600	1	1,200
G	4	1,000	2	1,500
H	2	250	1	450
I	2	200	1	300

11. The activities required to service a car at Zippy-Lube can be viewed as a mini-project as summarized below.

| Activity | Description | Predecessor Activity | Time Required | | |
			Min.	Avg.	Max.
A	drain oil	—	2	3.5	5
B	replace filter	A	1	2	3
C	refill oil	B, E	1	2.5	4
D	check tires	—	2	3	4
E	wash windows	D	2	3	5
F	fill fluids	E	2	3	4
G	final test	C, F	0.5	1	1.5

The variability in the time required to perform each activity is due to the different types, sizes, and condition of the cars to be serviced.

a. Draw the activity network for this problem.

b. Use PERT to identify the expected time and variance for each activity.

c. What is the critical path? What is the expected time and variance of the critical path?

12. Refer to question 11. Create a spreadsheet model to simulate the completion times for servicing cars. Assume that activity times follow a triangular distribution, and perform 300 replications on the model.

a. Estimate the probability of each activity falling on the critical path.

b. On average, how long should it take to finish servicing a car?

c. Suppose that the manager of this business wants to guarantee that your car will be ready within 10 minutes or you will receive a coupon worth $5 off your next visit. What proportion of customers would receive the coupon?

13. The activities summarized below must be performed by the promoter of a country music concert in Dallas.

| | | | Days Required | | |
Activity	Description	Predecessor Activity	Min.	Avg.	Max.
A	find location	—	2	4	7
B	hire opening act	A	3	6	10
C	hire technicians	A	1	2	3
D	set up radio ads	B	2	4	6
E	distribute tickets	B	2	3	5
F	rent sound and lights	B, C	3	4	6
G	set up newspaper ads	B	1	2	4
H	hire security	F	2	3	4
I	conduct rehearsal	F, H	1	1.5	2
J	final details	I	2	3	4

a. Draw the activity network for this problem.

b. According to PERT, what is the expected length of time required to accomplish these activities?

c. Assume that the durations of the activities are random variables that follow triangular distributions. Create a spreadsheet model of the project and use simulation to create 300 replications of the project. Rank the activities according to how critical they are.

d. When should the promoter begin working on the concert to have a 99% chance of completing the project by August 15?

14. Consider the following set of activities:

Activity	Days Required	Predecessor Activities	Activity	Days Required	Predecessor Activities
A	3	—	G	6	B
B	4	A	H	5	F, C, E
C	4	A	I	6	G, H
D	3	A	J	4	F, C, E
E	3	D	K	2	D
F	4	B	L	6	I, J, K

    a. Draw the CPM network for this problem.

    b. Use LP to identify the earliest start time for each activity.

    c. What is the earliest time that the project can be completed?

    d. Use LP to identify the latest start time for each activity.

    e. Create a spreadsheet to summarize the earliest and latest start and finish times, the slack for each activity, and the critical activities.

15. The following data summarize the per-day cost of crashing the activities in the problem described in question 14.

Activity	Crash Cost per Day	Maximum Crash Days	Activity	Crash Cost per Day	Maximum Crash Days
A	$50	2	G	$65	5
B	60	3	H	55	2
C	57	1	I	28	4
D	45	2	J	33	3
E	25	3	K	40	1
F	30	2	L	37	2

    a. Create an LP model to determine the least costly way of crashing the project to complete it within 20 days.

    b. By how much should each activity be crashed, and what is the total crashing cost?

The Imagination Toy Corporation A Case in Project Management

AMY White is the director of marketing for the Imagination Toy corporation (ITC). She just received a phone call from her boss indicating that the company's board of directors gave final approval for the production and marketing of the Might Morphin' Monkeys—a new product line of action play toys for ITC. Amy worked hard in developing the concept for this product line and is thrilled that her ideas will become reality. But this news also means that she must get busy developing the marketing and sales force training materials needed to launch this new product line successfully. Amy's boss wants to know how soon she can have the sales staff trained and equipped to handle the new line.

The development of marketing materials and training of the sales staff for the new product line constitute a project. Amy identifies 10 specific project tasks that need to be accomplished before she can roll out the marketing program for this product line. First, Amy needs to collect information about the details of the decisions made by the board of directors. She can start this task (task A) immediately, and she estimates that it will take 5 days to determine exactly which items and accessories will be included in the first offering of the product line. After she completes this task, she will request prototypes of all items from the engineering department (task B), which she expects will take 10 working days. While waiting for the prototypes, she can begin laying out the marketing program (task C). She expects this activity to take 8 days. Once the prototypes (task B) are available, Amy estimates that it will take 7 days to prepare instructions (task D) on the operation and use of the items in the product line and 9 days to design its packaging (task E). When the marketing program (task C) is finished, it must be approved (task F) by the president of the company. Amy expects this approval to take 3 days.

Amy plans to hold a 2-day training course (task G) for the sales force once the operating instructions (task D) and the packaging design (task E) are completed. When the operating instructions (task D) are finished and the marketing plan is approved (task F), Amy will develop an information guide (task H) that the sales force can distribute to retailers. Amy expects to take 8 days to complete the information guide. Also, as part of the marketing plan, Amy wants to hire a number of actors to portray Mighty Morphin' Monkeys (task I) at various promotional events around the country. Hiring and training these actors is expected to take 8 days and can be done only after the marketing plan is approved (task F). Finally, after the marketing plan (task F) has been approved and the packaging for the product has been designed (task E), special point-of-sale display racks must be manufactured (task J). Amy expects this activity to take 12 working days.

1. Develop and AON network for this problem.

2. Use Solver to determine the earliest and latest start and finish times for each activity.

3. Identify the critical path.

4. If Amy starts working immediately, how long will it take her to complete this project?

5. Suppose that the engineering department can create the prototypes in only 8 days if the engineers work overtime on this activity. Would this help reduce the length of time required to complete this project?

CHAPTER 16

Decision Analysis

THE PREVIOUS CHAPTERS in this book describe a variety of modeling techniques that can help managers gain insight and understanding about the decision problems they face. But models do not make decisions—people do. Although the insight and understanding gained by modeling problems can be helpful, decision making often remains a difficult task. The two primary causes for this difficulty are uncertainty regarding the future and conflicting values or objectives.

For example, suppose that when you graduate from college you receive job offers from two companies. One company (company A) is in a relatively new industry that offers potential for spectacular growth—or rapid bankruptcy. The salary offered by this company is somewhat lower than you'd like, but would increase rapidly if the company grows. This company is located in the city that is home to your favorite professional sports team and close to your friends and family.

The other job offer is from an established company (company B) that is known for its financial strength and long-term commitment to its employees. It has offered you a starting salary that is 10% more than you asked, but you suspect it would take longer for you to advance in this organization. Also, if you work for this company you would have to move to a distant part of the country that offers few of the cultural and sporting activities that you enjoy.

Which offer would you accept? Or would you reject both offers and continue looking for employment with other companies? For many, this might be a difficult decision. If you accept the job with company A, you might be promoted twice within a year—or you could be unemployed in six months. With company B you can be reasonably sure of having a secure job for the foreseeable future. But if you accept the job with company B and then company A grows rapidly, you might regret not accepting the position with company A. Thus, the uncertainty associated with the future of company A makes this decision difficult.

To further complicate the decision, company A offers a more desirable location than company B, but the starting salary with company A is lower. How can you assess the trade-offs between starting salary, location, job security, and potential for advancement in order to make a good decision? There is no easy answer to this question, but this chapter describes a number of techniques that can help you structure and analyze difficult decision problems in a logical manner.

GOOD DECISIONS VS. GOOD OUTCOMES

The goal of decision analysis is to help individuals make good decisions. But good decisions do not always result in good outcomes. For example, suppose that after carefully considering all the factors involved in the two job offers, you decide to accept the position with company B. After working for this company for nine months, it suddenly announces that, in an effort to cut costs, it is closing the office in which you work and eliminating your job. Did you make a bad decision? Probably not. Unforeseeable circumstances beyond your control caused you to experience a bad outcome, but it would be unfair to say that you made a bad decision. Good decisions sometimes result in bad outcomes.

The techniques for decision analysis presented in this chapter can help you make good decisions, but cannot guarantee that good outcomes will always occur as a result of those decisions. Even when a good decision is made, luck often plays a role in determining whether a good or bad outcome occurs. However, using a structured approach to make decisions should produce good outcomes more frequently than making decisions in a more haphazard manner.

CHARACTERISTICS OF DECISION PROBLEMS

Although all decision problems are somewhat different, they share certain characteristics. For example, a decision must involve at least two alternatives for addressing or solving a problem. An **alternative** is a course of action intended to solve a problem. The job selection example described earlier involves three alternatives: you could accept the offer from company A, accept the offer from company B, or reject both offers and continue searching for a better one.

Alternatives are evaluated on the basis of the value they add to one or more decision criteria. The **criteria** in a decision problem represent various factors that are important to the decision maker and influenced by the alternatives. For example, the criteria used to evaluate the job offer alternatives might include starting salary, expected salary growth, desirability of job location, opportunity for promotion and career advancement, and so on. The impact of the alternatives on the criteria is of primary importance to the decision maker. Note that not all criteria can be expressed in terms of monetary value, making comparisons of the alternatives more difficult.

Finally, the values assumed by the various decision criteria under each alternative depend on the different states of nature that can occur. The **states of nature** in a decision problem correspond to future events that are not under the decision maker's control. For example, company A could experience spectacular growth, or it might go bankrupt. Each of these contingencies represents a possible state of nature for the problem. Many other states of nature are possible for the company; for example, it could grow slowly, or not grow at all. Thus, an infinite number of possible states of nature could exist in this, and many other, decision problems. However, in decision analysis, we often use a relatively small, discrete set of representative states of nature to summarize the future events that might occur.

AN EXAMPLE

The following example illustrates some of the issues and difficulties that arise in decision problems.

> Hartsfield International Airport in Atlanta, Georgia, is one of the busiest airports in the world. During the past 30 years, the airport has expanded again and again to accommodate the increasing number of flights being routed through Atlanta. Analysts project that this increase will continue well into the next century. However, commercial development around the airport prevents it from building additional runways to handle the future air traffic demands. As a solution to this problem, plans are being developed to build another airport outside the city limits. Two possible locations for the new airport have been identified, but a final decision on the new location is not expected to be made for another year.

> The Magnolia Inns hotel chain intends to build a new facility near the new airport once its site is determined. Barbara Monroe is responsible for real estate acquisition for the company, and she faces a difficult decision about where to buy land. Currently, land values around the two possible sites for the new airport are increasing as investors speculate that property values will increase greatly in the vicinity of the new airport. The spreadsheet in Figure 16.1 (and in the file FIG16-1.XLS on your data disk) summarizes the current price of each parcel of land, the estimated present value of the future cash flows that a hotel would generate at each site if the airport is ultimately located at the site, and the present value of the amount for which the company believes it can resell each parcel if the airport is not built at the site.

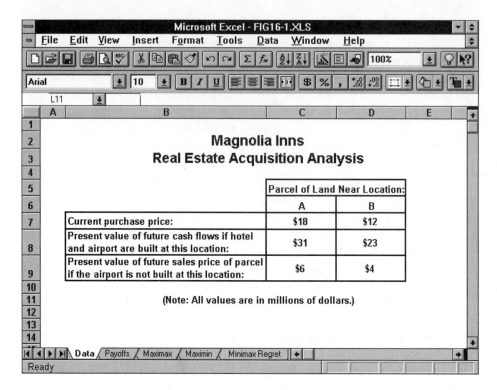

Figure 16.1: *Data for the Magnolia Inns decision problems*

The company can buy either site, both sites, or neither site. Barbara must decide which sites, if any, the company should purchase.

THE PAYOFF MATRIX

A common way of analyzing this type of decision problem is to construct a payoff matrix. A **payoff matrix** is a table that summarizes the final outcome (or payoff) for each decision alternative under each possible state of nature. To construct a payoff matrix, we need to identify each decision alternative and each possible state of nature. The following four decision alternatives are available to the decision maker in our example problem:

Decision Alternatives

1. Buy the parcel at location A.

2. Buy the parcel at location B.

3. Buy the parcels at locations A and B.

4. Buy nothing.

Regardless of which parcel or parcels Magnolia Inns decides to purchase, two possible states of nature can occur:

States of Nature

1. The new airport is built at location A.

2. The new airport is built at location B.

Figure 16.2 shows the payoff matrix for this problem. The rows in this spreadsheet represent the possible decision alternatives, and the columns correspond to the states of nature that might occur. Each value in this table indicates the financial payoff (in millions of dollars) expected for each possible decision under each state of nature.

Figure 16.2: Payoff matrix for the Magnolia Inns decision problems

THE PAYOFF VALUES

The value in cell B5 in Figure 16.2 indicates that if the company buys the parcel of land near location A, and the airport is built in this area, Magnolia Inns can expect to receive a payoff of $13 million. This figure of $13 million is computed from the data shown in Figure 16.1 as:

Present value of future cash flows if hotel and airport are built at location A	$31,000,000

minus:

Current purchase price of hotel site at location A	$-18,000,000$
	$13,000,000$

The value in cell C5 in Figure 16.2 indicates that if Magnolia Inns buys the parcel of land at location A (for $18 million), and the airport is built at location B, the company would later resell the parcel at location A for only $6 million, incurring a loss of $12 million.

The calculations of the payoffs for the parcel near location B are done using similar logic. The value in cell C6 in Figure 16.2 indicates that if the company buys the parcel of land near location B, and the airport is built in this area, Magnolia Inns can expect to receive a payoff of $11 million. The value in cell B6 in Figure 16.2 indicates that if Magnolia Inns buys the parcel of land at location B (for $12 million), and the airport is built at location A, the company would later resell the parcel at location B for only $4 million, incurring a loss of $8 million.

Let's now consider the payoffs if the parcels at both locations A and B are purchased. The value in cell B7 in Figure 16.2 indicates that a payoff of $5 million will result if both parcels are purchased and the airport is built at location A. This payoff value is computed as:

Present value of future cash flows if
hotel and airport are built at location A $31,000,000

plus:

Present value of future sales price for the
unused parcel at location B $ 4,000,000

minus:

Current purchase price of hotel site
at location A   – $18,000,000

minus:

Current purchase price of hotel site
at location B $\underline{-\$12,000,000}$
                                                            $5,000,000

The value in cell C7 indicates that a loss of $1 million will occur if the parcels at both locations A and B are purchased, and the airport is built at location B.

The final alternative available to Magnolia Inns is to not buy either property at this point in time. This alternative guarantees that the company will neither gain nor lose anything, regardless of where the airport is located. Thus, cells B8 and C8 indicate that this alternative has a payoff of 0 regardless of what state of nature occurs.

DECISION RULES

Now that the payoffs for each alternative under each state of nature have been determined, if Barbara knew with certainty where the airport was going to be built, it would be a simple matter for her to select the most desirable alternative. For example, if she knew the airport was going to be built at location A, a maximum payoff of $13 million could be obtained by purchasing the parcel of land at that location. Similarly, if she knew the airport was going to be built at location B, Magnolia Inns could achieve the maximum payoff of $11 million by purchasing the parcel at that location. The problem is that Barbara does not know where the airport is going to be built.

Several decision rules can be used to help a decision maker choose the best alternative. No one of these decision rules works best in all situations and, as you will see, each has some weaknesses. However, these rules help to highlight different aspects of a given problem and, together, can help us make more informed decisions.

NONPROBABILISTIC METHODS

The decision rules we'll discuss can be divided into two categories: those that assume that probabilities of occurrence can be assigned to the states of nature in a decision problem (probabilistic methods), and those that do not (nonprobabilistic methods). We'll discuss the nonprobabilistic methods first.

THE MAXIMAX DECISION RULE

As shown in Figure 16.2, the largest possible payoff will occur if Magnolia Inns buys the parcel at location A and the airport is built at this location. Thus, if the company optimistically believes that nature will always be "on its side" regardless of what decision it makes, the company should buy the parcel at location A because it leads to the largest possible payoff. This type of reasoning is reflected in the **maximax decision rule**, which determines the maximum payoff for each alternative and then selects the alternative associated with the largest payoff. Figure 16.3 illustrates the results of the maximax decision rule on our example problem.

Figure 16.3: The maximax decision rule for the Magnolia Inns decision problem

Although the alternative suggested by the maximax decision rule enables Magnolia Inns to realize the best possible payoff, it does not guarantee that this payoff will occur. The actual payoff depends on where the airport is ultimately located. If we follow the maximax decision rule and the airport is built at location A, the company would receive $13 million; but if the airport is built at location B, the company would lose $12 million.

In some situations, the maximax decision rule leads to poor decisions. For example, consider the following payoff matrix:

Decision	State of Nature		MAX	
	1	2		
A	30	−10000	30	← maximum
B	29	29	29	

In this problem, alternative A would be selected using the maximax decision rule. However, many decision makers would prefer alternative B because its guaranteed payoff is only slightly less than the maximum possible payoff, and it avoids the potential large loss involved with alternative A if the second state of nature occurs.

THE MAXIMIN DECISION RULE

A more conservative approach to decision making is given by the **maximin decision rule**, which pessimistically assumes that nature will always be "against us" regardless of what decision we make. This decision rule can be used to hedge against the worst possible outcome of a decision. Figure 16.4 illustrates the effect of the maximin decision rule on our example problem.

Figure 16.4: The maximin decision rule for the Magnolia Inns decision problem

To apply the maximin decision rule, we first determine the minimum possible payoff for each alternative and then select the alternative with the largest minimum payoff (or the maximum of the minimum payoffs—hence the term "maximin"). Column D in Figure 16.4 lists the minimum payoff for each alternative. The largest (maximum) value in column D is the payoff of $0 associated with not buying any land. Thus, the maximin decision rule suggests that Magnolia Inns should not buy either parcel because, in the worst case, the other alternatives result in losses whereas this alternative does not.

The maximin decision rule can also lead to poor decision making. For example, consider the following payoff matrix:

| | State of Nature | | | |
Decision	1	2	MIN	
A	1000	28	28	
B	29	29	29	← maximum

In this problem, alternative B would be selected using the maximin decision rule. However, many decision makers would prefer alternative A because its worst case payoff is only slightly less than that of alternative B, and it provides the potential for a much larger payoff if the first state of nature occurs.

THE MINIMAX REGRET DECISION RULE

Another way of approaching decision problems involves the concept of **regret**, or opportunity loss. For example, suppose that Magnolia Inns decides to buy the parcel of land at location A as suggested by the maximax decision rule. If the airport is built at location A, the company will not regret this decision at all because it provides the largest possible payoff under the state of nature that occurred. However, what if the company buys the parcel at location A and the airport is built at location B? In this case, the company would experience a regret, or opportunity loss, of $23 million. If Magnolia Inns had bought the parcel at location B, it would have earned a payoff of $11 million, and the decision to buy the parcel at location A resulted in a loss of $12 million. Thus, there is a difference of $23 million in the payoffs between these two alternatives under this state of nature.

To use the minimax regret decision rule, we must first convert our payoff matrix into a regret matrix that summarizes the possible opportunity losses that could result from each decision alternative under each state of nature. Figure 16.5 shows the regret matrix for our example problem.

The entries in the regret matrix are generated from the payoff matrix as:

Formula for cell B5:   =MAX(Payoffs!B$5:B$8)–Payoffs!B5
(copy to B5 through C8)

Figure 16.5: The minimax regret decision rule for the Magnolia Inns decision problem

Key Cell Formulas

Cell	Formula	Copied to
B5	=MAX(Payoffs!B$5:B$8)–Payoffs!B5	B5:C8
D5	=MAX(B5:C5)	D6:D8

Each entry in the regret matrix shows the difference between the maximum payoff that can occur under a given state of nature and the payoff that would be realized from each alternative under the same state of nature. For example, if Magnolia Inns buys the parcel of land at location A and the airport is built at this location, cell B5 indicates that the company experiences 0 regret. However, if the company buys the parcel at location B and the airport is built at location A, the company experiences an opportunity loss (or regret) of $21 million $(13 - (-8) = 21)$.

Column D in Figure 16.5 summarizes the maximum regret that could be experienced with each decision alternative. The minimax regret decision corresponds to the alternative with the smallest (or minimum) maximum regret. As indicated in Figure 16.5, the minimax regret decision in our example problem is to buy the parcels at both sites. The maximum regret that could be experienced by implementing this decision is $12 million, whereas all other decisions could cause a larger regret.

The minimax regret decision rule can lead to peculiar decision making. For example, consider the following payoff matrix:

	State of Nature	
Decision	**1**	**2**
A	9	2
B	4	6

The regret matrix and minimax regret decision for this problem are represented by:

	State of Nature			
Decision	1	2	MAX	
A	0	4	4	← minimum
B	5	0	5	

Thus, if the alternatives are given by A and B, the minimax regret decision rule would select alternative A. Now, suppose that we add a new alternative to this decision problem to obtain the following payoff matrix:

	State of Nature	
Decision	1	2
A	9	2
B	4	6
C	3	9

Notice that the payoffs for alternatives A and B have not changed—we simply added a new alternative (C). The regret matrix and minimax regret decision for the revised problem are represented by:

	State of Nature			
Decision	1	2	MAX	
A	0	7	7	
B	5	3	5	← minimum
C	6	0	6	

The minimax regret decision is now given by alternative B. Some decision makers are troubled that the addition of a new alternative, which is not selected as the final decision, can change the relative preferences of the original alternatives. For example, suppose that a person prefers apples to oranges, but would prefer oranges if given the options of apples, oranges, and bananas. This person's reasoning is somewhat inconsistent or incoherent. But such reversals in preferences are a natural consequence of the minimax regret decision rule.

PROBABILISTIC METHODS

Probabilistic decision rules can be used if the states of nature in a decision problem can be assigned probabilities that represent their likelihood of occurrence. These probabilities are often assigned subjectively for unique, one-time decision problems (such as our example problem). For decision problems that occur more than once, it might be possible to estimate these probabilities from historical data.

EXPECTED MONETARY VALUE

The **expected monetary value decision rule** selects the decision alternative with the largest expected monetary value (EMV). The EMV of alternative i in a decision problem is defined as:

$$EMV_i = \sum_j r_{ij} p_j$$

where

r_{ij} = the payoff for alternative i under the jth state of nature

p_j = the probability of the jth state of nature

Figure 16.6 illustrates the EMV decision rule for our example problem. In this case, Magnolia Inns estimates a 40% chance that the airport will be built at location A and a 60% chance that it will be built at location B.

Figure 16.6: The expected monetary value decision rule for the Magnolia Inns decision problem

The probabilities for each state of nature are entered in cells B10 and C10, respectively. Using these probabilities, the EMV for each decision alternative is calculated in column D as:

Formula for cell D5:   =SUMPRODUCT(B5:C5,$B$10:$C$10)
(copy to E6 through E8)

The largest EMV is associated with the decision to purchase the parcel of land at location B. Thus, this is the decision suggested according to the EMV decision rule.

Let's consider the meaning of the figures in the EMV column in Figure 16.6. For example, the decision to purchase the parcel at location B has an EMV of $3.4 million. What does this figure represent? The payoff table indicates that Magnolia Inns will receive a payoff of $11 million if it buys this land and the airport is built there, or it will lose $8 million if it buys this land and the airport is built at the other location. So there does not appear to be any way for the company to receive a payoff of $3.4 million if it buys the land at location B. However, imagine that Magnolia Inns faces this same decision not just once, but over and over again (perhaps on a weekly basis). If the company always decides to purchase the land at location B, we would expect it to receive a payoff of $11 million 60% of the time, and incur a loss of $8 million 40% of the time. Over the long run, then, the decision to purchase land at location B results in an average payoff of $3.4 million.

The EMV for a given decision alternative indicates the average payoff we would receive if we encounter the identical decision problem repeatedly and always select this alternative. Selecting the alternative with the highest EMV makes sense in situations where the identical decision problem will be faced repeatedly and we can "play the averages." However, this decision rule can be very risky in decision problems encountered only once (such as our example problem). For example, consider the following problem:

| | State of Nature | | | |
Decision	1	2	EMV	
A	15,000	−5,000	5,000	← maximum
B	5,000	4,000	4,500	
Probability	0.5	0.5		

If we face a decision with these payoffs and probabilities repeatedly and always select decision A, the payoff over the long run would average to $5,000. Because this is larger than decision B's average long-run payoff of $4,500, it would be best to always select decision A. But what if we face this decision problem only once? If we select decision A, we are equally likely to receive $15,000 or lose $5,000. If we select decision B, we are equally likely to receive payoffs of $5,000 or $4,000. In this case, decision A is more risky. Yet this type of risk is ignored completely by the EMV decision rule. Later, we'll discuss a technique—known as the utility theory—that allows us to account for this type of risk in our decision making.

EXPECTED REGRET

We can also use the probability of the states of nature to compute the **expected regret**, or expected opportunity loss (EOL), for each alternative in a decision problem. Figure 16.7 illustrates this process for our example problem.

Figure 16.7: The expected regret decision rule for the Magnolia Inns decision problem

Cell	Formula	Copied to
B5	=MAX(Payoffs!B$5:B$8)–Payoffs!B5	B5:C8
D5	=SUMPRODUCT(B5:C5,$B$10:$C$10)	D6:D8

The calculations in Figure 16.7 are identical to those used in computing the EMVs, only here we substitute regret values (or opportunity losses) for the payoffs. As shown in Figure 16.7, the decision to purchase the parcel at location B results in the smallest EOL. It is not a coincidence that this same decision also resulted in the largest EMV in Figure 16.6. The decision with the smallest EOL will also have the largest EMV. Thus, the EMV and EOL decision rules always result in the selection of the same decision alternative.

THE EXPECTED VALUE OF PERFECT INFORMATION

One of the primary difficulties in decision making is that we usually do not know which state of nature will occur. As we've seen, estimates of the probability of each state of nature can be used to calculate the EMV of various decision alternatives. However, probabilities do not tell us which state of nature will occur—they only indicate the likelihood of the various states of nature.

Suppose that we could hire a consultant who could tell us in advance and with 100% accuracy which state of nature will occur. If our example problem were a repeatable decision problem, 40% of the time the consultant would indicate that the airport will be built at location A, and the company would buy the parcel of land at location A and receive a payoff of $13 million. Similarly, 60% of the time the consultant would indicate that the airport will be built at location B, and the company would buy the parcel at location B and receive a payoff of $11 million. Thus, with advance perfect information about where the airport is going to be built, the average payoff would be:

Expected value *with* perfect information = 0.40*$13 + 0.60*$11 = $11.8 (in millions)

So how much should Magnolia Inns be willing to pay this consultant for such information? From Figure 16.6 we know that *without* the services of this consultant, the best decision identified results in an EMV of $3.4 million. Therefore, the information provided by the consultant would enable the company to make decisions that increase the EMV by $8.4 million ($11.8 – $3.4 = $8.4). Thus, the company should be willing to pay the consultant up to $8.4 million for providing perfect information.

The **expected value *of* perfect information** (EVPI) is the expected value obtained *with* perfect information minus the expected value obtained *without* perfect information (which is given by the maximum EMV); that is:

$$\text{Expected value } of \text{ perfect information} = \text{Expected value } with \text{ perfect information} - \text{maximum EMV}$$

Figure 16.8 summarizes the EVPI calculation for our example problem. Cell D6 in Figure 16.8 shows the calculation of the maximum EMV of $3.4 million, which was described earlier in our discussion of the EMV decision rule. The payoffs of the decisions made under each state of nature with perfect information are calculated in cells B12 and C12 as:

Formula for cell B12:   =MAX(B5:B8)
(copy to C12)

The expected value *with* perfect information is calculated in cell D12 as:

Formula for cell D12:   =SUMPRODUCT(B12:C12,B10:C10)

Finally, the expected value *of* perfect information is computed in cell D14 as:

Formula for cell D14:   =D12–MAX(D5:D8)

Notice that the $8.4 million EVPI figure in cell D14 is identical to the minimum EOL shown earlier in Figure 16.7. This is *not* just a coincidence. The minimum EOL in a decision problem will always equal the EVPI.

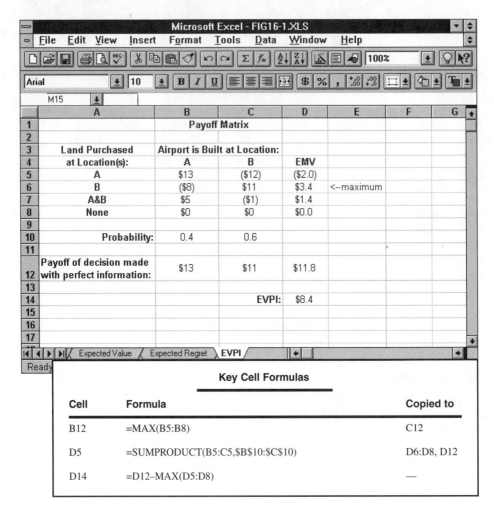

Figure 16.8: The expected value of perfect information for the Magnolia Inns decision problem

Cell	Formula	Copied to
B12	=MAX(B5:B8)	C12
D5	=SUMPRODUCT(B5:C5,$B$10:$C$10)	D6:D8, D12
D14	=D12–MAX(D5:D8)	—

Key Point

The expected value of perfect information (EVPI) is equivalent to the minimum expected opportunity loss (EOL).

DECISION TREES

Although some decision problems can be represented and analyzed effectively using payoff tables, we can also represent decision problems in a graphical form known as a **decision tree**. Figure 16.9 shows the decision problem for Magnolia Inns represented in this format.

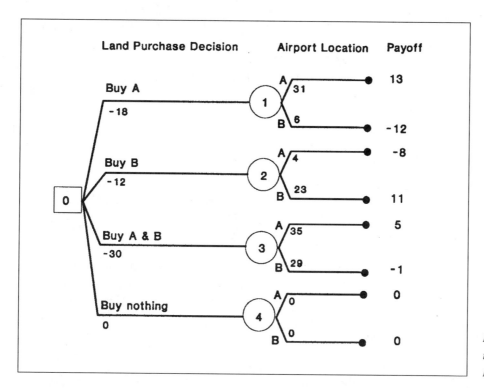

Figure 16.9: *The decision tree representation of the Magnolia Inns problems*

As shown in Figure 16.9, a decision tree is composed of a collection of nodes (represented by circles and squares) interconnected by branches (represented by lines). A square node is called a **decision node** because it represents a decision. Branches emanating from a decision node represent the different alternatives for a particular decision. In Figure 16.9, a single decision node (node 0) represents the decision Magnolia Inns faces about where to buy land. The four branches coming out of this decision node represent the four alternatives under consideration. The cash flow associated with each alternative is also listed. For example, the value –18 below the alternative labeled "Buy A" indicates that if the company purchases the parcel at location A, it must pay $18 million.

The circular nodes in a decision tree are called **event nodes** because they represent uncertain events. The branches emanating from event nodes (called **event branches**) correspond to the possible states of nature or the possible outcomes of an uncertain event. Figure 16.9 shows that each decision alternative emanating from node 0 is followed by an uncertain event represented by the event nodes 1, 2, 3, and 4. The branches from each event node represents a possible location of the new airport. In each case, the airport can be built at location A or B. The value next to each branch from the event nodes indicates the cash flow that will occur for that decision/event combination. For example, at node 1 the value 31 next to the first event branch indicates that if the company buys the parcel at location A and the airport is built at this location, a cash flow of $31 million will occur.

The various branches in a decision tree end at the small black dots called **leaves**. Because each leaf corresponds to one way in which the decision problem can terminate, leaves are also referred to as **terminal nodes**. Each leaf in Figure 16.9 corresponds to an entry in the payoff table in Figure 16.2. The payoff occurring at each leaf is computed by summing the cash flows along the set of branches leading to each leaf. For example, following the uppermost branches through the tree, a payoff of $13 million results if the decision to buy the parcel at location A is followed by the new airport being built at this location (−18 + 31 = 13). You should verify the cash-flow values on each branch and at each leaf before continuing.

ROLLING BACK A DECISION TREE

After computing the payoffs at each leaf, we can apply any of the decision rules described earlier. For example, we could identify the maximum possible payoff for each decision and apply the maximax decision rule. However, decision trees are used most often to implement the EMV decision rule—that is, to identify the decision with the largest EMV.

We can apply a process known as **rolling back** to a decision tree to determine the decision with the largest EMV. Figure 16.10 illustrates this process for our example problem.

Figure 16.10: Rolling back the decision tree for the Magnolia Inns decision problem

Because the EMV decision rule is a probabilistic method, Figure 16.10 indicates the probabilities associated with each event branch emanating from each event node (that is, a 0.4 probability exists of the new airport being built at location A, and a 0.6 probability exists of it being built at location B). To roll back this decision tree, we start with the payoffs and work our way from right to left, back through the decision tree, computing the expected values for each node. For example, the event represented by node 1 has a 0.4 probability of resulting in a payoff of $13 million, and a 0.6 probability of resulting in a loss of $12 million. Thus, the EMV at node 1 is calculated as:

EMV at node 1 = 0.4*13 + 0.6*–12 = –2.0

The expected value calculations for the remaining event nodes in Figure 16.10 are summarized as:

EMV at node 2 = 0.4*–8 + 0.6*11 = 3.4

EMV at node 3 = 0.4*5   + 0.6*–1 = 1.4

EMV at node 4 = 0.4*0   + 0.6*0   = 0.0

The EMV for a decision node is computed in a different way. For example, at node 0 we face a decision among four alternatives that lead to events with expected values of –2, 3.4, 1.4, and 0, respectively. At a decision node we always select the alternative that leads to the best EMV. Thus, the EMV at node 0 is 3.4, which corresponds to the EMV resulting from the decision to buy land at location B. The optimal alternative at a decision node is sometimes indicated by "pruning" the suboptimal branches. The pruned branches in Figure 16.10 are indicated by the double vertical lines (‖) shown on the suboptimal alternatives emanating from node 0.

The relationship between the decision tree in Figure 16.10 and the payoff table in Figure 16.2 should now be clear. However, you might wonder if it is necessary to include event node 4 in the tree shown in Figure 16.10. If Magnolia Inns decides not to buy either property, the payoff it receives does not depend on where the airport is ultimately built—regardless of where the airport is built, the company will receive a payoff of 0.

Figure 16.11 shows an alternate, and perhaps more efficient, way of representing this problem as a decision tree where it is clear that the decision not to purchase either parcel leads to a definite payoff of 0.

Figure 16.11: Alternate decision tree representation of the Magnolia Inns decision problem

USING TREEPLAN

A spreadsheet add-in called **TreePlan** can help us create and analyze decision trees in Excel. We will use TreePlan to implement the decision tree shown in Figure 16.11 in Excel.

To attach the TreePlan add-in, choose the Open command from the File menu and open the file named TREEPLAN.XLA provided on your data disk. To create a decision tree using TreePlan, open a new workbook, then invoke TreePlan by choosing the TreePlan command from the Tools menu (or by pressing [Ctrl][t]). In response, TreePlan displays the dialog box shown in Figure 16.12.

Figure 16.12: Initial TreePlan dialog box

If you click the New Tree button, TreePlan creates a tree diagram with one initial decision node and two decision branches. As shown in Figure 16.13, this initial tree diagram is inserted in the spreadsheet near the cell that is active when TreePlan is invoked. Also note that TreePlan uses the triangular symbols shown in cells F3 and F8 to denote the leaves (or terminal nodes) in a decision problem.

TreePlan automatically labels the branches in the tree as Decision 1 and Decision 2. Later, we'll change these labels to describe more accurately the decisions in our example problem. First, we'll add two more decision branches to the initial tree shown in Figure 16.12.

ADDING BRANCHES

To add a new decision branch to our tree:

1. Click the decision node (cell B5).
2. Press [Ctrl][t] to invoke TreePlan.

Figure 16.13: Initial decision tree created by TreePlan

The dialog box shown in Figure 16.14 appears. Because we selected a decision node before invoking TreePlan, this dialog box displays the options for working on a selected decision node. Different dialog boxes appear if we select an event node or terminal node and then invoke TreePlan. It is important to understand that TreePlan is context-sensitive—that is, the dialog box that appears when you invoke TreePlan depends on what cell is selected when TreePlan is invoked.

Figure 16.14: TreePlan Decision dialog box

To add a branch to the currently selected decision node, click the Add branch option, then click OK. A third branch is added to the tree, as shown in Figure 16.15.

Figure 16.15: Modified tree with three decision branches

To add the fourth decision branch to the tree, we can follow the same procedure:

1. Click the decision node (cell B8).

2. Press [Ctrl][t] to invoke TreePlan.

3. Click Add branch.

4. Click OK.

The four decision branches for this problem appear as shown in Figure 16.16. Notice that we changed the label on each branch to reflect the decision alternatives for Magnolia Inns.

ADDING EVENT NODES

Each of the first three decision branches in Figure 16.11 leads to an event node with two event branches. Thus, we need to add similar event nodes to the decision tree shown in Figure 16.16. To add an event node:

1. Select the terminal node for the branch labeled Buy A (cell F3).

2. Press [Ctrl][t] to invoke TreePlan.

Because we selected a terminal node before invoking TreePlan, the TreePlan Terminal dialog box appears as shown in Figure 16.17.

Figure 16.16: Modified tree with four decision branches labeled for the Magnolia Inns decision problem

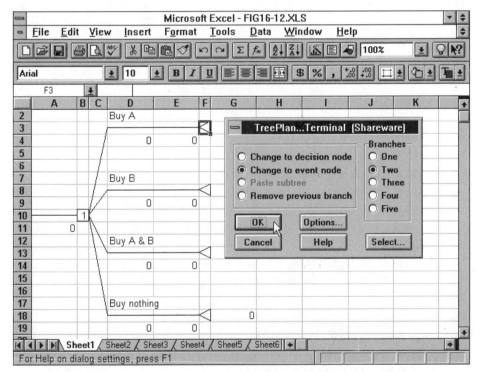

Figure 16.17: TreePlan Terminal dialog box

This dialog box displays the options for working on a terminal node. In this case, we want to change the selected terminal node into an event node with two branches, as shown in Figure 16.17. The resulting spreadsheet is shown in Figure 16.18.

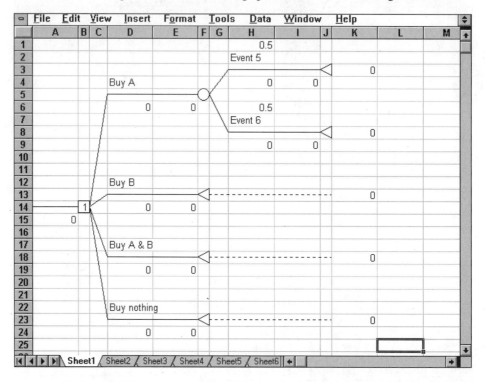

Figure 16.18: Modified tree with an event node

In Figure 16.18, an event node with two event branches now follows the decision to purchase the parcel at location A. TreePlan automatically labels these branches as Event 5 and Event 6, but we can change the labels to whatever we want. The cells immediately above each event branch label (cells H1 and H6) are reserved to represent the probability of each event. By default, TreePlan assumes that the events have equal probability (0.5), but we can change these values to whatever is appropriate for our particular problem.

In Figure 16.19, we changed the labels and probabilities of the event branches to correspond to the events occurring in the Magnolia Inns problem. The procedure used to create the event node for the Buy A decision could be repeated to create event nodes for the decisions corresponding to Buy B and Buy A & B. However, because all of the event nodes are identical in this problem, we can simply copy the existing event node.

You might be tempted to copy and paste the existing event node using the standard Excel commands—but if you use the standard Excel commands, TreePlan cannot update the tree settings properly. As indicated in Figure 16.19, TreePlan provides a built-in option that allows you to copy a section, or **subtree**, of a decision tree to another part of the tree. It is important to copy subtrees using this command so that TreePlan can update the appropriate formulas in the spreadsheet. To create a copy of the event node:

1. Select the event node you want to copy (cell F5).

2. Press [Ctrl][t] to invoke TreePlan.

3. Click Copy subtree.

4. Click OK.

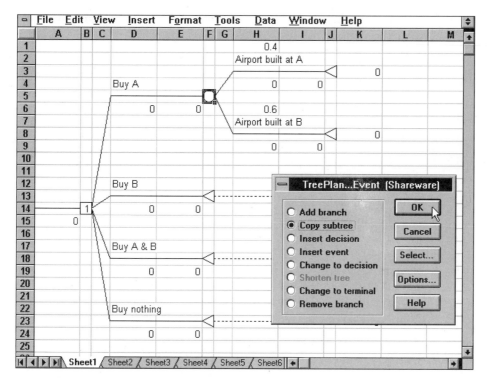

Figure 16.19: *Using TreePlan to copy a subtree*

This creates a copy of the selected event node on the clipboard. As shown in Figure 16.20, to paste a copy of this subtree into the decision tree:

1. Select the target cell location (cell F13).

2. Press [Ctrl][t] to invoke TreePlan.

3. Click Paste subtree.

4. Click OK.

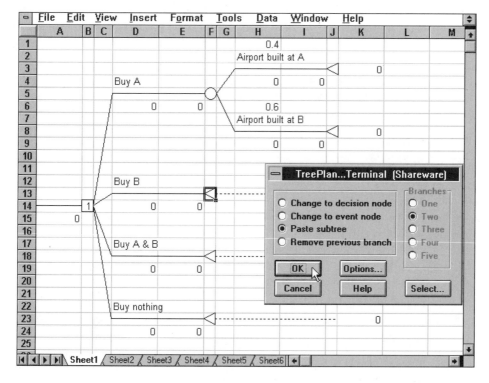

Figure 16.20: *Using TreePlan to paste the copied subtree*

We can repeat this copy and paste procedure to create the third event node needed for the decision to buy the parcels at both locations A and B. Figure 16.21 shows the resulting spreadsheet.

Figure 16.21: Decision tree with three event nodes

ADDING THE CASH FLOWS

To complete the decision tree, we need to add the cash flows that are associated with each decision and event. TreePlan reserves the first cell below each branch to represent the partial cash flow associated with that branch. For example, in Figure 16.22 (and in the file FIG16-22.XLS on your data disk) cell D6 represents the partial cash flow that occurs if Magnolia Inns buys the parcel at location A, and cell H4 represents the partial cash flow that occurs if the company buys the parcel at location A *and* the airport is built at that location. The remaining partial cash flows for each decision are entered in the appropriate cells in Figure 16.22 in a similar manner.

DETERMINING THE PAYOFFS AND EMVS

Next to each terminal node, TreePlan automatically created a formula that sums the payoffs along the branches leading to that node. For example, cell K3 in Figure 16.22 contains the formula =SUM(H4,D6). Thus, when we enter or change the partial cash flows for the branches in the decision tree, the payoffs are updated automatically.

Immediately below and to the left of each node, TreePlan created formulas that compute the EMV at each node in the same way as described earlier in our discussion of rolling back a decision tree. Thus, cell A20 in Figure 16.22 indicates that the largest EMV at the decision node is $3.4 million. The value 2 in the decision node (cell B19) indicates that this maximum EMV is obtained by selecting the second decision alternative (that is, by purchasing the parcel at location B).

Figure 16.22: Completed decision tree for the Magnolia Inns decision problem

OTHER FEATURES

The preceding discussion of TreePlan was intended to give you an overview of how TreePlan operates, its capabilities, and some of its options. Most of the other TreePlan options are self-explanatory, and you can obtain descriptions of them by clicking the Help button available in all the TreePlan dialog boxes. The Select and Options buttons available in all the TreePlan dialog boxes presented earlier lead, respectively, to the two dialog boxes shown in Figure 16.23.

Figure 16.23: TreePlan Select and TreePlan Options dialog boxes

At times we might want to select all the instances of a certain type of element in a decision tree. For example, we might want to select all the partial cash flows and display them in a currency format, or we might want to hide all the EMV values. The TreePlan Select dialog box shown in Figure 16.23 is designed to simplify this process. By selecting an option in this dialog box, all the elements of the type chosen will be selected automatically in the spreadsheet, enabling us to format them all at the same time.

The TreePlan Options dialog box serves two purposes. By default, TreePlan assumes that we want to analyze the decision tree using expected values. However, another technique (described later) uses exponential utility functions in place of expected values. Thus, this dialog box provides options for selecting whether TreePlan should use expected values or exponential utility functions. Also by default, TreePlan assumes that the EMVs it calculates represent profit values and that we want to identify the decision with the largest EMV. However, in some decision trees the expected values could represent costs that we want to minimize. Thus, this dialog box provides options for maximizing profits or minimizing costs.

About TreePlan

TreePlan is a *shareware* product. The developer of this package graciously allows it to be distributed with this textbook at no charge to you. If you like this software package and plan to use it beyond the context of this textbook, you are expected to pay a nominal registration fee. Details on registration are available near the end of the TreePlan help file, which you can access by clicking the Help button in any TreePlan dialog box.

MULTI-STAGE DECISION PROBLEMS

To this point, our discussion of decision analysis has considered only **single-stage** decision problems—that is, problems in which a single decision must be made. However, most decisions that we face lead to other decisions. As a simple example, consider the decision of whether or not to go out to dinner. If you decide to go out to dinner, you must then decide how much to spend, where to go, and how to get there. Thus, before you actually decide to go out to dinner, you'll probably consider the other issues and decisions that must be made if you choose that alternative. These types of problems are called **multi-stage** decision problems. The following example illustrates how a multi-stage decision problem can be modeled and analyzed using a decision tree.

The Occupational Safety and Health Administration (OSHA) has recently announced it will award an $85,000 research grant to the person or company submitting the best proposal for using wireless communications technology to enhance safety in the coal mining industry. Steve Hinton, the owner of COM-TECH, a small communications research firm located just outside of Raleigh, North Carolina, is considering whether or not to apply for this grant. Steve estimates he would spend approximately $5,000 preparing his grant proposal and that he has about a 50-50 chance of actually receiving the grant. If he is awarded the grant, he would then need to decide whether to use microwave, cellular, or infrared communications technology. He has some experience in all three areas but would need to acquire some new equipment depending on which technology is used. The cost of the equipment needed for each technology is summarized as:

Technology	Equipment Cost
Microwave	$4,000
Cellular	$5,000
Infrared	$4,000

In addition to the equipment costs, Steve knows he will spend money in research and development (R&D) to carry out the research proposal, but he doesn't know exactly what the R&D costs will be. For simplicity, Steve estimates the following best case and worst case R&D costs associated with using each technology, and he assigns probabilities to each outcome based on his degree of expertise in each area.

	Possible R&D Costs			
	Best Case		Worst Case	
	Cost	Prob.	Cost	Prob.
Microwave	$30,000	0.4	$60,000	0.6
Cellular	$40,000	0.8	$70,000	0.2
Infrared	$40,000	0.9	$80,000	0.1

Steve needs to synthesize all the factors in this problem to decide whether or not to submit a grant proposal to OSHA.

A MULTI-STAGE DECISION TREE

The immediate decision in this example problem is whether or not to submit a grant proposal. To make this decision, Steve must also consider the technology selection decision that he will face if he receives the grant. So this is a multi-stage decision problem. Figure 16.24 (and the file FIG16.24.XLS on your data disk) shows the decision tree representation of this problem where, for clarity, we have temporarily hidden the roll-back EMVs at each event and decision node in the tree.

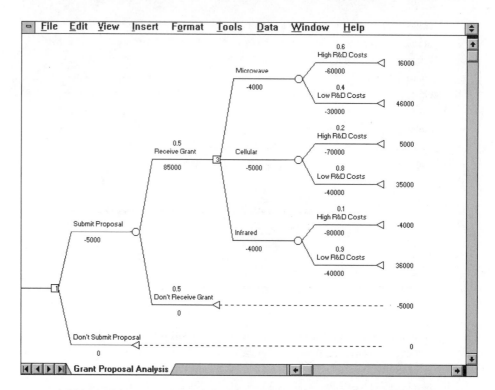

Figure 16.24: Multi-stage decision tree for COM-TECH's grant proposal problem

This decision tree clearly shows that the first decision Steve faces is whether or not to submit a proposal, and that submitting the proposal will cost $5,000. If a proposal is submitted, we then encounter an event node showing a 0.5 probability of receiving the grant (and a payoff of $85,000), and a 0.5 probability of not receiving the grant (leading to a net loss of $5,000). If the grant is received, we then encounter a decision about which technology to pursue. Each of the three technology options has an event node representing the best case (lowest) and worst case (highest) R&D costs that might be incurred. The final (terminal) payoffs associated with each set of decisions and outcomes are listed next to each terminal node. For example, if Steve submits a proposal, receives the grant, employs cellular technology, and encounters low R&D costs, he will receive a net payoff of $35,000.

In Figure 16.24, note that the probabilities on the branches at any event node must always sum to 1 because these branches represent all the events that could occur. The R&D costs that would actually occur using a given technology could assume an infinite number of values. Some might argue that these costs could be modeled more accurately by some continuous random variable. However, our aim is to estimate the *expected value* of this random variable. Most decision makers probably would find it easier to assign subjective probabilities to a small, discrete set of representative outcomes for a variable such as R&D costs rather than try to identify an appropriate probability distribution for this variable.

Figure 16.25 (and the file FIG16-25.XLS on your data disk) shows the completed decision tree for our example problem, including the EMV at each node. According to this decision tree, Steve should submit a proposal because the expected value of this decision is $13,500 and the expected value of not submitting a proposal is $0. The decision tree also indicates that if Steve receives the grant, he should pursue the infrared communications technology because the expected value of this decision ($32,000) is larger than the expected values for the other technologies.

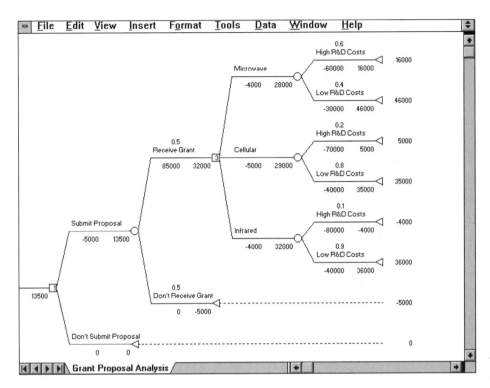

Figure 16.25: Multi-stage decision tree with EMVs for COM-TECH's grant proposal problem

SIMULATING A DECISION TREE

Before implementing the decision to submit a grant proposal as suggested by the previous analysis, Steve would be wise to consider how sensitive the recommended decision is to changes in values in the decision tree. For example, Steve estimated that a 50-50 chance exists that he will receive the grant if he submits a proposal. But what if that probability assessment is wrong? What if only a 30%, 20%, or 10% chance exists of receiving the grant? Should he still submit the proposal? Earlier, we noted that a broad range of R&D costs could occur depending on the technology decision made. So Steve might also wonder how sensitive the recommended decision is to variation in the R&D costs. How can Steve assess the impact of these uncertainties in making a final decision?

Chapters 12 and 13 discussed how simulation can help decision makers deal with uncertainty in spreadsheet (and other) models. Simulation can also help assess the effects of uncertainty in a multi-stage decision problem represented as a decision tree. Figure 16.26 (and the file FIG16-26.XLS on your data disk) shows how this might be done for COM-TECH's grant proposal decision problem.

IMPLEMENTING THE RNGS

To use simulation, we must first replace each of the uncertain values in our model with an appropriate random number generator (RNG). Let's assume that Steve wants the probability of receiving the OSHA grant to vary uniformly between 0.10 and 0.50. We created an RNG to implement this by entering the following formulas in cells H7 and H17:

Formula for cell H7:   =0.1+RAND()*0.4

Formula for cell H17:   =1–H7

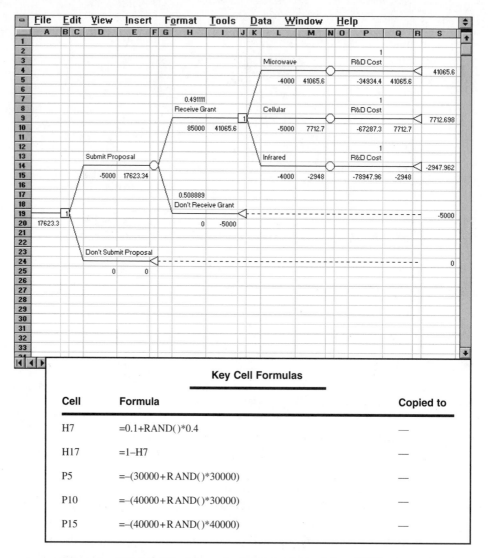

Figure 16.26: A modified decision tree to simulate COM-TECH's decision problem

Cell	Formula	Copied to
Key Cell Formulas		
H7	=0.1+RAND( )*0.4	—
H17	=1–H7	—
P5	=–(30000+RAND( )*30000)	—
P10	=–(40000+RAND( )*30000)	—
P15	=–(40000+RAND( )*40000)	—

Whenever the spreadsheet is recalculated, the formula in cell H7 returns a random value between 0.1 (if RAND() returns 0) and 0.5 (if RAND() returns 1). Because this value represents the probability of receiving the grant, 1 minus this value (the formula in cell H17) must represent the probability of not receiving the grant.

To generate random R&D costs for the technology choices, we first modified the event nodes associated with each choice to have a single branch on which we'll generate a random R&D cost. For simplicity, let's assume that Steve believes the R&D costs associated with each technology choice will vary uniformly between the best case and worst case values identified earlier. The RNGs for the R&D costs are implemented in Figure 16.26 as:

Formula for cell P5:   =–(30000+RAND( )*30000)

Formula for cell P10:   =–(40000+RAND( )*30000)

Formula for cell P15:   =–(40000+RAND( )*40000)

Each time the spreadsheet is recalculated, the formula in cell P5 generates random numbers uniformly distributed between −30,000 (if RAND()=0) and −60,000 (if RAND()=1). Similarly, the formula in cell P10 generates numbers between −40,000 and −70,000, and the RNG in cell P15 returns values between −40,000 and −80,000.

RUNNING THE REPLICATIONS

With the RNGs in place, the next step is to create a large number of replications of the model. We can do so using the procedures described in the earlier chapters on simulation. However, before performing the replications we must identify the performance measures we want to track. In our example problem, two performance measures are of interest to Steve. First, cell B19 indicates which of the two grant proposal decisions should be made (where 1 = Submit Proposal, and 2 = Don't Submit Proposal). If we track the value in this cell, we can compute the percentage of replications in which submitting the proposal is the preferred decision—or the probability that submitting the proposal is the best decision. Second, cell E15 represents the expected value of submitting the proposal for a given replication of the model. This figure will change whenever the spreadsheet is recalculated. Thus, if we also track the value in this cell, we can compute the expected (average) payoff associated with the decision to submit the proposal.

The Data Table command was used to generate 100 replications of our model (using the simulation techniques discussed in chapter 12). In Figure 16.27, columns B and C show the values assumed by cells B19 and E15 in the Grant Proposal Analysis spreadsheet during each replication. If you scan down column B, notice that decision 1 (Submit Proposal) seems to occur most frequently, but some replications also recommend decision 2 (Don't Submit Proposal). Column C lists the expected value of submitting the proposal in each replication.

ANALYZING THE RESULTS

As mentioned earlier, we might want to estimate the probability that submitting the proposal is the best decision. We can approximate this probability by the proportion of replications in our simulation that recommend decision 1 (Submit Proposal) as the optimal decision. This is calculated in cell F3 as:

Formula for cell F3:   =COUNTIF(B3:B102,1)/COUNT(B3:B102)

This formula uses the COUNTIF function to count the number of values in the range B3 through B102 that are equal to 1, and divides this quantity by the total number of values in the same range. The result indicates that decision 1 is the optimal decision in 88% of the replications we performed. Therefore, Steve could conclude that the probability that submitting the proposal is the best decision is roughly 0.88.

We can estimate the expected value of submitting the proposal by taking the average of proposal payoffs listed in column C. This is calculated in cell F5 as:

Formula for cell F5:   =AVERAGE(C3:C102)

The resulting value in cell F5 indicates that the decision to submit the proposal has an EMV of $7,043.

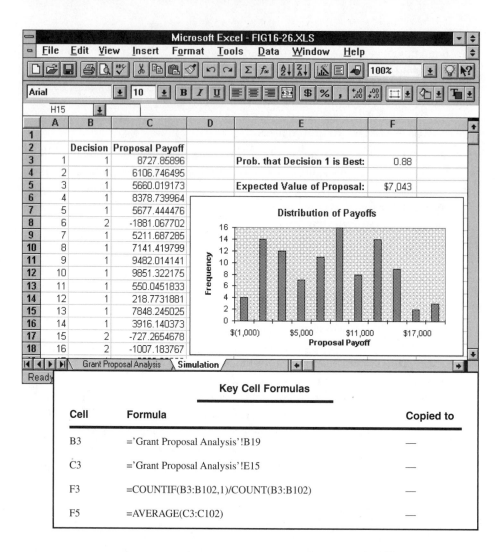

Figure 16.27: *Simulation results for COM-TECH's decision problem*

USING SAMPLE INFORMATION IN DECISION MAKING

In many decision problems, we have the opportunity to obtain additional information about the decision before we actually make the decision. For example, in the Magnolia Inns decision problem, the company could have hired a consultant to study the economic, environmental, and political issues surrounding the site selection process and predict which site will be selected for the new airport by the planning council. This information might help Magnolia Inns make a better (or more informed) decision. The potential for using this type of additional sample information in decision making raises a number of interesting issues that are illustrated using the following example.

Colonial Motors (CM) is trying to determine what size of manufacturing plant to build for a new car it is developing. Only two plants sizes are under consideration: large and small. The cost of constructing a large plant is $25 million and the cost of constructing a small plant is $15 million. CM believes a 70% chance exists that the demand for this new car will be high and a 30% chance that it will be low. The following table summarizes the payoffs (in millions of dollars) the company expects to receive for each factory size and demand combination (not counting the cost of the factory).

	Demand	
Factory Size	High	Low
Large	$175	$95
Small	$125	$105

A decision tree for this problem is shown in Figure 16.28 (and in the file FIG16-28.XLS on your data disk). The decision tree indicates that the optimal decision is to build the large plant and that this alternative has an EMV of $126 million.

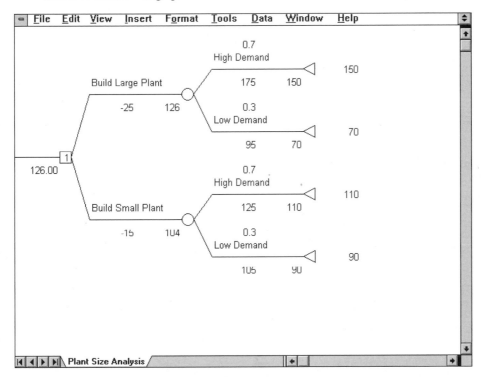

Figure 16.28: Decision tree for the CM plant size problem

Now suppose that before making the plant size decision, CM conducts a survey to assess consumer attitudes about the new car. For simplicity, we'll assume that the results of this survey indicate either a favorable or unfavorable attitude about the new car. A revised decision tree for this problem is shown in Figure 16.29 (and in the file FIG16-29.XLS on your data disk).

The decision tree in Figure 16.29 begins with a decision node with a single branch representing the decision to conduct the market survey. For now, assume that this survey can be done at no cost. An event node follows, corresponding to the outcome of the market survey, which can indicate either favorable or unfavorable attitudes about the new car. We assume that CM believes that the probability of a favorable response is 0.67 and the probability of an unfavorable response is 0.33.

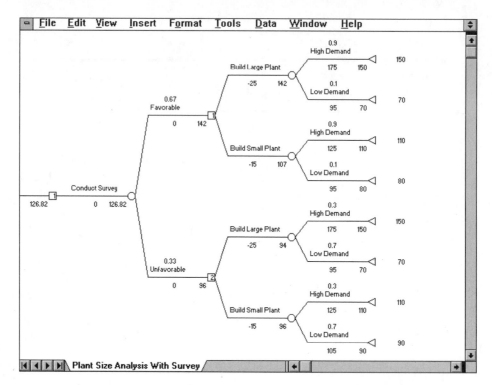

_**Figure 16.29:** Decision
tree if consumer survey is
conducted before CM makes
plant size decision_

CONDITIONAL PROBABILITIES

Once the survey results are known, the decision nodes in the tree indicate that a decision must be made about whether to build a large plant or a small plant. Following each decision branch, event nodes occur with branches representing the market demands for the car that could occur. Four event nodes represent the market demand that might occur for this car. However, the probabilities we assign to the branches of these nodes are likely to differ depending on the results of the market survey.

Earlier we indicated that CM believed a 0.70 probability exists that demand for the new car will be high, expressed mathematically as:

P(high demand) = 0.7

In this formula P(A)=X is read, "the probability of A is X." If the market survey indicates that consumers have a favorable impression of the new car, this will raise expectations that demand will be high for the car. Thus, given a favorable survey response, we might increase the probability assessment for a high market demand to 0.90. This is expressed mathematically as the following _conditional_ probability:

P(high demand | favorable response) = 0.90

In this formula P(A | B)=X is read, "the probability of A given B is X."

As noted earlier, the probabilities on the branches at any event node must always sum to 1. If the favorable survey response increases the probability assessment of a high demand occurring, it must decrease the probability assessment of a low demand given this survey result. Thus, the probability of a low demand given a favorable response on the survey is:

P(low demand | favorable response) = 1 – P(high demand | favorable response)
= 1 – 0.90 = 0.10

These conditional probabilities are shown in Figure 16.29 on the first four event branches representing high and low demands given a favorable survey response.

If the market survey indicates consumers have an unfavorable response to the new car, this will lower expectations for high market demand. Thus, given an unfavorable survey response, we might reduce the probability assessment of a high market demand to 0.30:

P(high demand | unfavorable response) = 0.30

We must also revise the probability assessment for a low market demand given an unfavorable market response as:

P(low demand | unfavorable response) = 1 − P(high demand | unfavorable response)

$$= 1 - 0.3 = 0.70$$

These conditional probabilities are shown on the last four demand branches in Figure 16.29. Later, we'll discuss a more objective method for determining these types of conditional probabilities.

THE EXPECTED VALUE OF SAMPLE INFORMATION

The additional information made available by the market survey allows us to make more precise estimates of the probabilities associated with the uncertain market demand. This, in turn, allows us to make more precise decisions. For example, Figure 16.29 indicates that if the survey results are favorable, CM should build a large plant; and if the survey results are unfavorable, it should build a small plant. The expected value of this decision-making strategy is $126.82 million, assuming that the survey can be done at no cost—which is unlikely. So, how much should CM be willing to pay to perform this survey? The answer to this question is provided by the expected value of sample information (EVSI), which is defined as:

$$\text{EVSI} = \begin{pmatrix} \text{Expected value of the best decision} \\ \textit{with} \text{ sample information} \\ \text{(obtained at no cost)} \end{pmatrix} - \begin{pmatrix} \text{Expected value of the best decision} \\ \textit{without} \text{ sample information} \end{pmatrix}$$

The EVSI represents the *maximum* amount we should be willing to pay to obtain sample information. From Figure 16.29, we know that the expected value of the best decision *with* sample information for our example problem is $126.82 million. From Figure 16.28, we know that the expected value of the best decision *without* sample information is $126 million. So for our example problem, the EVSI is determined as:

EVSI = $126.82 million − $126 million = $0.82 million

Thus, CM should be willing to spend up to $820,000 to perform the market survey.

COMPUTING CONDITIONAL PROBABILITIES

In our example problem, we assumed that the values of the conditional probabilities were assigned subjectively by the decision makers at CM. However, a company often has data available from which it can compute these probabilities. We'll illustrate this process for the CM example. To simplify our notation, we'll use the following abbreviations:

H = high demand

L = low demand

F = favorable response

U = unfavorable response

To complete the decision tree in Figure 16.29, we determined values for the following six probabilities:

- $P(F)$
- $P(U)$
- $P(H|F)$
- $P(L|F)$
- $P(H|U)$
- $P(L|U)$

Assuming that CM has been in the auto business for some time, it undoubtedly has performed other market surveys prior to introducing other new models. Some of these models probably achieved high consumer demand, whereas others achieved only low demand. Thus, CM can use historical data to construct the *joint probability* table shown at the top of Figure 16.30 (and in the file FIG16-30.XLS on your data disk).

	A	B	C	D	E	F	G
1							
2		**Joint Probabilities**					
3		High Demand	Low Demand	Total			
4	Favorable Response	0.60	0.07	0.67			
5	Unfavorable Response	0.10	0.23	0.33			
6	Total	0.70	0.30				
7							
8							
9		**Conditional Probabilities**					
10		**For A Given Survey Response**					
11		High Demand	Low Demand				
12	Favorable Response	0.90	0.10				
13	Unfavorable Response	0.30	0.70				
14							
15							
16		**Conditional Probabilities**					
17		**For A Given Demand Level**					
18		High Demand	Low Demand				
19	Favorable Response	0.86	0.23				
20	Unfavorable Response	0.14	0.77				
21							
22							
23							
24							
25							

Key Cell Formulas

Cell	Formula	Copied to
B6	=SUM(B4:B5)	C6
D4	=SUM(B4:C4)	D5
B12	=B4/$D4	B12:C13
B19	=B4/B$6	B19:C20

Figure 16.30: The calculation of conditional probabilities for the CM decision problem

The value in cell B4 indicates that of all the new car models CM developed and performed market surveys on, 60% received a favorable survey response and subsequently enjoyed high demand. This is expressed mathematically as:

$$P(F \cap H) = 0.60$$

In this formula $P(A \cap B) = X$ is read, "the probability of A *and* B is X." Similarly, in the joint probability table we see that:

$P(F \cap L) = 0.07$

$P(U \cap H) = 0.10$

$P(U \cap L) = 0.23$

The column totals in cells B6 and C6 represent, respectively, the estimated probabilities of high and low demands as:

$P(H) = 0.70$

$P(L) = 0.30$

The row totals in cells D4 and D5 represent, respectively, the estimated probabilities of a favorable and unfavorable response. These values correspond to the first two of the six probability values listed earlier; that is:

$P(F) = 0.67$

$P(U) = 0.33$

With these values, we are now ready to compute the necessary conditional probabilities. One general definition of a conditional probability is:

$$P(A|B) = \frac{P(A \cap B)}{P(B)}$$

We can use this definition, along with the values in the joint probability table, to compute the conditional probabilities required for Figure 16.29 as:

$$P(H|F) = \frac{P(H \cap F)}{P(F)} = \frac{0.60}{0.67} = 0.90$$

$$P(L|F) = \frac{P(L \cap F)}{P(F)} = \frac{0.07}{0.67} = 0.10$$

$$P(H|U) = \frac{P(H \cap U)}{P(U)} = \frac{0.10}{0.33} = 0.30$$

$$P(L|U) = \frac{P(L \cap U)}{P(U)} = \frac{0.23}{0.33} = 0.70$$

We can calculate these conditional probabilities of the demand levels for a given survey response in the spreadsheet. This is done in the second table in Figure 16.30 using the following formula:

Formula for cell B12:   =B4/$D4

(copy to B12 through C13)

Although not required for Figure 16.29, we can also compute the conditional probabilities of the survey responses for a given level of demand as:

$$P(F|H) = \frac{P(H \cap F)}{P(H)} = \frac{0.60}{0.70} = 0.86$$

$$P(U|H) = \frac{P(H \cap U)}{P(H)} = \frac{0.10}{0.70} = 0.14$$

$$P(F|L) = \frac{P(L \cap F)}{P(L)} = \frac{0.07}{0.30} = 0.23$$

$$P(U|L) = \frac{P(L \cap U)}{P(L)} = \frac{0.23}{0.30} = 0.77$$

The third table in Figure 16.30 calculates conditional probabilities of the survey responses for a given level of demand using the following formula:

Formula for cell B19: =B4/B$6
(copy to B19 through C20)

BAYES'S THEOREM

Bayes's Theorem provides another definition of conditional probability that is sometimes useful. This definition is:

$$P(A \mid B) = \frac{P(B \mid A)P(A)}{P(B \mid A)P(A) + P(B \mid \overline{A})P(\overline{A})}$$

In this formula, A and B represent any two events, and $\overline{A}$ is the complement of A. To see how this formula might be used, suppose that we want to determine $P(H \mid F)$ but we do not have access to the joint probability table in Figure 16.30. According to Bayes's Theorem we know that:

$$P(H \mid F) = \frac{P(F \mid H)P(H)}{P(F \mid H)P(H) + P(F \mid L)P(L)}$$

If we know the values for the various quantities on the RHS of this equation, we can compute $P(H \mid F)$ as in the following example:

$$P(H \mid F) = \frac{P(F \mid H)P(H)}{P(F \mid H)P(H) + P(F \mid L)P(L)} = \frac{(0.86)(0.70)}{(0.86)(0.70) + (0.23)(0.30)} = 0.90$$

This result is consistent with the value of $P(H \mid F)$ shown in cell B12 in Figure 16.30.

UTILITY THEORY

Although the EMV decision rule is widely used, sometimes the decision alternative with the highest EMV is not the most desirable or most preferred alternative by the decision maker. For example, suppose that we could buy either of the two companies listed in the following payoff table for exactly the same price:

	State of Nature			
Company	1	2	EMV	
A	150,000	−30,000	60,000	← maximum
B	70,000	40,000	55,000	
Probability	0.5	0.5		

The payoff values listed in this table represent the annual profits expected from this business. Thus, in any year a 50% chance exists that company A will generate a profit of $150,000 and a 50% chance that it will generate a loss of $30,000. On the other hand, in each year a 50% chance exists that company B will generate a profit of $70,000 and a 50% chance that it will generate a profit of $40,000.

According to the EMV decision rule, we should buy company A because it has the highest EMV. However, company A represents a far more risky investment than company B. Although company A would generate the highest EMV over the long run, we might not have the financial resources to withstand the potential losses of $30,000 per year that could occur in the short run with this alternative. With company B, we can be sure of making at least $40,000 each year. Although company B's EMV over the long run might not be as great as that of company A, for many decision makers, this is more than offset by the increased peace of mind associated with company B's relatively stable profit level. However, other decision makers might be willing to accept the greater risk associated with company A in hopes of achieving the higher potential payoffs this alternative provides.

As this example illustrates, the EMVs of different decision alternatives do not necessarily reflect the relative attractiveness of the alternatives to a particular decision maker. **Utility theory** provides a way to incorporate the decision maker's attitudes and preferences toward risk and return in the decision analysis process so that the most desirable decision alternative is identified.

UTILITY FUNCTIONS

Utility theory assumes that every decision maker uses a **utility function** that translates each of the possible payoffs in a decision problem into a non-monetary measure known as a utility. The **utility** of a payoff represents the total worth, value, or desirability of the outcome of a decision alternative to the decision maker. For convenience, we'll begin by representing utilities on a scale from 0 to 1, where 0 represents the least value and 1 represents the most.

Different decision makers have different attitudes and preferences toward risk and return. Those who are "risk neutral" tend to make decisions using the maximum EMV decision rule. However, some decision makers are risk avoiders (or "risk averse"), and others look for risk (or are "risk seekers"). The utility functions typically associated with these three types of decision makers are shown in Figure 16.31.

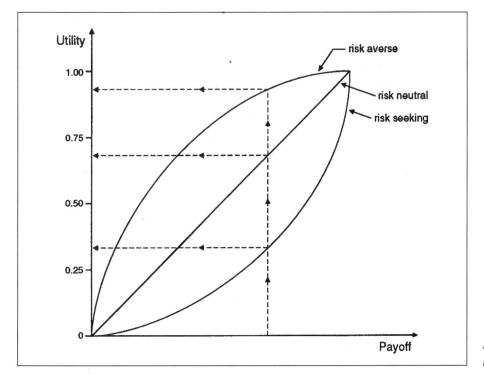

Figure 16.31: Three common types of utility functions

Figure 16.31 illustrates how the same monetary payoff might produce different levels of utility for three different decision makers. A "risk averse" decision maker assigns the largest relative utility to any payoff but has a diminishing marginal utility for increased payoffs (that is, every additional dollar in payoff results in smaller increases in utility). The "risk seeking" decision maker assigns the smallest utility to any payoff but has an increasing marginal utility for increased payoffs (that is, every additional dollar in payoff results in larger increases in utility). The "risk neutral" decision maker (who follows the EMV decision rule) falls in between these two extremes and has a constant marginal utility for increased payoffs (that is, every additional dollar in payoff results in the same amount of increase in utility). The utility curves in Figure 16.31 are not the only ones that can occur. In general, utility curves can assume virtually any form depending on the preferences of the decision maker.

CONSTRUCTING UTILITY FUNCTIONS

Assuming that decision makers use utility functions (perhaps at a subconscious level) to make decisions, how can we determine what a given decision maker's utility function looks like? One approach involves assigning a utility value of 0 to the worst outcome in a decision problem and a utility value of 1 to the best outcome. All other payoffs are assigned utility values between 0 and 1. (Although it is convenient to use endpoint values of 0 and 1, we can use any values provided that the utility value assigned to the worst payoff is less than the utility value assigned to the best payoff.)

We'll let $U(x)$ represent the utility associated with a payoff of \$$x$. Thus, for the decision about whether to buy company A or B, described earlier, we have:

$U(-30,000) = 0$

$U(150,000) = 1$

Now suppose that we want to find the utility associated with the payoff of \$70,000 in our example. To do this, we must identify the probability p at which the decision maker is indifferent between the following two alternatives:

Alternative 1. Receive \$70,000 with certainty

Alternative 2. Receive \$150,000 with probability p and lose \$30,000 with probability $(1 - p)$

If $p = 0$, most decision makers would choose alternative 1 because they would prefer to receive a payoff of \$70,000 rather than lose \$30,000. On the other hand, if $p = 1$, most decision makers would choose alternative 2 because they would prefer to receive a payoff of \$150,000 rather than \$70,000. So as p increases from 0 to 1, it reaches a point—p^*—at which the decision maker is indifferent between the two alternatives. That is, if $p < p^*$, the decision maker prefers alternative 1, and if $p > p^*$, the decision maker prefers alternative 2. The point of indifference, p^*, varies from one decision maker to another, depending on their attitude toward risk and according to their ability to sustain a loss of \$30,000.

In our example, suppose that the decision maker is indifferent between alternative 1 and 2 when $p = 0.8$ (so that $p^* = 0.8$). The utility of the \$70,000 payoff for this decision maker is computed as:

$$U(70,000) = U(150,000)p^* + U(-30,000)(1 - p^*) = 1p^* + 0(1 - p^*) = p^* = 0.8$$

Notice that when $p = 0.8$, the expected value of alternative 2 is:

\$150,000*0.8 − \$30,000*0.2 = \$114,000

Because the decision maker is indifferent between a risky decision (alternative 2) that has an EMV of $114,000 and a non-risky decision (alternative 1) that has a certain payoff of $70,000, this decision maker is "risk averse." That is, the decision maker is willing to accept only $70,000 to avoid the risk associated with a decision that has an EMV of $114,000.

The term **certainty equivalent** refers to the amount of money that is equivalent in a decision maker's mind to a situation that involves uncertainty. For example, $70,000 is the decision maker's certainty equivalent for the uncertain situation represented by alternative 2 when $p = 0.8$. A closely related term, **risk premium**, refers to the EMV that a decision maker is willing to give up (or pay) in order to avoid a risky decision. In our example, the risk premium is $114,000 – $70,000 = $44,000; that is:

$$\text{Risk premium} = \begin{pmatrix} \text{EMV of an} \\ \text{uncertain situation} \end{pmatrix} - \begin{pmatrix} \text{certainty equivalent of} \\ \text{the same uncertain situation} \end{pmatrix}$$

To find the utility associated with the $40,000 payoff in our example, we must identify the probability p at which the decision maker is indifferent between the following two alternatives:

Alternative 1. Receive $40,000 with certainty

Alternative 2. Receive $150,000 with probability p and lose $30,000 with probability $(1 - p)$

Because we reduced the payoff amount listed in alternative 1 from its earlier value of $70,000, we expect that the value of p at which the decision maker is indifferent would also be reduced. In this case, suppose that the decision maker is indifferent between the two alternatives when $p = 0.65$ (so that $p^* = 0.65$). The utility associated with a payoff of $40,000 is:

$$U(40,000) = U(150,000)p^* + U(-30,000)(1 - p^*) = 1p^* + 0(1 - p^*) = p^* = 0.65$$

Again the utility associated with the amount given in alternative 1 is equivalent to the decision maker's indifference point p^*. This is not a coincidence.

Key Point

When utilities are expressed on a scale from 0 to 1, the probability p^* at which the decision maker is indifferent between alternatives 1 and 2 always corresponds to the decision maker's utility for the amount listed in alternative 1.

Notice that when $p = 0.65$, the expected value of alternative 2 is:

$150,000*0.65 – $30,000*0.35 = $87,000

Again this is "risk averse" behavior because the decision maker is willing to accept only $40,000 (or pay a risk premium of $47,000) to avoid the risk associated with a decision that has an EMV of $87,000.

For our example, the utilities associated with payoffs of –$30,000, $40,000, $70,000, and $150,000 are 0.0, 0.65, 0.80, and 1.0, respectively. If we plot these values on a graph and connect the points with straight lines, we can estimate the shape of the decision maker's utility function for this decision problem, as shown in Figure 16.32. Note that the shape of this utility function is consistent with the general shape of the utility function for a "risk averse" decision maker given in Figure 16.31.

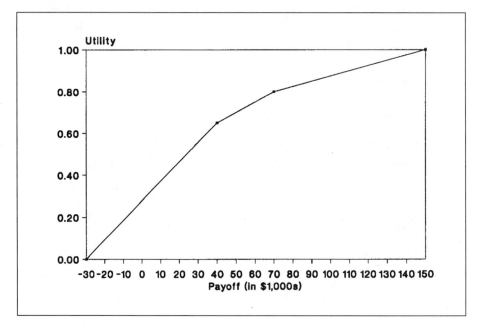

Figure 16.32: An estimated utility function for the example problem

USING UTILITIES TO MAKE DECISIONS

After determining the utility value of each possible monetary payoff, we can apply the standard tools of decision analysis to determine the alternative that provides the highest expected utility. We do so using utility values in place of monetary values in payoff tables or decision trees. For our current example, we substitute the appropriate utilities in the payoff table and compute the expected utility for each decision alternative as:

	State of Nature			
Company	1	2	Expected Utility	
A	1.00	0.00	0.500	
B	0.80	0.65	0.725	← maximum
Probability	0.5	0.5		

In this case, the decision to purchase company B provides the greatest expected level of utility to this decision maker—even though our earlier analysis indicated that its EMV of $55,000 is less than company A's EMV of $60,000. Thus, by using utilities decision makers can identify the alternative that is most attractive given their personal attitudes about risk and return.

THE EXPONENTIAL UTILITY FUNCTION

In a complicated decision problem with numerous possible payoff values, it might be difficult and time consuming for a decision maker to determine the different values for p^* that are required to determine the utility for each payoff. However, if the decision maker is "risk averse," the **exponential utility function** can be used as an approximation of the decision maker's actual utility function. The general form of the exponential utility function is:

$$U(x) = 1 - e^{-x/R}$$

In this formula, e is the base of the natural logarithm ($e = 2.718281 \ldots$) and R is a parameter that controls the shape of the utility function according to a decision maker's risk tolerance. Figure 16.33 shows examples of the graph of this function for several values of R. Note that as R increases, the shape of the utility curve becomes flatter (or less "risk averse"). Also note that as x becomes large, $U(x)$ approaches 1, when $x = 0$, then $U(x) = 0$; and if x is less than 0, then $U(x) < 0$.

Figure 16.33: Examples of the exponential utility function

To use the exponential utility function we must determine a reasonable value for the risk tolerance parameter R. One method for doing so involves determining the maximum value of Y for which the decision maker is willing to participate in a game of chance with the following possible outcomes:

Win $Y with probability 0.5

Lose $Y/2 with probability 0.5

The maximum value of Y for which the decision maker would accept the above gamble should give us a reasonable estimate of R. Note that a decision maker willing to accept this gamble only at very small values of Y is "risk averse," whereas a decision maker willing to play for larger values of Y is less "risk averse." This corresponds with the relationship between the utility curves and values of R shown in Figure 16.33.

INCORPORATING UTILITIES IN TREEPLAN

The TreePlan add-in provides a simple way to use the exponential utility function to model "risk averse" decision preferences in a decision tree. We will illustrate this using the decision tree developed earlier for Magnolia Inns, where Barbara needs to decide which parcel of land to purchase. The decision tree developed for this problem is shown in Figure 16.34 (and in the file FIG16-34.XLS on your data disk).

Figure 16.34: Decision tree for the Magnolia Inns land purchase problem

To use the exponential utility function, we first construct a decision tree in the usual way. We then determine the risk tolerance value R for the decision maker using the technique described earlier. Because Barbara is making this decision on behalf of Magnolia Inns, it is important that she provide an estimated value of R based on the acceptable risk levels of the corporation—not her own personal risk tolerance level.

In this case, let's assume that $4 million is the maximum value of Y for which Barbara believes Magnolia Inns is willing to gamble winning $Y with probability 0.5 and losing $Y/2 with probability 0.5. Therefore, R = Y = 4. (Note that the value of R should be expressed in the same units as the payoffs in the decision tree.)

TreePlan requires that we enter the value of R in a cell named "RiskTolerance." (This cell must be outside of the rectangular region containing the decision tree.) Cell D36 in Figure 16.34 serves this purpose. To assign the name "RiskTolerance" to this cell:

1. Click cell D36.

2. Click the Insert menu.

3. Click Name.

4. Click Define.

5. Type RiskTolerance (do not type a space in the name "RiskTolerance").

6. Click OK.

We can now instruct TreePlan to use an exponential utility function to determine the optimal decision. To do this:

1. Click cell D3.

2. Press [Ctrl][t] to invoke TreePlan.

3. Click the Options button.

4. Click Use Exponential Utility Function.

5. Click OK.

TreePlan automatically converts the decision tree so that the roll-back operation is performed using expected utilities rather than EMVs. The resulting tree is shown in Figure 16.35. The expected utility at each node appears in the cell directly below and to the left of each node (previously the location of the EMVs). The certainty equivalent at each node appears directly above and to the left of each node. According to this tree, the decision to buy the parcels at locations A and B provides the highest expected utility for Magnolia Inns.

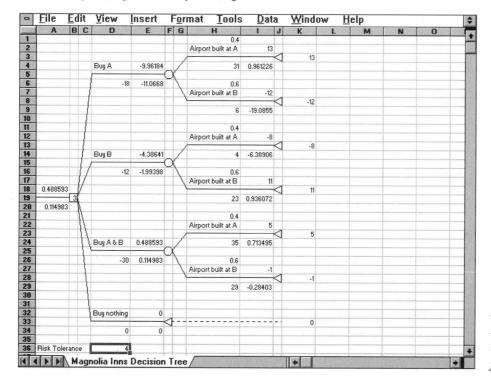

Figure 16.35: Analysis of the Magnolia Inns decision tree using an exponential utility function

MULTI-CRITERIA DECISION MAKING

A decision maker often uses more than one criterion or objective to evaluate the alternatives in a decision problem. Sometimes these criteria conflict with one another. For example, consider again the criteria of risk and return. Most decision makers desire high levels of return and low levels of risk. But high returns are usually accompanied by high risks, and low levels of return are associated with low risk levels. In making investment decisions, a decision maker must assess the trade-offs between risk and return to identify the decision that achieves the most satisfying balance of these two criteria. As we have seen, utility theory represents one approach to assessing the trade-offs between the criteria of risk and return.

Many other types of decision problems involve multiple conflicting criteria. For example, in choosing between two or more different job offers, you must evaluate the alternatives on the basis of starting salary, opportunity for advancement, job security, location, and so on. If you purchase a video camcorder you must evaluate a number of different models based on the manufacturer's reputation, price, warranty, size, weight, zoom capability, lighting requirements, and a host of other features. If you must decide whom to hire to fill a vacancy in your organization, you will likely have to evaluate a number of candidates on the basis of education, experience, references, and personality. This section presents two techniques that can be used in decision problems that involve multiple criteria.

THE MULTI-CRITERIA SCORING MODEL

The **multi-criteria scoring model** is a simple procedure in which we score (or rate) each alternative in a decision problem based on each criterion. The score for alternative j on criterion i is denoted by s_{ij}. Weights (denoted by w_i) are assigned to each criterion indicating its relative importance to the decision maker. For each alternative, we then compute a weighted average score as:

$$\text{Weighted average score for alternative } j = \sum_i w_i s_{ij}$$

We then select the alternative with the largest weighted average score.

The beginning of this chapter described a situation that many students face when they graduate from college—choosing between two job offers. The spreadsheet in Figure 16.36 (and in the file FIG16-36.XLS on your data disk) illustrates how we might use a multi-criteria scoring model to help in this problem.

In choosing between two (or more) job offers, we would evaluate criteria for each alternative such as the starting salary, potential for career development, job security, location of the job, and perhaps other factors as well. The idea in a scoring model is to assign a value from 0 to 1 to each decision alternative that reflects its relative worth on each criterion. These values can be thought of as subjective assessments of the utility that each alternative provides on the various criteria.

In Figure 16.36, the starting salary offered by company B provides the greatest value, but the salary offered by company A is not much worse. (Note that these scores do not necessarily mean that the starting salary offered by company B was the highest. These scores reflect the *value* of the salaries to the decision maker, taking into account such factors as the cost of living in the different locations.) The remaining scores in the table indicate that company A provides the greatest potential for career advancement and is in the most attractive location, but provides considerably less job security than that offered by company B.

Figure 16.36: A multi-criteria scoring model

Next, the decision maker must specify weights that indicate the relative importance of each criterion. Again, this is done subjectively. Hypothetical weights for each criterion in this example are shown in column F in Figure 16.36. Note that these weights must sum to 1. Weighted average scores for each alternative are calculated in cells C9 and D9 as:

Formula for cell C9: =SUMPRODUCT(C5:C8,$F$5:$F$8)
(copy to D9)

In this case, the weighted average scores for company A and B are 0.82 and 0.77, respectively. Thus, this model indicates that the decision maker should accept the job with company A because it has the largest weighted average score.

THE ANALYTIC HIERARCHY PROCESS

Sometimes a decision maker finds it difficult to subjectively determine the criterion scores and weights needed in the multi-criteria scoring model. In this case, the analytic hierarchy process (AHP) can be helpful. **AHP** provides a more structured approach for determining the scores and weights for the multi-criteria scoring model described earlier.

To illustrate AHP, suppose that a company wants to purchase a new payroll and personnel records information system and is considering three systems, identified as X, Y, and Z. The systems differ with respect to three key criteria: price, user support, and ease of use.

PAIRWISE COMPARISONS The first step in AHP is to create a pairwise comparison matrix for each alternative on each criterion. We'll illustrate the details of this process for the price criterion. The values shown in Figure 16.37 are used in AHP to describe the decision maker's preferences between two alternatives on a given criterion.

Value	Preference
1	Equally Preferred
2	Equally to Moderately Preferred
3	Moderately Preferred
4	Moderately to Strongly Preferred
5	Strongly Preferred
6	Strongly to Very Strongly Preferred
7	Very Strongly Preferred
8	Very Strongly to Extremely Preferred
9	Extremely Preferred

Figure 16.37: Scale for pairwise comparisons in AHP

To create a pairwise comparison matrix for the price criterion, we must perform pairwise comparisons of the prices of systems X, Y, and Z using the values shown in Figure 16.37. Let P_{ij} denote the extent to which we prefer alternative i to alternative j on a given criterion. For example, suppose that when comparing system X to Y, the decision maker strongly prefers the price of X. In this case, $P_{XY} = 5$. Similarly, suppose that when comparing system X to Z, the decision maker very strongly prefers the price of X, and when comparing Y to Z, the decision maker moderately prefers the price of Y. In this case, $P_{XZ} = 7$ and $P_{YZ} = 3$. We used the values of these pairwise comparisons to create the pairwise comparison matrix shown in Figure 16.38.

The values of P_{XY}, P_{XZ}, and P_{YZ} are shown in cells D4, E4, and E5 in Figure 16.38. We entered the value 1 along the main diagonal in Figure 16.38 to indicate that if an alternative is compared against itself, the decision maker should equally prefer either alternative (because they are the same).

The entries in cells C5, C6, and D6 correspond to P_{YX}, P_{ZX}, and P_{ZY}, respectively. To determine these values we could obtain the decision maker's preferences between Y and X, Z and X, and Z and Y. However, if we already know the decision maker's preference between X and Y (P_{XY}), we can conclude that the decision maker's preference between Y and X (P_{YX}) is the reciprocal of the preference between X and Y; that is, $P_{YX} = 1/P_{XY}$. So, in general, we have:

$$P_{ji} = \frac{1}{P_{ij}}$$

Figure 16.38: Pairwise comparisons of the price criterion for the three systems

Thus, the values in cells C5, C6, and D6 are computed as:

Formula for cell C5:   =1/D4

Formula for cell C6:   =1/E4

Formula for cell D6:   =1/E5

NORMALIZING THE COMPARISONS The next step in AHP is to normalize the matrix of pairwise comparisons. To do this we first calculate the sum of each column in the pairwise comparison matrix. We then divide each entry in the matrix by its column sum. Figure 16.39 shows the resulting normalized matrix.

We'll use the average of each row in the normalized matrix as the score for each alternative on the criterion under consideration. For example, cells F11, F12, and F13 indicate that the average scores on the price criterion for X, Y, and Z are 0.724, 0.193, and 0.083, respectively. These scores indicate the relative desirability of the three alternatives to the decision maker with respect to price. The score for X indicates that this is by far the most attractive alternative with respect to price, and alternative Y is somewhat more attractive than Z. Note that these scores reflect the preferences expressed by the decision maker in the pairwise comparison matrix.

Figure 16.39: Price scores obtained from the normalized comparison matrix

CONSISTENCY In applying AHP, the decision maker should be consistent in the preference ratings given in the pairwise comparison matrix. For example, if the decision maker strongly prefers the price of X to that of Y, and strongly prefers the price of Y to that of Z, it would be inconsistent for the decision maker to indicate indifference (or equal preference) regarding the price of X and Z. Thus, before using the scores derived from the normalized comparison matrix, the preferences indicated in the original pairwise comparison matrix should be checked for consistency.

A consistency measure for each alternative is obtained as:

$$\text{Consistency measure for X} = \frac{0.724 * 1 + 0.193 * 5 + 0.083 * 7}{0.724} = 3.141$$

$$\text{Consistency measure for Y} = \frac{0.724 * 0.2 + 0.193 * 1 + 0.083 * 3}{0.193} = 3.043$$

$$\text{Consistency measure for Z} = \frac{0.724 * 0.143 + 0.193 * 0.333 + 0.083 * 1}{0.083} = 3.014$$

The numerator in each of these calculations multiplies the scores obtained from the normalized matrix by the preferences given in one of the rows of the original pairwise comparison matrix. The products are summed and then divided by the score for the alternative in question. These consistency measures are shown in Figure 16.40 in cells G11 through G13.

Figure 16.40: Checking the consistency of the pairwise comparisons

If the decision maker is perfectly consistent in stating preferences, each consistency measure will equal the number of alternatives in the problem (which, in this case, is 3). So there appears to be some amount of inconsistency in the preferences given in the pairwise comparison matrix. This is not unusual. It is difficult for a decision maker to be perfectly consistent in stating preferences between a large number of pairwise comparisons. Provided that the amount of inconsistency is not excessive, the scores obtained from the normalized matrix will be reasonably accurate. To determine whether or not the inconsistency is excessive, we compute the following quantities:

$$\text{Consistency Index (CI)} = \frac{\lambda - n}{n - 1}$$

$$\text{Consistency Ratio (CR)} = \frac{\text{CI}}{\text{RI}}$$

where:

λ = the average consistency measure for all alternatives

n = the number of alternatives

RI = the appropriate random index from Figure 16.41

n	RI
2	0.00
3	0.58
4	0.90
5	1.12
6	1.24
7	1.32
8	1.41

Figure 16.41: Values of RI for use in AHP

If the pairwise comparison matrix is perfectly consistent, then $\lambda = n$ and the consistency ratio is 0. The values of RI in Figure 16.41 give the average value of CI if all the entries in the pairwise comparison matrix were chosen at random, given that all the diagonal entries equal 1 and $P_{ij} = 1/P_{ji}$. If CR ≤ 0.10 the degree of consistency in the pairwise comparison matrix is satisfactory. However, if CR > 0.10 serious inconsistencies might exist and AHP might not yield meaningful results. The value for CR shown in cell G15 in Figure 16.40 indicates that the pairwise comparison matrix for the price criterion is reasonably consistent. Therefore, we can assume that the scores for the price criterion obtained from the normalized matrix are reasonably accurate.

OBTAINING SCORES FOR THE REMAINING CRITERIA We can repeat the process for obtaining the price criterion scores to obtain scores for the user support and ease-of-use criteria. Hypothetical results for these criteria are shown in Figures 16.42 and 16.43, respectively.

Figure 16.42: Spreadsheet used to calculate scores for the user support criterion

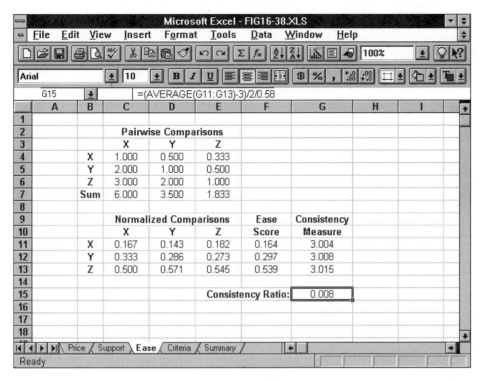

Figure 16.43: *Spreadsheet used to calculate scores for the ease-of-use criterion*

We can create these two spreadsheets easily by copying the spreadsheet for the price criterion (shown in Figure 16.40) and having the decision maker fill in the pairwise comparison matrices with preferences related to the user support and ease-of-use criteria. Notice that the preferences given in Figures 16.42 and 16.43 appear to be consistent.

OBTAINING CRITERION WEIGHTS The scores shown in Figures 16.40, 16.42, and 16.43 indicate how the alternatives compare with respect to the price, user support, and ease-of-use criteria. Before we can use these values in a scoring model, we must also determine weights that indicate the relative importance of the three criteria to the decision maker. The pairwise comparison process used earlier to generate scores for the alternative on each criteria can also be used to generate criterion weights.

The pairwise comparison matrix in Figure 16.44 shows the decision maker's preferences for the three criteria. The values in cells C5 and C6 indicate that the decision maker finds user support and ease of use to be more important (or more preferred) than price, and cell D6 indicates that ease of use is somewhat more important than user support. These relative preferences are reflected in the criterion weights shown in cells F11 through F13.

IMPLEMENTING THE SCORING MODEL We now have all the elements required to analyze this decision problem using a scoring model. Thus, the last step in AHP is to calculate the weighted average scores for each decision alternative. The weighted average scores are shown in cells C7 through E7 in Figure 16.45. According to these scores, alternative Y should be selected.

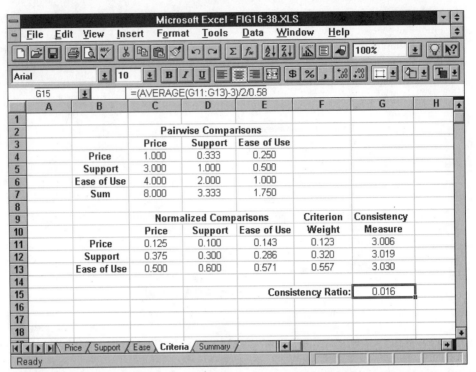

Figure 16.44: Spreadsheet used to determine the criterion weights

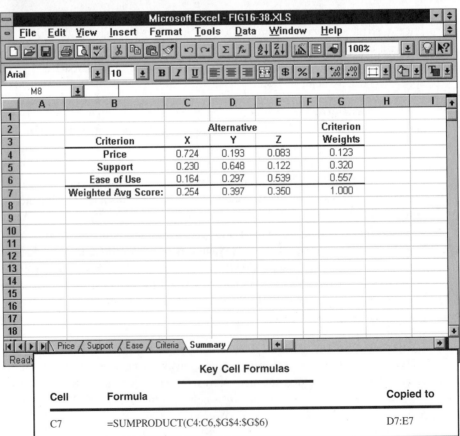

Figure 16.45: Final scoring model for selecting the information system

Key Cell Formulas

Cell	Formula	Copied to
C7	=SUMPRODUCT(C4:C6,$G$4:$G$6)	D7:E7

SUMMARY

This chapter presented a number of techniques for analyzing a variety of decision problems. First it discussed how a payoff table can be used to summarize the alternatives in a single-stage decision problem. Then a number of nonprobabilistic and probabilistic decision rules were presented. No one decision rule works best in all situations, but together, the rules help to highlight different aspects of a problem and can help decision makers make more informed decisions. When probabilities of occurrence can be estimated for the alternatives in a problem, the EMV decision rule is the most commonly used technique.

Decision trees are particularly helpful in expressing multi-stage decision problems in which a series of decisions must be considered. Each terminal node in a decision tree is associated with the net payoff that results from each possible sequence of decisions. A roll-back technique determines the alternative that results in the highest EMV. Because different decision makers derive different levels of value from the same monetary payoff, the chapter also discussed how utility theory can be applied to decision problems to account for these differences.

Finally, the chapter discussed two procedures for dealing with decision problems that involve multiple conflicting decision criteria. The multi-criteria scoring model requires the decision maker to assign a score for each alternative on each criterion. Weights are then assigned to represent the relative importance of the criteria, and a weighted average score is computed for each alternative. The alternative with the highest score is the recommended alternative. AHP provides a structured approach to determining the scores and weights used in a multi-criteria scoring model if the decision maker has difficulty specifying these values.

REFERENCES

Clemen, R. *Making Hard Decisions: An Introduction to Decision Analysis*. Boston: PWS-KENT Publishing Company, 1991.

Coyle, R. *Decision Analysis*. London: Nelson, 1972.

Heian, B. and J. Gale. "Mortgage Selection Using a Decision-Tree Approach: An Extension." *Interfaces*, vol. 18, July-August 1988.

Keeney, R. and H. Raiffa. *Decision With Multiple Objectives*. New York: Wiley, 1976.

Keeney, R. *Value-Focused Thinking*. Cambridge, MA: Harvard University Press, 1992.

Wenstop, F., and A. Carlsen. "Ranking Hydroelectric Power Projects with Multicriteria Decision Analysis." *Interfaces*, vol. 18, no. 4, 1988.

Zahedi, F. "The Analytic Hierarchy Process—A Survey of the Method and its Applications." *Interfaces*, vol. 16, no. 4, 1986.

Decision Theory Helps Hallmark Trim Discards

Source: Barron, F. Hutton, "Payoff Matrices Pay Off at Hallmark," *Interfaces*, vol. 15, no. 4, August 1985, pages 20-25.

MANY ITEMS DISTRIBUTED by Hallmark Cards, Incorporated can be sold only during a single season. Leftovers, or discards, must then be disposed of outside normal dealer channels. For example, table items such as napkins can be used in the company's cafeteria, donated to charity, or sold without the brand name to volume discounters. Other items have no salvage value at all.

A product manager deciding the size of a production run or quantity to purchase from a supplier faces two risks. First is the consequence of choosing a quantity that is larger than the eventual demand for the product. Products that have been paid for must be discarded, and the salvage value (if any) might not make up for the cost. The second risk is that the quantity might be less than demand, in which case revenues are lost.

A substantial increase in the dollar volume of discards prompted Hallmark management to initiate a training program for product managers and inventory controllers. They were taught to use product cost and selling price together with a probability distribution of demand to make order quantity decisions. The format for conducting the analysis was a payoff matrix in which rows represented order quantities and columns represented demand levels. Each cell in the payoff matrix contained a computed contribution to profit.

Salvage values and shortage costs were not included in the values of the payoff matrix cells. Instead, sensitivity analysis provided ranges of values within which the order quantity was still optimal.

Although some probability distributions could be estimated from sales data for previous years, it was sometimes necessary to use subjective probabilities. This was especially true for special promotions that had no relevant product history. For this reason, product managers were trained in specifying subjective probabilities. Although direct assessment of a cumulative distribution function would have tied into the order quantity decision more efficiently, it turned out that the managers became more adept at estimating a discrete probability function.

Enough managers adopted the payoff matrix technique, with positive results, that the training program has been continued and expanded within the company.

Questions and Problems

1. This chapter presented the problem of having to decide between two job offers. The decision maker could accept the job with company A, accept the job with company B, or reject both offers and hope for a better one. What other alternatives can you think of for this problem?

2. Give an example of a national business, political, or military leader who made a good decision that resulted in a bad outcome, or a bad decision that resulted in a good outcome.

3. Consider the following payoff matrix:

Decision	State of Nature 1	2	3
A	50	75	35
B	40	50	60
C	40	35	30

Should a decision maker ever select decision alternative C? Explain your answer.

4. Brenda Kelley runs a specialty ski clothing shop outside of Boone, North Carolina. She must place her order for ski parkas well in advance of ski season because the manufacturer produces them in the summer months. Brenda needs to determine whether to place a large, medium, or small order for parkas. The number sold will depend largely on whether the area receives a heavy, normal, or light amount of snow during the ski season. The following table summarizes the payoffs Brenda expects to receive under each scenario.

Size of Order	Amount of Snow Heavy	Normal	Light
Large	10	7	3
Medium	8	8	6
Small	4	4	4

Payoffs (in $1,000s)

Brenda estimates the probability of heavy, normal, and light snowfalls as 0.25, 0.6, and 0.15, respectively.

a. What decision should be made according to the maximax decision rule?

b. What decision should be made according to the maximin decision rule?

    c. What decision should be made according to the minimax regret decision rule?

    d. What decision should be made according to the EMV decision rule?

    e. What decision should be made according to the EOL decision rule?

5.   One of Philip Mahn's investments is going to mature, and he wants to determine how to invest the proceeds of $30,000. Philip is considering two new investments: a stock mutual fund and a 1-year certificate of deposit (CD). The CD is guaranteed to pay an 8% return. Philip estimates the return on the stock mutual fund as 16%, 9%, or –2%, depending on whether market conditions are good, average, or poor, respectively. Philip estimates the probability of a good, average, and poor market to be 0.1, 0.85, and 0.05, respectively.

    a. Construct a payoff matrix for this problem.

    b. What decision should be made according to the maximax decision rule?

    c. What decision should be made according to the maximin decision rule?

    d. What decision should be made according to the minimax regret decision rule?

    e. What decision should be made according to the EMV decision rule?

    f. What decision should be made according to the EOL decision rule?

    g. How much should Philip be willing to pay to obtain a market forecast that is 100% accurate?

6.   The Fish House (TFH) in Norfolk, Virginia, sells fresh fish and seafood. TFH receives daily shipments of farm-raised trout from a nearby supplier. Each trout costs $2.45 and is sold for $3.95. To maintain its reputation for freshness, at the end of the day TFH sells any leftover trout to a local pet food manufacturer for $1.25 each. The owner of TFH wants to determine how many trout to order each day. Historically, the daily demand for trout is:

Demand:	10	11	12	13	14	15	16	17	18	19	20
Probability:	0.02	0.06	0.09	0.11	0.13	0.15	0.18	0.11	0.07	0.05	0.03

    a. Construct a payoff matrix for this problem.

    b. What decision should be made according to the maximax decision rule?

    c. What decision should be made according to the maximin decision rule?

    d. What decision should be made according to the minimax regret decision rule?

    e. What decision should be made according to the EMV decision rule?

    f. What decision should be made according to the EOL decision rule?

    g. How much should the owner of TFH be willing to pay to obtain a demand forecast that is 100% accurate?

    h. Which decision rule would you recommend TFH use in this case? Why?

7. Refer to question 6. Suppose that TFH receives a quantity discount that reduces the price to $2.25 per trout if it purchases 15 or more. How many trout would you recommend TFH order each day in this case?

8. Bob Farrell, owner of Farrell Motors, is trying to decide whether or not to buy an insurance policy to cover hail damage on his inventory of more than 200 cars and trucks. Thunderstorms occur frequently and they sometimes produce golfball-sized hail that can severely damage automobiles. Bob estimates the potential damage from hail in the next year as:

Hail Damage: (in $1,000s)	0	15	30	45	60	75	90	105
Probability:	0.25	0.08	0.10	0.12	0.15	0.12	0.10	0.08

Bob is considering the following three alternatives for dealing with this risk:

- Bob can buy an insurance policy for $47,000 that would cover 100% of any losses that occur.

- Bob can buy an insurance policy for $25,000 that would cover all losses in excess of $35,000.

- Bob can choose to self-insure, in which case he will not have to pay any insurance premium but will pay for any losses that occur.

a. Construct a payoff matrix for this problem.

b. What decision should be made according to the maximax decision rule?

c. What decision should be made according to the maximin decision rule?

d. What decision should be made according to the minimax regret decision rule?

e. What decision should be made according to the EMV decision rule?

f. What decision should be made according to the EOL decision rule?

9. Morley Properties is planning to build a condominium development on St. Simons Island, Georgia. The company is trying to decide between building a small, medium, or large development. The payoffs received for each size of development will depend on the market demand for condominiums in the area, which could be low, medium, or high. The payoff matrix for this decision problem is:

	Market Demand		
Size of Development	Low	Medium	High
Small	400	400	400
Medium	200	500	500
Large	−400	300	800

Payoffs in $1,000s

The owner of the company estimates a 21.75% chance that market demand will be low, a 35.5% chance that it will be medium, and a 42.75% chance that it will be high.

a. What decision should be made according to the maximax decision rule?

b. What decision should be made according to the maximin decision rule?

c. What decision should be made according to the minimax regret decision rule?

d. What decision should be made according to the EMV decision rule?

e. What decision should be made according to the EOL decision rule?

10. Refer to question 9. Morley Properties can hire a consultant to predict the most likely level of demand for this project. This consultant has done many similar studies and has provided Morley Properties with the following joint probability table summarizing the accuracy of the results:

Forecasted Demand	Actual Demand		
	Low	Medium	High
Low	0.1600	0.0300	0.0100
Medium	0.0350	0.2800	0.0350
High	0.0225	0.0450	0.3825

The sum of the entries on the main diagonal of this table indicates that the consultant's forecast is correct about 82.25% of the time, overall.

a. Construct the conditional probability table showing the probabilities of the various actual demands given each of the forecasted demands.

b. What is the EMV of the optimal decision without the consultant's assistance?

c. Construct a decision tree Morley Properties would use to analyze the decision problem if the consultant is hired at a cost of $0.

d. What is the EMV of the optimal decision with the consultant's free assistance?

e. What is the maximum price Morley Properties should be willing to pay the consultant?

11. MicroProducts, Incorporated (MPI) manufactures printed circuit boards for a major PC manufacturer. Before a board is sent to the customer, three key components must be tested. These components can be tested in any order. If any of the components fail, the entire board must be scrapped. The costs of testing the three components are given below, along with the probability of each component failing the test:

Component	Cost of Test	Probability of Failure
X	$1.75	0.125
Y	$2.00	0.075
Z	$2.40	0.140

a. Create a decision tree for this problem that could be used to determine the order in which the components should be tested to minimize the expected cost of performing the tests.

b. In which order should the components be tested?

c. What is the expected cost of performing the tests in this sequence?

12. Refer to question 11. A manufacturing engineer for MPI collected the following data on the failure rates of components X, Y, and Z in a random sample of 1000 circuit boards:

X	Y	Z	Number of Boards
p	p	p	710
p	f	p	45
p	p	f	110
p	f	f	10
f	p	p	95
f	f	p	10
f	p	f	10
f	f	f	10
			Total: 1000

(p = pass, f = fail)

For example, the first row in this table indicates that components X, Y, and Z all passed their inspections in 710 out of the 1000 boards checked. The second row indicates that 45 boards passed inspection on components X and Z, but failed on component Y. The remaining rows can be interpreted similarly.

a. Using these data, compute conditional probabilities for the decision tree you developed in question 11. (Note that $P(A|B) = P(A \cap B)/P(B)$ and $P(A|B \cap C) = P(A \cap B \cap C)/P(B \cap C)$.)

b. According to the revised probabilities, in which order should the components be tested?

c. What is the expected cost of performing the tests in this sequence?

13. The Banisco Corporation is negotiating a contract to borrow $300,000 to be repaid in a lump sum at the end of 9 years. Interest payments will be made on the loan at the end of each year. The company is considering the following three financing arrangements:

- The company can borrow the money using a fixed rate loan (FRL) that requires interest payments of 9% per year.

- The company can borrow the money using an adjustable rate loan (ARL) that requires interest payments of 6% at the end of each of the first 5 years. At the beginning of the 6th year, the interest rate on the loan could change to 7%, 9%, or 11% with probabilities of 0.1, 0.25, and 0.65, respectively.

- The company can borrow the money using an ARL that requires interest payments of 4% at the end of each of the first 3 years. At the beginning of the 4th year, the interest rate on the loan could change to 6%, 8%, or 10% with probabilities of 0.05, 0.30, and 0.65, respectively. At the beginning of the 7th year, the interest rate could decrease by 1 percentage point with a probability of 0.1, increase by 1 percentage point with a probability of 0.2, or increase by 3 percentage points with a probability of 0.7.

a. Create a decision tree for this problem, computing the total interest paid under each possible scenario.

b. Which decision should the company make if it wants to minimize its expected total interest payments?

14. Refer to question 13. Suppose that the financing options available to Banisco are:

- The company can borrow the money using a fixed rate loan (FRL) that requires interest payments of 9% per year.

- The company can borrow the money using an adjustable rate loan (ARL) that requires interest payments of 6% at the end of each of the first 5 years. At the beginning of the 6th year, the interest rate could increase to any value in the range from 7% to 11% with equal probability.

- The company can borrow the money using an ARL that requires interest payments of 4% at the end of each of the first 3 years. At the beginning of the 4th year, the interest rate on the loan could change to any value in the range from 6% to 10% with equal probability. At the beginning of the 7th year, the interest rate could change by any amount from a decrease of 1 percentage point to an increase of 3 percentage points, with equal probability.

a. Create a decision tree to simulate this problem, computing the total interest paid under each possible scenario.

b. Replicate the decision tree 100 times, keeping track of the optimal decision that would minimize the total expected interest payments in each replication.

c. Based on this analysis, which financing option would you recommend to Banisco? What is the probability that this decision will result in the lowest total interest payments?

15. Refer to question 13. The present value (PV) of a future cash-flow value (FV) is defined as:

$$PV = \frac{FV}{(1 + r)^n}$$

where n is the number of years into the future in which the cash flow occurs and r is the discount rate. Suppose that the discount rate for Banisco is 10% ($r = 0.1$).

a. Create a decision tree for this problem, computing the PV of the total interest paid under each possible scenario.

b. Which decision should the company make if it wants to minimize the expected PV of its total interest payments?

16. Medical studies have shown that 10 out of 100 adults have heart disease. When a person with heart disease is given an EKG test, a 0.9 probability exists that the test will indicate the presence of heart disease. When a person without heart disease is given an EKG test, a 0.95 probability exists that the test will indicate the person does not have heart disease. Suppose that a person arrives at an emergency room complaining of chest pains. An EKG is given and indicates that the person has heart disease. What is the probability that the person actually has heart disease?

17. From industry statistics, a credit card company knows that 0.8 of its potential card holders are good credit risks and 0.2 are bad credit risks. The company uses discriminant analysis to screen credit card applicants and determine which ones should receive credit cards. The company awards credit cards to 70% of those who apply. The company has found that of those awarded credit cards, 95% turn out to be good credit risks. What is the probability that an applicant who is a bad credit risk will be denied a credit card?

18. Suppose that you are given the following two alternatives:

Alternative 1: Receive $200 with certainty

Alternative 2: Receive $1,000 with probability p or lose $250 with probability $1 - p$

a. At what value of p would you be indifferent between these two alternatives?

b. Given your response to part a, would you be classified as risk averse, risk neutral, or risk seeking?

c. Suppose that alternative 2 changed so that you would receive $1,000 with probability p or lose $0 with probability $1 - p$. At what value of p would you now be indifferent between these alternatives?

d. Given your response to part c, would you be classified as risk averse, risk neutral, or risk seeking?

19. Refer to question 9. Suppose that the utility function for the owner of Morley Properties can be approximated by the exponential utility function:

$$U(x) = 1 - e^{-x/R}$$

where the risk tolerance value R = 100 (in $1,000s).

a. Convert the payoff matrix to utility values.

b. What decision provides the owner of the company with the largest expected utility?

20. Refer to question 10. Suppose that the consultant's fee is $5,000 and the utility function for the owner of Morley Properties can be approximated by the exponential utility function:

$$U(x) = 1 - e^{-x/R}$$

where the risk tolerance value R = 100 (in $1,000s).

a. What expected level of utility is realized if Morley Properties hires the consultant?

b. What expected level of utility is realized if Morley Properties does not hire the consultant?

c. Based on this analysis, should Morley Properties hire the consultant?

21. The president of Pegasus Corporation is trying to decide which of three candidates (denoted as candidates A, B, and C) to hire as the firm's new vice president of Marketing. The primary criteria the president is considering are each candidate's leadership ability, interpersonal skills, and administrative ability. After carefully considering their qualifications, the president used AHP to create the following pairwise comparison matrices for the three candidates on the various criteria:

Leadership Ability	A	B	C
A	1	3	4
B	1/3	1	2
C	1/4	1/2	1

Interpersonal Skills	A	B	C
A	1	1/2	3
B	2	1	8
C	1/3	1/8	1

Administrative Ability	A	B	C
A	1	1/5	1/8
B	5	1	1/3
C	8	3	1

Next, the president of Pegasus considered the relative importance of the three criteria. This resulted in the following pairwise comparison matrix:

	Criteria		
	Leadership Ability	Interpersonal Skills	Administrative Ability
Leadership Ability	1	1/3	1/4
Interpersonal Skills	3	1	1/2
Administrative Ability	4	2	1

a. Use AHP to compute scores for each candidate on each of the three criteria, and to compute weights for each of the criteria.

b. Was the president consistent in making pairwise comparisons?

c. Compute the weighted average score for each candidate. Which candidate should be selected according to your results?

22. Kathy Jones is planning to buy a new minivan but, after narrowing her choices down to three models (X, Y, and Z) within her price range, she is having difficulty deciding which one to buy. Kathy has compared each model against the others on the basis of four criteria: price, safety, economy, and comfort. Her comparisons are summarized as:

Price	X	Y	Z
X	1	1/4	3
Y	4	1	7
Z	1/3	1/7	1

Safety	X	Y	Z
X	1	1/2	3
Y	2	1	8
Z	1/3	1/8	1

Economy	X	Y	Z
X	1	1/3	1/6
Y	3	1	1/3
Z	6	3	1

Comfort	X	Y	Z
X	1	1/4	1/8
Y	4	1	1/3
Z	8	3	1

Kathy wants to incorporate all of these criteria into her final decision, but not all of the criteria are equally important. The following matrix summarizes Kathy's comparisons of the importance of the criteria:

Criteria	Price	Safety	Economy	Comfort
Price	1	1/7	1/2	1/5
Safety	7	1	4	2
Economy	2	1/4	1	1/2
Comfort	5	1/2	2	1

a. Use AHP to compute scores for each minivan on each of the four criteria, and to compute weights for each of the criteria.

b. Was Kathy consistent in making pairwise comparisons?

c. Compute the weighted average score for each minivan. Based on this analysis, which minivan should Kathy buy?

23. Identify a consumer electronics product that you want to purchase (for example, a TV, VCR, camcorder, personal computer, and so on). Identify at least three models of this product that you would consider purchasing. Identify at least three criteria on which these models differ (for example, price, quality, warranty, options). Use AHP to determine scores for each model on each of the criteria, and to determine weights for the criteria. Which model should you choose according to the AHP results?

The Spreadsheet Wars
A Case in
Decision Analysis

SAM Ellis is worried. As president and CEO of Forward Software, Sam introduced a new spreadsheet product, Cinco, to the market last year. Forward Software has been developing and marketing high-quality software packages for more than five years, but these products are mostly computer software language interpreters, similar to Pascal, FORTRAN, and C. These products received excellent critical reviews, and because of Forward's aggressive pricing and marketing, the company quickly captured a major share of that software market. Buoyed by its wide acceptance, last year Forward decided to enter the applications arena for the IBM and compatible audience, leading off with Cinco and following up with a word processing application, Fast.

The spreadsheet market is dominated by Focus Software, whose product—Focus A-B-C—has an 80% market share. Focus A-B-C was released in 1981, shortly after the IBM personal computer (PC) was introduced, and the two products had an immediate symbiotic effect. The spreadsheet was a major advance over what was available at the time, but required the extra 16-bit processing power that IBM PC offered. IBM, on the other hand, needed an application that would make its PC a "must buy." Sales of Focus A-B-C and the IBM PC took off as a result of their near-simultaneous release.

At the time of its release, Focus A-B-C was a superb product, but it did have flaws. For example, because the software was copy-protected, it could be installed on a hard disk, but the original floppy disk had to be inserted each time before the software could run. Many users found this step an annoyance. Another problem with A-B-C was printing graphs. In order to print a graph, users had to exit the software and load a new program, called Printgraf, which would then print the graph. Finally, the product had a list price of $495, and the best discounted price available was approximately $300.

However, Focus A-B-C had a unique menu system that was intuitive and easy to use. Pressing the slash key (/) displayed the menu system at the top of the spreadsheet. The menu allowed the user to make choices and provided a one-line explanation of each menu option. Compared to the cryptic commands or keystrokes users had to enter in other products, the Focus A-B-C menu system was a model of simplicity and clarity. Millions of users became accustomed to the menu system and hailed its use.

Contributed by Jack Yurkiewicz, Lubin School of Business, Pace University, New York.

Another advantage of Focus A-B-C was its ability to let users write their own macros. Literally a program, a macro allowed a user to automate spreadsheet tasks and then run them with a keystroke or two.

In 1985, a small company named Discount Software introduced its own spreadsheet to the market. Called VIP Scheduler, the product looked and worked exactly the same as Focus A-B-C. Pressing the slash key displayed the identical menu as found in Focus A-B-C, and the product could read any macros developed with Focus A-B-C. VIP Scheduler was designed to look and work exactly as Focus A-B-C so that users would not have to learn a new system, and could start productive work immediately. VIP Scheduler also offered two advantages over Focus A-B-C: its list price was $99 and the software was not copy-protected. Sales for VIP Scheduler were strong, but many consumers, perhaps feeling safer with the Focus name, did not buy the product, even though critical reviews were positive. VIP Scheduler did find a receptive market in academia.

When Forward released its first spreadsheet product, Cinco, it was hailed by critics as a better all-around product than Focus A-B-C. It had better graphics, allowed users to print graphs from within Cinco, and was 100% compatible with Focus A-B-C. Cinco had its own menu system, which was as flexible as the Focus A-B-C system, but the menus and options were arranged more intuitively. For users who did not want to invest the time to learn a new menu system, Cinco could emulate the Focus A-B-C menu system. Both menus were activated by pressing the slash key, and users could specify easily which menu system they wanted. All macros written for Focus A-B-C ran perfectly on Cinco, provided that the Focus A-B-C menu system was being used. Because of favorable reviews and aggressive marketing by Forward, Cinco quickly gained market share.

In a move that surprised the industry, Focus recently sued Discount Software, publisher of VIP Scheduler, for copyright infringement. Focus claimed that its menu system was an original work, and that VIP Scheduler, by incorporating that menu system in its product, had violated copyright laws. Focus claimed that the look and feel of its menu system could not be used in another product without permission. Sam is certain that Focus initiated this lawsuit because Cinco has made such dramatic progress in gaining a share of the spreadsheet market. Sam also is sure that Focus's target is not really VIP Scheduler, because it has such a small market share, but Cinco.

After discussions with Forward's attorneys, Sam thinks that if he makes a quiet overture to Focus to settle out of court, Focus would be amenable to such a proposal. This would stave off potential negative publicity if Focus wins its suit against Discount Software and then follows up with a lawsuit against Forward. Based on projections of Cinco's sales, Forward's attorneys think that Focus could ask for $5, $8, or as much as $15 million in damages. Sam believes that the probability of Focus agreeing to $5 million is 50%, $8 million is 30%, and $15 million is 20%.

Sam knows that settling now means an immediate loss of income, in the amount of one of the three estimates given, plus an admission of defeat and guilt for Forward. On the other hand, Sam could wait for the outcome of the Focus versus Discount Software suit. Forward's attorneys believe that Focus has a 40% chance of winning its lawsuit against Discount Software. With a win, Focus would have its legal precedent to sue Forward. It is by no means certain that Focus would institute a lawsuit against Forward because Forward is a much larger company than Discount Software and could afford a vigorous legal defense. Also the case against Forward is not as clear cut because Cinco has its own menu system as the primary mode of operation and offers the Focus A-B-C menu system for those who want to use it. VIP Scheduler provides only the Focus A-B-C menu system. However, Forward's attorneys believe there is an 80% chance that Focus would initiate a lawsuit against Forward if Focus wins its suit against Discount Software.

Sam believes that even if Focus sues Forward, he could still try to settle the case out of court at that time or decide to go to trial. An attempt to settle out of court at that time would be more expensive for Forward because Focus would feel secure that it would win its case against Forward, having already won its lawsuit against Discount Software. Thus Forward's attorneys think that

Focus would settle for no less than $7 million, possibly asking for $10 million or even $12 million. The respective probabilities that Focus would settle for these amounts ($7, $10, and $12 million) are estimated to be 30%, 40%, and 30%. Also, Forward would have to pay its attorneys roughly $1 million to go through the settling process.

However, if Focus sues Forward and Forward decides to go to trial instead of initiating settlement proceedings, Forward could lose the case. Forward's attorneys estimate there is an 80% chance that Forward would lose the trial, resulting in a judgment of either $10 million, $12 million, or $18 million against Forward, with probabilities of 10%, 20%, and 70%, respectively. The attorneys also estimate that their fees for a trial could run as high as $1.5 million.

Use decision analysis to determine what Sam's optimal strategy should be. Create the decision tree for this problem, including all costs and probabilities, and find the optimal decision strategy and expected cost for that strategy. Consider Sam to be "risk neutral" in this analysis.